Hermetic Behmenists: Writings of Dionysius Andreas Freher and Francis Lee

Copyright 2017 Topaz House Publications

No part of this book may be reproduced except brief quotations and scholarly usage except by permission of the publisher.
All medical information is for historical interest only. No guarantee is given for the efficacy of any of the practices described herein.

ISBN: 978-0-9988213-1-3

Visit Topaz House Publications at www.topazbooks.pub

Hermetic Behmenists,

writings of

Dionysius Andreas Freher
Francis Lee
Richard Roach, and
Christopher Walton.

Comprising an elucidation of the scope and contents of

The Writings of Jacob Boehme,

Intoduced and edited by
John Madziarczyk

Topaz House Publications
Seattle, WA
2017

Table of Contents

Preface 1

Introduction 3

   1. Boehme and the Background of Theosophy 5
   2. Rosicrucians and Para-Rosicrucians 23
   3. The Philadelphian Society 41
   4. Freher, Walton, "Notes and Materials", Texts in This Volume 56

Part One: Dionysius Andreas Freher

                Foundational Texts

   1. God Without Nature or Creature [from Serial Elucidations A, section 1] 97
   2. How the Nothing Brings Forth Something [From Serial Elucidations F, part 1] 101
   3. God in Unity and Trinity Before and After Eternal Nature [Serial Elucidations G, part 1] 145
   4. General Positions on Divine Nature in Unity and Trinity [Serial Elucidations G., part 2] 171

                Intermediary Texts

   5. Two Questions Answered, [Serial Elucidations G part 7] 183
   6. Considerations on Lucifer and the Third Principle [?][Serial Elucidations B Section 5] 209
   7. Rubens' Manuscript [Extract from the Commentary on the "Three Tables"] 225
   8. [Thirty Propositions, Fragment] 233

9. Of the Further Manifestation of God Through the Creation of Angels[?] [Serial Elucidations B section 4]   243

10. Process in the Philosophical Work [Serial Elucidations G], part 10   249

12. Growing Vegetables [Serial Elucidations G, part 11]   273

Observations on Waple

11. Observations on Waple [Serial Elucidations H]   281

Highlights within Waple

[Seven Spirits]   289

[Nature of Angels]   297

[Seven Spirits in Nature]   308

[Formation of the Planets]   314

[Alchemy]   323

[Breath in Man]   337

[Adam in Paradise]   341

[Eve and the Serpent]   352

[Reproduction]   360

[Partial Esoteric Anatomy]   375

[Esoteric Meaning of Jesus]   390

[God and the Nature of Evil]   403

[Thirty Positions on God]   407

[Spiritual Discernment]   433

[The Ten Commandments]   440

[Baptism]   444

[Eucharist]   447

[The End Times] 457

Final

13. Freher's Confession, [Three Tables, Table One] 467
14. Walton's Summaries of Serial Elucidations A-E 485
15. Discourse by William Law, Compiled from Freher's Works 517
16. List of Freher's Works by Walton 537

Part Two: Francis Lee

Philadelphian Society Era Texts:

1. Letter to Dodwell 553
2. [Comments on the Seven Spirits.] 631
3. Introduction to the First Volume of "A Fountain of Gardens" by Jane Lead 633
4. Excerpt from Theosophical Transactions 647
5. Questions to Edward Hooker. About Pordage 663

Post-Philadelphian Texts:

6. Concerning Wisdom 665
7. Short Reflections on the Universal Matter, 687
8. [On the Book of Revelation] 691
9. [On Moses] 695
10. [Paragraph on Mystical Theology] 696
11. One Hundred Questions on the Mosaic Cabbala 697

Organizational Texts and
Texts on Contemplation and Prayer:

15. [Lee on the Contemplative Way] 709

16. [Two Commemorations and Three Prayers by Lee]. 721
12. [Plan for a Publishing Company] 729
13. Model of a Society for Reviving the Spirit and Life of Christianity 731

Part Three: Richard Roach & Christopher Walton

Richard Roach

1. Solomon's Porch. 737
2. [Chapter on Magical Prayer] 763
3. Index of Philosophical and Theosophical Terms 767

Christopher Walton

4. [Comments on the Philadelphians] 781
5. [On Enthusiasm.] 787
6. [Walton's Reading List on Magic] 791

Appendix 797

Preface

"Hermetic Behmenists"? Aren't all of Jacob Boehme's writings Hermetic? Perhaps, but there are several ways of responding to Boehme's thought. One of them documents mystical experiences and the work of pursuing the Behmenist path, another analyzes Boehme's thought in ways that are closer to those of occultism—moving back from the personal and looking at the writings in relation to the occult and hermetic thought that informed Boehme's work. Of the two ways, the writings included here come at Boehme's work from the latter perspective. Although Behmenist writings such as those of Jane Lead, where she recounts her mystical visions and transmissions from spiritual beings, are very enlightening, they wouldn't fit into the category of "Hermetic Behmenism" unless the descriptions in them intersected with the alchemical, Paracelsan, Hermetic, or perhaps kabbalistic, traditions, as well as with the Theosophical.

This book is based on writings published by Christopher Walton in "Notes and Materials for an Adequate Biography of William Law", specifically those by Dionysius Andreas Freher, Francis Lee, and Richard Roach. "Notes and Materials", published in 1856, contains transcripts of writings that had never appeared before in print, and for the most part still have not. Unfortunately, "Notes and Materials" is chaotically organized, with much of the book set in nine point font, and footnotes that are, in one case, over a hundred pages long. The material is difficult to physically read, there are no table of contents and no index, and writings that should be placed in the main part of the text are instead put into very long footnotes.

The book itself was never put for sale on the open market, but was only printed in an edition 500 copies, then given to friends and distributed to university libraries. This has not made the work, and its otherwise unpublished contents, nearly as available as they should be. The work you're holding in your hands aims to change that.

Dionysius Andreas Freher was a brilliant commentator and expositor of Jacob Boehme's philosophy, whose work is almost entirely unpublished and in manuscript form. None of it appeared during his lifetime. Many of the short works that have occasionally appeared by Freher have been transcribed from Walton's book itself, not from his manuscripts. With the very notable exceptions of Adam McLean's publication of two graphical works by Freher, the "Three Tables" and "Paradoxical Emblems", and some of the excerpts of Freher in Robert Faas' "The Divine Couple", there have been no new editions of Freher's works from manuscript in the last one hundred and fifty years.

Likewise, Francis Lee was also a brilliant follower of Boehme, although in his later years he left the Behmenist current and went on his own way on the mystical path. He was one of the founders of the Philadelphian Society, a Behmenist group oriented around the prophecies and visions of Jane Lead. While a great deal of work by Lee was published by his daughter over thirty years after his death, she left out Lee's earlier Behmenist works, and no mention was made of the Philadelphian Society, or of Behmenism in the accompanying biographical essay. Happily, Walton's book contains Behmenist writings by Lee that were otherwise unpublished. They were included along with a selection of other writings in manuscript form from across Lee's career. All of these have been reproduced here.

Richard Roach was a member of the Philadelphian Society and a friend of Lee. Part of his poem "Solomon's Porch", about Sophia, Prophecy, Alchemy, and the Philadelphian Society, was reproduced in Walton's book. It was originally published in full as part of the introduction to a Philadelphian Society publication. The full poem appears here, with the partial text of Walton completed by a copy of the full poem created as part of the Early English Books Online Text Creation Partnership. Two other pieces of Roach have been added from his later work "The Imperial Standard". These consist of a piece on magical prayer and a dictionary of Theosophical terms, which I believe may be of great value and use to the reader.

An essay by Walton himself, about religious enthusiasm, has been included, along with Walton's recommendation of books on magic that people should read, and miscellaneous notes about the Philadelphian Society. Also included is an appendix containing a comparison of one of Jane Lead's works with a later Rosicrucian text.

The following introduction will take the reader into the world of Jacob Boehme, into Theosophy as it existed in the 17th-18th centuries, to the world of our authors, and into the Philadelphian Society itself. Along the way we will also trek down the path of Rosicrucian thought, it's myths and truths, and how it relates to Boehme's vision, as well as to our authors. Hopefully, this will prove to shed some light on these topics. Unless otherwise indicated, "Theosophy", as used here, refers to a system of Christian mysticism, combined with Paracelsan and Hermetic occult thought, and is not related to the later Theosophical Society.

Introduction

Why, in this day and age, should occultists consider the thought of an obscure Christian mystic?

First, I believe that the mystics of all religions have fragments of the greater truth in their writings. This includes the Christian as well as the Islamic and Judaic, the Hindu and Buddhist. Secondly, Christianity was the lingua franca for philosophical and mystical discourse in the West previous to the Enlightenment, even through the changes of the Renaissance. Outside of the Kabbalah, any actual non-Christian thought in the West at this time was most likely very, very deeply concealed, and even there may have been influenced by Christianity itself.

Thirdly, while it may upset individuals who integrate Boehme into more mainstream Christian thought, Boehme's thought is radically different from that of the majority of Christian philosophers. It takes in so many elements of contemporary occult thought from outside of Christianity that it's not simply heretical, but resembles a split off from Christianity into another religion altogether. To say that Boehme writes outside the lines of conventional Christianity is an understatement.

Boehme's Theosophy is a florid arrangement of cosmogony not contained in the Bible, alchemical principles, Paracelsian ideas, magic taken in a broad sense, Renaissance Hermeticism, and other currents, contained within a nominally Christian context. Boehme narrates a creation of the world which diverges substantially from that contained in the Bible and outlines a version of the esoteric functioning of the world which likewise has no Biblical basis. There are angels with free will, fountains of light, a world of fire and wrath, a world of light and meekness, hermetic signatures that link all of it together, Lucifer as the first Adam, and much much more.

Indeed, while speaking of the broader current of Theosophy, which includes but is not defined by Boehme, Antoine Faivre points out that there were two currents within it: that of those who pursued the route of mystical contemplation, and those who pursued the route of alchemy and more magical activities[1]. The followers of Boehme fall into both categories. I believe that Freher's writings belong more to the latter category, with most of the English Behmenists falling into the former. This differs from Faivre in that he believes that Freher fits into the former category as well.

While from an orthodox Christian perspective the thought of Boehme might be highly heretical, taken on its own it forms a coherent and unique whole. It's consistent within itself, as a general system of magical mysticism that flows from a Christian base. Boehme's thought is a portrait of the mystical world as perceived through the mystic vision itself, and it also functions surprisingly well as a guide for those who are pursuing Renaissance Hermeticism and what could be called the 'traditional' Western magical worldview.

The word 'traditional' has in recent times come to be associated with unsavory currents of thought, but what is meant is that magical worldview based on the Ptolemaic cosmos that existed from late antiquity to the beginnings of the Enlightenment. Boehme represents a transitional point of view: he incorporates the new Copernican doctrines into his mystical thought, which is Heliocentric instead of Geocentric, while retaining the ideas of planetary influences, and the existence of a super-celestial world, that typifies the Ptolemaic understanding of the universe. Boehme's thought, as well as that of his interpreters such as Freher and the Philadelphians, can be a great help to people trying to navigate that world.

Boehme incorporated some of the most radical and provocative esotericism of his day into his thought, including the thought of Paracelsus and the Paracelsans. This, in general, also approved of magic, if used in a circumscribed way, and Paracelsan grimoires were in fact produced. The "Arbatel" is an example of a Paracelsan grimoire, written by a Paracelsan[2], and published by a Swiss Paracelsan[3].

Boehme and Mysticism in general.

As for the other fork, I believe that Boehme's work favorably compares with the mystical understanding of the world contained in Hinduism and Buddhism, as well as in the more esoteric sides of the Abrahamic religions. As a mystical system parallels can be drawn between Boehme's thought and Mahayana Buddhism, as well as the more mystical sects of Hinduism. Indeed, the author of the only book devoted to Dionysius Andreas Freher, wrote in the late '40s, in talking about Freher's attitude towards the relationship between texts and practice, that his attitudes were like those of Vivekananda on Bhakti yoga[4].

Systems such as Buddhism and Hinduism contain parallels to notions in Boehme and Freher, such as the idea that venoms can be transformed into positive virtues. The venoms are evil distortions of otherwise natural impulses, and when processed through meditation and ritual can be transformed into perfected virtues. This idea is represented in the physical object of the Vajra of Mahayana Buddhism, which gives the current of 'Vajrayana Buddhism' its name. One side of the object has five arms that signify the five venoms, while the other has five arms that embody the five perfected virtues. A major difference between Vajrayana Buddhism and the thought of Freher is that in the thought of Freher the impulses to wrath have parallels in impulses to love, and what is advocated is to apply these impulses to the wrathful impulses, thereby tempering them and returning them to their healthy forms. By applying the light to the wrath, the wrathful impulses are transformed into virtues. Similarly, many of the processes of Tibetan Buddhism that depend on manipulating the internal esoteric anatomy are parallel to the internal spiritual alchemy that appears to have been pursued by the Behmenists, including Freher. All of the leading members of the Philadelphian Society, which Freher was loosely associated with and of which France Lee was a part of, that is to say John Pordage, Jane Lead, Francis Lee, and Richard Roach, wrote pieces about spirituality that incorporate alchemical symbolism.

Boehme's biography.

Jacob Boehme was born in 1575, in Alt-Siedenberg[5], near the town of Görlitz, in Upper Lusatia in Germany, which later became part of Prussian Silesia, and died in 1624. Görlitz is currently located on the border between Germany and Poland, with its sister city of Zgorzelec in Poland connected to it by bridge, while Alt or Old Seidenberg is now known as Stary Zawidów, and is located in Poland. Görlitz is also close to the Czech province of Bohemia. However, during Boehme's time, these political entities did not exist. Neither did the connotations of nationality implied by them, although differences between Slavic speakers and German speakers existed, with German speakers dominating the region.

Andrew Weeks, in his "Intellectual Biography of Jacob Boehme" has done a very thorough job of documenting Boehme's social and cultural place in Görlitz. Weeks documents that Görlitz in the late 16th century was a unique place[6]. He documents that the area been subject to successive waves of activism by the new Protestant sects, and that some of the aristocracy adhered to radical Protestant doctrines[7], which contributed to the ecumenical nature of the town, and that the merchants of the town as well as the aristocracy were free thinking, both in religious matters and in the new philosophies of the Renaissance. As a consequence they didn't allow the persecutions that happened elsewhere to happen in their town[8].

It's often stated that Boehme was a "simple shoemaker". The story appears in to be much more complicated than that. Freher's biographer Charles Muses, and, implicitly, Andrew Weeks, note that the notion of a "simple shoemaker" has been misinterpreted[9]. "Simple" in this case doesn't mean uneducated, or worse, unintelligent, it means not being part of the aristocracy, and not having benefitted from the extensive primary and university education that members of the aristocracy went through. Instead, Boehme's knowledge came from a basic education such as was deemed appropriate for tradesmen to receive, as well as from self-education and avenues of knowledge attained through more working class means. Muses[10], and others, also state that Boehme was familiar with the spiritual thinkers of his day, although he said he didn't think much of them. However, this may be a rhetorical device on the part of Boehme, who preferred his philosophy to that of others.

Additionally, Weeks demonstrates that there was actually a Paracelsan physician and alchemist in Görlitz named Abraham Behem[11], who corresponded with Valentin Weigel[12], and speculates that he might have been some relation to Boehme, and possibly a teacher[13]. Abraham Behem was the brother in law of the mayor of Görlitz, Bartolomeus Scultetus[14], who in turn was a former Gymnasium teacher and Renaissance Humanist[15]. Weeks also reports that Paracelsus' writings were being compiled and printed in Görlitz, and that Scultetus worked on the editing of one of these writings[16]. Weeks speculates that Boehme could have been exposed to all of these currents in Görlitz, and that they may have fundamentally shaped his thought. They also provided the context within which Boehme's mystical experiences took place.

Boehme had a mystical experience in 1600 that left a life long impression on him. He stated that it only lasted fifteen minutes but that it contained enough to base his later philosophy on[17]. Boehme had other mystical experiences later in life. Boehme kept his revelation to himself, but eventually created a manuscript "Morgenrothe", or "Morning Redness", translated as "The Aurora", which laid out what he had gotten from the vision. "The Aurora" was first circulated privately in 1612. The circulation, even in manuscript form, caused so much controversy that the main pastor of Görlitz demanded that Boehme not write any more. Boehme obeyed this command for six years, until he started writing again in 1618. He subsequently produced an amazing amount of works on a great diversity of theological, biblical, and philosophical topics. The only book that was published in his lifetime was "The Way to Christ", in 1624. All of the rest of Boehme's works circulated in manuscript while he was alive. Boehme passed on in November of 1624.

As for what Boehme believed, there are several ways of describing it. However, because Theosophy as a whole will be dealt with below, for now I'll start with a leading theme in Boehme's thought, followed by a thumbnail presentation of his cosmology.

The leading theme is one that Weeks points to as one of the essential features of Boehme's philosophy, the contrast between "historical faith" and "mystical faith"[18], which is also what Boehme saw as the difference between the "Steinkirche", or "stone church"[19], bound by outer conformity, but lacking the spirit of true religious experience, and the path of true religiosity itself. For Boehme, the mystical experience and real Christianity existed beyond the world of the "stone church". Boehme appears to have seen the Protestant, mostly Lutheran, discussions of the nature of the Bible, of the meaning of Christianity, and of the world in general, as dominated by formalisms that lacked a true understanding of the realities behind them. Boehme's writings, then, can be seen as a manifestation of the opposite: as writings in touch with the living realities of Christianity, the Bible, and the world, incorporating communication with God, the angels, as well as visions and revelations, into its reality.

Boehme's Theosophy.

What, exactly, then, did Boehme believe? The following cosmology is heavily influenced by Freher's interpretation of Boehme.

God, at first, subsisted complete in himself as a monad. This monad wanted to manifest the potentialities in itself, and so generated the Son. The Son is a circle, with the monad as the center point. The circle is a figure of completeness anchored by the point at its center. The Son, in turn, perceives the point in the center, and this act of perception is what the Holy Spirit consists of.

Once the Son perceives the Father, the point in the center of the circle, the cycle is closed and a fourth being is created, Eternal Nature. Strictly speaking, before the creation of Eternal Nature, the Trinity is only imperfectly perceived. Individuals can only get fleeting images of it, and in the main it is unknowable. Eternal Nature can be said to be the thoughts of God, and is the first quality that can be concretely perceived by humans.

Within Eternal Nature, the Trinity manifests itself again, producing lesser versions of the Father, the Son, and the Holy Spirit. Because the first impulse of manifestation is force, the force of pushing forward and manifesting reality, this part of Eternal Nature carries the force and character of the Old Testament God, which is closer to wrath than love. After these three lesser principles of the Trinity manifest in Eternal Nature, their cycle closes, and another cycle starts. This time, the Trinity manifests within a field of Love and Light, characteristic of the New Testament, as opposed to the wrath of the father of the old. So, in the end, you have two copies of the Trinity, first manifesting in what Boehme, Freher, and Behmenists refer to as the principle of Wrath, and then manifesting within the principle of Light.

Together, the two principles contain six hypostasis, or lesser versions of the trinity. After the three versions of the Trinity manifest in the Light world, the circle closes and a seventh is produced. This seventh incorporates the qualities of both the Light and the Wrath worlds. It reconciles them, and binds them together into a stable whole. This seventh entity is the foundation of Heaven itself. The seven principles as a whole are also referred to as the seven "Fountain Spirits", because as principles of manifestation they flow forward like fountains, constantly generating more from themselves. This seventh fountain spirit is parallel to the Holy Spirit, as the Wrath world is parallel to the Father and the Light world to the Son.

Within the seventh entity, or fountain spirit, the Heaven of the angels is created, with Lucifer as the head angel. All the angels, as created beings, contain images of Eternal Nature within them, meaning that they all have elements of Wrath and elements of Love. They also have free will. Lucifer decided to try to seize the throne of God, which existed beyond Eternal Nature, in the realm of which people can only get a fleeting glimpse. He failed, but in deciding to try to seize the reigns of heaven, Lucifer chose to act on his Wrathful principle to the detriment of his Light principle, and this produced a disharmony which destroyed the unity of Eternal Nature.

The seventh fountain spirit of Eternal Nature, the world of Heaven, broke in two. The Light principle and the Dark principle separated into their own respective worlds. Lucifer, and the angels who sided with him were banished to the Dark world. By deciding to act on their Wrathful impulses they also destroyed the principle of Light within themselves and became beings solely dominated by Wrathful impulses. The angels who stayed loyal to God retained both natures in themselves, and came to reside in the Light world.

After this, God decided to create Adam as a replacement for Lucifer, and to create Paradise, the Garden of Eden, as a replacement for the seventh fountain spirit in Eternal Nature. Paradise was likewise an attempt at balancing the world of Light and Darkness, but the Fall of Lucifer had already happened. Lucifer existed in the Wrath world, and could influence the Garden of Eden. Lucifer tempted Eve, who gave into the Wrathful or lower nature and accepted the apple, and gave it to Adam, who likewise gave into his Wrathful or lower nature in eating it. The harmony of the Garden of Eden was destroyed, and the world as we know it was manifested. This is a place where the Light World and the Dark World interpenetrate, but without any harmony or proportion, a place of imbalance. Adam and Eve were banished into this new world. Much later, Jesus was sent as a means for salvation of the individual and for the world as a whole.

Boehme states, and Freher amplifies, that the Wrathful principle where the demons and Lucifer live is not evil in and of itself, but is instead a legitimate function of God's character that has been distorted out of proportion, causing it to produce evil. A re-harmonization of the wrathful and loving tendencies in the human being, and in the world, is therefore necessary for spiritual regeneration. Unlike some present day Protestants, particularly in the United States, who believe that simply receiving the spirit or allowing Jesus into your heart 'saves' you, and signifies the end of spiritual work, both Boehme and the Behmenists saw this state as a preface to new stages of purification and self-work, aimed at getting closer to God.

On another level, the seven fountain spirits, or replications of the parts of the Trinity in Eternal Nature, also correspond to the characteristics of the seven planets. Mars, Saturn, and Mercury are labeled by Freher, following Boehme, as the Trinity of the Wrathful principle. Venus, Jupiter, and the Moon are labeled as the Trinity of the Light Principle, with the Sun standing as the reconciling principle between the Light world and the Wrath world.

Now, let's look at the foundations of Boehme's thought. I've divided this background into four sections: Hermeticism, the thought of Paracelsus, Theosophy itself, and the concept of Sophia or Wisdom as it intersects with the thought of the Theosophists. After the background, we'll discuss the Rosicrucians and the Philadelphian Society.

Hermeticism

Before defining Theosophy, let's look at the 'Hermetic' in 'Hermetic Behmenists'. To start with, Hermeticism as it was understood in Western Europe during the Renaissance and after should be distinguished from Hermeticism as it existed in the first centuries C.E. The original Hermeticism refers to a series of writings and dialogues composed in the Middle East in the first centuries C.E.

These expository writings consist of a master, Hermes Trismegistus, explaining the structure of the world, its development, and humanity's place within it, to disciples. These dialogues are both philosophical and religious. Hermeticism is a product of the Hellenistic intellectual tradition as it existed at the end of the Roman Empire, and consists of a mixture of late Neo-Platonic, Stoic, and pagan Greek religious, philosophical, and mystical thought, combined with elements of Semitic, Judaic, Egyptian and possibly Christian, religious beliefs. Although there was likely an extensive Hermetic literature at the time, the main texts that survive are the Corpus Hermeticum, and the Asclepius.

Now, in looking at what 'Hermeticism' means in the context of Western Occultism, I would argue that what's important is what people knew of Hermeticism in the Middle Ages and the Renaissance, as opposed to Hermeticism as it existed originally. Scholars and others in the West didn't have access to the majority of the Hermetic documents until the last years of the 15th century; therefore their concept of Hermticism was shaped by the documents that they actually had. These were the Asclepius, the Emerald Tablet, and miscellaneous treatises on astrology, alchemy, and magic attributed to Hermes Trismegistus. These miscellaneous texts include the "Liber Hermetis", a treatise on practical astrology.

I believe that the Emerald Tablet and the Asclepius were the documents that established the popular meaning of 'Hermeticism' in Western Europe, which continues down to our day. Although the landmark translation of the Corpus Hermeticum by Ficino was a wonderful accomplishment, and helped to spark the Renaissance, Ficino's translations entered into a world where the concept of Hermeticism was already established. In fact, one of the reasons that the Corpus Hermeticum was eagerly received by scholars and esotericists was because they were already familiar with the contents of the Asclepius.

The distinction between the Hermeticism of the Corpus Hermeticum and that of the Asclepius is important to note, because otherwise several very important aspects of occultism in the 16th and 17th centuries remain obscure. The Corpus Hermeticum is much more mystical than the Asclepius, and those who look at the Corpus rather than the Asclepius may be puzzled about how tracts about mysticism could have given rise to a very practical occult tradition. By contrast, the Asclepius contains much more of what was called 'Natural Philosophy', information about the development and functioning of the world outside of the mystical experience of the individual.

The Asclepius outlines the functioning of the elements, the planets, the mystical signatures and correspondences, the animating spirit of the universe, and the cosmos as a whole. It's approach can be summed up by a phrase from its beginning: Many in One, One in Many[20], meaning that it treats of the unity of the (pagan Greco-Roman) divine realm in combination with the forms which that world takes in reality as we know it. This would have easily combined with the teaching of the Emerald Tablet, such as the phrase "that which is above is like that which is below". What that means is that, despite outward differences, there is a unity to the universe, and the various parts of the universe are connected by sympathy and antipathy to each other. This principle of sympathy also applies to the human being, considered as a small version of the cosmos. The astrological and other qualities found in the macrocosm are found in the human being, and they exist in sympathetic relation with those qualities in the cosmos itself. All of this makes the texts eminently interesting and useful for practical occultism, and in fact, the Asclepius may have been seen as a fuller exposition of the principles contained in the Emerald Tablet.

Also very important in the Asclepius is the concept of the "Anima Mundi" or Spirit of the World. The "Anima Mundi" is bound up with the creation, development, and subsequent interrelation, of the different parts of the world. The world of the Asclepius is made out of matter and spirit, with spirit being the animating Spirit of the World. This Spirit not only sustains life but is ultimately directed by the will of divinity, and proceded from the unity of creation to the prolifieration of the many kinds of beings that exist within the cosmos, animating them. It's one of the means by which the One and the Many are united.

As such, it plays a great part in what could be called the intermediate realm of Hermeticism. The intermediate realm is the space between Divinity and the manifest World, and on a cosmological level consists of the astrological realms. There's also an intermediate period in the creation of the World, and the Spirit of the World is present within that as an active force guiding the manifestation and creation of the universe. Because everything originally comes from unity, and everything is animated by the Spirit of the World, this means that everything is, in a sense, still united through the Spirit of the World. This means, among other things, that through sympathetic harmony, and the action of similar signatures, animated by the Spirit of the World, action at a distance can happen between disparate objects and creatures that possess these signatures.

As for the question of authorship and how the figure of Hermes was received in the Renaissance and the Middle Ages, a distinction is made in the Asclepius itself between the god Hermes and the writer of the texts. While authors associated with the Golden Dawn and related traditions were quick to associate Hermes Trismegistus with the god Hermes, and from there with the Egyptian Thoth, this is not how the texts themselves identify the author. Instead, Hermes Trismegistus in the

Asclepius directly says that Hermes was his divine ancestor[21]. The literature of both the Corpus Hermeticum and the Asclepius is in the form of a dialogue between a master and students, and the Asclepius is labeled a 'Sermon' by Hermes Trismegistus in many translations. This suggests that they fit, or were composed so as to fit, into a type of literature produced by the profusion of sects that existed in the first centuries C.E., often lead by a charismatic prophet.

Because the teacher appeared as a mortal with wisdom, as opposed to a god, in the writings themselves, this lead to the thinkers of the Renaissance to label Hermes Trismegistus as a prophet and teacher, and from there to make the leap that he lived either at the time of Moses or before it. By doing so, the scholars of the Renaissance were not overlooking the content of the Hermetica but were instead taking it at its word, and subsequently trying to figure out where the figure of Hermes Trismegistus fit into their timeline of history.

Paracelsus.

Paracelsus, the bombastic physician from Switzerland, was born in 1493, and died in 1541. Paracelsus criticized the classical medical tradition, and came up with a unique synthesis that was derived from Renaissance Hermeticism, his own ideas, and his experience as a physician. However, Paracelsus was contradictory. Although his thought wouldn't exist without Renaissance Hermeticism, Paracslsus turned his back on it. Instead of referring to thinkers like Marsilio Ficino, Paracelsus proclaimed that the Body, the Bible, the Book of Nature, and the Light of Nature, were the only things people needed to find the truth. Paracelsus' focus on the Bible as a basis for scientific thought may have encouraged some to adopt his philosophy, on the basis that, unlike the Renaissance Hermeticists, it wasn't based on pre-Christian thought. This allowed Paracelsus' ideas to be integrated into a heavily Lutheran context.

The philosophy of Paracelsus as it most concerns us here, intersecting with Boehme and the Theosophists, can be summed up under three headings. Paracelsus had unique opinions about the relationship of the Macrocosm to the Microcosm, about the Three Principles of Alchemy, and about the idea of a life giving energy, or spirit, in the world.

Like the Renaissance Hermeticists, Paracelsus declared that man was a small version, or microcosm, of the whole, meaning that the principles of the planets, the signs, and the faculties attributed to the celestial realm could be found in the human body and the human mind. Paracelsus, though, put his own spin and emphasis on the relationship between the two, pointing to the microcosmic nature of man as signifying man's great power in the universe, as opposed to signifying his subjection to astral influences. In this, Paracelsus echoes[22] the thought of Pico della Mirandola in his "Oration on the Dignity of Man", which declares that man contains within him all the potentials of nature, and that he can make use of them as he wishes[23]. In the philosophy of Paracelsus, man is radically independent, and possesses a fragment of the Book of Nature within himself[24].

Paracelsus' idea of the Microcosm was intimately associated with his idea of a Book of Nature, and with the Light of Nature derived from it. The idea of Nature as a book within which people could read eternal principles was a development of the medieval notion that theological principles could be seen manifested in nature. These thinkers were more poetic than Paracelsus. An example of their notion of the Book of Nature is that of the meaning of the Rose. The Rose was thought to have been created with thorns to demonstrate that the pain of the thorns were necessary to get to the beauty of the flower, an allegory for the suffering and resurrection of Jesus. The "Book of Nature" contributes to "The Primacy of the Mythic"[25], which Faivre describes as an essential part of the Theosophic current, within which Paracelsan thought would play a large part. Paracelsus partially scientificized the idea, making it amenable to occult interpretations.

The "Book of Nature" in Paracelsus' thought is the same as the Macrocosm, and reading the "Book of Nature" is the same as gaining an understanding of the Macrocosm, which is used to understand the Microcosm. Paracelsus very forcefully argues in his "Paragranum" that the physician needs to find explanations of what happens in the body through looking at what happens in nature[26]. What this means is finding parallels between natural processes and biological phenomenon. For instance, Paraelsus finds a parallel between an earthquake and severe fevers, which can lead to trembling[27]. This preserves the metaphorical nature of the medieval "Book of Nature", but changes the emphasis from religious symbolism to physical phenomenon.

Now, Paracelsus' understanding of the relationship between the Macrocosm and the Microcosm wasn't functional but cosmological. The functional interpretation is closer to the thought of Ficino and other Renaissance Hermeticists who saw the influence of Divinity or God working from the top down, as being transmitted to the earth through astrological influence, among other methods. In this, the main Macrocosm is a combination of the zodiac and planets with a basic understanding of the elements. This has the potential for ignoring Nature taken as a whole, which presents itself as a greater thing than the sum of elemental and astrological signatures.

Paracelsus' ideas are cosmological in that he doesn't rely on astrological influence for the functioning of the universe, but implies that the correspondences of the Microcosm to the Macrocosm were introduced in the creation of humanity. They appear as a physical fact. While the Macrocosm and the Microcosm correspond, in this picture there aren't causal rays connecting the two. We have the signatures of stars, as well as plants, within us, which correspond to properties in the body, but this does not mean that the stars therefore act on these signatures through rays. Paracelsus, despite admitting some astrological influence on diseases, specifically says that "Their radii have no impact on the human being"[28], where "radii" is a synonym for rays. Practically, this stance appears to have contributed to an understanding of the Macrocosm by later authors that didn't focus on the stars so much as on the earth as a whole, with the earth itself seen as a functioning being whose action was parallel to that of the human body.

The "Book of Nature" also leads into the "Light of Nature". Paracelsus was a great supporter of experimental knowledge, and, in giving an example of how craftsmen find the principles of their trade, uses the term "Light of Nature" to describe the guidance that nature gives the individual who conducts an experiment. The results of the experiment, and the consequences that can be drawn from it, contain the guidance of the Light of Nature[29]. This activity, experimental activity, can be seen as "Reading" the "Book of Nature" and letting the "Light of Nature" therefore guide the individual. What this also means is that by conducting experiments, those metaphorical parallels between the Macrocosm of Nature and the human body are discovered, and finding these parallels is a manifestation of guidance from the "Light of Nature".

The preference for the power of the Microcosm by Paracelsus may have also been influenced by his Protestant beliefs, such as "Scriptura Sola", the belief that people only need the Bible combined with guidance from the Holy Spirit to understand Christianity. As Weeks says, the idea of man as book, and nature as a book, parallels the Lutheran idea of the Bible as a book that anyone can read[30]. This would be the Bible in the vernacular, which in Protestant thought would be open without the need for intermediaries to guide the individual in interpretation. This, no doubt, was one of the factors that contributed to the popularity of Paracelsus with the mostly Protestant Theosophers.

In this way, also, Paracelsus set the stage for what Antoine Faivre describes as the three fold connection in Theosophy between God, Man as Microcosm, and Nature[31]. What appears to be unique is that all three of these factors appear in Theosophical thought. Most practical occultism, though at times concerned with the super-celestial realm, can be said to focus more on the Microcosm in concert with Nature than on God. Theology, on the other hand, sees the relationship of Man with God as being primary, sometimes not devoting as much time to Nature. Praising all three, the Book of Nature, God, and the Microcosm, as well as the potential relationships between them, combines the two approaches into one.

Next, Paracelsus developed a doctrine of three basic alchemical principles, Salt, Sulphur and Mercury. This was in opposition to the prevailing notion, which according to Debus was based on the two substances of Sulphur and Mercury[32]. The three principles included and went beyond the physical substances they were named after. The spiritual Salt, Sulphur, and Mercury, were flexible enough principles that they were thought to be located spiritually within substances that didn't have physical Salt, Sulphur, or Mercury in them. They also were separate from the elements of water, fire, earth, and air. These too were considered in metaphorical, spiritual, terms, but they also appear to have been regarded as an outer reality within which the inner reality of the Principles was concealed. Debus reports that the three principles correspond to three different products that are generated in laboratories when a substance is distilled[33], and that this may have caused the prestige of the principles to greatly increase. Here, the presence of a hidden set of principles behind apparent nature may have suggested to Boehme a parallel with the spiritual reality that lay behind apparent reality. The alchemical principles were potent and living, and they could also be found in men as well.

Finally, Paracelsus believed in a pervasive life giving force. One of the theories that Parcelsus had about what made it function as a life giving force was that it possessed a substance called "Sal Niter", a kind of nitrous salt[34]. Sal Niter, in the literal sense, referred to a kind of Saltpeter that could be mined as the mineral Nitre. The "Sal Niter" was incorporated into Boehme's "Aurora" as the "Sallitter"[35]. Boehme's concept spiritualized the idea of the Sal Niter far, far, beyond what Paracelsus originally meant. Though successors to Paracelsus incorporated the concept of Sal Niter into that of the Anima Mundi, or the Spirit of the World, from Hermeticism, it was not originally incorporated into that idea.

The "Sallitter" or Sal Niter is a good example of Paracelsan concepts that are between alchemy and chemistry. Paracelsus invented these, based on experimental observation, to explain various aspects of the world. Sal Niter, or Nitrous Salts were not chosen by him at random. Instead, the nitrous salts of Paracelsus were likely linked to two phenomenon: gun powder[36] and fertilizers[37]. The explosive potentials in gunpowder suggested that there was a secret energy contained in the substance, while nitrous salts increased the yield of crops, and are still used today as fertilizers. Because they contained related substances, the life giving action of fertilizers could be seen as drawing from the same source of energy that caused explosions.

Also, air itself was known to be a substance, and people like Paracelsus were already theorizing that it could contain other substances within it[38]. Paracelsus theorized that the air contained a substance analogous to that contained in gunpowder, which nourished the body[39]. Though Paracelsus was mistaken about the nourishing element, at least physically, it is striking that much of the air we breath is in fact made up of inert nitrogen. Through this, Sal Niter proves to be something found in fertilizers, in gunpowder, in mineral form in the ground, and in the air.

Another similar term used by Paracelsus, and sometimes Boehme and his commenters, was Tartar, which was a negative principle consisting of congealed humours that appeared like a stone[40]. Like the Sal Niter, this too was taken from observation, in this case from the fermentation of wine[41]. Wine fermenting leaves a salt of tartaric acid on the walls of the wine cask. The fermentation of wine was thought to be similar to an alchemical transformation, in that it produced a living spirit from the grapes in the form of alcohol. Tartaric acid, by analogy would be an unhealthy byproduct of a similar process in human beings. This parallel process was thought to take place in the digestion of food, which played a much larger role in Galenic medicine than it does in current day medical thought.

One more Paracelsan concept that entered into Boehme's thought was that of the Archeus. The Archeus was a concept that Paracelsus developed in order to explain the complex functioning of the organs. As presented in Grame Tobyn's portrait of the Galenic worldview, the humours and their vessels were understood fairly straightforwardly[42], but the actions of the internal organs were more mysterious. As opposed to the world of the humors and their vessels, which were ruled by the elements, the more complex internal organs were under the control of "faculties" that in turn corresponded to the planets[43]. For Paracelsus the Archeus, actually several Archei, were coordinating intelligences that lived in, ruled, and directed the actions of internal organs like the liver and stomach[44].

Many of the functions of the internal organs in the Galenic worldview had to do with digestion. This included organs that today are thought to have nothing to do with digestion, like the Spleen and Pancreas. Food was considered to undergo different stages of digestion, fermentation, and combustion, in the process of transformation from the food we ingest to what is ultimately used for bodily nourishment.

* * *

Boehme and Freher were partially products of their age, and this means that they also took it for granted that their audience would be familiar with certain terms, particularly medical terms, that have since fallen out of use. While both Freher and Boehme spend quite a lot of time defining and working with the Paracelsan principles, many concepts from the Galenic system of medicine are much less defined. The Galenic system as a whole goes far beyond what's been described here, and reading up on it is highly recommended.

Graeme Tobyn's book "Culpeper's Medicine: A Practice of Western Holistic Medicine" is an ideal place to start. Nicolas Culpeper was a 17th century English physician and herbalist whose works became standard references in their time, and Tobyn does an excellent job in explaining their medical concepts to a contemporary audience. Another idea familiar to people of Boehme's time that has been lost is the pre-modern theory of vision. This says that what we see is generated by rays that come from our eyes, bounce off of objects, and then come back to them. There were variants of this theory that allowed light to come into the eyes but also said that the eyes generated a force that bounced off of objects and was received back into them.

Theosophy

Antoine Faivre describes Theosophy as a fusion between Christian contemplative traditions, Renaissance Hermeticism, and Paracelsan thought[45]. In Theosophy, techniques of Christian meditation and contemplation are fused with both the Renaissance Hermetic and the Paracelsan understandings of the Macrocosm and Microcosm, and the correspondences between them. This anchors Christian meditation and contemplation in the body as Microcosm, as the space in which visions take place. As such, what happens in contemplation and meditation can be seen as the interaction of forces present within the body, which in turn represent Macrocosmic principles. Because of this combination, something wonderful happens in the thought of Boehme.

By being anchored in the body, in the Microcosm, the inner perception now has access to the Macrocosm as well. This means that through the doctrine of correspondences, the inner spiritual vision can now examine, and unfold the meaning behind, the entirety of phenomenal reality. Everything can be linked together in a grand spiritual system—elements, alchemical principles, astrological principles, the five senses, bodily organs, humors, animals, vegetables, minerals, metals. This, in turn, can be linked with the perceptions of super-celestial reality, which is represented by the angelic realm, as well as sub-elemental reality, represented by the hell-like wrath universe where Lucifer and the demons dwell, to present a complete vision of the divine principles behind phenomenal reality.

Andrew Weeks points out another tension as fundamental to Boehme's thought, which may be said to apply in a limited form to Theosophy itself. This is the tension between the Scholastic, more conventional, Aristotelian Protestant thought of Boehme's day and the Platonic or Neo-Platonic, Hermetic, thought which also circulated during this time[46]. In Weeks' presentation, part of Boehme's writing is an attempt to reconcile the two, with Neo-Platonic ideas of secret animating spirits explaining the inner meaning present behind apparent Aristotelian reality. This, in turn, is linked with the Boehmean understanding of the difference between the "Stone Church" or dead church of the exterior world and the living spiritual reality, the true spiritual church, that exists behind phenomenal reality.

This theme can be merged with Faivre's, and taken one step further. The hidden Neo-Platonic, or Hermetic, life of the world could be experienced through visions and inner contemplation. By this, through a combination of Biblical study with interior contemplation anchored in the body, it would be possible to rightly read the "Book of Nature" as contained in the human body, and then use this as a jumping off point for the perception of the spiritual essence of the universe, as well as higher religious truths. This, though, would be anchored in communication with and guidance by the Holy Spirit. This linking of inner reality with outer reality conforms to the "Primacy of the Mythic" described by Antoine Faivre as one of the essential characteristics of Theosophy, along with the triad of God-Nature-Man[47]. In this, the mythic melds with the actual, represented by the "Nature" part of the Triad.

The series of visions and perceptions received, combined with the individual's personal spiritual development, would also eventually generate a kind of "Hiero-History", or sacred history, which would refer to events happening in the spiritual universe over time. This would be understood as the inner reality underlying the apparent events of the mundane world. That this type of Theosophic belief emerged in Protestant circles first is potentially connected to the doctrine of "Scriptura Sola", the belief that the only thing necessary for understanding the Bible was the Bible itself with guidance from the Holy Spirit.

This would likely be condemned as an example of how Protestant theology can go wrong by Catholic apologists. This is because "Hiero-Histories" of this kind, as well as many of the doctrines we've been discussing, are examples of spiritual guidance that has given birth to new revelations, which in one way or another conflict with acceptable Biblical doctrine. In that worldview, all of these things are examples of what can happen when Biblical tradition, how the Bible had been interpreted for centuries, is discarded.

More particularly, in relation to Theosophy in general, Antione Faivre labels Valentin Weigel as the direct precursor of German Theosophy, by the connection he made between Christian contemplative thought and Paracelsan ideas about the nature of the world[48]. Weigel's synthesis is well worth looking into, and common themes can be identified between his writing and that of Boehme's. It was objected by Charles Muses, the scholar of Freher, that Weigel could not have influenced Boehme because his writings were only published after Boehme had his fundamental mystical experience in 1600[49]. However, Andrew Weeks documents that Weigel corresponded with an individual in Görlitz, Boehme's home town. Weigel devoted a whole book, "Der Güldene Griff", or 'The Golden Grasp' to the functioning of the inner eye and to the possibility of reading the equivalent of the Book of Nature within the Microcosm[50].

Taking it one step back, though, Weigel in turn was elaborating on the thought of Johannes Tauler, who was a student of Meister Eckhart. Tauler added what could be called a roughly neo-platonic interpretation to Eckhart's inner mysticism, which prefigured in certain ways the synthesis that Weigel would produce. Tauler's neo-platonism comes out in his discussions of the path, and intermdiate world, between the individual and ultimate union with the Godhead, which, though not using the particular doctrinal points of neo-platonism, nevertheless recalls the intermediate world of emanations between ultimte Divinity and human reality characteristic of neo-platonism. Like Weigel, Tauler speaks too of the interior perception, and of purifying the mind, and withdrawing into that inner perception, so that wisdom and the Holy Spirit can come in, specifically mentioning it in a sermon produced for Christmas[51], as well as elsewhere.

Tauler, however, was writing in the 14th century, roughly two centuries before the Reformation, and was careful to limit the scope of the use of inner perception for guidance in his sermons. In Tauler's sermons, the advocacy of inner perception is balanced by appeals to obey the Church hierarchy and not to create innovations in practices and doctrines[52]. Weigel, on the other hand, puts his synthesis of inner perception and Paracelsan thought, as well as general Hermetic thought, into a stridently Protestant context, emphasizing that the insights into the spiritual universe produced by inner perception meant that individuals didn't need guidance from Priests, scholars, or other ecclesiastical figures in order to arrive at an understanding of Christianity and of the spiritual universe.

Weigel goes even farther than that, though. For Weigel, the fragment of the Book of Nature inside of man can supercede scripture itself. Weigel goes beyond "Scriptura Sola" to the reception of divine wisdom and insights into supernatural reality through inner perception, where Scripture is reduced to a testimony supporting what the heart knows[53].

Weigel, in "The Golden Grasp", presents a picture of cosmology where Adam was originally endowed with the full knowledge of both sacred and mundane reality[54], which was obscured when the Fall happened. All of Scripture, all of the laws that preceded Jesus, were reminders of aspects of this divine reality within that man had lost access to. This was still there, just waiting for something to catalyze it and bring it to the surface. With the coming of Jesus, the path for a full restoration of the divine image, which is the same as the knowledge of the Microcosm and the Book of Nature inside of Man, became possible[55]. Therefore, Weigel states that what's essential is to make contact with sacred reality and invite Jesus to come down into a person and sanctify the divine image within, opening the sealed book[56]. Once that is done, communion with the higher realities through meditation and inner perception is possible, and these experiences become more valid than outward scripture.

There are connections between this idea of the fragment of the Book of Nature as Microcosm and the idea of the Book of Raziel as the primal book of wisdom that Adam had access to in the Garden of Eden. In this, that particular book is the Book of Nature within the Microcosm.

Sophia.

The word "Theosophy" can be interpreted to mean "Theological Philosophy" or as a theology specially devoted to the figure of "Sophia" or Wisdom. This latter is a cosmological figure, a faculty or aspect of God which is, in various presentations, everything from an aspect of the creation of the universe, to the means of communication between God and man. I believe that the idea of Theosophy as a particular fusion of Theology and Philosophy, and as devotion to Sophia, are interrelated, and that they can both be traced in part back to the "Book of Wisdom", also known as "The Wisdom of Solomon". "The Book of Wisdom" is an extra-canonical book that was excised from the Anglican cannon, but that, according to Arthur Versluis, retained its importance in the Lutheran version of the Bible[57].

The main geographical foci for the theosophical authors of Boehme's time, and to a great extent after, were the German speaking, Protestant, lands. I believe that because of this, the "Book of Wisdom" was absorbed into the synthesis between inner Christian meditation and Renaissance Hermeticism that produced the Theosophical current as a whole. As Versluis says, it appears to be absolutely central to the understanding of Wisdom by the Theosophists.

Written in the first century A.D., the "Book of Wisdom" introduces Wisdom as a figure who inspires Solomon, and is connected to the general notion of the Wisdom of Solomon. Wisdom, in this case, includes both practical wisdom and religious wisdom. Of the types of knowledge that Wisdom can grant, the author describes knowledge of the functioning of the universe, of the world itself, how to be a good ruler, and how to be a good person. Wisdom, in this case, includes "Gnosis", if this is defined as religious or mystical knowledge, but goes far beyond it into non-mystical areas of knowledge. This capacity of Wisdom to grant knowledge is similar, but not identical to the idea of the Holy Spirit.

Like the Hermetica, the "Book of Wisdom" was also produced in a Hellenistic context. In fact, like Ecclesiastes, it appears to be influenced by Stoic philosophy, as well as Neo-Platonic philosophy. In particular, the list of types of knowledge that the spirit of Wisdom can grant includes subjects covered by the Hermetica, particularly by the Asclepius. A notable contrast, though, between the "Book of Wisdom" and the Asclepius is the extensive condemnation of idols in "The Book of Wisdom", but here as well, the details of why exactly the author thinks idols or statues are wrong implicitly contains elements of Hermetic thought.

This personification of Wisdom is not found in similar detail in other parts of the Bible. I believe that the unique aspects attributed to Wisdom in the "Book of Wisdom" suggested to receptive readers a secret, or obscure, tradition regarding the nature of divinity, one that was associated with a feminine aspect of God. There are parallels between the cosmology of the "Book of Wisdom" and the Hermetica as well, in that the Asclepius refers to the Cosmos as the second of God, or as the manifestation of God's potentiality, while the "Book of Wisdom" labels Wisdom as a mirror of divinity. If Cosmos is taken as a parallel of Wisdom, the manifestation of the potentials of God in it can be seen as a mirror of God, where the attributes contained in it are reflected. This is very similar to the notion of "Eternal Nature" in the thought of Freher and Boehme. There are also similarities between Wisdom and the Anima Mundi, or Spirit of the World, and it's very, very, possible that some writers may have combined the two concepts into one. I believe that all of this made the Book of Wisdom attractive to occultists and mystics of a Hermetic bent.

Valentin Weigel, for instance, fused the idea of Wisdom with that of the powers of the Microcosm. Specifically, in "The Golden Grasp", Weigel points to the Hermetic types of knowledge that Wisdom can grant, and says that what Wisdom actually does is activate the innate knowledge of these things that's contained within the Microcosm[58]. Wisdom in this telling doesn't simply instruct people on how to be a good person, a good governor, or a spiritual individual, but facillitates the remembrance of these sorts of knowledge that are already in the individual.

This attractiveness is also confirmed by Welling's "Opus Mago-Cabbalisticum", which has four sections labeled "Eternal Wisdom"[59], Although in the first chapter of the section on Wisdom, Welling identifies Wisdom with Christ, in the second chapter, "On the Seekers of Wisdom", Welling quotes from exactly the parts of the "Book of Wisdom" labeled here as "Hermetic", that indicate what knowledge Wisdom can give the seeker[60.] This is balanced against injunctions that the true Philosopher doesn't seek personal gain from the use of this knowledge, but instead seeks to use it to approach God and the divine realms in general, as the ultimate purpose of the work.

Another theme of Wisdom, comes from the incorporation of the Song of Songs into the tradition. The "Song of Songs" was allegorized in the Middle Ages to refer to man's relationship with divinity, with the longings of Sheba to Solomon interpreted as being the kind of spiritual longing necessary to truly unite with divinity. Through this, devotion to Wisdom in later texts assumed a love role that can be described as erotic in approach.

However, qualifications need to be made. Though the "Song of Songs" was allegorized as representing the individual's longing for union with God, the main allegorical commentaries, such as that of St. Bernard of Clairvaux, picture the individual seeking union with divinity as Sheba, not as Solomon[61]. Solomon is pictured as the groom that the aspirant desires and seeks union with. In this, Solomon is Wisdom, and Wisdom is an aspect of Jesus. However, this does not mean that those who adopted this position were advocating a homosexual interpretation of the union of the individual with Wisdom. Instead, the interpretation appears to not involve conventional gender at all.

There is another alternative, though, which is found in the writings of Boehme himself. In "The Way to Christ", as excerpted by Versluis in "Wisdom's Book", Boehme talks about the wooing of Sophia or Wisdom not in the erotic terms of the Song of Songs, but in terms reminiscent of the Troubadours and the tradition of Courtly Love[62]. Here, Sophia, Wisdom, is the granter of a kiss, while the aspirant is described by Boehme as a "Knight". In another example, in "The Three Principles", the rose serves as a gift that the Holy Sophia gives to an aspirant who reaches her[63]. This too draws from the tradition of Courtly Love where the aspiring knight would be granted a rose by the lady to which he was devoted.

Section II

Rosicrucians and Para-Rosicrucians

I believe that Dionysius Andreas Freher fits into the para-Rosicrucian current of thought. However, before going into that, I have to define what I mean by the term "para-Rosicrucian", and by the term Rosicrucian itself. I believe it's been established that there was no "Rosicrucian" organization. The "Rosicrucians" were a literary device that was accidentally released into the world as a truth. The "Fama Fraternitas", that is the first Rosicrucian document, circulated in manuscript form, until it reached the hands of Adam Haslmyr. According to McIntosh, Haslmyr first wrote a response to the Rosicrucians [1], which ended up being published before the Fama itself, and then passed the manuscript of the Fama onto one Benedictus Figulus, who arranged for it to be published[2], in 1614.

Johann Valentin Andreae most likely wrote the Fama Fraternitas as a story embodying the kind of values, spiritual, social, and otherwise that he would have liked to see exist. The "Fama", then, fits into the world of allegory, as well into that of utopian allegorical literature. Allegory in this case can be seen as a positive complement of satire. Writers used to produce fantastic satires, such as Gulliver's Travels and the works of Rabelais, that criticized society through the means of unrealistic stories where the situations the characters encounter, and participate in, are meant to portray the vices and failings of contemporary society. The same devices used in satire to criticize society can also be used to construct an ideal view of society, to construct a positive vision that contains values and ideals that the author would like society to reflect. This, though, is different than wanting to literally implement the structure of the allegory in reality. When read in this sense, the "Fama" and the other original Rosicrucian literature becomes much more comprehensible. In fact, Antoine Faivre in his essay "The Rosicrucian Manifestos [1614-1615] and the Western Esoteric 'Tradition'", looks at the first Rosicrucian pieces both from the perspective of literary history and from that of occultism[3].

However, saying that the Rosicrucians were fictional is not the end of the story. After all, Andreae lived in a specific period of time, and in a specific location, Tübingen in Germany, and the currents of thought that he wanted to promote were not invented by him. Instead, they were part of the broader world of Protestant mysticism, magic, alchemy, and medicine, of which he was also a part. Theosophy was a part of it too, as were Renaissance Hermeticism and Christianized Kabbala. Mention should also be made of the contemporary project of "Pansophy" or the unification and reconciliation of all knowledge into a coherent whole, which also contributed. Although the "Rosicrucians" themselves were fictional, the currents of thought that the "Rosicrucians" were based on were not.

What Andreae was doing, and the relationship which at first existed in the milieu where the Rosicrucian idea got started, can be seen as a parallel to how thematic categories of music, film, and art are sometimes established. Often, new genres of art, new artistic movements, don't formally name themselves or introduce points of common beliefs. Instead, the names and categories are often introduced from the outside, by writers and critics that are looking at the material, who see that something new is going on, and want to invent a category that describes what exactly is happening.

An example of this is the coining of the term "Jazz". The term was not invented by the musicians themselves, but was applied to what they were doing by an outside journalist. In fact, some of the musicians who played jazz objected to the use of the term, because at the time the word had a sexual connotation. Yet, despite objections, the term stuck, and evolved to refer to a group of musicians whose work had common characteristics.

I believe that a similar situation exists with the "Rosicrucians". Even though there was no Rosicrucian Brotherhood, nevertheless, esotericists, mystics, and magicians, existed whose work and thought fit with that which was described in the "Fama" and other documents. Because "Rosicrucian" was an invented category, many of these likely didn't adopt the term for themselves, and in some cases died before the Fama was written.

Where, on the whole, though, does Boehme intersect with the Rosicrucians? Theosophy was a core strand of the Rosicrucian idea, although the manifestos themselves were the product of the pre-Boehme Theosophical world. I believe that Johann Arndt was the pre-Behmenist Theosopher that Andreae was closest to. Boehme himself had his mystical experience and composed his first writings before the Rosicrucian fervor hit. However, while there may not have been an initial connection, Boehme's thought came to be integrated into that of the Rosicrucians of the 18th century.

What I believe happened was that those individuals who were pursuing the types of mysticism and magic that Andreae had first identified and lauded in the manifestos as "Rosicrucian" were swept up with the popularity of Boehme, as were many people of their time. When Boehme's writings burst onto the scene, he appears to have displaced other Theosophers such as Arndt as the main Theosophical focus of the current. Consequently, when individuals pursuing this kind of mystic thought decided to formulate themselves as actual Rosicrucians, with or without an overarching organization behind them, they naturally incorporated Boehme's thought into what they were doing.

The story of the Rosicrucians comes full circle in the self-labeled Rosicrucians of 18th century Germany. These were individuals and groups that attempted to found actual, Rosicrucian brotherhoods. On the one hand, these groups, particularly the "Gold und Rosenkreuzers", or Gold and Rosicrucians, were using a structure that didn't originally exist. On the other, the Gold and Rosenkreuzers can be convincingly argued to have developed from the original currents of thought that Andreae was describing, and praising, as "Rosicrucian" in the manifestos. In a way, the "Gold und Rosenkreuzers", though taking fiction as reality, were actually more Rosicrucian than many of the later self-identified Rosicrucian groups, because of their connection, and emergence from, German Theosophical, occult, and alchemical currents.

This is where Freher connects to the "Rosicrucian" tradition, and where the term para-Rosicrucian comes in. Though Freher never labeled himself a Rosicrucian, his thought connects to that of the Gold and Rosenkreuzers, and to the Rosicrucian current in Germany in the 18th century in general. The reasons include, but go beyond, Jacob Boehme's influence on the Gold and Rosenkreuzers.

To understand why Freher can be classified as a para-Rosicrucian, you have to look at his background. Dionysius Andreas Freher was born in Nurnberg in 1649 and died in London in 1728[4]. Before coming to London, Freher had already studied Boehme in the original German, and had made contact with Behmenist circles on the continent. Freher was loosely associated with the Philadelphian Society, although it appears that he kept his own opinions about Boehme. Indeed, Freher's familiarity with Behmenist philosophy impressed the Philadelphians, with Freher possibly looked on by them as someone who had a more thorough understanding of Boehme's philosophy, which could be shared with them. Consequently, Freher's great work, the "Serial Elucidations", was reported by Walton to have been written in response to questions about Boehme's philosophy by Behmenists in Great Britain.

However, while Freher may have been looked at as an interpreter of Boehme, he was also separated from Boehme's work by roughly a century, and came into the Theosophical world two generations later. This new context also shaped Freher's perspective, and I would argue that part of the clarity of Freher's interpretation of Boehme was also due to the benefit of several layers of Theosophical interpretation that had happened since the Boehme's original writings. Like everyone else, Freher was a product of his times, and those times also gave birth to Behmenist influenced Rosicrucian thought.

The overlap between Behmenist influenced Rosicrucian thought and Behmenism itself can be seen by a quote by Harmsen in his paper "Reception of Jacob Böhme and Böhmist Theosophy in the Geheime Figuren der Rosenkreuzer", about the "Secret Symbols of the Rosicrucians". Harmsen, in looking at the sources of the "Secret Symbols of the Rosicrucians", finds it significant that the graphical works of Freher, along with other Behmenists, weren't included[5]. Harmsen attributes this to the editors of the "Secret Symbols" possibly not wanting their work to be associated with any well known personality, in order to make the work non-partisan, as it were[6]. What's remarkable is that Harmsen takes it as a matter of course that Freher's graphical works would be appropriate for the "Secret Symbols", which we'll examine in more detail later. Instead of justifying why Freher's works might have been appropriate for the "Secret Symbols", Harmsen finds the question of why they weren't used a more interesting one.

Also significant is that while Freher was writing his "Serial Elucidations", Samuel Richter, also known as "Sincerus Renatus", published his work "Die wahrhaffte und volkommene Bereitung des philosophischen Steins der Brüderschaft aus dem Orden des Gulden und Rosen Kreutzes", or "The True Preparation of the Philosophical Stone, by the Brotherhood of the Gold and Rosy Cross", in 1710, which on top of alchemical speculations also included supposed statutes and laws of a "Gold and Rosicrucian" order. Freher wrote his "Serial Elucidations" between 1699 and 1712. Richter is described in McIntosh's "The Rose Cross in the Age of Reason" as a (potential) Pietist preacher who had "Paracelsan and Böhmistic views"[7]. Harmsen labels Richter's later book "Theo-Philosophia Theoretica-Practica" as a "Böhmist" work[8]. Richter's work was one of the initial spurs to the development of an actual "Gold and Rosicrucian" order.

Similarly, Richter also published the first volume of Georg von Welling's "Opus Mago-Cabbalisticum", which was both influenced by Boehme and influential on the actual Gold and Rosenkreuzer organization. This first volume of Welling's work, "On Salt", was apparently issued without the author's permission in 1719. Welling's full book, with all three volumes, plus appendices, was published in 1735, by one Chritsoph Schütz, described by Harmsen as a Radical Pietist influenced by Boehme[9], who also authored a book called "Die Güldene Rose", or "The Golden Rose", which though having a suggestive title was not a Rosicrucian work.

Though Freher never called himself a Rosicrucian, I believe that there is significant overlap between his explication of Boehme and the Behmenist thought that influenced 18th Century German Rosicrucianism. Freher, in this, provides valuable documentation about, and guidance within, a current of thought that is otherwise obscure in the English language, despite having produced a number of valuable and provocative works.

We can see the connection between Behmenist thought and the 18th century Rosicrucians by looking at three pieces of literature associated with the Gold and Rosenkreuzers, and with the Rosicrucians in general. One of these is Georg von Welling's "Opus Mago-Cabbalisticum et Theosophicum", another is the "Geheime Figuren", or "Secret Symbols of the Rosicrucians", published by Gold und Rosenkreuzer circles in 1784, although it has a long history preceding that. A third is a supposed list of "Secret Signs" of the Rosicrucians published by Franz Hartmann, that, on examination reveals itself to be derived from a work by Jane Lead. This document was part of a mass of material compiled by Hartmann as a "Key" to his edition of the "Secret Symbols", which, never published, was included as an appendix to "In the Pronaos of the Temple of Wisdom", published in 1890. We'll look at two sections from Welling's "Opus Mago-Cabbalisticum et Theosophicum" and three figures from the "Geheime Figuren".

As for the Gold and Rosicrucians themselves, they appear to have been the end result of a growing interest in Rosicrucianism and alchemy in the 18th century that was, in part, inspired by Richter's work. Christopher McIntosh has traced the influence of Richter's treatise on alchemy, with its supposed description of the statutes of the Rosicrucians, through manuscript works of individuals who pursued alchemy in a Rosicrucian context. Though there's a great likelihood that Richter's description of a Rosicrucian organization was fantasy, it appears to have inspired actual activity by individuals and small groups, who took up these statutes of Richter's Rosicrucians as their own. The next phase in the development of the Gold and Rosenkreuzers came with the publication of "Aureum Vellus", or "The Golden Fleece", in 1749, by "Herman Fictuld", a pseudonymous author.

Fictuld also talked about Gold and Rosicrucians, but connected the gold to a chivalric order connected to the Golden Fleece[10], which was supposedly the origin of the Rosicrucians themselves. In this interpretation, the gold of the Golden Fleece was a metaphor for the perfected gold of the great work of the alchemists. Like Richter, Fictuld's work appears to have served as a catalyst for people who wanted to pursue works like those of the "Rosicrucians", and to have built on Richter's work.

Finally, in the 1760s the Gold and Rosencreuzers emerged as a combination alchemical, theosophical, and Masonic organization in southern Germany, Austria, and lands held by the Habsburgs in central Europe[11]. In this, the various ideas about organization that were floating around in the world of the Rosicrucian theosophers and others combined with the rituals, organization, and grade systems of Masonry to create a solid organization. From its base in Austria and southern Germany it spread throughout the German speaking world, and then established branches in nearby Poland and further off Russia[12]. Christopher McIntosh lists 1,000 members as a plausible number[13]. According to surviving documents, the Gold and Rosenkreutzers applied a theosophical interpretation to their physical alchemy, seeing it as a means of spiritual realization. They also applied a theosophical, and alchemical, interpretation to Masonic ritual.

Repeatedly, Welling's "Opus-Mago Cabbalisticum" is labeled by scholars as a textbook of the order. This is most forcefully done in a paper by Westlund[14], who, in looking at the grades, rituals, and work, of the

Gold and Rosicrucians, states that from the grade of "Practicus", Welling's work was a textbook. Sunderland thereafter goes on to offer concrete summaries of just what alchemical work, and ideas, were associated with the particular practical grades of the Gold and Rosicrucians[15].

Much more could be said about other aspects of the Gold and Rosicrucians, especially concerning episodes at the court of Frederick the Great and his successor, but those are immaterial here, as this work is centered on the ground, on practice as well as theory, rather than on political intrigue. However, it is one of life's ironies that a current of thought associated with radical Protestant doctrine was smeared with the slander of being a tool of the Jesuits[16]. That charge was brought against the Gold and Rosenkreuzers as part of a 'culture war' that took place in the Prussian court between Rosenkreuzers who were champions of conservative politics and others who were champions of the radical Enlightenment, including members and supporters of the actual, as opposed to fictitious, Illuminati[17].

Opus Mago-Cabbalisticum

The structure and context of Welling's work is Theosophical, with influences from Boehme and others. The volumes of Welling's work, devoted to each of the Paracelsan Principles, Salt, Sulphur, and Mercury, start out with investigations into that Principle, both physically and spiritually, and end with theological material. The Principles in Welling's thought were also linked to Behmenist ideas. Welling's Salt is a non-dual substance that divides or decays into Sulphur, standing for Boehme's Wrathful principle, and Mercury, standing for Boehme's Light principle[18]. Welling's work has recently been translated into English and is available from Red Wheel/Weiser Books.

Welling's work, as embodied in Volume 1 of "Opus Mago-Cabbalisticum", can be looked at through the lens of natural philosophy and through the lens of theology and theosophy. The natural philosophy provides a picture of how the world currently works, while the theology and theosophy provide the background for that current functioning. First, let's look at the natural philosophy.

To begin with, there are terms in Welling's book derived from Paracelsan thought that make no sense unless you recognize the unique meaning Paracelsus put on them. The first book, on Salt, describes Salt as a life-giving agent[19]. It categorizes the different types of Salt, making it clear that the author is talking both about common table salt and about something higher. In actuality, Welling's concept of Salt is derived from that of Paracelsus' "Sal Niter", or Nitrous Salts, referred to before. The "Sal Niter" was thought to be the source of life, and was based on Paracelsus' observation of the action of nitrous salts on plant growth, as fertilizers, and as gun powder. However, as in Boehme, the idea of the Sal Niter does not appear in its original form, but has instead been fully fused with that of the Anima Mundi of Renaissance Hermeticism. Welling very thoroughly integrates the concept of the Sal Niter into a cohesive cosmological system.

Welling generalizes the powers of Sal Niter into the power of astral energy, and says that among other sources, the life giving power of the sun was due to Sal Niter streaming from the Sun onto the earth, through the medium of light[20]. The difference between the Anima Mundi and Welling's concept of the Sal Niter is that the Anima Mundi was thought to unite disparate phenomena across space, while the action of the astral or sidereal energy, on the other hand, was more localized, and its method of transmission resembled that of light, albeit in an invisible form. This astral or sidereal energy, was thought to be the medium for the influence of the stars, to contain the energies that sustain life, and to be the medium of magic. Stars and planets transmit the astral light to the earth, where it influences nature and humanity.

Welling presents a version of the functioning of the earth that echoes that of the human body. The Salt is transmitted to the earth by the sun, the moon, and the stars, and is absorbed through the oceans into the earth itself[21]. Then, it travels to the center of the earth, where the fiery core heats it like an alchemical furnace, which causes the salt to assume a solid form, whereupon it travels back to the surface[22]. Once it gets there, it serves as nourishment for vegetables[23], and through them, and the animals that eat them, it reaches human beings as nourishment. This parallels the process of digestion in the Galenic system, where the point is to take food from the outside of the body and transform it into a substance fit for nourishing the body itself.

The Theological system of Welling's "Opus Mago-Cabbalisticum" is understandable as a modification and elaboration on Boehme's Theosophy. To give an example of the similarities, what follows is a summary of the cosmology that Welling puts forward in Volume 1 of "Opus Mago-Cabbalisticum".

Welling sees the first manifest world as the throne of God, with Jesus standing in God's place, and like Boehme, sees the heavenly throne surrounded by seven spirits[24]. This is an upper heaven, with the original heaven of the angels created below. In creating this latter area, God creates the angelical world, with Lucifer as its center, through a Fiat, or declaration of the word[25]. After the creation, the archangel Sachariel, associated with Jupiter, was deputized to continue the flow of light from the Throne of Jesus to Lucifer, serving as a kind of pipeline for the sustaining light from the throne to the angelic world[26]. This angelic world itself was then suffused with both light and darker principles. Lucifer was originally king of this angelic realm.

When Lucifer decided to rebel, the pipeline was severed, which deprived Lucifer of the light, leaving him with only the dark principle[27]. He, and the dark principle were expelled from heaven, and the dark principle collapsed into itself, forming a thick chaos[28], which served as the first matter of the Earth[29].

However, in Welling's reading of the creation of the universe as described in Genesis, God separated Lucifer and his angels from the chaos and imprisoned them in the fiery world of the Earth's core[30]. He then raised up dry land from the remaining chaos and started creating anew[31], and the plants and animals that were created existed in perfection[32]. Here, you see the creation of Boehme's Third Principle, only described in a different way. Just like in the account of creation by Boehme, the original harmony of the angelic realm was destroyed, which lead to the realm itself being destroyed and separated into a wrathful principle and a light principle in the super-celestial realm of the angels, which were then reconciled to a certain degree to form a reconstituted Earth. Next, Welling deals with the Garden of Eden and the creation of man and woman. Like other commentators, Welling treats the exact relation of the Garden of Eden to the pre-Fall earth in an unclear way. The Garden of Eden is portrayed by Welling as occupying a space above the upper atmosphere of the earth[33], though likely underneath the Moon.

Through several different steps, Adam, and then Eve fell into the temptations of Lucifer, ate the fruit of the Tree of Knowledge, and were expelled from the Garden. They were expelled from the Garden to the earth, which at this point was still paradisal itself[34]. As an accompaniment to their expulsion, God cursed the earth, and this caused the spiritual harmony that had been created by God on earth to be broken. Welling describes the differences that existed between plants as they were first created, and as they existed after the curse, saying that before the curse, plants gave forth fruit easily, the fruit was very nourishing, and its spiritual essence was easily available, while after the curse, the spiritual nature of the same plants went inwards and concealed itself[35], making toil and labor necessary to get sustenance. This is basically a Behmenist version of the story of the Garden of Eden mixed with naturalistic scientific concepts current in Welling's day. The world after the Fall is still a mixture, but one which is not harmonious. It's one where Satan, previously contained in the center of the Earth, now has free reign over the Earth.

At this point, Biblical history starts, culminating with the coming of Jesus, who opens up the way for individuals to achieve spiritual regeneration[36], and who will regenerate the universe as a whole after severe purification by fire[37]. While Welling declares that all creatures will be redeemed in the end, that does not mean that the process of redemption will, therefore, be easy. Instead, Welling outlines a program of punishment as purification for the demons, and for Lucifer himself, which at its end will cause them to have repented of their ways[38]. After that, the world will be made anew in perfection. This is a fundamentally Universalist position, Universalism being a doctrine that says that ultimately all damned souls, and demons, will be redeemed and welcomed into Heaven.

Both Welling and his publisher, the Radical Pietist Schütz, were Universalists[39]. This tendency was shared both with Jane Lead and with two of the Philadelphian Society's followers in Continental Europe, Johann and Johanna Petersen[40]. Hessayon, in discussing Jane Lead's influence, comments on the reception and influence of her universalist beliefs on prominent German Pietists, including the Petersens, who went on to promote Universalism in the German speaking world. Francis Lee also translated one of the Petersen's works into English[41]. Commenting on the influence of Boehme on the Radical Pietists, McIntosh suggests that the influence of Boehme was responsible for the interest of some Pietists in alchemy[42]. Incidentally, Schütz' work was influential on the Ephrata Community of Pennsylvania, which, though not Rosicrucian, was certainly Theosophical, its founder Conrad Beissel being directly influenced by the writings of Jacob Boehme. Like Schütz, Beissel was also a Universalist[43].

Although Welling explains it in a different way, the basic structure of his account of creation and the Fall of Man is the same as what Freher outlines in his explication of Boehme, as well as what Boehme himself outlines. While the ideas are not identical, it's possible to figure out where Welling is coming from through taking Freher and Boehme as your base and working out from there. Just as the notion of "Salt" and its importance in Welling's thought is made clearer by the idea of Paracelsus' "Sal Niter", which helps to make sense of Welling's seeming inexplicable praise for the common substance, Boehme's philosophy, and particularly Freher's explication of it, helps to make order from the chaos, and aids in approaching and understanding Welling's work as a unified whole. The thought of the Philadelphians may also be helpful in this regard. Although

I do not classify the Philadelphians as para-Rosicrucians, it's notable that every single one of the major Philadelphians, that is to say John Pordage, Jane Lead, Francis Lee, and Richard Roach, wrote pieces using alchemical language, as we'll see in due time.

"Secret Symbols"

The "Geheime Figuren" or "Secret Symbols of the Rosicrucians" are notable because they incorporate Behmenist themes. Formally published in 1785, Theodor Harmsen has done a wonderful job of reconstructing their pre-history in his two essays "The Reception of Jacob Böhme and Böhmist Theosophy in the Geheime Figuren der Rosenkreuzer", and "Fiction or a much stranger Truth. Sources and Reception of Geheime Figuren der Rosenkruezer" where he he traces their history from manuscript circulation to print. The "Geheime Figuren" are figures that, in a complicated fashion, combine Theosophical, Alchemical, Rosicrucian, Christian, and Kabbalistic imagery and text into a series of diagrams describing the nature of the universe and of humanity's place within it.

The symbols in "Geheime Figuren" were taken from previously published sources, and developed over the course of decades, during which they circulated in manuscript form, with symbols added and revisions made along the way. The book was in circulation before the Gold and Rosenkreuzers existed. Harmsen points to the editors of the 1785 version as likely Gold und Rosenkreuzers[44], and theorizes that the editor made the "Geheime Figuren" more Behmenist[45]. Harmsen, after examining other alchemical authors, puts Boehme alongside Sendivogius and Basil Valentine as influences on the Gold und Rosenkreuzer's alchemical thought[46]. He also refers to a Gold und Rosenkreutzer publisher who issued an edition of Jacob Boehme's work in the same period that the "Geheime Figuren" were published[47]. Additionally, Harmsen also states that copies of emblems from the "Geheime Figuren" have been found copied in archival materials related to the Gold und Rosenkreutzers[48]. Harmsen has also traced one of the "Geheime Figuren" to an edition of Boehme's works printed by one Van Beyerland[49]. This is the "Gnaden-Wahl", which translates out into Mercy (or Grace) and Choice, which we'll look at below.

We'll look at three of the symbols in the "Geheime Figuren". I'm using the AMORC version of "Secret Symbols", as opposed to Hartmann's, because it's more complete. Unfortunately, two of the most Behmenist symbols are not found in Hartmann's edition. The "Geheime Figuren" as a whole aren't a unified system, but present at least three different, fundamental, versions of reality, of which the purely Behmenist is only one.

One of the most direct borrowings from Boehme comes in the figure on page 10 of the first part, headed by the words "Mercy, Choice, WilllliW" on the top of it. This is the "Gnaden-Wahl" referred to above. This plate has two parts. The first directly portrays the world of Wrath and the world of Light of Boehme, with a third circle composed of their intersections portraying the Third Principle of the universe. The text indicates that the dark world is the world of woe, while the light world is the world of good, and that on earth we have the choice of which principle, and which world, we want to honor. The second diagram portrays the planets that correspond to the hypostases in the dark and light worlds.

This diagram is located on the bottom of the page, and consists of a circle divided in half: the left half is dark, the right is light. Within that circle are seven other circles: three on one side, three on the other, and one in the center. The circles are labeled with planetary symbols. The planets associated with the dark principle are Saturn, Mars, and Mercury, while the planets associated with the light principle are the Moon, Venus, and Jupiter. The Sun stands in the center of the two principles, combining light and dark within it. This is exactly the way that Freher corresponds the planets with the light and dark principles of Boehme, which exist within Eternal Nature, with the Sun in the pre-Fall world acting as the reconciling principle. The dark principle is labeled as being of Fire and of God, while the light principle in the diagram is labeled as being of Light and of the Son.

This figure has a parallel with Freher's Paradoxical Emblemata #100[50]. Freher's figure represents the same information as the figure at the bottom of the diagram: a circle divided into two, with the light world on one side, and the dark world on the other, with the corresponding planetary hypostases. Paradoxical Emblemata #100 is different from the "Geheime Figuren" figure in that the light world is on the left side and the dark world is on the right, and instead of the sun in the center of the circle, it's towards the bottom on the center line. The trinity, represented by an eye in a triangle, is at the center. Considering that Harmsen has traced this symbol back to an edition of Boehme's work, it's possible that this Paradoxical Axiomata might actually have been based on the proto-type of this "Secret Symbol".

The same motif of the interpenetrating worlds or principles is also present in the diagram on page 6, labeled in English "Figurative Image of how within this World Three Worlds [are] within each other." This presents three very large circles, with the third produced by the interpenetration of the two. Additionally, the three worlds or circles are contained within a larger circle. Here, the dark world is associated with the realm under the earth, while the light world is associated with the heavens. The AMORC translation specifically says that the three worlds are the "heavenly world" and "hellish world" and "earthly Sun-World". The larger circle that contains the three is labeled "God", while the light circle is labeled "Jesus" and "God's Right Hand", and the dark circle is labeled "Lucifer" and "God's Left Hand". The part of the third circle where the Light circle overlaps is labeled "2nd. Principle", while the part of the third circle where the Dark circle overlaps is labeled "1st Principle".

This is modified version of Boehme's interpretation of the world, where the Wrath or Dark world is the first principle, and Light world is the second principle. The conflation of the Light principle with the Heavens and the Dark principle with the world under the earth echoes the scheme presented in Welling's "Opus Mago-Cabbalisticum". It appears to be an attempt, in both cases, to reconcile Boehme's mystical cosmology with a more practical physical one. Unlike in the previous diagram, there are no planetary or other astrological symbols.

The third symbol is "De Septeneriis Mysteriis", on page 29. It provides a fascinating variation on Boehme's philosophy in diagram form. Despite having the number seven in the title, the first thing that stands out is the fourfold symmetry of the diagram. The diagram consists of four figures, one inside of the other. Each figure is made out of circles. At the center is one circle. This circle is surrounded by four circles in a symmetrical cross form. These four circles are surrounded by eight circles, which in turn are surrounded by twelve. Each of the circles is labeled with the names of the Trinity, but there are variations in some of the names, which, though like the conventional names of the Trinity, aren't exactly the same.

What appears to be happening is this: opponents of Boehme, and of the Philadelphians, often accused them of promoting a quarternary, as opposed to a trinity, because of their veneration of Sophia as a principle. Lee, Freher, and others, went to pains to argue that this was not the case. Here, on the other hand, the creators of the diagram appear to have embraced the idea of a quarternary, composed of God the Father, the Son, the Holy Spirit, and Sophia, as opposed to the Trinity. They appear to have represented in their diagram the procession of this quarternary from unity into manifest reality. It starts with a single point, which generates the first four powers from it. These four generate eight, and the eight generate twelve. The twelve corresponds to the world of the zodiac. The names in the circles represent the particular hypostases of the quartenary. This diagram is related to one on page 57, that is labeled as having to do with the "Septenariis", and which provides more concrete information on the significance of the first figure.

The "Septenariis Mysteriis" illustrates how some of the basic ideas and approaches of the Behmenist theosophers can be altered and extended. I think that, fundamentally, while all of this might not be completely Behmenist, nevertheless, reading Freher, as well as Lee, gives one the tools to go further and to figure out the variations that people like the authors of the "Geheime Figuren" made within the field of Theosophy.

Eternal Wisdom

Welling's "Opus", as published in its full form, also contains an entire section devoted to Eternal Wisdom, which comes after the first three volumes. This is the Sophia of Theosophy, discussed earlier. Overall, this section agrees with the general Theosophical interpretation of Wisdom, and with the "Book of Wisdom", but diverges from that of the Philadelphians, and others, who traditionally saw Wisdom as a female figure. The last section of the work, a song in praise of Wisdom, goes in the opposite direction, explicitly labeling Wisdom as female and talking about the relationship of the seeker to Wisdom in ways that are very near to being explicitly erotic. However, it's not clear whether Welling himself inserted this, or if it was added by his publisher Schütz. Nevertheless, the Theosophical interpretation of Wisdom rises through the chapters before reaching a crescendo in the Song.

In the first chapter, "On Eternal Wisdom, What and Who It actually is", Welling unequivocally states that Wisdom is Christ[51]. This follows another train of thought that identifies Wisdom with the Logos, due to the latter's description as a power moving on the waters in the first chapter of Genesis. This moving power was assimilated to the movement of Wisdom portrayed in later documents.

In the next chapter, about the "Seekers of Wisdom", Welling presents Wisdom according to the Hermetic understanding of what knowledge Wisdom can grant the seeker. Welling quotes the "Book of Wisdom" itself, chapter 7, verses 15-22, reproduced here according to the New International Revised Version of the Bible:

> "May God grant me to speak with judgment,
> and to have thoughts worthy of what I have received;

for he is the guide even of wisdom
and the corrector of the wise.
For both we and our words are in his hand,
as are all understanding and skill in crafts.
For it is he who gave me unerring knowledge of what exists,
to know the structure of the world and the activity of the elements;
the beginning and end and middle of times,
the alternations of the solstices and the changes of the seasons,
the cycles of the year and the constellations of the stars,
the natures of animals and the tempers of wild animals,
the powers of spirits and the thoughts of human beings,
the varieties of plants and the virtues of roots;
I learned both what is secret and what is manifest,
for wisdom, the fashioner of all things, taught me."

This exhortation about what Wisdom can teach is followed in Welling by the statement that despite the potential worldly benefits of such knowledge, the true seeker of Wisdom seeks it for spiritual benefit, not for material gain[52].

Chapter Three is entitled, "By Which Means and in What Ways can Wisdom be Attained?". Here, even though Wisdom is identified with Christ, the means of approaching Wisdom are similar to that of previous Theosophists. Welling not only recommends prayer[53], but also states that we should approach Wisdom with a spirit of purity, suffering, and self-renunciation[54], in order for the seeker to become the bride and Wisdom the bridegroom , and unite in love[55]. In fact, Welling makes reference to prayers containing the "desire, longing, and moaning of the spirit in love."[56] This echoes the tradition of incorporating allegorized motifs from the "Song of Songs" into the devotional approach of the individual to Wisdom. What is unique here is that this desire and longing is specifically attributed to seeking the blessings of Wisdom, as an aspect of Christ, as opposed to simply seeking those of Christ himself.

There are also familiar themes from Weigel in the Third section, such as the necessity of retreating into a purified interior space and praying[57] for communion with the spirit of Wisdom[58], as opposed to looking for guidance in outward books, rituals, and traditions. Welling declares that the individual must become a "book yourself"[59].

The fourth section, the Song, or, 'Addendum', is labeled "A Song of Praise in Honor of Divine Wisdom". In this, Sophia is exclusively referred to as female, and not labeled Christ. Although at one point in the song the author refers to her as having a "loving mother's heart"[60], in other places he refers to "the embrace of your warm, loving breast"[61], her kiss[62], her beauty[63], to her eyes which "make my heart surrender"[64], as well as how "my passion cannot help but grow"[65]. The author also states that she should not put him to the test, but instead "let me suckle at your breast"[66], and later says that after he's passed on there will be a "wedding night" where "I shall embrace you as my wife."[67]

The "Song" is immediately followed by a selection of alchemical texts that Schütz announces he's adding himself. Because of these texts, as well as because of the difference in attitude between the "Song" and the rest of "Eternal Wisdom", it's unclear if the song too was added by Schütz. Schütz appears to have added unlabeled material in other cases, such as the preface to Volume 2, on Sulphur, which is essentially an advertisement for his book "The Golden Rose", and other writings.

Hartmann and the Philadelphians.

Though there are similarities between the Philadelphians and the continental Rosicrucians purely because they share a Behmenist background, there's also a direct connection between the Philadelphians and Rosicrucian thought: a Rosicrucian document published by Franz Hartmann's in his book "In the Pronaos to the Temple of Wisdom" derived from a work by Jane Lead.

As part of the appendix to "Pronaos", which is about Rosicrucians, Hartmann includes several documents purporting to be the statutes, aims, and laws of the Rosicrucians. One of these is "Secret Signs of the Rosicrucians"[68]. "Signs" in this case are not the same as "Symbols", but are moral qualities that a Rosicrucian should embody. Looking at it, surprisingly, it's directly derived from Jane Lead's "The Messenger of an Universal Peace or a Third Message to the Philadelphian Society", published in 1698. The "Third Message" contains sixteen points labeled "Marks of a True Philadelphian"[69]. It's prima facie apparent that Hartmann's text is derived from Lead's, with the word "Rosicrucian" substituted for "Philadelphian,", among other differences. The titles of the sixteen points are very similar. The explanations of the points in Hartmann's document are clearly derived from those of Lead's. I've reproduced the titles of Hartmann's text and those of Lead's, side by side, and have included the full text of both Lead's text and that of Hartmann's in the appendix. There, the documents are lined up, with point one of the Philadelphian text being followed by point one of Hartmann's Rosicrucian text.

Table 1
Comparison of Lead's document with Hartmann's.

1. A Philadelphian suffers long.
2. A Philadelphian is kind.
3. A Philadelphian envies not.
4. A Philadelphian vaunts not himself.
5. A Philadelphian is not puffed up.
6. A Philadelphian does not behave himself unseemly.
7. A Philadelphian seeks not his own.
8. A Philadelphian is not easily provoked.
9. A Philadelphian thinks no evil.
10. A Philadelphian rejoices not in iniquity.
11. A Philadelphian rejoices in the truth.
12. A Philadelphian conceals all things.
13. A Philadelphian believes all things.
14. A Philadelphian hopes all things.
15. A Philadelphian endures all things.
16. A Philadelphian never fails.

1. The Rosicrucian is Patient.
2. The Rosicrucian is Kind.
3. The Rosicrucian knows no Envy.
4. The Rosicrucian does not Boast.
5. The Rosicrucian is not Vain.
6. The Rosicrucian is not Disorderly.
7. The Rosicrucian is not Ambitious.
8. The Rosicrucian is not Irritable.
9. The Rosicrucian does not think evil of others.
10. The Rosicrucian loves justice.
11. The Rosicrucian loves the truth.
12. The Rosicrucian knows how to be silent.
13. The Rosicrucian believes that which he knows.
14. The Rosicrucian's hope is firm.
15. The Rosicrucian cannot be vanquished by suffering.
16. The Rosicrucian will always remain a member of his society.

Lead's "Third Message" was translated into German in 1698, and published as "Der Himmlische Bottschaffter eines Allgemeinen Friedens: oder Eine dritte Bottschafft an die Philadelphische Gemeine." What I think happened is this: Lead's writings were circulated in continental Europe, among the Theosophical community there, and this particular writing made its way into Theosophical circles that were also sympathetic to Rosicrucian thought, whereupon they adopted Lead's sixteen points and changed their vocabulary to reflect the Rosicrucian context. Somewhere along the line they were rewritten. Eventually, Hartmann got access to them. Though it's possible that they both came from acommon source, I believe that Lead's text is the source of Hartmann's, because the explanations that are given in Lead's text are much more thorough and composed than in Hartmann's document.

Hartmann states that these "Secret Signs", along with the other material in the section, were originally going to be part of a book called "Key to the Secret Symbols of the Rosicrucians"[70], which would have been a companion to Hartmann's edition of the "Secret Symbols". Hartmann, in his introduction to this material, quotes Blavatsky as saying that the "Golden and Rosy Cross"[71] are a powerful spiritual brotherhood. Also, Hartmann, in the introduction to his edition of the "Secret Symbols" themselves, speaks of the "Brothers of the Golden and Rosy Cross" as true adepts[72]. I believe that it's very possible that Hartmann got this material, as well as the other material in this section of "Pronaos", from manuscript sources and/or very obscure books relating to Rosicrucian circles, possibly from those related to the Gold and Rosenkreuzers themselves.

However, there are complications with this, which make little sense. Namely, that despite emphasizing the "Gold and Rosicrucians", Hartmann in "Pronaos" dismisses the Gold and Rosenkreuzers around the court of Frederick the Great as "Pseudo-Rosicrucians"[73]. This has to do with the political events around the Gold and Rosenkreuzers referred to earlier. It's possible that Hartmann, who was a leader of Blavatsky's Theosophical Society, felt that these individuals weren't "True" Rosicrucians. His introduction to the "Secret Symbols" repeats the Theosophical Society doctrine about the Rosicrucians, which links them to a long line of adepts that preceded Andreae and the manifestos of the early 17th century , so it's possible that in his mind there were other criteria by which to judge whether or not one was a "True" Rosicrucian, other than being a member of a Rosicrucian organization.

Introduction 41

If Hartmann didn't derive the document from a Gold and Rosenkreuzer or other Rosicrucian source, a number of perplexing questions present themselves: Why, out of all the documents available, would Hartmann pick this one? Why would he then take it, rewrite parts of it, and substitute "Rosicrucian" for "Philadelphian"? Both docuements are available in German, and comparing the two shows deep differences between the texts, which suggests that Hartmann did not just come across Lead's document and repurpose it for his work. Hartmann did write a book about Jacob Boehme, and presumably had access to a variety of Behmenist Theosophical writings, and Jane Lead's writings did circulate in Europe, but even taking that into account, picking this section out of a book by an English Behmenist still looks like plucking a needle from a haystack. If Hartmann wanted to adapt Theosophical documents to the Rosicrucian cause, surely there would be closer ones at hand.

Section III

The Philadelphian Society, Lead, Pordage, Lee, and Freher.

The Philadelphian Society was a theosophical group at the end of the 17th and the beginning of the 18th century, headed by Jane Lead, Francis Lee, and Richard Roach. The Philadelphian society was officially launched in 1697 when Jane Lead decided to present her revelations to the public and engage in a public ministry. In scholarship, the beliefs and history of the Philadelphians have been chronicled by Arthur Versluis in "Theosophia", "Wisdom's Children" and "Wisdom's Book", the last of which contains excerpts from both the Philadelphians and a wide variety of other Theosophists. Versluis' books are absolutely foundational for our understanding of the Philadelphian Society and Theosophy as a whole.

However, these books were published between 1994 and 2000. With the possible exception of Adam McLean's excerpts from Philadelphian thought on the "Alchemy Website", as well as graphical works from Freher issued by McLean through "Magnum Opus Sourceworks", as well as excerpts from Philadelphians in Richard Faas' anthology "The Divine Couple", there appears to have been a very long dry spell in scholarship and publications devoted to the group. Happily, this has recently changed.

What has changed is the publication of the landmark book "Jane Lead and her Transnational Legacy", a collection of papers produced in the wake of an academic conference about Lead. Edited by Ariel Hessayon, who also contributes three papers, the book is essential reading for anyone who wants to understand the origins, flourishing, and outcome of the Philadelphian society. Notice should be taken also of Paul Kléber Monod's groundbreaking work on British occultism in general in the 17th-18th centuries, "Solomon's Secret Arts", which also treats the Philadelphians within their greater historical context, as well as Gibbons's "Gender in Mystical and Occult Thought". The latter book presents a great deal of primary research about the backgrounds of the main Philadelphians, although its scope is restricted. Much of what follows is taken from the research of Hessayon, as well as from the paper in "Jane Lead" by Lionel Laborie[1] about the later years of the Philadelphian Society.

History of the Philadelphian Society.

The history of the Philadelphian Society can be broken down into two phases: that of the proto-Philadelphians, who existed before the society was formally established in public, and that of the Philadelphian society proper.

Each of these two phases was dominated by a man, in combination with women who served as prophets: John Pordage, in the first phase, and Francis Lee in the second. Mary Pordage and Jane Lead were the prophetesses of the first period, and Lead served as the main prophetess of the second period.

Pordage was a preacher and religious radical during the English Civil War years and the Interregenum, between the winning of the Civil War by Cromwell and the Restoration of the monarchy. Pordage continued his radical preaching afterwards. Lee, on the other hand, was an Oxford educated theologian who had made contact with Behmenist groups during wanderings in continental Europe[2] prior to contacting Lead back home. Similarly, Dionysius Andreas Freher was also a highly educated scholar who had studied Boehme in the original German, and also had contact with continental Behmenist groups before moving to England. Because of this, while Lee approved of and collaborated with Lead, the writings of Lee himself, as well as those of Freher, are somewhat separated from those of Pordage and Lead.

However, looks can be deceiving. Although Pordage was a preacher and someone who participated fully in religious radicalism, he too was an educated man. Pordage also graduated from Oxford with a doctorate in divinity[3], and had gone to Leiden in the Netherlands to study medicine[4], as had Lee. Though he may not have gotten a degree in medicine[5], according to Arthur Versluis, Pordage in his later years partially made his living as a doctor and an herbalist[6]. I believe that the difference between Lee and Pordage comes from Pordage being fully engaged with millenarian faith, receiving visions, prophecies, talking to angels, encountering demons that are fought against, perhaps witnessing miracles, and Lee, whatever private spiritual practices he engaged in, not being motivated by the same type of spirit.

That the difference appears to have been in basic orientation towards spirituality can also be seen by comparing the career of Lee with that of his co-leader in the Philadelphian Society, Richard Roach. Roach, like Pordage, was an Oxford educated doctor of divinity[7], but unlike Lee he threw his lot in with the French Camisard prophets in the years after Lead's death. Thes French Prophets were religious refugees from France who had a spirited religious life that resembled the radical millenarians of Pordage's time.

Pordage was appointed vicar of the parish of Berks in Bradfield in the 1650s, and a group of spiritual devotees grew around him who were sympathetic to a mystical and millenarian version of Protestant spirituality. This group included his second wife, Mary, who was prone to mystical visions and served as a prophetess for the group. During this time, Pordage hosted some of the most radical Protestant millenarians of his day. These included Abiezer Coppe, who was one of the leading Ranters, as well as the Digger William Everard, and the translator John Everard, among others[8]. The activities of Pordage's group as well as his visitors were so scandalous that they lead to an inquiry being formulated, and Pordage's dismissal from his ministry.

What the Church found objectionable appears to have been what can only be called a full-scale engagement with the spirit world on the part of Pordage and his associates. This includes receiving visions, talking to angels, having angels appear, prophecies, spiritual battle between demons and angels, and manifestations of poltergeist like activity[9]. It also included accusations that Pordage and his wife Mary saw themselves, at least for a period of time, as being embodiments of various Biblical figures[10], which might be interpreted as having these figures speak through them. Other accusations were that Pordage conjured demons, denied the divinity of Christ, and fathered an illegitimate child[11]. This was too much, even during the Interregenum, when the Puritans and Parliament dominated the country, and when the monarchy had been abolished. Pordage wrote several pamphlets in his defense, including "Innocensie Appearing", but they were not successful. It should be noted that, being born in 1608, Pordage's time at Berks was not one of youthful enthusiasm. The trial happened in 1654, when he was 46 years old.

Raymond in "Conversations with Angels" reproduces parts of "Innocensie Appearing", as well as Pordage's testimony, that indicates there were Behmenist aspects to his belief at this early period[12]. In particular, a large section of Innocensie Appearing talks about the Dark World and the Light World of Boehme, and gives interpretations of what happened at Bradfield that cast it as a battle between the forces of the Dark World and the Light World.

It's notable that the parish Pordage was appointed to was endowed by the alchemist and antiquarian Elias Ashmole during Pordage's time there, but it appears that Ashmole kept his distance from Pordage. Among other differences, Ashmole was a monarchist, and is cast as a crypto-Catholic by Tobias Churton[13]. Yet, Ashmole remarked on Pordage's knowledge of "astronomy", which in this context means astrology[14]. According to Monod, Ashmole also sent Pordage a gift of a copy of his English translation of "Fasciculus Chemicus", an alchemical treatise by Arthur Dee, John Dee's son.

After losing his position at Bradfield, Pordage moved to London, where he lived until temporarily reappointed to his former position. This, ultimately, ended in 1662, after the Restoration, when the "Act of Uniformity" was passed, which dictated that clergy in the Church of England had to use the Book of Common Prayer. Previous to this, a much wider lattitude of beliefs was allowed to the clergy. The "Act of Uniformity" caused a great nunmber of clergy to be kicked out of the Church, and established the term "Nonconformist" as the label for the new Protestant denominations formed by these clergy in wake of the act. Subsequently, Pordage moved back to London[15] with his wife, and most probably with some of his children. Versluis describes Pordage's London years as ones of much hardship[16].

It was in London that the circle that would eventually give rise to the Philadelphian Society was formed. There was continuity between this group and the group at Bradfield because, at the very least, Mary Pordage was also a member, and appears to have remained a leading visionary. Mary Pordage passed on in 1666, and two years later, in 1668, Jane Lead, who had also recently been widowed, became one of the central members, and a visionary. Lead had been associated with the circle in some capacity since 1663[17]. She moved into a collective housing arrangement with Pordage and other members of the community[18], and, though chaste, appears to have eventually become a spiritual partner to Pordage. She stayed with Pordage till the end of his life[19].

That the millenarian environment of Pordage's time at Berks was carried over in some capacity to Pordage's later groups, ultimately influencing Lead, can be seen from the "First Message to the Philadelphian Society", published in 1696, which declared that the Philadelphian Society was the seventh Church mentioned in Revelations, but that the

Fifth Monarchy Men were the fifth[20]. The "Fifth Monarchy Men" were a radical millenarian sect in and after the English Civil War that agitated for the execution of Charles I as necessary for clearing the way for the coming of the millennium. Not only that, but the Anabaptists are listed as the fourth church[21]. Interestingly enough, in the third message to the Philadelphian society, published two years later in 1698, the identity of the seven churches is removed from the context of the English Civil War and put into a global one, with the orthodox churches as well as others named as predecessors.

Pordage passed on in 1681, but already at that time some of the literature generated by the circle had started to be published. Jane Lead's book "The Heavenly Cloud" appeared in the year of Pordage's death, and Lead's book "Revelation of Revelations" appeared within a year after[22]. Pordage's own writings were collected in "Theologia Mystica" and printed in 1683. There are questions, however, about how faithfully what appeared in "Theologica Mystica" actually represented Pordage's thought. Joad Raymond, in "Conversations with Angels", cites an unpublished version of the book located in the papers of a Philadelphian at the Bodleian Library in Oxford, which states that part of "Theologia Mystica" is just a summary of manuscripts by Pordage written by others[23]. Presumably, the manuscript this is contained in includes a fuller version of "Theologia Mystica".

Nevertheless, the work of the Philadelphians started to circulate. It appears that after Pordage's demise, the proto-Philadelphians consisted of four groups, or congregations, loosely associated with each other[24]. The next phase in the evolution of the group was made possible by the international circulation of Lead and Pordage's writings within the European Theosophical community. Connections were made with Theosophical groups in the Netherlands, and Hessayon has labeled the husband of one of the prominent female proto-Philadelphians, Anne Bathhurst, as the likely individual who introduced Lead and Pordage's writings to the community there[25]. This was John Bathhurst, a merchant whose business took him to the Netherlands.

Members of the Theosophical community there must have been impressed by the writings, because one of the readers wrote to Lead, striking up a correspondence which also lead to the translation of her works and those of Pordage into German[26]. This was a Baron Knyphausen, who also paid for both the translating of Lead and other Philadelphian's writings in German and Dutch, and their publication in general. These translations appear to also have made an impression.

What appears to have happened next is that, sometime later, a young doctor of Divinity named Francis Lee was engaged in an extended tour of the Continent, where he also studied medicine in Leiden, and practiced medicine in Venice[27]. During his stay on the Continent, Lee also made contact with Theosophical circles that had copies of Lead's work, and that introduced him to it. Lee liked what he read, and when he returned to England he looked the author up. At the time that Lee contacted Lead, she was living in a home for aged widows, with her living provided by a charity that sponsored the women[28].

Lee and Lead began a collaboration that would first produce many books by Lead and then the Philadelphian Society itself. Lead appears to have had quite a lot of unpublished writings, which consisted both of treatises, and of diary entries that she compiled with John Pordage. Lee edited these and, with the help of the Baron on the Continent, arranged for them to be published[29]. Lee also attracted at least one acquaintance from Oxford to the group, Richard Roach, who would go on to have a major role in the Society. Lee also married one of Jane Lead's daughters, which is the reason why in writings such as his letter to Dodwell, Lee occasionally refers to Lead as 'Mother'[30].

It appears that many of Lead's published writings were composed during Lead and Pordage's collaboration. This includes the spiritual diaries that were published in several volumes as "A Fountain of Gardens". Sarah Apetrei, in her contribution to "Jane Lead and Her Transnational Legacy", reproduces some very rare manuscript fragments by Lead from the time that "A Fountain of Gardens" covers, and while tentative, they suggest that the original revelations as recorded by Lead differed from what was eventually published. As part of her research, Apetrei also reproduces a manuscript fragment by Lead where she appears to make reference to Pordage and others making additions to her texts[31], saying that others, presumably Pordage, can do a much more efficient job of explicating her texts than she could.

It should be noted that Lead isn't objecting to their explications. Instead, she appears content to let them explicate them, noting that it would take a lot of time for her to do the same thing. While Lead may have approved of it, this manuscript fragment does suggest that many of Lead's writings were collaborations between herself and Pordage. I should add that the evidence doesn't indicate what sort of working relationship the two had. While it's possible that Pordage altered Lead's writings according to his own ideas, it's also possible that Pordage and Lead, as longtime collaborators, had worked out an understanding of the meaning of the visions, and that Pordage was putting interpretations into Lead's work that she agreed with. Additionally, Lead's writing didn't stop with the demise of Pordage.

On a more personal level, whatever the provenance of "A Fountain of Gardens", the entries in the diary are often very profound and beautiful statements about spirituality. It's also possible that some of her later writings were influenced by her work with Francis Lee, and, while this is speculation, I believe that some of her later writings, such as "The Laws of Paradise", reflect Lead moving away from the interests of Pordage and towards those of Lee.

What appears to have happened next is that in 1696 Lead experienced a vision of the holy Sophia, or Holy Wisdom, who commanded her to form a public group that would serve as the groundwork for a coming Church. This church would be last church of the ages, that would gather up all the fragments of Christianity into itself, and set the stage for the end times[32]. Holy Wisdom referred to this church as the Philadelphian Church, taking the name from the last of the churches mentioned by St. John in the Revelations. This was integrated into a prophecy that talked about six predecessor churches that had paved the way for the Church of Philadelphia. Some time later in the year, Lead experienced another vision of Wisdom that gave her further instructions. The two revelations were published as "A Message to the Philadelphian Society, Whithersoever dispersed over the whole earth." in 1696, and the actual Philadelphian Society was announced to the public in 1697.

The sense in which they were to be organized as a Church appears to have included an inner structure, as well. Wisdom announced, in the "First Message to the Philadelphian Society", that the Church would have an anointed priesthood[33], and that it would have established oracles[34]. Propsition 35 of the "Forty Four Propositions extracted from the reasons for the foundation and promotion of a Philadelphian Society" clarifies this. It states that ther will be a Priestly Order, a Prophetical Order, and a Royal or Davidical Order[35].

The 1701 reprint of Lead's "Revelation of Revelations" also provides more concrete information on the three orders. This comes in sections added to the new edition, one at the end of the main text, the second in the form of questions by readers appended to the main text. The first section, from pages 165-166, gives advice to the members of the first and second orders, while the seond, from page 188-190, consists of questions about the use of the term "Magi" as well as about the orders themselves, which are answered[36]. The idea of three orders of priesthood preceded the Philadelphian Society—it can be found in the original edition of

"Revelation of Revelations", where it's associated with the "Melchizadeck Priesthood"[37]. However, it appears that the concept at that point was not codified in the way that it would later become. In the "Postscript" to the "First Message", Lead declares that the church will have a "strict law and discipline" for believers[38]. The "Messenger of An Universal Peace, or a Third Message to the Philadelphian Society" is more explicit. Here, you have a catechetical section called "Marks of a True Philadelphian", which consists of 16 statements such as "A Philadelphian Thinks No Evil" and "A Philadelphian Seeks Not His Own"[39], which have explanatory paragraphs attached to them outlining the meaning of the statements.

Laborie, in looking at documents and diaries from Roach and others, paints a picture of the state of the proto-Philadelphians before their public announcement. They were divided into four groups, or congregations, who were grouped geographically in similar neighborhoods in London and met regularly[40]. Hessayon, in talking about Lead's decision to form a public group, points to Lead as primarily representing one of these groups, not all, and also points to dissatisfaction from other members in the formation of the Philadelphian Society[41], which also saw Lead assume the status as the primary prophet of the Society for the public. Of the four groups, one, the "Bow Lane Church", that was anchored by Radical Quakers who had become Philadelphians, objected so much that they essentially separated from the other three. The "Bow Lane Church" is sometimes called a successor to the Philadelphian society but in reality was a proto-Philadelphian group that went on its own way.

As opposed to their previous private theosophical study circles, the Philadelphians organized public meetings, which look suspiciously like Church services, where the message was shared and where the Philadelphians explained their beliefs to the public. These were, presumably, Behmenist. Also during this time works by Pordage that were never printed in English were translated into German and Dutch and published on the Continent. During this time the Society also started a magazine, called "Theosophical Transactions". Hessayon states, that while the name "Transactions" might seem somewhat scientific, another possible interpretation of the name is as "Actions" in the sense of the "Acts of the Apostles", one of the books of the New Testament[42]. "Theosophical Transactions", which is at present a very rare publication, appears to have been strangely heterogenous, and to have included references to ceremonial magic as well as Theosophical doctrine.

Commentators on the Philadelphians, as well as on related Theosophical groups, almost unanimously point to the public, formalized, nature of the Philadelphian Society as causing problems within the greater Theosophical community. The idea of forming an outward Church was very much frowned upon by the greater Theosophical world. It was also something that Lee himself would deny the Philadelphian Society was doing in his defenses of the society. The Theosophical movement grounded itself in part on being a non-sectarian movement where what was important wasn't formal creeds but instead inward work and contemplation.

Why the Theosophers felt that forming Churches and Denominations was wrong can be seen in Valentin Weigel's treatise "The Golden Grasp". In it, Weigel distinguishes between different "Eyes", or faculties, with the highest being that which perceives spiritual reality, and the second highest being reason[43]. Weigel strongly condemns sects as being an outcome of individuals using the rational eye, or rational understanding, rather than the eye of spiritual understanding[44]. Weigel states that individuals who perceive things through the mystical eye have no disagreement among themselves[45]; they all perceive the same religious truths through direct experience. It's only when people turn away from this direct experience, and start examining scripture and doctrine according to the rational eye that disagreements come.

Weigel contrasts with the perception of the real living spirit behind scriptural passages and the perception of the form alone, and says that, when reading scripture rationally, anyone can use passages to justify any position, but that this process of justification misses the point[46]. It misses the point because reason cannot solve theological questions. Only the perception of spiritual reality, and the perception of the spirit behind the scriptures, can provide concrete answers to them. Weigel intimates that this knowledge of spiritual reality is such that individuals who perceive it will not fixate on language and unnecessary worldly arguments. This fits in well with the emphasis in Theosophy on metaphorical and symbolic understandings of scripture and of religious principles in general, which by their nature are inexact.

Jane Leade's messages from Sophia, then, instructing her to found the Philadelphian Society, could be seen through this lens as evidence that Lead had fallen away from the true perception of things, and instead had become dominated by concerns from the rational faculty. On the other hand, the messages that Lead received instructed her to build a universal church from the various churches that were in existence, in preparation for the Millenium, which isn't quite the same as simply forming a new denomination. It does, though, require that those who subscribe to it believe that the end of the world is imminent, and that Lead was the one person chosen out of all of humanity to deliver this message of the need for the formation of the final church.

Versluis, in "Wisdom's Children", makes the case that some of the resentment to the Philadelphians in the greater Theosophical community was produced by an intermediary between the Philadelphians and the Dutch communities who apparently believed that the Philadelphians already were a Church, and who asked his Dutch contacts to sign up as affiliates. Versluis believes that the emissary was mistaken as to the nature of the Society in doing this[47] but I don't think that's necessarily the case.

One of the problems in studying the Philadelphian Society is that, as Ariel Hessayon points out , most of the apologetic literature generated by the Society does not line up with the facts about what the Society was actually doing[48]. This literature portrays a much more modest, and less millenarian, society than appears to have been the case. This also goes for Lee's writings, his defenses of the Philadelphian Society, as well as his letter to Dodwell, included here.

However, while motivation is very hard to impute to someone three hundred years after the fact, I believe that the evasiveness of Lee can be seen as an attempt to shield the Society from harassment by a government that still had an interest in religious affairs. Lee was a co-founder of the society, and the editor of most of Lead's published works. It can be assumed that he believed in and approved of the millenarian message of Lead, even if he publicly tried to minimize the parts of it that would have been controversial to the religious and political establishment of his time. Nevertheless, while Lee's letter to Dodwell, for example, might not be accurate as a picture of the society, it is very enlightening for the presentation of Behmenist philosophy that it gives, which is on the level of Freher's analyses, although much briefer.

There was another theological matter that divided both Theosophers and others regarding Lead. In 1693, after Pordage's death but before the foundation of the Philadelphian Society, Lead adopted the doctrine of universal salvation, which said that at the end of times all sinners, and all demons, would be redeemed[49] . This contrasted with Boehme's notion of the end times. Versluis[50] suggests that a reason why this would be disagreeable is that in Behmenist thought Lucifer and his angels had free will, and chose to do evil. Because of this, there would be no guarantee that any sort of torture or forced purification would, in the end, cause them to change their opinions, no matter how long it lasted. While divisive, it appears that a number of Theosophers in continental Europe came to agree with her, which contributed to a small movement that combined Philadelphian Theosophy and Pietism with Universalism.

There is also the matter of the relationship between the Philadelphian Society and practical occultism. While most of the works of Lead and others make no reference to practical work, there are excerpts from the "Theosophical Transactions", by Francis Lee, which show a keen interest and familiarity with these subjects. One document, which is reprinted in "A Sorcerous Anthology, Magical and Occult Writings from the Publications of Robert Cross Smith", answers questions about a vision where a spirit leads a person to a mountain, where they entered inside and were offered treasure by the spirit. This document is included here as well.

While Theosophical Transactions stems from Lee's time, the question of the relationship of magic to the Philadelphians goes into the period before the society was formally announced. As noted, Pordage was accused of practicing magic, and his household appears to have experienced much supernatural phenomenon associated with angels and demons, as well as communication with angels themselves. Something to be noted in accounts of Pordage's testimony, as Joad comments, is that while he denies conjuring demons, he says very little about the angelic side[51]. However, this is not the extent of it.

Though it hasn't been commented on before, the diary entries in "A Fountain of Gardens" contain extensive references to spiritual alchemy, as well as instructions given by the angels on how to make alchemical herbal medicinal preparations. This comes after extensive metaphorical instructions on internal alchemy.

The spirits, for example, give a recipe for an oil to make out of herbs that will be good for health, and an annointing oil for spiritual warfare. This is the full recipe for the annointing oil:

"First then come with me into my secret Lebanon, where the Beds of Spices are, and take thee seven Ounces of the Mace of Grace, of like quantity of the Spikenard of Love; the Camphore of Peace; the Heart-cheering Cloves, of the Saffron of Joy; the Noble Frankincence of all Faith; the Myrrh of Triumphant Victory; the Cassi of a Sound Mind and Perfect Heart. Take all these and put them under the grinding Wheel which maintaineth its uncessant working Motion within thee, till they come to be an Oily Substance, mixed into one perfect Lump, then diffuse all in the Juice of the Pomegranat for a certain time, adding hereunto the Powder of Gold of Pervilium, which is to be mixed with the Magistery of Pearl, and the Ruby-Spirit; all which close in a pure Crystalline Bottle, into which nothing ever before was put, and set it constantly under the

Sun-shine of thy Heavens for the perfect Clarification thereof: Which at the tenth number will attain to the full height of a Life-quickning Spirit." [52]

It should be noted that according to Versluis, Pordage made his living in his later days through herbal medicine[53]. Versluis also includes a letter that Pordage wrote to a follower about attaining the Philosopher's Stone in his collection "Wisdom's Book"[54]. This is a piece of writing by Pordage that was translated into German and circulated on the continent, but was never published in English. Versluis had to translate it back into English to include it in the collection.

Similarly, Adam McLean has reproduced on the "Alchemy Website" an article by Francis Lee from "Theosophical Transactions" called "On the Philadelphian Gold." This is a dialogue between a lover of gold and a Philadelphian on the true nature of alchemy[55]. In it, Lee expresses the opinion that all of nature is polluted because of the consequences of the fall, and that both nature itself and the individual have to purify themselves to fully realize the spiritual forces that live inside of them, which are concealed by fallen nature.

Again, the poem "Solomon's Porch", by Richard Roach, which was affixed to the beginning of volume one of "A Fountain of Gardens", and which is reproduced here, uses extensive alchemical imagery, and blends it with praise of the holy Sophia. Like much relating to the Philadelphian Society, Pordage, Lead, and Lee, there is much work to be done around these topics.

The Philadelphian meetings eventually caught the eye of the public, and people increasingly hostile to the group started turning up at them, disrupting them[56]. This lead to a change of venue, where the same disruptions started happening again, and further moves after that[57]. Despite this, the Philadelphians continued their public presence until 1703, when a now sick and dying Lead announced that the group had fulfilled their six days of activity and now was engaged in a seventh day of rest[58]. Lead passed on the next year, in 1704. Then, not much heard of the Philadelphians for several years. During that time, it appears that Francis Lee drifted away from the group.

The Revived Society.

In 1707 the group made a reappearance. Laborie reports that the group pointed to 1707 as a pivotal year based on prophecy and biblical calculations[59], and in 1707 a group of religious refugees from France appeared, who became known as the French Prophets.

The French Prophets were part of the Protestant group known as the Camisards, who had been engaged in a war against the French government. This was because the Edict of Nantes, which had established toleration for Protestants in France, had been repealed by Louis XIV, who sent armies into heavily Protestant regions to demand conversion, or, failing that, expulsion.

The Camisards that appeared in England were enthusiasts in the religious sense of the word. They too were Prophets. They believed that the end times were at hand, and that the Holy Spirit spoke through them at meetings. Laborie describes meetings of the French Prophets where people trembling were possessed by the Holy Spirit, who gave forth prophecies about the end times as well as castigated the world for its sinfulness[60]. They also claimed miraculous cures happened at their assemblies, and bestowed public blessings, related to faith healing, on favored individuals. Laborie also documents extreme practices by the Prophets that included public humiliation and public corporal punishment inflicted on followers who had engaged in transgressions[61].

Richard Roach sought out an audience with the French Prophets, while the group was still new and while, perhaps, their extreme enthusiasm wasn't fully visible, and negotiated a merger between them and the remaining Philadelphians[62]. This constituted the revival of the Philadelphian society. The association with millenarian spirituality and religious enthusiasm was not out of character, if you consider the ultimate origin of the Philadelphians within Pordage's group at Berks at Bradfield. Like the French Prophets, Pordage and his associates received prophecy, and experienced other full on manifestations of spiritual phenomenon. Indeed, the current of thought that some of Pordage's visitors, such as Abeizer Coppe, were associated with is sometimes called "Spiritualism", which is a less perjorative version of "Enthusiasm".

Shortly after the merger, according to Laborie, Francis Lee and other members of the first Philadelphian Society wrote to Roach advising him against involvment with the French Prophets[63]. Later, in 1710, Lee would pseudonymously write a long essay called "The History of Montanism", which was affixed to a work denouncing the French Prophets. "History of Montanism" was a tract against a heresy from the first centuries A.D. which revolved around a charismatic male prophet who had a number of female prophetesses around him. It was implicitly a rejection of both the enthusiasm of the Prophets as well as of the visions of Lead, and marks the conventional point of Lee's final separation from the Philadelphians, although he appears to have kept in contact with other Philadelphians socially.

Roach fell into merging the society. One of the French Prophets, who would be soon dead, announced that he would be resurrected from the dead in five months, and that this would signify the beginning of the end times[64]. The time, May 1708, came and went and the member was not resurrected, which caused a loss of support for the Prophets. In this, it should be noted that the man who claimed he would be resurrected, Thomas Emes, wasn't one of the Camisards from France, but an Englishman who had become part of the Prophets. Laborie reports that in the wake of the failure of the prophecy, the Prophets went looking for people who were possessed with a bad spirit, who were subsequently expelled[65]. He also reports that in the aftermath of the failed prophecy the two groups started to meet separately, though they still remained associated[66].

In 1710, one of the female Philadelphians appeared at a meeting of the Prophets and made a speech calling for more of a spirit of love in their doctrine, and more of a connection between the two groups. In return, she was physically attacked by one of the Prophets, who beat her[67]. Beyond this abhorrent violence, the nature of the event also points to a theme that looms large in Laborie's account of the two groups: the French Prophets preached fire, brimstone, and condemnation, while the Philadelphians favored love[68].

Though the relationship of the Philadelphians with the Quakers was complicated, perhaps the Quaker ethos parallels that of the Philadelphians in some ways. John Pordage condemned the refusal of Quakers to take oaths in one work, but, nevertheless the Bow Lane congregation of the Philadelphians came from an association of Quakers. More research needs to be done, but it's significant that the Bow Lane congregation came from Reading, and that Reading was Pordage's first appointment as vicar[69], before Berks at Bradfield. Perhaps the Bow Lane congregation came from followers of Pordage from those days. If it did, despite condemning Quakers for not taking Oaths[70], Pordage would have had an association with Quakers going back to the start of his religious career.

This incident of violence, followed by warnings and further condemnations by the Prophets, led to the final severance between the two groups. Laborie reports that in 1713 the Prophets declared that Richard Roach was guilty of blasphemy[71]. Laborie notes that the Prophets were observed to have been very quiet from 1713 on[73], perhaps signaling a crest to the public activity of that group. He also indicates that after this the remaining groups within the Philadelphia society still continued meeting for some time, in some capacity[72]. However, practically, this also spelled the end for the revived Philadelphian Society.

Despite personal acrimony, Roach still maintained friendly relations with some of the Prophets through the end of his life[74]. Roach continued to have a millenarian perspective through the 1720s, writing his books "The Imperial Standard" and "The Great Crisis" during that time, which predicted the imminent end of the world. Roach passed on in 1730.

Strangely enough, some of the French Prophets, and their English members, were also active in alchemy. Paul Kléber Monod documents that one of Isaac Newton's assistants in alchemy, Nicholas Fatio, was a Prophet[75]. Fatio is mentioned by Laborie as one of the Prophets that Richard Roach both knew and kept contact with after the separation of the two groups[75]. Another of the French Prophets, Moult, was also an alchemist[76], a member of the Royal Society, and also a friend of Roach[77]. Additionally, Monod documents that the Prophet who claimed that he would rise from the dead in five months, Dr. Emes, was also an alchemist who had written several pamphlets on the subject[78].

Lee in his later years appears to have continued to be a mystic, but to have dropped Boehme and arrived at a philosophy that combined Kabbalism with Neo-Platonism. Lee's interest in these currents took place in a Christian and Biblical context. Although actual kabbalistic texts had started to be translated into Latin at this point, such as those contained in "Kabbalah Denudata", Lee was proficient enough in Hebrew that he was able to not only read the Bible in the original but to also read the Midrash and other commentaries on the Old Testament in their original Hebrew.

Evaluating Lee's later positions as a whole is difficult. This is because those writings which were posthumously published appear to only discuss mysticism in a sub-rosa way. One of the literary devices used in the 17th and 18th centuries was to take a seemingly simple, obvious, or mundane, topic, examine it, and trace out hidden implications from it. This Lee used to great effect, as many of the essays published in "Apoleipomena, or Essays Theological, Mathematical and Physical", volumes 1 and 2, are about seemingly non-mystical topics which Lee uses as a basis for launching into mystical speculations. Nevertheless, in the end, it's often unclear just what larger system of belief the concepts that Lee is describing belong to. The essays are often, in the end, very ambiguous, which is a high contrast to the works contained in this volume, which are explicit about the mystical concepts they're describing. They also do not contain Behmenist content, at least content that's explicitly Behmenist. Lee died of fever in 1719, in Flanders, Belgium, while traveling to meet the French mystic Madame Guyon[79].

Through all of this, the role of Dionysius Andreas Freher appears to have been that of someone in the background, someone who was part of the general Behmenist community, who was in contact, presumably, with the Philadelphian groups that survived, but who didn't take part in the revived society or the activity of the French Prophets.

Part III

Freher, Walton, and the Texts

Freher's background.

The stories of Lee and Roach are entwined with that of the Philadelphian Society, but that of Freher is less so, at least outwardly. Though a part of the original Philadelphian Society, Freher did not publish any works under his own name, and did not take a public role. Who, then, was Dionysius Andreas Freher?

Freher was a native of Nurnberg who was born in 1649, and died in 1728. He came from a prominent judicial family. One of Freher's cousins, Paul Freher, composed a work on the prominent intellectuals of his time, whose short title is "Theatrum Virorum Eruditione"[1]. Dionysius Andreas Freher had a classical education, and also studied Jacob Boehme while in Germany, before moving to London. Muses has tracked down an uncle of Freher's who already lived in London, who had a diplomatic posting[2], and speculates that it may have been this connection that paved the way for Freher to move to Great Britain.

Hessayon has documented that Freher had contact with the society from 1697, and that he translated Lead's "The Laws of Paradise" into German in 1701[3]. That said, because of a documented presence of Freher in Great Britain in the final years of the 17th century, it is possible that he's the person that Roach referred to in "Solomon's Porch" as being a person who could shed light on Boehme for them[4]. Walton notes that Freher's early works appear to be answers to questions that other Behmenists had about Boehme's doctrines[6], and it's possible that he was seen as a potential resource for the Behmenist community in London as a whole.

Freher also appears to have known Lee very well. As the general editor of the Philadelphian publications, Lee would have worked with Freher on his translation of Lead's "Laws of Paradise". Also, both Freher and Lee are named in Rev. Waple's will[7], Waple being the author of the now lost Behmenist work whose commentary by Freher makes up the whole of "Serial Elucidations" volume H. Additionally, the Alchemy website reproduces a listing of a document held in the Rawlinson Manuscripts at the Bodleian Library at Oxford that records the receipt of £31 16s by Roach, Lee, and Freher collectively[8]. Lee also appears to have possessed a full set of Freher's "Serial Elucidations", which Freher composed between 1699 and 1712. We know this because Lee's copies made their way into the hands of Walton, via William Law and his descendants[9].

Freher is known to have assembled a small theosophical circle around him, which consisted in part of J. D. Leuchter and Allen Leppington. Leuchter was an engraver, and collaborated with Freher on his graphic works. He also was the individual who made most of the initial copies of Freher's manuscripts, copying them long hand. Considering that Freher's complete works in manuscript form most likely total several tens of thousands of pages, this is quite impressive.

Beyond this, we really don't know much about Freher. How he supported himself while in Great Britain, what profession Freher studied for in Germany, none of these are currently known. Walton makes a comment on Freher living with Rev. Waple during the last years of Waple's life[10], but there's not much more. Perhaps there are hitherto unexploited manuscript sources, in the United Kingdom and Germany, that could shed light on Freher's life.

As for Freher's work, Charles Muses divides it into three periods[11]. The first period includes that of Serial Elucidations, volumes A-I. These are Freher's commentaries on Jacob Boehme, and consist of a number of different sorts of works. The majority of the works by Freher included in this book come from Serial Elucidations. These were composed between 1699 and 1712. The period also contains the graphical works "Hieroglyphs" and "Three Tables". Both of these works also have commentaries, with that of "Three Tables" being 500 manuscript pages.

Next, there is the Conference period. The Conferences are dialogues about predestination. They start with a thorough grounding in Boehme's thought before going on to treat the subject itself and the opinions of contemporary thinkers on it.

Finally, there's the last period, that of the Treatises, and of Freher's last graphical work, the "Paradoxical Emblemata". The "Treatises" are Freher's treatise against Universal Restoration, championed by Jane Lead, as well as his treatise on Good and Evil. The Paradoxical Emblemata are Freher's final graphical work, and consist of emblems embodying theosophical concepts accompanied by short texts.

Running through these periods are the extant letters of Freher. These include his letters to and about the Bow Lane Church, a split off from the proto-Philadelphian Society. They also include letters written on miscellaneous religious topics then current in England.

One work that Freher is most known for, and that, anonymously or not, was to get quite a bit of circulation, is his engravings of the various states of Man—before the fall, after the fall, and on his way to regeneration. Freher, with the help of his associate Leuchter, executed these engravings in a form that was both beautiful and interactive. They were interactive because each table was composed of several different engravings that were fixed one atop of the other, and that had small 'doors' that could be lifted, revealing the prints beneath.

These three "Tables" were of the human body, and showed the correspondence of the various organs to the planets, as well as to other components of Boehme's theosophical understanding of the universe. They would be reproduced anonymously twice, first as an appendix to the book "Works of Jacob Behmen", volume III, by William Law, and second as part of "A New and Complete Illustration of the Celestial Science of Astrology" by Ebenezer Sibly, who likely got them from Law's book. One of the illustrations in Sibly's book, that of man before the fall, appeared on the cover of "The Station of Man in the Universe: Ebenezer Sibly on the Spirit World and Magic", published by Topaz House Publications.

Freher also produced a commentary on the "Three Tables". This commentary is listed as having five hundred manuscript pages. The commentary also contains the personal discussion about the Bow Lane Church that has been labeled as Freher's "Confession". Excerpts from the commentary found their way into "The Astrologer of the Nineteenth Century" as the "Rubens Manuscript", said to have belonged to the painter Peter-Paul Rubens and collected by the artist Richard Cosway, who was a fan of Rubens. Part of it was also summarized and paraphrased by William Law as part of volume III of "Works of Jacob Behmen", although Muses comments that the paraphrase is "really inadequate"[11]. Walton links both Freher's tables and his commentary to a book by Johann Gichtel, a Dutch Behmenist, which is often mis-labeled "Theosophia Practica"[12], and which very famously gives similar placements of the powers of the planets within the human body, and may very well have been the prototype for Freher's work.

Whether the book by Gichtel was the original inspiration or not, the diagram format that Freher used was a natural extension of Boehme's correspondences. Boehme had produced a document called "Four Tables", which in a style reminiscent of Henry Cornelius Agrippa's "Four Books of Occult Philosophy", as well as the "Magical Calendar" of Trithemius, presented his system of correspondences in tabular form.

Walton, his life, and the book.

Walton (1809-1877) was a jeweler in London who was associated with the circle around the Behmenist James Pierrepont Grieves[13]. As described by Joscelyn Godwin, Grieves was more conventional in his Behmenist interests than most of the writers we've discussed[14]. This circle was notable for also including Mary Anne Atwood, who was the author of "A Suggestive Inquiry Into the Hermetic Mystery"[15]. Walton, in his list of book recommendations, includes "A Suggestive Inquiry" as part of the section on "Magic", included here.

Walton, in addition to conducting research into the life of William Law, also had aspirations to found a Theosophical College, as well as a larger publishing project which would reissue a great number of Christian spiritual classics. Unfortunately, these didn't come to fruition, but as Jocelyn Godwin reports, Walton did attract a couple into his circle who studied with him, and that would go on to be commentators on Boehme and on Theosophy itself, the Penny's. These were A.J. Penny and her husband Edward[16].

A.J. Penny went on to write "Studies in Jacob Boehme", while Edward would translate "Man, His True Nature and Ministry" by Louis-Claude de Saint-Martin, as well as a collection of Saint-Martin's letters, into English[17]. A.J. Penny, presumably with her husband as well, was one of the few people in the late 19th century to be familiar with Freher's work. In her book on Boehme, she comments on a biography of Boehme by a Dutch clergyman, and states that Freher dealt with Boehme's thought much better[18], elsewhere pointing to "Notes and Materials" as a source to look at for Freher's writings[19] . A.J. Penny was also unique in that she was of the younger generation and lived into the era of the Theosophical Society, with which she became associated, making a her a unique, but non-influential, connection between the world of Behmenist Theosophy and that of the Theosophical Society itself.

Where was Christopher Walton coming from, ideologically, in putting together "Notes and Materials"? Walton came from a background in a stable Protestant denomination, Methodism, before finding William Law through the latter's correspondence with John Wesley, the founder of Methodism[20]. Walton not only praises Law, but repeatedly refers to him as 'Elias'[21], one of the Biblical figures that should arrive before the end-times, and sees Law's writings as a preface to a restored and perfected Church. Within this, Walton also praises Boehme and the commentators that are included in "Notes and Materials".

It's difficult, personally, for me to understand what Walton saw in Law. Law's writings, in my opinion, are derivative, light weight, and much less insightful than Boehme's writings themselves, not to mention Boehme's commentators. Law plagiarized Boehme, as well as Freher, and was not forthcoming about his sources until fellow authors noted his plagiarism and pointed out the similarities[22]. However, Walton appears to view Law's actions not as plagiarism but as inspiration. Boehme, and Freher, supposedly inspired Law to produce his works.

I believe that Walton's overall vision was of a reformation of the Methodist denomination that would have combined the thought of Wesley with that of Law. The writings of Boehme, Freher, and others, would have served as advanced material for students. Walton's projects, establishing a Theosophical college, as well as Theosophical study circles, would have been within the church, and would not have disturbed the unity of it.

Walton compiled "Notes and Materials" over a long period of time, working in his spare time, as a labor of love. Muses states that the book was written and printed between 1847 and 1853[23]. The particular time frame that Walton was working with is evident from the citations that he gives in his recommendations about books on magic to read. This list, which is reproduced here, is part of a much longer list of Christian mystics and theologians that Walton compiled. Walton was writing after the Spiritualist movement had started but before the Theosophical Society was founded, and his recommendations include Spiritualist writers, possibly better ones as a whole, as well as thinkers who talk about Vital Magnetism.

"Notes and Materials for an Adequate Biography of William Law" is a mess, but it's important to recognize what the intent of the book was. It is, as the title indicates, notes and materials for a biography. That means that it's a time capsule of Walton's research into the origins of Law's thought, preserved for a future biographer of Law. Preservation, not readability, appears to have been Walton's main goal. Not only that, but the ultimate point of all the texts that are excerpted is to help understand William Law, not to present the texts as they are for independent researchers. This means that individuals using the book for that purpose are working somewhat at crossed ways to what Walton was intending.

Nevertheless, the compiling and printing of the book was a great accomplishment, without which the works of Freher in particular would be even more distant and inaccessible than they are today.

Besides "Notes and Materials", Walton also edited and introduced "Introduction to Theosophy" in 1855. This consisted of two works by William Law. Walton also shows himself to be a capable Theosophist in the preface to the latter work. Unfortunately, the same problems that plague "Notes and Materials" are present in his preface to the "Introduction": there's an enormous footnote that underlines most of the preface, and there are even multiple page footnotes in the "Advertisement" to found a Theosophical college located in the back of the book.

What did Walton think about Lee, Freher, and Roach, though, and Lead? Walton's thought appears to be nuanced. Walton has a much more positive view of Freher than of Lee, most likely because Freher was claiming to be explicating Boehme's work instead of announcing a new revelation. The announcement of a new revelation appears to be the main problem that Walton sees with Jane Lead. Says Walton:

"If Lead had solely meant by her 'visions and revelations' this circumstance of the apprehension of the deep points of Behmen's philosophy, (which also applies to Pordage) then the writer would fully approve of the term, though by no means of the Muggletonian fanatical parabolic garb in which she invests them[...]"[24]

With regards to Richard Roach, though Walton mislabels the poem "Solomon's Porch" as by Lee, he significantly cuts the poem off just before it starts to use alchemical symbolism, ironically stating at the point he cuts it off:

"The poem here takes a fresh wing and direction; but we have not room for further sublimities and annunciations of this soaring evangelical prophet of the latter days' glory."[25]

On the other hand, Walton sees Lee's preface to the first volume of Lead's "A Fountain of Gardens" as reflecting the enthusiasm of a new convert[26], but he also condemns Lee for writing "The History of Montanism" later in life.

"Upon which, the editor of this treatise, as incumbent upon him, would additionally remark, That it appears to him quite paradoxical, how Lee, so eminently devoted and spiritual an individual, so experienced in deep communion with God, and so cognizant of the super-rational operations of the Spirit, could have written(even anonymously) the history of the Montanists as he has done in the above work; after what is contained in the above-mentioned letter to Dodwell, in his prefaces to Lead, and in his other writings in connection with the Philadelphians. Contrasting the spirit of these latter, with the cool, sembiant-impartial, yet, in effect, condemnatory tone of the same writer, in the above-mentioned work, an ordinary reader would suppose the author to have been a menial crafty advocate, acquainted, as a backslider, or growing lukewarm professor, with the spiritualities of high Christian experience, and, at the same time, with what may be plausibly urged against them by sober orthodoxy and rationalists, and yet ready to write on either side, as hired."[27]

Though much of the book revolves around William Law, Walton's own contributions are fascinating, although largely beyond the scope of this introduction. Particularly, in the never ending footnote under the Freher section, there's a long discourse by Walton on magic in relation to scientific ideas that were popular in his day, particularly magnetism, but also some others. One of Walton's writings, from a different section, that I've labeled "On Enthusiasm", has been included here.

Lastly, another author that Walton excerpts is the little known Mary Pratt[28]. Pratt was a theosopher who lived in the late 18th century, who was also an advocate of Vital Magnetism[29]. Walton excerpts Pratt's theosophical letters, which deal with her own inner mystical experience of divinity. Pratt was an unusual person, in that she was a Behmenist who was married to a Swedenborgian (who she complains doesn't believe in Boehme)[30], but was also linked to the mystic, stage crafter, and painter Philip James de Louthenbourg[31]. The latter was a Mason, an advocate of Vital Magnetism, a mystic, and a friend of Cagliostro[32]. Cagliostro and his wife actually stayed at the de Louthenbourg's house in London[33], and de Louthenbourg accompanied Cagliostro's wife on her voyage to Switzerland to join her husband[34].

It's unclear what de Loutherbourg's personal spiritual beliefs were, but Hessayon writes that he painted a portrait of Swedenborg, from already made engravings[35], and possessed books by Jane Lead and other Behmenists[36]. Hessayon reports that Pratt read Lead and other Philadelphians, such as Roach[37], which Pratt also alludes to in the letters printed by Walton[38]. Pratt, who wrote two pamphlets defending Vital Magnetism, devoted one of them to the specific defense of the healing activities of de Louthenbourg and his wife.

The structure and contents of the book.

As said, the book is "Notes and Materials for an Adequate Biography of William Law". In this, Walton is writing to a future individual looking to take up the work, who he refers to as "The Candidate". Much of the book outside of the large extracts of manuscripts and other material consists of recommendations of works that "The Candidate" should read, in order to have the appropriate background necessary to complete the work. Later on in the book, Walton gives a theoretical curriculum for a Theosophical college. The two lists are very similar. Additionally, the lists of books are duplicated in the different sections, so that large portions of the material that aren't excerpts of other writers are in fact lists of books, which are almost identical, that appear in sections one, two, three, and four.

Schematically, the book is divided into four sections. I say "Schematically", because in practice the majority of the book is made up of section two, which dwarfs the others in size. The book as a whole is 688 pages long. Section I consists of a bibliography of Boehme's works that gives way to long excerpts from Boehme's work, and then to excerpts from Law's work, as well as Walton's comments on both Law and Boehme. It's 121 pages long.

Section II is where all but two of the writings by Freher and Lee in this volume come from. Walton explains that there were originally only going to be three sections in the book, and that what has become Section II was intended as a note to Section III. As a section that was originally going to be a note, it's 510 pages long, within the book's 688 pages. Section III is 32 pages long, and consists of book recommendations, advice for "The Candidate", and extracts from William Law's works. Section IV is 20 pages long, and is Walton's 'Conclusion', which contains excerpts from William Law's works that the author feels get to the heart of Theosophy. This is followed by an advertisement that repeats information that is also included before the Preface of the book.

As for Section II, this note-cum-section was intended by Walton to be a kind of dictionary of mystical writers and their works that would be useful for the future biographer of William Law. It was supposed to consist of a list of writers and works, plus a small entry describing who the writers were and what their philosophy was. The list of writers proper, with annotations, comments, and footnotes consists of 66 pages. However, at some point, Walton decided that there needed to be included larger extracts of writings by certain authors, especially where the writings were generally unavailable. So, Walton included a very, very, long postscript to

Section II, which is where the Freher and Lee writings are located. This postscript, to the section that was originally supposed to be a note itself, is 488 pages long. All of the writers cited in Section II are part of Behmenist and Christian mysticism, as well as Neo-Platonism, in ways that Walton felt intersected with William Law's thought.

Walton also, in Section III, gave extensive descriptions of the manuscripts that he'd collected of Freher and others, how he came by them, what they consisted of, notes on the manuscripts, and also declared that they were going to be available for the student to look at. They are available, at Dr. Williams' Library in London. Presumably, if someone found the book, and was interested enough in the topic to want to carry the project of a biography through to fruition, they would see that there was more material available in London and be clued in on where to find it.

That said, there is no index to "Notes and Materials", and no table of contents. There's no way to find the main sections of Lee and Freher, which aren't in footnotes, besides looking through the book itself. As for the footnotes, the sections by Lee and Freher that are contained in them are even more difficult to find. I'm indebted to the work of Charles Muses, who, so far, has been the only individual to write an entire book devoted to Freher, for listing the sections in the book where Freher's work appears. Unfortunately, no such guide exists for the writings of Lee in Walton's work, which appear much more often in footnote form than those of Freher.

The writing is, on the whole, microscopic. Though there are some sections that have normal sized type, the majority of the book uses type sizes reserved for footnotes as its main font. This has contributed to the book's obscurity. Incidentally, with regards to the very small type, Joscelyn Godwin reports that A.J. Penny complained about the type to Walton, and Walton replied that she should get special reading glasses, recommending a place in that could manufacture them for her[39].

Walton also excerpts very long pieces of French language Theosophy, including a large part of a biography of Louis-Claude de Saint Martin. At times the juxtapositions in language can be jarring, as when, in his dictionary of recommended authors at the beginning of Section II, he includes a large French language reading list of, and commentary on, Theosophical authors, where the names, the titles, and the commentaries on the authors are left untranslated. There are also sections of untranslated Latin text. Strangely, there's very little German. Be that as it may, though jarring for the reader, especially when the untranslated biography of Saint-

Martin appears over completely unrelated footnotes in English, it does offer further possibilities for researchers who possess the necessary language skills.

At times, it's difficult to know just who the author is of a given section. This is because Law, outside of the dialogue form, adopted formats for his writing that resemble those of Freher and Boehme, and Walton continued the practice by putting his own writing in formats that resemble those of Freher and Boehme, and Law. Because of this, and because almost inevitably anything not labeled as Freher or Lee has turned out to be by Law, Walton, or sometimes Boehme himself, the only writings excerpted here from the book, and included in the corresponding author's sections, are ones that have been explicitly labeled as such by Walton. It's possible that there are fragments of Freher and Lee in the never-ending footnote that are not labeled as such.

The footnotes under the post-script to the second part are constant, and they often take up half the page, sometimes taking up all the page except for one or two lines at the top. They also often do not correspond to what's above them. There are a few reasons for that. One is that the things that Walton has to say, and the excerpts that he marshals in order to support them, are very long. This leads to situations where Walton comments on a section of Lee or Freher in a footnote, but his explanation and excerpts are so long that at the end of the note Lee or Freher have since moved on to other topics. Sometimes, the documents that Walton is commenting on have ended and new, unrelated, documents are above the footnotes. In at least one case, though, the difference is intentional, though ill advised.

This section is underneath the series of pieces by Freher in the post-script to Section II. Walton says that he's inserting the footnote "As a relief to the uniformity of these pages"[40], i.e. in order to make things more interesting; and so he includes as footnotes information that has absolutely nothing to do with the text above it. These are biographical documents and information about William Law. This includes a docment that traces the history of Law's place of birth from the time of the Roman occupation of Britain, through to his birth[41].

This leads to situations such as the following, on page 338, where the last part of the top text reads

"Page 73. Q. 1. To these several ends of their creation belongeth also this—that they should form, or concur to the formation and multiplication of God's wonders in his formed Wisdom, viz. Each of them in his station, and according to the different names and powers which they represented."

while the bottom text starts off:

"In the year 1315, it was in the hands of Margaret, Queen of England, second wife of Edward the First, and eldest daughter of Philip the Third, King of France, then a widow. She died in 1317."[42]

There are also many other materials included, which, though interesting to students of Law, have absolutely nothing to do with the text above them. I believe that Walton wanted to fit in as much as he possibly could, and that preservation was more important than organization.

Walton also inserts his own comments directly into the excerpts that he reproduces. These comments often relate to William Law and Methodism, pointing out connections between Freher or Lee and Law, or stating that what Freher or Lee is saying is misguided. These comments have been edited out, with only the comments that Walton provided that actually help in the understanding of the texts being preserved. Like the footnotes, these comments, that are contained in brackets, are sometimes very long, and in those cases make the texts they're located in harder to read. In one case, a text by Francis Lee, Walton inserts comments almost after every sentence of Lee's, albeit only towards the end of the piece. This, in particular, interferes with reading the text, and has been excised.

I should say, again, that in all of this Walton appears to have been very good natured, and to have had the best interests of his project at heart. The problem is that that project was wrapped up in the interpretation of Boehme by William Law, and rather than just let the pieces be, Walton inserted comments that to him were no doubt helpful statements that would guide the reader to the connections between Law, Freher, and Lee.

Texts by Freher, Lee, and Roach Included in this Volume, and their Descriptions.

Freher's Texts

The sources of Walton's selections, thankfully, can be easily identified, because of the list of Freher's writings that Walton also includes in "Notes and Materials". This list takes its section names directly from the titles of the pieces.

In total, fourteen pieces by Freher are included here. Additionally, there are two pieces of writing derived from Freher: a summary of the contents of "Serial Elucidations A-E" written by Christopher Walton, and a list of Freher's writings compiled by Walton. Additionally, there is a discourse by William Law, that is largely a paraphrase of Freher's writings.

Of the different writings of Freher included here, the largest sources are "Serial Elucidations H" and "Serial Elucidations G". The entirety of Serial Elucidations H, which is Freher's comment on Waple's now lost Behmenist work, is included here, while five of the other selections come from "Serial Elucidations G". Serial Elucidations A is represented by one text, while Serial Elucidations B is represented by two texts, that were originally inserted into Walton's summary of Serial Elucidations A-E. Walton appears to have arranged his extracts of Freher in a particular sequence to cover Boehme's philosophy from its start to its full development, and while Walton's particular scheme has not been replicated, I've followed the idea faithfully.

The texts start with selections talking about the start of the universe and the creation of the Three Principles, which I call 'Foundational' texts. They are followed by 'Intermediary' texts that deal with cosmology in ways that incorporate astrology and the elements, as well as the human body and esoteric physiology. After these are the 'Final' texts, which deal with issues common to other parts of Christianity. These include discussions of the Behmenist notion of Jesus, the Eucharist, issues of sin and free will, and others. This pattern is actually repeated within Freher's "Observations on Waple". "Observations on Waple" is a book in itself, and was composed that way. The "Foundational" and "Intermediary" selections are placed before "Observations on Waple". Unfortunately, there are few "Final" texts outside of the end of "Observations". Freher's "Confession" is placed after the "Observations", and is the best representative.

The three categories start with the hardest texts and become easier as they go along. The 'Foundational' texts are the most difficult, because the ideas that they present are purely Behmenist, and have very little relation to ideas outside of the world of Jacob Boehme and Theosophy. The 'Intermediary' texts are easier because they share a common vocabulary with Renaissance and post-Renaissance occultism, such as planetary influence, the Three Principles of Paracelsus, the elements, and esoteric physiology. This consists of discussions about how all of these macrocosmic components correspond to different parts of the body, as well as to Boehme's ideas. Uniquely, these texts include a Behmenist piece on the growth and development of plant life. The 'Final' texts are the easiest, because the ideas that they discuss are common to religious discussions that have been going on in Protestant Christianity for quite a long time. With regards to Freher as a para-Rosicrucian, the texts which most clearly show this are those in the 'Intermediary category.

Following Walton, the 'Foundational' texts start with a section from the very beginning of Serial Elucidations A about God considered before time, space, and eternal nature, and go forward from there in a sequence that roughly parallels the creation of the universe. After the text discussing God before the creation of time and space the next pieces discuss how the creation of the universe could have happened from nothing, followed by pieces about how God can be pictured in a way drawing on the via negativa as well as the positive path, and several pieces on the idea of the Trinity in Boehme's thought, as well as the concept of Eternal Nature.

The 'Intermediary' section starts with "Two Questions", which is a letter on the nature of the fire and wrath worlds. This is followed by a selection about the Fall of Lucifer. After that is an excerpt from outside of Walton's book, about the nature of Adam. This is part of Freher's commentary to his "Three Tables", labeled by Walton as "Microcosmos", and comes from a previous Topaz House publication, "A Sorcerous Anthology: Magic and Occult Writings of Robert Cross Smith". It originally appeared in a book called "The Astrologer of the Nineteenth Century", supplied to Smith by the mysterious "Philadelphus".

Following this, there's "Thirty Propositions", a fragmentary work that deals with Adam and Eve, their expulsion from the Garden of Eden, and their posterity. After that is the somewhat misleadingly titled "Of the further Manifestation of God through the Creation of Angels". In actuality, this piece focuses more on personal spiritual work than on the creation of angels, and instead serves as an introduction to the next piece, Freher's "Process in the Philosophical Work".

"Process" is perhaps better known than other pieces due to its being transcribed by Adam McLean and posted on the Alchemy Website. It is a piece that parallels the alchemical process with the suffering and resurrection of Jesus. "Growing Vegetables" follows, with "Observations on Waple" coming next.

Freher's Observations on Waple, the whole of Serial Elucidations H, is a masterpiece in and of itself. Uniquely, while it's a commentary on a now lost text, one doesn't have to be familiar with that text to follow what Freher is saying. The commentary deals with the entirety of Boehme's thought, and is framed in a style where Freher states something that Waple has said, then declares how he thinks that Waple has or hasn't gotten it correct, and why. The "Highlights" in the Table of Contents are purely my own work. "Observations" has no chapter or section headings, despite being almost two hundred pages long, and I wanted to give some indication to readers of where information potentially very interesting to them was located.

Freher's "Confession" comes next. This consists of a comment appended to Freher's commentary on his first "Table" dealing with his conflicts with the Bow Lane Church and his personal spiritual development.

Finally, the Freher section ends with two secondary texts and a list of Freher's works composed by Walton. The secondary texts are Walton's summary of the contents of Serial Elucidations A-E, and a discourse made from Freher's texts by William Law. The first text, though derivative, demonstrates a very thorough understanding of Freher's writings, and provides information on Freher's ideas in "Serial Elucidations" that goes far beyond a list of the contents of the works.

The second text is a discourse that Law wrote, in the form of a letter, where he extensively quotes from Freher's works without attribution. The text is a combination of Law's writing and Freher's. Properly, it belongs to the 'Foundational' division of texts. Judging by its style, the first pages of the text are largely Law's own take on Freher and Boehme's ideas, which are followed by more direct paraphrasing and quotations from Freher's works themselves.

Finally, Walton's list of Freher's works is the last selection in the section, and gives an idea of the scope of Freher's still unpublished works. A more complete bibliography of Freher can be found in Charles Muses' "Illuminations on Jacob Boehme: the Work of Dionysius Andreas Freher".

Freher's Works:

Foundational Texts

1. God without nature or creature [from serial elucidations A, section 1]

2. How the nothing brings forth something [From serial elucidations F, part 1]

3. God in unity and trinity before and after eternal nature [Serial Elucidations G, part 1]

4. General comments on divine nature in unity and trinity [Serial Elucidations G., part 2]

Intermediary Texts

5. Two questions answered, from Serial Elucidations G part 7

6. Considerations on the fall of Lucifer, creation of third [Serial Elucidations B Section 5]

7. Rubens' Manuscript [Extract from the commentary on the "Three Tables"]

8. Thirty Propositions [Fragment]

9. Part of discourse on angels. [Serial Elucidations B section 4]

10. Process in the philosophical work [Serial elucidations G, part 10]

11. Growing Vegetables [Serial Elucidations G, part 11]

12. Observations on Waple [Serial Elucidations H]

Final

13. Freher's Confession, from the commentary on the "Three Tables".

14. Walton's Summaries

15. Law Extracts

16. List of Freher's Works

Lee's Texts

The pieces that Walton included, that are reproduced here, appear to span a number of years, and include both pieces from Lee's years as a Philadelphian and those from after he left the society, and after he had published "History of Montanism". Because of this, there are some very interesting parts of the writings that can be viewed as transitional between the Behmenist perspective and the later kabbalistic, neo-platonist, Christian perspective Lee would adopt. Particularly, "Concerning Wisdom" includes terms from both, being most like Boehme in its beginning while transitioning to a kabbalistic discussion of Wisdom as the Shekinah, associated with Malkuth, in the later part. Other later pieces include two long sets of questions or queries about the kabbala in relation to ideas about both the creation of the world and the meaning and significance of particular words in Hebrew used in Genesis and elsewhere. Unfortunately, there is no standard bibliography of Francis Lee.

Besides those writings associated with the Philadelphian Society, Lee's post-Philadelphian works were printed via his daughter over thirty years after his death, in 1752. Someone, presumably his daughter but possibly not, wrote an introductory biography for the two volume set that left out any events happening between the 1694 and the 1708[43], that is to say the period in which he pursued Philadelphian and Behmenist work and writing. The author of the introduction also mentions a life of Lee that was written by the Rev. Haywood, who came into many of Lee's writings after his death, that she says contained "many mistakes", and so would not allow to be printed[44]. Luckily, this biography, with the other papers, found its way into Christopher Walton's hands. Through this, it was preserved, along with all the other material that Walton collected. Ariel Hessayon has used this fugitive biography, with its "many mistakes", as one of his sources for information on Lee in his papers contained in "Jane Lead and Her Transnational Legacy"[45]. It should be remembered that Lee had married one of Jane Lead's daughters, and so the daughter of Lee who compiled the collected works, and presumably wrote the introduction, was Jane Lead's granddaughter. Many of the pieces that Walton printed appeared in print for the first time.

Of the pieces that are being printed here, I've divided them between Philadelphian and post-Philadelphian, and writings on prayer and organization. However, because many of the pieces that Walton printed are not dated, this is inexact. They've been split up according to content, to the period I personally think they belong to. In the case of the five texts attributed to the Philadelphian period, four of them are explicitly linked to it, while one is linked to it based on content. This last piece is the one I've labeled "Seven Fountains". Because it's a presentation of a Behmenist concept, and uses phrases from Pordage's thought, specifically "Still Eternity", I've labeled it as Philadelphian. The post-Philadelphian writings are basically everything else, exclusive of the short pieces on organization and prayer.

Of the pieces, the centerpiece is Lee's reply to Henry Dodwell about the Philadelphian Society. This letter, in which Lee defends the Society from charges of heresy, also includes explanations of Boehme's ideas as understood by Lee. The explanations are very valuable, although the letter, while still very long, is shorter than Freher's parallel writing, that is to say his comment on Waple's writing. These two are the centerpieces of the respective authors' writings within this book.

The writings identified as post-Philadelphian are much different, in that the cosmologies they describe aren't Behmenist, but reflect a combination of "Mosaical Philosophy", or Christianized Cabbala, along with Neo-Platonism, as well as influences from the current scientific and philosophical thought of Lee's day. Some, such as "One Hundred Questions on Mosaic Cabbala", appear to have very little to do with the Philadelphian writings, while others, such as "Concerning Wisdom", appear to belong to a period where Lee was still pursuing some of the themes in Philadelphian literature in new contexts. "Concerning Wisdom", is about Sophia, Wisdom, and while it isn't an orthodox Philadelphian text, it certainly draws on the broader current of Theosophy with regards to the idea of Wisdom.

Another highlight is the "Short Reflections on the First and Secondary Universal Matter." This is because Lee discusses some of the same topics as Georg von Welling in "Opus Mago-Cabbalisticum". Particularly, Lee discusses the Sal Niter, as well as the model of its transmission from the Sun, in line with Welling's philosophy. There is no date on the piece. Lee died the year that the first volume of Welling's work was released, but may possibly have still read it. Alternately, Lee could have gotten parts of the model from some of the sources that Welling drew on, such as the alchemist Sendivogius.

The Lee texts that have to do with prayer are six: a short commentary about contemplative prayer, two memorial prayers for Lee's friends, two prayers against sickness for those friends, and one prayer against sickness not addressed to anyone. The comment on contemplative prayer appears in two sections in "Notes and Materials", separated by close to four hundred pages. The first section appears as a footnote to one of the book lists, specifically to the part of the book lists that detail the works of Madame Guyon and Antoinette Bourignon, two mystical thinkers. The second half is inserted as part of the never-ending footnote under the Lee section. The two memorial prayers, put together by Walton, are of Hickes and Nelson, two figures associated with the Church of England that Lee befriended after he left the Philadelphian Society. Hickes was the author of the essay that Lee's "History of Montanism" accompanied.

Lee also left a selection of texts that relate to a proposed structure of study circles for Theosophy. These Walton reproduces, and they are included here. They consist of a discussion of the subject, and of an example agreement that people seeking to form a study circle should sign off on. These are the short "Model of a Society for Reviving the Spirit and Life of Christianity", and "A Specimen or Agreement […] for forming a society for the revival of Christianity". Both are in the form of numbered propositions. Walton also includes a paper by Lee about creating a publishing company for reprinting classics by mystical writers, in the same format. Unfortunately, there are no dates to these documents.

Lastly, one of the texts that is definitely Philadelphian is an excerpt from "Theosophical Transactions", a series of answers to questions about a dream that a correspondent had where he was lead into a mountain and presented with treasure. This does not appear in Walton's text, but appears in a previous Topaz House publication, "A Sorcerous Anthology: Magical and Occult Writings from the Publications of Robert Cross Smith". It originally appeared in "The Astrologer of the Nineteenth Century", supplied by the enigmatic "Philadelphus". This excerpt is notable for several reasons, but one of them is that it appears to show that Lee was familiar with contemporary practices of using magic to find treasure.

Definite Philadelphian Society Texts:

1. Letter to Dodwell

2. [Short Piece on the Seven Fountains.]

3. Introduction by Lee to the First Volume of "A Fountain of Gardens"

4. Selection from "Theosophical Transactions"

5. Questions about Pordage to Edward Hooker.

Possibly Post-Philadelphian Mystical Texts:

6. "Concerning Wisdom"

7. "Short Reflections on the Original Matter",

8. [On the Book of Revelation]

9. [On Moses]

10. [Paragraph on Mystical Theology]

11. "One Hundred Questions on the Mosaic Cabbala"

Organizational Texts and Texts on Contemplation and Prayer:

12. [Comments on Contemplative Prayer]

13. [Two Commemorations and Three Prayers]

14. [Piece about Creating a Publishing Company]

15. "Model of a Society for Reviving the Spirit and Life of Christianity"

Roach's Texts.

The texts by Richard Roach come from the beginning and end of his writing career. The first selection is "Solomon's Porch", a poem that was originally placed at the beginning of Jane Lead's "A Fountain of Gardens", volume 1, published in 1696. The other selections, on magic prayer and on Theosophical and Philosophical terms, comes from "The Imperial Standard", published in 1726. This latter publication was written after the second iteration of the Philadelphian Society had ended, but still contains Behmenist thought and ideas. Some of the terms defined by Roach, such as "Ectypes", are terms that are also used in previous Philadelphian literature, such as in the short piece on the "Seven Fountains", by Lee, included here. The terms also include interesting definitions of the Behmenist conception of "Magia".

Solomon's Porch, as reproduced here, is a combination of Walton's version and the full version. Walton did not include the whole book, and cut the poem off before it started to talk about alchemy. The remainder of the poem has been reconstructed from texts created by the Early English Books Text Creation Partnership, checked against copies of the original "Fountain of Gardens" volume 1.

Roach's Texts

1. "Solomon's Porch"

2. [Divine Magia, Prayer]

3. "Index of Philosophical and Theosophical Terms"

Walton's Texts.

There are three short texts by Walton. The first consists of two long comments about Freher, Lee, and the Philadelphian Society, based on knowledge that Walton had come by both through participating in the Theosophical world of his time and through his research. The second is an interesting essay on "Enthusiasm". Also included are the part of Walton's book recommendations that have to do with magic and the occult. This was originally part of the list of books that the "Candidate" who would complete the biography of William Law should have read. It's unique in that it presents a picture of what books on magic and the occult were considered valuable in the 1850s, before the rise of the Theosophical Society. There are also other, very small, pieces of writing by Walton included before and after some of the texts by Freher and Lee. These were located before and after the pieces in "Notes and Materials", and are those comments that serve to give context to the writings. The numbering of Roach and Walton's texts has been combined due to the small quantity of them.

Walton's Texts

4. [Comments on the Philadelphians]

5. [On Enthusiasm]

6. [Reading List on Magic]

Appendix

Finally, there is the Appendix. This consists of a paragraph by paragraph comparison of Jane Lead's "Marks of a True Philadelphian", from the "Third Message to the Philadelphian Society", with the "Secret Signs of the Rosicrucians" published by Franz Hartmann as part of "In the Pronaos of Wisdom". The "Marks" and "Signs" are positive moral qualities that a Philadelphian or a Rosicrucian should seek to emulate.

Notes

Section I

Boehme and occultism

1. Faivre, Antoine, *Theosophy, Imagination, Tradition, Studies in Western Esotericism* trans. Christine Rhone, (Albany, NY: State University of New York Press, 2000) , p.15.
2. Peterson, Joseph, *Arbatel: Concerning the Magic of the Ancients*, (Lake Worth, FL, USA: Ibis Press, 2009) p. XI
3. ibid., p. XIII-XIV

Boehme and Mysticism

4. Muses, Charles, *Illumination on Jacob Boehme, the Work of Dionysius Andreas Freher*, (New York: King's Crown Press, Columbia University, 1951) p.9

Boehme Biography

5. Weeks, Andrew, *Boehme: an Intellectual Biography of the Seventeenth-Century Philosopher and Mystic*, (Albany, NY, USA: State University of New York Press, 1991) p. 35
6. ibid., p. 27
7. ibid., p. 21
8. ibid., p. 29, 31
9. Muses, *Illumination*, p. 29-32
10. ibid., p. 32
11. Weeks, *Boehme*, p.30
12. ibid., p. 30
13. ibid., p. 30
14. ibid., p. 30
15. ibid., p. 27
16. ibid., p. 30-31
17. Versluis, Arthur, *Wisdom's Children, A Christian Esoteric Tradition*, (Albany, NY, USA: State University of New York Press, 1999) p. 4
18. Weeks, *Boehme*, p. 36
19. ibid., p. 21

Hermeticism

20. Copenhaver, Brian, *Hermetica: The Greek Corpus Hermeticum and the Latin Asclepius in a new English Translation with Notes and Introduction*, (New York, NY: Cambridge University Press, 1992) p. 67

21. ibid., p. 90

Paracelsus

22. Weeks, Andrew, *Paracelsus Theophrastus Bombastus von Hohenheim, 1439-1541. Essential Theoretical Writings*, (Boston, MA, USA: Brill Publications, 2008), p.183
23. Mirandola, Pico della, "On the Dignity of Man", trans. Charles Glenn Wallis, in *On the Dignity of Man, On Being and One, Heptaplus*, (Indianapolis, IN, USA: Hackett Publishing Company, 1965) p. 4-5.
24. Weeks, *Paracelsus*, p. 163-165
25. Faivre, *Theosophy*, p.8
26. Weeks, *Paracelsus*, p.117-121
27. ibid., p. 129
28. ibid., p.179
29. ibid., p. 309
30. Weeks, Andrew, *Paracelsus: Speculative Theory and the Crisis of the Early Reformation*, (Albany, NY, USA: State University of New York Press, 1997), p. 13
31. Faivre, *Theosophy*. p. 7-8
32. Debus, Allen G., *The Chemical Philosophy*, (Mineola, NY, USA: Dover Publications, 1977) p. 79
33. ibid., p. 80
34. ibid., p. 87-88
35. Boehme, Jacob, *The Aurora, That Is, The Day-Spring*, trans. John Sparrow, ed. C.J. Barker, D. S. Hehner, (Edmonds, WA: Sure Fire Press, Holmes Publishing Group, 1992) p. 92
36. Debus, *Chemical Philosophy*, p. 107-108
37. ibid., p. 88-89
38. ibid., p. 107-108
39. ibid., p. 107-108
40. ibid., p. 107
41. ibid., p. 362-363
42. Tobyn, Graeme, *Culpeper's Medicine, a Practice of Western Holistic Medicine*, (Rockport, MA, USA: Element Books, 1997) p. 62-64
43. ibid., p. 74-75, 85, 86 diagram, 91-92
44. Debus, *Chemical Philosophy*, p. 107

Theosophy

45. Faivre, *Theosophy*, p. 6, 7
46. Weeks, *Boehme*, p. 62-63

47. Faivre, *Theosophy*, p. 8,
48. ibid., p. 50
49. Muses, *Illumination*, p.31-33
50. Weigel, Valentin, *Valentin Weigel: Selected Spiritual Writings*, trans. Andrew Weeks, (Mahwah, NJ, USA: Paulist Press, 2003) p.143
51. Tauler, Johannes, *Johannes Tauler: Sermons*, trans. Maria Shrady, (Mahwah, New Jersey, USA: Paulist Press, 1985) p. 36, 37-40
52. ibid., p. 42-44
53. Weigel, *Selected Spiritual Writings*, p. 204
54. ibid., p.152, 159
55. ibid., p. 182
56. ibid.,p. 208-209, 206-207

Sophia

57. Versluis, Arthur, *Wisdom's Book, the Sophia Anthology*, (St. Paul, MN, USA: Paragon House, 2000) p. 27
58. Weigel, *Selected Spiritual Writings*, p. 189-190, 206-207
59. Welling, Georg von, *Opus Mago-Cabbalisticum et Theosophicum*, trans. Joseph G. McVeigh, (San Francisco, CA: Red Wheel/Weiser 2006), Kindle Edition, Eternal Wisdom, Chapter 1, Kindle Location 10908
60. ibid., Eternal Wisdom, Chapter 2, Kindle Locations 10975-10977
61. Clairvaux, Bernard of, *Bernard of Clairvaux: Selected Works*. Trans. G.R. Evans, (Mahwah, New Jersey, USA: Paulist Press, 1987) p. 216
62. Versluis, *Wisdom's Book*, p. 47
63. Boehme, Jacob, *Concerning the Three Principles of the Divine Essence, of the Eternal, Dark, Light and Temporary World*, trans. John Sparrow, (London: Watkins, 1910), Chapter 18, Paragraph 58, p. 449

Section II

Rosicrucians and Freher

1. McIntosh, Christopher, *The Rosicrucians: The History, Mythology, and Rituals of an Esoteric Order*, third rev. edition, (San Francisco: Red Wheel/Weiser, 1998) , p.66
2. ibid., p.66
3. Faivre, *Theosophy*, p. 171
4. Muses, *Illumination*, page 1.

5. Harmsen, Theodor, "The Reception of Jacob Böhme and Böhmist Theosophy in the *Geheime Figuren der Rosenkreuzer*", in *Offenbarung Und Episteme: Zur Europaischen Wirkung Jakob Bohmes Im 17. Und 18. Jahrhundert (Fr He Neuzeit)*, ed. Kühlmann, Wilhelm / Vollhardt, Friedrich, (Berlin, Germany: De Gruyter, 2012) p. 201
6. ibid., p.20
7. McIntosh, Christopher, *The Rose Cross in the Age of Reason, Eighteenth-Century Rosicrucianism and its Relationship to the Enlightenment*, (Albany, NY: State University of New York Press, 2011), pg. 32
8. Harmsen, *Reception of Jacob Böhme*, p. 193
9. ibid., p. 194
10. McIntosh, *The Rose Cross in the Age of Reason*, p.46
11. ibid., p. 50
12. ibid., p. 50
13. ibid., p. 57-58
14. Westlund, Tommy, *AN OVERVIEW OF THE ALCHEMICAL AND MAGICAL SYSTEM OF THE GOLD- UND ROSENKREUZ ORDER*, http://www.alkemiskaakademin.se/gurc.pdf, 2007, p.6,
15. ibid., p. 6-12,
16. McIntosh, *Rose Cross in the Age of Reason*, p. 135, 138, 140,
17. ibid., p. 133-136, chapter eight in general.

Opus Mago-Cabbalisticum

18. Welling, *Opus Mago-Cabbalisticum*, Volume 2, chapter 1, part 3, Kindle Locations 3676-3678.
19. ibid., Volume 1, chapter 1, part 9, Kindle Location 381
20. ibid., Volume 1, chapter 1, part 8, Kindle Locations 360-361
21. ibid., Volume 1, chapter 1, part 10, Kindle Locations 395-396, 408-409
22. ibid., Volume 1, chapter 1, part 10, Kindle Location 408-409
23. ibid., Volume 1, chapter 1, part 10, Kindle Locations 409-410
24. ibid., Volume 1, chapter 4, part 3, Kindle Locations 2293-2294.
25. ibid., Volume 1, chapter 4, part 3, Kindle Locations 2296-2303.
26. ibid., Volume 1, chapter 4, part 4, Kindle Locations 2313-2317
27. ibid., Volume 1, chapter 5, part 3, Kindle Locations 2436-2440
28. ibid., Volume 1, chapter 5, part 3, Kindle Locations 2464-2467
29. ibid., Volume 1, chapter 5, part 5, Kindle Locations 2476-2481
30. ibid., Volume 1, chapter 5, part 10, Kindle Locations 2592-2597
31. ibid., Volume 1, chapter 5, part 19, Kindle Locations 2857-2858
32. ibid., Volume 1, chapter 5, part 25, Kindle Locations 2989-2991

33. ibid., Volume 1, chapter 5, part 33, Kindle Locations 3178-3181
34. ibid., Volume 1, chapter 5, part 36, Kindle Locations 3378-3380
35. ibid., Volume 1, chapter 5, part 36, Kindle Locations 3381-3384
36. ibid., Volume 1, chapter 6, part 3, Kindle Locations 3539-3541
37. ibid., Volume 1, chapter 6, part 6, Kindle Locations 3602-3605
38. ibid., Volume 1, chapter 6, part 6, Kindle Location 3618-3621
39. Bach, Jeff, *Voices of the Turtledoves: The Sacred World of Ephrata*, (University Park, PA, USA: Pennsylvania State Press, 2003), p. 43
40. ibid., p. 43
41. Gibbons, B.J., *Gender in Mystical Thought: Behmenism and its Development in England*, (New York, NY: Cambridge University Press, 1996), p. 167
42. McIntosh, *Rose Cross in the Age of Reason*, p. 32
43. Bach, *Turtledoves*, p. 43

Secret Symbols

44. Harmsen, *Reception Jacob Böhme*, p. 199-200
45. ibid., p. 199-200
46. ibid., p. 201
47. ibid., p. 200
48. Harmsen, Theodor, "Fiction or a much stranger Truth. Sources and Reception of the *Geheime Figuren der Rosenkreuzer* – Secret Symbols of the Rosicrucians in the 18th, 19th and 20th Centuries", in *Aufklärung und Esoterik: Wege in die Moderne (Hallesche Beitr GE Zur Europ Ischen Aufklärung)*, Ed. by Neugebauer-Wölk, Monika / Geffarth, Renko/ Meumann, Markus, (Berlin Germany: De Gruyter, 2013) p. 739
49. Harmsen, *Reception of Jacob Böhme*, p. 202-203
50. Muses, *Illumination*, frontispiece

Eternal Wisdom

51. Welling, *Opus Mago-Cabbalisticum*, Eternal Wisdom, Chapter 1, Kindle Locations 10929-10930
52. ibid., Eternal Wisdom, Chapter 2, Kindle Locations 10984-10986
53. ibid., Eternal Wisdom, Chapter 3, Kindle Locations 10996-10997
54. ibid., Eternal Wisdom, Chapter 3, Kindle Locations 11038-11040
55. ibid., Eternal Wisdom, Chapter 3, Kindle Location 11042
56. ibid., Eternal Wisdom, Chapter 3, Kindle Locations 11016-11018
57. ibid., Eternal Wisdom, Chapter 3, Kindle Locations 11075-11076
58. ibid., Eternal Wisdom, Chapter 3, Kindle Locations 11076-11079
59. ibid., Eternal Wisdom, Chapter 3, Kindle Locations 11079-11081

60. ibid., Eternal Wisdom, Addendum, Stanza 8, Kindle Locations 11209-11212
61. ibid., Eternal Wisdom, Addendum, Stanza 9, Kindle Location 11218
62. ibid., Eternal Wisdom, Addendum, Stanza 9, Kindle Locations 11227-11228
63. ibid., Eternal Wisdom, Addendum, Stanza 10, Kindle Locations 11235-11236
64. ibid., Eternal Wisdom, Addendum, Stanza 10, Kindle Locations 11238-11240
65. ibid., Eternal Wisdom, Addendum, Stanza 12, Kindle Locations 11259-11263
66. ibid., Eternal Wisdom, Addendum, Stanza 13, Kindle Locations 11273-11276
67. ibid., Eternal Wisdom, Addendum, Stanza 15, Kindle Locations 11319-11323

Hartmann and Lead

68. Hartmann, *In the Pronaos of the Temple of Wisdom, Containing the History of the True and False Rosicrucians* (London: Theosophical Publishing Company, 1890), p. 105-110, also *Rosicrucian Symbols*, (Sequim, WA, USA: Holmes Publishing Group, 2005), p. 7-12
69. Lead, Jane, *Messenger of An Universal Peace, a Third Message to the Philadelphian Society*, orig. 1698, http://www.janelead.org/files/115240200.pdf p. 49-53
70. Hartmann, *Pronaos*, p.100
71. ibid., p. 102
72. Hartmann, Franz *Cosmology, or Universal Science*, (Whitefish, MT, USA: Kessinger Publishing, n.d.), p.8
73. Hartmann, *Pronaos*, p. 93, 94, 97-98

Section III

Philadelphian Society

1. Laborie, Lionel, "Philadelphia Resurrected: Celebrating the Union Act (1707) from Irenic to Scatological Eschatology", in *Jane Lead and Her Transnational Legacy*, ed. Ariel Hessayon, (London:Palgrave Macmillan, 2016)
2. Hessayon, Ariel, "Lead's Life and Times (Part Two)", in *Jane Lead and Her Transnational Legacy*, ed. Ariel Hessayon, (London:Palgrave Macmillan, 2016) p. 58-59

3. Gibbons, *Gender in Occult and Mystical Thought*, p. 106
4. ibid.p. 106
5. ibid., p. 106
6. Versluis, *Wisdom's Book*, p. 66
7. Hessayon, "Lead's Life and Times (Part Two)"p. 60-61
8. Raymond, Joad, "Radicalism and Mysticism in the Later Seventeenth Century: John Pordage's Angels", in *Conversations with Angels: Towards a History of Spiritual Communication, 1100-1700*, ed. Joad Raymond, (London: Palgrave Macmillan, 2011)p. 409
9. ibid., p. 409-410, 411-413
10. Gibbons, *Gender in Occult and Mystical Thought*, p. 108
11. ibid., p. 107
12. Raymond, Joad, "Radicalism", p. 411-413
13. Churton, Tobias, *The Magus of Freemasonry: The Mysterious Life of Elias Ashmole—Scientist, Alchemist, and Founder of the Royal Society*, (Rochester, Vermont, USA: Inner Traditions, 2006) chapter 9, sec."The Antiquarian", Kindle Locations 3009-3012
14. Gibbons, p. 106
15. ibid., p. 107
16. Versluis, *Wisdom's Book*, p. 66
17. Hessayon, "Lead's Life and Times (Part Two)" p. 42
18. ibid., p. 43
19. ibid., p. 48.
20. Lead, Jane, *A Message to the Philadelphian Society, Withersoever Dispersed Over the Whole Earth*, London, 1696, original p.8, http://www.janelead.org/files/115240200.pdf, p.9
21. ibid., original p.8, http://www.janelead.org/files/115240200.pdf, p. 9
22. Hessayon, "Lead's Life and Times (Part Two)"p. 49
23. Raymond, p. 419
24. Laborie, "Philadelphia Resurrected", p. 214-215
25. Hessayon, "Lead's Life and Times (Part Two)", p. 55
26. ibid., p. 55-56
27. ibid., p. 58
28. ibid., p. 59, 55, 52-53
29. ibid., p. 55-56
30. Gibbons, *Gender in Occult and Mystical Thought*, p. 165
31. Apetrei, Sarah, "Mystical Divinity in the Manuscript Writings of Jane Lead and Anne Bathhurst", in *Jane Lead and Her Transnational Legacy*, ed. Ariel Hessayon, (London:Palgrave Macmillan, 2016), p. 183-184

32. Lead, *Messages to the Philadelphian Society,* original p. 6, http://www.janelead.org/files/115240200.pdf , p. 8
33. ibid., original p. 34, par 19
34. ibid., original p. 40, par 25
35. Anonymous, *Forty-Four PROPOSITIONS EXTRACTED From the REASONS for the Foundation and Promotion of a Philadelphian Society,* orig. 1698, http://www.janelead.org/files/121513288.pdf, p. 6, par. 35,
36. Lead, Jane, *Revelation of Revelations,* 1701 edition, original p.175-176, 188-190, http://www.janelead.org/files/57309565.pdf, pages 109-110, 121-122
37. Lead, Jane, *Revelation of Revelations,* 1683 edition, http://www.passtheword.org/Jane-Lead/revelatn-3.htm, end of first paragraph.
38. Lead, Jane, *Messages to the Philadelphian Society,* original p. 74-75, http://www.janelead.org/files/115240200.pdf , p.24
39. ibid., http://www.janelead.org/files/115240200.pdf, p. 49-53
40. Laborie, Lionel, "Philadelphia Resurrected", p. 214
41. Hessayon, Ariel, "Lead's Life and Times (Part Three)", in *Jane Lead and Her Transnational Legacy,* ed. Ariel Hessayon, (London:Palgrave Macmillan, 2016) p. 73
42. ibid., p. 74
43. Weigel, *Selected Spiritual Writings,* p. 161
44. ibid., p. 198-199
45. ibid., p. 184
46. ibid., p.199
47. Versluis, *Wisdom's Children,* p. 67
48. Hessayon, "Introduction, Jane Lead's Legacy in Perspective", in "Jane Lead and Her Transnational Legacy", p. 14 , "Lead's Life and Times (Part Two): the Woman in the Wilderness", p. 42, "Lead's Life and Times(Part Three): The Philadelphian Society" p.78
49. Hessayon, "Lead's Life and Times (Part Two)" p. 53
50. Versluis, *Wisdom's Children,* p. 74
51. Raymond, Joad, "Radicalism", p. 411
52. Lead, Jane, *A Fountain of Gardens,* vol. 1, (London, 1697), p. 111-112
53. Versluis, *Wisdom's Book,* p. 66
54. Pordage, John "A Philosophical Epistle on the True Stone of Wisdom", in *Wisdom's Book, the Sophia Anthology,* ed. Arthur Versluis, (St.Paul, MN, USA: Paragon House, 2000), p. 67-76,
55. Lee, Francis, "On the Philadelphian Gold", originally in *Theosophical Transactions,* http://www.alchemywebsite.com/philadel.html

Introduction 85

56. Hessayon, "Lead's Life and Times(Part Three): The Philadelphian Society", p. 75
57. ibid., p. 75-76
58. Laborie, "Philadelphia Resurrected",p. 215
59. ibid., p. 216
60. ibid., p. 224
61. ibid., p. 219
62. ibid., p. 221
63. ibid., p. 227-228
64. ibid., p. 226
65. ibid., p. 227
66. ibid., p. 228
67. ibid., p. 227-228
68. Gibbons, *Gender in Occult and Mystical Thought*, p. 106
69. Hessayon, "Lead's Life and Times(Part Two)", p. 58
70. Laborie, "Philadelphia Resurrected" p. 229
71. ibid., p. 229
72. ibid., p. 230
73. ibid., p. 230-231
74. Monod, Paul Kléber, *Solomon's Secret Arts, the Occult in the Age of Enlightenment*, (New Haven, CT, USA: Yale University Press, 2013), p. 205
75. Laborie p. 230
76. Monod, p. 205
77. Laborie p. 230-231
78. Monod, p. 205
79. Gibbons, Brian, "Francis Lee", in *Oxford Dictionary of National Biography: in association with the British Academy : from the earliest times to the year 2000*, vol. 33., (New York: Oxford University Press, 2004), p. 62

Section IV

Freher's background.

1. Muses, p. 4
2. ibid., p. 6
3. Hessayon, "Lead's Life and Times(Part Two): The Woman in the Wilderness", p. 59
4. Muses, p. 20
5. Walton, Christopher, *Notes and Materials for an Adequate Biography of William Law*, (London, 1856), p. 491, "Postscript"

6. Hessayon, "Lead's Life and Times(Part Three)", pg. 78.
7. McLean, Adam, *Database of alchemical manuscripts - Bodleian - Rawlinson*, http://www.alchemywebsite.com/almss6.html , #586
8. Muses, p. 54
9. Walton, p. 491, "Postscript"
10. Muses p. 55
11. ibid., p. 70
12. Walton, p. 686-687

Walton's background

13. Godwin, Joscelyn, *The Theosophical Enlightenment*, (Albany, NY: The State University of New York Press, 1994) p. 228
14. ibid., p. 232
15. ibid., p. 235
16. ibid., p. 239-240
17. Versluis, *Wisdom's Children*, p. 118.
18. Penny, A.J. *Studies in Jacob Boehme*, (Whitefish, MT, USA: Kessinger Publishing, 2010) p. 27
19. ibid., p. 194
20. Godwin, p. 237
21. Walton, p. 113
22. Muses, p. 25
23. ibid., p. 45
24. Walton, p. 234, footnote.
25. ibid., p. 257, footnote.
26. ibid., p. 233
27. ibid., p. 331, footnote
28. ibid., p. 587-591
29. Monod, p. 326.
30. ibid., p. 328
31. Godwin, p. 101
32. Monod, p. 298
33. Godwin, p. 101
34. ibid., p. 101
35. Hessayon, Ariel, *Jacob Boehme, Swedenborg, and their Readers*, https://www.researchgate.net/publication/27225165_Jacob_Boehme_Emanuel_Swedenborg_and_their_Readers, (2007), p. 38
36. ibid., p. 40
37. ibid., p. 40-41
38. Walton, p. 590, footnote

Walton's Book

39. Godwin, p. 238
40. Walton, p. 334
41. ibid.n, p. 334-342,
42. ibid., p. 338

Lee's texts

43. Lee, Francis, *Apoleipomena, or Dissertations Theological, Mathematical, and Physical*, vol. 1, (London: Alexander Strahan, 1752), p. xvi
44. ibid., p. xviii
45. Hessayon, "Lead's Life and Times(Part Two): The Woman in the Wilderness", p. 58

Works Cited

Anonymous, *Forty-Four PROPOSITIONS EXTRACTED From the REASONS for the Foundation and Promotion of a Philadelphian Society*, orig. 1698, www.janelead.org/files/121513288.pdf

Apetrei, Sarah, "Mystical Divinity in the Manuscript Writings of Jane Lead and Anne Bathhurst", in *Jane Lead and Her Transnational Legacy*, ed. Ariel Hessayon, London:Palgrave Macmillan, 2016

Bach, Jeff, *Voices of the Turtledoves: The Sacred World of Ephrata*, University Park, PA, USA: Pennsylvania State Press, 2003

Boehme, Jacob, *The Aurora, That Is, The Day-Spring*, trans. John Sparrow, ed. C.J. Barker, D. S. Hehner, Edmonds, WA: Sure Fire Press, Holmes Publishing Group, 1992

Boehme, Jacob, *Concerning the Three Principles of the Divine Essence, of the Eternal, Dark, Light and Temporary World*, trans. John Sparrow, London: Watkins, 1910

Churton, Tobias, *The Magus of Freemasonry: The Mysterious Life of Elias Ashmole—Scientist, Alchemist, and Founder of the Royal Society*, Rochester, Vermont, USA: Inner Traditions, 2006, Kindle Edition

Clairvaux, Bernard of, *Bernard of Clairvaux: Selected Works*. Trans. G.R. Evans, Mahwah, New Jersey, USA: Paulist Press, 1987

Copenhaver, Brian, *Hermetica: The Greek Corpus Hermeticum and the Latin Asclepius in a new English Translation with Notes and Introduction*, New York, NY: Cambridge University Press, 1992

Debus, Allen G., *The Chemical Philosophy*, Mineola, NY, USA: Dover Publications, 1977

Faas, Robert J., *The Divine Couple, a Christian Book of Mystery on Eros-Love*, St. Paul, Minnesota, USA: Grailstone Press, 2001

Faivre, Antoine, *Theosophy, Imagination, Tradition, Studies in Western Esotericism*, trans. Christine Rhone, Albany, NY: State University of New York Press, 2000

Gibbons, Brian, "Francis Lee", in *Oxford Dictionary of National Biography: in association with the British Academy : from the earliest times to the year 2000*, vol. 33., New York: Oxford University Press, 2004

Gibbons, B.J. *Gender in Mystical Thought: Behmenism and its Development in England*, New York, NY: Cambridge University Press, 1996

Godwin, Joscelyn, *The Theosophical Enlightenment*, Albany, NY: The State University of New York Press, 1994

Harmsen, Theodor, "The Reception of Jacob Böhme and Böhmist Theosophy in the *Geheime Figuren der Rosenkreuzer*", in *Offenbarung Und Episteme: Zur Europaischen Wirkung Jakob Bohmes Im 17. Und 18. Jahrhundert (Fr He Neuzeit)*, ed. Kühlmann, Wilhelm / Vollhardt, Friedrich, Berlin, Germany: De Gruyter, 2012

Harmsen, Theodor, "Fiction or a much stranger Truth. Sources and Reception of the *Geheime Figuren der Rosenkreuzer* – Secret Symbols of the Rosicrucians in the 18th, 19th and 20th Centuries", in *Aufklärung und Esoterik: Wege in die Moderne (Hallesche Beitr GE Zur Europ Ischen Aufklärung)*, Ed. by Neugebauer-Wölk, Monika / Geffarth, Renko / Meumann, Markus, Berlin Germany: De Gruyter, 2013

Hartmann, Franz *Cosmology, or Universal Science*, Whitefish, MT, USA: Kessinger Publishing, n.d.

Hartmann, Franz, *Im Vorhof des Tempels der Weisheit*, Kindle Edition, München, Germany: Verlag Heliakon, 2014

Hartmann, Franz, *In the Pronaos of the Temple of Wisdom, Containing the History of the True and False Rosicrucians*, London: Theosophical Publishing Company, 1890.

Hartmann, Franz, *Rosicrucian Symbols*, Sequim, WA, USA: Holmes Publishing Group, 2005

Hessayon, Ariel "Introduction: Jane Lead's Legacy in Perspective", in *Jane Lead and Her Transnational Legacy*, ed. Ariel Hessayon, London:Palgrave Macmillan, 2016

Hessayon, Ariel, *Jacob Boehme, Swedenborg, and their Readers*, https://www.researchgate.net/publication/27225165_Jacob_Boehme_Emanuel_Swedenborg_and_their_Readers, 2007

Hessayon, Ariel, "Lead's Life and Times (Part Two)", in *Jane Lead and Her Transnational Legacy*, ed. Ariel Hessayon, London:Palgrave Macmillan, 2016

Hessayon, Ariel, "Lead's Life and Times (Part Three)", in *Jane Lead and Her Transnational Legacy*, ed. Ariel Hessayon, London:Palgrave Macmillan, 2016

Laborie, Lionel, "Philadelphia Resurrected: Celebrating the Union Act (1707) from Irenic to Scatological Eschatology", in *Jane Lead and Her Transnational Legacy*, ed. Ariel Hessayon, London:Palgrave Macmillan, 2016

Law, William, *Works of Jacob Behmen, the Teutonic Theosopher*, volume 3, London: G. Robinson, 1772

Lead Jane, *A Fountain of Gardens*, vol. 1, London, 1697

Lead, Jane, *A Message to the Philadelphian Society, Withersoever Dispersed Over the Whole Earth*, London, 1696, http://www.janelead.org/files/115240200.pdf

Lead, Jane, *Messenger of An Universal Peace, a Third Message to the Philadelphian Society*, orig. 1698, http://www.janelead.org/files/115240200.pdf

Lead, Jane, *Revelation of Revelations*, 1683 ed. http://www.passtheword.org/Jane-Lead/revelatn.htm

Lead, Jane, *Revelation of Revelations*, 1701 ed. http://www.janelead.org/files/57309565.pdf

Leade, Jane, *Der Himmlische Bottschaffter eines Allgemeinen Friedens: oder Eine dritte Bottschafft an die Philadelphische Gemeine*, Amsterdam, 1698

Lee, Francis, *Apoleipomena, or Dissertations Theological, Mathematical, and Physical*, vol. 1, London: Alexander Strahan, 1752.

Lee, Francis, "On the Philadelphian Gold" orig. *Theosophical Transactions*, http://www.alchemywebsite.com/philadel.html

McIntosh, Christopher, *The Rose Cross in the Age of Reason, Eighteenth-Century Rosicrucianism and its Relationship to the Enlightenment*, Albany, NY: State University of New York Press, 2011

McIntosh, Christopher, *The Rosicrucians: The History, Mythology, and Rituals of an Esoteric Order*, third rev. edition, San Francisco: Red Wheel/Weiser, 1998

Mirandola, Pico della, "On the Dignity of Man", trans. Charles Glenn Wallis, in *On the Dignity of Man, On Being and One, Heptaplus*, Indianapolis, IN, USA: Hackett Publishing Company, 1965

Monod, Paul Kléber, *Solomon's Secret Arts, the Occult in the Age of Enlightenment*, New Haven, CT, USA: Yale University Press, 2013

Muses, Charles, *Illumination on Jacob Boehme, the Work of Dionysius Andreas Freher*, New York: King's Crown Press, Columbia University, 1951

Penny, A.J. *Studies in Jacob Boehme*, Whitefish, MT, USA: Kessinger Publishing, 2010

Peterson, Joseph, *Arbatel: Concerning the Magic of the Ancients*, Lake Worth, FL, USA: Ibis Press, 2009

Pordage, John "A Philosophical Epistle on the True Stone of Wisdom", in *Wisdom's Book, the Sophia Anthology*, ed. Arthur Versluis, St.Paul, MN, USA: Paragon House, 2000

Raymond, Joad, "Radicalism and Mysticism in the Later Seventeenth Century: John Pordage's Angels", in *Conversations with Angels: Towards a History of Spiritual Communication, 1100-1700*, ed. Joad Raymond, London: Palgrave Macmillan, 2011

Tauler, Johannes, *Johannes Tauler: Sermons*, trans. Maria Shrady, Mahwah, New Jersey, USA: Paulist Press, 1985

Tobyn, Graeme, *Culpeper's Medicine, a Practice of Western Holistic Medicine*, Rockport, MA, USA: Element Books, 1997

Versluis, Arthur, *Wisdom's Book, the Sophia Anthology*, St.Paul, MN, USA: Paragon House, 2000

Versluis, Arthur, *Wisdom's Children, A Christian Esoteric Tradition*, Albany, NY, USA: State University of New York Press, 1999

Walton, Christopher, *Introduction to Theosophy, or the 'Mystery of Christ'*, vol. 1, London, 1855

Walton, Christopher, *Notes and Materials for an Adequate Biography of William Law*, London, 1856

Weeks, Andrew, *Boehme: an Intellectual Biography of the Seventeenth-Century Philosopher and Mystic*, Albany, NY, USA: State University of New York Press, 1991

Weeks, Andrew, *Paracelsus: Speculative Theory and the Crisis of the Early Reformation*, Albany, NY, USA: State University of New York Press, 1997

Weeks, Andrew, *Paracelsus Theophrastus Bombastus von Hohenheim, 1439-1541. Essential Theoretical Writings*, Boston, MA, USA: Brill, 2008

Weigel, Valentin, *Valentin Weigel: Selected Spiritual Writings*, trans. Andrew Weeks, Mahwah, NJ, USA: Paulist Press, 2003

Welling, Georg von, *Opus Mago-Cabbalisticum et Theosophicum*, trans. Joseph G. McVeigh, San Francisco, CA: Red Wheel/Weiser 2006, Kindle Edition

Westlund, Tommy, *AN OVERVIEW OF THE ALCHEMICAL AND MAGICAL SYSTEM OF THE GOLD-UND ROSENKREUZ ORDER*, http://www.alkemiskaakademin.se/gurc.pdf, 2007

Part One:
Dionysius Andreas Freher

Selection One.

"God Without Nature or Creature", from "Serial Elucidations, A, part 1"

[The first work by Freher in Walton's book, prefaced by Walton's introduction to the Freher selections. —Ed.]

FREHER.

Having, doubtless, excited in the mind of the reader a just curiosity to see something of what Freher has written,—of whose discourses Law, as observed, had the full benefit, which therefore will require to be perused by the candidate, to enable him to apprehend the elementary formulation of Law's mind, in its theosophic development; and as the present section is to be regarded as indicative of the highest philosophical, mystical, and theological science extant in this country, at the commencement of the last century; we propose to devote the remaining portion of this POSTSCRIPT, to a few illustrations of the genius and talent of Freher.

We have already incidentally described the character of Freher's works. It will therefore be merely needful to repeat, in this place, that they contain a systematic exhibition and demonstration of the truths and principles of Behmen's philosophy; the author, as he proceeds, inviting or anticipating objections to particular points of his subject, either as not clearly apprehensible to the honest enquirer, or seemingly inconsistent with the received orthodox truth, or with other portions of Behmen's writings; which he fails not to clear up before continuing his discourses, having only at heart the interests of truth, and the setting it forth in its full natural light.

It will be out of question, by any extracts which could here be inserted, to afford an adequate conception of the universality and profundity of Freher's philosophical science: the only object that can be attempted, will be to present a few glimpses therof; and this, also, in the hope of inducing a demand for the publication of his entire works, according to the advertisement to be annexed to this treatise. For an example, therefore, or illustration of the merits of Freher's writings, as most appropriate for insertion on the present occasion, we have, amid the difficulty of selection, fixed upon two or three of the above-mentioned Discourses, in answer to the above-mentioned offered or supposed entertainable objections, and as containing a summary of his preceding elucidations of the subjects in question.

The first of these extracts, which treats briefly "Of GOD considered without NATURE or CREATURE," may be considered as a kind of introduction to the rest, and is as follows:—

I.—It is a deep grounded central axiom of immovable and unquestionable truth, firm and solid throughout all principles, and most worthy of being exactly pondered, as in the very beginning of all these writings, so also chiefly in the beginning of this first head thereof, that *no eye can see beyond its own sphere, or world, wherein it is born, or wherein it doth exist, and hath its only essence, and all its seeing faculty.* THREE PRINC. ii. 1–4, etc.; vii. 1, 2, etc. BAPTISM, i. 14. SIGN. RER. iii. 6, 7, 8. EPISTLES, v. 2, 3, etc.; xxxii. 3–8.

II.—According, then, to this fundamental position, it is an absolute impossibility for all created intellectual eyes to look essentially into that Abyss which is beyond eternal nature; or to apprehend distinctly, and to declare positively, in an affirmative way, *what God is without all nature and creature.* Truly, if we would say, that either men or angels were able to do it, our saying would bear the self-same absurd and contradicting nonsense, as if we did say, that this or that can act without or beyond its own sphere of activity.

III.—For every created eye or intellect is a particular thing, having a distinct existence from other things; being posterior to, and standing, as to all its faculties within the sphere of eternal nature. Whereas, without eternal nature, there is and must be an eternal *nothing*, in comparison to all created things in nature: and an eternal *chaos*, or *temperature*; or an eternal *oneness*, in comparison to that divisibility and innumerable multiplicity that is in nature. In which eternal *nothing*, *temperature*, and *oneness* no creature can exist, nor ever be brought forth; seeing it is self-evident that something and nothing, distinction and temperature, multiplicity and oneness, cannot stand together in one and the same sphere, but do imply the very highest, and most irreconcilable contradiction. THREE PRIN. i. 21, 22. PREDEST., ii. 56–63.

IV.—But, nevertheless, the created intellect, both in men and angels, considering things *a posteriori* as they are in nature, and knowing they came into natural existency from such a deeper original or foundation-essence, as is itself ALL things in a most eminent sense, must needs on one side own all things to have been in that same original fountain, before eternal nature: because they came forth from out thereof; and must also on the other side disown any thing to have been therein so, as it is now in its created existency, after eternal nature: or else we would say, that it hath been a creature before it was created.

V.—This we are able to apprehend; but to declare, further, distinctly and positively, What this original or foundation-essence is in itself, and how all things have been therein before eternal nature, will be much more impossible for us, than to apprehend distinctly, and to declare positively, what and how we have been in the loins of our father Adam. FORTY QUES. i, 341, 347.

VI.—All what we can conceive and say thereof is this: that we all, when yet in the loins of Adam, have been nothing, lying in one only chaos, without all distinction from each other: which in a sense, and with respect to what we are now, is very true. And yet it is not without all limitation true, in an absolute transcendent sense. For we may see, that even from this same nothing the apostle can, and doth draw forth a most excellent and emphatical argument, to demonstrate thereby the great pre-eminence of the Melchisedech priesthood above the Levitical, saying that Levi, who received tithes after he was in existency, *payed tithes in Abraham*, when he was yet so nothing, as to be only in the loins of his father.

VII.—Though, therefore, our Author hath written most deeply and solidly, as of nature and creature; so also even of God himself without all nature and creature; yet we are not to think that he had, or could have had an essential prospect, or looking as it were *a priori* into that most incomprehensible Abyss of all abysses. For no illumination, though never so high, can afford such an one unto any created eye; but only a sight *a posteriori*, whereby, (in a comparative or negative way and manner,) he could and did express that first Original Being, out of nature, with natural words; being made able to find out the fittest expressions that could be found in outward nature. And of these, I think those three, mentioned before, are the most accommodate to every capacity.

VIII.—But this must yet especially be taken notice of, that these three expressions, (and chiefly that of *oneness*,) relate not only to the creatures, but also to all what God hath manifested through eternal nature, to be himself. Which will be so much as to say, that here in this place, where God is considered without all nature and creature, no distinct idea may be had, (and shall also not be desired to be had) of the Holy Trinity: no Father, Son, nor Holy Ghost; no Wisdom, no light, glory, majesty, goodness, holiness, are yet here brought forth into distinct manifestation. For though all these things have been verily there also, and must not be said to have had a beginning after, much less to be generated by eternal nature; yet they were as yet unknown, incomprehensible, and unmanifest.

And this expression, They were then so, and are now so, doth not import that ever any change, turning or alteration was made, for all is eternal, and co-eternal, without any beginning or shadow of turning: but we, that live and understand in time, and are used to periodical distinctions, cannot express what we conceive thereof otherwise, but by a *before* and *after*: which yet doth signify nothing else, but our own distinct idea of one and the self same eternal object. Which idea is another thing when we consider this eternal object abstractively, as it is *in itself* without all nature: for then it is to us, that are in nature, unknown, hid, and unintelligible; and is another again, when we consider it *as manifested* through the concurrence of eternal nature: for then we are able to have an apprehension or sight thereof, more or less, according to that degree, in which our eye is illuminated by the eternal light.—In respect now to that former consideration, we cannot express it better and nearer, than by saying, All these things were, (or rather are) an eternal incomprehensible *nothing*, when compared to that which we now, after their manifestation through eternal nature, can apprehend them to be: They are an eternal unintelligible *oneness*, in opposition to our distinct manifold ideas, we can now have of them: they are an eternal inconceivable *temperature*, in comparison to that distinction we can now conceive therein.—He, therefore, that hath but a due apprehension of these three expressions, may easily be freed from being disturbed by such seeming contradictions, as might appear in some of these places, where JACOB BEHMEN writes of *God considered without Nature and Creature*, and may also easily discern, what here and there is intermixed, relating to his eternal manifestation. Which places are these following: THREEFOLD LIFE, i. 33. FORTY QUEST. i. 24–48., 262–265. INCARN. PART II. i. 29. ii. 1–25.; iii. I, 2, etc. PREDEST. i. throughout. CONTEMPL. DIV. i. 17–22. BAPTISM, i. 1–9. MYSTER. MAG. i. 2; iii. 1–8; xxix. 1–6 (*N. B.*) x lx. 38–48.; lxi. 23–66(*N. B.)*; lxvi. 63. APPENDIX.1–4, etc. SIX POINTS, i. 8–37 (N.B.). HEAV. EAR. MYST. i, ii., iii. CLAVIS, r. I -3, etc. TABLE, v. 13–35. APOL STIEF. i. 199–212; iii. 34–45. SECD. APOL. B. TYLK. v. 86 and 146. SIGNAT. RER. iii. 1–5.; vi. 1–4."

And so the writer proceeds, in successive chapters, to open out the orderly elucidation of the mystery, according to its birth and description in Behmen; [...]

Selection Two.

"How Nothing Brings Forth [...] Something, in and Through [...] Eternal Nature", "Serial Elucidations F, part 1"

[...] the next following chapter being thus headed, "Of the Two Eternal Principles: of the Seven Properties of Nature: and of Darkness, Fire and Light."

The next extract we propose to insert, is "A DISCOURSE concerning the true SIGNIFICANT SENSE of TEUTONICUS's deepest, eternal, or ABYSSAL NOTHING: HOW this NOTHING brings forth itself into SOMETHING, in and through the PROCESS of ETERNAL NATURE. But more especially, how all his DIFFERENT DESCRIPTIONS of the DIVINE BEING, in UNITY and TRINITY, before or without, and then as in or after ETERNAL NATURE, may be found standing without all contradiction in a most HARMONIOUS CONCORDANCE:"

"Preface or introduction.—It is unquestionable that TEUTONICUS, in almost all his books considereth the Divine Eternal Being distinctly; sometimes (1.) as all unmanifest, as abyssal in the deepest sense, much different from that wherein the dark world it called abyssal, both in his own writings and in the holy Scriptures; as transcending all created capacities, and utterly excluded from any possibility of being an object either of a human, or of an angelical understanding; and as it was, still is, and will be for ever and ever, above, without, beyond, and before eternal Nature; notwithstanding that this nature is, in a sense declared formerly, co-eternal unto that Divine Being, so that all priority, or successiveness, is totally excluded. And sometimes, again (2.) he considereth this Divine Being, as manifested in and through eternal nature, as byssal, or as that which from the former unformed, beginningless and endless Abyss, hath introduced itself into a ground, or byss; into perceptibility, or into beginning and end; as capable only now of being understood and enjoyed, in a measure and degree, by understanding creatures, created for that purpose; and as it was, still is, and will be for ever and ever, in and with eternal nature. Notwithstanding that this nature was always, is still, and shall be for ever, distinct from, and in no wise to be confounded with that Divine Being.

So then, therefore, (3.) it is unquestionable also, and obvious in all the books of Teutonicus, that he useth several various expressions, and maketh most different descriptions of the Divine Being, which are not applicable promiscuously unto both these considerations, but must be referred either unto that former, or unto this latter in due distinction.

Though it cannot be denied, but that he useth also many times the same words, both of the one and of the other, and this chiefly because of the insufficiency of our capacities and speeches, which both are after and under eternal nature, and cannot either reach unto, or be furnished with words able and sufficient to express that which is beyond and before it. Such expressions, therefore, as are used both in that former, and in this latter consideration, must, in the sense, be distinctly taken and regulated according to what he so frequently and plainly hath premonished, and laid as a foundation for a further superstructure. For this foundation, if observed, cannot but presently direct the reader to that distinction, always to be had in the sense, though it cannot always be had in outward words; and thus in every expression which is dubious or common (as to the outward sound) unto both considerations: but if neglected, much confusion and seeming contradictions cannot be avoided.

The first result from these three fundamental unquestionable assertions, justly here to be taken notice of in the beginning, is this: When Teutonicus considereth of the Divine Being as before, or without all nature and creature, the *generation of eternal nature*, in its seven properties, is not implied in that consideration, *neither tacitly nor explicitly*, and must not be conceived as if the mention thereof were only left out for brevity's sake. But this generation of eternal nature in all its properties, is utterly and absolutely excluded therefrom, and must be *conceived* as *quite posterior* to this first consideration; yet so, that this posteriority be not referred to the thing itself but only to our narrow capacity and confined understanding.

If, in the *first* consideration of the Divine Being, the generation of eternal nature in its properties should be looked upon as tacitly implied, all the distinction between the first and second consideration, is wholly done away; which yet was laid down, as the first foundation, most plainly and clearly, in more than twelve or fifteen places. And besides this, many hundred noble expressions are rendered senseless, nay, the whole superstructure of all his building is thereby overthrown. Pray, how can God be considered as without and before all nature, if the generation of nature is said to be only left out in the written words, but is to be conceived in the mind as already done? Or how could Teutonicus have said: *so far is God considered without all nature and creature?* Truly, that *so far* can bear no other sense but this, *unto* (or till it cometh to) *the generation of the properties of nature, is God considered without all nature.*

But here two objections may be made. The first is this: since there is neither *before* nor *after*, in the consideration of God and eternal nature, we cannot but think that these two expressions, *before* and *without* nature, must be all equivalent. And since now God is considered by Behmen only as in the second principle of light and love, wherein he is distinct from, and superior to his dwelling place, he could rightly have said, that God is considered without nature, notwithstanding that in this consideration the whole generation of nature is tacitly implied, though not always distinctly mentioned.

It is answered, first, as to the priority, it was granted already, that we ought not to say of any *before* or *after*, with relation to *the thing itself*, but that we must say so with respect to our *apprehension*: which is to conceive all these things orderly, since we are not able to apprehend there as they are in themselves, all at once. And secondly, as to the two expressions, *before* and *without*, though they are, upon one account, commonly and rightly joined together, are yet, upon another, not at all equivalent, but greatly different from each other in their sense and relation.

For when I say, God is considered as *before* eternal nature, this nature is always utterly excluded, and must be conceived as absolutely posterior to that consideration, which the natural and common sense of that word doth show sufficiently. But when I say, God is considered *without* nature, as Behmen doth sometimes, the whole eternal nature is not always utterly excluded, but only the left, or inferior restless part of nature, which is frequently by Behmen called nature, absolutely, without addition, and in a stricter sense excluding the other, right, superior, transmuted part; which, as in opposition unto that former, is not by Behmen called nature, but most significantly the end of nature, or the fulfilling, or satisfying of nature, or also the holy or the tinctured nature.

So now it is true indeed, that when he thus considered God, as in that second superior transmuted principle of light and love, the generation of the first principle in all its foregoing properties, is verily implied, and must be conceived as already done. But what can this signify or make against our position? All this consideration of God, is not a consideration of God as abyssal and unmanifest, and unintelligible; but as intelligible by creatures, as byssal and manifested in and through eternal nature; and may be called without nature also,—not that the generation of nature is utterly excluded, or were to be looked upon as posterior, but only because it is done *through* the inferior and restless, *in* the superior harmonized part of nature; and is so verily *without* (but not before) that lower disharmonized part of nature, which properly and strictly is called nature.

But further it is absolutely false, that Behmen considereth God only so. For though he hath the same expressions that are in this objection mentioned, viz., that God is considered *only* in the second principle of light; yet it is clear as the day at noon, that this *only* is, by himself, limited and confined to eternal nature, and especially to the three tinctured and harmonized properties thereof. So that it is to say, that God, as manifested in eternal nature, is considered only in the second principle. And so this *only* doth not at all import that there is not a deeper and more central consideration of God, since it is notorious, that he considereth God also as unmanifest, in that abyss wherein there is neither darkness nor light, etc.; that is before eternal nature.

The second objection is this: If, in that consideration of the Divine Being, which Behmen calleth before and without nature, we do not look upon the generation as tacitly implied, Behmen shall be found full of contradictions; but if we do, all what he saith thereof in plain. Answer:— The quite contrary to this is true. For, as it cannot be denied, that there is something deeper, more central, and unintelligible than eternal nature is; which something is the very same eternal or Abyssal Nothing, which the Divine Being is before eternal Nature: if it be either wholly taken away, or not observed as it ought to be; or if it is mixed and confounded with what should be conceived as posterior to it, no marvel that there appear in Behmen contradictory expressions. So, then, this mentioned erroneous position cannot be a proper means to reconcile such contradictions; and though it may make a *plainer prospect* of one superior part of Behmen's building, yet it cannot give a plain and full view of the whole structure, nor show the coherence between the foundation and that which is built upon it. But let everything, and every expression thereof, be placed and looked upon as in its own proper station, as it is either more distant from, or nearer unto the centre, or as it is even that deepest and most individual centre itself, and all will be free from contradictions.

When two opposite winds do meet each other, in the same height of our atmosphere, there must needs be opposition and strife; for each of them is resisted by the other, and neither can go its own way, till the weaker be driven back, or swallowed up by the stronger. But let the one blow from east to west, in such or such a height as, for instance, of a certain mountain, and then the other one may go freely forth his own quite contrary way from west to east, in a region above it. This is known to be so, many times in this our macrocosm, and is truly a fine emblem, able to give us a good direction, in our constructions we put upon these deep spiritual matters, to imitate these orders and regulated courses of nature. And this the more, because we have before us a plain pattern of this our enlightened author, who constantly did so himself, throughout the whole progress he made from the deepest and most central, unto the highest and most outward circumferential thing. Needs therefore, if these shall be understood what he hath so orderly and gradually declared, we must do the same thing, by looking upon everything in its own place wherein it standeth, and wherein it is by him expressed. So doing, every lower and more external expression will open a free and plain way unto every other that may be either more central, or the deepest centre itself; and we shall plainly find, that as eternal nature is in the second consideration to the Divine Being, plainly and necessarily implied, so from the first consideration thereof it is wholly and absolutely excluded: which, in the following discourse, shall be made out, I hope and trust, to the assistance of God sufficiently.

IN THE FIRST PLACE, then, I shall say something concerning the Abyssal Nothing, and declare the reason why this is so called by BEHMEN.

IN THE NEXT PLACE, I shall say something especially concerning the Trinity, showing (1.) from Behmen's own expressions, that a Trinity both before and after eternal nature (but with a great difference of sense), is inseparable from the Unity. (2.) What difference in the Trinity, thus considered in this twofold respect. And (3.) that, notwithstanding this difference, there are not two Trinities, but only one. IN THE THIRD PLACE, I shall go forth to the delineation of these four figures, showing (1.) that they do, if all four unitedly taken together, stand in a good conformity to that single figure, which Behmen himself made in the FORTY QUESTIONS; notwithstanding that their outward form might appear as quite another thing.

(2.) That the first and fourth are to be looked upon as only one; notwithstanding that in the fourth several things are added, which were wanting in the first. (3.) That the addition of those things in the fourth, is caused only by the second and third; which both, and even distinct from each other, must have been inserted between the first and the fourth. (4.) That nothing in Behmen's writings (as to this matter concerning the Divine manifestation), may be found, which could not be referred unto the one or other of these four. (5.) That nothing, as to all this matter is omitted, but everything is set in its due place and order (though this was impossible, that every particular should have been distinctly expressed by a peculiar character), and that by every one of them that are expressed, something of consideration was intended to be represented. This I say, as far as I can judge, will be the best method.

If there should be said anything making for the honour of God, declaring the truth, and being beneficial to the reader, all praise and glory shall be given unto Him alone, without whose assistance we can do nothing. Amen.

Ex NIHILO NIHIL FIT: This was a saying of that famous heathen philosopher, almost idolized by many learned among the people, called Christians. And though it was said by him as in opposition to the Christian doctrine, is yet true enough in some sense, limited unto that notion, which a corrupt natural reason, or earthly wisdom could have afforded him of that common expression of *nothing*. But yet it is not here received, either upon account of his authority, or in his heathenish sense, but in that of TEUTONICUS, who saith that very same in these formal words: *out of nothing, nothing can come forth, but everything must have its root*. And who giveth not only a far deeper declaration, but maketh also a far better use thereof, than by any natural philosopher could have been done.

If he then saith so plainly, that out of nothing nothing can come forth: and if he, notwithstanding this, calleth the Divine Being (out of which angels and men came forth as an offspring), an eternal nothing: it is as clear as anything can be, that there must be the greatest difference between that former, and this latter nothing.

Whenever Teutonicus says, Out of nothing nothing can come forth, it is certain that he taketh this nothing in that common sense, wherein there is said generally, that the whole creation is brought forth by the Creator out of nothing. If he now had said, that this Creator himself was in this same sense nothing before he created: could anything be more foolish or mad?

If it is thus foolish and abominable a thing to form such a negative ides, as mentioned, of that which was, or rather which is to be conceived, before eternal nature, this eternal nothing before nature must certainly be something. For if we do not conceive it as nothing, we must conceive it as something, there being no third notion either distinct from these, or partaking of them both. But we must of necessity take one, and deny the other. And since it is not nothing, according to Teutonicus's own plain words, it must needs be something.

But I would not here be misunderstood, as I easily might, if this dilemma should be extended beyond its sphere, and so beyond the sense and intent, wherein and for which it is here taken. For I know very well that, according to the principles of Teutonicus, in various senses, upon different accounts, and with several respects, that which is by him considered as before eternal nature, may be called both something and nothing, and may be said again to be neither nothing nor something.

And truly he cannot be blamed for such variety, and seeming contradictory expressions.

He could not help it, and no man living upon earth shall be found, able to represent these things to the understanding of another, with such expressions as never should seem to cross and contradict each other. If the Spirit of God in the revelation could have said of one and the same thing, it was, and was not, and yet was, nay, could have added, that *here is wisdom*, etc., who can justly complain of Teutonicus? The understanding must supply that which is wanting in the expressions, which may be done in part, by duly considering that this matter, with its expressions of nothing and something, cannot be referred unto one only world, or universe, which would make no difference in the sense, but unto two extremely different from each other; which is therefore, and must be, the chief cause for which one and the same expression is true, with relation to the one, and false, or at least much altered in the sense, with reference to the other.

This, then, is an evident position of Teutonicus, that the Divine Being, considered as *before* eternal nature, is an eternal *something*, though he so frequently calleth it an eternal nothing, which will appear by the following particulars.

We may ask reasonably, what was before the creation of angels and of this world? And we may answer, *God*. Which will be enough for a common or superficial understanding; but more distinctly and theosophically we must answer with Teutonicus, *God and eternal nature*. Now, we cannot ask farther, what was before God? But we may ask (in a sense limited as above), what was before eternal nature? meaning not, thereby, that there was any instant in which eternal nature was not, and after which it came to be what it is; but meaning only that there was, and still is, something deeper, or something more internal and central, which is eternal *nature's root, ground*, and *original*, since out of nothing, nothing can come forth. And asking what that was, and is, which like as now, so also from eternity, *causeth* eternal nature to be what it is, and gave it to have what it hath? We must, with Teutonicus, answer, that this is *God, an eternal nothing, a still eternity, an eternal liberty*, a resting quiet temperature, a serene light:

An unintelligible softness, meekness, stillness, humility; an abyssal Being; a chaos, comprehending itself, or comprehensible by itself; a Wonderful Eye, wherein all the colours, powers, and virtues, lay together in such a mixture, as that they are indeed undiscernable, so that none can tell what it is; and make nevertheless a most terrible, awful prospect, confounding and consuming every sight that looks thereon. An eternal mirror of wonders; an abyssal powerfulness, all-sufficiency, omniscience, something which is and is not; (N.B.) which is, and dwells in itself, and is not manifest without itself; something which is nothing and all; a single eternal life or good; and a single will without *desire*. A spiritual, substantial power, working in itself, (N.B.) a sensibility of love; a pleasant, loving taste; a delightsome moving of the Holy Ghost, in the eternal wisdom; an eternal love, and only love generating and introducing itself in pure love into trinity; which trinity as yet is not distinguished according to what we can call a distinction in and after nature, and is not therefore a proper object of our understanding. JE-HO-VA: Father, Son, and Holy Ghost; a threefold opening, and breathing out, working in itself, generating itself, finding and perceiving itself; a divine eternal unity. An infinite Triune Being, past all finding out, etc:

All these expressions may be found in Behmen, for an answer to that question, what was before eternal nature. And so we may now see, not only that he expresses it so variously, but also by expressions negative and positive. Nay, sometimes his expressions do so notoriously contradict each other, that it might seem as if they were designedly used to frighten away from these mysteries all ill-natured and unworthy readers, and to raise up an attention and inquiry after truth in such as had but so much or consideration and reasonable judgment as to think, that this author had anything of reality in him, and was not quite a mad and drunken babbler. For instance, when he saith in one place, that which is before eternal nature, is an eternal life and good: and in another, that the abyss hath no life and good; and in another, that there is light and clearness in the abyss, and that there is neither light nor darkness therein. Again, that before eternal nature is no finding, no perceiving, no knowing itself; no activity, no mobility, and yet that there is perceiving, knowing, loving, tasting, opening, generating, breathing out, working and moving, etc., before and without eternal nature. And again, when he saith plainly, (N.B.) that all the powers, colours, and virtues lay together in one (without distinction), and yet adds in the same place, that one power, colour, and virtue knoweth or perceiveth the other, in distinction; and that this is a manifold generating harmony, well tuned and concordant with every sound thereof. Or a speaking word, wherein all the languages, powers, colours, and virtues, do lay together, and with or by the speaking do unfold and introduce themselves into a sight or seeing eye.

These seeming contradictions shall be cleared up hereafter, they are here only presented to prove that Teutonicus doth not represent that which is before eternal nature, as a nothing, but as a something, or true substantial Being.

For since he speaketh thereof so variously, now in a negative, and then again in a positive way, it is undeniable, that he would not have us to conceive it, as non ens, or nothing, but as a real something.

It was necessary, also, for him to use these seemingly contradictory expressions, and to represent it both as nothing and something, neither this nor that alone could have served his ends.

If he had represented it as a something only, he would not have sufficiently declared the infinite distance between that abyssal centre, and all its outflown, lesser and greater circumferences. He would not have exalted it duly, above all what can be named, thought on, spoken of, or comprehended. He would have misled us dangerously, and given occasion for to conceive it only as the greatest and most particular something, when it is not such a something, as had any other something besides it, from which it could be distinguished, as a peculiar something by itself, but must be quite exempted from the number and order of something, and exalted far above it, as an universal ground, source or centre, out of which all somethings, with all their order, are originated.

Like as we see a fine resemblance thereof in a *centre* and its *circumference*. The circumference consists of innumerous little points, answering fitly unto so many particular somethings, placed by each other.

But the centre is only one individual *point*; as to its quantity not bigger than any of all the rest, but as to qualities the most considerable of all, and in a sense so big as all the circumferential points taken together; nay, upon another account, even infinitely bigger.

For upon this only, all the circumferential points do depend, having only from that one all that they are, and have; nay, there is none of them, though never so little, which hath not something answering thereto, and corresponding therewith, in the central point, as their original; seeing that even this also may be considered not only as a centre of its circumference, but also as a circumference of itself. Wherefore, then, we may conceive it as to *qualities*, so big as all the points together in the whole circumference. And when we consider that, from this only central point, without any addition thereto, diminution thereof, or any change of place and number, innumerous other circles, first lesser and then wider, even in infinitum, may be conceived coming forth, this one original central point may well be conceived as infinitely larger than all the circumferential points can be. Which all are confined to number, order, and place, and subject to various mutations of increase and decrease, when that central point alone is immutable in itself, free from all such imperfections, and hath nevertheless in itself more eminently all what there is in all of them, for all what is in them displayed, is in that concentrated.

Further, we may conceive a visible circumference wherein no centre doth visibly appear at all, and yet we are always sure there is, and must be, a fixed unalterable *point*, which made all the points in this circumference to stand in the order they do, and to have such a connexion with each other. And again, all the points in this circumference stand in divisibility, and multiplicity, as so many particular parts; so that each of them filleth but its own place, and is but that which it is within its own narrow compass, but nothing more; and none or them can be considered anyways as a whole, and when, taken even altogether, are but a whole circumference, wherein no centre is implied as a part thereof.

But the central point only is a single, indivisible universe and can be truly called a whole; since not only it can never be divided into two, but also never can admit a second or third besides it; and is moreover, in a sense and manner, both centre and circumference itself. So that it is, and abideth unalterably in the whole circumference an only perfect whole, and all fulfilling, all sufficient all.

Let now a due application of all this, and more the like, be made to that Abyssal Being, and we shall see, that like as a centre is no less, but more really something that any point of the circumference; and as it is nevertheless also really nothing at all to all the point thereof, because it doth not belong to their number and order, but is that which maketh them to have such a number and order, it is incomprehensible to them; but itself doth in a sense comprehend them all, and had them in itself, before they were set forth in number and order out of it; it is excluded from all the circumference, and keeps only its own central residence, where none of all the other points can approach unto. It is quite of another nature, condition, and properties; and so may be called on one side a real being in itself, but on the other quite a nothing unto them. So also that abyssal being before eternal nature, which is the only original of all things that are thereafter, may be called nothing most significantly, with respect to all that is originated therefrom, when yet it is a substantial being in itself. Wherefore then, if he had represented it only as something, by mere positive expressions, he would have taught us to conceive it, not as an abyssal, incomprehensible, (N.B.) Universal Centre, but as an outflown, particular something, which we might have looked upon as if it were belonging to the number and order of other particular somethings. And so he should thereby have led us to form thereof such or such images, as we could have thought the fittest and most appropriable thereto, when they all would be no better than idols of gold and silver.

But now, by telling us not only in one respect, by positive expressions, that it is a Being, but also by negative descriptions, that it is nothing to us, and unto all things that are posterior and exterior, he prevents (if we understand him) all such mistakes. For he will most earnestly call us to mind, that in our enquiry after that which is before eternal nature, we be very cautious, modest, and sober, not running out too far, and not thinking that we have, or can have, any ability to find out such pertinent notions, as might be answering thereunto, and might afford us words, fit to declare affirmatively what it is. But that we shall be sure that it utterly vanisheth away out of all our sight, thoughts, and ideas, so that by none of them it can be apprehended, imaged, or expressed. Nay, that even the nearest and best we can have thereof lawfully, must be denied again, and quite abstracted from all that sense which they can have or bear in this world. This is to say, it is nothing, and is the reason why he so frequently calleth it an eternal nothing.

But now again, on the other side, if he had represented it always and absolutely as nothing, by only negative expressions, without affirming anything, he had erred himself and misled others, and quite contradicted his own axiom, that out of nothing nothing can come forth.

HAVING THUS PROVED, I think sufficiently, from Behmen's manifold own expressions (1.) that the generation of eternal nature in all its properties, is not implied, but totally excluded from that first consideration of the Divine Being, which he useth to call, without all nature and creature. (2.) That this Divine Being without nature, is not to be conceived according to the usual absolute sense of this latter expression (nothing), but according to the most eminent sense of that former (being); which sense must be abstracted indeed from all conceivable beings, in and after nature. Yet not abstracted by way of a strict and direct opposition, which would lead us into that common notion of nothing, but by way of a great exaltation above it, in such an eminent manner, that we may say it is a being indeed, but a being only in and to itself, having no communion in properties or qualities with any other being; and belonging not to the number and order wherein all particular beings stand with a mutual relation to themselves. (3.) That consequently these two expressions, nothing and being, must needs be joined together in all our discourses and conceptions thereof, and that neither by this, nor by that alone, the whole truth can be declared in its fullness. And (4.) that this taking these two expressions in the sense here mentioned, is the only true middle way, leading safely through two most dangerous extremities, and making us to avoid on one side our forming images of that divine abyssal Being, which we are naturally so much inclined to conceive in forms and figures; and on the other to avoid dishonouring our only true eternal root, or central being, without which no creature could exist. And that, therefore, we must not place it in the circumference, which is belonging only unto things brought forth, in which circumference this divine abyssal being is nothing; but that we must place in its own central residence, wherein this eternal nothing is a true substantial being, not brought, but bringing forth all whatever may be called something, in and after eternal and temporal nature: where innumerable somethings do represent themselves to our eye and understanding, and are yet (only by reason of there being many) nothing else but small particulars, all confined to their own narrow compass; when that central nothing alone is a whole universe, and an individual, all filling and all sufficient all:

We must now consider, a little more distinctly, some of our Author's chiefest *affirmative* expressions, in order to approach thereby nearer to the most principal matter, which is the consideration of the Trinity, both before and after eternal nature. Some, I say, of his affirmative, not negative, expressions; setting this down as a considerable foundation of what is to follow, that his affirmative expressions must prevail in our consideration, and must be more looked into, observed and insisted upon, than his negative ones. Because by so doing, we shall find ourselves enabled to save all his negative expressions also, so that none of them shall be lost, or left as useless or insignificant.

When, on the contrary, if we regard chiefly his negative expressions, and insist upon them absolutely and universally, not minding in what particular respect they are used so and so, we can no way save his affirmative expressions, but lose and make them empty and insignificant, as if they were but a frivolous pratling.

We will therefore choose out some of his affirmative expressions, as shall lead us the nearest way to a decision of these two principal points, inseparable from each other, and do concern (1.) the Divine Abyssal Being's finding, knowing, or perceiving itself; and (2.) its generating itself in Trinity before the generation of eternal nature.

(1.) Then I do recommend justly, to a serious consideration, that description of the *wonderful eye of eternity*, which we meet with in the Second Part of the Book of the Incarn. iii. 1, which is to be compared with the following places:—Myst. Mag. i. 7, 8; Predest. i.4–9; Forty

Quest. i 14–21; Contemp. Div. iii. 6, 7. [The references of this discourse are to the German original, from which our English translation differs in the arrangement of the paragraphs.]

All these places declare one and the same thing, viz., the Divine Being before and without eternal Nature.

This is evident, also, from his own declarations in the Div. Contempl. iii. 6., according to the German original. *We cannot*, saith he, *say* (N.B.) *that herein a nature or creature is to be understood, but it is the eternal forming of the Divine word and will,* where the *Spirit of God* (N.B.) *in such an object, in the powers of wisdom, and by such formings of similitudes hath played with himself.*

Now this denomination (of an eye) doth sufficiently show, that we are to conceive it in a sense as *something*, which is also still more evident from the attributes he ascribes to it. He says, that this EYE is like as (in the sight of a created understanding) *a prospect of great wonders, wherein all colours, powers, and virtues* (N.B.) *appear as a most dreadful being, etc*:

That no man indeed can discern distinctly this from that, and that nevertheless it may be looked upon, (N.B.) yet so that this eye as a terrible lightning is confounding and consuming all created sight.

That the wonders *in this eye have no number, no ground, and no end*; and that *the soulish spirit only, which hath its original from thence, can be able to understand it.* Further, that this is the *moving, or the life* of the Deity, an eternal seeing, an abyssal eye, wherein one colour, power, and virtue (N.B.) *perceiveth the other in distinction*:

That this is a most concordant generating harmony: that the eternal nothing without nature and creature introduced itself into an eye, or an eternal seeing, for to find and contemplate itself: That in the unnatural, uncreatural Deity, (i. e. without all nature and creature), there is but one will, which is called the one only God, willing in himself nothing else but to find and contemplate himself; and that herein (N.B.) the Trinity and the looking-glass of wisdom, or the eye of eternity is understood. That this eye is not to be compared to a circle, but to a globe, and that therein all beings were seen from eternity, without being, or before they had a being. That the spirit of eternity introduced the eye of the soul thereinto, or openeth unto the spirit a prospect thereof, and that only then it can be seen:

That in the abyss there is (N.B.) no finding, but that the finding is in this abyssal eye, wherein there is made manifest what the eternity is.

That this *eye maketh beginning and end*; That there is in this first world an opening; a moving, an outbreathing, a multiplication, a forming similitudes, etc., all which the author doth represent in a simile taken from the mind, will, senses, and thoughts of man. Which different things he placeth expressly and considerately before the magnetical impression (*i.e.* the first form of eternal nature) out of which afterwards joy and sorrow (the first and second principle) cometh forth.

(2.)—The second affirmative expression here to be taken notice of, is this, that Teutonicus calleth this *eternal Eye* the *first world*, whereof no creature knoweth anything. It is plain enough that a world is not an empty region, as that it could be conceived as a mere nothing in opposition to something; but that it is an universe, containing in itself all, without exception in one sense, and all, with limitation, in another; viz. all what it can be capable of, according to its own particular kind. So we find it both in the dark world, and in the holy light world, and in our four elementary world also.

(3.) He says, in more than a hundred places, that there is a Divine Being therein, a being of all beings, a foundation being, nay that this being is that first abyssal world itself, etc. And though he saith expressly that this world or being is ineffable and incomprehensible, yet it is deeper than any thought can reach; that it is without properties, without inclination to this or that, and that it hath no other being besides, before, or behind itself, which it could be discerned from, or touched and affected by, etc. Yet all this, and much more the like, cannot make this Divine Being a nothing in itself, but a nothing to all those exterior and posterior beings which are derived down from that, in and through the generation of eternal nature.

This he says himself in the plainest words: *The Divine Being, before and without nature, is an eternal nothing, though we ought not to say a nothing, since this nothing is God, an eternal All.* And again, *This eternal being is a pure Nothing, unto all whatever there is posterior to itself.* What can be plainer than these two expressions? Doth he not directly limit this denomination of nothing only to the creatures and to their understanding? And that he will not have them to call this abyssal being an eternal nothing with relation to himself, but permits them only to call it so with respect to themselves, and to all their narrow capacities; to the end that none presume to form such or such ideas and images thereof, etc.

Further; when Behmen saith, that in this first abyssal world there is the greatest stillness, meekness, quietness, etc., he not only distinguisheth plainly this first world from all other posterior worlds, wherein there is more or less, and in each according to its kind and order, some stirring, moving, working, comprehensibility, thickness, palpability, etc.; but he doth also grant expressly that even in this first world also, there are all these things now named, though not according to the sense these names can bear in any of the other worlds, but according to its own central station.

And though he saith plainly that of this first world, no creature knoweth anything; yet he limiteth this by saying again, that the spirit of soul, which is a creature, may be introduced thereinto, and may be made able to see, *that it is*.

(4.) See especially the Book of PREDESTINATION, i. 4, 7, 20, 21, where we shall find this first Abyssal Being before and without eternal nature, is a *substantial* spiritual power, working in itself lovingly, etc.

(5.) What Teutonicus saith concerning especially the Trinity in this Abyssal world, see the Second PAR. INCARNATION, ii. 4, 7; MYST. MAG. viii. 5, 10.

We find that in the Chaos (which is the first abyssal world), is the Trinity also, nay that there must be owned a Trinity therein, as soon as is granted a living, understanding Being. That as there is in this first world an eternal seeing, so also an eternal imagination and impregnation of the first will, and further, an eternal generation in the Three (commonly called persons), so distinct (N.B.) from each other, that none of them is that which the other is, but each only that which it is itself. That the first groundless will generateth in itself a grounded comprehensible will, co-eternal indeed to the first will, and having nevertheless in a sense, an eternal beginning. Which *second grounded will is the first will's eternal something, or essentiality and perceptibility*, through which that first will goeth out, and introduceth itself into an eternal contemplation of itself, which outgoing is the *third* (person), and is a moving life of the first and second.

That this Tri-une Being, in its outgoing and contemplation of itself, hath been so from all eternity, and hath been but one life, one will, *without desire*. That in this eternal generation, three things are to be understood. (1.) A groundless will; (2.) an eternal mind of that will; and (3.) an out-breathing, speaking forth, or out-going from the will and mind, (or, as he saith sometimes, from the will through the mind, which both is right and true,) which is the spirit of them both. That this Trinity before eternal nature cannot yet be called properly Father, Son, and Holy Ghost, and is not yet an object of our understanding, but that the Trinity is only understood rightly in that exterior manifestation of this abyssal being, which is made in and through the generation of properties of eternal Nature, wherein all the understanding creatures stand, and beyond which therefore, none of them can reach.

Concerning these contradictory (viz., affirmative and negative) expressions of the first divine Abyssal Being, I shall further consider and explain these two things, (I.) *how they are both true with respect to two different worlds.* (II.) *how they are both also true in one and the same abyssal world, with respect only to two different degrees or parts thereof.*

I.—Concerning understanding, knowing, and perceiving itself; both these are affirmed and denied of the first abyssal being, by Teutonicus, and both are consistent with each other, with respect to two different worlds.

We heard above, that all what there is before and without the generation of eternal nature, is, by Behmen, called the *first world*. Upon this foundation, I do call the *second world* all that which followeth immediately upon the first, and this is the *whole generation of eternal nature*.

And this denomination of the second world, in such a distinction from the first, is to signify no more, and nothing else, but that this or that is so and so; not with respect to that which is before nature, in the chaos or abyss, but to that which is in the generation of eternal nature, and to even that generation itself, conceived in a general idea, and extended to all the several properties thereof, without descending to a particular notion of darkness, fire and light.

But it may be objected against this distinction of a first and second world, that Behmen expressly saith and confineth this finding and not finding to the abyss, or first world, without any mention of a second. Answer: This is granted. But then it must be granted also, that very frequently he speaks of the Divine Being's knowing and perceiving itself, with a manifest relation to that, which is not in the first world, but in the generation of eternal nature; declaring that only therein is generated that which creatures call understanding, knowing, feeling, etc.: so that here lieth a sufficient reason and ground for looking at his expressions with a different respect to two most different worlds.

Secondly, Behmen doth, indeed, speak only of the abyss, referring unto that only both his affirmative and negative expressions; but that this denomination of abyss is to be taken in two greatly different senses, which are carefully to be distinguished, according to what the matter, then considered, doth require. These two senses do both indeed belong to the first world; so that we cannot say, the abyss in one sense is in the first world, and in the other sense in the second; but that the abyss is in that first world only, and is that first world itself.

But yet these two senses do belong to that first world, with a great deal of difference.

The one sense belongs so entirely to the first world, that it can in no sense be referred to the second. The other sense belongeth to that first world also, yet so that it implyeth a certain relation to the second world; which relation is all inseparable from that sense.

For abyss is with Behmen a relative expression, and cannot be conceived, according to his mind, without its correlate, which is byss, no more than father without a son. As now abyss is taken in a twofold sense, so it hath also a twofold relation, or byss, to be taken in a twofold sense, each of which must be conformable to that world whereof it is then spoken.

The whole second world, or the whole generation of eternal nature, in the seven chief properties thereof, is byss, though the principal reflection aims at the light world only, and terminates therein. And the abyss of this byss is the whole first world, or all what there is before, without any particular notice taken of what by Behmen is represented therein more distinctly, and is called the Divine Abyssal Being; and this is the one sense of this word abyss.

Which sense, because of the byss corresponding with this abyss, implyeth not one, but two different worlds, vastly different from each other.

But now, again, in that first world only, before eternal nature, there is, according to Behmen's own plain words, and large deduction, both abyss and byss together; for that Divine Abyssal Being is its own both abyss and byss.

Since, therefore, this twofold sense of the abyss is plainly founded in Behmen's writings, the reason for looking upon his contrary expressions, first, with respect to two different worlds, and secondly, with respect to the first abyssal world only, is also plain and solid.

For to come now to our first purpose, it will be most proper to represent but briefly several circumstantial things relating to those negative expressions, and to recommend them all together to a serious consideration; viz., who it was, that uttered these negative expressions, and unto what end he uttered them. Of what he speaketh; upon what account; in what manner, and to what end.

(1.) He that uttered these negative expressions was a creature, and, notwithstanding his extraordinary gifts, but a small particular of the innumerable products of eternal nature, calling himself but a little point or spark. Consequently then, he had all his understanding and knowledge from the Divine Being indeed; but so, as this is considered not before, but in, or after that eternal generation of the properties of eternal nature. Moreover, he was a man who, from his natural birth, was as simple and ignorant as any other, which he frequently confesseth; a man who not only owned to know nothing of himself, but who felt also, and understood experimentally, in a very high degree, himself to be nothing, in a sense quite different from that, nay, even (N.B.) opposite unto that, wherein he useth to say, the Divine Being, before the generation of the properties of nature, is an eternal nothing. But a man also, who, notwithstanding all his nothingness, *was really permitted to have a prospect into that eternal nothing, and to see that it IS*; though his sight must have been immediately confounded, so that he could not see, much less declare affirmatively, what or how it is. And such an one was it, that uttered these negative expressions

(2.)—Unto creatures, all of the self-same nature and condition, as himself; which all therefore are capable, more or less, of understanding his mind and sense: yet so, that none of them can pretend to be sufficient of himself, for understanding him. And among these, he directs himself especially to the simple ones, calling himself a philosopher of the simple, and saying of them, that their simplicity is not to hinder, but much gather to further them, and make them more fit for understanding these deep things; which is to say chiefly and especially, more fit to be admitted, as he was, into the sight of eternal nature, and of that eternal nothing also, which is before it. Where they cannot but meet with that same entertainment which he met with, viz., to be dazzled and confounded, so as to be not able to see distinctly what or how it is, though they may see plainly that it is. Now, unto such he speaketh

(3.) Of their deepest abyssal original; of that which dwelleth, and is what it is only in and to itself, without any relation or tendency towards anything without. Of that which desireth not to be *understood* by creatures, but only to be owned, and in a deep internal silence, awe, and reverence, to be *adored*, as the deepest and most internal centre of all whatever was, or is, or shall be hereafter; of that which is most different from the consideration of all *the Divines* therein, that they all conceive and describe an infinite, good, just, holy, gracious, etc. Spirit. Which is a consideration of God as manifested in and through eternal nature, unto creatures; when in this first consideration of his, God is not only without all creature, but all nature also: and is infinitely superior to all conceivable properties, and to all words or names, though they were to signify (N.B.) the greatest imaginable perfections.

If all the perfections we can conceive to be so, or use to express by such or such denominations, are much rather lies than truth, when attributed to the Divine Being, considered as manifested in eternal nature, and with relation to creatures, according to what is plainly said by many mystical writers: how much more must they all be lies, when attributed to that Divine Abyssal Being, which by Behmen only, is considered as dwelling in itself, before and without all nature and creature?

Though both in this consideration and in that, they may be owned to be true, in a sense relating to the stammering creatures; for they are not said to be true in the one consideration, and false in the other, but, both in that former and in this latter, they may be tolerable, and owned to be true, in a sense wholly relating to creatures. And again, both in this and that they are false, in a sense relating unto that Divine Eternal Being itself; though much more false, when this is considered as before, than when it is as in or after eternal nature; seeing that all conceptions, words, and names, have each of them their own peculiar sense, originated in the generation of the properties of nature, and determined by particular understanding creatures. Wherefore, then, no such sense can be attributed unto, or spoken of that abyssal being before all nature and properties, so as to declare how or what it is, in and to itself. Of that abyssal central being he speaketh now

(4.) Upon that account, which was mentioned several times, and is of the greatest consequence, viz., that a creature, in a sense and manner, may be admitted into the sight thereof, so as to see that it is, though no creature can fix its eye upon it, nor bear the sight thereof, so as to see what and how it is. Which is, and must be so, of all necessity, not only because of the creature's weak and narrow constitution, but also because of that abyssal being's own nature; which cannot but be melting down, confounding, and consuming everything that is belonging unto another world.

If the creature itself could be brought (as to its own particular created existency) into this first abyssal world, it must immediately be dissolved and annihilated as to all its created being, and could not be preserved in its particular created existency.

But now the creature itself is not brought into that first world, but only the creature's sight, or as it were a ray of the creature's seeing or understanding faculty is admitted thereinto; or rather, a little opening of this abyssal depth is made in the spirit of the soul, through the which opening this spirit must needs be made sensible of something appearing in that central depth, and even appearing like as it were a most terrible lightning; because his ray of seeing or understanding is immediately confounded and swallowed up thereby, so far as it hath looked into that abyssal depth. And this terrible something he cannot express nearer, nor more significantly, than by calling it an eternal abyssal nothing, in consideration both of its own particular being, which is in a sense and manner, or as it were in part, annihilated thereby, and in comparison of so many millions of other particular beings, which all may be looked upon without danger, as so many proper objects of his understanding. But seeing the creature itself, as to its own existency, doth continue to be that same which it was before, and cannot be annihilated; its seeing faculty must continue also, forasmuch as it proceedeth forth from that created natural being.

This, therefore, may now justly be said both to have seen and not to have seen. It hath seen, because it was really touched, and made sensible of such an abyssal being's existency in itself, or its own central world: and it hath not seen, because it was immediately, as it were, killed, driven back, and confounded, so that it cannot say what it was, or how it was, but only that it was not this nor that, nor anything that could be named in all these worlds, which creatures can have any access unto.

For all what can be looked upon by understanding creatures, can also be declared more or less what, or how it is, and may have a name more or less convenient unto its nature and properties, whereby it is not only distinguished from all other somethings, but is also placed in the number and order of all those other somethings.

But of this abyssal being, all must be denied, whatever is affirmed of all other things in other worlds. It must absolutely be exempted from all and every number and order, and cannot be named by any proper name, whereby it were to be distinguished from other somethings; seeing that there is none besides itself in that first abyssal world.

And this is plainly to say, that it is *nothing* at all with respect to creatures, yet something in and to itself. And this makes it plain why Teutonicus must have spoken of that Divine Abyssal Being

(5.) In a human way or manner, like as a little stammering child, delivering, indeed great true, heavenly, deep, eternal things, but with an earthly tongue; having no other words but such as are of this low, four-elementary world; which are much more insufficient to represent that which cannot be looked upon, and is therefore beyond expression, than the colours of a painter are to represent lively such or such a visible object. That he speaketh thereof in such a manner, even when he declareth things much inferior to this, he freely confesseth.

In such a manner therefore, and with such expressions as he could have had in this world, he speaketh unto his fellow creatures

(6.) To this end and intent, that he may not only exalt (according to his duty) that Divine Abyssal Being, above all nature and creature, and set it in its own place, exempt from all the number and order of all posterior somethings; but also that he may, according to his command, inform his fellow creatures, as he did seriously, to be cautious in their enquiry, to watch over their own motions, to restrain their curiosity so natural unto them, and chiefly, to make no images of that first central or abyssal being, by representing it in such or such a particular similitude, without which we can conceive thereof nothing at all. Nay, to know also surely that, notwithstanding all his declarations, they cannot come to have any true, proper, affirmative conception thereof; which might be in a sense and manner excusable in the second consideration of God, as manifested in eternal nature; but is here in this first all intolerable, without any limitation, and which he never intended to prescribe to any, as shall appear by and by.

Let now all these six circumstances be duly considered, and it will plainly enough appear not only why Behmen called this Divine Abyssal Being an eternal Nothing, but also why he said there is no finding, knowing, and understanding therein.

If we understand the generation of eternal nature in its properties, we cannot but grant that all what we apprehend of such and all the like expressions, and whatever we are able to say thereof with any other words, *are originated in eternal nature*, together with all our being, knowing, understanding, etc. So that all this wholly depends upon that eternal generation, as a product, result, or consequence thereof; which by no means can be conceived as antecedent to the properties of eternal nature; or if we would presume to conceive it so, we should presume to conceive a nature antecedent to eternal nature.

If there is before eternal nature an eternal chaos or temperature, wherein all things lie in stillness and equality, without order, number, measure, properties, qualification; without being distinguished from each other, (according to our author's simile) like as fire, light, heat, smoke, air, water, etc., lay in a candle without distinction. And if all distinction relating unto and perceivable by creatures, hath its original in eternal nature, like as the distinction of leaves, branches, fruits, hath its original in temporal nature, so that they cannot be brought forth in distinction, except there be first performed an actual moving and concurrent operation of its properties, in every particular plant or tree; how can there be, or be conceived, a finding, perceiving, knowing, etc., before eternal nature, where that which is supposed to be found, perceived, known, understood, seen, etc., is not yet distinguished from that which findeth, perceiveth, knoweth, understandeth, seeth, etc. And where that ray, which is to go forth from the one to the other, is not yet generated between them, but lieth still in its own nothingness?

It is certainly true and plain, that all these expressions mentioned, bear a relation to the second world, and further also, a relation to the creatures, and to their understanding after this second world, it must therefore be true and plain also, that all these, and the like expressions, are justly to be denied of that first abyssal being or world, and that it cannot be strictly and significantly enough expressed and imprinted into the hearts of men, that there is in that first central world, no such thing at all, as by any creature, in any other circumferential world, can be understood, apprehended, or declared by words.

For so that first abyssal being is duly exalted above and totally excluded from all the capacity, of men and angels. They are all confined to their proper station in due humility: eternal nature is distinguished from and subordinated to that central being, which it had its eternal original of; and this is declared to be always the same in itself, and absolutely incommunicable unto anything, but what is itself in its own abyssal world, which never any creature can approach unto, neither with its being, nor by its understanding.

All this is plain; for every one that doth but so much as own an invisible spiritual world will readily grant, that things in this world, wherein we now live in such a blindness and ignorance, and even in that sense which they bear with relation to creatures, cannot be attributed unto that internal world. How much more, then, must he that owns Behmen's abyssal world, be ready to grant, that nothing of this external world, in that sense wherein it is taken therein, can be attributed to that first eternal one.

But now if any one should hence conclude, that Behmen, by denying so positively that perceiving, knowing, etc. is in the first abyssal world, or in the Divine Being before eternal nature, that therefore he has denied that same in all and every sense, absolutely, without any limitation in the very largest extent, he would certainly be mistaken, and guilty of having stretched out his words beyond his scope, and contrary to all his affirmative expressions.

Let it not seem contradictory, that above, and here again is said of affirmative expressions, when there was said expressly a little before, that Behmen never intended to prescribe his readers any true, proper, affirmative concept of that first abyssal world.

And again: let it not seem contradictory, that above is said, the creature is not capable of any other sense, perceiving, knowing, etc., but what is after and hath its original in the generation of eternal nature, when there now here is said, that knowing, perceiving, etc., is denied indeed of the abyssal being in that sense which hath any relation unto creatures, but that it is not denied in all and every sense. For this doth plainly suppose that there is another sense, which hath no relation unto creatures, and is nevertheless conceivable by creatures; which with that former saying cannot be reconciled.

Answer 1st. As to the affirmative expressions, I say, they are called only so with respect to their verbal construction, wherein they stand opposite to this or that, and are called negative. And so it is true, indeed, in a very low, inconsiderable, and outward sense, that they make an appearance of a fixed and solid position or affirmation. But we are not to stick to that, if we intend to be more intimately acquainted with Behmen's sense. For it is certainly true, also, in a much deeper, and most considerable sense, that all those (so called) affirmative expressions, are turned by him into negative, and that he never had any design to prescribe unto, or to raise up in his readers, such an affirmative idea of the Divine Abyssal Being, as could be called so, in an eternal true reality.

And this doth appear plainly from so many limitations, cautions, restrictions, etc., obvious everywhere in all those places where he speaketh of that first abyssal world.

Whereby he sheweth sufficiently, that all his expressions are negative in their true internal sense, though many of them in their outward shape, and in a sense of this world, appear as affirmative, which neither he was, nor any other can be able to remedy.

Every affirmative saying doth attribute something particular unto that first abyssal world, which in this our outward world must be tolerated, since the creature cannot do otherwise. But the creature, if it hath any understanding from a higher principle, will of itself observe a due distinction between world and world, and will not presume to bring any particular thing or sense passable in the one, into the other, as if it were passable therein also; but will see itself, that nothing that is affirmative in this world, wherein there is all particularity, division, and contrariety, can be affirmative in the first abyssal world, wherein there is a whole and total, undivided universality.

Affirmative expressions in this world may indeed be attributed to the second world, and may be tolerable, if their sense be refined and exalted above what they signify here below; because there is a connexion between them, consisting therein, that they both are in and after nature. But as to the first abyssal world, no affirmative saying from this world can be admitted into that, though never so much refined and exalted; because there is no *coherence*, *no analogy*, and *no mutual answerableness* between them, the one of them being in nature, and the other without nature.

Which immense distance makes all affirmative expressions in nature to be negative, or false, when applied to what is without nature. Every affirmative expression maketh an image or representation of a thing in such a form or figure, either finer and more spiritual, or grosser and more corporeal.

If then, of this first abyssal world, no image in nowise sense or manner shall be made (though in some sense or manner it must be made of the second world), no affirmative expression hath here any place, but must (since we cannot help using them in our speech and writings) be always restrained and confined; whereby then, in our mind, that same is made negative, which in outward words appears affirmative.

All affirmative expressions have a natural inseparable relation unto nature and creatures, and are all born in this low four-elementary world.

If then, all this world, and all nature and creature can show and give us nothing that could be applicable to the first abyssal world; and if no created understanding can be found able to reach unto that world, and to form from ten thousand affirmative expressions but so much as one true, positive idea thereof; all affirmative expressions, must be denied again, and are turned thereby into negative, let their outward appearance in a grammatical construction be what it will.

If we suffer them to make an affirmative idea in our mind, this idea will certainly be false, and contrary to Behmen's sense and intent.

But if we can come to have, a right negative idea, this will be the best, the nearest unto truth, and the most conformable unto our creatural state and duty. For it is a negative idea which Behmen presseth upon his readers, even in the midst of all his affirmative sayings; and beyond a negative idea we cannot climb up higher.

But I would not here be mistaken; for I know and freely grant that of this first abyssal world, there is and must be had one general idea, which may be called (in a half and broken sense) affirmative, viz. *that it is something in and to itself.*

And by saying, that beyond a negative idea we cannot climb up any higher, I understand, according to Behmen's own direction, that of this first world we can only say that it is neither this nor that, etc.; but cannot go forward to a sure, determined position, declaring what or how it is. And though we could, or did, by the very best and most accommodable expressions, yet none of them would be without all relation to nature and creature, and to this outward world also. Wherefore then, they all must be denied again, and could leave nothing behind them, in our mind, but an obscure, and as it were, a broken shadow of an affirmative representation. Which I could make out further, from a consideration of all those attributes that are usually given to the Divine Being, considered as in and after eternal nature, if I were not apt to think it is already evinced sufficiently, that Behmen is all for negative ideas, and that there is not such a contradiction to be found, as was objected above, concerning his affirmative expressions. Let us now

Answer 2ndly, Unto that other part of the objection, viz. that knowing and perceiving is denied indeed of the abyssal being, in that sense which hath any relation to creatures, but that it is not denied in all and every sense.

This seems to suppose, that there is a certain sense conceivable by creatures, which hath no relation to creatures.

But herein is no contradiction nor difficulty at all. It is easily to be understood, that a creature cannot be capable of any other sense, but what hath a relation unto creatures, and what is posterior to eternal nature. But seeing that a creature can know and own, there is still another and deeper world beyond its reach, which is not therefore an object of its understanding; the creature can know also certainly, that this or that may be affirmed or denied of that world, in an human way or method, and by such a person as hath had, a prospect thereof, as Behmen had.

And if the creature can know and own so much, it can certainly also know more, that all such words and expressions as are thus spoken thereof, must have a sense in them. If then, there is a sense in them, this sense must be as it were proportionable, not unto the second natural, but unto the first abyssal world, although it be expressed by natural words, inferior and posterior not only to the first, but also to the second world. And if so, the creature can also easily apprehend of itself, that this sense is not proportionable to its understanding, and that it is not expressed or included in words, for to be found out and understood, what or how it is in itself (which is deeper than any thought can reach), but that it is only mentioned or shadowed out by natural words, all taken *a posteriori* from things derived thence, to be known that it is, and to be owned that it is the deepest, central original of all the posterior worlds.

Teutonicus speaketh of the second world, viz., of eternal nature and its two eternal principles, all with words taken from temporal nature; giving, indeed, unto eternal invisible things, the same names which are given unto temporal and visible things; because these came forth from them, and are their visible representatives, and he had no other words to use, cautioning us at the same time, that we must observe a distinction in the sense, lest we should set cows and calves into heaven, and charge him undeservedly with gross absurdities.

So he speaketh also of the first abyssal world, with the same words he useth in the descriptions of the second world, which certainly he doth not, that we should make a confusion of these two worlds, so carefully by him distinguished, but he doth it only upon the same account as mentioned, which alone might be sufficient to show us, that we must observe a distinction in the sense, which he could not observe in words; and which we can easily observe, if we but mind which world it is he speaketh of, whether the second together with its temporal outbirth, wherein all things are displayed in distinction, or the first only, wherein all things are concentrated.

Whatever now is understood from his words, by any reader from the lowest to the highest degree, that is a sense which hath a relation unto creatures, and a sense which is natural; and though it be an illuminated understanding, yet this sense is natural, i. e. posterior unto, and originated from eternal nature; and though it may be good and true in its kind, with respect to the creature, and to the illumination, yet this sense must not be applied to that first abyssal world, as if it were able to declare what it is, but must absolutely be denied, since this first world is deeper than any natural sense or thought can reach.

But now, when such a sense as this is denied, the question is, What is then left, or what benefit can we reap from such descriptions?

Answer: There is left a deeper sense, excluding the generation of eternal nature, and therefore not conceivable by creatures, what, or how; but only knowable that it is. The words of Behmen signify that all our ideas of this first abyssal world must be negative; and that no affirmative one, truly to be called so, can be had thereof by any creature.

And our benefit is, that we are by his descriptions, advised what, and from whence we are, and how far we can reach; and be cautioned also to put a stop to our natural curiosity, etc. Thus much concerning this objection.

Proceed we now in our designed method. When Behmen saith first negatively, that perceiving, knowing, etc., is not in this first abyssal world, by perceiving and knowing we understand that which is natural unto ourselves, and presupposeth the generation of eternal nature, upon which, with all our senses and perception we do depend, and are not able to have any deeper sense of these things than what this generation of eternal nature hath endued us with. So that we must own that all this, and whatever might be named the like, in this particular and natural sense, is not and cannot be in that first abyssal world, which excludeth nature.

But when Behmen saith again affirmatively, knowing and perceiving, etc. is in the first abyssal world; must this affirmative expression be false, by reason that the former negative was true? God forbid! That former negative must have been true, because of its implying a relation to the second world, which in the first can have no place at all, and must therefore absolutely be denied, nay cannot be denied strictly and vigorously enough.

And this latter affirmative must be true also, because of its not implying any relation neither unto nature nor creature, but reflecting only upon that first world as it is in itself. And so both this and that is true, with different respects, to two most different worlds.

Our greatest stumbling block lieth in this, that the same words, knowing and perceiving, etc. are used both in the affirmative and negative expressions; and because we cannot form in our minds any difference between knowing and knowing, we are apt to think there can be no foundation for it.

But let us but mind only this, often told us by Behmen, that none of our senses, thoughts, concepts, can reach that first abyssal world; because we are with all our being, only natural, and cannot rise, or raise up in us, nor send forth any thought beyond eternal nature. We might be apt to fancy, indeed, that we send beyond eternal nature such or such of our thoughts or ideas, when we are trying to conceive in our minds that first abyssal world. But if we stick here, our thoughts are very low, and unacquainted with Behmen's sense in this deep unexpressible matter.

None of our thoughts can be free from eternal nature, nor reach beyond its limits, no more than the sound of our words, when we speak at London of the East Indies, can exceed that compass, which our voice is able to reach. But all our thoughts are generated in and by eternal nature, are inferior to it, and are confined thereby to mere particulars, as they are all particulars themselves; wherefore, then, none of them can be able to break through its borders, and to enter that first central world, which alone is a whole and universal all.

Now, if all that natural sense which we have about these expressions of knowing, perceiving, etc., be utterly denied of the first abyssal world, there will presently (without our forming, or being solicitous about another sense,) this position result from his words, that there is, in his affirmative expressions, a sense, not conceivable what or how, but knowable that it is.

Which being knowable, will be found grounded upon that seeing of the spirit of the soul; when that other, not being conceivable, is grounded upon that right's being dazzled, confounded, etc.

He that made the eye and prepared the ear, shall he not see see and hear?

I know it will be here replied, the *causa efficiens* of knowing, etc. in creatures, is to be sought after in the generation of eternal nature, i.e. in the second, and not in the first world, which hath no relation unto creatures.

This is granted: but then we must ask further, Whence comes knowing in this second world? If it be the second, then there is another first and deeper, even that which Behmen expressly calleth God in himself, the first world; then certainly this second in the generation of eternal nature, is descended down from the first. We know that God and nature are not to be confounded. God in himself is free from nature, and is not generated by it, but is prior and superior to it; notwithstanding that in another sense, neither of them is prior, nor posterior, but both are co-eternal. But seeing that it cannot be said of God, that he had an eternal beginning in nature, when it can be said of nature, that she had an eternal beginning in God: and seeing again, that something is by Behmen, placed and considered as before and without eternal nature, which he calleth God, Nothing and All; we must allow that this eternal nothing and all, is the only *causa efficiens* of that second world, and the knowing therein.

It will still be replied, That knowing, etc. is not denied absolutely and in every sense of the first abyssal world, but that it lieth therein only potentially, and so, as Behmen saith, all powers, colours, and virtues do lie therein, as in a chaos or temperature, without distinction.

Answer: This chaos, or temperature without distinction, is rightly so called in one sense, with reference to the second world, and to creatures depending upon it, but cannot be called so in another, with respect to the first world itself. Seeing we heard above, that Behmen plainly saith, that in this first abyssal world, the one power, colour, virtue, etc., perceiveth the other in distinction.

Forasmuch then, as in this first world is distinction, let it be in what sense soever, this first world is not a chaos, nor a temperature in and to itself, though it is still so with respect to the second world.

For if this distinction in the first world, is not, according to the distinction in eternal nature, conceivable by creatures, but according to the first world, only knowable that it is; and if that spirit of the soul which is admitted into the sight thereof, can see that powers, colours, and virtues (three distinct things) do lie therein, and yet not see them distinctly, so as to discern the one from the other, this first world must be a chaos or temperature with respect to that soulish spirit that looks thereon, and to the second world wherein all things are so distinct as to be discernable;

but must also again not be a chaos or temperature, with respect to what it is in and to itself. For seeing Behmen saith that in the first abyssal world, that which he calleth the Father, is not that selfsame in all and every sense, which he calleth the Son; that which he calleth Spirit, is not that which he calleth Wisdom; and so the powers are not colours, etc. All and every distinction cannot be absolutely denied.

It is known that Behmen describeth the eternal chaos as a most terrible appearance, which, like as a dreadful flash of lightning, confoundeth instantly and consumeth the sight of the soulish spirit, so that he cannot see what it is, but only know that it is. What shall we now think of this description? Can we think, that it is given forth by Teutonicus, in order to declare what this wonderful thing is in itself? Hath it not a manifest relation unto creatures, and even unto creatures only, by saying that it is confounding and consuming? For certainly this cannot be applied to that Eye of eternity, with respect to what it is in and to itself, seeing that none will say, it is itself, and by itself, confounded in its sight? Wherefore then, it must be quite another thing in, and to itself, than what it appears to be to a created eye, looking upon it from without.

If this eye seeth something, and seeth so that it can bear the sight without being confounded at it, it cannot see (like as the spirit of the soul seeth) only one something, or one confuse chaos; but it must see a numberless number of things, and must in this seeing, perceive them so as they are, viz. as not yet in being, and so also as not yet distinguished in themselves, but as standing in a possibility to be brought forth into so many distinct beings; and so also as distinguishable in the sight of this eye. For this is plain,, when we but consider what from this sight, or in this eye, doth arise, viz. a delightful play, and further, a design to bring forth these wonders into being, that that they might appear into a distinct existency, etc.   Again,

If perceiving, knowing, etc. should be absolutely denied of the first abyssal world, pray what could the name of Wisdom signify?

It is certain that Behmen placeth Wisdom not only in the second world, or in and after the generation of eternal nature, but also in the first; and that he saith expressly, in a Clavis never to my knowledge printed in English: *The Mysterium Magnum without nature, and Wisdom, are utterly one and the same thing.*

We know, indeed, that he speaks of a *Mysterium Magnum* in and after Nature; but this is plainly distinguished from that, by this notorious mark of distinction, *without nature*.

Now as to that other denomination of wisdom, he saith indeed plainly, that Wisdom is properly so called in the second world, implying and presupposing the generation of eternal nature; and that before nature in the first world, it is more properly called a *mirror of eternal wonders*. But even this twofold denomination showeth us, that one and the same thing ought to be considered in a different sense, relating to two different worlds. For though he hath given us this twofold denomination, as proper, yet he useth almost always the selfsame name of wisdom, both in his first consideration before, and his second after the generation of eternal nature. And what is this else, but to say, that we must not make two quite different things, of that which is but one; but must look upon that one thing in two different respects, senses, and degrees, according to the different conditions of the first and second world.

Wisdom, then, is indeed more properly to be called so, in and after the generation of eternal nature, wherein it is Mysterium Magnum, with respect to its being unfolded and displayed afterwards in the creation, chiefly of angels and men, and is presupposing its having been unfolded and displayed in another degree already, in the generation of eternal nature.

And Wisdom is indeed more improperly called so before and without nature, where it is Mysterium Magnum, with respect to its becoming unfolded and displayed the first time, or in the first degree, in the generation of the seven chiefest, and innumerous lesser properties of eternal nature; and is presupposing no other antecedent unfolding or displaying.

But yet it is still both before and after nature only one and the same thing, and the two different denominations are only to give us notice of two different degrees, wherein this one thing is to be considered, if we will not confound the first world with the second.

Wisdom implieth in its idea, perception, knowledge, and understanding; therefore these are with wisdom both before and after eternal nature.

In the first world, God is considered only *as in himself, abstractively* from all relation, respect, or tendency towards anything without himself. And in the second, he is considered as *in eternal nature*, or with respect to something, which is in a sense without him, and is not himself, but is to be distinguished from him. When, nevertheless, this twofold consideration made by the creature, doth not make a twofold God, as it doth also not bring in a confusion between the first and second world. So then, according to this distinction, wisdom also must be considered both as in the first world, before, and as in the second, after eternal nature; when yet there will not be made thereby two wisdoms, but only one, and no confusion shall be brought in, but a great difference between the first and second consideration of wisdom will be found, consisting chiefly therein, that as wisdom in the second world, implyeth a knowing and understanding what it is, to have actually unfolded and displayed the first deepest central world, in and through the generation of eternal nature, to have introduced himself out of the still eternity, or first temperature, which is without all properties, into the second temperature, full of harmonised properties and qualifications; to have brought forth his eternal tender Lubet through the three first restless properties of nature, to have exerted his omnipotent all-sufficiency in the generation of the fourth, by opening therein his own eternal liberty, or central groundless world, and to have introduced that eternal lubet, through this most dreadful magic fire, into that most majestic habitation, which is the second principle of light and love and glory, etc:

So also wisdom in the first world, implyeth a perceiving, knowing, and understanding what it is to live and dwell only in himself, in the calm still eternity or liberty, without fire and light, and the properties of nature. But especially and chiefly also, what it is (N.B.) to be in himself alone all-sufficient for all the things performed in the generation of eternal nature. If we own that wisdom in the second world implyeth perception and knowing, in that former more exterior sense, we must own also, that wisdom in the first world implyeth perception and knowledge, etc. in this latter more interior sense. For these two can no more be separable from each other, than the second world can be separable from the first, or a circumference from its centre.

If there is in the first world before and without nature, no perception, knowledge, etc., then there is also not only no wisdom, but also no God, in no sense and manner. But how contrary is this to our CENTRALIS PHILOSOPHUS, who says, God is in himself the first world: *God is both the byss and abyss, and yet nothing apprehendeth him, except the true understanding or intellect:* and (N.B.) this intellect is *God himself.* Again,

If there were no understanding in this abyss, eternal nature must be looked upon as the only mother of wisdom. But nature is not the mother of wisdom, not even of that wisdom which is considered in the second world: but nature is only that medium *sine qua non*, or that instrument by the use of which, the first original mother, or the deepest central womb, which is wisdom before nature in the first world, hath introduced itself into such a perceptibility, knowledge, and understanding, as can be had in the second world only, and as wisdom therefore in the first world could not have at all.

Wisdom cannot conveniently be called a mother, for as she never hath borne any other thing, wherefore Behmen calleth her a Virgin; so we can also not say, that wisdom in the first world hath borne any other or younger wisdom different from herself, as a child differs from its mother. But we say only that wisdom in the first world, wherein she was only in and to herself, hath in the second world unfolded and displayed herself and all her secret riches, which were concentrated in the first world:

That so she might be made sensible of what it is to have them thus displayed, and to behold and enjoy them distinctly, in fire, light, glory, joy, etc.: And she might also make herself thereby intelligible, accessible, and communicable, in a sense and manner unto creatures; all which she could neither have had nor could have been in the first world, before and without nature.

And though it may be said, if rightly understood, that eternal nature is the mother of wisdom, yet to say so absolutely and universally, without restriction, is nothing less than abominable nonsense. And to conceive that eternal nature hath brought forth wisdom, properly so called in the second world, out of itself, or from its own sufficiency, without concurrence or direction of a deeper antecedent wisdom, and without a foregoing intent, is utterly inconsistent with Behmen's Theosophy. Which not only placeth wisdom as well before nature in the first world, as after it in the second, but tells us also, that the first Abyssal world will not be such an imperceptible nothing as it is before Nature, but will perceive itself in and through the properties of nature; and that it hath therefore a *fixed intent* and purpose to flow forth out of its still eternity, and to introduce its tender lubet into strength, power, glory, majesty, fire, and light.

All which doth show us sufficiently, that wisdom in the first world is not an empty name, but that it implyeth not only a perceiving its abyssal state, but also a finding itself able and all-sufficient for performing its intent, viz., for going through the three first properties of dark nature into the fire, and through the fire into the light.

For this is its going into the second world, and its becoming in this world that which it will be, and not yet can be, in the first world. Further,

Behmen saith plainly, that *in the Mysterium Magnum before and without Nature* (which is wisdom, as we heard above), *there laid eternal nature itself, as a hidden fire, which (N.B.) is and is not. It is not,* for it is in that first world, not only nothing unto creatures, but also nothing unto itself. And yet *it is,* for it is in the first world unto the eye of eternity that, which wisdom finds herself sufficient, for to fit and to prepare as a proper instrument, for her own use and advantage.

If then, nature laid thus hidden in wisdom, wisdom is not brought forth by nature, but nature by wisdom. And wisdom is but unfolded, displayed, manifested and glorified by nature, which is but as an instrument in her hand. And if so, it cannot but be evident sufficiently, not only that wisdom in the first world before, and wisdom in the second world in and after nature, are not two, but only one; but also that this one wisdom must be considered with a different respect to these two different worlds, and must be taken in such a twofold sense, as mentioned before.

Our simile we had above, taken from a *centre* and its *circumference*, may help to illustrate this matter very much.

First we are to take good notice thereof, that the two names centre and circumference are both relative, so that neither of them can be, nor be conceived, without or with exclusion of the other. There may be, and may be conceived indeed, a single point, which can be made a centre, but cannot be called a centre, nor be conceived so, as long as the notion of a circumference is not implied. And again: there cannot be, nor be conceived any circumference, if a centre is not implied and presupposed; though there can be, and be conceived an individual point without relation to a circumference, and even that selfsame point which afterwards is made and called a centre, as soon as it hath drawn about it its circumference.

So then we have now a notable distinction between a POINT and a CENTRE: which distinction, as it doth not make neither two points nor two centres, so it doth also not bring in any change or alteration upon that point, but gives it only a new relation, which it had not before, and obliges us to consider one and the same thing in two different respects. First, as it is only in and to itself, without any relation to this or that without itself; in which consideration it is called a point, but not a centre. And secondly, as it is with this relation to the circumference without itself, in which consideration it is called a centre, not a point, notwithstanding that it still is in itself that very same without any alteration, which it was before, when it not yet could have been called a centre.

And so this distinction is not generated in our brain, nor laid upon the thing by our contrivance, but is generated in the thing itself; hath its ground in an actual generation, done without us; and is brought from thence into our idea, which cannot change or place the order of these names according to its own pleasure, but must needs conceive them as they are in their natural order; according to which, the notion of a point is prior to the notion of a centre, and the notion of a centre prior again to the notion of a circumference.

For every centre is a point, but not every point a centre; and no circumference can be, if there be not first a centre, from which it may have its being.

Like as also no centre can be, which could not first have been a point before it was a centre, and which could not still be that same point, though the circumference thereof were utterly removed. Seeing that the circumference depends only upon the centre, and cannot be without it what it is, but must lose all its being if the centre is abolished. But the centre depends not so upon the circumference, for it hath something in its own essence, which is deeper and more substantial than this accessory relation. This therefore it keeps and represents under the primary name of a point, and can by abolishing all the circumference, lose nothing but that secondary relative name of a centre.

Now in this distinction we shall find a fine and proper emblem of the first world before and without, and of the second world in or after eternal nature; and of those things also that are or may be attributed both unto this and that. The *point* shall be an emblem of the first abyssal world, considered only and purely as in and to itself. And the *centre* of that first abyssal world again, yet no more considered as before, but as bearing a relation to its being outflown, and unfolded in the generation of the eternal nature, which fitly may be represented by the *circumference*.

Now further, this circumference may be considered so as we did above, viz. as consisting of numberless little points, all surrounding their centre and all standing in equal distance therefrom, and all being connected to each other in an exact order, number and proportion.

And in this consideration we may find a fine emblem of the creatures, but especially of angels and men, all standing round about the central throne of majesty, in the second world; and so also round about their only common deepest original in the first abyssal world; and all being made able to know and understand, not only their own condition they are in, with a mutual relation to themselves, but also more or less to their common centre, or abyssal original.

A large application of this simile is not intended, seeing that so many particulars thereof were declared and insisted upon above.

Let but them, and what more may depend upon them duly be considered, and it will appear of itself, that all that which holy angels, and men of Behmen's understanding, will say in this matter, that same (viz. in a shadowy resemblance thereof, and answerableness thereunto) all the particular points of a circumference would say also, both of themselves and of their centre, if they were understanding creatures, and able to declare their mind by speech; all which saying would certainly be to this elect. Since there is perceiving, knowing, etc. in the circumference, which is granted by every one, there must also be perceiving, knowing, etc. in the centre, with that distinction only, which was mentioned so frequently. But again, since there is perceiving, knowing, etc. in the centre, as centre; which knowing and understanding hath a relation unto creatures, and is so much as to say: An understanding what it is to be a centre, and to have brought forth actually a circumference; there must also be perceiving, knowing, and understanding in that central point, considered only as a point, and before it came to be a centre. Which understanding hath not such a relation unto creatures, but is only so much as to say: An understanding what it is to be an individual point in itself, or an *all* and *one*, and to be all-sufficient of itself, for to become a centre. The plain reason of this consequence may appear from these two considerations. (1.) The generation of the circumference hath not brought any change upon that point, but only hath occasioned a new relation, expressed by that new relative name of a centre, when it was before that very same, in and to itself, under the name of a point. For the circumference, in its generation having not been able to give anything unto its centre, but only to receive from its centre, all what it is and hath, could not have given knowledge and understanding unto its center, but could only have been instrumental for unfolding and displaying that understanding, which in the centre was before, and so also in the point before the centre, (2.) In the abyssal point, before it was a centre, there was an aim, an intent, (as we have heard from Behmen above) to become a centre, by flowing forth and introducing itself into the generation of eternal nature; and further, by means of this, into the creation of angels and men. Which intent doth imply a perceiving, knowing, etc. (called so by denominations taken from after eternal nature, because none can be had from before it) both what it is, to be in and to it itself, an individual point, and to have an all-sufficiency for performing all that is required, for to be called a centre, and to be praised so, throughout the whole circumference.

So therefore it may be said, not only in a particular sense, that understanding is generated (not out of but) in or through the circumference of eternal nature; but also in a general one, that understanding was before the generation of eternal nature; and that this nature (unless understanding had been so before) could not have been generated at all. Which understanding in this latter sense, is plainly understood by that eternal seeing in Wisdom's glass, which is before and without eternal nature, according to many places in Behmen, already quoted.

So I think it is made out sufficiently, that all the expressions of Behmen about this matter, both negative and affirmative are true, with a different respect to two worlds. In those that are called negative, saying, that no perception, etc. is in the Divine Abyssal Being, the creature speaketh in its own sphere unto creatures, and of created things, having in its idea of perception, knowing etc. nothing else but what what is generated in and through the process of eternal nature. For beyond that it is not able to raise up any thought, much less to form any affirmative idea. Justly therefore the creature denyeth all these things of the Divine Abyssal Being, saying positively and absolutely they are not therein, and exalting thus that first Central Being above all what can be conceived, what is particular, circumferential, and standing in number and order. But in those expressions that are called affirmative, the creature speaketh as it were, in imitation of that Abyssal Being, which all alone knoweth and understandeth not only that, but also what, and how it is, in and to itself. And which is rather to be conceived therefore, as speaking of itself, and saying: I am the Lord thy God, but one God, etc. which how it is declared by Behmen, and applied to that first central being in the first world, before and without all nature and creature, may be seen and taken into deep consideration from the first chapter of PRAEDESTINATION. Unto which for a conclusion this only question may be added: What is that which holy angels not only adore, but also so adore, that they hide and cover their faces from?

Which we must needs answer unto (1.) that their honouring and adoring is chiefly to be referred to that infinite, most glorious Being in fire and light, which is so near unto them, that they are themselves also partakers of that divine nature, as so many particular images or representatives thereof, and related thereunto as children unto their father. And (2.) the hiding and covering their faces, hath a plain relation to that deepest, central and abyssal being, before and without its manifestation in eternal nature, or in fire and light.

For this they are not so near unto, but stand in a sense, as it were at an infinite distance from it, and can never be able to be admitted thereinto, though they may be able to look upon it. But like as our natural sight is instantly dazzled and confounded by looking into the bright shining sun, so that our eyes must be shut or covered; so theirs also, by looking into that first central world, which, from such a looking upon it, they can know no more of, but that it is, and must leave the knowledge and understanding, what or how it is, unto this first abyssal being itself.

Now all these things calmly and without prejudice considered, are enough to show, that both the affirmative and negative expressions of Teutonicus, are just and true, by minding only such s different respect to two different worlds.

But though thus far all is right, yet all this is not yet far enough, nor doth it reach the bottom, or represent the full sense and mind of our author.

From whose words there will still be objected, *In one will can be no knowledge of itself.* Wherefore we must now further in a second consideration, show also, that all his expressions both affirmative and negative are sound, true, and consistent with each other, in and with respect to the first abyssal world only, without any relation, or reflection, made upon the second world, or generation of eternal nature. * * *

II.—In this our Second Consideration then, wherefrom the generation of eternal nature with all its properties is utterly excluded, the denomination of this first world, and especially that of *abyss* and of *will*, or the first Abyssal Will, are to be considered.

It is true indeed, that if this first world, or God in himself is called by Behmen *abyss* only, and nothing else or more but abyss, we cannot attribute any knowing, etc. to it, and his negative expressions only must be true, with exclusion of all them that are affirmative.

And again, if in this abyss, there is asserted by Behmen *One only Will, absolutely* and *in every sense*; his plain expression, that *in one will there can be knowledge* of itself, must be true absolutely and without any limitation:

But if we can show from his plain words, that in this first world (which is abyss and nothing but abyss with respect to the second world) there is not only abyss, but byss also, in another sense and respect appropriable to the first world. And again that in this first world, (wherein there is one will, in one sense) there is also in another, both a first and second will, answering to that abyss, and byss, which both are in the first world, which are inseparable from each other, are that first world themselves, it will be evident, that with a different relation to this abyss and byss, and to this first and second will, answerable thereunto, all his negative and affirmative expressions must be true both together, not only without any loss, but also without any contradiction. The negative must be true of the abyss, or first will, and the affirmative of the byss or second will, and so they shall be both true of this first world, without any relation to the second.

I shall represent an abstract of the first chapter of his Mysterium Magnum, making such observations as plainly and undeniably arise from his expressions.

So then he says, ch. i. 2. *God is an eternal nothing; he hath neither ground, nor beginning, nor place, and possesseth nothing but himself.*

This is certainly spoken of God before and without eternal nature, for he saith that he *possesseth nothing but himself:* ergo no eternal nature, and none of all the properties thereof; for all these are not himself, but after and under him.

Now of this first world, or of God, considered as in himself only, he saith further, *He is the will of the abyss; He is in himself but one.*

Again, *He generates himself in himself,* (*ergo* not in nature) *from eternity to eternity.*

Objection. No generation can be without motion; now motion is a property of nature, *ergo*, the generation of eternal nature is here implied.

Answer. No natural generation, distinctly conceivable and intelligible by creatures, can be without that motion, which is the second property of eternal nature.

But a supernatural (called in other places the intellectual life, or) generation, not conceivable distinctly by angels and men, what or how it is, but only knowable that it is, can be without that motion, which is the second property of nature.

But there will be asked, What distinction can we conceive to be between motion and motion? Or why must we call one natural and the other supernatural? Is not this a distinction of our own invention?

No, this distinction is delivered us by Behmen, and is grounded upon the whole harmonious analogy of all his writings.

For we can conceive such a distinction between motion and motion, as we can and ought to conceive, between God dwelling in himself, in the first world, and as manifested without himself, in the second world; between *lubet* and desire, neither of which can be conceived without all motion, when yet this latter only is natural, or in nature, and that former supernatural, or above and antecedent to nature. And again, such a distinction as is between generation and generation, or which here is all the very same, between *generation* and *manifestation*.

Read attentively the tenth, eleventh, and twelfth verses of the seventh chapter in the Mysteriums Magnum, where these two positions are distinctly expressed and explained, viz. (1.) *God generates himself in Trinity:* and (2.) *the Trinity is rightly understood only in his eternal manifestation, or generation of eternal Nature.*

Is it not here undeniably plain, (1.) that he speaks of a generation in himself, before nature, and (2.) of a manifestation, or generation in eternal nature; and that he distinguishes the one from the other, by saying, that the generation in nature, only is an object of our understanding, but not so the generation before and without nature. Again, he saith

He hath no peculiar room, or place, where he might dwell: The eternal Wisdom, or intellect is his habitation: He is the will of wisdom, and wisdom is his manifestation.

Now that which is here called wisdom, is above called the Mysterium Magnum without nature, and the seeing Eye of eternity; and this wisdom is called again the *habitation* of the first will, and the *manifestation* thereof.

Now who does not see that he speaks here of a manifestation antecedent to nature, though in other places, and in another sense and respect, he saith right and true that without nature no manifestation could be? Nay who does not see, that such a manifestation and in such a sense, must be in God, of an absolute necessity, before and without nature. For truly a seeing eye implyeth all this manifestation.

But let us follow our author further.

v. 3. In this eternal generation, three things are to be understood: (1.) *an eternal will,* (2.) *an eternal mind of that will, and* (3.) *the outgoing from this will and mind, which is a spirit of the will and mind.* * * *

Before I proceed any further, it will be useful to make the following observations:

(1.) That whenever Behmen declareth the generation of eternal nature, considering the same, not only as to the distinct properties and different operations thereof, but also chiefly as to its coming forth out of the abyssal deep, or eternal temperature, or eternal nothing; he considereth that *nothing* chiefly as an UNITY, making in the most places no mention at all, and in some few, but a short mention of the Trinity.

But contrariwise, when he considereth that abyssal deep, or eternal nothing, only as in itself, he makes but little mention of the Unity, and insists chiefly, distinctly, and sometimes largely upon the Trinity.

(2.) The next observation is this, that in some places, Behmen gives us a description of God and Nature taken together in conjunction; wherein as to God, he represents both unity and trinity, and as to nature, he considers it as generated already, or as generating actually, so that he declareth the whole process of this generation, in all the seven properties. So, for instance, he doth in the AURORA, in the THREEFOLD LIFE, in the CLAVIS, etc.

And again in other places he describeth God and Nature together, but so, that he considereth nature as not yet generated, but as still lying in the first abyssal will, as a hidden fire, which is, and is not; taking no notice of its distinct properties, but only of its being eternally distinct from God, its only co-eternal original; which nevertheless he considers and represents not only as to the Unity, but also and chiefly, as to the Trinity. This he doth in the EARTHLY AND HEAVENLY MYSTERY, from the first text to *v.* 5 of the fifth text. So also in the SIX POINTS, i. 1–33. These places are thought to be the most against all knowledge, etc. and all Trinity before and without nature, though at the bottom they are strictly concordant with this first chapter of MYSTERIUM MAGNUM, and the first chapter of PREDESTINATION. * * *

Here I will only observe of these two places, in general.

If Behmen, in the *Nine Texts,* and in the SIX POINTS, considereth God and nature, so, that as to God, he tells us, *What the Divine Being is in itself without a principle or what the deepest Divine Being is without nature*, which are his own words. SIX POINTS, i. 22, and 30. And so, that as to nature, he looks upon it, as not yet nature or not actually generated, but as *lying still in the first abyssal will, as a fire which burneth not, which is, and is not—*. And if he nevertheless distinguisheth God from nature, or from that which is to be nature afterwards, and says of a *generation in God, a generation in Trinity, a threefold Spirit*, etc. after the same manner as he doth in the first chapter of MYSTERNIUM MAGNUM and PREDESTINATION, it is certain that he giveth us in all these places but one and the same description of the Divine Being, containing a generation in Trinity, antecedent to nature, and excluding all its properties.

And again, if Behmen in the *Nine Texts*, gives us a description of the *spiritual* and *essential* or *natural life*, or of God and nature, so, that he not only calleth the one as well as the other a *life*, expressly speaking of *two lives*,

But also, that answerably to these two lives, he speaks of a twofold *desire. Text* iv. *v.* 8; the one of which is after the generation of the word or heart, and the other after the generation of nature. Declaring that first generation in the spiritual life, after the same manner, as he doth in the MYSTERIUM MAGNUM and PREDESTINATION, and saying moreover, that *in the natural life no intellect would be, if the spiritual life were not* (N.B. 1.) *desiring, in which desire* (not that which is after the generation of nature) *the Word is generated from eternity to eternity: from which* (N.B. 2.) *the desiring will goeth out eternally, into the natural life, and openeth*, etc.;

It is as plain as anything can be, that he asserts in the *Nine Texts* an Intellect, and generation in Trinity before and without nature.

But to return to the Mysterium Magnum. There then he says, that *In this eternal generation three things are to be understood*. As to the word *generation* we must observe, that as it differs from *manifestation*, in every common sense and matter, so it differs also therefrom in Behmen's sense, and in this deep spiritual matter;

Wherein the generation must needs go before the manifestation. Now in that first consideration of the Divine Being, he useth always the word *generation*, and in the second, implying and presupposing nature, that of *manifestation*.

The generation in Trinity is done and is still doing before and without nature, from eternity to eternity. But the manifestation of this Trinity, is done and still doing in the generation of nature.

We cannot say that the Trinity is generated in or through nature, though in a certain limited sense it might be said so, but we cannot say so in an absolute sense without any limitation, if we will not make nature the original of the Triune Being: But we can say absolutely and in every sense, that the Trinity, which was, and still is generated in Itself, before and without nature, is *manifested* in and through nature, without itself; and is by this manifestation made intelligible, first unto God himself, (in a certain sense relating unto nature, spoken of above sufficiently) and further unto creatures also. For, though there are not yet in this consideration, any creatures to be implied, yet there is implied so much, that this manifestation in and through nature, made a way for the production of creatures, which without it could not have been produced; and that it made also the Trinity able to be an object of a created understanding; which it could not have been, if this manifestation had not been made.

We know, not only that the generation of nature, is in its three first properties, represented by Behmen as a $\triangle$, and called expressly the triangle of nature; but also, that these three are by him referred distinctly to the father, Son, and Spirit.

Now we cannot say, that they are referred unto them, only so far, as Father, Son and Spirit are manifest in this generation of nature; but we must say also, so far as Father, Son, and Spirit are in this *eternal generation* before and without nature, where they are not yet properly to be called Father, Son, and Spirit (see Mysterium Magnum, vii. 10, 11,) and are yet called so most frequently.

For if that Father, Son and Spirit, which Behmen calleth so before nature, by denominations taken from after nature, is the Trinity in this eternal generation, represented by Behmen in such a character as a $\triangle$ or $\curlywedge$

Further if this Trinity is that one eternal life, good, or God, which he commonly calleth so, in his first consideration of God: And if nature with all its properties, hath its eternal original from that one eternal life; the $\triangle$ in nature cannot but be originated from Father, Son and Spirit, or from that Trinity which is before and without nature. Seeing that this same triangle in nature is the beginning of its manifestation or the manifestation thereof itself, according to the inferior restless part of nature. Which manifestation therefore of the Trinity must needs be placed in nature, when the generation thereof must be before and without it; so that we rightly conceive this generation to be prior, and that manifestation to be posterior, yet both co-eternal and without beginning, but in such a difference of sense, as there was mentioned above.

Now further, this distinction and difference between generation and manifestation, can she show us plainly, how we are to conceive rightly, to place in due order the Unity and Trinity.

But first we must here observe, of the expression *Unity*, that it is here taken in that strict and narrow sense, wherein it is used by Behmen with relation to the Trinity only; and not in that larger, wherein he useth to say of an unity, or, if I may say so, of a chaotical oneness of all things, in the first Mysterium Magnum. Which latter unity hath a relation, or is rather opposite, not to the Divine Trinity, but to the variety and multiplicity produced in nature, and further in the creation of angels and men and of all this third principle. Which observation is well to be taken notice of, that we may not confound this unity with that, or else we shall confound the Trinity with multiplicity, and God with nature.

This latter unity, with relation to nature and creatures, and to the variety and multiplicity therein, is or was an unity before and without nature only, but in the generation of nature and creature, it is utterly lost, is turned into multiplicity, and hath ceased to be what it was before nature, so that it cannot be found in nature and creature, considered as nature and creature; for it is their own essentiality to stand all in division, distinction, particularity and variety, which if they stood not in, they were not nature and creature.

But that former Unity, with relation to the Trinity only, is an unity always, and everywhere, and ceaseth not to be in the generation or the Trinity; it is not lost at all therein, nor is turned into the Trinity, but continueth still an individual unity, diffused as it were through the whole Trinity, and to be found whole without diminution in each of the Three, and whole also without alteration in all Three together. For as much as it is the inseparable essentiality of God, both before and after nature, to be but one, in an universal individual Unity.

And though the properties of eternal nature do continue also, in a sense, all seven to be but one, yet this oneness of them is already so much different and declined from its former unity, which it had when it still laid as a hidden fire in the first abyssal will, and is now so abolished in the distinct generation of nature and the seven different properties thereof, that it can no more be found in nature, considered as nature generated, but only in a reflection made upon its first original.

Now this unity is here not considered, but only that former Unity in its strict and narrow sense, with relation to the Divine Trinity.

And of this Unity, we say according to Behmen, that we cannot place it before and without nature, and the Trinity, as if before eternal nature, there were nothing but an unity, and as if this unity were only in and through nature displayed, or unfolded into a Trinity.

For he says expressly, that *in this generation* (N.B.) *three things are to be understood*. And again, the *triangle denotes* (N.B.) the *hidden God* (or God unmanifest) viz. *the word or Divine Intellect, which* (hidden God) *in his eternal beginningless generation, is threefold, and yet but one in all manifestation.*

Here we see again and again, (1.) that the generation is different from the manifestation of God. (2.) That there is a generation in Trinity, (asserted by Behmen) in God himself from eternity to eternity. (3.) God unmanifest (which is nothing else but God before and without nature) is here denoted by a *triangle*, and expressly said to be threefold in the beginningless generation. (4.) That this God unmanifest in one sense, relating to nature, is manifest to himself according to his own eternal generation in himself.

For seeing there is in this unmanifestedness, mention made of a *Divine Intellect*, a manifestation of God unto himself is plainly implied, though he be unmanifest in nature.

Before and without, nature, in the first place the Unity and in the second the Trinity are to be conceived, both as unmanifest to nature, but manifest unto themselves.

In or after nature, we must place first, the Unity again, and then the Trinity, but now as manifest and able to be an object of a created understanding, which, both as to angels and men, is and abides for ever and ever in nature, and in nature only.

And so we place no nature between the Unity and Trinity, but only between the Tri-unity unmanifest and the same Tri-unity manifest. Again,

If we own, as it cannot be disowned, that Behmen makes a distinction between an eternal generation of God in himself, and an eternal manifestation in nature, saying, in this latter of *three persons*, and in that former of *three things*, we cannot refer the Trinity to this latter as also not unto that former only, but must refer it unto both; seeing that not only the three things before nature answer unto the three persons after nature, which are not generated by nature, but only manifested: but also that the three things before nature must needs be an unfolding of the Unity, as well as the three persons in or after nature, though not in an equal sense, manner or degree.

Selection Three.

"Points concerning God in Unity and Trinity Before and After Eternal Nature"

[This is possibly an incomplete copy of "Ninety Seven Points", from Serial Elucidations G, part one. —Ed.]

The Third of the selected Extracts and abstracts from Freher is headed, "POSITIONS CONCERNING GOD in UNITY and TRINITY, considered both as BEFORE and AFTER ETERNAL NATURE, according to BEHMEN's CENTRAL THEOSOPHY," thus:—

I. —The first and deepest consideration of God in unity and trinity, is not that which JACOB BEHMEN hath delivered in his *Aurora*, declaring always together and intermixing with it the generation of eternal nature in its seven properties, or fountain spirits.

But that is the first and deepest, which afterwards he gave us in the most of his following books, where he calleth it an eternal generation of God in himself, in trinity, without all nature.

II. —In this first and deepest consideration, God is not to be conceived according to any such definitions, as usually do ascribe unto him all the highest and most glorious attributes, be they either such as are generally found out and owned by all created spirits, to be truly divine perfections, or also such as are expressly mentioned in the holy Scriptures.

III. —This is the ground of Behmen's saying so much of an eternal nothing, oneness, chaos, temperature, etc.; of his denying in God thoughts, deliberations, decrees, consultations, predestinations, etc. about things to be created, or governed in such or such a manner; and farther of his taking wisdom in different senses, and placing it now before, and then again after the trinity.

IV. —None of the true perfections imaginable are hereby denied in God, even not in this first and deepest consideration without all nature. But the meaning is only this, that in this consideration, they cannot yet be a *distinct* object of our understanding. Because they are still to be looked upon, as not yet unfolded out of their root, or centre, which he calleth an universal all, no less than eternal nothing. And if we do conceive them by distinct ideas, we show but forth thereby, that our consideration doth not go beyond the generation of eternal nature.

V. —It is not hereby asserted, that such definitions of God, as may be seen in all the systems of Divines, are to be rejected as erroneous and hurtful; rather they are freely owned to be good, profitable, and sufficient to instruct men in what they are to know of God, for their eternal salvation. But it is asserted only, that they are not central, and do not declare, as Behmen doth, what God is in himself, without nature.

VI. —When God is considered by Behmen without all nature, but yet still with some relation and comparison to creatures, He is said to be an eternal nothing, an ineffable and unintelligible oneness, a most internal ground, root or source of all created beings, which by none of them can be named, found out or understood.

VII. —When God is considered without all nature, and as in himself only, without any relation or comparison to creatures, we must say, according to Behmen, that God is a beginningless and endless beginning, delighting in himself, and playing with himself, in the wonders of his eternal wisdom.

VIII. —In this definition, the trinity in unity without all nature is contained and expressed. By God delighting in *himself*, a single individual being, or an unity without distinction is expressed; when yet from the second consideration of God, as in and after nature, it doth appear, that here also before and without nature, in this same individual being three things are to be understood, so that we can say thereof truly, in some, but not in every sense, the first is not the second, and the second not the third.

IX. —For that which delighteth is to be conceived, as answering to that, which in and after eternal nature, is called Father. That which is delighted in, as answering to that which afterwards is Son. And this delight itself, as answering unto that, which afterwards is called Holy Spirit, but here, as before and without nature, a moving life of Father and Son.

X. —These three are not to be conceived as if they were three distinct beings, persons, or intellectual spirits, existing besides one another, each having his own understanding, will, etc. This would be making three Gods.

XI—These three are but one intellectual being, having but one intellect, will and life. When nevertheless there is such a distinction between them, as is not imaginary, nor also arbitrary. But it is a distinction *cum fundamento in re*, representing rightly three and neither more nor less. Behmen distinguisheth them thus: he calleth them an eternal nothing, and an eternal ens, or something. Again, a beginningless and endless abyss; an eternal beginning and end, or a byss coeternal to the abyss; and an *outgoing* or proceeding from that abyss and byss, or also from that abyss through that byss. Again, he calleth them the first or abyssal will, the second will, or with the Scripture the eternal *Word*, and the *moving life of the Deity*. And sometimes Father, Son, and Holy Spirit.

XII. —The eternal nothing, answering or appropriable to that which after nature, is called Father, may be safely conceived so, but with this caution, that we do not think it so (nothing) in and to itself, but only so to all and every created understanding.

And when this nothing itself openeth upon the spirit of a soul, it instantly confoundeth and consumeth all its sight, and reduceth it in a sense and manner, into its own nothingness. The generation of the fourth property of eternal nature, wherein this nothing openeth, and which is to be met with more or less in the process of regeneration, is of all this not only an unexceptionable witness, but also an instructor, able enough to inform us, how we are to conceive of this eternal nothing.

XIII. —The eternal ens, or something, answerable or appropriable to what in and after nature is called Son, may safely be conceived so, as we can conceive an endless, substantial being, but with this caution, that we do not say or think, it is so to nature and creature, but only, in itself, and to that former nothing. For as to all created spirits, it is still but nothing, because it is still before, above, and without nature, and can by none of them be seen, found out, and entered into; notwithstanding that it is, in a sense, to be distinguished from that nothing, and that this nothing doth see, find and manifest itself therein, and delight in it as in its own expressed image.

XIV. —Behmen's frequent expressions of abyss and byss, are all equivalent in sense unto those of nothing and something. But because he speaks more distinctly and explicitly of abyss than of nothing, more is also to be said thereof.

When he speaketh of this abyss, declaring what it is in and to itself, he never says, that it is a nothing, but plainly and expressly in more than twenty-five places, that it is a *beginningless endless Eye*. This eye seeth all nature and creature, before either this or that can be called so. It seeth all the powers, products, numbers, etc. that ever are or can be brought forth into being. But it seeth none of these things as without, or as really distinct either from itself, or from one another; and seeth therefore itself only, that is in a word, its own central all-sufficiency for all these things.

XV. —Here now is the Divine intellect or Wisdom in its first and deepest sense, which Behmen also calleth wisdom expressly and in many places. And here therefore that objection saying, He placeth preposterously the will before wisdom, and wisdom after the will, contrary to sense and reason, is answered sufficiently, and must be looked as risen only from a misunderstanding him.

For though he placeth wisdom in another sense, and upon another account, not only after the will, but after the trinity, as he doth for instance in his *Table of the Principles*; yet here standeth wisdom, in this sense, before the will, and the will followeth immediately upon it. For

XVI. —Thirdly, when Behmen intends to proceed further, and to declare that eternal generation in three, which goeth, as it were, on the one side, from this abyss towards within; when that of eternal nature in seven tendeth on the other side, from the same abyss towards without,—he saith, This abyss is, or also, hath a will, which he calleth the first abyssal will, in distinction from the second will that of the byss. This expression of a first and second will, doth not say that there are two wills in the Divine Being, they are one as the Father and Son are one.

The first will is not to be conceived as a will by itself, for it is not yet that which we use to call a will, but it is to be conceived as the first imperceptible disposition to the will. Which disposition is in the abyss, but as in the abyss cannot come to its maturity.

XVII. —The reason why Behmen calleth it the first will, when it cannot properly be called a will, is this: That which is in the abyss, is that self-same, which is in the byss; in the abyss in its deepest root, in the byss in a full-grown tree. If then that which is in the byss is a will rightly and properly so called; that same in the abyss may aptly though not so properly called a will, with this distinction of first. This second will he calleth also with Scripture the eternal Word, because this second will is not only an offspring produced out of the first, but chiefly such an offspring, as is an express image, manifestation, unfolding, outspeaking, or declaration of all (neither more nor less) what the first will was, or had in its own central depth.

XVIII. —The generation of our own word, within the particular sphere of every one's created being, can be in a manner, or in part, a fine though but shadowy representation thereof. For though we use to call only that a word, which is distinctly formed and pronounced; yet we know, that every such formed word hath a much deeper root, in the inmost recesses of our soul and spirit, even before it cometh to be perceptible in our mind.

Further, we know, that such a formed word is nothing else, but an opening, or manifestation or declaration of what our soul first had unformed in its own depth, or what our will first in itself, and first even insensibly was inclined or disposed unto. And then also we know, that this is nothing else but that; and that by the formation of an express word, the first disposition thereto in the will, doth only bring forth and exalt itself, and nothing but itself, unto such perfection, as it could not have had, as long as it was unformed in its first original depth.

If then that which is expressly formed and spoken forth is rightly called a word, that which this same word was, before it was thus formed, may well enough be called a word also.

XIX. —In one will, says Behmen, no knowledge of itself can be. And this is not to say, That for a knowledge of itself two wills in two distinct intellectual beings are required. But only, in this first abyssal will, if it were alone, without having brought forth and exalted itself into its own formed expressed image, viz. the second will, no perception nor knowledge of itself could be.

XX. —The abyss is all-power concentrated, and the byss the same all power unfolded. Now this all and that all must needs be one, and no distinction can be found out between all and all; neither can there be two different alls.

XXI. —The communion between these two, which is a living beam, proceeding from the first into the second, and through the second, (and so from first and second into the eternal wisdom, delighting and playing in and with its wonders.) is the Spirit, called here by Behmen a moving life of the Deity. And this completes this holy most adorable number Three.

XXII. —Unto these three no fourth can be added, and by Behmen's saying never so much of an eternal Virgin Wisdom, no quaternity is made.

Immediately after these three, Behmen in his *Table* placeth Wisdom, distinguishing the outgoing from that which is gone out, and saying, that the outgoing, or proceeding forth is the spirit, and that which is gone out is wisdom.

Wisdom stands rightly both in the beginning and end, or both before and after this Trinity, concluding as it were the circle of this eternal generation, which was also begun with wisdom.

Wisdom is compared by Behmen not only to a seeing Eye, but also to a Mirror full of wonders. And though he sets these two comparisons commonly together, yet he distinguished them also plainly enough here and there, so that this twofold comparison may not only show us that twofold sense in which he looks upon wisdom, but also direct us to that twofold place, wherein he placeth it, and show also why he speaketh before the will, and also again after the Trinity.

When he considered the abyss, not yet as a father, but as abyss only, he saith affirmatively of it, that it is an eternal seeing eye. Here now in this place there is not yet any mention made of the will, which will makes the first beginning of the abyss's being called a father; and so also there is not yet a generation of the son, nor a proceeding of the spirit to be conceived: but this wisdom or seeing eye, is considered only and strictly as by itself, in its own eternal centre, wherein it seeth purely in itself, its own radical all-sufficiency for all whatever is in any sense posterior; and so not only what may concern nature and creature, but also what belongs to the next following generation itself.

In this first consideration therefore, the comparison of an eye is more fit, than that other of a looking glass, which implied notoriously two things, a certain object, and then also something that it can be an object to.

When Behmen had declared the eternal generation in Trinity, so that now Father, Son, snd Spirit are considered in that distinction, wherein they stand so for, that we can say, The Father as father is not the Son, and the Son as son not the Spirit, though all three but one and the same intellectual being; then only, but not before, according to this distinction, a distinction also between wisdom and wisdom doth appear, and the comparison of a looking glass full of wonders is now more fit and proper than before. Notwithstanding that wisdom is both now and then the same.

For it is now no more considered by itself alone, as an abyssal eye, in its own internal centre, but as outgone and dilated in the byss, and as in conjunction with this byss; between which two, abyss and byss, there is now a mutual relation, so that it is no more the abyss's, but the Father's and the Son's wisdom. And something there is now also which the wonders of this looking-glass can be a passive subject to, viz. a moving active life of the Father and Son, which is the Spirit. For,

XXIII. —In the consideration of the eternal generation only, and not before it, the abyss is considered as outgoing or proceeding forth from itself. If then this abyss is a seeing eye in and to itself, this seeing eye goeth out, and makes itself more external than it was before; viz. in that sense strictly, and not any further, in which we can say, The Spirit gone out from the abyss, is to be considered as more external than the abyss, as in itself only. When therefore this eye considered as abyssal only, had more strictly, or as it were more narrowly for an object, its own central and radical all-sufficiency, it hath now, considered as more external, as it were in a larger dilatation, an infinite multiplicity and variety of wonders; which are to be looked upon not only as distinct from the Spirit, but also as a passive subject of this spirit, wherein he moved, playeth, and delighted. Which indeed is to be such an object as they could not be before, when the Spirit was not yet a moving life, outgone from the abyss.

And with relation therefore to this spirit, that same eternal wisdom, before abyssal only, but now in conjunction with the byss, is more fitly than before compared to a looking glass, standing as an object before the Spirit, and representing all its infinite variety of figures, powers, wonders, etc.

This distinction between wisdom and wisdom is so much *cum fundamento in re*, as that is between the first and second will, or that also between Father, Son and Spirit. And if therefore it is needful to consider the eternal unity, antecedent to the trinity, and again the eternal generation in trinity as subsequent to the unity; there is also needful such a distinct consideration of Wisdom and wisdom, and a placing wisdom in the one sense before, and in the other after the Trinity.

XXIV. —Wisdom in that first sense and place is by Behmen called Mysterium Magnum without nature, considered as in its most internal root or centre. And this second sense and place it is that *same* Mysterium Magnum without nature, but considered as more external, as gone out, or displayed out of that root.

Wisdom in that first sense and place can be considered neither as active nor passive, because abyssal. But in this second sense wisdom is rightly considered as passive only, and as incapable of activity; for it is in subordination to the spirit, like as a body to its life. A body may be living indeed, and full of vigour and activity, and can for all that never be that life or principle of activity itself: so also wisdom is indeed not without life and hath nevertheless no life without the spirit, which is the only life therein, and from which, wisdom in this second sense, is so inseparable, as wisdom in the first sense is from the abyss.

Wisdom in the first sense, compared to a seeing Eye, is the divine intellect, that is, God himself considered only and purely as in himself, but not yet as in Trinity. And in this second sense, compared to a Mirror full of wonders, wisdom though still divine, is not purely God himself, neither as in Unity, nor as in Trinity, but it is as it were a habitation of God, considered now in Trinity. Which habitation without all nature, answers to that in and after nature, which is called a most glorious, majestic habitation, or temperature in substantiality, which also is not God himself but under God, as every habitation is under its inhabitant.

Yet in all these and the like distinctions, the eternal wonders of wisdom, relating principally to the second sense, are inseparable from that seeing Eye in the first. The wonders of wisdom are in the first sense thereof, tacitly implied, and in the second more explicitly represented. For the Spirit is now that which seeth them, and delighteth in them. And his seeing is no more as in himself only, but as something gone out and distinct, though not separate from himself.—The next consideration is concerning the divine Trinity, both as before and in and after nature.

XXV. —As soon as the first Abyssal Will is conceived or named, there is also conceived on the one side, the Father of the Byss, and on the other the Father of Eternal Nature. Which are not two fathers, but only one, though the generation, upon several accounts, is twofold. For like as from the first abyssal will towards *within*, proceedeth forth, from eternity to eternity, a generation in Three; so also from the *same* abyssal will proceedeth forth an eternal generation into Seven, which is the generation of eternal nature. Wherein the three do manifest themselves more externally, and come thereby not only into a clearer distinction, but also into a nearer, as it were approaching towards the creation of living intellectual beings, to be made after their own tri-une image, that they might by them be known and glorified. For none of them could have been brought forth by or from the three only, without the seven, generating themselves mutually and perpetually in that constant process, called by Behmen the generation of eternal nature. Why this eternal generation is rightly called an eternal manifestation of the Divine Tri-une Being, is most worthy and needful to be examined.

The name of a manifestation implieth (1.) that there is something, which hath a being in and to itself; (2.) that this something is unmanifest, hid and covered, etc. (3.) that there is also something unto which this manifestation is to be made. Now then, that the Divine Tri-une Being without nature, is not a nothing in and to itself, and is not by nature to be brought forth from not being, into being, has been enough proved.

But since, in this Tri-une Being, the byss is a manifestation of the abyss unto itself, it maybe justly asked, What is then further hid, secret, or unmanifest?

And what is that unto which a manifestation is required to be made? Answer. Notwithstanding all this manifestation of the abyss, by its byss, the whole Tri-une Being without nature is still unmanifest unto itself. And this manifestation is therefore a manifestation of this Tri-une Being made unto itself only, though it is also consequently, a manifestation, made in order to the production of intellectual creatures: none of which this Tri-une Being could have been made manifest unto; nay none of which could have been brought forth, unless this Tri-une Being had first been manifested to itself, through the generation of eternal nature.

XXVI. —The byss is a manifestation of the abyss unto itself. For the abyss's eternal finding, perceptibility, etc. is the byss. And in the mirror of wisdom, an infinite variety and multiplicity of wonders, figures, colours, virtues, etc. do appear, to that moving life of Father and Son, which is the Spirit. All this is true in its sense and degree; yet all this will not yet do. For all these things are still merely nothing in and to themselves, and have no activity in or with them, but are only as transitory or shadowy images in a looking glass, which are and can do nothing to themselves, though they are something to that Eye which looketh upon them. No properties therefore no qualifications are in motion, no sound from them is heard, no harmony ariseth, no fire burneth, no light can shine, etc. And though there is a clearness and serenity, yet there is no splendor, lustre, and glory.

And upon this account, the Spirit cannot, in a full sense, be said to perceive and know himself, or to be manifest unto himself, before he knoweth effectually what it is to have passed through all the inferior properties of nature, and to have exalted himself through the fire into the light of glory. If then this is done in and by the generation of eternal nature, and if it cannot be done any other way, this generation is rightly called a manifestation of the Spirit, and so of the whole Tri-une Being, made only to itself.

XXVII. —It is plain from hence, that this manifestation is not, as it were the removing of a vail, or the like impediment, from a thing, that is covered or concealed by it, no such thing is here to be imagined. For as it is not a manifestation, made either to, or by any other, but made only by and to that being itself: so is it also an eternal impossibility, that this Being could be manifest unto itself (in that sense which Behmen takes this word) without or before an actual performance, of all what is for this manifestation required. Which is in short a raising up the properties of nature, a passing through them, and an exalting itself thereby into glory and majesty.

This cannot be done by three, and not by less than three: and though the properties of nature are in one respect but three, nay in another also but one; yet in their full dilatation, they are also seven; and by three only, this raising, passing through and exalting cannot be performed.

For that which will thus exalt and manifest itself is in a manner three already; and this manifestation is not a going backwards, or decreasing, but an increasing: and though this Tri-une Being doth not itself increase, yet its manifestation is and must be a fruitful progress, laying as it were a foundation for an infinite multiplication.

XXVIII. —As in this eternal manifestation must be more than three, so by the same necessity, there can be neither more nor less than seven.

For the three in the eternal generation may be conceived, the first as a *terminus a quo*, than which is nothing sooner or deeper; the second as a *terminus ad quem*, beyond which is no going further, and the third as a medium between them, both distinguishing and combining them. And this threefold degree of progress must in the generation of the properties of nature distinctly be expressed and represented, if the three without nature shall be manifested, and gradually exalted in and by the progress of nature; as it is accordingly expressed in the three principal regions, or parts of nature. And it is this same distinct expression, which bringeth in, or carryeth along with it of all necessity, the full and perfect number seven, without having less, or wanting more. For when in the eternal generation the *terminus a quo* is but one, the same cannot be one but must be three; in this eternal manifestation thereof, because there are three in the completed eternal generation, which all three together are to be manifested and exalted in this progress of nature.

All three therefore are, as in the end of this progress, so in this beginning thereof also, wherein all three do consequently leave behind them, as it were, these footsteps, which are the three first properties of eternal nature, distinctly by Behmen ascribed to Father, Son and Spirit.

Now further: as the Three in the eternal generation are not to stand still in this beginning, but must go on unto a full manifestation, and exaltation in the light of glory and majesty: so these their first footsteps in nature cannot be left in that state, wherein they are in this beginning; but must be fixed and appear in the end of nature also, which is the *terminus ad quem*, beyond which is no going further.

And these are the three superior properties of nature, not only answering in one sense, unto the three first, but also one with them in another. And so there are now six of them.

But now as to the medium between them, which is both to distinguish and to unite them, this cannot be neither three nor two, but must be one. Two cannot be an exact distinguishing mark, between these three and three, for if they are two, they not only can, but also want still to be distinguished themselves by a third.

Three can also not be such a true distinction, for they are themselves distinguished already by a third standing between one and one. This third therefore would be the distinguishing, not between three and three, but between four and four. Again, neither two nor three can be duly uniting these three and three, for this uniting must be done in or by one only indivisible point: The three on the one side, stand as it were by themselves in a circle or globe, so do the three on the other also. As then two circles cannot touch one another in more than one point, so it is here to be conceived also. And this one point must be such a one, as may be able, not only to keep in itself an exact neutrality between the three and three, but to have also an equal communion with both sides, so as to keep them not only from each other in one respect, but also to bind them both together in another. All which cannot be done by two, or three, but by one only. And this is now the fourth property in the generation of eternal nature, standing in the midst between three and three and making up the full and perfect number seven; by which the whole manifestation of the three without nature is all accomplished. So as nothing can be taken from or added to it.

XXIX.—By this eternal generation in seven, the Tri-une Being without nature is manifested unto itself, and all the Divine attributes are out of their root unfolded.

For all what for this manifestation is required, is now performed by the generation of these seven. The fire burneth, the light shineth; that in strength and power, this in splendor and brightness, the air uniteth and keepeth them in union, being itself neither this nor that. And so the former stillness is turned now into a most glorious region, full of living, moving, working and all harmonized properties and qualifications; wherein God in Trinity dwelleth and perceiveth what it is, to have actually exalted himself from an abyss into glory and majesty.

XXX.—The Divine Tri-une Being was never without this eternal generation in seven, which is therefore all inseparable therefrom, though it may be separately by itself considered, and though Behmen ascribeth an eternal beginning unto this sevenfold generation; yet this is not to say, that the Divine Being was by itself alone, before a beginning thereof was made; but only that this generation in seven is not the first, and deepest, or inmost original centre.

And this saying therefore of a beginning, is to be taken only in such a sense, as in which the Byss or Son himself, though equally co-eternal to the Father, is rightly said to have an eternal beginning in the will, which beginning he had not once in such or such an instant, but hath it still from eternity to eternity.

XXXI.—All what creatures can know, perceive, enjoy and understand of God, is only in and by this eternal generation in seven; which is therefore not to be looked upon, as if it were a thing strange unto, or separable from God, or not of so great an importance in the consideration of God. For it is the Divine nature, which all the creatures, that are made after his image, must be partakers of, if they shall be able to stand before his throne: and without which he can much less be known and understood by them, than any particular thing can be known without knowing the nature thereof. Wherefore then in a true definition of God, not only the number three ought to be expressed, but also the number seven.

Without the three the seven could not be, and without the seven, the three could not be manifest. For the seven do make in their generation those two eternal principles, which are fire and light. And these two are that same, wherein the manifestation of the Divine Tri-une Being without nature is accomplished; the Father's in the fire, the Son's in the light, generated and shining forth out of that fire, and the Spirit's in them both.

XXXII.—After the three first properties, called by Behmen the triangle in nature, and referred distinctly to Father, Son and Spirit, in the generation of the fourth, which is the fire, the first Abyssal Will is opened as an eternal nothing, consuming, melting down, turning, and traumatize, in one sense, into nothing, but in another into something better and more noble, all what by the three first properties in their fighting and whirling was made up. And this is the Father, whom the Scripture also calleth a consuming fire. If then this first abyssal will is God, viz. the Father, considered as in himself only without all nature, this same abyssal will, now opened in the generation of this fourth form, is *God in nature*.

From this first manifestation which is the Father's in the fire, the second, viz. the Son's in the light, is all inseparable. And so is also from these two the third, which is the Spirit's, called or compared, as in the Scripture, so by Behmen also, to a wind or air, not only proceeding forth from fire and light, but also keeping them both in union, according to that outward representation thereof in temporal nature, wherein we see, that without air proceeding from the fire, no fire can burn and consequently no light can shine.

XXXIII. —From this different consideration of the Trinity cannot be inferred, that Behmen makes two Trinities, the one before and the other after nature. For the first abyssal will, the eternal word, and the out-going from this and that, before and without nature, are the three selfsame, that in and after nature, are called Father, Son, and Holy Ghost. And if his speaking of a first and second will, does not make two wills in the Divine Being, which was made out above, his speaking of a Trinity without, and a Trinity in nature does also not make two Trinities. For as the second will is but an opening, manifestation, and exaltation of the first, having neither more nor less in it than that first; so also the Trinity in nature is but an opening, manifestation and exaltation of the Trinity without nature, and hath in it neither more nor less.

XXXIV. —When we say with Behmen of an opening, manifestation, or exaltation in the Divine Tri-une Being, we say that same in substance, but more explicitly, which the Scripture saith more implicitly, when it calleth the Son an express image, character and brightness of the Father's glory. For if we are thus to conceive of the son, we must needs conceive also of the father, that he hath no brightness of glory without the Son. And if so, must we not conceive the Father without the Son, as a centre sealed up, not manifested unto himself, and not exalted into a brightness of glory?

The Son's generation therefore, which is from eternity to eternity, is nothing else but the Father's manifestation unto himself, made by his own opening, proceeding forth, and exalting himself from a low or deep abyss, into the highest seat of glory.

XXXV. —Though there are not two Trinities, the one before and the other after eternal nature, yet there are several considerable differences between the Trinity considered as without and as in and after nature; some of which have a relation to creatures, but the chiefest is that which concerns the Trinity as in and to itself.

The Trinity without nature cannot have any created representative, made after its own image and likeness. When the Trinity considered as in and after nature, can have, and hath such in an innumerable number; even angels and men, all having (if not by their own fault fallen away from it into disorder) in themselves, this eternal generation in seven, and so also the two eternal of fire and light, in their most harmonious union, answering unto that wherein they stand in this eternal manifestation of the most holy Trinity. The deep ground and reason, why the Trinity before nature cannot have any created representative of itself, is shown us by Behmen sufficiently. — Again,

The Trinity without nature cannot be a proper and direct object of any created understanding, and can never be seen, felt, or enjoyed, either by angels or men: when the Trinity in nature can and is by them understood, seen in a manner, nay *felt* and *enjoyed* even so, that Father, Son and Holy Ghost, in their *distinct communications*, or influences, *can be discerned* by such souls and spirits, as stand with them in a nearer and more intimate union. The reason both of this and that can easily be given: for if the whole created being of angels and men is and must be inferior and posterior to this eternal generation of nature in its seven properties, all their understanding, feeling, enjoying, must be strictly confined thereunto, so that there is an impossibility for them to reach beyond it.

And if all their created being is of the same nature, which the trinity is manifested in and by, even of this eternal nature in its seven properties, they cannot but understand, see, feel, and enjoy God in Trinity, after whose tri-une image they are made, and of whose Divine nature they do partake, even so that he is not ashamed to call them *sons, children, gods,* etc.

XXIV. —The chiefest difference, between the trinity considered as before, and as in and after eternal nature, is this, that in the second consideration it can properly and directly be called a trinity; because there is a plain and manifest distinction between the three, which is fitly figured out and represented, even in outward nature also, by that distinction which is therein between fire and light and air. And though we say, with Behmen, that three things are to be understood is this eternal generation without all nature, and again God generates himself in trinity. In which expressions a distinction is implied, so that we cannot understand them at all, without thinking more or less of some distinction between the three, yet we are to say also, according to his instruction, that all intelligible distinction in the trinity, depends upon a raising up of the three first properties of nature by the first abyssal will, which is Father; further upon the generating and passing through the fire; and then also upon a manifesting the brightness of the Father's glory in the light or Son. So then we are permitted indeed to conceive the three in the eternal generation, with a distinction, because we cannot do otherwise; yet we are charged also to abstract our mind again from all this concept, and to deny all our affirmative ideas, according to what he plainly says. —*Mysterium Magnum*, cap. vii. 11, 12.

Seeing that we are not able to understand any distinction before and without the distinct generation of eternal nature in its seven properties, etc.

XXXVII. —It is not so much our knowing, there are three without nature, but it is rather this perceptible distinction in nature, which makes us to call it a trinity. For though the three without nature are naturally prior to the trinity in nature, yet as to *our knowing*, we cannot but say, that the trinity in nature is prior to the three without nature, because our understanding ariseth after nature, and goeth not forward from what is unmanifest without, to its manifestation in nature, but contrariwise from this unto that, so far, that we are directed by what is manifest in nature, to know that same must have been unmanifest without nature. Because we now find in nature a plain intelligible distinction between the three, we call it rightly and properly a trinity. And because further we know from hence, that three also are and must be without nature, we take this denomination of a trinity from nature, and attribute it unto that which is without nature also. Though we cannot do it so properly, because as soon as we go beyond nature, and what is manifest in nature, all distinction is lost, and vanisheth away out of all our sight and perception.

XXXVIII. —A simple and rude similitude may perhaps declare the meaning hereof a little nearer. When we conceive a little grain, of such a quantity as is but discernible to the eye, we can visibly distinguish therein, a superior, an inferior, and a middle part. But when we now suppose, is lessened and reduced to the quantity of an invisible and impalpable atom, we can perceive nothing more of a distinction, when nevertheless, so long as we can conceive it to be an atom, we can conceive also that it hath still the same three parts, which before were visibly to be discerned. And this notion of its three parts is all inseparable from our idea, whereby we conceive an atom, and must needs continue so, though we should think it to be lessened, even in infinitum. But if we could suppose, this atom were at length all spiritualized, and so thereby totally taken away out of the number of all corporeal beings, which all are confined to their dimensions, though never so little; then only all the distinction in our idea would be totally lost together with the name of atom, and nevertheless there would remain in us the notion of a certain spiritual something, which we could no more conceive with any distinction.

XXXIX. —So also in a tree, when we see three branches, we see them in a plain and manifest distinction; but when we go back first to the stock, considering that they laid therein, before they came forth thereout, all the manifest distinction is disappeared, and nevertheless, from their being manifestly three, we can justly conclude, there were three also in the stock, because there must needs have been a threefold disposition thereto; which as long as it is, or can be conceived threefold, it cannot be conceived without all kind of distinction, though no distinction is or can be obvious to any of our outward senses. But when we go now deeper, to a consideration of the very seed, out of which all this tree, with all its branches came forth, we can be said in a sense and manner to go beyond the generation of nature, because in this seed, the actual strife of the first three properties of nature, must be conceived as not yet raised up, and so this seed lieth in a state of stillness, rest, and nothingness, with respect to what afterwards is brought forth thereout. There now the distinction may be said to be lost totally, for, what distinction can we possibly imagine, when we must conceive, the three first properties of nature themselves, which are by their actual strife the beginning of all growth in every tree, are not yet entered into their distinction? But nevertheless, again, from our having observed three branches, in the outward manifestation, we cannot but conclude, three also must have been in the first original centre of this manifestation, which centre we may justly think, had in its own sphere no sufficiency for more and no disposition for less than three. And thus so long as we do so think thereof, or speak of three, not all distinction in all and every sense can be excluded from our idea, notwithstanding that we are not able to find out, or to perceive a distinction in the thing itself.

This now may show us, though never so obscurely, that it is no contradiction, when we say on one side, the three in the Divine Eternal Being, without nature, are distinguished; and when we say again on the other side, they are not distinguished. For we say that former, with respect to our apprehension, wherein we cannot separate all and every distinction from an idea of three; and this latter we say with respect to such a distinction, as properly may be called so, according to our common sense and manner of expression, wherein every distinction is and must be posterior to the generation of eternal nature with its seven properties.

XL.—A hand or foot of a child in the womb, saith Behmen, groweth forwards from within, and before it hath any visible figure, it hath already its own proper form or signature in the spirit. If then this be so, as it certainly cannot be otherwise, we must of all necessity conceive, that the spiritual signature of the one cannot be that of the other, but must be, in a manner so distinct therefrom, as a full grown hand is from a foot, and this even long before it can properly be called a hand or foot, and before any distinction between them can appear. And he therefore that was able, *as Behmen was*, to declare this wonderful generation and formation in the womb, from the first beginning in the Spirit, to the manifest and visible outbirth thereof, should find himself necessitated, not only to take the names of the parts or members, for instance, those of hands and feet, from the visible outbirth, and to give them unto that, which is but an invisible disposition thereto in the spirit; but also to tell us sometimes, these members, (hands or feet) are distinguished even in this spiritual disposition, sometimes, again, they are not distinguished, before their distinct figure and formation in fingers and toes can appear.

And by so saying, such a declarer would not contradict himself at all. For they are not distinguished with respect to our sight, and yet they are distinct and must be conceived as distinct, because when they can but upon any account be called hands and feet, we are not able to conceive them without all and every distinction, especially when we know, that each of them hath already in the spirit, before it cometh to the outbirth, its own proper form or peculiar signature; for this constrains us to apprehend and own, that the signature of a hand cannot be that of a foot, though as yet neither this nor that can properly be called so.

So, therefore, we are to conceive every distinction, as it were, in different degrees of increase and decrease, for in the first stirring of the properties of nature, every distinction takes its begining, and from thence it goeth forwards, increasing gradually, till at length in the outbirth it cometh to be manifest and plainly discernible. But in our sight and apprehension, going backwards, from the outbirth to the first root in the spirit, every distinction decreaseth more and more, till at length it is totally lost. Which is done so soon as we presume to go beyond the generation of nature, in its distinct properties.

Thus now was the case of Behmen, when he declared the Trinity, considered both as without and as in eternal Nature. And accordingly he hath not contradicted himself, when he not only gave us three distinct names of Father, Son, and Spirit in the Trinity without nature, but told us also expressly, that we are to understand three things in this eternal generation: and yet tells us again, in outward appearance, quite the contrary. As *Mysterium Magnum*, cap. vii. 11, 12.

XLI. —The conclusion of this matter will now be this, That we are to conceive the first disposition in the spirit, to be, as it were, a hidden, invisible, imperceptible root, of that manifest distinction, which can be perceived in an outbirth; and this manifest distinction, as it were the fruit or product of that root. And that we say, concerning this twofold consideration of the Trinity, (1.) The Trinity considered as in nature, differs chiefly from the Trinity without nature, in this, that the Trinity in this eternal manifestation is manifestly, and as to creatures intelligibly distinguished, when contrariwise all the creatures are not able to find out, or understand a distinction in the eternal generation without nature. (2.) As the first stirring in the properties of nature, which makes a distinction intelligible to creatures, is to be conceived as an invisible root, of which that visible distinction in its following outbirth, is a fruit or product; so the three in the eternal generation without nature, are to be looked upon, as an unintelligible root of that intelligible distinction, which is made in the first stirring of the said properties of nature; for without that Triune root, the distinction in the first properties of nature could not have been brought forth.

And therefore, (3.) the three in the eternal generation without nature are distinguished, by such a distinction as is perceptible and intelligible by and to themselves, but absolutely imperceptible and unintelligible unto creatures.

(4.) A distinction, or root of distinction must there be in these three in the eternal generation, because the first is not the second, the second not the third, and the third neither the first nor second. (5.) This distinction must be perceptible by themselves, because the second of these three is an eternal perceiving, finding and enjoying of the first, caused by intervention of the third, which is a moving life, both of the first and second, and because the Divine Intellect, or Wisdom, which is not the Father's only, but also the Son's, exerted and manifested in this eternal generation, by the proceeding forth of the Spirit, cannot but imply an eternal understanding of what it is to the first, to find, perceive and enjoy himself in the second, by that moving life which is the third. And if so, this can be nothing else, but an intellect touched and affected by, or an eternal understanding of this distinction. (6.) But absolutely imperceptible and unintelligible must this distinction, or rather this root of distinction be, to all created spirits; because it is before, without and above that distinct manifestation of these three, made in and by the properties of eternal nature; wherein they live and move; from which they are, and have all that they can be said to have, and be; and which, therefore, all their perception and understanding strictly must be confined to, as to a sphere of their activity. So that there cannot be conceived in them any ability, proportion, or capacity of perceiving and understanding that which is beyond this sphere; which is, and can be extended no further than to that eternal manifestation of these three, which is made, and could not be made otherwise, but by a distinct generation of nature in its seven properties, rightly called the Seven Fountain Spirits, with respect to all posterior created things, flown forth from them, descended down, or breathed out.

XLII. —Whether this eternal manifestation, in and by the seven properties of nature is to be looked upon, *as purely voluntary or as absolutely necessary*, cannot positively be defined from plain express words or Teutonicus. But many things may be observed from his writings, whereby it can be plain, that it is more consistent with his sense, and much more conformable to the whole construction or coherence of the eternal generation in three, with the eternal manifestation thereof, in seven, to declare for this latter, than for that former.

XLIII. — All what, for this eternal manifestation's of the three in seven being purely voluntary, can be brought forth, will, as I think, summarily be this:

That the Divine Tri-une Being, in the eternal generation without nature, stands in a full accomplished perfection, is all sufficient for, and in, and to itself, enjoyeth itself in a fullness of love and delight, rest and acquiescency with itself, and wanteth nothing to be superadded unto it which could increase its ever blessed happiness, etc.

And from hence is now inferred, that if this be so, no necessity can be thought upon, for a more exterior manifestation of the three in seven; but this manifestation must be looked upon as purely voluntary, so that it be wholly and only referred to his good will and pleasure. And if he would not have been pleased to condescend thereto, he should still have wanted nothing, like as nothing is added unto him thereby.

Answer. What is here said against a necessity of the eternal manifestation of the three in seven, that same almost could be reasoned against a necessity of the eternal generation in three itself, by saying, The Father is all, and hath all in himself, for the Son hath no more but what the Father hath. And that which is and hath all, cannot but acquiesce with its own fulness, etc. What necessity therefore of this Father's generating a Son? But as this reasoning is not good here, so not there.

XLIV. —From what was said above concerning an exaltation of the Divine Triune Being, and such a manifestation as is made only by and to itself, as also of its being still but central, not manifest unto itself, not unfolded, etc., it can be plain, that such an idea of the Divine Being without nature, as here in this objection is expressed by the words of a *full* and accomplished perfection, and enjoyment of love, delight, and acquiescency, etc., is all inconsistent with Behmen's ground. For though we do not deny, that all the Divine perfections are in the Triune Being without nature, yet we say, that in this first consideration of God, which is not *total*, but only *partial* they are not yet exerted, and cannot become exerted, but by the raising up and passing through the properties of nature.

And though, therefore, we rightly say, in one sense, The Tri-une God without nature wants nothing, but hath all, and is all-sufficient in and to himself, so that nothing can be given or super-added unto him, which could make him more perfect. Yet without contradicting this, we may rightly say also, in another sense, The Tri-une God, considered as without nature, wants something, which he hath not in this first consideration, for he wants a fit and proper medium or subject, wherein his all-sufficient perfections may exert, display, and show forth themselves, that so thereby he may come to *perceive himself*, viz. to perceive what he is in that state, wherein they are actually exerted, which medium is the generation of the properties of nature.

And this expression, though gross and rude enough, can give offence unto any man of sense no more than this, The Father considered as Father only, though he is, and hath all in himself, stands yet for all this, not in a full accomplished perfection, for he hath no brightness of glory, and wants therefore, a son, or express image of his substance, that he may thereby come to know, and perceive himself, viz. what he is in that state, wherein the brightness of his glory is actually generated, displayed and manifested unto him. Which expression is, in itself, all innocent and true enough.

XLV. —It can be plain and evident of itself, that by necessity, we do not understand, There is this or that coming in upon the eternal will from without, and binding it down; so that this will were to be conceived first as indifferent, further as moved and drawn, and at length brought away from his former indifferency. But here is no such thing.

The eternal will, which is next to the abyssal eye, and is even that abyssal eye itself, considered as in its first disposition towards a progress or proceeding forth, cannot be considered first as standing indifferent between YEA and NO, and then as moved and drawn to the YEA, by something coming in from without, or from besides, and representing its motives to that eye, or will, causing thereby first a consideration, or deliberation, and then a consent, which the will must now condescend unto, lying as it were impotent under a necessity, and not altogether free from weakness. etc. Away with all such and the like thoughts!

In the first central Abyssal Being itself, not without it, that is, in that eternal Eye and Will itself, or in its own internal, inseparable essentiality, that thing must be implied, which we call a necessity, for want of a more convenient expression.

And if so, it is plain, that as this eye or will is most internal and essential to the Divine Being, so that also must be so, which we call a necessity. And which, therefore, cannot be conceived as a thing different from the will, or standing besides it, moving or persuading it, and in a manner overruling it. But must be conceived as in a most harmonious union and concord with the will, nay as the will itself, considered in this necessity, as in a peculiar and eminent perfection.

For as there is an absolute necessity, implying the highest perfection, that God must be a living God, knowing, feeling, and enjoying himself, so that the will stands not indifferent, and wants no foregoing consultation, whether or no he shall be a living God: so also is there such an absolute necessity, full of perfections, and necessarily implied in the Divine essentiality, that the Divine Tri-une Being must go forth to the generation of eternal Nature, whereby his omnipotent life and power may be unfolded, displayed and manifested, wherein his infinite perfections may be exerted and exalted through the fire in the light of glory.

XLVI. —If we but consider the first abyssal will, and the first stirring thereof, wherein the eternal generation and manifestation are inseparably connected, and from whence go both together the one towards within, and the other towards without: according to what Teutonicus declareth thereof in many places, and especially in the *Earthly and Heavenly Mysterium*, we shall find plainly enough, such an absolute necessity as mentioned, though he himself never hath expressed it so.

For the Will intends a manifestation of its own central and radical all-sufficiency, which manifestation is nothing else but an unfolding of his infinite perfections, and an exaltation thereof, from their being concentrated all at one, as it were, into a glorious circumference, wherein they may appear and work in their distinction. Now this will can do nothing to its purpose without a stirring, which is self-evident. And if then this very stirring, for as much as it is in a sense and manner, exterior than the still and resting will in itself, is nothing else but a beginning of raising up the properties of nature; we cannot conceive it otherwise nor can we perhaps express it better, than by saying:

There is for the generation of eternal Nature such an absolute internal necessity, as cometh not upon the will from without, or from anything besides itself, but lieth in the will, and is so near and so essential to the will, so harmoniously united with the will, and therefore also so inseparable from the will, as this will is near and essential unto, united with, and inseparable from itself. Seeing that if we conceive, this will intends its manifestation, we must needs conceive also, that this will knoweth, not only that he cannot obtain it without a stirring, but also that this same stirring is the beginning of a raising up that fire, which before laid hid in the will, and was not burning, nay that this stirring is made in order thereunto. And if we must conceive it so, it must needs evidence itself, that this will, intending its manifestation, intends by that self-same intent, as by one single act both to stir, and also by this stirring to raise up that fire, for to be manifested thereby, and to be exalted through it into the light of glory. So therefore none of these three can be considered as superfluous, but all three must be owned to stand in an equal degree of necessity, if but the will is supposed to intend its own manifestation, the necessity whereof cannot be questioned.

XLVII. —Another argument for such a necessity could be brought forth, from a consideration of the Divine Goodness, and communicability thereof. For, as the eternal Will in his infinite wisdom, knoweth himself to be good, so he knoweth also, and cannot but know, this goodness to be communicable, outflowing, and giving forth itself. And as it is not indifferent to the will, whether he be good or not, but is his intrinsical essentiality, that he must be the supremest good, so it can also not be thought to be indifferent to him, whether or no his goodness shall flow out and communicate itself; but as these two, to be good, and to be communicable, or willing to communicate himself, are inseparable from the will, and have both an equal ground in the Divine Being, so also a necessity for them must be equal in them both. When yet, like as there is nothing besides him, which might make or cause him to be good, so also is there nothing besides which might cause him to communicate his goodness, but this goodness itself upon its own account, and from its own internal nature or moving principle floweth out, and cannot but flow out, without denying, or forsaking its own nature and name. And there lieth the necessity of the generation of eternal nature. For though all this communicability is directly to be referred to creatures, created after the image of God; yet it presupposeth necessarily the seven distinct properties of eternal nature, without which no creature could have been, and so also nothing of the divine goodness could have been communicated.

XLVIII.—Almost that same, but as to several particulars with a greater emphasis and evidence, could be said concerning the Divine Omnipotence. We cannot say properly, in the first consideration, without all nature, that God is omnipotent, for there is not only nothing wherein his omnipotence could appear unto himself; but there is also nothing, wherein or whereby he might feel and perceive himself to be omnipotent. When yet this saying doth not bring upon him any weakness, impotence, or imperfection: for we do not say, that it is eternal nature which makes him to be omnipotent; but that he himself raiseth up the properties of eternal nature, for to afford unto himself thereby, that necessarily requisite subject, wherein and whereby his radical omnipotence may be exerted and made perceptible unto himself. And further we say, That it is the generation of the fourth property of nature, or the enkindling the fire; the dwelling therein in one respect, and the passing through it in another, wherein and whereby he can and doth perceive himself to be actually and effectually omnipotent, which he cannot without this generation. Wherefore then without this generation we say rightly, He hath the ground and root of omnipotence, in and purely of himself, but without a manifestation thereof, and without feeling and perceiving what this root is in its manifestation.

And so we cannot so properly say, He is omnipotent without all nature, but more properly we say, He is all sufficient for to show forth his omnipotence in the generation of nature, which all-sufficiency cannot raise in us any idea of defect or imperfection but rather of all and every perfection; only considered as still concentrated, and not yet out of that centre unfolded and displayed.

If we then cannot think it is indifferent to the eternal will, whether or no he be actually exerting, feeling and perceiving himself as an omnipotent God, but if we must conceive a necessity for the affirmative, we must needs say also, There is implied in the first abyssal will, such an *absolute necessity*, as declared, for the *generation of eternal nature* in its seven properties.

All the Divine attributes would likewise furnish us with further proofs of this necessity, especially those that have more or less a relation unto creatures; and that never could have been manifested or exerted, if intellectual creatures had not been created by the Father, redeemed by the Son, and fitted by the Holy Ghost for a communion with Father and Son.

Moreover also, many expressions might be found in the holy Scriptures which would afford such arguments. As for instance, a threefold, very considerable one might be formed from the words of St. John in the *Revelation*, concerning the seven spirits, which are, as he saith (1.) before the throne of God, from which (2.) he wisheth grace and peace unto the churches, and which (3.) he placeth in the middle between the Father and Son, wishing grace and peace, first from him which is, and is to come; in the next place from the seven spirits: and then in the third from Jesus Christ.

But since, it is I think made out sufficiently enough, that such a necessity lieth in the very deepest root, even in the first Abyssal Will itself, it is needless to gather arguments from this and that, which all is but posterior to that abyssal root.

XLIX.—Like as in the first consideration of the Divine Being without nature, Wisdom was considered immediately after the Trinity, where it was represented as a looking-glass full of wonders, and in distinction from the Spirit: so it is here also in this second consideration of God, manifested in nature, to be considered after and under the Holy Trinity. Nay even much more properly here than there, because not only was it there, not yet a proper object of human understanding, but also, because all the denominations, which Behmen giveth unto wisdom in the first consideration, without nature, when he calleth her *an eternal Virgin, a mirror full of wonders*,—the Spirit's *corporality, clothing, habitation, instrument*, etc. are all taken from this second consideration, wherein they are significant and intelligible unto creatures; when, nevertheless with respect to them they are not so in that first consideration, but yet are used therein also, for want only of more convenient ones, and for to declare thereby, that wisdom in the first consideration is not another thing, but that same which it is in the second; though it stands now in another, more external and more intelligible condition, state and degree, wherein it can be a proper object of our understanding, like as the Trinity itself.

And moreover all what was said before concerning a distinction between the outgoing, and that which is gone out, or between the Spirit and wisdom, was to be understood only according to what was declared, concerning a distinction between the Three in the eternal generation without nature. But here now, in this second consideration, the distinction is plain enough, and can be understood by intellectual creatures.

For there it must needs have been unintelligible, and past all their finding out; because it was without that sphere wherein they live and move and have their being.

But here it must needs also be intelligible, obvious and familiar unto them, because it is not only within their sphere, but also so nearly related unto them, that they are endued themselves therewith, and called expressly the *children of wisdom*.

L. —This distinction between the Spirit and wisdom, or according to Behmen's expression, between the outgoing and that which is gone out, is the chiefest point in this consideration. And seeing that Behmen himself, in a few words, hath pointed as it were with the finger upon a certain simile, I shall lay it open into its particulars. Which will sufficiently show that Behmen is absolutely guiltless of that crime, which many charged him with, that he made a *Quaternity* in the Divine Being.

A wise and potent king seeth in his wisdom, considered with himself, and without any advice from his counsellors, pondereth in his own mind such things, as he knoweth can promote his own honour and glory, and the prosperity of his kingdom. Now so long as this is only a seeing, contemplating, and pondering in his own mind, it is what it is, only in, and to himself, but it is nothing at all to his counsellors, and of no effect in his government; for it is still, in a sense and manner, separated as it were from his royal power and authority, which cannot yet exercise or show forth itself therein, nor do any good thereby to any other, etc.

And this may represent to us the Divine Wisdom, taken in its first and deepest sense, wherein it is Divine Intellect compared to a seeing Eye, and not distinct from God, but God himself.

This king, having thus seen and found out in his wisdom, how to promote and exalt his glory and the good of his kingdom, settles now further himself into a will or resolution, for to put out a proclamation, and to declare thereby his will.

Now this will is indeed the first step towards the declaration of those things, that in his wisdom were seen, and found expedient and necessary. But as long as it is only a will, antecedents a real act and deed, it is still but nothing, and of no benefit to all what is without and posterior to it, which all nevertheless doth depend upon it, as upon its original. And this will may be looked upon as a representation of the eternal Father.

When now further, this will goeth actually forth, by putting out this intended declaration of itself, we may plainly therein discern three things more, as so many distinct figures of the Son and of the Spirit, and of that which Behmen calleth wisdom in a second, inferior, and more external tense. For,

The declaration of this royal will, considered as to the sense and substance thereof, which is not visible, but intelligible unto his subjects, and in itself nothing else but an express image and manifestation of what the will had first in itself conceived, approved of, and disposed itself unto; nay even strictly such a manifestation as hath neither more nor less in it than that very same, is a fit representation of the Eternal Son; which hath an eternal beginning in the will, as in the Father, of which he is an express image and manifestation, having all that which the Father hath, snd neither more nor less.

The actual putting out of this declaration, which is an active moving, and proceeding forth of this royal will unto its manifestation, and is distinct both from the will itself, and from the declaration of the will also; and yet inseparable from the one so well as from the other, because it is participating with both, and combining them both, represents to us the Spirit, which is an active moving life of the Deity, and a band of union between the Father and the Son.

The declaration of this royal will, considered as it is visible also, and more external; or as a thing which passively can be said, that it is gone out from the royal will, and which is a writing subscribed by the king's hand, and sealed with his seal, is a representation of the eternal wisdom, taken in the second, more external sense, wherein it is compared to a looking-glass, and is not God himself, but distinct from and under him; as this writing is also distinct from, and under the king, and distinct also from his will, and from the declaration thereof, considered as to its invisible sense and substance.

Like as this writing is purely passive, having no life, motion, power, or operation, or efficacy, and doing neither good nor evil of itself, or from its own ability: So is wisdom in this latter sense also.

But like as the king's will, power, and royal authority, declared in the going out thereof, or in the putting forth this declaration, is the only life, activity and power therein, for which it is honoured, esteemed, and justly styled royal, and by which it is able and sufficient to do good unto the kingdom; seeing that the king's will and royal authority doth own it, as its own product; is joined therewith, doth operate therein, and doth in a manner quicken it, and keep it alive, by maintaining it, and executing the ordinances contained therein, etc. So also is and doth the Spirit of God in and with this wisdom, which here most properly in this distinction from the Spirit, is compared to a looking glass, full of wonders.

Besides this distinction between going out, and that which is gone out, or between the Spirit which is God, and wisdom which is under God, there is yet another distinction to be taken notice of, between this Wisdom and wisdom itself, or rather (which is more proper according to Behmen's expressions, who giveth the name of wisdom only to what is in the holy Light World) between this looking-glass, and Looking-glass.

For as the Spirit itself cometh now in a two-fold consideration, according to the Two Eternal Principles, and in answerableness to that distinction, which is now intelligible between the Father and the Son; so doth this looking-glass also. And as the Spirit is in each of these two eternal worlds, according to the property of each; so is this Looking-glass also, in each according to its condition, representing only that, which to that part of eternal nature doth belong, and having no ability to admit of anything that is of, or appertained to the other part.

For in the very nature of a Principle, if taken in Behmen's sense, this is most necessarily, and absolutely implied. That it hath its own dominion, in, and by, and for itself, according to its own natural constitution, and that it cannot be concerned with any thing that is without its own sphere.

And hereby that great objection, cast in against Teutonicus, when he had written, *God knew not beforehand the fall of Lucifer*, is answered sufficiently: as may be seen from his own words in the *Aurora*, and in his *Apology against Balthasar Tilken*.

Selection Four.

"General Positions on Divine Being in Unity and Trinity". "Serial Elucidations G, part 2

The Fourth Extract, selected for insertion on the present occasion, consists of "GENERAL POSITIONS CONCERNING the DIVINE BEING in UNITY and TRINITY, and ESPECIALLY the GENERATION of ETERNAL NATURE, gathered from our FORMER WRITINGS, according to the MIND of TEUTONICUS; and all taken either IMMEDIATELY FROM his own plain UNQUESTIONABLE WORDS, or by means of an EVIDENT CONSEQUENCE flowing forth freely OUT OF THEM," thus:—

The first and deepest concept, the human mind can have of the Divine Being, according to the Scripture, is justly said to be that of Unity: because in our going back from the multiplicity of things, inquiring after their originals, we must needs stop and rest in the unity, without proceeding any further.

This concept of the unity doth not import, that, at any imaginable moment of eternity, the Unity hath been so alone by itself, without or before the Trinity; but only that our weak and finite understanding cannot but apprehend it so, and speak thereof so separately. For if the generation of the eternal Word, was and is from all eternity, without beginning (which Behmen expressly asserts with the Scripture), the unity never was without or before the trinity, yet must be conceived of as before, for natural reasons.

This Unity, belonging not unto the number and order of divided, outflown, and multiplied things, but being infinitely deeper than all things, and all our possible ideas thereof, and having as yet no manner of relation unto them, is to be conceived of, much rather so, as we conceive of that negative original, preceding all the numbers, and expressed in arithmetic by an O. than so as we do of the first positive number 1. And therefore chiefly is it that Behmen useth to call this unity, an eternal nothing. *Predestination.* i. *Theosoph Quest.* i.

In the concept of this unity, still considered as to itself alone, is necessarily implied, that it is without and before all manifestation, still, unmoveable, quiet, silent, hid and dwelling in itself; and therefore well enough expressed by *still eternity*, and by Behmen's *temperature* (the first), *abyss*, and *eternal liberty*; which latter expression denotes with him a freedom from, and a priority to all the properties of Nature. For all what in our concept implieth anything of moving, speaking, breathing, etc. implieth a receding from the true concept of this unity, and representeth more or less implicitly, instead thereof, a trinity.

All this again doth not import that at any imaginary moment of eternity, there hath been such a state of rest and silence, which by Behmen is expressly contradicted:

But only, that our understanding, in its gradual process backwards, and inquiry after the deepest original of things, cannot but apprehend it so. For, if by nature we understand with Behmen in general, a moving stirring life, and ask thereupon what is without or before it? we must needs answer, a rest and stillness; or else we would say, there is a moving and stirring, without and before motion or mobility.

All what was said hitherto, was in consideration of the Unity, as only and strictly in and to itself. But now of this same Unity, Abyss, Nothing, or eternal Liberty, considered as with some respect, or as in order to eternal nature, Behmen saith it *hath a Will*, and is a *Will*, both which is right, and neither this nor that is inconsistent with the other (*Deus est quod habet*), if we but look upon that former as more accommodate to our manner of apprehension and speech, and upon this latter, to the internal reality of the thing itself, this wherein there is no distinction.

Considering this, we may find Behmen reconciled sufficiently with himself, when he says in one place, *God dwelleth in himself*, and in another, *he dwelleth in an abyss*, and in a third, *the abyssal nothing is a dwelling-place of the divine Unity*, because here, before and without nature, there is no difference between the abyss and the will, or the dwelling-place and its inhabitant.

This abyssal Will is here not yet considered as in its act, or as a perceptible will, but as in its root. For else Behmen could not call it abyssal, and could not have said, That in this will, *nature lieth as a hidden fire, which is and is not*. Seeing that in the will, considered as in its set nature doth no more lie as a hidden fire, but rather as a fire now manifesting out of the abyss, by the generation of gradual properties.

This abyssal Will is now further considered by Behmen as Father, both of the eternal Word, in the eternal generation within, and of eternal Nature also, in the co-eternal manifestation without.

To the question lately proposed, How can one and the same will move or go forth at one instant both towards within and towards without? The answer is, according to Behmen's ground, plain and easy, viz. this: a will in *actu* cannot do so, because there is already a certain determination implied in the notion thereof, by which determination it is either to go in, and then it cannot go out, etc. But this will, still here considered as abyssal, can do so, because there is not yet in the notion thereof, a distinct determination implied, neither to this side nor that. And if a root, in its gross manner and way can spread forth itself, at once, and by one motion, both to the right hand and to the left, why not much more eminently so, this most universal root of all divided things?

The so called, by Behmen, eternal generation and co-eternal manifestation, are as it were two collateral branches, out of one and the same root. Though therefore we cannot say, the same *actual will* that goeth out, goeth also in, which Behmen never said, yet we can say with him, *the same abyssal will* goeth both out and in at once, and displayeth itself in these two branches, of which it is the common root, having not yet in it any distinction, as long as abyssal; nor can we conceive in it any determination to this or that, according to Behmen's plain words, saying, *It is without all properties, and hath no inclination to this or that, for it hath nothing before, behind, nor besides itself, which it could be inclined to.* The two places of Behmen quoted above, will justify this answer in almost all their expressions, convincing us, that if we conceive of any inclination or determination in this abyssal will, we do no more conceive an unity, but a duplicity: no more a temperature, but a distinction and inequality; no more an unsearchable nothing, but two conceivable somethings, the one inclining and the other inclined to; no more an eternal liberty, but a being tied to this, in opposition to that; no more an abyss, where this no searching, finding, etc., but a byss, having found already something, which it tendeth to, and uniteth with in its will.

Now further: out of this abyssal Will, by its moving and flowing out, Behmen says, All cometh forth whatsoever there is, both in the internal generation in trinity, and in the co-eternal manifestation in nature.

As to that former there is no objection made, for therein is generated according to the Scripture, God out of God. But concerning this latter, there is first brought in a question, and then from this a great objection.

It is asked, Is eternal Nature out of the abyssal will, so that this abyssal will, is the (*quasi*) material cause thereof? Or is it only brought forth out of nothing, by an *omnipotent power* of this will, *commanding* that it should be so?

The answer must be, according to Behmen, *affirmative* for that former, and *negative* to this latter. Though there must needs be observed, that according to Behmen's ground, and the whole construction of his writings, that the concept of a *material cause*, however refined by the addition of a *quasi*, is here in this matter much more impertinent, than ever an ell can be to measure the height etc. of the wind.

He expressly calleth this Abyssal Will a *father of* nature; not a *former*, nor *maker*, nor also *creator*, but a father, in which name, his having generated, or brought it forth out of himself, is absolutely implied. But,

The reasons for which an *out of* nothing is all inconsistent with Behmen's ground, and an *out of himself* is expressly asserted, may be these following:

(1.) The Abyssal Will, as it is here considered in this beginning of the gradual generation of nature, hath no power, to command that anything should come forth out of nothing. And though there is all power therein concentrated, yet there is not any ability for to exert any power; but this first out-flowing into desire, and further into the other properties of nature, is made for this selfsame end, that the powers might be exerted and displayed and brought forth into activity, Which is not done before the generation of the fire. And though there is in the Divine Being, neither a *before*, nor *after*, yet it might be so in our distinct apprehension. In the *fire* therefore, not before it, Behmen placeth properly the Divine omnipotence. If we place such an omnipotent commanding power in the first Abyssal Will, we understand him not, and run all into confusion.

(2.) The first step of the Abyssal Will, out of its abyss into nature, is a *desire*. Nothing can be nearer to the will, than its own raising itself, for to take in that which it willeth. And this raising, or as Behmen styles it, this sharpening itself, is, in this beginning part of nature, called by him desire. Who now can say, with any sense, that a desire is brought forth out of nothing, by the will's omnipotent command, and is thus joined to that will from without? Must we not say, That out of the still and resting will, the stirring desire floweth out? That is, a desire of that will, which intendeth to manifest itself thereby. And the will itself bringeth forth itself into desire. For truly the will conceiveth a desire in itself, in one respect, and sendeth it forth out of itself in another, as an exterior offspring.

(3.) This generation (in its full perfection) is the *Divine nature*, even that which we shall be made partakers of again in our regeneration, according to Scripture. It is the manifestation of God in his powers and wonders, And what shall hinder us to say, in one particular sense, It is God himself, (though we say rightly again in another, it is not God, but his manifestation, instrument, etc., of which seeming contradiction hereafter,) seeing that the Scripture expressly saith, *our God is a consuming fire*.

Now then the Divine nature, or that which the Scripture calleth *our God*, is not brought forth out of nothing, by a commanding omnipotent power of another God, that liveth before and without nature.

(4.) This generation of eternal nature is not to be conceived as arbitrary, but as necessary, therefore it cannot be out of such a nothing as is without, or different from the first Abyssal Will; but out of that Nothing, which is not only nothing in one respect, but also an universal All in another; and which will not bear that former name and being only, but must necessarily manifest and display itself in multiplicity and variety, for to shew forth its own abyssal Allness.

(5.) Of created and visible things the Scripture no where saith, that they were brought forth out of nothing, but that the *invisible things of God were made visible*. If we then with the Scripture, are to call them his invisible things, we are not to conceive of them as of nothing, though they were nothing to themselves before they came to be visible. And if this be right and true as to the lower things of this world; how much the more, and in what a higher degree of truth and regularity, must it be right and true also, concerning these invisible things themselves, viz. the properties of eternal nature?

Which therefore, when we conceive them with Behmen as having laid in the first Abyssal Will, like as a hidden fire, which was and was not, are not to be conceived of as nothing, nor as having laid in nothing, but must be called with him, his *imperceptible things*, and said to be made perceptible, in, and by this outflowing eternal generation.

(6.) Angels and men are the children and offspring of God (according to Scripture,) partakers of the Divine nature; bearing his name written upon them; having that life and light in them, which was in the eternal Word, which Word was in and with God, and was God; having a natural kind of omnipotence in them, for to faith nothing is impossible, etc.: and of man especially the Scripture saith, that he came to be a living soul, (not by God's saying, *fiat*, out of nothing, but) by his breathing (out of his own mouth) into him the breath of life; that we must be born again from above, and out of God; that his seed remaineth in us; that he is not only our creator, with respect to the body, but also *father*, with respect to soul and spirit; that Christ the only begotten Son, in whom the Father is well pleased, called us his *brethren*, etc:

Let now all these things and many more the like, be duly pondered, and then the conclusion must needs be this, That angels and men are generated out of God, and not brought forth out of a nothing, by God's commanding will. And if so, they must needs be so many *living witnesses*, that this eternal nature, with all its properties, is out of God also, considered here but as the first Abyssal Will; and this because they have in all their nothing else, but what is and was before them in eternal nature.

Hereupon two objections are now cast in: the one taken from the notion of a *material cause*, and the other from an apprehension of the darkness its being in God, which is said to be directly contrary to the Scripture.

The first objection is this, If eternal nature is not produced out of nothing, by the abyssal Will, commanding that it should be so, but is brought forth out of that will itself, then it must be either God or a part of God: because this out of imports a (quasi) material cause, and makes God to be not only an effective, but also a constitutive principle of nature; and so God and nature are confounded, which is all intolerable.

To this first objection distinctly, it may be answered: (1.) Such an objection was not made to Behmen himself, but yet what he would have said, if occasion had been given him, may be apparent enough, even from that simile he made use of in this matter.

He bids us to consider our mind and thoughts, because we bear in us, and are ourselves the nearest representation of the Divine Being, that may be had. By our mind he understandeth not a formed, determinate, or particular thing, which could be described to be so, or so: or distinguished by this or that from other things of the same kind, but an universal, unformed, still, silent, unmanifest, free and undeterminated ground; or as he expresseth it sometimes, an invisible, or imperceptible *well-spring*, in itself neither good nor evil, neither light nor darkness, neither joy nor sorrow, but antecedent to all these distinctions, and a mere nothing with respect to all our sensations or perceptibility; until it be made sensible and perceptible in and by our thoughts and senses, which out of it arise and multiply themselves *in infinitum*.

The mind he compareth to the eternal nothing, the first temperature, the abyssal stillness,etc. for as this, so also that, is in itself unmoveable, imperceptible, and without properties: and the thoughts he compareth to the perpetually generating properties of nature; for as the former are a stirring life of the mind, so also these latter, of the abyssal still eternity.

Now if we consider how the contents of this simile do agree, or disagree, with the notion of a material cause, we shall easily find what Behmen would have said thereof.

Three only particulars can make enough for this present purpose:

(*a.*) Nothing can be called a material cause, nor be looked upon as running, in a higher sense, parallel therewith, but that which hath in, by, and for itself (before or considered as abstracted from its effect) its own peculiar and particular essences; and them so really as ever afterwards, that material, or *quasi* material effect hath, which is made up thereby.

(*b.*) Those essences, at least in part, if not wholly, must be communicated, or translated from the cause to its effect.

(*c.*) This translation or communication doth import of all necessity, that the material, or *quasi* material cause must always lose, or be deprived of just so much of its matter or essences, as it hath communicated to its material or *quasi* material product.

Now none of these three requisites can here be applicable to this present simile, and much less to that eternal generation of nature, which is thereby as in a shadow represented. And therefore Behmen would certainly have rejected this notion of a *quasi* material cause as altogether impertinent, and no more fit to conceive thereby anything of this matter in reality, than an earthen vessel is, to contain such or such a quantity of human thoughts. For he expressly declareth, that like as

(*a.*) Our mind hath not its own *peculiar and particular* essences, in and by itself, before or considered as abstracted from its thoughts, so also the first abyssal Will hath none, and is therefore by Behmen called an *unessential will.* As our thoughts themselves are the essences of the mind, which is but an universal root or ground of them, so also the properties of eternal Nature themselves are the essences of their universal root, which is the first abyssal Will.

As our mind cannot be distinguished from its essences, except only thereby, that it is in itself a whole, unchangeable and unmoveable being, prior and superior to its essences, but in itself without distinction and perceptibility; seeing that our thoughts are but so many particulars, distinct from the mind and from themselves, because generating themselves in a perpetual motion and alteration, and making thereby the mind perceptible of itself: so also is it declared by Behmen concerning the first abyssal will, and the eternal properties of nature, perpetually generating themselves.

(*b.*) If then our mind, as in and to itself, without its thoughts, is unessential, no essences thereof, neither wholly, nor in part, can be communicated from this imagined *quasi* material cause to its product or effect.

And as our mind is never broken to pieces, nor divided into parts, by sending forth out of itself so many thoughts: and what is more, as our mind itself, is never changed or transmuted into the thoughts, so as to cease to be what it was, and to be no more an universal fruitful root or ground thereof: so also all this is rightly applied by Behmen to the first abyssal Will; and all this declareth again sufficiently, that as our mind, so also this abyssal un-essential will can have no manner of communion with what we call a material cause.

(*c.*) As our mind, communicating no essences to its thoughts, can lose nothing at all of its being, nor be deprived of anything, by their arising and coming forth out of it, But rather on the contrary, as it (in a sense and manner) winneth and getteth thereby; seeing that it cometh thereby into manifestation and perception of itself, and that it sheweth forth thereby, for its own delight, the endless fullness of its own hidden treasury: so also this third particular is largely declared in many places, and elegantly applied by Behmen to the first abyssal will. And this then sheweth again, (first) that the notion of a material cause, though never so much refined by a *quasi*, and though never so useful in the lower region of natural things in this our Third Principle, is here, in this consideration of this beginning of eternal nature, altogether impertinent. And (secondly) that nevertheless as it is rightly said, Our thoughts arise, and come forth out of our mind, have no other thing for their original, and are not formed out of nothing by a commanding power of the mind: so also is it rightly said, The properties of eternal nature arise out of the abyssal will, have no other original but this will, and are not brought forth out of nothing, or barely effected by the will, commanding that it should be so.

Hereupon is now replied, If our understanding of this matter is to be thus directed by this simile, we shall at length lose all the distinction between God and nature; for it is generally agreed upon, that our thoughts are nothing else, but the mind itself, variously modified.

If we then shall say accordingly, That eternal nature is in like manner God himself, will not this be to take away all distinction?

Answer. This exception against Behmen's simile is of no consideration; because the contents thereof make in reality very much for his sense, but nothing at all against it: But this will evidence itself, by what now further is to be answered to that former great objection, viz.,

(2.) There was said above, What shall hinder us to say in one respect and sense, eternal nature is God himself, seeing that this saying is supported by these plain expressions of the Scripture, *our God is a consuming fire*; and again, *God is light*? Though we may say rightly also in another sense, Eternal nature is not God himself, but only his manifestation, or his instrument.

Both this and that is said by Behmen in plain words. Affirmatively he saith, *Aurora,* Chapter xi, *This light is the true Son of God, whom we Christians honour and adore, as the second person in the holy Trinity,* etc. And negatively he says again, in plain words, of the three first properties of eternal nature, That they have their ground in the Trinity, but are not to be understood, as that they are God, hut only his manifestation. And so of eternal Nature in general, That it is to be distinguished from God, and is his instrument, or an instrument of the still eternity.

Now from the whole system of all his writings about this matter, it appears sufficiently, that he hath not thereby contradicted himself in sense, though the words run directly contrary to each other. For like as we can rightly say, in one respect of his usual simile, Our thoughts are the mind itself, because without our thoughts, we cannot be sensible of the mind; all our sensation is confined, and all our perception of the mind restrained to our thoughts; and without or abstracted from our thoughts, the mind is as it were quite nothing, etc. And as we can nevertheless rightly say also, according to Behmen's declaration, Our thoughts are not the mind itself, because the mind is their ground and root, which if it were not, the thoughts could not arise, nor change, nor multiply; the thoughts are particular things, posterior and inferior to the mind; and the mind is a whole universe, prior, and superior to the thoughts.

The thoughts are a moving stirring life, when the mind, abstracted from the thoughts, is still unmoveable rest: in the spirit of our mind (not our thoughts) the Scripture saith, we shall be renewed; and though even as to the thoughts also, we shall certainly be renewed, yet the Scripture, speaking in this place of the mind, and requiring in other parallel places, the very bottom, or the inmost ground of the heart, sheweth sufficiently that the thoughts are not the deepest ground in the sight of God, and therefore (in so good a sense as ever that other can be,) not the mind itself.

Though the thoughts are the deepest in our sight, or perceptibility, and make us therefore to say tolerably, they are the mind itself, because we can have no apprehension, nor sensation of what the mind is without our thoughts.

So also now all this is rightly applied by Behmen to God and nature; and this simile can safely direct our understanding of this matter, so that nothing of a due distinction between God and nature is lost thereby, and no contradiction in sense is found. For we can rightly say with Behmen in one sense and respect, Eternal nature is God himself, because it is *that which of the Divine Being is communicable* to the creature, (according to Scripture,) both with respect to our understanding, and to all our constituent essences. It is that deepest, inmost ground (expressly called God in the Scripture) wherein we live and have our being; which ground we are confined to, and deeper than which we cannot reach, but must needs say in Behmen's sense, that which is beyond it, is an eternal Nothing. It is *that which we are commanded to worship, as our only God in Trinity*; seeing that the Scripture tells us of no other Father, but him that calls himself a consuming fire; of no other Son, but him, that is this Father's light and brightness; and of no other Holy Spirit, but him that proceedeth from this fire and light. And lastly, it is that, wherein our highest good, eternal happiness and glory, and our ultimate end consists, or that wherein we are to rest and acquiesce for ever. Rightly therefore is it called and owned to be God, *our* God, But all this notwithstanding, we can rightly say also with Behmen, in another sense and respect, Eternal nature is not God himself, because it is not that most supreme, all-abyssal, all-unsearchable, and altogether incommunicable being, which generates himself in himself in Trinity. It is not that (in every imaginable sense) beginningless, and endless Unity, which, before and without its outflowing can be conceived of, if not properly as a centre, yet as an indivisible point; but it is rather to be likened to a circumference, which in some sense hath a beginning and an end:

It is not altogether that groundless ground, which hath nothing before it, out of which it could come forth, which it could depend or rest upon, and which is itself the ground of all what is posterior; but it dependeth upon this ground, is out of this ground what it is, and if this groundless ground were not, this eternal nature also could not be. What distinction now between God and Nature can we desire more; and where is the confusion, pretended to be brought in by Behmen's simile? But with him, and according to Behmen's sense, we say now further:

Of that first, all-abyssal, all-incommunicable, beginningless, endless, groundless, Triune Being (which because it is in itself only what it is, must needs be hid and unmanifest), this eternal Nature, in the perpetual generation of its seven chief properties, all intelligible and communicable more or less, is a perpetual *manifestation*. And this is called also by Behmen significantly, with another peculiar respect, A sounding harmonious instrument, which the Spirit of eternity playeth upon; and with another again, A tool wherewith he worketh, etc.

But here is now replied again, Generation and manifestation are two expressions, not well consistent with each other, in one and the same thing. If eternal nature is a generation, how can it be a manifestation? And if it be a manifestation, what sense can there be in calling it a generation?

Answer. Eternal nature is a *manifestation* with respect to what is before and without it, for this is made manifest thereby; and a *generation* it is chiefly with respect to itself, for it is not only generated once, as we might conceive of it, but is also generating perpetually, that is, standing perpetually in the same incessant, unalterable generation of its properties. When it is considered as in the first abyssal Will, wherein Behmen says, It laid as a hidden fire, which is and is not, it is unmanifest; but when it is considered as coming forth, in the three first properties, out of that hidden ground, this same coming forth is its *generation*, significantly called so, because it cometh not forth from besides that will, but out of it, which in common speech cannot be otherwise expressed, but by saying, that it is generated, or born out of that womb, wherein it laid. And this same generation is a *manifestation* also, no less significantly called so, (1.) with respect to itself, because that which was a hidden fire, which was and was not, is now a manifest and freely-burning fire, of which it cannot be said, It is, and is not, but only, It is. And (2.) with respect also to the first abyssal Will, which was not manifest, but also could not be manifest without this generation, but is now manifested by the same, because it hath not only showed forth thereby its own hidden central all-sufficiency for such a generation; but is also now itself this manifested free-burning fire, which it was not, and could not have been, without this generation of the three first properties of nature. But this I have reason to hope will be more cleared by what I have still further to answer to that former great objection. For

III. [Here the matter was interrupted, nay broken off with violence.]

Selection Five.

"Two Questions Answered", Serial Elucidations G, part 7

The Fifth of these progressive Extracts, consists of the following LETTER to a Clergyman, in which are "TWO QUESTIONS ANSWERED:—

Revd. Sir,—Your first Question is, Whether Jacob Behmen asserts, that there was a motion of the central fire with its own self desire, whereby the will of God was stirred in both fires, and the anger-fire broke forth, *before the fall of angels?* This now I cannot but answer unto directly, saying, God forbid! No such thing may be found, neither said, nor implied in any place of his writings. But the contrary may be demonstratively shown not only from a great many of his plain expressions, free from all ambiguity, but also from the whole order and connexion of God's eternal manifestation, made first as to himself through eternal nature, and further as to creatures through their creation. And especially in his fourth theosophical question, wherein you say, that he seems to assert it so, he saith no such thing at all. How it may be translated into English, I know not, but if your expressions are taken from that translation, it is directly contrary to the high Dutch original. For,

(1.) The author saith not, that the *central fire moved with its own self desire*. But so he saith, When the central fire of the own will (that fire which is, if divorced from the light, the matrix or mother of own will) moved, and when it introduced itself into a *greater desire*, for its contemplation and formation, then the creation was done. Which greater desire is so plain as the day at noon, that it was not that evil, accursed, own self-desire, or selfishness, which he saith, v. 4, was cast out from the working of God, and was shut up into darkness; but it was a good, needful, regulated, and blessed desire, not cast out from the working of God, but made use of in his work; and not shut up in darkness, but brought forth to the light. For when the central fire moved, and introduced itself into this greater desire, the eternal ideas came to be figured or formed creatures, to the praise of the wonders of God.

(2) He saith not, that by this motion of the central fire, the eternal will of God *was stirred* (passive) in both fires. But he saith the pure contrary, viz. that the eternal will of God *stirred* (active) the central fire, (that one only substance or being, v. 2.) and that he stirred it in or as to both fires: into which this One Being is distinguished in the Two eternal Principles.

If he had said that former, he would on one side have dethronized the eternal will of God, raising up above him, a motion of eternal nature; and especially of the inferior fiery part thereof. And on the other, he would have showed himself a kind advocate to the apostatized angels, instructing them how to plead their cause against the Creator. But since he saith the latter, he is clear and free both from this and that.

(3.) He speaketh distinctly of two, nay I may say, (knowing what and how, though I cannot presume to make it intelligible enough) of three much different things, which you seem, Sir, to take out for one and the same, or at least to make but a little distinction between them; mentioning indeed both the central and anger-fire, but considering not how they are two, notwithstanding that they are also but one, and thinking, that in this single expression of anger-fire you have the whole matter perfectly implied. Whereas our author hath not such a single and general expression in this place, but speaketh very circumspectly and circumstantially, saying v. 4, In this motion (of the central fire) the hellish *foundation of God's anger* broke forth *also along with it.*

Whether it be so distinctly expressed in the English translation I cannot tell; but this I can, that none of these circumstances is to be neglected, if his sense shall not be wronged; for none is superfluous, they are altogether significant, and sufficient to demonstrate that he asserted no such thing, as in your question is expressed.

Of this two or threefold distinction then, we must have got an idea in our mind, if not from a deep internal ground, yet at least from having much conversed with his style, or manner of expression. If we have got that former, he cannot at all, and if this latter, not easily, be misapprehended. The central-fire and anger-fire are in one remoter sense, but one indeed; but in another nearer, they are also really two.

Like as on one side the central-fire is but one substance with the light-fire, v. 2, when there is yet also a great distinction between these two: so on the other, the central-fire is also one with the anger-fire, and yet there is a far greater distance between these latter, than between the former two. For the former two can and do actually consist together, both in God and in creatures, but the latter two can by no means consist together, neither in God, nor in creatures.

In God there is a central-fire, but not an anger-fire, neither before nor after the fall of angels; and in creatures if there be an anger-fire, there is no central-fire, for by falling into that, they are immediately banished out of this; and that which before was a central-fire in them, is now become an anger-fire, not in God, but in themselves.

The central-fire is properly the First Principle, the great strong city of God the Father, the residence of his living power and almightyness. And this was never and can never be an anger-fire, if we will not think, that the eternal Father is angry with his only begotten Son.

Nay we cannot say, that it is an anger-fire in him, even now, after the fall of angels and men. For God is not angry with the devil, he is still the same from eternity to eternity, and changeth not; but the devil is angry with God, and so the anger-fire is only the devil's residence, for he hath changed the central fire into an anger fire, not in God, but in himself.

If they both were angry with each other, they lived both within the same residence, which without blasphemy cannot be asserted.

And so far I think it is intelligible enough, but there is still yet another and more subtle distinction to be made, reaching much deeper, and not easily without experience to be really apprehended.

And this lieth therein, that our author saith not in your single expression, The anger fire broke forth, but the *hellish foundation of God's anger*, which he calleth also especially Satan, or the dragon, whereof there may be seen what he saith, Question xiii. 10, 11, compared to xi. 3–6. For if this be understood, it will show forth itself in the clearest evidence, that he doth not assert what your question, Sir, expresseth. But fearing justly that I might not be able to explain myself intelligibly enough, as to this particular, and seeing that it can by other means be evidenced sufficiently, I shall lay this aside; being moreover well enough sensible thereof, that nothing can suffice you for evidence, except this particular expression, of *breaking forth* be cleared up, so that you may acquiesce with what he understandeth, by saying, The hellish foundation of God's anger *broke also forth along with the motion of the central fire*, and this in the creation of angels, certainly before their fall.

For here, I think, lieth the only knot, which gave occasion to this Question, and which the English translation of this third and fourth verse (which I have now seen) gave you just occasion for, seeing that it is very wrong, and must mislead the reader.

Wherefore I am the more concerned in my mind, how to lay open most plainly our author's sense in this serious matter, which is truly of great importance, and of many considerable consequences.

And I think I cannot do it better, than by considering first the whole order and connection of all what here is said in this fourth Theosophical Question. For so there will appear manifestly not only that his sense is good, conformable to all his writings, simple and child-like; but also, that it is well and significantly expressed, and even so, that it doth not justify nor excuse the fallen angels, but only exalt the glory of their Creator.

The whole order and connexion is this: before the creation of angels, there was only God, with the two central fires, an eternal generation of wonders, etc. as he declareth *v.* 1. Now it is asked,

Which was the first original or principal cause of the creation of angels, or that which made the first beginning in order thereunto? To say it was a motion of eternal Nature, or of one part thereof, as the fire is, and this with its own self-desire too, by which motion the will of God was stirred, caused, or perhaps necessitated to the creation, would be the greatest nonsense of the world.

But it was the eternal Will himself, desiring those eternal ideas should be substantial living creatures, formed for his praise and glory. And this, but not that former can be shown conformable to all our author's writings. But further.

Could the eternal ideas come to be substantial created beings, without an actual moving of that whereout they were to consist, or which there was to make up their being? To say they could, would be a great nonsense again. Truly that whereout they should come forth, which was eternal Nature, must both have been moved, and must have moved itself also, in a different respect. But that being moved must have been prior; and this moving itself posterior, as an effect of that former. For we know that eternal nature was itself, in its own essentiality, a perpetual moving without rest, or an eternal never-ceasing generation. But if this eternal moving (without being moved particularly by the only supremest power) could have been sufficient to bring forth the creation of angels, the angels altogether must have equally co-eternal with eternal nature, and could not own any other superior creator. It was then the eternal Will of God himself, who first moved and stirred this eternal nature, which there was to make up their created being; and then only, not before, but after it was thus moved and stirred, it was able to move itself, also further effectually to the creation.

No creation then was, nor could have been, until first the eternal will had actually stirred eternal nature.

In eternal Nature now, there were before the creation of angels, the two central fires, the anger fire and love fire; now so called (N.B.) *a posteriori*, after they both are manifested by the fall in a divorce from each other;

but as then they could not have been called so, but their only name was, fire and light in a most harmonious union, one only substance, *v*. 2. If then eternal nature was that which must have been moved or stirred by the eternal will, it must have been moved in, or as to both fires; not as to an anger and love fire (because not so before the fall), but as to fire and light.

For these two, and not only this or that thereof alone, but both together jointly and in union with each other, were to break forth. Which is properly and emphatically expressed so, for it was most really a *breaking forth*, out of, or through their own sphere, wherein they were before without living substantial creatures, into an *exterior manifestation*, or into innumerable self-subsisting beings, all bearing that one eternal fire and light within themselves, and all being nothing else but glorious fire-flames illuminated by the light, as so many little particular representatives of their Father and Creator, that great universal All in All, both in fire and light.

No living creature can there be generated in this Third Principle, except it have the fire of temporal nature, united to the light thereof in the generation of its life; and these two cannot be separated from each other, except this creature die.

So also out of eternal nature no living creature could have been brought forth, except it had its eternal fire and light, united to each other in its generation or creation; which it also must keep in that union, if it will live, and fall not into eternal death. And as these two, after they are broken forth in union into the creature, cannot be separated from each other, without its destruction: so they could also not have been separated from each other, before or in their breaking forth; for the life is in the fire, and without the fire the light is dead. And again, out of the fire only without the light, no glorious holy angels could have been brought forth, (we might say, devils could, if there had been such a creator, as could have delighted to create devils, which God forbid we should so much as think;) for holiness and glory is in the light, and without the light, the fire is but dark, obscure, and unholy, profane and strange to the most Holy and Almighty, whose dwelling-place is fire and light in union, but neither this nor that alone. But further,

When now thus eternal nature was moved and stirred as to both fires by the eternal will, what was the consequence or effect thereof? We see there were several and different effects, all linked together, and so succeeding each other (at least as to our manner of apprehension) that always the following depended upon its next preceding.

The first was, That eternal Nature moved itself also, and why should it not move to the creation, when it was moved thereto by the only superior eternal Will?

It is certainly nothing else but an instrument in his hand, and must nevertheless not be conceived as a dead, senseless, unmoveable instrument, like as an axe or hammer is in the hand of a carpenter, for it was itself in its own essentiality an eternal moving generation: wherefore it must be conceived as a living, faithful and obedient servant, who hath the principle of life and motion in his own members indeed, but is nevertheless only an instrument of his master, moving not to this or that design, except he be first moved and stirred himself thereto, by his command, as having also not ability enough to perform it, without being commissionated and empowered thereto by his authority.

This moving now in eternal nature was in, or as to both fires, for as to both it was also moved, for both were in union and both were one, like as Father and Son are one.

But as the fire is naturally prior, because of its being the root of the light, and the light posterior, because of its coming from the fire; so the first or chiefest, or beginning-motion is also ascribed to the fire, and not to the light. Before, the author had spoken of two central fires, and had said they were but one, but now he must also speak distinctly, of that central fire in particular, wherein there lieth the principal efficacy, or the foundation power of formation or generation. And this being in the fire, and not in the light, he saith Justly, that the *central fire of the own will moved*, Showing thereby, that the beginning of moving to the creation in eternal nature, was and must have been made in the fire and not in the light.

And this fire, he saith not, moved with its own self desire, nor saith he that it moved in its own will, for it was declared sufficiently that it moved not, until it was moved and so commanded to move by the eternal Will; but he saith plainly, that it moved and introduced itself into a greater desire, which sheweth quite another sense than the English translation expresseth. But why he calleth it the central fire of the *own will*, several good reasons might be given, but this is the chiefest, viz. that he now must have distinguished the two central fires, if he should have declared distinctly what he intended. If he then must have distinguished the first central fire from the second, he could not have done it better than by a denomination taken from its own proper, essential, and inseparable character, not common to both fires, but proper in particular to that first alone.

But seeing that there was not yet such a character manifested, neither before nor in the creation, both fires standing then as one only Being, in the most harmonious union, he must have taken a convenient distinguishing denomination *a posteriori*, from after the fall of angels. And there he found the proper character of this first central fire was *own will*, immediately after or in the fall of angels. Which character is absolutely proper to the fire, but incommunicable to the light.

For in the fire, and not in the light, the *own will* ariseth, and liveth, whenever and as soon as a divorce is made between them. In the fire, and not in the light, is that eternal substantial life, which cannot die nor cease, being an indissolvable circling band of the four first properties of nature, generating themselves always mutually, and therefore also perpetually, if but once knit together by the kindling of the fire. When contrariwise, that life which is in the light can die, or cease and pass away, as it died also actually in the fall of angels, when own will arose in the fire, wherein it liveth also still as in its proper residence. And so that first central fire is justly called the fire of own will; though I grant freely that *all* is not yet said hereby, but it is called so, with another and deeper respect also. Which if I should bring forth, I could neither do it in few words, nor perhaps so as to be enough understood. Seeing then (1.) that this which is now said is not contrary unto that, (2.) that it is a great deal plainer, and (3.) exactly conformable to all our author's writings, I shall pass it by, and proceed.

The next consequence depending upon the first, and almost coincident therewith, is this, That when the central fire moved, it introduced itself into a greater desire. As the moving before was ascribed peculiarly to the fire, and not to the light, because of its priority, and of its having the principal power of formation or generation in itself above the light; so this greater desire is ascribed also peculiarly to the fire, and not to the light, though neither here nor there the light may be excluded. As eternal Nature in its own intrinsical essentiality, from eternity was a moving generation as to both fires, so it was a desire also from eternity as to both fires.

How *will* and *desire* in a true and real sense, may and must be attributed to all its seven fountain properties, nay, to all its lesser subordinated innumerable powers also, shall be said in the consideration of the second question. Here we are only to say, That eternal nature in general was and had (for being and having cannot here be distinguished) a desire from eternity; and that this desire is not that, which is ascribed peculiarly to the first attracting form thereof, whose proper sphere of activity was only the perpetual generation and multiplication in infinite, of the forms and powers of eternal nature, within its own circumference.

But this desire here now spoken of, which became a greater desire, by its being stirred by the eternal will, was stretching forth as it were beyond that sphere, for its object was to break forth into an exterior manifestation, and to bring forth living, intellectual, substantial, and self-subsisting creatures, wherein it might display and show forth, the infinite variety of its powers and wonders. And though this desire was kept under both on the side of the eternal will, by his absolute sovereignty, until he was pleased to move; and on the side of eternal nature also, by its submission and faithful obedience to its Lord and Master; yet nevertheless there was in its own internal ground a desire, and continued such a desire, till it became a greater, more living and vigorous, nay, a more exerted and efficacious desire, by its being moved and stirred in both fires. For thereby it was now raised up as a spark of fire that before was covered with ashes; it was commisionated thereby, and mightily empowered to break forth as to both fires, according to its desire, into an exterior, substantial manifestation.

Wherefore then it cannot but be manifest, that this greater desire is not that own self-desire, which beareth the number and mark of selfishness, but so distant therefrom as the south is from the north, or the day from the night. For when that is an untimely, monstrous birth, and even from the womb a professed enemy to the eternal will of God, this is surrounded for its defence, both from before and after, by the eternal will itself. Seeing that, from before it hath the foregoing moving of the eternal will, of which moving it is the proper intended effect and offspring; and after it, it hath its own immediately following effect and offspring also, which tended again to the praise and honour of the eternal will. For,

The third consequence, depending upon the former two, and especially upon the second, is now this, That the eternal ideas became substantial creatures, to the glory of their Creator. Here then is now the actual breaking forth of the two central fires, out of eternal nature into an exterior manifestation, to be considered; and that which is further said, *v.* 4. to have *also broken forth along with them, viz. the hellish foundation of God's anger*, is here as to its breaking forth, to be considered also.

For they are inseparably joined together, as in reality itself, (when the great wheel of eternal nature in its whole universality is considered, comprising all whatever laid therein and came forth thereout,) so also in these expressions of our author, wherefore then they must be joined also in our consideration.

Before, there was spoken only of two things, which were called two central fires, but now there cometh also forth a third, which laid indeed always implicitly under the former two, as their root and ground, but came not then explicitly into consideration.

For it is one and the same thing, whether there be named two central fires, or darkness, fire, and light. Only this is the difference, that now that former double, and then this latter threefold expression is more accommodate to such or such a state of things, that may be differently considered. As now these three make up the whole eternal nature, and are three such essential parts thereof, as body, soul, and spirit are of man; so they must also all three have broken forth into the creation of angels, if they should have been really children of the Living God, generated out of eternal nature, after the likeness of their Father. But not all three in the same sense, degree, and manner, but each in such a sense as it is able to bear, and each according to its own order and degree, wherein it stood from eternity, with respect to the other two; either deeper into the bottomless centre, or higher exalted, in the conspicuous superficies.

As to the two central fires, it can now be plain enough, from what there was said thereof before, That their breaking forth was a most glorious, real and visible manifestation of fire and light, in a most intimate union, displayed in a numberless variety and multiplicity of illustrious shining fire-flames, which were so many living, intellectual, blessed, and holy-substantial creatures, all bearing the holy name of trinity and unity, both in and upon themselves, and all being the natural children of God, generated in eternal nature, after his own image and likeness, which is (in eternal nature) nothing else but fire and light.

But what shall we further say, as to the breaking forth of darkness, represented in such dreadful expressions, as the *hellish foundation of God's anger?* In what sense can this have broken forth also, and even along with fire and light? What communion between them can be so much as dreamed of?

Answer. Let there first be well taken notice of, and attentively remembered, that and how, darkness was from eternity, that it was not, and yet was; in what place or station it was, with respect to fire and light; in what condition it was considered as in and to itself, and chiefly that it was good, no less than fire and light in its own kind, and rank, and order. Let but all this be well considered and understood, it must of itself appear, what this breaking forth of the darkness was, and that there must indeed be given another definition thereof, than that of the former breaking forth, but that nevertheless, all what our author saith thereof, is properly, well, and significantly expressed; and especially that this expression of breaking forth is justly used as well with respect to darkness, as with respect to fire and light.

If we should see a ladder of three steps, and consider it as a semi-diameter of a circle, and as breaking forth into a circular motion, we could not but say, that this same and single breaking forth is common unto all the three steps, and so properly applicable unto the lowest as unto the highest, but not unto every one promiscuously in the same wise, seeing that each of them must keep to its own place and order. The highest toucheth the outmost circumference, and there it breaketh forth into motion, making the greatest and most considerable circle of all. The middle is lower, and lesser, its breaking forth into motion is in its own inferior degree, and its circle cannot be of the same extent. But the lowest must still keep the centre, and can make no perceptible circle at all, when it doth nevertheless in that centre break forth at the same instant, into motion also, no less than the superior two, none of which can break forth alone; as also the two superior cannot by themselves alone, without assistance and concurrence of this third and lowest, if the whole ladder shall not be spoiled and broken into pieces.

Let now these three ladder steps be darkness, fire, and light, and let this circle be that universal wheel of eternity, so considered as it ought to be, viz. that only circumference thereof, and that which reacheth the circumference, to be visible and manifest, but its centre, and that which lieth therein, or is annexed thereunto, to be altogether invisible, secret, and unknown. And then this rude simile may easily show forth of itself its true application, so far as it hath in it any shadow of resemblance, for much more is not to be expected. For it is not an improper resemblance, and may at least declare us so much, that as really as there were brought forth many legions of living, substantial creatures in eternal nature, by its breaking forth into an exterior manifestation; so really also, and in the same degree of reality, all these holy angels must have had in themselves the three essential parts of eternal nature, standing in every particular microcosm of density in the selfsame order, in which they stood in the macrocosm thereof, and in which order they were also all three harmoniously broken forth into motion, for to make up so many representatives of that greatest universal All in All.

And so therefore from this united and harmonised breaking forth, they must have had an eternal light, in the supremest, excellentest, most manifested circumferential place of their created being; where they had it also, and have it still (as many of them as there kept their habitation in the light), giving and being unto them, all their glory, beauty, delight, and happiness.

Further, they must have had also, an eternal fire in the middle place of their being, united to the light, and generating it, but standing lower and in an inferior degree of dignity; as they had and have it also, giving and being unto them, all their life, strength, power, and activity. Thirdly, they must have had also an eternal darkness in the lowest, most hidden, and central place of their being, united to the fire, and affording unto it its essences, but standing not with it in the same degree of nobility. And so they have it also, giving and being unto them the central foundation, and root of their fire and light, keeping these two in their order, and preserving them in their union and glory, as long as it is itself kept by them under, and affixed to the centre.

Like as the lowest ladder-step only by means of its being fixed to the centre, is the only cause of a regulated circular motion, which must become irregular and all disordered, as soon as this is turned aside from the centre, and will break forth to move in, or nearer to the superficies.

If then they had these three things in such an order, they had the darkness under their feet, according to what is said of their eternal Father himself, whose children they are, and whose likeness therefore they must bear, if they shall be his representatives. And if so, this darkness was not evil, not hell, and not anger or anger-fire, as long as under their feet; and nothing to this sense or purpose was ever said by Behmen.

He saith indeed here, The hellish foundation of God's anger broke forth, but how can there be spoken of these three things distinctly, in an earthly language, now after the fall, and by such creatures as do participate themselves of that lamentable fall, but by such distinct denominations as of necessity must be taken from what these things are now, unto creatures, in their disorder sad divorce? He saith not. The hell broke forth, not the anger-fire broke forth, for that would be saying, God was angry with his creatures, prepared hell for them, before he created them, and cast then thereinto in their creation. And from whence could hell and anger have broken forth into the creation, when there was neither this nor that in all the vast extent of eternity? If we believe there was nothing else before the creation, but God in fire and light, how or where, from whence or to what end could there have been hell and anger? Could that central fire of God the Almighty have been hell? And what could there have been angry with each other, seeing there was nothing else but himself alone in fire and light?

But this is the thing: there was in eternal Nature that, which after the fall, could have had nothing else but hell and anger-fire unto rebellious creatures. Not that it had been changed in itself; but because they manifested it in themselves in disorder.

And this broke forth in the creation; but in this breaking forth, it was but fire and light, or life and glory: and not hell and anger, no more than it is now unto those holy angels that kept their habitation in the light. And though it was darkness in and to itself, as to its own particular essentiality, yet it was not, and could also not have been manifested as darkness, seeing that it was kept under by fire and light, so that there could not appear what it was, and needs must be, when separated from fire and light. And therefore Behmen calleth it not positively hell, nor anger-fire itself, but only the hellish foundation of God's anger, or that which must of necessity have been hell itself, superstructured as it were, upon this dark foundation, as soon as it was raised up out of its bottomless pit.

And this, he saith, broke also forth along with fire and light: intimating significantly, that it broke not forth alone in its own strength and power, and so not in its own dark shape; that it broke not forth in disunion from fire and light, and so not with its own self-desire, which it was not permitted, as now shall follow.

And that it broke not forth in the first place, but in its lowest order and degree, or as it were after them as an appendix.

And this hellish foundation, he saith further, God hath cast out from his working, and hath shut it up into darkness. How could he have plainer expressed, that this hellish foundation broke not forth into such a manifestation as fire and light?

Truly, if God hath cast it out, it could not have crept or broken in, and if God hath shut it up into darkness, then certainly it came not to be manifested in the light. And so this breaking forth as to the darkness, must have quite another sense, which we shall find out by and by.

But it will be asked and said, What is here meant by this casting out and shutting up in darkness? If there was not an evil thing in eternal Nature, intending to break forth unto destruction, why must it have been thus resisted by God, and cast forth from his working? If it was good and useful, why was it not permitted to stand in its lot? And if evil and hurtful, from whence had it its original? Or how could it have been said, that all was good in eternal nature before the fall?

Answer. There was said before, that eternal Nature had and was a *desire*, to bring forth its wonders in a more exterior manifestation. If now this was so, it was not so in this or that particular part thereof, but in the *whole* in general, and in *each part* thereof in particular. So that it must have been in the fire as well as in the light, and in the darkness as well as in them both. And if so, even reason itself may tell us, that if each of these three desired to be made manifest, none of them could desire to be made so, according to the nature and condition of the other, but each only according to that which was its own. Each could but desire to bring forth its own wonders. As the light could not desire to be darkness, so could it also not, to bring forth the wonders of darkness, and so *vice versa*.

But as each is confined to its own particular essentiality, whereby it must be what is, so this desire of each must also be naturally confined to its own proper essentiality, as being a proper consequence thereof, annexed thereunto inseparably, and wholly depending thereupon. So that it be inclined only to bring forth that which it hath in itself, as sufficient only for that, and further for nothing more.

As also each of these three desireth still, and is not only naturally inclined, willing, and ready to manifest its own secret wonders, but doth it also effectually, each in its own region, being now enabled to do so, by the fall of angels and men: and this both in the Two Principles of eternal nature, and in this Third also, as in their bipartite temporal outbirth.

All this desiring now, (considered as in eternal nature before the fall and creation, and as purely abstracted from all relation and reference unto creatures,) is good, and must be so, if eternal nature shall be what it is to be.

No own will, no self-desire may be found therein; which only then might be said, when we could imagine that the light desired to be fire, and the darkness to be light, or the fire either this or that. Nothing is here inordinate, and so nothing also hurtful, or noxious, but all is profitable and useful, because all in its order, and so also serviceable to the whole manifestation of the eternal Will. Nothing is here to be restrained, cast out, shut up, or pressed down, but each must stand in its lot, and each must have its share in that eternal first seven-fold and further infinite generation, which there was before the creation of angels. And as each must be what it is, so each must also be for that which it hath, in its own peculiar ground and bottom.

But now, as soon as there is spoken of this desiring with any respect to creatures, or to their creation, there is immediately made a digression from that pure, abstracted sense; and this goodness faileth more or less, growing weaker and weaker, and declining always gradually so much from its primeval purity, as much as the creature is considered in conjunction therewith.

If all these things that are in eternal nature, always and in every respect good, both unto God, and unto each other, and unto themselves, could be good in and unto creatures also, always and in every respect, wherein were the creature lesser or inferior than God? what prerogative could the Creator have above the creature? what distinction could there be between order and disorder? and what could it signify, that God is called a God of order? To say, This God of order could according to his omnipotence, have manifested all these three things, according to their threefold desire, in that order wherein they stood from eternity, and so this goodness must have continued, is true indeed, in that sense which before was spoken of, and as I think sufficiently declared, but it is false in this, which we now are speaking of. For even therein consisted their eternal order, that the light only was manifested, shining into the darkness, and that the darkness was unmanifest, comprehending not the light, and being nevertheless subservient to the generation of fire, out of which the light could shine and could manifest, in its own manifestation, all the powers both of darkness and fire, but not in their own dark fiery qualifications, but transmuted, according to its own soft, meek, and tender essentiality.

It is the first fundamental truth, That there was nothing evil in eternal nature. Like as also nothing (properly) good, because of this same reason, That it had not any evil in opposition against it, from which it could be distinguished by such a denomination of good. But since this opposition is effectually in the fall, we have no expression nearer unto the truth than this, that we say, All that there was in eternal nature was good, not with opposition to any evil that then was, but to that which afterwards was manifested in the fall.

But nevertheless, there is also further a second fundamental truth, well consistent with, and immediately annexed thereunto, viz. *There was that in eternal nature which must have been evil in end unto creatures, as soon as they manifested it in themselves;* when it was good and profitable before, in and to itself, and to them also, so long as it was unmanifest in them. And here we shall find that which must have been restrained, cast out from the working of God, and shut up in darkness. For therein laid all the danger, and the root of declining from good into evil, when it cannot nevertheless be attributed to the thing itself, considered as in that former abstracted sense, but only to this conjunction with the creature, in this latter relative sense.

But how, and what was this? It was that natural desire, inclination, and readiness to bring forth its own dark powers. And how could this have been evil and dangerous in the very creation, and yet have been good in eternity abstracted from the creation? If this be not apprehended, all the rest will for the greatest deal remain obscure, and therefore, being certainly much concerned therewith, I must make it as plain as I can.

We must then according to the direction of Teutonicus, (though he doth not propound it after such a way or method,) conceive it thus:

(1.) In that pure abstracted sense from all creatures and creation, these three things in eternal nature were all three manifest and all three hid, in a different respect. All three were manifest, but each only in and to itself, and therefore all three must also have been hid, each with respect to the other two. When we then find this expression in Teutonicus, which he hath frequently, The darkness was manifested in itself from eternity, it is not inconsiderately to be passed by, for it hath its deep, true, significant and wide reaching sense, which I know not how to express nearer by other words, than by saying, As the darkness was in and to itself, when it was not, or nothing to the light, so it was also, and must have been manifest in and to itself, when it was not manifest in and to the light. For it was, and if it was, it was but that same which it was, and nothing else. And this being what it was, cannot but imply a manifestation of what it was, answerable to that sense wherein it was, and relating only to itself.

In that sense then wherein it was, and wherein it was manifest, it had also an inseparable desire of being manifest, or of continuing to be what it was. And this desire now was therein good, needful and profitable, not bringing in any evil or disorder. For it was not a desire reaching beyond its own sphere, or intending to destroy the light, by breaking forth out of its own limits into the light's region, but only to generate and bring forth its own dark powers, and so to preserve its own being in its own region. Which all must have been so, and continued so without alteration, for it was subservient to the light. If it had not been so, no fire could have been generated, having no essences but from its root, and so the light could not have shined out of the fire, and could have had nothing to shine into. For its essentiality is to shine into the darkness, and that of the darkness to comprehend not the light. But,

(2.) As soon is there is spoken of creatures and their creation, there is a digression made from this pure abstracted sense, and this desire can no more be so considered in a singleness, or by itself alone, but all three must now be considered as in conjunction, breaking forth and entering each from its own deeper particular sphere into one only compounded, lesser, lower, and weaker, for to make up all three together every particular angelical being. Wherein, or with respect to which, this desire of darkness cannot further be considered so single, pure, and close to itself, for it hath now an external object, which it can lay hold on, and make a pretension to, no less than fire and light, seeing it is no less than they a third essential part thereof.

And as by the moving of the eternal Will in both fires, the central fire especially introduced itself into a greater desire, so did also the *light*, and so no less the *darkness*, each in its order and place, and according to its condition. When, nevertheless, even in this greater desire also, there was no evil, nor any danger, as far as it can be conceived by itself alone, abstracted from the creature, for it had not, nay, could also not have changed itself, and no alteration was brought upon it from without; but only in its conjunction with this external object, there was an evil danger of disorder and confusion conceived as it were in the womb, not as an absolute necessity, but as a possibility of being brought forth into real existency. And so the former goodness, consistent with that pure abstracted sense, is now inconsistent, at least as to the same decree thereof, with this latter relative; not because of its being changed, but because of its now having ability and possibility, in this external object to be changed, by this dark desire's being stirred, raised up, and manifested beyond that sense wherein it was manifest before: which before could not have been done by itself without the creature, but could now by the creature, as it was also done soon thereafter, by some of them in their fall.

But could not this dark desire have been kept under or in order, in and by the creature, that so its goodness and profitableness had been continued without alteration? Certainly it could, for so it was also, and is yet still, with all those holy angels that kept their habitation in the light. For it could not have broken forth into manifestation of itself, neither could it have necessitated any creature to raise it up. Certainly no more than fire lying hid in a flint stone can break forth to consume houses if not brought forth by a living agent, and no more than it can necessitate or constrain any living to strike it out of steel and flint. But if now this is done by a living creature, and evil consequences come forth from this doing, who can be blamed as an author of evil?

So therefore, all and every evil hath its only original in the creature, and not in this dark desire, considered in itself without the creature; for in its conjunction with the creature the danger was conceived, and by the creature's *own activity*, the evil was effectually born. This desire of darkness implieth as in and to itself nothing else but a bringing forth of its own powers, that is a preservation of its own being; and this is good, for it is consistent with order, and is according to its own natural and eternal right. But this same desire of darkness, as in conjunction with the creature, implyeth also further disorder, and destruction, rebellion and insurrection, against the light, and this is evil. If then that former can be separated from this latter, as it really can and did before there was any creature, there can be no evil, and *none could have been* in eternity, *before the creation*. But if this latter cannot be separated in the creature from that former, as it certainly cannot by any means that former goodness faileth, when this desire is considered in conjunction with the creature, and faileth so, that the fault is on the side of the creature, and not on the side of this desire.

Which even in the creature itself, intendeth not properly and directly the destruction of the creature, but only its own manifestation and increase.

Nay what is much more, even now after the disordered manifestation of this dark desire, when it is really hell, darkness, torment, anguish, and anger-fire, we may still find some evident and most considerable footsteps of this distinction, declaring plainly, that all what there is or can be conceived of evil, lieth only on the side of the creature, and not on the side of that which came out of eternal nature to be manifested by the creature. For hell-darkness and anger-fire would immediately be good and only good, without any mixture of evil, and could bear no more such dreadful names, if but the own will of creatures, with respect to which they are and must be evil, could be taken away, abolished and annihilated. Which certainly as it is a sure and solid truth, so it is most worthy to be taken into deep consideration.

But I think it can now from hence be plain enough, what is here meant in our author, *by the breaking forth of the hellish foundation of God's anger.* And that there must be spoken thereof in different senses, which I see not how to represent better in their difference, but by saying, It broke forth, and broke not forth, and yet broke forth. Far we may find in this fourth theosophical question, compared with the fourteenth question, such a threefold sense, as is according to this threefold expression, though we find not such a construction of words.

(1.) *It broke forth,* seeing that all the holy angels must have been made up, in their creation, by darkness, fire and light; according to the likeness of their Father in eternal nature. But it broke forth in its due order, for it was not made manifest, entering not into the superficies, or supremest risible circumference of the angelical beings, but kept below to the centre, as the lowest step of this eternal ladder.

And entered nevertheless into them, and into every one of them, to be the root and ground of their fire and light.

Which entering into them, was its breaking forth, from its own uncreated eternity, into a lower and exterior degree of many particular created beings.

(2.) *It broke not forth,* in that sense which implieth hell, or anger-fire, properly so called now after the manifestation thereof. For here it was cast out and shut up: which is not so grossly to be conceived, as if the darkness had had a rebellious will or desire, to be hell, and to break forth in flames of anger-fire, to destroy the light, and to disturb the whole creation of God; which rebellious will, as a raging, furious devil must have been resisted by force and violence, and bound with eternal chains of darkness.

For what a ridiculous nonsense would this be, and what strange monsters would not be generated therefrom?

Certainly not so much as the least shadow thereof may be found in all the writings of Teutonicus, if not ignorantly, or maliciously perverted.

The darkness had a will or desire indeed, or a natural internal propensity and inclination to enter into manifestation, and to bring forth in and by the creature its own powers and wonders: Which was so natural unto it, as it is unto fire and light. And this was good and not evil, as far as it can be considered without conjunction with the creature; for it implieth no rebellion against the light, no disorder, or destruction of anything in eternal nature, but only its own generation, manifestation, and preservation of its own being. Which must be preserved in its own state and condition, and is, by the concurrence of fire and light themselves, preserved in eternal nature.

But it was not good in this conjunction with the creature, for there it implieth, and carryeth along with it, of all necessity, an undoing of the light in the creature, and so the creature's destruction, and insurrection against the eternal will of their Creator, who would not have had them creatures of darkness, but of light.

Here then in the creation of these creatures, this will and desire of darkness, was not made use of by the Creator, in such a sense as he made use of that desire of light, but he cast it out. From whence? From his working saith our author, not absolutely from the creature, for darkness must have been the third essential part thereof, hid in its inmost deepest centre, but from his working he cast it out. What is this else, but to say, He opened not the dark bottomless pit, but shut it up in its own abyssal centre, he brought forth no hellish wonders, and created no devils, but all holy angels of light, being all bright and glorious shining flames of fire, and having the darkness, together with all its dark will, desire and inclination under their feet.

So therefore this hellish foundation of God's anger broke not forth, and could also not have broke forth in the creation of angels; but afterwards it did in their fall, when this desire of darkness was stirred, raised up, assisted mightily, and brought forth effectually by their own activity, working in the dark and false magia of their own will. But nevertheless again,

(3.) *It broke yet forth* even in this creation itself.

And what is now this breaking forth else or more, but a nearer advancing, not from not being unto being, but from a state of pure absolute impossibility of coming ever into being, to a state of possibility, or if it might be said so, to a good hope for being. For before the creation, there was an eternal impossibility that darkness ever should have been manifested, beyond that sense and degree wherein it was and must have been manifested in and to itself;

Seeing that not only, it could not have manifested itself any further, but also, that it could not have desired, or not have been inclined to do so, because there was nothing which it could have been manifested in or unto. But now there were so many millions of exterior living objects, all capable of receiving its manifestation into their own ground, wherein it laid unmanifest, and all also able themselves to bring it forth into manifestation, both within and without themselves.

There was then now a possibility, and a door as it were was opened in the creation, through which it could creep in, and come into manifestation; not indeed by its own sufficiency, but by the creature's assistance, and concurrence, if these might be so curious and desirous as to unlock its secret pit, and so to enter into a manifest conjunction with it. Which that they could by their own will and desire, experience hath shown us in the fall of angels, and can still daily shew in our own actual transgressions, that these two desires, of darkness and of living creatures, can enter into, unite and mingle with each other, more easily than black can unite and mingle with black.

And here that *greater desire*, whereinto eternal nature, after its being stirred up in both fires, introduced itself, may be found with respect to darkness. For when this had before, according to its eternal right, a desire to be manifest, and to continue so, in that sense wherein it was to in and to itself; it got now a greater desire, to be manifest in the creation also. Which greater desire was cast out by the Creator; not because of its having been evil in itself abstracted from the creature, but because of its being inconsistent in the creatures with that state, wherein he would have had for his own praise and glory, and their own happiness.

And this, saith Teutonicus now further, *v.* 5, was the ground and cause of Lucifer's fall.

But if we would imagine such a cause as whereby he were made excusable in the least, we should be quite out of the way. It drew and tempted him indeed, but in him only, and not without him. So that it was but his own lust that tempted him; and tempted he must have been as well as Adam, and as all the rest of holy angels. It drew and tempted them all, but it necessitated none, and could also not, or else they must all have fallen, no less than Lucifer with his legions. But as the greater part stood unmoveable in the truth and light, so could he also have stood and kept his own lust under foot.

And then this darkness would with all its drawings so little have darkened him, as his fire could have burned him, or could have consumed his shining light.

Of man saith the scripture, Thy perdition is from thyself: notwithstanding that man had in his temptation this same, living, strong and mighty prince of darkness against him. For it was but his own lust which he could have been sensible of, and this therefore was properly that which tempted him; had he prevailed against this, all what there was without him, should not have hurt him.

And if it was so with man, how much the more is Lucifer's perdition from himself; who had not such a living, strong, and cunning adversary against him from without, as he was afterwards himself unto man. He abode not in the truth, and he kept not his habitation in the light, saith the Scripture, and maketh so himself only, and nothing without him the cause or causer of his destruction.

I shall now but try, whether I could illustrate a little more all this matter, as to its chiefest particulars, by a convenient similitude, obvious unto reason and senses.

From the creation of this world all that there ever since was manifested therein, both good and evil, laid hid and secret in the manifold powers and energies of temporal nature. And so, that all things successively and gradually, each in its appointed time, should be brought forth into manifestation. Of so many others let us consider only that evil, noxious and destroying invention of gunpowder, certainly not flown forth from the properties of light and love, but out of darkness, from this hellish foundation of God's anger; seeing it is notoriously made up of the three first properties of darkness, and only by the concurrence of the fourth it is enabled to show forth its stupendous effects.

As really now as this laid in the powers of temporal nature from its very beginning, so really also this nature had a desire to bring it forth into manifestation. As it hath still such a desire for all what may yet be behind, and shall have it unto the end of time. All the powers, properties, and energies of stars and elements, and all what there is set at work, or hath a share in the government of this principle, from the supremest officer down to the lowest, is capable of this desire, each in its order, and degree, and according to its ability. But especially the spirit of this world (according to the plain expressions of Jacob Behmen) is created with a natural inclination, to bring forth into manifestation, all what there lieth hid in the secret recesses of his kingdom. For therein his government and the execution of his office consisteth; he being ordained to manifest both good and evil in this his mixed third principle, wherein yet all is good, if considered as in and to itself.

This desire then in the spirit of this world, with reference especially to the manifestation of gunpowder, was absolutely good in him, (in such a goodness as this principle can be capable of) as far as it can be considered only in itself, and purely abstracted from men. For though we may say of the devil, yet we cannot of the spirit of this world, that he desired or intended so many thousands of living men and beasts should be killed and destroyed thereby; but his desire implieth nothing else, but that a faithful execution of his office might be made by manifestation of those powers and wonders, which he was ordained to manifest. But as soon as it is considered in conjunction with man, this goodness faileth immediately, not that it had been changed in itself; but because it is inconsistent in its manifestation with the condition of sinful man.

This manifestation with its effects could not have broken forth of itself, or by own sufficiency of this desire, though it had been never so strong, and notwithstanding that all the materials requisite thereto, were in their being; but it wanted a living agent, or such an intellectual instrument as could be able and fit to make a proportionable mixture and composition thereof, and to prepare what there was more required for its pernicious use. And this could have been no other but man. Beasts were not able, and the devils also not, because of there being cast out from this principle, so as to have no power therein at all.

It could therefore not have broken forth before the creation of man; there it was in a state of absolute impossibility. But in his creation we may say, it advanced nearer, or made as it were the first step of advancing from a state of impossibility to possibility, for that external living agent, whom this desire could come into conjunction with, was now in being. But in his fall the conjunction between them was actually made; and in this conjunction all evil that ever arose therefrom, was actually conceived in the womb.

What here might be objected, That thus it seems a necessity is laid upon man, by which he was constrained to fall; for that else the spirit of this world could not have manifested its wonders and secret powers, and that so his being created with a natural inclination thereto, must have been in vain, is of no consideration at all. Man was free, and not necessitated to join in his imagination with the spirit of this world, and if he had kept him under, he should himself nevertheless have manifested his wonders, quite in another and much more glorious way; not as a foolish captive and servant, but as a wise ruler and master thereof. But now in his fall, or joining with him, a wide gate was opened, through which this hellish invention could get a ready entrance into this world, after such a pernicious way as it is still therein unto this day.

But nevertheless it was still unknown to mankind for several thousand years, during all which time it could not have been called evil, if purely considered in and to itself, as it is a wonder of the powers of nature. And, which is the chiefest thing, and the conclusion of all, when it broke forth at length, after such a long period of ages into an actual manifestation, it carried no killing and destroying evil along with itself, of an absolute constraining necessity, but all that evil laid there already before in man himself. For it could not have forced any body to kill his fellow-creature thereby, though it may have occasioned and tempted many, who yet all were free, so that they could have left it alone: and if they all had kept under foot their own evil lusts of hatred, envy, anger, pride, and covetousness (which properly was that which tempted them), it would have done no more hurt in the world, than it did before it was in being.

But this is enough. What further might be said and applied conveniently to our purpose, can easily represent itself, if duly considered and compared.

I shall now say something in short, concerning, Sir, your second Question, which was this,

What is the true notion of own self-desire as it relates to fire and forms, and such like things of themselves inanimate; will and desire, in propriety of speech belonging only to intellectual and rational beings?

Answer. Several things are here expressed, which first a little distinctly must be taken notice of, before a direct answer can be given to this question. But, though there many things properly belonging and subservient thereunto, come into my mind, yet I shall for brevity's sake set down only some of them in the following positions:

I.—It is not the right way for truth and wisdom to make or settle outward notions, and to fix our mind upon spoken or written words; but the only way is, according to the direction of the Scripture (repeated and insisted upon most earnestly by Teutonicus), *to ask of God, that giveth to all men liberally, and upbraideth not.*

II. —If this is given by God, and is *obtained* in the soul internally, it is authorised by its giver to regulate the propriety of outward speech, by which itself cannot be regulated reciprocally. For,

III. —It is unquestionably true, that our propriety of outward speech must be subject to a propriety of inward sense; seeing that upon this only, it must depend, and that it ought not to aspire to any higher dignity, but to be a faithful interpreter thereof.

IV. —It is no less true, that all what we can call a good, nay the very best propriety of speech, is but earthly, imperfect, impotent, shadowy (in comparison to inward light and substance), full of confusion (because our Jerusalem speech is lost, and this but born in Babel), and always subject to be taken differently, according to the different constitutions of hearers or readers, none of whom can take any outward expression nearer unto truth, than himself *standeth therein*.

V. —Many things are said in a good propriety of speech (according to our sense and apprehension), even in the Scripture itself, condescending to our capacity, which yet are all improper, and if regulated by that outward propriety of speech, utterly false; when they are really true in their own internal propriety, which if it should or could be exactly represented, should be all inconsistent with the propriety of earthly speeches. Instances would make a prolixity. This only, concerning the deliberation or consultation of God, and his decrees, following thereupon, could evidence it sufficiently.

VI. —It must justly be asked, By what ground, or in what sense, the Seven spirits of God before his throne, can be placed in the number of things inanimate? or what the true notion is of being inanimate? Seeing that the prophet Ezekiel testifieth of those four which he saw as a fourfold wheel full of eyes, they had a living Spirit within them; and seeing further that they are the original of so many thousand animate beings. For that they are called seven wheels, and seven burning lamps, and that neither wheel nor lamp upon earth is animate, can signify nothing at all.

Truly our author had found a true propriety of internal real sense, which cannot be outdone by any propriety of earthly speech.

VII.— He that made the eye, should he not see? and should he not hear that prepared the ear? saith the Scripture of God, who nevertheless hath neither eyes nor ears; when yet he hath them both for above all propriety of earthly speech, in such a true propriety of inward sense as is consistent with eternity, and with his transcendent being.

And as this is said of God, so it may be said also in its lower, subordinate sense of eternal Nature.

VIII. —All the forms thereof *see, hear, feel, smell*, and *taste* each other, truly, really, and properly, in such a truth, reality, and propriety as is consistent with their eternity, though not with the capacity of sinful man; who lost his intellectual eye, and all internal senses, and is but able to look into time, and this moreover but so, that there justly might be doubted, whether he more properly should be called blind or seeing.

IX. —How these five senses are appropriable to the forms of eternal nature? or how they see and feel each other, is asked in vain, and should be declared in vain, though it were by an angel from heaven, if we are not ourselves *acquainted inwardly* with the movings and operations of eternal nature, in its *restored harmonious union*. All what our author saith thereof, is not to declare it to any other so as that it should be understood from his outward words, by bringing them into regular notions, but only to stir up every one that complaineth of unintelligibility, to seek and ask the understanding of *God*, where he may certainly find it, according to his appointed measure, like as he found it, who before was so ignorant thereof as any other can be upon all the earth. For,

X. —So impossible as it is to be understood, if we are not acquainted with the operations of eternal nature within ourselves, so possible and easy is it, if we are; for then it declareth itself most sensibly, and wanteth no declaration from without. It is seen and felt in the mind of man, as a *living word* of God is spoken, heard, and understood without any outward sound, and without means of any language.

XI. —If then these things be so, *will* and *desire* cannot be so strange to the seven forms of eternal Nature as they might seem, if we would think, that the propriety of earthly speech, which we are used to, is a good and proper *norma* for these eternal, immeasurable things to be regulated by.

XII. —A little new-born child, Whether it hath will and desire, and especially own will, and self-desire? might here justly be asked. I am sure enough, directly and positively it can neither be affirmed nor denied, but a harmonious mixture and union must be made of Yea and No. If we should consider this a little deeper, much would be found therein, convenient to this present matter, concerning the Seven forms of eternal nature.

XIII. —Each of them, considered as by itself alone (though none can be alone), hath its own will and desire.

And this (1.) is its own immutable essentiality. (2.) It lieth in its own immutable essentiality. These two cannot in eternal nature be distinguished from each other, they are one and the same thing, but from the effects and consequences we find the distinction after the fall in creatures. It is rightly said (1.) that it is its own immutable essentiality; for it is that, whereby it is, and continueth to be what it is, and cannot be any other thing or property; and can also have no inclination, no possibility, nor any kind of ability, to be, or to become any other thing, but what it is. And so it is not an acting, stirring, or working activity, as we conceive in the notions of will and desire, for there is no occasion for it. It is quietly what it is, and need not be busied with a moving will, or desire to be, or to maintain its being, for there is no opposition, which it could or must resist by exerting any act of will or desire.

It standeth (notwithstanding that it hath really its own particular essentiality for itself) in the nearest union with all the others, making up with them, one only harmonised substance. But seeing further, that this same afterwards in fallen creatures, is own will and self desire, with respect to these seven disharmonized properties, when scattered and brought in opposition against each other in creatures; it is also rightly said (2.) that will and desire laid in the immutable essentiality of each of these seven forms: for it ariseth only from thence, and showeth forth itself immediately. Each is departing from union, and withdrawing into that which is its own; each is contrary to all the other, and hath now a natural strong desire, (inclination or propensity is not here enough,) or a fixed, obstinate will, to stand by itself, upon its own bottom; to exclude all the other, to prevail against all and every one; and only to preserve and maintain its own particular being. Which could not be so, if in the first harmonized original (when they all seven were united into one only substance, and ruled by one only will, of light and love), each of them had not its own particular, immutable essentiality.

So THEN there was no own will, nor any own self-desire in eternity, before the fall of angels; nothing the like was ever said by Teutonicus, who declareth expressly, in more than fifty places, not only that it had its original in the fall, but also, that it could not have been in eternity before the fall. But *that* must have been therein, which, when introduced into an exterior manifestation, and so communicated up to creatures, could, in and by them have been stirred and raised up in discord and opposition. And this was that seven-fold, particular, immutable essentiality of the Seven eternal Properties, whereby each of them, must have been only that which it was. For the one could not have been the sixth, nor the second the fifth, etc. But they altogether could have given up their will and total being into the whole; all loving, desiring and embracing each other, in union and harmony, and so making up one only will and substance.

But when they were now stirred up in the deepest central root by Lucifer and his angels, this union and submission to the will of light and love, was broken and disturbed; each recalled as it were that which was its own unto itself, acted according to what it was able in its own essentiality, and showed forth what it was, when departed from union.

And so there must arise seven particular, not only different, but also contrary wills and desires, which the *Revelation* of St. John represented by the emblem of *seven heads of the dragon, by seven mountains, and seven heads of the scarlet-coloured beast, thereupon the whereupon the whore sitteth,* etc.

Selection Six.

"Considerations on Lucifer and the Third Principle"[?] From Serial Elucidations D, Section 1. Walton Section VII:

(VII.)—OF THE CREATION OF THIS OUTWARD THIRD PRINCIPLE, WHEREIN WE LIVE AND MOVE AND HAVE OUR OUTWARD BEING.

[On account of its importance, we give the entire of the above section, up to the dissertation on Gen. i. 1, thus:—]

"From what was said before it might now be plain already, but is here to be made plainer, that the fall of Lucifer was the only (*causa sine qua non*) cause, or rather the only occasion of the creation of this our third principle, which is nothing else but a temporary, coagulated out-breathing or exhalation, and so a visible representation and manifestation of the two interior, eternal and invisible principles, brought forth into war and opposition to each other by Lucifer, but settled again in this world, by the infinite wisdom and power of God in such a combination, order, proportion, and harmony, that (notwithstanding all their contrarieties, wherein they both act their parts upon this one only visible stage,) they must both be subservient to the keeping out and under their former prince, and to the greater manifestation of the glory of the omnipotent Creator. And so, this creation is not a bringing forth of any such new or strange thing as had not been before in any wise or manner; but is only an alteration of that state which was before the fall, in the particular kingdom or region of Lucifer. Which alteration was made by God for the better, after that Lucifer had brought forth an alteration upon it, for the worse. For he had utterly spoiled, darkened and wasted it, and made out of a pleasant angelical garden, a dark den of lions, dragons, and tigers, a habitation of devils, and a hold of every foul, unclean, and hateful spirit. Which it would still be, if God (the Father especially, unto whom this first moving in the creation is properly and fundamentally attributed) had not moved himself, and had not made another opposite alteration of the whole state of this kingdom; and this chiefly by the light and water in this third principle, which he produced again, but of an inferior and exterior kind and degree to what it had been before it was spoiled by Lucifer. For thereby on one side, the prince of darkness was utterly cast out from all his former possessions; and thereby also on the other, the pure transparent materiality, or the seventh form of eternal nature (as to this particular region darkened, obscured, said grossly compacted by him,) was taken away from under his tyrannical dominion, and instated in such (as it were) a middle state or tolerable condition, as from which (though it must now during the time of this mixture of good and evil be subject unto vanity) it can and shall be purified and refined by fire again; and so be restored into its primeval glorious transparency, wherefore it is that this first creation, brought to pass by a foregoing spoiling, carrieth along with it of all necessity, a second or new creation, or restoration into the primeval state; and this beginning of time implieth absolutely an end of time also: and this even so naturally and inseparably that Teutonicus had no scruple to say, that *if we knew exactly the hour and minute of that sixth day wherein the creation was accomplished, we could also know the year and day of that fiery trial whereby it shall be delivered again from the bondage of corruption;* for the beginning and the end are thoroughly alike to each other, and this latter is most naturally, or according to the immutable laws of eternal nature, contained in the former. But the eternal Father hath reserved in his own power the knowledge both of this and that; and it is not at all for us to know his secret times and seasons.

Here then to have a due conception of what the creation is in general, before we come to consider it particularly, that *vulgar opinion* which is generally had thereof, is in the first place to be removed. For though it may be pleaded, that it is not only consistent with the outward letter of the Scripture, but it may be granted also that it can be consistent with piety and integrity of heart, so as to do no hurt unto them that hold it in simplicity of mind, because not able to look into the deeper ground; yet, nevertheless, it is inconsistent with the *recondite wisdom of God*, which is behind the *veil of Moses*, and may do such hurt unto an enquiring mind, as to keep it out from the understanding of those secret mysteries that were implied indeed from the very beginning in the outward letter of the Scripture, but not unfolded to the generality of mankind, except only now in this latter age of the world; wherein they *will manifest themselves*, though not unto all sorts of people promiscuously, but unto them only that seek the wisdom there where it can be found, and that cannot be contented with a broken superficial knowledge, but desire instantly to look deeper into the *eternal ground*, to understand the *whole connexion between eternity and time*, and to apprehend how, and why the latter of an absolute necessity (viz. after the fall of Lucifer,) must have been brought forth out of that, and why it must also of the same necessity be swallowed up into that again.

This vulgar opinion then, considered the creation of this world, as a work of the free, predeterminate or fore appointed will and pleasure of God only and solely, without making any reflection upon the foregoing fall of Lucifer, as if it had no communion nor connexion therewith at all; and thinketh that by saying, God was pleased in his infinite wisdom to make this third principle, and all the creatures therein, so as they are now, or (if it is able to look a little further) so as they were before the fall of man, and the curse was pronounced upon them, it hath expressed the whole mystery so solidly and deeply as that nothing more can be added, but that we must fully acquiesce with this free will and pleasure of God, and ought not to enquire any further. Let now this superficial opinion stand in its place for the *common people*, to whom it may be sufficient and well enough, if they make but a good use and application thereof to a Christian-like behaviour; but as to *Christian philosophers*, it is certainly very short of being sufficient to reach the ground and bottom. For these (to mention only two or three general instances, and to pass over an innumerable multitude of particulars) will never say, That it was the free, fore-appointed will and good pleasure of God, the *Father of Light, with whom is no darkness at all, nor any variableness nor shadow of turning*, that there should have been *darkness upon the face of the deep;* nor that the earth, but for so much as one single moment, should have been *without form and void:* nor can they grant that it was his prefixed holy will and intention, (arisen and established absolutely in his own counsel, before and without any reflection upon what was actually done by his rebellious creatures,) that there should be such dry, barren, howling wildernesses upon earth, full of tearing beasts and venomous worms, insects and serpents, and such rough, hard, and horrid rocks and stones, which never were nor can be of any use to man, whom yet all the creatures of this world were designed to be put in subjection unto. But that the cause of all such and the like things, and most especially of that never-ceasing strife and war, whereby both living and lifeless creatures upon earth do continually persecute, murder, and destroy one another, must certainly be found out somewhere else, and not be attributed to the absolute holy will and good pleasure of God the Almighty, who is the only goodness itself, and in nowise good and evil. This is the sentiment of *Christian philosophers*, who yet will not proclaim it publicly to the promiscuous multitude of (as well divines as laics) because they know that it cannot be understood nor accepted by any, unless it be such as are able to look into the ground of eternal nature, and to give a satisfactory answer to that objection which here doth presently arise.

For our dark natural reason, having no true idea of what the creation was, cannot but say, If God had not himself alone created all visible and invisible things, without all exception, then there must have been some other creator besides him. And if he had not created them according to his own unlimited will and fore-appointed pleasure, so as they now are, then there must have been some creature that hindered his absolute sovereign will, and constrained him to make them so and so, when otherwise he could have made them better, and settled them in a state of perfect concordance, without any contrariety, hurtfulness, war, and opposition. This creature now could not be supposed to have been any other, but even Lucifer himself with his angels; which yet to say or think would be an abominable thing, etc. This same was not only objected unto Teutonicus by some that misunderstood his writings, and could not apprehend the *generation of eternal nature,* but it was also most perversely laid to his charge by others, that he held such a doctrine as that Lucifer had made the earth, rocks and stones, and the venomous and hurtful creatures, and was thus a creator of them, besides Him, of whom the Scripture saith, that *he created heaven and earth and all that is therein:*— whereby we are the more confirmed (said those ignorant opposers) that this shoemaker intended to teach us afresh that old damnable doctrine of *Manes,* babbling of two contrary Gods, a white or good, and a black or evil one. But truly this altogether is so far from his mind and sense, that it hath no communion therewith at all, as may plainly appear unto everyone that hath but a small understanding of the process in the *mutual generation of the forms of eternal nature,* and will but search a little into this matter. But I think it most proper and necessary that this objection should be examined and answered unto, before we descend to a particular consideration of this creation; and this for a defence of the truth, and innocence of our author. It hath two parts, both which are to be considered distinctly: for it saith (1.) that Teutonicus made Lucifer a maker or creator of earth and stones: and (2.) that he makes him a binder or controuler of the free sovereign will of God, whom he constrained to bring forth the creatures of this world in such or such a condition.

Concerning the *first* part, the whole matter is easily thus to be conceived. Before the revolt of Lucifer, as long as he was a holy angel of light, all the *seven forms* of eternal nature stood in the most perfect union and harmony, both in himself, and without him in his whole kingdom. The *six properties* therefore, generated the *seventh* most gently, softly, and sweetly, in a clear, pure, crystaline transparency, according to the nature of the *light;* which then had the predominance over all the rest, as they do still throughout all the other kingdoms and regions of all the holy angels, that kept their habitation in the light, and as they shall do again in the place of this now defiled and cursed third principle also, when they shall be re-harmonised, and the whole principle be purified by fire, and so be restored into its former glorious condition. When now Lucifer, in unanimous concurrence with all his angels, by his perverse will, desire, faith, or magia, stirred up the fourth form of fire, first and chiefly within himself, intending to raise it up above all the rest, and to exalt himself therein as an almighty, most sovereign monarch, the whole harmonious order of eternal nature in his created being, was presently broken. But this could not have been done as in and to his own particular creature only; but by this selfsame act and deed, his fiery spirit went also actually forth from him in his false magia, into all that was without and besides him, intending to conquer and to trample all under his feet, and so to be alone the supremest all in all. Thus now he poisoned, infected, and polluted all what he could enter into; all that gave him any admittance, or in anywise condescended to his will. He stung as a *fiery serpent*, not only into the other angelical thrones, and provoked them to do the same which he did, from whence came the *war in heaven between Michael and the Dragon;* but he went also out against God himself, his father and creator, intending to bring him under into subjection. The whole harmonious order therefore of eternal nature, wherein darkness and fire had stood from all eternity in subordination to the light, was thus immediately broken without his particular creature also, wherever he could get any admittance; not broken indeed as to God his creator, for this was really too strong for him, nor was it broken as to the rest of the holy obedient angels, for they resisted him and kept him out, but it was broken in his own whole region or kingdom, for there only he could prevail, seeing that this stood in subjection under him, and was by birthright, his natural due possession, whereof he then was the only king and ruler. There, therefore, he found a free admittance and condescension to his will, with the four first forms of nature, which he could raise up, and so subdue the rest. Throughout all his dominion therefore, but nowhere else beyond it, though he designed it everywhere, the harmonious order of eternal nature was actually broken. For *that* which before stood in the midst between *three* and *three*, was now by his false magia dislocated and removed from its appointed place, and could no more keep under the darkness beneath, nor any more give forth a shining glorious light above. So, therefore, the three inferior forms on the left hand, swallowed up before from all eternity, by the three superior on the right, came to be raised up out of their hidden deep, and were set in opposition, and enabled to act according to their own will and inclination. Wherefore also, they exerted presently their own peculiar qualifications, most intrinsical and natural unto them when not kept under by the lightness of light and love. What now their peculiar qualifications were, was formerly mentioned sufficiently, and is now here plainly to be seen by those fruits or products they brought forth immediately. To generate the seventh form of materiality, is common unto all the six, and none of them can be excluded therefrom; whether they stand in union or in disharmony, they can never cease to generate the seventh. Materiality therefore, must still have been generated in all this disorder and confusion, no less than before, in their concordance. But what kind of materiality could now here have been generated, when these three inferior forms of darkness had got the predominion? All the former purity, sweetness, clearness, softness and meekness was abolished: the whole region had before been full of light and glory; but now that was extinguished, and *there was darkness upon the face of the deep*. Before, it was a dwelling-place of meekness, tranquility, and love; but now, it was turned into fierceness, tumult, wrath, envy, hatred and anger. The *harshness* having now the greatest hand in the generation of the seventh form, attracted, astringed, and compacted, without any resistance or restraint, in the extremest force and vehemence; and this still so much the more and stronger, as it was more stirred up and exasperated, on one side by its own stinging prickle, and on the other side, by its own turbulent whirling wheel. The seventh form therefore, which should have been generated sweetly and gently, pure, transparent, thin, subtle, fine and crystaline, by the predominant concurrence of the three superior forms of light, could not have been so generated any more within the sphere of this disharmonised region; but must now have been generated only according to the predominant property of the three inferior forms of darkness, that is, it must have been made dark, thick, gross, obscure, hard, rough, ponderous, earthy, stony, and rocky. And this not only in such or such a particular place of this region, as now is this earthly globe, but everywhere throughout this whole kingdom, though not everywhere equally alike, but here more and there less, according to the various conditions of several places different from each other; and according also to the different activities of those diabolical agents that stirred and exasperated the forms of nature either more or less, or after this or that peculiar manner. Like as we may observe an outward resemblance thereof in the ice, congealed out of a soft water, or other liquid, which is done everywhere in all the world, whenever this astringing power can prevail; and yet is not done everywhere equally alike, but more in one place and less in another, according to the different conditions of those liquors that are capable of being congealed, and according also to the various degrees of this congealing force.

This now is a short abridgement of what Teutonicus saith of this matter throughout all his writings, but more especially in his AURORA from the xiiith to the xviith chapter, where he declareth this fall and work of Lucifer most particularly with all its circumstances, and with respect to all the forms of nature from the first unto the seventh; worthy indeed of all consideration. But who can say here with any sense, that he giveth unto him the character of a maker or creator? Is he not manifestly represented in all his pages and lines as a breaker and destroyer? For he is not said to have himself generated the dark, gross, impure materiality; but the three first forms of darkness, in their predominance over the three of light, have generated it so, as soon as they had extinguished and swallowed up the light. But Lucifer is only said to have been the chief agent, who stirred them up thereto, by his strong stirring and exasperating the violence of the harshness and fiery strength; and this the Scripture saith itself implicitly, when it calleth him *Apollyon*, and more explicitly, *a liar and murderer from the beginning*. And though he were even expressly said to have generated the dark and gross impure materiality, in such a sense as now in this world a dark, false magician may be said to produce or generate this or that material thing, (which he doth not so by himself, or by his own sufficiency, but by the forms of nature, which he disorderly and maliciously abuseth, and which alone can properly be said to have produced it,) yet even then also, this production made by Lucifer from the beginning, could not at all be called, nor be considered as a making or creating work; but only as a perverting, breaking, defiling, and destroying of that which before was holy, clear, and pure. Teutonicus therefore, made him not a maker of earth and stones, but he made him a spoiler and waster of that blessed crystaline earth, which he used to call *ternarius sanctus,* and which had been full of the light and glory of God, as well in his kingdom when he was an angel of light, as in the other angelical regions: and he saith that he was the *only cause* of that first spoiled condition of the earth, thus described in the beginning of the first chapter of Genesis, *The earth was without form and void, and darkness was upon the face of the deep.* But if these opposers think this to be contrary to the truth, let them declare more solidly what the Scripture means by calling him *a destroyer and murderer from the beginning,* and let them show us what he destroyed and murdered, before the creation of this world. Did he not murder the light in his own creature, and in his whole region, and raise up instead thereof the darkness, whose prince he is unto this day? And did he not waste his own kingdom, his glorious inheritance, his holy, clear, paradisical earth, the seventh form of eternal nature, his pleasant angelical garden, full of glory and delight, making it really dark and empty, void and without form, and destitute of all that beauty wherewith it had been adorned by his Father and Creator? So that Teutonicus might well say of him, *If all trees were writers, all their branches pens, all the mountains books, and all waters ink, they would not be sufficient to describe that lamentable condition which Lucifer with his angels, brought upon his region.* As little therefore, as he had created that former pure transparent earth, whereon he dwelt in the light before his fall, so little also did he create this outward earth. He caused indeed, the forms and powers of darkness to generate, in their predominance over the light, such a dark, dead, dry, rough, and gross materiality everywhere throughout his whole region; but it was God and he only, who created, that is, formed and settled together in one globe, this dispersed impure matter, and rectified it again, by restoring unto it light and water, in the same manner as it had before, (though not in the same internal degree of glory, beauty, and excellence, which was not to be done in this beginning of time, but to be reserved to the end thereof, as hereafter will appear) and replenished it with innumerable creatures of all sorts and kinds; altogether representing those that were also before upon that former paradisical earth: which certainly Lucifer would destroy and make void and without form again, if his power were equal to his will, for he is a destroyer of all the creatures of God, and a setter up of his own dark lying figures, formed by his own will, in his false magia. So that it is a great ignorance and misapprehension, if not a great perversity to say, that Teutonicus made Lucifer a maker or creator of earth and stones.

But now further, as to that *second* part of this objection, whereby it is said that if it was not the free fore-appointed will and full pleasure of God, that the creatures of this world should be so as they are, then Lucifer must have hindered and constrained him to make them so and so, when otherwise he could have made them better, and settled them in a state of perfect concordance without any contrariety, hurtfulness, venom, war and opposition, etc. This is quite erroneous, and stands upon that false hypothesis, that the creation of this third principle hath no connexion with the fall of Lucifer, but is a free, fore-designed work of God, to be considered without any reflexion upon what was done by this revolting angel; which is justly called a false hypothesis, inasmuch, as this creation is a work of God *a posteriori*, made only to rectify and restore that which was spoiled and destroyed. For if Lucifer had not fallen, no creation of this third principle would have been brought forth, nor could any alteration have been made in this region; for it stood already in the *highest degree* of glory, light and dignity, and must have continued the glorious inheritance and possession of their great prince and hierarch for ever and ever. Whether God would have been pleased to create some other things, and so to have manifested his goodness and glory unto some other creatures, besides the holy angels, or whether he would not, we are not to determine; but only this we may freely say, that if Lucifer had not revolted, and by his revolt laid waste his kingdom, no creation, no transformation, nor any alteration could have been made in this region. For the two eternal principles had then continued in their harmonious order: darkness and fire must have abode in their subjection to the light to all eternity, as they stood therein from all eternity. This third principle therefore, could not have been made, especially not in this region, a distinct representation and manifestation of their several divided properties, as it is and must be now. If then, there was no fore appointed will and decree in the counsel of God, before and without a reflection upon this sad apostacy of Lucifer, to create this third principle, and to manifest therein a visible figure of the two eternal principles in their opposition to each other, how could this will of God have been hindered or limited? And how can he, who is only to restore a thing spoiled by another, be said to be constrained by that spoiler to restore it so and so; especially when this restorer is all sufficient to show forth thereby his power and wisdom, and to make use of that same spoiling for the greater illustration of his own honour and glory? It may be said indeed, That he is occasioned to accommodate his wisdom to the condition and circumstances of that spoiled thing, and this in a sense, may be said also of God; but how can this be more derogating from his honour and glory, than it is when we say, and say rightly according to the truth, That he created such angels as could revolt against him, and that he gave unto them such thrones and possessions as could be spoiled and wasted by them? Seeing that by their revolt they did no hurt at all unto him, but hurt only themselves; and that he hath restored, and will restore what was spoiled, so as that even this spoiling itself shall serve to the greater exaltation of his might, honour and glory.

The fall then of Lucifer was foreseen indeed from all eternity in the mirror of eternal wonders, and so was the creation of this world also; and though there is or was no real before or after in that eternal all seeing eye, yet with respect to our understanding, the fall of Lucifer is fore-going, as it was also actually, and the creation of this third principle is following, and so following, that it depends upon that, and was not decreed beforehand, or without respect to that, but only in consequence and relation unto that. For when these things stood thus in this depraved state, what was there to be done, both with Lucifer and with his corrupted region? Should God have left him alone, so as to give over this whole kingdom into his absolute power, to exercise therein his sad tyrannical dominion, according to all his own will, in despite of God and all his holy angels? No, this could not have been done at all. For this region was not Lucifer's propriety, but his Creator was the only proprietor thereof; and it was only given unto him by birthright for an inheritance, if he would continue an obedient son. When he therefore departed from obedience, it was but just with God to thrust him out, and to take from him his inheritance. And moreover also this region, considered especially as to the seventh form of nature therein, neither had, nor could have revolted, nor committed any iniquity against its Creator; seeing that it stood only in mere passiveness, and must suffer itself to be defiled and polluted, having no ability to resist, because it was only a generated body, without any activity of itself, and could therefore not hinder its alteration and pollution, brought in upon it by the now predominant forms of darkness. How then, or by what equity could it have been punished with being given over into the arbitrary government of this apostatised prince of darkness? Unto whom it must now (until the power of omnipotence in the following creation appeared for its deliverance) have been subject indeed, but this constrainedly, not willingly; for it is natural and intrinsical unto every, even the most senseless thing, to incline to continue in its own state, rather than to be brought down into a lower and worse condition. It was then not only justice and equity with God, but was also of the highest necessity for the maintaining of his honour and glory, to take this region away from under the subjection of this rebellious angel. But this could not yet have been sufficient for its restitution, but it must further also be refined and purified by fire, and so restored into its former beauty and excellency; for it was defiled and corrupted so that the glory of God could not appear, nor dwell, nor represent and manifest itself therein. But now further, this purification by fire, and so this full restoration into the primeval glory, could not have been done then immediately, for it was a vacant throne, destitute of its natural prince, and in the counsel of the most Holy Trinity it was decreed, that another king should be raised up instead of Lucifer, after quite another way and manner, unto whom this region should be given for an eternal possession: for so saith the Scripture to this purpose, that we *were chosen in Jesus Christ before the foundation of the world;* and though this king should have been Adam the First, yet it was also seen and known beforehand that he would not stand firm in the hour of his temptation, but fall back, and so bring thereby another defilement upon this region again. And therefore (though not therefore only, but for several deeper, fundamental reasons, which could be produced if this did not suffice) it was not, nay it could not have been purified then, by such a purification as it is to pass through at the end of time, and so neither could it then have been restored into that same light and glory wherein it stood before, but another expedient was in the meanwhile found out in the wisdom of God, whereby his whole will and counsel most wisely could be performed; and this was the creation of this our outward third principle, wherein the two interior principles are left indeed in their contrariety to each other, (not by any necessity or constraint laid upon the creator by his rebellious creature, but by his own wisdom, for the greater manifestation of his glory, and the greater confusion of this spoiler,) and do both actually send forth their influences thereinto, according to their several divided properties, but are nevertheless so far harmonised and knit together in order, measure, weight and proportion, that neither of them can entirely prevail against the other; that the dark and fiery principle, which is destroying in its own nature when alone predominant, cannot alone exert its power and dominion, but must only serve the principle of light, for to move and stir it up, that so they both concurrently may be subservient to produce and manifest the secret wonders of God, whose shadows shall appear hereafter in eternity; and that they both may keep out and under their former prince, who is now only a prince of darkness. For though he may have an access in that dark and fiery part, with respect to which he is also still called a prince of this world; yet seeing that this is nowhere alone, but hath always and everywhere more or less an opposite part of light and water with it, he is everywhere resisted and excluded, except where men by their own malice, give unto him an open door. And moreover this whole principle, seeing that it is quite of another and exterior condition, nature and order, than that wherein he was created, availeth him nothing at all, nor can he make any use thereof, though he still is and liveth within its sphere. He can see no more in the light of this principle than he can in his own darkness; and the water of this principle can refresh him no more than his own fire can. So therefore he only is disappointed and deluded in all his designs, but the glory of his Creator exalted in all his works. And there is rejoicing even in heaven also among the holy angels because of the creation of this outward world, whereby the whole region is delivered from his tyranny, and is set in such a state as from which, (after the time shall be accomplished wherein it must be subject unto vanity, because of the transgression of man,) it maybe restored into its primeval dignity, and so re-united to the other two angelical hierarchies.

So then the creation of this third principle is not at all such a work as is commonly apprehended by *the vulgar*, but quite another thing; to declare and demonstrate which much more might indeed be added, but it will still evidence itself more and more hereafter. Here therefore it may suffice only to have said in general, That it is nothing else but a transformation of the whole polluted kingdom of Lucifer into another exterior state, and inferior degree of goodness, light and dignity, made in order to bring it up in due time again, through the purifying fire into that primeval glory wherein it stood before the fire was stirred up, and the darkness set in opposition against the light.———

Having thus seen the connexion between the fall of Lucifer and the creation of this third principle, and what this creation is in general; and having given, I think, a sufficient answer to that twofold objection, we are now further to consider this whole outward creation more particularly, according to the description given forth thereof by Moses. *In the beginning then God created the heaven and the earth*, saith Moses. *By the word of the Lord were the heavens made, and all the host of them by the breath of his mouth*, saith David: and *In the beginning was the word, and the word was with God, and God was the word; the same was in the beginning with God: all things were made by him, and without him was not anything made that was made, etc.*, saith the apostle John. All three say concordantly one and the same thing of the creation, though the words of the Apostle reach further, and imply much more than those of Moses and of David. For this *beginning* which Moses speaketh of, is only the beginning of time; which according to his following description, must of necessity have been brought forth after the fall of Lucifer. But the *beginning* mentioned by St. John is not this beginning of time only; for he saying that without the Word, which was in the beginning with God, not anything was made that was made, includeth manifestly the creation of angels also, which verily had its beginning before the beginning of the creation of this third principle: whereas Moses saith nothing at all neither of the creation of angels, nor of their fall explicitly, but was only, and (for reasons declared elsewhere) very shortly and obscurely too, to describe the outward creation of this our visible world.

So then we have now here already two beginnings, different from each other by degrees of being more exterior and more interior. For the creation of angels belongs not at all unto time, nor was the beginning thereof a beginning of time; but the time of this third principle is such a necessary unavoidable consequence of their fall, as an earthly room or place is of a gross compacted body. We must say indeed, that the creation of angels had a beginning, for though their essences were eternal, yet they were not formed or figured creatures from eternity; but we cannot say this beginning imports a time, no more than we can say, that it imports such or such a determinate extension of room and place; though really something answering unto both is imported, which because it is surpassing our outward condition, wherein all things are grossly compacted, our earthly tongue hath no denomination to express or represent it by conveniently: for though it imports not a time yet it imports a lower state than eternity is, when considered absolutely as to itself, without any respect to creatures. The mighty angel in the Revelation, sware *by him that liveth for ever and ever, who created heaven and earth, and the things that are therein, there should be time no longer, but in the days of the voice of the seventh angel, the mystery of God should be finished.* Now this mystery of God is wholly relating unto man, created after the creation of heaven and earth, and all of the things that are therein. If then there shall be time no longer, after the finishing of this mystery of God, there was also no time before this mystery of God had its actual beginning in the creation of heaven and earth and the things therein, though there had been another beginning already before in the angelical creation.

It may seem superfluous to insist so much upon this difference, the notion whereof may be plain and notorious enough, but I think it not so, because these two beginnings are not yet all that the words of St. John are applicable unto; but we shall find *two other beginnings more*, both which are much deeper, and far more intrinsical, because without any relation unto creatures, and which do differ also from each other by such a difference as might be said in this or that respect, to bear some analogy to this, whereby the beginning of time differeth from the beginning of the creation of angels. Seeing then that these two posterior beginnings are nearer to us (because both relating unto such creatures as stood originally in the same degree of excellency, having both been treated after the image and likeness of God), and are therefore more comprehensible, we must needs look upon them with attention, and procure in our mind a true idea of that difference whereby they are to be distinguished from each other, if we expect to have any good apprehension of those other two beginnings that are much more abstruse and remote from our eyes. For they are all four to be taken notice of, if the expression of the Apostle, and that excellent explication which Teutonicus giveth forth thereof, shall be fully understood.

If we then look deeper, beyond both this and that creation into the generation of eternal nature, we shall find that something like to a beginning is to be understood there also, which is implied in the denomination of a principle, and which has been spoken of sufficiently before, where it was called an *eternal beginning* or a *beginning without beginning*. And this is the lower beginning of these latter two, answering in different respects both to the beginning made in the angelicall creation, and to the following beginning of time in the outward creation also. For as to both these, eternal nature is as it were successively and gradually descended—down lower and lower, and hath manifested in the former more secretly and unitedly, and in the latter more openly and separately all its hidden powers and energies. Seeing that in the beginning of the angelical creation, its darkness and fire, though both co-operating indeed subserviently, were still hid and kept under in subjection, and the light only was made manifest in all the holy angels. When contrariwise in the beginning of time, or in the outward creation, it hath openly displayed both darkness, fire and light, in a plain distinction and division, obvious everywhere, and made even a visible and transitory representation of each of them particularly.

But further, if we now look deeper again beyond eternal nature and its eternal beginning itself, into that transcendent, abyssal, incomprehensible generation of God, who there generateth God, or spreadeth forth himself into Father, Son and Spirit, spoken of lately in the explication of that Scheme or Table, which considered God without all nature and creature, even there also there is still in a higher and more recondite sense, a *beginning*, or rather something as quite afar off, and only with relation to our apprehension answering thereunto, to be conceived, which more than any of all the former wanteth indeed a *peculiar* and *more convenient denomination*; for this of a beginning is much too gross and low; but seeing we have no better, we must call it a beginning too, and be contented with that difference whereby we can distinguish it from all the others in the apprehension of our mind. For it is rightly said, that in our apprehension only it answers to a beginning; and yet it is rightly said also, that a real ground of this our apprehension is in the thing itself; which would be plainer on both sides, if we could have another and more significant denomination than that of a beginning is. And this is the inmost or deepest beginning of all, beyond which there is no other to be looked out for more, and is answering in different respects to all the following three, but nearer and more especially to that next eternal beginning made in the generation of eternal nature; seeing that these two are both relating to the manifestation of God unto himself only, when the other two have their only relation to the manifestation of God made by and unto creatures. Wherefore also this answerableness whereby this deepest abyssal (or rather byssal) beginning answers to the beginning in the generation of eternal nature, is as far above that whereby it answers to the angelical beginning, as God the creator is above the creatures; and infinitely more different from that whereby it answers to the beginning of time, than a bright shining light is different from a dark shadow, caused by the interposition of an obscure body, which was even actually done by the fall of angels in this outward creation. When it doth nevertheless truly answer more or less to all the three following degrees of beginning successively, and unto each according to its own either nearer or more remote condition. So that therefore as to all these four, the words of St. John are to be understood, when those of Moses speak of the most outward and lowest beginning of time in the temporal creation only. Which apostolical words we shall now further take into more particular consideration, beginning from that which is the deepest and inmost, and so proceeding down to that which is the lowest and outmost of all; which also alone is to have an end, not in any deeper, but only in such a sense, and according to such a manner as is directly opposite unto those circumstances, in the consideration of which it can alone properly be said to have had a beginning, nay, which made, or even were themselves this very beginning of time." [To resume the Summary.]

Selection Seven.

[Exercpt from the commentary on "Three Tables", originally printed in "Astrologer of the 19th Century", 1835, reprinted in "A Sorcerous Anthology, Magic and Occult Writings from the Publications of Robert Cross Smith", Topaz 2017. The annotations are from "Philadelphus". —Ed.]

AN EXTRACT FROM THE TRANSLATION
OF
Ruben's Latin Manuscript.[1]
Communicated by Philadelphus.

EXTRACT I.

"If, then, love, in union with humility, is, in an inferior sense, perfection in this world already, it must needs be that which is perfect in the highest fulness of perfection in the world to come: when this mysterious and prophetical character (said to have been the seal of David, that great warrior, and of Solomon, that prince of peace, and that eminent lover of wisdom, — when this character, *denoting*

hieroglyphically the spiritual signature both of David and of Solomon; denoting the two eternal principles *in union*; denoting the creation of the *third principle*; denoting the six working properties of *eternal* nature in their everlasting *rest*; denoting fire

---

1 A translation of the famous Latin MSS. by Sir P. Rubens, annexed to his treatise on the Proportions of the Human Figure, Cabalistic Principles, &c. &c. This valuable morceau of antiquity was sold at Hugier's famous sale at Paris, and purchased by the late Richard Cosway, Esq. R. A.

and water in an harmonious union; denoting the *two tinctures* restored into ONE, who is ALL in ALL, or without whom there can be nothing; denoting that all whatever was, or is, or shall be, is of, and through, and to, that ONE; denoting *almost the whole* instance of time and eternity, as the same, in our age, is laid open by Jacob Behmen, that blessed instrument in the hands of the Spirit of God; on which account, I may justly call this seal or character *prophetical*:) when this character, I

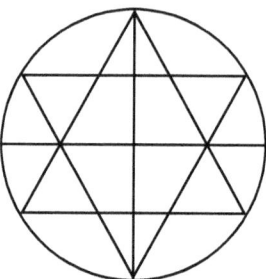

say, spiritualized, and only with *addition of a cross*, which is not expressed therein directly (and no wonder that it was not in those days), shall be the broad seal, not only of the eternal King of kings, but also of *every one* of his subjects; and not only of that everlasting kingdom of Light and Glory, but also of *every individual* inhabitant thereof; although *not in all of the same size*, but in some broader, and in others narrower, yet, *in all of them*, from the highest to the lowest, the very same, as to its spiritual shape and figure. Amen, Hallelujah!"

EXTRACT II.

Being Part of an Explanation of three wonderful Tables, representing the three States of Man, viz. his Perfect State, his Fallen State, and his Restored State.

"Though Adam was really created in this world, even upon earth, and introduced into Paradise, which was upon, or was greening or budding forth through this earth, yet still his distance from, and his height above it, was so great, that no spirit of reason—no, not in the best mathematician, shall ever be able to measure it; for that paradisaical earth, of which his body was made, was so distant from, and above, what we now call earth, as Paradise (which is still extant in the same place where it was then, and is not destroyed by the deluge, as reason fancies, but is only *covered by the curse*) is distant from, and as high above, the beastlike body of an earthly man that is to be turned into dust, though he may be buried upon the same spot of ground which Paradise did formerly green upon. So, therefore, what is here meant, is not such a distance, nor such a height, as may be measured by measuring lines, and may, nevertheless, be justly so called; but it is such a one as runs (in an inferior sphere) parallel with that superior sense which we take in mind, when we consider the *three principles* in a mutual relation. The first principle is still in the second, and the second in the first; and we may truly say, that heaven is in hell, and hell in heaven, seeing they are *both within ourselves*; and yet the second is at such a height above the first, and the first at such a distance under the second, and such a great gulf is fixed between them, that none (as Abraham said to Dives) can pass, neither from the one side nor the other. The *two eternal* principles are both together in *this temporal third* principle (or outward world), and in everything therein; and yet this third is in the same distance under them, and they in the same height above it in which time is under eternity, and eternity above time; and GOD himself, 'in whom we move and have our being,' *is nearer to us than we are to ourselves;* and is yet at such a distant height above us, that only the *true spirit of the soul* can attain to a *real perception* of Him; and that the Scripture calls the earth his footstool, and says that heaven, and the heaven of heavens, cannot contain him. The place of man's nativity in the middle, between time and eternity, wherein he was touched by this or that, is the only thing, on account of which it was said in the beginning, that this (the first) table did represent him in his primitive state of his integrity. For all his graces, perfections, virtues, powers, and glories, he was endowed and gifted with, and especially all those excellent particulars related and declared by Jacob Behmen, concerning the manner of his eating, drinking, seeing, never sleeping, &c. are all found necessarily depending hereupon, and flowing freely forth from this his standing in the middle, and being touched from that which was above, *as well as from that which was under him*. So that, by naming only this place of his nativity, all his perfections are named also implicitly, and want not at all to be enumerated distinctly to the spirit of understanding, to whom it is plain and clear that Adam could not have had them, if his station had been either higher or lower. For, if it had been lower, and he had not been touched by the Spirit of eternity, he must needs have been a creature belonging only to this third *temporal* principle, and a subject of the astral spirit of this world, though he might have been the noblest, and of the highest rank and quality among all his subjects; he could not have had such a dominion, as really he had, over all the creatures of this third principle, and over the astral spirit of this world: and, what is of the greatest consideration, he could not have had the *two tinctures* united in one in his own single person; but must, of all necessity, *have been made* male and female in two distinct and divided bodies, after the manner of all those living creatures that are subjects to the astral spirit of this world. And if his station had been higher, and he had not been touched by time, he would entirely have been cut off, or quite excluded from this third principle, and *could not have been an entire image of God, after his own likeness*. But here may be objected and queried—Are not the holy angels *entire* images of God, notwithstanding that they have nothing of this third principle in their created being?—*Ans*. The holy angels are *entire* images of God, as manifested then when they were created, viz. before the creation of this third principle, when God was manifested only in the two eternal principles of fire and light; but Adam was to be an *entire* image of God, as manifested in the three principles *after the fall of Lucifer*, not in eternity only, but also in time, which entire image of God, after his own likeness, he could not have been, if the third principle had not been a third constituent part of his being. Upon this account it is that Jacob Behmen rightly said, men shall, after the end of time in eternity, even excel the angels, whom we know the Scripture calls 'ministering spirits, sent forth to minister for them who shall be heirs of salvation.' The primitive state of integrity is commonly said, by the spirit of natural reason (human wisdom), to have been the state of Adam and Eve in Paradise; but, as this spirit is a fool *in these matters*, so he speaks both foolish and nonsensical things thereof.

"Can that be primitive which was not first, but had something antecedent to it, of which itself is but an appendix, or a necessary consequence? Can that be an integrum or a whole, which is divided into two, and so divided that these two can never more be made that whole or that one again, which they were before they were divided? These two here spoken of may indeed be joined and copulated together *from without*, and upon that account (yet in quite another sense wherein they were one before) they may be called one, as they are called in Scripture one flesh. But what is this state and condition to that wherein they were one in one only person? This primitive state of integrity was only then in being, when God (having made but one Adam) saw every thing that he had made, and found it very good. But when he said afterward, 'It is not good that man should be alone,' his state of integrity, alas! was faded away already, for he had already transgressed his limits, he was departed from his eminent station, he was sunk down into time, he had opened a door for the astral spirit of this world to come in; he had hearkened to his suggestions, he had stooped down with his will and affections to embrace the love of this third principle; and so he had already dealt treacherously against the wife of his youth, which had been his companion, and the wife of his covenant *within himself,* and had longed for a helpmate besides and without himself; he was infected with a desire after the knowledge of good and evil, and had eaten already of the forbidden tree of that knowledge, not indeed outwardly with his mouth, yet magically with his lust and imagination; and so he had really begun and carried on that same transgression, *which afterward was consummated* by that same helpmeet that was *made in this transgression* of his; and, therefore, first, it was now not good that he should be alone; *the plain reason thereof could be given distinctly,* but it is enough to say only, that he himself had made *not good* what God had made very good *before.* And therefore, secondly, like as afterward, the end of this transgression consummated was death, so the end of this foregoing preparation and disposition towards it was a 'deep sleep,' justly to be called a forerunner of, or a brother-in-law to, that death; and therefore, also, thirdly, when the transgression was consummated by his helpmeet, *he showed forth the inward signature of his own mind,* which he had in the beginning thereof, by calling his wife 'the mother of all living,' which certainly hath no manner of sense in it, except only with a close respect to this transitory world, wherein he had now settled himself according to his newly-framed own contrivance, and wherein, according to the Apostle's word, but contrary to his sense, he forgot the things behind him, and minded only that which was before him; for, if he had a sober serious remembrance of his primitive station, or a mournful sense of what he was departed from and was deprived of, he could not but call his wife the mother of all dead. But this denomination he could not reasonably have liked so well as that of the former, because, first, he was now for begetting children, which all were to have of him that life he now himself lived in, viz. in the region of stars and elements, when his former true life, which he now was dead unto, could not be propagated by him into any one of them. He must needs, therefore, be more pleased with such a denomination as denoted a life in this world, after his own likeness, and obvious to his senses, than by such a one as implieth, only tacitly, a life lost, gone, and vanished away, so that he could have no more any true sensation thereof, and expresseth downright and directly the very contrary of every life. And because, also, third, he must needs have likened better to please his wife, whom he loved, and to flatter her, than to make such an affronting reflection upon her, as to lay all the blame upon her alone, extenuating, at same time, if not quite denying, at least implicitly, his own fault and guilt, seeing especially that he could not be ignorant of the next immediate consequence thereof, which needs must have been this, that his own conscience would have risen and shown in his own face, and told him that *he himself had been the father of death* before ever his wife had got a personal existence. For this is true,—by one man (says the apostle, not by one woman, but by one man, even Adam the first, not by Adam and Eve, for, though this be true in a second posterior sense, yet it is not so in this chief original sense) sin entered into the world, and death by sin, which one man is always in the Scripture put in a diametrical opposition over against that other one man, Jesus Christ, for this very reason called the second Adam very frequently, but never the second Adam and Eve. And so, likewise, when God called to our first parents after the fall, he did not say in the plural number, 'Where are ye, Adam and Eve;' but he called in the singular only, 'Where art thou, Adam? Hast thou eaten,' &c. which-plainly showeth, that God called to an account chiefly, and in the first place, him whom he knew to have been the first author and original agent in the transgression, *before even the woman was taken out of him*, which never could have had a personal being in this world, if he, by his own lust, imagination, and desire, had not himself spoiled, perverted, and *caused to be not good*, what God had made very good in the beginning.

"In the primitive state of integrity, all the senses, thoughts, imaginations, and enjoyments of man, and all his magical operations in the spirit of his soul, could not but have been thoroughly pure, holy, and heavenly, because both the glass of his mind, and the eye of his understanding, were so too; and therefore, as this tree was, so must its fruits and products have been also. Accordingly, then, he could not have had any other sensations but such as could, and did, arise in the *spirit of the soul*, from a union with, and full obedience to, the spirit of God in his light and love, from an intuition and fruition of his infinite goodness, from a profound contemplation and deep understanding of the wonders and riches of his wisdom shown forth in the creation of this world, from an intimate acquaintance with the holy virgin Sophia (designated by Solomon, wisdom), from the mutual embraces of the two eternal tinctures of fire and light united in his own single person, from a familiar conversation with holy angels, from his own personal perfections, which he was endowed with as a sovereign prince ruling over all things in this whole third principle, &c. What those senses, sensations, and enjoyments were, in particular, no living soul can be found able to declare, because this primitive state is lost, and was never attained again, — neither can it be attainable by any during this mortal life; and Adam himself could not have declared it to his offspring, *after his transgression and fall*; for of that single primitive image of God, in which he was in the beginning, he himself knew nothing more after his 'sleep.'

"In the paradisaical or middle state thereof, all the former senses, or heavenly sensations, had left, and were departed from him, or rather he had left, and was departed from them, and had removed himself into a lower and more exterior station, wherein his senses were still indeed pure, holy, and paradisaical, yet no more so, as they had been before; for he, having now some other inferior objects before his mind, must needs also have had a lower and inferior understanding. Seeing that, instead of his former intimate acquaintance with the holy virgin *within himself* and instead of the loving mutual embraces of the two tinctures within his own single person, he was now wholly taken up, without himself, with such a visible helpmeet as he had longed for; which alone can show sufficiently an exceeding great difference between his senses in the primitive state, and his senses in this inferior state, wherein he was after he had awakened from his ' deep sleep.' But even these paradisaical senses also continued not very long with him; for, in the fallen state, when the transgression was consummated, all those paradisaical senses and enjoyments were *utterly extinct*, and, instead of them, all the sensations of Adam and Eve were no other but terrors, dread horrors, fears, anguish, trembling, and despair; and, although the promise of the woman's seed put a stop to the extremity of those terrible sensations, yet it did not restore them their lost paradisaical enjoyments, much less

Adam's primitive heavenly senses; but it laid only in the inward ground of their souls a foundation of faith and hope, which they should keep up, strengthen, and corroborate in themselves, as a means to have this restoration performed in them successively, gradually, and always in the same proportion in which they should be found steady, faithful, and true to this *new-laid* foundation."

Selection Eight.

Thirty Propositions (Fragment).

[No extant version of the whole is known. –Ed.]

"XCV.—That the corruption of human nature, reaching to the very bottom thereof, did indeed show forth itself mightily by the answer Adam and Eve gave to their Creator herein, that neither he nor she would find and own the cause of their fall in their own bosom;-Adam laying the same upon the woman, which God (as he said) had given him, and the woman upon the serpent; which, by not removing the fault from himself upon the devil, but silently as it were owning and bearing it, behaved himself better than both of them. But that notwithstanding this, into this human nature so thoroughly corrupted, grace was spoken again by the promise of the blessed woman's seed, or serpent treader.

[Note.—The antecedent A and B *signatures* of this piece, containing Positions "1" to "94" inclusive, in quarto MS., (the present *signature* being marked C, and consisting of forty-two pages of German and English face to face, in the author's own hand-writing,) with the subsequent signatures D &c., are no longer to be found; nor have they been with the remainder of the author's MSS. since the year 178*. If these MISSING SIGNATURES be in the possession of any reader, will he please to communicate to the address given at the foot of p. 51.]

XCVI.—And of this, we believe, that it was not only a bare promise of a thing that should come to pass after several thousands of years, but also a grace even then already beginning and actually showing forth itself. Whereinto Adam and Eve with all their posterity, were not only received again to be children of grace, but had also so much of power given unto them, as that they could rule over the sin dwelling in them, by the assistance of that grace, laid hold on by faith and taken in into their spirit; as this ruling over sin was soon after thus required of Cain.

XCVII.—Also that not only the eternal Word, the Father's only begotten Son, had here already set himself actually as a mediator, in the middle, between the fallen humanity and the anger of God enkindled therein, to withhold the same from devouring these two poor creatures; but also that the heavenly Virgin, which was departed from Adam in his sleep, did now again in union and communion with the eternal Word, approach to the fallen humanity: yet that she gave not herself into the soul, comprehensibly, much less into the soul's own will; but only that she stood in her own principle of light, over against the soul, or in the inmost deep of the human mind, showing forth herself therein, and opening as it were a door of possibility for all men, through which they can come again to their lost heavenly image. Because in this inspoken grace of the serpent treader, and in the promise of the blessed woman's seed, she hath espoused herself afresh to the human soul, and promised to walk with the soul through the dangerous valley of this world, to warn, to conduct and guide it safely, and at length in the perfect regeneration, to take the same into her arms, as her espoused bridegroom.

XCVIII.—But especially we believe that this holy woman's seed, which alone is the true serpent treader, was inspoken chiefly and directly into the woman, not into the man, that is, not into the masculine fire-ground, or Adam's fiery tincture separated from the light, but into that light and water tincture which in Eve was disappeared: and that so it was set in opposition against the fiery will of the soul in Adam, and against that sinful spring which first had taken its beginning in him. Nay, that in such a manner it could not have been spoken into the man; because this same fiery will and tincture of the soul in Adam, separated from the holy light and soft water, was and is still that serpent in the humanity, whose head was to be bruised by the soft tincture of holy light and water,—that is, whose power was to be broken thereby, and whose predominion was to be taken away. And that therefore in the regeneration, the man is not to apply unto himself any more that which was said unto Eve, with relation to the outward natural life and order, viz., Thy will shall be subject to thy husband, and he shall rule over thee; but that contrariwise, the sentence against the man is now this, according to the true ground and substance, viz., Thy masculine fiery will shall be subject to the wife of thy youth, or to thy heavenly Virgin, and she shall rule over thee.

XCIX.—This inspoken grace or covenant of grace, we believe, was propagated from generation to generation, yet only in its own inward ground and not in flesh and blood, until the time was fulfilled and had run unto its end. (scope, limit, period,) in the blessed Virgin Mary. Though we cannot properly call it a propagation, because it was not done from the efficiency of men, nor by their concurrence (assistance), but from the efficiency of this covenant of grace which here was made, and by virtue of the promise made therein: according to (in performance of) which, this inspoken grace moved itself freely, and opened itself out of its centre, more or less and in different degrees, from generation to generation.

C.—We hold that herein, one of the strongest arguments lieth against a particular and partial election of some only unto life, and reprobation of others unto damnation. Because this grace was inspoken, and this promise made to the whole life of the humanity, which as yet was still but one, as one only stock or a tree, before the same could have spread forth itself in boughs and branches; nay before these two first parents (which with respect to propagation are to be looked upon as only one) were cast out from the garden of Eden. Which grace and promise therefore can press forward upon all their children, no less than death hath done so from one upon all.

CI.—After the sentence was passed upon Adam and Eve, and this promise was made unto them, they were, we believe, as Moses saith, cast out (driven out) from the garden of Eden, (for paradise they had lost already before,) by a cherub with a flaming sword, turning every way. And though we believe the relation of Moses, even in the literal sense thereof, to be fully true, yet we believe also and have it by experience, that this cherub with his sword, hath something in it much greater and deeper than what in that time was outwardly done; and are besides also well assured, that every man born of man and woman without exception, upon his way returning home to paradise, shall find this cherub and his sword in their own souls, yet every one according to his peculiar state and condition.

CII.—With St. Paul we believe, God would have it so, that all the generations (families) and nations upon earth should come forth from one only blood; and that therefore, this only stock of the human tree hath propagated and spread forth itself successively into innumerable boughs and branches. But especially, that not only from the beginning of the first world, with the children of Adam, but also and even more conspicuously in the beginning of the second world, with the three sons of Noah, it hath divided itself into three great, principal branches; so driving forth still unto this day, its growth in three lines or parties and sorts of people. And that these three lines or generations of men, have divided themselves, and still do so, according to the manner and property of the three principles, divided in the humanity.

CIII.—The first we call justly the line of the serpent's seed, which showed forth itself in Cain, the first born of Adam, and afterwards in Ham, who was accursed by his father. The second, the line of the woman's seed, the line of grace or of the covenant of grace, which opened itself in Abel, further in Seth, and among the sons of Noah in Shem. And the third we call the line of nature, or of the natural wonders, which in the first world, so much as we have an account thereof given us by Moses, had not yet so distinctly separated and manifested itself in sundry persons and families, but kept most to Cain's posterity; but in the second world, it distinctly opened itself in Japhet, and displayed itself in the heathen (gentiles) that were of his posterity.

CIV.—With the third line of nature or of natural wonders, we understand the honest, wise and prudent among the heathen, which, according to the letter knew nothing of the grace, and were not taken outwardly (like as the Jews) into the covenant of grace, but lived as rational men, according to the testimony of their consciences or to the light of nature; wherein many of them made a great progress in the knowledge of God, of outward nature and of themselves. And these we say have the promise, that 'they shall dwell with Japhet in the tabernacle of Shem.'

CV.—The second line, which is that of the woman's seed or of the covenant of grace, we take either in a narrower sense only, for the seventy-two generations that follow orderly the one upon the other in the genealogy of Christ, down from the first Adam unto the Virgin Mary; or also, in a larger and more extensive one, for all those collateral generations, tribes, or even single persons, that were contained (included) in the covenant of grace, and behaved themselves accordingly in their life and conversation.

CVI.—But with the first line of the serpent's seed, we understand the thoroughly wicked crew of them that despise, nay mock both the light of grace and that of nature, and live after their own lusts like brutes, if not worse; and these (we say) are excluded from the tabernacle of Shem, and accursed with Ham. Though we do not mean that Noah cursed his son Ham thoroughly in soul and body, but only the serpent's seed and spirit, dwelling in him and operating through him.

CVII.—These three lines we do not so distinguish, or separate so far, as that we should say on the one aide, All the children of grace stand through and through, from within and without in the grace, and have nothing on them neither of the serpent's seed nor of the outward corrupt nature; or that we should say on the other side, All the children of nature and of the serpent's seed are totally in body, soul and spirit, excluded from the covenant of grace, and have no possibility for grace to be obtained in them. No, but we distinguish them only so for, that we say on the one side, The children of nature, but more especially the children of the serpent's seed, have not the covenant of grace in a moving (working) life in them; because the corrupt nature and the serpent's life in them, keepeth under and as much as it can, killeth the motion of the covenant of grace which liveth in itself or in its own internal principle in them: but they have still the possibility in them, to draw back their will and to sink it down into the grace which lieth in them, though in many of them deeply shut up, and which calleth upon them in their consciences, and will manifest itself in them; because no man was ever born out of a serpent's seed only and solely, but all are born out of the one only human seed, into which indeed the serpent's seed was crept in, but into which also the grace was inspoken, even before any man was generated out of it. And on the other side we say, that all the children of grace and of the covenant bear also on them from without, the serpent's seed and the corrupt nature; and that there is none to be found, even not the most sanctified, who dare boast himself to be wholly free therefrom; but that they do not suffer these to rule in them, because the grace is in them moveable, stands in a working life, keeping under continually and casting out all what is not in and from itself.

CVIII.—For we believe and confess, that herein as to the outward life, if the same be considered only as to itself, as abstracted from the grace living and operating therein, there is no other difference between men and men but only this, that one man sticks perhaps more and deeper than another in this or that peculiar kind of dirt and mire, when contrariwise the other may stick more and deeper in another sort thereof; whereby the one as well as the other is so polluted, that neither of them is able to come into that city, wherein nothing of pollution is admitted. And that therefore, none hath any reason to upbraid another with his defilement, and to boast of his own purity, though, in the sight of others as well as in his own eyes, he might be truly pure of this or that particular dirt (filth), wherewithal he seeth his neighbour is abominably defiled. Because the one as well as the other is out of the serpent's seed, and both together belong but to the corrupt nature; because also, the one as well as the other must of himself confess and say, Behold I am generated out of a sinful seed, and in iniquity hath my mother conceived me.

CIX.—Of this generating and conceiving in sin we believe, that it doth *conclude all under sin*, that is, not only them that generate, conceive and bear, but also them that are generated and born. For seeing that sin is already acting and working in them that generate, conceive and bear, and that it cannot work-out or bring forth anything else but what is alike unto itself; there must needs therefore be sin in them also that are generated and born, though it cannot presently from their birth, act and work in them after the same or the like manner. From whence then, that well known distinction ariseth between the so called *original* sin and *actual* sin.

CX.—Concerning original sin we believe, that though in itself it be not a doing, acting and working, as actual sin is, it nevertheless bears the name of sin. Justly and properly; because it is the inward root, ground and bottom, and the universal original of all those outward evil works that can be called sins.

CXI.—That in short, it consists in nothing else but in that disorder and corruption, which the first Adam, quite contrary to his creation and to the will of his creator, introduced into all the properties of human nature, and manifested in all his essences. Whereby he dislocated in himself the three principles from their due place and order; giving so much room and leave to the spirit of this world, that the same could exalt himself above the paradisical life in him, and make out of the heavenly image of God, an earthly beast as to the outward life. Whereout then nothing else could arise, but darkness in the intellect, perversity in the will, a false love turned unto himself in the heart, and a great impotence in all the powers and faculties.

CXII.—That this disorder and corruption is in and for itself indeed, without activity with respect to children in their conception and birth, so that it cannot presently break forth in actual sins; but that nevertheless it is the true and only root, out of which necessarily and unavoidably, the actual sins must spring up and break out when the child comes to an age, though in one it may be more and in the other less: and that absolutely nothing else but sin and what followeth upon sin, but nevermore anything good and pleasing unto God, can be generated out of it. Nay that this is much less possible, than it is for a thistle to bring forth figs, or for a thornbush to bear grapes.

CXIII.—That Adam must necessarily and unavoidably have brought upon, and communicated unto his children in their conception and natural birth, all this disorder and corruption, together with all that belongs to this fruitful root of sin; because he could not have generated out of himself any other image but what he was himself, and could not raise up another and better life in them than he had in himself. And that again, his children most necessarily have propagated upon their children and children's children from generation to generation, this root of sin; because none of them all could in this case, have given unto his children a better portion than what himself before had received of his father.

CXIV.—We hold that, if a proper name should be given unto this original sin, a fitter and more convenient one could hardly be found than selfhood of selfishness, provided only that something deeper be understood thereby that commonly is done. It is commonly apprehended that selfhood or *selfishness* is to say so much as own-will and self-love, and that all these three together are to be accounted as actual sins: which in a certain sense we grant, and do not censure it, but leave willingly unto every one the apprehension he hath thereof. But we do here understand by *selfishness*, the human nature as it is broken-off from its right and true inward centre, as it is entered into its own government of the divided and contrary (fighting) properties of life, as it stands upon a ground and bottom of its own making, and as it hath settled itself as it were to rest only in and upon itself. Which nature is such in every man, even from his conception and birth; and is in its own inward spiritual signature in the sight of God so qualified and conditioned even before any will or love can move or stir therein perceptibly, or can act and operate in the least.

CXV.—For we cannot but conclude rationally thus: all what the corrupt human nature, by means of its sinful activity in every man born of man and woman, operates and effects, that very same it hath received already in the mother's womb a natural inclination, disposition and ability to operate and effect; or else it could not work those sins which it worketh. Like as no tree in this world could bear such or such fruits, if the peculiar kind and property thereof, together with a natural disposition or tendency for bearing of such fruits, had not been before in the seed. Or like as no man in this outward macrocosm, could either inwardly contrive anything with his thoughts and senses, or outwardly make any works with his hands, if he had not received within his own microcosm, when the same was prepared in his mother's womb, such senses and hands, together with a natural genius, inclination and disposition for this or that, even before he was able to employ them, nay, before he knew anything either of the one or of the other.

CXVI.—This sinful inclination and disposition to actual sins, we know not how to express or represent by words better, than by saying, When the sinful seed is sown by the male and conceived by the female, then already all the disordered and corrupted properties, nay the whole fallen human nature doth lie therein: like as a whole tree with all its boughs, leaves, fruits and qualities doth lie in a kernel, though these things are then not yet unfolded in a distinguibility. And this human nature, as well in this sown sinful seed as in the parents from whom it comes, is even then already formed in itself, as it were in a circle like a serpent in a spire; for instead of stretching forth and tending directly to the Creator of the true paradisical life it bends and turns itself crookedly or in a round, enters into itself, combines firmly its own end with its beginning, makes in this circle both its own circumference and its own centre, and settles itself therein exactly in the property of a serpent, which, out of the midst of his spire, lifts up his head and prepares himself to shoot forth like an arrow from a bow. Such a signature we say, the human nature hath even in the seed sown in the mother's womb, and before the rising of its natural life. And this we call *selfishness*, with respect to its own spiritual figure; and with respect to parents and children together, we call it *original sin*.

CXVII.—This selfishness, propagated upon us all from the first Adam, or this seed or character by our parents imprinted in us all when we still were but a seed, which seal hath not only engraven upon it, as it were from without, an image of the serpent, but is also in its own selfish being a true image of the old serpent; the impression of which makes us all to be the first corrupt Adam's natural children, nay children of wrath and guilty of death,—this selfishness, I say, we own to be the *deepest ground* of our corruption, and compare it justly to the root of a tree firmly fixed wide and broad, stretching forth itself, or rather comprising all in itself, and bringing forth all out of itself but continuing itself always deeply hidden under ground: and this tree we call the tree of death.

CXVIII.—But own-will and self-love, which denote already and carry along with them a more outward and more perceptible activity of sin, sprung up out of that root, we compare to a gross, thick and twofold stock of the same tree; yet so, that these two are strongly grown together, firmly united (interwoven) and inseparable from each other. Which stock is indeed the next immediate ground of all the branches and fruits that stand above it; but hath itself nevertheless also still a deeper ground under it, standing between this and them in the midst, like as the stock of every natural tree.

CXIX.— But all the other activities, together with the outborn works, or actual sins, not only of the gross earthly flesh but also of the subtle senses and reason, nay of the whole natural life and of all the powers and faculties thereof,—we compare according to their differences and degrees, partly to the greater or lesser branches, partly also to the blossoms, leaves and fruits of this tree; saying, that death is the end of them all like as also death was their beginning.

CXX.—But here we do include also expressly, all those good works that were wrought out before the regeneration, and did thus not proceed from a renewed ground; where they might have had indeed a form of goodness, nay more also than a bare form thereof, and might have been called good in a sense of this outward world, and in comparison to those that were notoriously evil. For, because they came not out of faith, which faith belongeth to the regeneration, and to the inspoken (incorporated) grace; because also without faith no man can please God, they must needs be sins, as the Apostle witnesseth.

CXXI.—Yet we hold that, between these so-called good works before the regeneration, there is still a considerable difference to be observed, because the persons that wrought them out must needs be distinguished. For first, some abide in their unregenerate state, and so depart this life, and fall into death. Secondly, others return, enter into repentance, attain at least to the beginning of regeneration, and sink down through death into life. And thirdly, others again may backslide from their good beginning of regeneration, wherein they had wrought good works, turn with the dog to their own vomit again and with the sow that was washed to their wallowing in the mire, and continue to lie therein unto their end, and then fall into a deeper damnation. And the works of all these three follow after them, but with a great difference.—Of the *first*, we believe that all their good works falsely to called, which were not good before God but originated from the evil root of self-hood, and coloured over, as it were only from without, with a shining form of goodness out of the astral light,—such works we say, as well as those other of theirs that were notoriously evil, shall go together with themselves into perdition. Concerning the *second*, we believe that all their works, washed in the Lamb's blood, separated from all the evil, and made white as snow though before they might have been red as blood, shall stand before them for ever, to an eternal hymn of praises and thanksgivings for their redemption. And of the *third*, we believe that all their truly good works shall be remembered no more, but shall be taken from them and put up into that good principle whereout they were born, when they themselves shall go without them into their place; because every principle is to gather its own fruits into its barn, and neither of them can take in anything but what is grown out of, and according to its properties.

CXXII.—Of this tree of death, whose root is *selfishness*, whose stock is *own-will* and *self-love*, and whose whole superior part is *all other actual sins*,—we further believe and have it by sure experience, that many of these evil fruits may be plucked off and cast away, nay, that a man through assistance of the Spirit of God may resist powerfully, and prevent the coming forth of others the like instead thereof; and that nevertheless, that stock which beareth them all, may still abide in itself unaltered and unknown also to such a man. Further still, that even this stock also, which is much thicker and stronger than to be shaken by human strength, may be truly shaken by an Almighty arm and hand stretched out from on high, so that all what stands upon it in that man must tremble; and that nevertheless, the root of this tree may still stand fast and unmoveable in the ground, and may still also, as to its proper serpentine figure and properties, continue unknown unto such a man. And lastly, that this root in its own figure (signature), cannot be seen and known by any living, except a strong spiritual earthquake, out of the first principle, do violently shake his whole ground; and that then only, the very foundation pillars of all his natural being are moved and weakened, all what is in him to the very deep is denudated, and all must tremble, both what is above and what is beneath howsoever it might be called.

CXXIII.—And this same *root* we believe, was chiefly that which made in the *second Adam*, our only Saviour and Redeemer, the most difficult battle in his *spirit*, caused the greatest and most vehement anxiety in his *soul*, and forced out a bloody sweat from his holy *body*, when he was to lay hold on the human nature he had taken upon him, to pull it up by this root powerfully out of its own selfish ground, and to transplant it again into its right field, or into its first Divine original. For to this same end he was sent by his heavenly Father, that he might destroy the works of the devil, (which altogether, so for as they concerned the corrupt humanity, did concentre in *this root,*) and that he might procure a perfect redemption to the whole human nature. Nay for this same end, God made him who knew no sin, to be not only a sacrifice for sin, as St. Paul says in one place, but also, as he says in another place, he was made sin for us, that we might become in him, not only righteous but also righteousness."

CXXIV. [We possess this position in the German, but the English translation of it in face, with the remainder of this invaluable piece in MS, as we have stated, is no longer to be found.]

Selection Nine.

"Of the Further Manifestation of God Through the Creation of Angels"[?] From Serial Elucidations B, Section 4.

(V.)—OF THE FURTHERMORE EXTERIOR MANIFESTATION OF GOD, THROUGH THE CREATION OF ANGELS. Wherein is treated of *material causes.*

[The remainder of this dissertation, as confirmatory of the intimations of this treatise, touching some of the evangelical wonders shortly at hand, and which may be expected to ensue from the establishment of *Theosophic Colleges,* (in regard to pure sanctity, theosophic or intellectual light, and the re-investiture of the soul with the omnipotent powers of faith,) we give in its entireness, so far as that particular subject is concerned.]

"This being *out of God* was now the chiefest thing that, with a particular respect to holy angels, must have been declared and demonstrated. Besides which, seeing now nothing more in Behmen that could have had either difficulty or obscurity in it, if this, and especially if the *generation of the seven forms* of eternal nature be apprehended, I would not have enlarged further, but intended only to set down his principal places, treating of their creation, glorious condition, order, and distinction, with respect both to the *number three* and *seven* etc. But since I am desired further to give a short abstract of those several particulars, which he states concerning them here and there in his writings, I shall do it accordingly; though it can hardly be so done, as that all his places could be recited touching every particular thing, because they are so dispersed, and the greatest part of them would require to be repeated several times, which I think would cause both confusion and tediousness: wherefore I shall put them all together in the conclusion.

FIRST, then, as to *their creation,* he saith, They were created *out of God;* out of his powers and wisdom, out of his eternal essences, out of fire and light, out of eternal nature, out of the seventh form of eternal nature, out of all the powers and virtues of God, etc. All which different expressions may easily be found to agree with each other, without any contradiction, if the *seven-fold generation* of eternal nature be more or less understood.

He saith, that God, by moving himself, (*the ground of which moving on the side of God,* as hath been mentioned already several times, *is that only thing which we know not, and which shall not be inquired after by the creature*,) hath figured an image of himself, like as a *little God*. Or that the word of God, *verbum Domini* laid hold on the fountain spirits, apprehending them by the *fiat* in his will, and compacting them, or as it were driving them together, like as from a displaying into narrowness. By which compacting and driving together, (so again done afterwards, more outwardly and grossly, as to the materiality of this third principle,) their creation was effected, where of especially may be considered what he saith, Aurora, xvi. 13–21, and i. Incarnation, ii. 1–25.

But if there should be objected, and said, What Behmen saith in these two places is unintelligible—why could he not have declared it plainer, to remove offences and obstacles, and to make an end of controversies—it must be an absolute impossibility to understand this creation distinctly, and so he may be suspected of having not understood himself etc.? It may be answered with confidence and verity, That these two places, and so also all his others, are much more intelligible than all the *chymical writers* are, in their enigmatical descriptions of the process of their *philosophical work:* who indeed are altogether unintelligible to everyone that is not himself a true philosopher and possessor of the art, and hath not the spirit of understanding in himself, for unto such they are intelligible enough. But why should others complain of their darkness and unintelligibility; or how can they say, that there is an absolute impossibility to understand and to declare this *philosophical process* plainly? seeing that the only reason of their being so abstruse and retired in their words, is that exceeding great danger, which manifestly lieth in a plain publication of this secret work, not only with respect to the world, but also to themselves; whereof they are wont to say, that they should lose even their eternal salvation, if they should go beyond their limits, in making known unto the world that, which God will have kept secret from its eyes. If now this can sufficiently excuse their enigmatical way of writing thereof, why shall it not also much more excuse the abstruse expressions of Behmen, used in this matter especially; and not only because no other utterance was given unto him, but also willingly and purposely, as to several circumstances thereof? seeing that this is indeed of a far greater importance, and of much more dangerous consequences to the children of men, than ever that can be. *If Lucifer had not known* (these are his plain words) *the manner and method of the creation, and the whole working process of the magical powers, he might have been a holy angel unto this very day.* And so he saith also further, *that God placed another exterior king into the room of Lucifer, in this third principle, whom he could name indeed, but would forbear it, because of the dark magia;* and though he named him afterwards in another place intelligibly enough, because this is not of such great importance, yet he was so cautious in his expressions, that he said no more but what he was permitted to say: of which kind there could also be produced several further instances from his writings, if necessity did require it. But, to return to our present matter; the whole tenth and eleventh chapters of his MYSTERIUM MAGNUM are worthy to be taken into a serious consideration, and may be found to be a great deal plainer as to this or that particular, than are the two former alleged places.

There he saith expressly, that *this great danger was always and is yet still the only reason, why this magical generation is as kept so very secret from the beginning of the world, until this present day;* when we nevertheless cannot say, that it was altogether unknown and unintelligible, in a whole universality to all the children of Adam, which would not be true. Like as he also saith it not, but granteth plainly, that for instance, *Moses had, indeed, a true knowledge and understanding thereof, though not always according to his own pleasure, nor in his own reason and capacity, yet he had, and must have had it in that instant time, when those magical powers were opened in him, and when the spirit of his will and imagination was concurring with them, in an actual performance of those works, he was called and commanded to effect by them.*

To say therefore, It is absolutely unintelligible, is to deny that man's internal deep is a dwelling place of those magical powers and his will and imagination to be a living agent, capable of being instructed by the Spirit of eternity, the only supreme director of the divine magia how to act and do: which yet cannot be denied. If man really acts with them, and performeth this or that stupendous work by them, he certainly knoweth the way, manner and method, by which his work is done, and can also declare it unto others, if he be permitted. Or else, would it not be the same absurdity, as if we should grant on the one hand, that a skilful watchmaker can make and hath actually made a curious artificial watch; but would pretend on the other, that it is beyond his understanding, and quite unintelligible to him, and that he therefore cannot tell or declare unto anybody, how he made it? As to BEHMEN, it is with me, and I am sure with many others also, beyond all doubt and question, that he verily had a true and deep understanding, not in his reason, but in his eternal spirit, of the *manner* and *process* of the whole creation; nay that he really and fundamentally understood even the way and method of the *necromancy* itself, not in practice as the devil's agents do, but in the ground and depth thereof, wherein they are blind and ignorant. But none can pretend that he should have declared these *magical powers* so, as that the children of men could play with them according to their good pleasure. He hath done faithfully what he was commanded to do; that is, he hath declared them plainly and intelligibly enough, as to that which can serve us in the process of regeneration. There can be no difficulty to him, that desireth earnestly to follow that direction, given forth through him by the Spirit of God. Let us therefore first pass through this process, and arrive at *that gate* which he went through, and then, when this is *opened in ourselves*, we shall see what we see not now, and what he saw not also himself, before that time. But (N.B.) if we think we must understand these things *beforehand*, and want not such living, *self-experimental process* thereto in ourselves, we presume to look into the eternal world with a temporal eye, or to pierce with our firmamental eye through a thickstone wall. And if we would conclude, that he could not have seen and understood these secret things in the eternal world, because he could or would not declare them so plainly and intelligibly, as that we could understand them as well as he is said to have understood them himself, we make the same consequence as if we should say, that nobody ever understood the process of the philosophical work, because none would declare it so, that everyone could make gold according to his pleasure.

This as to Behmen himself. But as to others, that were more or less at all times, both under the Father's dispensation in the Old, and the Son's in the New Testament, called unto and exercised in the *divine magia*, it cannot be denied nor questioned at all that, if they were the children of God, and did the works of their Father, (as the Lord Jesus said unto his disciples, that they were to do *even greater works than he had done* himself upon earth.) they certainly knew their work, and the way, manner and method also how it was done, like as he knew it; for they were not dumb, blind or dead instruments in his hand, but living and understanding agents with him, though inferior to him. And if these *children of God* are, at such a time, in a peculiar manner in their Father's *workhouse*, and in his all-filling presence, they see and know also certainly the works of their Father, and the way and method how they are done by him; for though his works be infinitely superior to theirs, yet the manner of performance is quite the same, differing only by a degree of excellency, as an universal differs from particularity. And though their knowledge, in a mutual comparison of themselves, may be different also, so that it can be not only greater in one and less in another, according to their several different abilities, calling and capacity, but also that it may be in the same person greater at one time and less at another, according to their various practice and experience, and to that degree wherein the Spirit of God is pleased to open their understanding, to enable their faculties, and to set them either at this or at that work; yet of none, and so also not of the very least of them can it be said, that this manner and methodical process of the magical powers is unintelligible. But it is verily and really easier to them in such a state and time, to see and to understand, with their own seeing eyes, and internal intellect, (I say not reason and human wisdom, but *intellect*, which is as far above reason as eternity is above time,) the way and manner *how God their Father made all things out of himself*, by his omnipotent will and *verbum Fiat*, than an external earthly man can see, know and understand, how a painter hath painted such or such an image with his hand and pencil. If this only be excepted, which hath been already several times expressly excepted, and again but recently, which doth also not appertain to the actual work, or process of the magical powers itself with respect to the creature *a posteriori.*

And this I may say confidently, knowing that I say the truth, and knowing it, not only because Behmen saith the same by other expressions, (whose authority is justly much esteemed and valued by me,) but because also *I know another testimony thereof*, which is of far greater authority than one thousand outward witnesses can be. Wherefore, I am also well assured with Behmen that this knowledge and understanding shall be raised up out of the dust and darkness, in the due time of God, and shall not be further so hidden, unknown and unintelligible to the children of man, as it hath been to the generality thereof, from the beginning of the world. And certainly this same manifestation through Behmen, (though still unintelligible to the greater part of mankind, nay to the outward reason and human wisdom of every one without distinction, as it also will be to the end of the world, yet intelligible enough to some or other internal eye and intellect, nay much plainer than it was declared before him at any time,) is a *sure preludium,* or forerunner, bringing the glad tidings of a clear approaching day. But as to this our present age, blessed be God omnipotent, those magical powers as to their *working process*, are still unknown unto men; but when another generation shall be upon earth, they that then live shall again bless and praise him, that he hath unlocked his secret treasures, and hath poured out the *Spirit of understanding* upon them that *know* him, and are deeply rooted in true love and profound humility! In the mean time I do not for my part, desire to know or understand anything more thereof, according to my own will and pleasure, but I can be satisfied with *that little* which he was pleased in his mercy to let me *see* and *know*, for I can acquiesce therein without offence, doubt or scruple; and so expect the coming of his appointed time. What offence could I take, if I am convinced on one hand, that angels and men are verily gods out of God, and that they are his children, generated out of his eternal essences, bearing his name, partaking of his nature, and being designed to be one with him eternally; and on the other, that they are not confounded with him, or he with them, any more, than Moses and Aaron were confounded with that serpent they made out of their rod, etc.; both which I think is made out hitherto sufficiently. But for the rest, I may also have great reason to be very circumspect as to all my own expressions, and especially about this dangerous matter, therefore I shall now lay it aside, and return to what is said further by Behmen of the *holy angels*.

He saith then further, that they were created after the image and likeness of God, no less than man, though with this difference, that man was also ordained into this third principle, created after the fall of angels, which they therefore have not."

Selection Ten.

"Freher's Process in the Philosophical Work", From Serial Elucidations G, Section 10.

The following curious and interesting Paper, as consonant with the tenor and spirit of this whole Treatise, has been likewise selected for insertion with the preceding extracts. It is entitled "The PROCESS in the PHILOSOPHICAL WORK, considered as thoroughly ANALOGICAL with that in MAN'S REDEMPTION through JESUS CHRIST; and REPRESENTED by POSITIONS given thereof, as to Its PRINCIPAL POINTS In BEHMEN'S SIGNATURA RERUM, chapters vii, x, xl, xii:"—

I. —Adam's primeval state in paradise, and the manner of his spoiling himself, his whole created being, by his lustful imagination after the knowledge of good and evil, is rightly by this author, not only spoken of in the first beginning of his description, but also frequently repeated and variously expressed throughout his whole discourse. For if man understandeth not his own corrupted nature, and that curse which he himself lieth under, how can he be imagined to be able for an understanding of the nature and curse of the earth? Or upon what ground can he presume to deliver such a particular thing from that curse; or to be instrumental in this deliverance? which is the true artist's only business.

II. —As long as Adam stood in a pure paradisical innocency, the eternal Word and power of life, (called by Behmen the heavenly mercury,) was his leader, and had predominance in him. His life, which was a clear flaming fire, burned in and was nourished by that pure spiritual oil of the Divine substantiality; which, together with the holy water of eternal life, is generated in the angelical world: and this, therefore, could not but give forth a glorious bright shining light.

III. —Through the power of his imagination, or lust after the knowledge of good and evil, that which then was still kept under in him, and so was hidden from him, viz. the outward watery property, came to be manifest in his holy oil, and got predominance therein. This oil therefore, now overpowered thereby, could no more be such an agreeable food, and well-doing to his fire, as it could and did before. And so his fire not only lost its shining light, but came also to be spoiled itself, for it was obscured, and made all impotent. And his mercury, which before in his holy oil, had caused and raised up paradisical joy and triumph, according to his moving and stirring property, was now made a stinging anguishing poison, according to his own natural constitution, which he doth and must stand in, when before or without the light.

IV.—Nothing of the Divine substantiality was hereby spoiled, poisoned, or turned into evil: though sometimes this or that expression, which must be made use of with respect to man, may seem in outward appearance, to say something the like. For that which was in man of the Divine substantiality, faded, disappeared, or died indeed, but only with respect to man; seeing that this disappearing, was but an entering again into its own secret original, and so but a returning unto God the giver thereof.

When contrariwise the creatural mercury, that is, man's own life, went forth with its will, desire and lust, out of eternity into time: so that the former union was broken, and upon this breach, its own natural property and propriety could not but be made manifest immediately: and because of this manifestation, which never should have been made, according to the will of God, it is now rightly called, spoiled, poisoned, and turned into evil; when yet all this doth not reach the Divine substantiality, nor the holy life of God, but only that of man.

V.—This is the substance of what Behmen largely declareth concerning man's paradisical state, and falling away from it under the curse. Where he brings in also for a clearer illustration hereof, not only the fall of Lucifer, saying of him, that his desire was to try the fiery mercury, like as man desired to try the watery; but also the serpent with its poison, saying, that in the strongest and most poisonous mercury, the highest tincture lieth, yet not in its own natural property, etc.: all which he represents as a most proper, and pertinent introduction to this discourse of the philosophical work.

VI. —Immediately after the fall of man, God said unto the serpent, I will put enmity between thee and the woman, and between thy seed and her seed: her seed shall bruise thy head, and thou shalt bruise his heel. And herein the philosopher's stone or tincture lieth implicitly. For though this primarily concerneth man, yet secondarily it concerneth the whole creation also; and this bruising of the serpent's head is done both spiritually and corporeally, and both in time and in eternity, and though in different degrees, yet in a parallel process or method, both here and there.

VII. —The serpent's sting points at the wrath-fire, and the woman's seed at the light and love-fire. These two are in every thing; and in the curse that former came to be predominant in outward nature. This latter now must be raised up again, and, by its shining through the wrath, it must subdue and keep it under, and take away from it its predominant power, so that it may keep and exercise only its true natural office, as a servant in and to the light And that these two may no more stand in contrariety and opposition to each other, but be one only thing, reharmonized by light and love, and re-introduced into paradise. And when now thus the dark poisoned mercury is tinctured, his anguishing death is turned into triumphing life and joy, and his former dark desire into a new light and love desire; which of itself is now able to make in itself a pure love and light substantiality, viz. a heavenly body out of an earthly.

VIII.—The whole work consists summarily therein, that two things must be reduced back into one, even into such a one as they were from the beginning before they came to be two; a heavenly thing and an earthly one are to be joined. That former must be admitted or received into itself by this latter, and must change it into its own heavenly quality. Earth must be turned in, and heaven out, etc. Which the mercury, that is therein, doth all himself; the artist is not to do it, neither can he do it: he is only to join together those ingredients that are requisite, and to leave the work to be done by that workman which is therein already.

Yet nevertheless Understanding and Faith is in him required; and by this latter especially he is to co-operate, if his design shall take effect. For his design is nothing less than to fetch out a body from the curse, and to raise it up from the dead; which never can be done by him, that is still dead himself, both in his understanding, and as to his internal life.

IX. —With all this, the process in the regeneration of man runs parallel exactly. Consider only with thyself the heavenly humanity of the regenerator, and the earthly of poor fallen man, that is to be regenerated: consider, that the former must be received or taken in by the latter, and that this must suffer itself to be subdued, changed, kept under, and turned in by that. Consider that faith in man is absolutely required, by which he must in a sense co-operate indeed, but that for all this, he cannot make himself a child of God; but must suffer himself to be made so by the eternal speaking Word, which in the philosophical process is called by Behmen, the heavenly mercury, which also at the end of time, as in the completest period of the regeneration, will raise up his body again, which then shall no more be earthly, but heavenly, and conformable to his own glorified body.

Consider all this in its true coherence, and dependence upon the only love and free grace of God: and you will certainly find, that all the description of this process, is nothing else but a sound true, solid, explanation of these words of St. John, *As many as received him, to them gave he power to become the sons of God, even to them that believe in his name.*

X. —In these words also lieth plainly, the possibility for obtaining the perfection in the philosophical work: which is rightly and firmly grounded here-upon by Behmen.

For if God gave us, out of his infinite love, that which is the greatest and highest, how could he have withheld from us, that which is much lesser and lower? If man, in this divine power, bestowed upon him by free grace, can verily rule and triumph again over sin, death, devil, and hell, whom he made himself subject unto by his lust, Why should he not also be enabled thereby, to rule and triumph again over the curse in the earth, he brought into it by the same lust? When this latter is but a natural consequence of that former; nay an inconsiderable ode in comparison to that. Truly it is inseparable therefrom, *if that former be really attained unto, and provided that all the qualities that are requisite thereto, be verily found in the artist or Philosopher.*

XI—All these qualities are, as in their principal sum and substance, concentrated in this, *that the artist first must have the curse transmuted in himself into the heavenly blessing, through that holy tincturing blood of Jesus Christ.* Which Behmen thus sometimes expresses, He must first be, and have really that same in himself, which he will make or introduce into metals without himself. And this he frequently presseth home unto every one, warning earnestly and calling heaven and earth to be witnesses, that *none shall presume to meddle with the curse in the earth, before he be really delivered*, as to his inward man, *from that curse in himself*; or else he may expect to earn nothing else but curse instead of blessing. Before this, his own internal deliverance, he may have indeed many fine notions of this work in his brain; but *the real process cannot be manifest in him, and so not understood by him, in that experimental fulness and exactness which is required.*

XII—This same he also offers to the serious consideration of such a one, under these and the like philosophical terms, He is to know that his Mercury is kindled in the fiery Mars, and burns in the eternal Saturn, in the terrible impression of darkness; his Venus is captivated, his water dried up, his Jupiter is become a fool, his Sun is darkened, and his Moon turned into a black night. And now there is no other remedy but to take Venus, (the eternal love of God) and to introduce that into his poisoned

Mercury and Mars, that they may be tinctured thereby, and then his sun will shine again and Jupiter rejoice, etc. Which he represents afterwards in plain words from his own way, *practice* and *experience*.

XIII. —Yet all this, though really attained unto, will not be yet fully sufficient. For there is not only such a sufficient *ability* for this work, and a sufficient *understanding* of its process required, which I doubt not but Behmen had: but there is also required an *especial calling* thereunto, which he had not. Without this calling the artist goes but in his own will; though his meaning and intent, as to his thinking were never so good and pure. And this call he must be able to discern, by its own internal character, which it carrieth along with and in itself, from his own natural impulse. Which easily may delude him, under the specious appearance of a divine call; and whereby the spirit of this world, which from its own internal constitution, is mightily for such an undertaking, will certainly mislead him into various dangers.

XIV. —When now these two more general requisites, viz.,

(1.) An experimental understanding, from the artist's process in his own regeneration, and (2. a Divine call for this undertaking, are truly found in him, two other more particular qualities will still be required in him, when he now is to make a beginning of his work.

And these are represented by Behmen from that parable of our Lord, concerning a man that went down from Jerusalem to Jericho, and was robbed and wounded by highwaymen;

Saying, That the artist must truly and wholly stand in the figure of the merciful Samaritan and must have both his *will* and *eyes*. His will, that he may desire nothing else, but to heal and restore that which is wounded and broken: his eyes, that he may be able to discern that wounded body which he is to heal, and which is not easily to be discerned, and not by every one, because of its great corruption.

XV. —These eyes he shall have the greatest need of in his very first beginning, to choose the proper matter for this work. This is called by Behmen and described parabolically, That evil child, which is run from its mother's house, (from Jerusalem to Jericho) and desired to be in self, or to stand by itself upon its own bottom. And this must be sought for in Saturn; which Saturn therefore, the artist must have sharp and piercing eyes to look into, both as to eternal and temporal nature. For the wrath of God, by its strong astringent impression, (says he) hath shut it up into the chamber of death. Not that it hath turned the same into Saturn.

But it keeps it imprisoned in the Saturninish death, in the first cold, hard, dark, astringent property; which is called the great still standing death, because as yet there is no mobility of life therein.

XVI.—When this proper matter is found in Saturn, the artist may go to work, but so, *that he do consider and follow that same PROCESS, which God observed in the redemption of mankind through Jesus Christ,* (in which twofold holy Name, the general process was clearly understood by Behmen from the language of Nature,) even from his conception and nativity, unto his resurrection and ascension. So doing, he may come to find the joyful feast of Pentecost, viz. that desirable tincture in outward nature, which is answering unto that holy spiritual tincture, whereby St. Peter, in his first public sermon, on the day of Pentecost, tinctured three thousand souls at once. Now observe,

XVII.—When the human mercury, the outspoken word of the human life, was infected and poisoned by the serpent, or made manifest in its own natural quality, which it hath in itself, before and without the light, God did not reject the humanity, so as to annihilate it wholly, and to make another new, and strange Adam, but he regenerated that which was spoiled. And this he effected not by any such new or strange thing, as which the humanity had not had in it before; but by that self-same holy divine mercury, which at first was breathed into Adam, for to make him an image and likeness of God.

This he re-introduced again into the poisoned humanity, and made thereby a good, sure and solid disposition to the new regeneration thereof. And this was done in the immaculate conception of Jesus Christ. For therein a conjunction was made, between the eternal speaking, and the human outspoken word, mercury, or human life, now poisoned in man, and full of self, or own will.

XVIII.—This must be the first consideration of the artist. Well to be observed, that so he may be sure to act accordingly, and to bring not his subject matter to the fire, without such a previous conjunction; if he will not work in vain, and make himself ridiculous. And for an illustration hereof this may serve: in the Second Principle, of light, the love-desire, that is, the first property of eternal nature, but considered as in the fifth, makes a pure christalline substantiality. And therein the divine mercury is the eternal holy Word and understanding: but in the first principle, wherein the harsh astringent desire makes a dark obscure substantiality, the same mercury is a principal part, or chief property of the wrath of God, and an original of all mobility, and moving power. This mercury therefore (considered as in the outspoken Word, or life of man,) after it was turned away from the second principle, of light and love, and was made manifest according to its own wrathful property in the first; could not have been restored or brought back again, but by that very same mercury, which was first breathed into man, and was not altered in the light and love of God, though it was altered in man, in whom it disappeared and lost its former pre-dominion. Now the getting this lost pre-dominion again, either in man, or in any other creature, according to its own kind, is nothing else, but *that same tincturing* and transmuting, which *in all this discourse* is spoken of; and which pre-dominion therefore of that heavenly mercury must needs reproduce again such a pure light's substantiality, as that which disappeared in man, by his fall, and in the earth by the curse.

XIX. —In the relation of St. Luke, concerning what the child Jesus did with his parents, in the twelfth year of his age, a representation is seen of the inward and outward world, and of their different wills. For the inward will in Jesus broke first the natural will of his parents, when he remained in the temple, without their knowing and consent, nay, said also like as rebuking them, How is it that ye sought me? Wist ye not that I must be about my Father's business?

And then again, the will of this outward world in his parents, broke the inward will in Jesus, for he went down with them to Nazareth, and was subject unto them. This showeth to the artist, that in his work he shall soon find such a two-fold will also. The will of the inward world, will not in the beginning presently condescend and be subject to his will.

But if he *ceaseth not to seek after it*, as Mary did, and *wrestleth with it all the night* like Jacob, with a *full resignation* of his own will, which is the will of this outward world, this Divine will, will at length condescend to him, and go down with him; for it is as it were broken or conquered by his will.

XX. —Here the artist, or magus is to know, that he is not to bring that will or tendency to the perfection, into this matter from without, but that it lieth therein already before.

He must only *first in himself* be capable of the Divine will, and then with his own renewed, or tinctured will, which here is his *magical faith*, he must handle his subject matter; that so thereby the will towards perfection, which lieth in the matter indeed, but still and unmoveable, may be stirred up and brought into conjunction with his human tinctured will, and so also with the Divine will. And that further this Divine will may press forward or outwards, meet with and bless that outward will, which presseth backwards or inwards from the corruption into God's love and mercy,

XXI. —*Highly is this point recommended* unto the artist, not only for to *consider and understand*, but also *to make it his continual practice. Because herein the Philosophical baptism, as to the greatest part consisteth*, and this *practice* is the *very first beginning thereof.* This only can make him able to baptise truly and rightly, for he is to baptize his matter, not only with the water of the outward, but also with that of the inward world. Of which more hereafter.

XXII. —The poor fallen humanity considered so barely as it was in, and to itself, viz. as broken, spoiled, poisoned, was not cast immediately into the fiery furnace, and melted down by the wrath of God; but, as said before, a conjunction was first made between the earthly and heavenly humanity.

Neither came the great fiery trial upon it, immediately after this conjunction; but a long and wonderful process was held, before it came to that great earnest. First, the humanity was to be baptized with water in the Jordan, and with water from above the firmament. Further, it was led into the wilderness, for to be tempted by the devil, which devil (N.B.) was not put into the humanity, but permitted to stand over against it, and to offer unto it all that the first Adam was tempted with. And all this time of forty days, no outward food was given to this new baptized humanity, but it was to live upon its own life's mercurius, viz. the eternal Word proceeding from the mouth of God, according to the answer the Lord Jesus gave unto the devil. After this he came forth in public, preached, and did great wonders in all the seven properties of nature. And though at length even his human body was really glorified upon the holy mount, and seen so by three of his disciples, yet by all this, the full perfection was not yet wrought out, but the very greatest, sharpest trial was still behind. Answerably to all this process, the Philosophical work also must be carried on, and the artist will see a continual parallelism; but at length he will find also, that all this, though it was shown him in never so glorious an appearance, is still short of perfection, and all but as it were preliminary.

XXIII. —By the Philosophical baptism, if it be truly performed, in the dead mercury, which lieth in impotence, and hungers only after its own property, being of itself not capable, either of desiring after, or of admitting into it any other, the hunger after the heavenly substantiality is stirred and raised up again.

And by this hunger, that heavenly substantiality is *drawn in*, with its own peculiar will, desire, or inclination, which is nothing else but a readiness, or tendency to become manifest with its life in the death. And herein is the first beginning of a new body, or rather of a seed, from which a new body is to come forth in its due time.

XXIV. —What this Philosophical Baptism is, and the absolute necessity thereof, may be thus represented. Every hunger is a desire after such a thing as is conformable to that hunger: for after that which is disagreeing and contrary to it, no hunger in anything can be. The dead corrupted mercury then hath a hunger indeed, but only (according to its own condition in the curse), after death, wrath and poison, etc. If now to this hunger such a dead and wrathful thing is given, as it hungers after, the death therein must needs increase, and its wrathfulness must be strengthened thereby. But if to this hunger the life is presented, or a living, heavenly property is offered, the death is not at all able to receive it. Unto this death therefore, the death and wrath of God must be given, but in this death and wrath the heavenly substantiality. And this is the Philosophical baptism, for this is that earthly and heavenly water, in the first of which is death, and in the second life: both which must be together; for the reason is now plain, why neither by this nor by that alone, this baptism can be performed. But when it is thus rightly done, this baptism, viz., that which is heavenly swalloweth up into death, that which is earthly and wrathful, and exalts its own new life therein; though not immediately, like as it also was not done in Christ immediately after his baptism.

XXV.—This Philosophical baptism is nothing else but a conjunction, to be made between the fiery and watery mercury. The fiery must be baptised with the watery. And this is what Behmen means by saying obscurely: have a care only for this, that thou baptisest the mercury with his own baptism. For this watery mercury is his own, viz. it is that, which [before—Ed.] the fall and curse he enjoyed and rejoiced in, as his most precious treasure; whereby his fiery poisonous wrath, was kept under, and prevented from being manifest. But when these two were separated from each other, a breach was made, which cannot be healed again, but by a renewed conjunction between them.

Like as it is in animals and in fallen man also the same thing, only different in degrees.

The conjunction of male and female, which is absolutely required, to the multiplication of every kind of living creatures (which hath in vegetables also something answering thereunto), may be a good illustration thereof. And therefore it is

XXVI. —That by Behmen this very same, which here now is called also the philosophical baptism, is called also a matrimony or espousal, when he plainly says, not only that to the earthly wrathful mercury, a fair loving virgin of his own kind must be given in marriage, but also that this same giving is the philosophical baptism.

And again says he, The woman's (not the man's) seed shall bruise the serpent's head. The man hath in his tincture the fire-spirit, and the woman in her's the water-spirit.

This latter must baptise, soften, and overcome that former, and so transmute its strong fiery hunger after wrath, into a tender love-desire; and herein lieth the baptism of nature. In this stedfast love-desire, these two are at last turned into one, so that they are no more male and female, fire and water in contrariety, but a masculine virgin with both tinctures in union. But before this be wholly effected, and as long as they are in the way and process thereunto, Behmen calleth them in all this discourse, the *young man* and the *virgin*, or also the bride and the bridegroom.

XXVII. —Immediately after the baptism of Christ, he was led by the Spirit into the wilderness, to be tempted by the devil. And a serious consideration of the whole process in this threefold temptation, is highly recommended to the artist. For in this philosophical work the same must be done also, in a total answerableness to the three particulars therein, relating to the three first properties. All which is largely declared by Behmen, the sum and substance whereof, is this:

XXVIII. —The human soul, or the whole humanity as an image of the eternal speaking Word, was now tried, after God had re-introduced into it a spark of his eternal love, whether it would enter again into its primeval state and place and be an instrument of God, to be played upon by the holy Spirit, in his love; or whether it would rather continue in his own will, and suffer the devil to play upon its instrument in the wrath and anger of God. And so in the philosophical work also, the earthly poisonous mercury, after he is now joined again to the heavenly, is tried, whether he will go out from his own natural wrathful property, and suffer himself to be turned into his first, pure and crystalline condition, wherein he stood before the curse: or whether he will rather continue in his own awakened and now predominant quality.

XXIX. —In our Lord Jesus Christ, the human will rejected all the devil's presentations and offerings, resigned itself, and entered wholly into the first mother's womb, according to his words to Nicodemus, etc. And so in the philosophical work, if it goes well and right the artist will see, that when the tempter comes on, the young man, or mercury gives himself up wholly into the first mother, and that this will swallow him up as into nothing. At which the artist will be amazed and terrified, thinking that all is lost and undone, for he sees nothing, and has lost all appearance of heaven. But he must have patience, that which is impossible in his sight, is not so in the powers of nature.

XXX. —The wilderness wherein this temptation is done, is, in this philosophical work, the outward, earthly, dry, desolate and barren body.

Wherein the young man, or the mercury is not able to stand against the devil, unless he lay hold on his virgin, and be by her supported. He is, therefore, to unite with her, to cast his will and desire into her love, and to eat of her bread, not of his own natural quality, like as Christ our Lord, all the forty days of his temptation, did eat only of the eternal speaking word, and would not eat of that bread, which he could have made out of the stones. All which is nothing else but that mercury must admit and receive into its own poisonous quality, the heavenly tincture, and suffer the serpent's head, the fiery, wrathful property, to be bruised thereby in himself. Which if he doth not, the devil will prevail, and detain him captive in that state, wherein he is, when separated from his virgin. But if he doth the devil must withdraw, and the virgin takes his seed from him into her womb.

XXXI. —What the devil is in this work, the artist (says Behmen) will easily know, but he calls him not by any plain or distinct name: doubtless it is such another wrathful dark and poisonous matter, as may be fitly compared to the devil, and may be able to do in this process, the devil's office, because of the qualities alike in both. Thus says he, he shall have a care, to suffer not, that this tempting devil be too furious, or too wrathful, but proportionable, etc.

And again, on the other hand, that he be not too weak, for else the mercury should not be assaulted by him sufficiently, and might as a hungry wolf, swallow up his baptism, return to his own wrathful property, and continue still that same poisonous thing, which he was before.

XXXII. —At the end of forty days, when the devil had ended all the temptation, he must depart from the Lord Christ, and the angels came and ministered unto him. This also the artist is especially well to observe, for he himself stood here in the fiery trial also, and may now perceive infallibly, whether or no, he be fit for, and accounted worthy of his work. If at the end of forty days, in answerableness to the process of Christ, the angels do not appear, he may surely think of himself, that he is not yet fit and worthy; and of his fiery masculine mercury, that this doth not yet stand in a due internal union with the watery feminine, but that it is still that same, in its own wrathful property, which it was before, and that the devil hath prevailed. But if he seeth the sign of the angels, he may rejoice and be sure, that the bridegroom is in his bride, and she in him, and that his work can prosper. What this sign of the angels is, the author saith not expressly; it must be some new delightful appearance, by its own character so intelligible to the artist, as that was intelligible unto him, when before he saw nothing, and had lost the appearance of heaven.

XXXIII.—Immediately after this temptation, and overcoming of the devil, the Lord Christ began his public office, not only by preaching, reproving and instructing the people, but also, by working many great miracles, through all the properties of nature. For instance: in Saturn, he raised up the dead; in Luna, he transmuted water into wine, and fed with five loaves of bread five thousand men; in Jupiter, he made out of the ignorant and simple fishermen, the most wise and understanding apostles; in Mercury, he made the deaf hearing, the dumb speaking, and healed the lepers; in Mars he expelled devils from the possessed: in Venus, he loved his brethren and sisters, as to the humanity, and gave freely his life for into death. Only six of the properties are here enumerated, and the seventh which is Sol, standing in the midst and uniting three and three, is here not mentioned, because this belongeth to the full perfection, which then only was attained unto, when he was risen from the dead, ascended up to heaven, and had poured out the holy tincturing spirit, on the day of Pentecost. But that Behmen hath a good ground for referring distinctly to all the seven properties of nature, all the miraculous deeds, could be made out sufficiently from him, were it needful.

XXXIV. —All this now the artist shall distinctly see, that it hath an exact answerableness in the Philosophical work, when the forty days temptation with good success is ended. In Saturn, he shall see, that now the mercury raiseth up from death, that same substance, wherein he was shut up before. In Luna, that he feedeth and nourisheth that substance, when there is nothing outwardly wrought, which it could be fed and nourished with: and again, that the deadly water is exalted and turned into wine, by having now got (like as wine hath) an union of a fiery and watery virtue. In Jupiter, he shall see the four elements each by itself, and their colours, and the rainbow upon which Christ sitteth for Judgment, in the outspoken mercury; so that he highly shall be amazed at it, and perceive that the wisdom of God playeth and delighteth therein. For the friendly Jupiter showeth forth his properties herein, after such a manner as that is, in which God will, in its time change this world, and transmute it into paradise.

In Mercury, he shall see that heaven separates itself from the earth, and that it sinks down again into the earth, and changeth the same into its own colour, and that mercury purifieth the matter, etc. In Mars, he shall see, that Jupiter in the Mercury, casts out from the matter upwards a black fire smoke, which will be coagulated like as soot in the chimney. And this is the poisonous hunger in the mercury, rightly to be compared to the devil, because it hath, according to its own kind, the devil's qualities. What Christ did in Venus, the artist shall see most gloriously in the Philosophical

Work. For as soon as this black devil is expelled from the matter, Venus in her virginity appears, in great beauty and glory, which is a fine type or emblem of the great love of Christ.

XXXV. —Now here, when this appears, the artist is rejoiced, and thinks reasonably his work is finished, and he hath got the treasure of the world; but soon shall he find himself extremely disappointed. For when he trieth it, he shall find, it is but Venus, still a female, and not yet a pure and perfect virgin, with both tinctures united into one. Like as in Christ, the eternal speaking Word had indeed wrought out through his humanity, all these wondrous deeds; and yet the full perfection could not be made manifest therein, his human body could not be glorified, and much less could he have poured out the Holy Ghost, before he was passed through the great anger of God or death and hell. So also in this philosophical work, though all these glorious things have appeared in the properties of nature, yet the universal tincture is not yet fixed and manifest, but all what was seen hitherto, was only transient, and the greatest work to be done, for this fixation and manifestation, is still behind. For all the seven properties must be made totally pure and crystalline, before they can be paradisical, and each of them hath its own peculiar process, when it is to go out from the wrathful into the paradisical life; wherein they must all seven have but one will, viz. that of love, and all their former own will, wherein each was for itself, in opposition to the others, must be utterly swallowed up. And then only they are fixed, and able to abide the fire, for then no Turba can be more therein.

Which is now further effected by a process answering to that which was observed in the suffering and death of Christ.

XXXVI. —As soon as the regenerator of mankind came into this world, from above, and had the name of a king given him, the *civil government* thereof could not endure him; but presently he was by Herod persecuted, and at length by Pilate crucified, though he had plainly declared that his kingdom was not of this world. And because this newborn king came not with a royal state and splendour, nor in such an outward power, as the Jews expected and hoped for, at the coming of their Messiah, the *ecclesiastical government* in the high priest and Pharisees, would not receive him.

And since he owned himself to be the Son of God, and a king of truth, and said he was come to save his people from their sins and darkness, and from the wrath to come, the *devil* also could not endure him. But he was immediately a strong opposition against all these three together in conjunction. So also in this philosophical work, as soon as Venus thus appears in her beauty, with her own natural character, and in order to perfection, there is a great alarum, opposition and insurrection against her, manifest in Saturn, Mercury, and Mars, the first of which is a true figure of the civil government, the second of the ecclesiastical state, and the third of the devil. And as these three jointly were the same chief agents, that brought the Lord of Life and Glory unto death; so in this philosophical work, the three inferior wrathful properties, Saturn, Mercury, and Mars, are rightly called by Behmen the murderers of Venus.

XXXVII. —This great opposition and uproar against the Lord Christ, had, in the internal truth and reality no other ground but this, that he was from above, when all these three were from beneath.

Deep, great, and many things are in these few words comprised, and the essential nature of a Principle (taken in Behmen's sense) is understood therein. If the Lord had been out of their own dark, harsh, bitter and wrathful root, and if he had appeared, for to preserve and establish the same, in its own selfish and wilful qualities, they would have received him very kindly, and no opposition could have been made.

But he was from another principle, and came only for to destroy the works of the devil in this world, and to recall its inhabitants unto light, love and truth. Now all this was bad news in the ears of all these three parties, for none of them was willing to be stript of its selfish greatness, dignity, strength and power, and therefore they all three at length agreed for his crucifixion. So also in this philosophical work, there is no other ground for this great opposition, but this very same, that Venus is from above, when these three are from beneath; united in one wrathful sphere, and unwilling to be deprived of their natural power and pre-dominion.

Heaven stands now in hell, upon earth, and will transmute them both into paradise; and hell perceiveth its ruin is inevitable, if it receives into it this child from heaven, and therefore it swelleth up against it, and opposeth all what it can. But by this same opposition, it must and doth but promote its own destruction; as it was done also in the process of Christ.

XXXVIII. —Here might be objected, How can all this be consistent with what was done and declared above, viz. that the matter was purified, the devil expelled, and the sign of the angels appeared, etc.?

For if so, whence can now such a wrathful, hellish opposition arise. The answer given to this by Behmen himself, (though but implicitly, and not so directly) is of the greatest importance not only in this philosophical process, but also especially in that of man's regeneration. When Mercury, says he, is awakened from the death of Saturn's strong impression, and receiveth manna (heavenly food, light's and love's substantiality, his own true virgin, the water of life, the philosophical baptism) into the mouth of his poisonous property, a joyful crack ariseth indeed; for it is like as if a light were kindled in the darkness, and a paradisical joy and triumph ariseth in the midst of the wrath. When now this mercury thus gets a twinkling glimpse thereof in Mars, the wrathfulness is terrified at the love, and sinketh back, like as in the generation of the second principle out of the first; and the angelical properties appear as in a glimpse.

And so this is (N.B. not yet a transmutation but) like as a transmutation, but only transient but not yet fixed.

If therefore a fixed and radical transmutation shall be done, the same process, that was in this like a transmutation, must be repeated again; but in a far higher or rather deeper degree. And the same can also be repeated, because the harsh, bitter, wrathful hellish properties were hitherto suppressed only in part, but not fully rooted out, and radically turned into one only will. And they therefore are now raised afresh by this appearance of Venus, nay even much more than they were before, they stand up in opposition against her, for to maintain their own natural right. So that here also, in a sense, the words of Christ are true, I am come to kindle a fire, and to bring upon earth a sword, enmity, etc.

XXXIX.—This opposition is, in this Philosophical work, between three and three; like as it is also in the generation or eternal nature.

Yet this is to be understood in such a sense, as the foregoing position can bear, wherein there was asserted, That here nothing as yet is permanent and fixed. So it was also in the process with the Lord Christ: when he was a going into the strong severity of the wrath and anger of God, in order to the full consummation of his great work, he said expressly of himself, I am not alone, but the Father is with me. He had then with him on the one side, or from above, the Father, and him unalterably, in one sense, though changeably in another, relating to the sensibility of his outward human person. Which may appeal, by his woeful crying out on the cross, My God, My God, why hast thou forsaken me? For that which here by some now is objected, concerning a wrong translation of these words, is not to be regarded, because the sense of them is not as they imagine. And on the other side, or as from beneath, he had with him, though in a very low degree, and in considerable sense, the common ignorant people, which received and accompanied him with great joy and acclamations, when he came riding upon an ass into Jerusalem. So also in this philosophical work, Venus is not alone, but, as it were, from above, Jupiter is with her, and from beneath Luna, which is a true figure of that vulgar, simple, ignorant crew. This Luna holds with Venus, so long as it goes well with her, that is so long as Saturn, Mercury, and Mars do not actually exert their malice against her, but when these three murderers arise, and will forcibly put her to death, or swallow her up into their wrathful pit, then Luna also changeth her colour and inclination; like as the vulgar people changed their will, and instead of their former hosanna, cried now out, Crucify, crucify him.

XL.—In the process of Christ, when it cometh to the great earnest, not only that which was done with him outwardly, by the Pharisees, High Priests, etc., but also that which was done within his own person, in body, soul, and spirit must be considered.

The Two eternal Principles, viz. the fire world with its properties of wrath and anger, and the holy light world, with the pure love and light's substantiality, or heavenly flesh and blood, were both manifest in him, and stood open the one against the other; and the great work of redemption could not have been performed, except they entered into one another *essentially*; for else no solid, fixed, permanent transmutation of the first into the second, could have been effected.

This now made an inexpressible terror in the humanity of Christ, viz. in his whole person, considered in all the Three worlds or Principles. For the love was struck with terror, and trembled at the rough, harsh, bitter death, which it was to give up itself into; so as to be swallowed up by the wrathful properties of anger, all now distinctly raised up and qualifying according to their own nature. And the anger also was struck with terror, and trembled at the appearance of love, wherein it was to lose its own wrathful and now predominant life. And so from hence the outward human body also, in this third principle, was so violently struck with terror and trembling, that the sweat thereof was, as it were great drops of blood, falling down to the ground. Yet he said then, Father, if it be possible, let this cup pass from me, yet not my will, but thine be done; which words are to be understood, as spoken by the whole person of Christ, viz. in each world and property, according to the different condition of each.

For the first principle, or anger said, Let this cup of love be removed from me, that I may keep my dominion in men, because of their transgression; like as we may see an excellent type thereof in Moses, when the wrath of God said unto him, Let me alone, that I may devour this disobedient people; but Moses in the figure of Christ, and Christ in the highest operation of love, would not let him, but replied, first indeed as it were to the same purpose, If it be possible let this cup pass from me, but added also immediately, Yet not my will, but thine be done. Whereby the human will of Christ as to this Third Principle resigned wholly and submitted itself to the will of the angry father and was obedient unto him, even unto the death on the cross.

So also in this philosophical work, when it cometh to this great earnest, the artist shall plainly perceive a great terror and trembling therein; he shall see, that Mercury especially, which is the principal agent against Venus, trembleth at the appearance of Venus, and that Venus also not only trembleth at this opposition of the three wrathful murdering properties, but also that it is with her like as if a sweat did break out from her body; and that nevertheless she is not stirring, but quiet and resigned to suffer all that they can inflict upon her, and to be wholly swallowed up by them into their wrathfulness.

XLI.—In the process of Christ, the devil said, or thought within himself, I am alone the great monarch in the fire, Saturn is my might, and Mercury is my life, and I am in, and through them, a god and prince of this world, and will therefore not suffer such a one as calls himself a Prince of Love, to rule therein, but I will devour him in my wrath, together with his love. This he intended indeed, with concurrence of the two principal properties of this outward world, Saturn and Mercury, the civil and ecclesiastical government. Thus also in the Philosophical work the artist shall plainly see, that Venus, which is all passive and wholly resigned to enter into the dragon's jaws, is surrounded on every side by Saturn, Mercury, and Mars, nay, also that they lay hold on her. and bind her, by injecting their poisonous rays upon her, etc.

XLII.—In the first place, Mars bringeth Venus to Mercury, like as the devil's agents in the anger of God, brought the Lord first to the high priest. But as this was already beforehand prepossessed with hatred against him, and did not duly or truly try him, nor could look into his internal will and work of love, but looked upon him only from without, examined him superficially, and concluded, that since he stood not with them, in the same will, way, and form, he was not to be tolerated among the living. But seeing that he could not execute his design, to kill him, he sent him to Pilate, with the character of an evil doer, that had deserved death. So also in this philosophical work, this very same is the true internal signature of Mercury, against Venus.

He was already before possessed with his own hateful quality, and stood in opposition against her, and is therefore not able to try, much less to approve of the loving property of Venus, but hath only a will and ability to murder her. But seeing that there is in Venus another living Mercury, from above, he cannot destroy her by his own power, but must confederate himself with Saturn; and unto him he delivereth this Venus, for to be killed, like as Christ was delivered to Pontius Pilate to be crucified.

XLIII.—Pilate, a governor or lord in the dark Saturnish impression, did little inquire after, or concern himself about the spiritual doctrine, light, love, and truth of Christ, but only about the government; and upon this only account of Christ's being against Caesar, and his own coveting to be accounted Caesar's friend, he sentenced him unto death. So here also in the philosophical work, Saturn, the dark astringent property, does not at all concern itself, with this or that internal loving quality of Venus, being not able to receive anything thereof into its own essence; but only for the pre-dominion in this great contest. Saturn will not lose the friendship of Mars and Mercury, which both are with him in the same sphere, and jointly make up therein their own government, which needs must be overthrown, if Venus should be permitted to arise, and shine therein, with her light and love. And therefore he puts in execution that which is well pleasing unto them, and which they think may make for their wrathful government.

XLIV.—Pilate sent the Lord Christ unto Herod, and this mocked him, and put on him a long white garment. In this philosophical work, Herod the king answereth unto Sol, who is a king also in his own principal. And this Sol puts upon Venus a simple, lunarish white colour; for it perceiveth that there lieth in Venus a solarish kingly power, and therefore it giveth unto her the white colour, from the eternal liberty's property, and would fain see, that she might open therein her powers from the fire's centre, and show forth herself in a golden lustre, which, if Venus did, she would be indeed a master over Mars and Mercury, but only in this outward world, a ruler in the wrath, like as this Sol is. But as the Lord said unto Pilate, My kingdom is not of this world, and would answer nothing unto Herod, nor his expectation by working a miracle before him, because in this white garment he stood only before the justice of God, and represented the poor, fallen Adam, in his false love of himself, whereof this white robe was a very significant figure, deeply declared by Behmen. So also in the philosophical work a breaking forth of the solarish power, in a golden lustre from the fire's centre, and tincturing this white lunarish appearance of Venus, is all in vain expected; because the pure union, and universal tincture cannot be made manifest, except first all the dark wrath and poison of Saturn, Mercury, and Mars, be wholly drowned and swallowed up in blood and death.

XLV.—Herod sent the Lord Christ back again to Pilate, and this, by his soldiers, stript him, put him on a scarlet robe, scourged him, put on his head a crown of thorns, and showed him to the multitude, who cried out, Crucify him, etc. So also in the philosophical work, Venus is delivered again unto Saturn, and he, with his strong, dark impression, lays hold of her, strips her of her fair robe, and puts on her a scarlet colour, wherein the wrath of Mars is lodged. This colour is from Saturn's and Mercury's property, mixed with the fiery Mars, as the artist shall distinctly see. When, now, the Lord Christ, in this royal robe, which was put upon him but in scorn, was presented to the pharisees, priests, and people, they all cried out, Away with him, we own no other king but Caesar. So also, when Venus, in this royal colour, appears unto Mercury, Saturn, and Mars, and Luna also, they all together, with one consent reject, that is, they dart forth their malignant, poisonous, fiery rays upon, and imprint the same in her, by the sharp impression of Saturn, so that the artist shall see distinctly, that Venus is like as scourged and full of spots. And moreover, which is indeed the greatest wonder, he shall exactly see the crown of thorns, with its sharp, stinging prickles, is put upon her.

For as the *whole process* in the suffering and death of *Christ*, is a *circumstantial representation* of all what the first Adam had acted in his transgression, in a *quite contrary way*, which is distinctly shown and declared by Behmen. And as the *condition of man in the fall*, is the same with the *earth's condition in the curse*, only different from it in degree, which he demonstrateth sufficiently. So also *the manner and process of their restoration, cannot but be alike in both*.

And as the Lord Christ in all his sufferings was most profoundly humble, and only passive, in a full submission to his Father's pleasure, so also, in this philosophical work, Venus is wholly quiet and passive, etc.

(*a.*) Many particulars more are by Behmen observed, but they shall be but mentioned in short. The three nails wherewith Christ was nailed to the cross, are referred to the three first sharp, piercing properties. (*b.*) The two figures of the Virgin Mary and St. John, standing under the cross, are referred to the young man's and the virgin's life, now appearing distinctly, (*c.*) The words of Christ, *Father, forgive them, they know not what they do*, are deeply and excellently declared by Behmen, (1.) as to the redemption of mankind, by showing, when Jesus destroyed death and selfhood in the humanity, he did not throw away that human property, wherein the anger of God was kindled before, but even then he took it truely unto himself, i.e. he took even then rightly the outward, out-spoken kingdom of wonders into the inward. (2.) As to the philosophical work, in showing that the three murderers when drowned in the lion's blood, do not pass away, but are forgiven, i.e, their former wrathfulness, as to its natural quality, is not annihilated, but turned in the highest love-desire, (*d.*) The two thieves are referred to the kingdom of the devil in the wrath, and to the kingdom of love in the light, which two kingdoms are now separated the one from the other. (*e.*) The words of Christ, saying to his mother, Woman, behold thy son, and to St. John, Behold thy mother, are excellently discoursed of by Behmen, not only with reference to the redemption of mankind, and to the universal church, but also to the philosophical work; wherein the artist is to know, that he must imitate St. John, that all his work is done only in or about the mother, that is, the kingdom of outward nature, from which Christ here departeth; that his work *in this world never will become wholly celestial,* that he cannot manifest therein the paradise, so as that God should appear therein face to face. But that he must abide all the time of this, in the mother only, though be verily obtaineth the universal tincture in this mother. Like as the mother of Christ also obtained it, in her being called by the angel, the Blessed among the women; notwithstanding which, she was afterwards to pass through temporal death, etc.

So also the artist obtaineth the blessing in this miserable world, so that he may tincture his corrupted earthly body, and preserve it in health, unto the termination or end of his highest constellation, which is after or under Saturn.

(*f.*) Concerning the words of Christ, I thirst, and the vinegar mingled with gall, which when he had tasted, he would not drink, are profoundly declared (1.) as an outward, most significant figure of what was transacted inwardly between the holy name Jesus, and the anger of God awakened in the human soul. The name Jesus thirsted after the salvation of men, and would fain have tasted the pure living water in the human property; but the anger of God in the soul, gave itself into this thirsting love desire, which the love would not drink, but yielded up itself, in a full resignation and obedience thereinto. Vinegar and gall are the proper figure of the human soul, viz. of these properties wherein the human soul essentially standeth, when without the light. The soul now here given again into the holy light's substantiality, which was in Adam, disappeared, etc. This caused such a two-fold crack, or shriek, as in the generation of eternal nature was explained.

The first terrible crack made the earth to quake, and rent the rocks asunder, etc. The second joyful crack raised the dead bodies of them that had hoped and waited for the coming of the Mesias, and rent also the vail in the temple, from the top to beneath, uniting now the human time with eternity, etc. And (2.) as to the philosophical work, wherein Venus also thirsteth after the manifestation and pre-dominion of the fire of love; but Mercury, in the sulphur of Mars and Saturn, presseth itself into her, with his killing menstruum, which is the greatest poison, or the dark, wrathful source. But Venus, instead of drinking the same down, yieldeth up herself wholly thereinto, as if she did actually die. And from hence the great darkness in the philosophical work ariseth, so that the whole matter cometh to be as black as a raven.

(*g.*) When the inward sun of the eternal light's principle, in the humanity, had given up itself into the dark wrath and anger of God, the outward sun in this third principle, which taketh all its glance and lustre from that inward, as a representation, or mirror thereof, could not shine. For if its root or deepest ground (considered as in the region of this world) was gone down into darkness, for to renew this principle into the light, the outbirth of this root, the outward sun, must needs have been darkened, contrary to the common course of nature, and this even from the sixth hour of the day unto the ninth, which was the time of the first Adam's sleep, etc. In the philosophical work, as the artist shall see, all what God hath done, in and with the humanity, when he was to redeem and bring it again into paradise; so he shall see also in answerableness to this great supernatural darkness, that when Venus thus yieldeth up her life, which all her glance and lustre dependeth upon, all her beauty must disappear, and darkness cometh up instead thereof. He shall see also, that not only Venus, in the three wrathful properties, but also that these three themselves, in Venus, do lose their life all together, and that all is now so black and dark as a coal. For here now life and death lie together still and quiet in the will of God, and to his only disposition. The whole is now reduced to the *beginning*, and standeth in that order, wherein it stood before the creation. Nature's end is now attained unto, and all is fallen home unto, or into, the power of the first Fiat.

(*h.*) After this, the Lord cried out, My God, why hast thou forsaken me? The eternal, speaking Word stood now still, in the humanity, *i.e.* it did not operate therein, so as to be sensibly felt thereby. For the heavenly humanity, which in Adam was disappeared, and in Christ quickened again, was to bruise the head of the wrath, in the fiery soul, and to change the soul's fire into a clear, shining sun. That now this might be done, the humanity must be introduced into this wrath, by the eternal, speaking Word, and by the same also, through this wrath and death, into the solarish or paradisical life. When now this was done, the humanity could not but feel that wrath in the soul, and in the same instant of this feeling, it could not feel the presence and power of the eternal speaking Word, so as it could and did before, etc. And this was the forsaking.

So also in the philosophical work, when the wrathful properties swallow up the life of Venus, which is to change them into Sol, and to make that all seven may be but one, Venus is forsaken.

And this makes her to lose her colour, and become dark, (*i.*) As the Lord Christ, after all his powerful works, overcoming of the devil in the temptation, and transfiguration of his human body, was to go through all these sufferings, and at length wholly to die on the cross, whereby he frustrated in a sense and manner, the expectation of all his disciples. And as he had no other gate or way, than death, through which he could have entered into his glory, and drawn after him his members: So also in this philosophical work, the artist hath hitherto seen indeed many wonderful things, and very glorious appearances, which made him to have a very great hope and expectation; yet for all this, now his expectation is in a sense quite overthrown. For now the whole nature dieth in his work, and he must see that all is changed into a dark night. All the properties, powers, and virtues, most now cease to be and do, what they were and did before, and must fall into the end of nature.

All yieldeth up its former life and activity, there is no more any stirring, moving, or operating. All the properties are in the crown-number, scattered in thousand, and so entered into the first mysterium, in that state wherein they were before the creation. The meaning is not, that the outward materiality is made invisible, or quite annihilated, but only, that all the powers therein which the outflown properties had from the eternal speaking Word, and which were raised up against each other, in contrariety, each of them according to its own nature, are now at the end of their activity in self-will, and earthly inclination, and are fallen home again into the power of the eternal speaking Word, having no other way, nor gate, but this death, through which they could enter from the curse into their primitive blessing. But when thus they are in death to themselves, and in the hand of the eternal Word, this cannot but raise them up again unto glory, as by a new creation, answering to the resurrection of Christ.

(*k.*) The Lord Christ died indeed, as to the humanity from this world, but he took the same human body again in his resurrection, and left nothing thereof behind, but only the government of the four elements, wherein the wrath, curse, and mortality lieth, etc. So in this philosophical work also, the first matter is not abolished, but only the curse therein is destroyed, in the four elements, and the first life in the one eternal element is raised up again; and therefore it is now six, and can abide the fire. A glorious new body is now raised up out of the black darkness, in a fair white colour, but such a one as hath a hidden glance in it, so that the colour cannot be exactly discerned, until it resolveth itself, and the new love-desire cometh up. And then in Saturn's centre, but in Jupiter's and Venus's property, the sun ariseth. This is in the Fiat, like as a new creation, and when this is done, all the properties cast forth unanimously their desire into Sol. And then the colour is turned into a mixture of white and red, from fire and light in union, i.e. into yellow, which is the colour of majesty.

(*l.*) The appearance of love, to the wrathful properties of darkness, causeth, as mentioned above, a great crack, shriek, or terror. The wrathfulness is mightily exasperated by this appearance of love, and presseth vehemently into her, for to swallow her up into death, which it doth also actually. But seeing that no death can be therein, the love sinketh only down, yieldeth up herself into these murdering properties, and displayeth among them her own loving essentiality, which they must keep in them, and cannot get rid of. But even this is a poison unto death, and a pestilence unto hell. For the wrathful properties are also mightily terrified at this entering of love into them, which is so strange and contrary to their own qualities, and which makes them all weak and impotent, so that they must lose their own will, strength, and pre-dominion, etc.

So was it done in the death of Christ, and after such a manner, (largely and excellently declared by Behmen.) Death and curse in the humanity, was killed and destroyed, in and by the death of Christ, who, after his resurrection, had no more the form of a male in his human body, but this of a paradisical virgin, as Adam had before his fall. And so also is it, in this philosophical work. In this terror, crack, and mutual killing (though there is properly no death, but only a transmutation, or union of two into one), when Venus yieldeth up her life to the wrathful properties, and when these, having lost their pre-dominion, are raised up again to a new life, the virgin giveth her pearl to the young man, for a propriety. And so the life of the anger, and the life of the love, are no more two, but only one; no more a male and female property, but a whole virgin, with both tinctures united into one. When then the artist seeth the red blood of the young man rise from death, and come forth out of the black darkness, together in union with the white colour of the virgin, he may then know that he hath the *great arcanum of the world*, and such a treasure as is inestimable.

Several more things might be added from Behmen, which would afford many excellent considerations. But these may be sufficient to show that *harmonious analogy* which is *between the restoration of fallen man, through Jesus Christ, and the restoration of cursed nature, in the Philosophical Work.*

The candidate will of course understand that the above extracts from Freher, are presented chiefly with regard to LAW, the great practical subject of the proposed biography, as illustrative of the theosophic or highest development of his *perfectly square,* masculine understanding; for they are all printed off from the MS. copies made by him for future reference, and the benefit of his friends. We use the term *practical* in connection with the biography, as the subject of it will necessarily be therein presented to the world, as an example of the right proporions of an universal intellectual cultivation, and as a kind of standard model (with reference to education,) of a learned and accomplished sober English gentleman, philosopher and Christian.

What is then so offered, may suffice for the candidate, and also serve to afford to the religious world a glimpse, if not a perfect conviction, of the eternal foundation and truth of Behmen's writings, as a revelation from God, however they may have been scoffed at by popular, unphilosophic religionists, practical infidels, and incipient idiots, as the reveries of an enthusiast or madmen.

For Behmen, as observed in the note of p. 630, and as, we trust, will be fully manifest through the instrumentality of the present treatise and the proposed biography, stands before the world in the character of the last great prophet of the gospel dispensation, commending himself, in such light, to all intelligent right-minded men, as supplying that desideratum of divine revelation, which has long been the demand of all nations, no less than of the Christian world, in the full open exhibition of truth from its deepest ground, and by consequence a strict and perfect demonstration of all the orthodox doctrines of the gospel.

To afford however the completest gratification that can be desired by the reader, we will present four or five sheets more of these writings, containing a kind of popular summary and specification of the leading contents and sense of Behmen's works, which will also form a fitting conclusion to the present POSTSCRIPT.

And we super-add this unpremeditated appendix the more cheerfully, as by it many worthy living students of Behmen, will obtain a fresh insight into numerous very generally unapprehended points of his writings, and so will be effected a still further reconciliation of his declarations with the received and progressing discoveries of practical science, or of these with the former.

Selection Eleven.

"The Growing of Vegetables", Serial Elucidations G, part 11.

The following paper contains a representation of "The GROWING of VEGETABLES, with RESPECT to their YEARLY RENEWING in the Spring-time, as described by BEHMEN:"—

I. —Heaven and earth make up but one principle and are the two chief constituent parts thereof, to be compared in a sense unto male and female: so that the concurrence of them both is necessarily required, for the generation of all sorts and kinds of earthly things.

II. —The properties of Nature therefore in the earth, which on the third day of the crestion, when they were in conjunction with the eternal Word moving them especially, could produce, with out concurrence of the sun, all sorts and kinds of vegetables, can now do the same no more. But, because of their being after the fall and curse, half dead and impotent, they want now the sun's heat and light, for to be thereby raised up, stirred and enlivened.

III. —All the Seven chief Properties of nature, together with their lesser subordinate qualities, are in every *seed*, but in various degrees and orders; so that some of them lay more or less deeply hidden therein, and others are more or less outward and nearer to activity, according to the different kinds thereof.

But all are without a manifest distinction, as if they were all but one and the same thing; wherefore then they must also be without qualifying or exerting their several distinct faculties, till the seed be *thrown into the ground*.

IV. —All the same properties are in the earth also, but in several degrees and orders, variously different, according to the different constitutions of places; and in the earth no less than in the seed, they are impotent, shut up into death, and overpowered by its cold astringency. Because then the earth hath its own centre precipitated down front the sun, nay set as it were in opposition over against it, so that it must be more passive than active, its properties could never be able to raise up any qualification to the seed, unless they were first raised up themselves, by the influence of heat and light from the sun.

V. —When this begins to be done, and goes then further on gradually, the Properties begin to be stirred, and are enabled gradually to operate, each of them according to its own nature; for the heat, which is the next degree to the light, is unfolded and raised successively more and more out of the cold astringency.

And so therefore an agreeable conjunction or union is made between the properties of the earth and those of the seed, which latter are taken in, and supported and strengthened by the former. Provided,

VI. —That the properties of that peculiar ground or place wherein the seed is sown, be not in their constitution too much contrary, but agreeing more or less with the properties of the seed in their condition and order, or kind. For else the grain or seed is taken in indeed by the earth, but not so the properties of that seed by the properties of the earth. Seeing that there can be no conjunction, or at least no agreeable living union between them. And from hence therefore ariseth a slow and weak vegetation, or also sterility, and a total corruption of the seed. This Behmen illustrates by a similitude taken from a mother's entire kindness and affection to her own natural son, and the same mother's lesser tenderness, or total carelessness towards a step-son.

VII. —These two then in conjunction, viz. the natural contrariety and strife of the three first properties, in the earth and seed; and (2.) the sun's influencing power, not only raising up that strife by its heat, but also gradually reconciling it in its light, are the cause of all and every vegetation.

And this in an harmonious answerableness to the two eternal principles. For like as Eternal Nature tendeth always forwards in and by the war and strife of the three first dark properties, to their transmutation into peace and light and glory, which it obtaineth in the second principle of light and love; so doth also Temporal Nature tend or press always forward, to its perfection in its kind, or to a transmutation of its inferior striving properties, to be made in and by the light or tincture of outward nature, which is hid in everything, and is fully obtained in the full maturity of every fruit.

VIII. —This conjunction between these two is always broken in the winter, by the then predominant astringent cold. But as soon as the properties of the earth can have the heat stirred and raised in them again, this conjunction is renewed, and their strife begins afresh. And so from hence it is, that in every tree yearly new twigs and branches are produced; and from every root or seed, a new vegetation springeth up, which is thus more particularly described by Behmen.

IX. —The sun's heat warmeth and stirreth the *quality* of water, or the water spirit, and so also the material water or sap, both in the earth and in the seed. And then the light of nature, in and with that sweet water spirit springeth up; which maketh all the other properties moving and stirring also. For there is now a mutual affecting, touching, penetrating, and working of the properties in one another, when nevertheless each or them keeps constantly to its own natural inclination, and cannot therefore but act accordingly.

X.—All the other qualities, besides the sweet water and light being in themselves but dark, harsh, cold, rough, astringent bitter, dry, etc. are thereby naturally made *sensible* of this light and water's being their end and aim, or their only desirable treasure, refreshing, softening, tincturing, and reconciling them. Wherefore then in this their sensibility of natural tendency, pressing towards perfection, the vegetation is now carried on by their own natural strife and contrariety. For the seed is now impregnated with a new life according to its kind.

XI. —This new life, being still surrounded with death, and encompassed with a gross, hard, unprofitable husk, shell, etc. cannot spring up beyond it, and so not manifest or exert itself, but by breaking through that dead inclosure, putting off the same, and leaving it behind in and to the earth. And here that death lieth, so much spoken of by Behmen, and applied to the regeneration, according to the words of Christ, The grain of wheat cannot bring forth fruit, except it fall into the ground and die.

XII. —In this mutual affecting and touching of all the qualities, the sweet water-spirit *tasting*, as it were, the bitter and harsh qualities, it naturally stretcheth forth itself, flying or retiring from them as much as it can, which Behmen illustrates by a similitude of a man tasting an astringent bitter gall, who naturally caggs at it, and wideneth his palate, showing thereby a natural antipathy against astringency and bitterness.

XIII. —But this sweet quality with its water and sap, thus flying and retiring in its antipathy, from the bitter and astringent, makes them but more eager to follow after it, and causeth the astringent spirit especially, to press more earnestly upon it: which causing is nothing else, but a more lively stirring and raining up its internal property, desiring to be by that sweet water refreshed, to satisfy its own natural dryness, and to have also such fit subject before it, as may be capable of its operation.

XIV. —This operation is, according to the natural inseparable constitution of this astringent quality, continual attracting, coagulating and (in conjunction with the heat) a drying and thickening the water or sap. Whereby this cometh to have such or such a visible colour, and palpable figured body according to the kind of the first seed.

XV. —This flying and pursuing after going on thus continually, until the water is all consumed, and the sweet quality is made all impotent, so that it can at length retire no further, is the true growing or vegetation in this four elementary world; wherein it cannot be done but so successively, gradually, and by little and little. For,

XVI. —This sweet quality with its water kindled more and more from above by the sun's heat, and pressed upon from beneath by the bitter and harsh qualities, cannot but fly and retire in its natural antipathy more and more, not only first springing up above the ground, and not only stretching forth itself on every side as in a circumference, but also pressing directly forwards, or rather upwards to the sun, for to escape as it were, their violence. But being always further and further pursued by the other contrary, and especially by the astringent quality, it cannot but be successively more and more coagulated and compacted: and so therefore successively a long and round stock or stalk groweth up.

XVII. —The stalk is always thicker below on the bottom, and thinner or smaller above in the height, decreasing in its quantity by little and little. And this is from the sweet water-spirit's having first its full strength, but losing it successively more and more; till at length it grows so weak and impotent, that it cannot retire any higher, but must submit, and be as it were captivated by the other properties.

XVIII.—The different colours and the alterations of them, made severally in one and the same vegetation, wherein we may see that first below the herb or plant appears whitish, and is then changed into green, brown, yellowish, etc. are from the various predominancies of the different qualities, in the outmost surface of the stalk, affected by the sun's heat and light.

XIX.—The branches, leaves, knots, etc. have all their original from that continual strife between the contrary qualities, which is sometimes carried on more regularly and gently, and sometimes as in a storm or violence: which latter especially is a cause of the knots, and must be supposed wherever we see a knot, that there hath been such a vehement assault made upon the sweet water, that it was like as if at its period, but that it had strength to escape and get through again. [In the *Signatura Rerum*, Behmen declareth this figuration of the knots, etc. much deeper, and more reflecting upon the generation of eternal nature, saying for instance, Each of the properties pursue the sweet water : Mars raveth and rageth. Mercury is terrified at it; and Saturn, by his strong impression, maketh this terror or crack (which is salnitral, according to the third property of nature,) corporeal; and thus the knots come to be. In this terror. Mercury goeth on a side, and taketh Venus along with him; which causeth a spreading forth of twigs and branches, etc.]

XX. —When the water is so far spent and dried up, or coagulated and compacted by the sun's heat from without, and the first astringent property within, and consequently the sweet quality hath so much lost its strength as that it can no more press forward to preserve itself, it is necessitated to yield to the contrary qualities. Which it doth by spreading out the little residue of its sweet watery essence, as in a round court or ball, and admitting all the other qualities thereinto. And this now is the generation of a round bud or head, which the astringent spirit compacteth, and wherein all the rest do further act their parts, each of them according to its own natural drift, until another grain or seed be therein produced in a perfect answerableness to that first, out of which this growth came forth.

XXI. —In this bud, the sweet quality with its water may now be compared in a sense to a pregnant woman, which having conceived a seed (the other crude qualities) into her womb, must now further herself bring it to maturity, and labour for an opening and bringing forth thereof for this sweet water must bring forth from hence the proper natural children of all the other properties.

XXII. —These children are the various leaves of the flowers and blossoms, of so various, and sometimes also mixed colours. All which are no more (like as the green leaves were on the stock below) of the water quality's nature and condition, but according to that of all the other qualities, and their manifold combinations, etc.

For the sweet water now impregnated with all these qualities, cannot bring forth children according to its own, but needs bring them forth according to the constitution of that seed, which it is impregnated with.

XXIII. —When these red, white, yellow, blue, etc. children are brought forth, the sweet mother thereof groweth all faint and weary, and is not able to nourish them very long. For they are not only very tender as to themselves, but also, with respect to this mother, are upon a certain good account, only as it were her step-children. Because not generated freely, nor from, nor according to her own natural quality, but according to the others, and as by constraint, when the sweet quality was decayed, and all the others had overpowered and captivated her.

XXIV. —When therefore the sun's heat from without presseth upon these tender flowers and blossoms, all the qualities in them are stirred up and enlivened. For the spirit of life, even that true vegetable life, which is in every vegetation, according to its kind, is now exalted in them to the highest degree. Seeing then that these tender flowers are for this strong spirit, too weak and cannot bear it, they must surrender their various noble virtues, which they send forth from them, in a lively pleasant smell or perfume; but they themselves must soon after fall away and wither. And so now from hence the vegetation decreaseth, and turneth back or downwards, in a good and true sense and respect, though in another it goeth still forwards, to the maturity of the seed or fruit

XXV.—For in this flourishing and blossoming of the vegetables, (even of thorns and thistles also.) a conjunction is made manifest more or less between time and eternity, or earth and paradise.

And eternity as it were beholds, or represents itself in time, by a visible image, partaking more or less both of the one and other. For in this smell especially, something of a paradisical property is opened: the meaning of which is not this, that the smell itself, forasmuch as it can be perceived by the earthly sense, or nose, were purely paradisical, for it is according to the condition of this third principle, but only that something of a paradisical property doth lie and open itself therein more or less, according to the different kinds of vegetables.

XXVI.—This paradisical property showeth forth also its own signature, by the manifold beautiful colours; when the temporal earthly property expresseth its character, by the subtle green leaves, surrounding the blossoms and flowers.

For the various colours are according to the various dispositions of all the other qualities, besides that of the sweet water, and are rightly also called their colours; yet they are not absolutely their own, so that they could produce them without a concurrence of the hidden *inward world*. But there is in this blossoming a transmutation (of the sulphur and its sal, says Behmen, wherein all the qualities are understood) into paradise, or into a paradisical property and joy.

XXVII.—In this conjunction now between time and eternity, or earth and paradise, that highest degree consisteth, which the spirit of life in all the vegetables, but in each according to its kind and capacity, is or can be exalted into; and which degree can now further not rise any higher. For though even afterwards also, in the full maturity of the fruits, something the like is opened again, and manifested after such a manner, in the pleasant smell and taste of the fruits; yet this which is here done in the blossoming, is the principal thing, with respect to the inward hidden world; though that other may be called the principal thing also, but only with respect to this outward four elementary world, and the chief benefit, which is brought forth thereby, unto creatures. From hence therefore the vegetation turns, as it were back or downwards, unto earthliness. For,

XXVIII.—Seeing that the kingdom of this outward world is but temporal, having its own dominion, or government, as a principle by itself, and lying moreover under the curse and vanity, this paradisical property with its image, character, and signature, cannot make a very long stay therein, but withdraws soon into its own centre. And this third principle according to its own natural right or privilege given unto it on the third day of the creation, and confirmed immediately after the deluge, is only for such a grain or seed to be brought forth from the blossom, as may be perfectly according to the sort and kind of the first, and may have in it the same quality and capacity of bringing forth and multiplying again after the same manner.

And thus the Circle of Vegetation is ended or concluded, by the end's returning into its own beginning.

Selection Twelve.

"Observations on Waple's Writings About Jacob Behmen"

[This is labeled as the entirety of Serial Elucidations H.—Ed.]

These further extracts then, consist of "MISCELLANEOUS OBSERVATIONS occasioned by the REVD. EDWD. WAPLE'S own WRITINGS about JACOB BEHMEN, which he desired ME to CORRECT ["and COMPLEAT", Walton marginal note—Ed.]" How these critical remarks display the universal and exact knowledge of Behmen's mind and writings, possessed by Freher, and justify Lee's poetic apostrophe, *In sum, second to thee* p. 253, will be for the reader to consider. They proceed thus:—

Page 33. *Question, Do they mean that the Father and Son, etc?* Answer. They take the words of the Scripture, calling God, fire and light not metaphorically but in their plain natural sense; and mean that the Father and Son (as *in nature*) are formally that spiritual fire and light, but as *without nature* they are in fire and light, as in somewhat distinct from themselves. For the Will as abyssal or without nature, is not yet fire, and the eternal liberty or that state of tranquillity, which is before or deeper and without nature, is not yet light; but in the process of nature, the will or rather the desire, or the will in and by its desire, cometh to be fire, and the liberty light, according to the large declaration of the seven properties of eternal nature.

Page 44. *Q. ult. What reason do they give for their translation of* John i. 1, *further than the order of the words?* A. They say that a translation of the apostle's words, as is done in the English version, by saying *the Word was God* instead of *God was the Word*, is inconsistent with the deep mysterious description of the Godhead, and with the sense intended therein, and inconsistent also (in this place) with the order of the eternal generation; and that it takes away the greatest emphasis and force of an argument that can be had from hence, and which lyeth in his own construction of these words. For, the apostle's intent is to shew by these words, both union and distinction in the Godhead, and even to shew it by going directly as it were forward, from the centre, *God*, or first abyssal will, to the circumference, *Word*, or express character of his substance; which order is perverted by transposing the words, and the weight thereof is lost. For the apostle's words in their order, import so much, as that the only true eternal *God*, considered as the Father, or first abyssal will, not indeed as being an abyssal will, but as having set forth himself in an express image of his substance, was himself that *Word*, which was with him in the beginning, he being himself both the first and the last, the beginning and the end: and this is not so imported, when these words are trajected. And so, the apostle, having said immediately before, *the Word was with God*, and having declared thereby a distinction between God, or the first abyssal will, and the Word or the byss; and saying now further, and *God was that Word*, declareth again the highest union between them, and this from the centre or abyssal will forwards, in the natural order of generation, towards that which is that centre's, as it were, circumference, and not backwards from the circumference to the centre: for this centre is that circumference eminently, as containing it, and being able to bring it forth; but this circumference is not that centre reciprocally, in the same sense, emphasis and consequence. And in short, Behmen's explication of this Scripture-place cannot have half so much of life and deep weighty sense, as it hath when these words are transposed, which in the German Bible are rightly rendered, according to the Greek original.

Page 45. *Q. But do they mean, that they have one and the self-same numerical or individual essence or substance—three essentialities are but one essence?* A. The two last similies mentioned in this question, are without doubt the best and fittest, because the first, of heat, light, and air, is that which Behmen useth frequently; and the second, of the three faculties of the soul (though I would rather say, fire, light, and tincture), is taken from the image of God, to the consideration of which Behmen useth to direct his reader. But whether now, or how these latter three, or those former three shall be called (in school expressions) numerically, individually, identically, specifically etc. the same, I am not able to say, being not acquainted sufficiently with the emphasis and importance of these words.

Page 48. *Q.* 1. *The eternal glorious Light do they take it to be God or a creature?* A. The asker of this question, before he can be answered, must needs be asked again, What he understands by *God?* or in which of the two senses (the very last time represented, and owned to be pretty plain,) he takes *God* in this question. For the answer to it must be accordingly. I cannot answer so simply and generally, *it is an eternal emanation from God*. For this answer is not distinct, but lies in confusion, breeds a world of other confusions, and leaves all together in the dark. In the question, *God* is taken in the second sense, which from all the following discourse, till page 62, and farther, appears sufficiently: when, in the answer, I cannot but take it in the *first* sense. If I say, *an eternal emanation from God*, I must understand *God* as an abyss, as not yet light, as not yet a most perfect being, but still as a central incomprehensible unity, which is not God in the *second* sense. All therefore what in the next following Question is discoursed of, makes nothing to the purpose, seeing that it opposeth something, which in the foregoing answer (according to Behmen's ground), is not asserted, and all but upon this mistake, that there is not minded what Behmen understands here by *God*.

Page 50. *Q.* and *A.* 1. This very same which now was said, evidenceth itself still more in the discourse, concerning a *necessary emanation, which is generally affirmed to be an undoubted error*. For, a necessary emanation from God, if God be taken in the second sense, as by them that oppose and contradict such a necessity, may indeed be granted to be an error; but if Behmen takes God here in the first sense, and they cannot or will not mind what he means by *God*, viz. only and solely the *abyss*, and how he declareth (N.B.) what this abyss is, and will nevertheless charge him with an undoubted error, they show themselves to be full of nonsense and unreasonableness. For, I suppose they will not deny, but that it is *necessary*, (not arbitrary nor contingent,) that God is light, in one sense, and that he dwells in the light, in another. And if so, it is *necessary* that the abyss should not continue in an abyssal state, but be unfolded, and bring forth such emanations as it doth. *Objection.* This unfolding is done in the eternal generation in Three, which we can grant to be necessary, but what necessity is there for an unfolding in Seven also? Answer. (1.) *This* unfolding is not done in the eternal generation in three, for if there is a Tri-unity rather than a Trinity, it is (I don't know how to call it) a . . . . rather than an unfolding. This unfolding therefore must needs be done in seven, by which the three are made known distinctly. (2.) If the central life and light is rather a rest and clarity (see page 62 at the end and page 64 at the beginning) without exulting joy, and a bright diffused glory; there is a palpable necessity for such an unfolding in seven, if we will not think it indifferent whether the Divine Being be in an exulting joy and glory, or whether it be not (3.) If the abyss is not a most perfect being in that sense in which generally and rightly God is called so; what error is it then to say, Out of the abyss the divine perfections must be unfolded? It is rather an undoubted error to leave it indifferent whether God be a most perfect being or not. To conceive therefore, in the first place, of this most perfect being, and then to speak in the second place, of necessary emanations from it, is directly contrary to Behmen, and is the true ground of all this confusion, and endless as well as needless controversy.

Page 54. *It is commonly asserted that nothing can emanate from God, except by . . . . which is not God in the highest sense of that word*. Here again all this now spoken of showeth forth itself as clear as the day. For they commonly take God in the highest or completed sense of that word, viz. in that which I called the second: if then Behmen takes it not so in this matter, but in the first and deepest, do they not fight against a shadow of their own making; and how can they pretend to an understanding of what he saith? Let it be as true as it can be agreed upon among themselves, that nothing can emanate from God, which is not God in the highest sense, (viz. when they take God, as they do, in the highest, fullest or second sense,) when Behmen takes it in the first or deepest, as he doth in this matter; such a position accommodated to that first sense is utterly false, and the direct contrary is true. Consider only what he saith of the abyss, and you may find, that something emanates from it (*not by way of creating efficiency out of nothing*) which is not abyss, nor can be abyss for this same reason, because it is emanated or unfolded out of the abyss, and which therefore is not God, and cannot be God in that sense in which the abyss is God, but on the one side in a higher, and on the other in a lower. *Summa summarum:* this unhappy dispute ariseth only from not minding what Behmen in this matter means by *God*, and yet presuming to try and judge him by what others have said from another principle; which indeed is not fair, but such a dealing with him as we would not be dealt with ourselves.

Page 66, *et seq*. Concerning what here is discoursed of *two Trinities*, I see, and say only so much, that even this controversy also ariseth, at least for a great deal, from the same ground of confounding the *one sense* of God with the *other:* and that after such a manner of arguing, it might as well be pretended, that Behmen makes two Gods, the one imperfect, and the other perfect, and the one within the other. In the order of our conceptions (yet *cum fundamento in re*), going from the creatures backward, or into the deep, there is a *Tri-unity* beyond or deeper than the *Trinity*; and further an abyssal *Unity* beyond or deeper than the *Tri-unity*. But as the Unity and Triunity makes neither two Gods, nor two unities, nor two tri-unities the one within the other, notwithstanding that the unity is verily in the tri-unity, and that both this and that is God: so the triunity and trinity makes neither two tri-unities nor two trinities, the one within the other, notwithstanding that this latter is represented as actually fire, light, and air, and that former not actually so, but only potentially; and notwithstanding also, that the unity and the tri-unity is in the trinity. Like as the Son is in the Father as in his original, and the Father in the Son as in his express image, which nevertheless makes not two Gods.

As to the Priscillians and Gnostics, and what they held hereof, I can say nothing. It may be they had a deeper understanding than the relation we have thereof imports; and their being condemned in a synod signifieth nothing at all to me, who am fully persuaded that at first the Lord of Life and Glory himself was condemned by the generality of the whole Jewish church, with as much, if not more outward appearance of right in the eyes of the high priests and pharisees; so also afterwards many of his members were so condemned by the Christian synods, in the time of which the church had lost already her true simplicity and virgin-purity, and was setting up more and more an outward form of words, instead of the inward teaching of the Holy Spirit of God.

Page 76, is to me very obscure, so that I can make nothing thereof. It is plain that the scripture saith, In God we live and move and have our being; and that here is meant God as in nature, seems to be determined by the words *more immediately*, for in God as in nature we live and move more immediately, and are not capable of being raised up beyond nature. Why then is it replied, *The scriptures attribute this to God the infinite spirit, from whom all things continue to have their being, or their* :TO:ESSE *immediately*, as if either God in the sense here taken by Behmen, viz. God in nature, were not an infinite spirit, or as if the creatures had their being immediately from God without nature, which cannot be and is no where said in the Scriptures.

Page 98. *A.* 1. *They may be said to be partakers—not necessarily.* It may be granted the creation of angels and men was done by God freely and contingently, not necessarily, but this *participation* upon a presupposition that God would have such creatures after his own image and likeness is not free nor contingent, but necessary. For he could not have created them after his image and likeness without making them partakers of his Divine nature, though it is true that this participation is only after a creatively manner, derivatively.

Page 100. *A.* 1.—*They assert the fire of this emanation to be immortal as well as the light.* This is true absolutely in eternal nature, but not so in the creature. And therefore I cannot say what further follows, *and consequently the soul as well as the Spirit.* For though the light and spirit dies not in or to God, yet it died in and to the creature, that is the creature lost it and was separated from it, and retained only its own natural principle of immortality, or continued only to be a living soul in its own fiery nature, but not a blessed image of God in the light.

Page 102. *A.* 1. Because here is asked. What they deliver concerning the manner of this emanation's coming out of God? I think it might be more distinct if it were answered thus: They say, that upon the desire's actual moving and attracting, divers such other properties or spiritual motions arise, as are necessary for the production of a spiritual fire, and further of the light, and that so this emanation is eternally produced or brought out of the unproduced, unmade, or self-existent abyss of all things, in which, considered as an abyssal will and Father of nature, it is to be conceived of as a hidden fire and light, not meaning that it was actually fire and light, and hid as it were behind a vail, but that it still was lying potentially in those not yet moving spiritual properties or motions, by the united concurrence of which it must have been manifested or brought into act.

Page 116. To the particulars of this answer could be added I think, in the first or second place (for it will be directly relating to the question, and is plainly Behmen's ground) That the desire is not in God, that is not in the abyss, nor in the Abyssal Will, and much less therefore in the Triunity or Trinity. For though we may say the fire is in the abyss, as a hidden and not yet burning fire; and so also the desire is therein, as a hidden and not yet desiring or actual desire; yet we must say also from the plain and contrary nature of abyss and desire, that the desire, as soon as it is conceived to be actual desire, and actually attracting is no more in the abyss, but is gone forth the first step out of it. And if then the desire, as hidden in the abyss, is not yet attracting, filling and darkening, this filling and darkening which is in the desire, as gone out already and attracting actually, can also not be in the abyss, but only in the first step from the abyss, which first step having never been without or separated from the fifth, sixth, and seventh, it never was also in that first step otherwise than as to our necessary conception.

Page 126. *A. 2. Out of their possible, uncreated, ideal state.* Seeing that in the next following answer, a reason is given why they cannot properly be called creatures, I think they should also, there not be said to having been in an *uncreated state*,—abyssal state, would be my expression.

Page 126. *Q. ult. What ground have they for asserting such a kind of production or generation?* In the answer no ground for it is shewn, but only is said, *they think it may be illustrated from what occurs in this world, etc.* Whereas Behmen had certainly a deep and solid ground for it, and had not taken it up by reasoning from what is in this world; which ground in short was his breaking in the Spirit through the gates of hell into the light-world, and having therefore this generation, as to both the principles, opened in his own soul. A ground certainly not to be shaken by devils, and much less by men, of which all his writings testily sufficiently.

Page 138. *Q*. 1. *What ground is there for their asserting that these seven Spirits are the instruments under God of the Divine nature in man?* This seems to me very obscure and ambiguous, for these seven spirits (as also is said in the next following answer) are God's eternal nature, and this nature, or these seven Spirits are by Behmen called God's instruments whereby he worketh, which is plain. But to call the seven Spirits, instruments under God of the Divine nature in man, seems to be so much as to say they are instruments of themselves, or nature is its own agent and its own instrument, or these seven spirits are so distinct from nature, that nature can be an agent, and these seven Spirits the instruments of this agent; which by Behmen is not asserted, nor could any ground be had for such assertion.

[Vol. II.] Page 1. *Q*. 1. Considering that *knowledge* is not the *manifestation* itself but rather an effect and consequence thereof, I should be apt to think that either this first question might be formed otherwise, or if it should stand so, that something more might be expressed in the answer, viz. this, or something the like,—it is such an efficacious and solid understanding (chiefly and summarily) of God and man, as cannot be had but by a manifestation of the Spirit from Christ, in whom are hid etc.

Q. 2. For considerable reasons, I would for my part change the order of these two particulars, saying, 1st, in the renewed spirit of the mind, from the Word and light of God as in its only true place; and 2ndly, in the Scriptures as in a direction thereto, and a testimony thereof. Job. r. 39, 40.

Q. 3. The words not *in the same measure*, I would either leave out wholly, or turn them into these—not in the same manner. Because the Word and light of God considered in the humanity and with respect to the several ages of the church, was from the beginning and will be unto the end of time increasing, unfolding and displaying itself more and more, like a tree in its boughs, greater and lesser branches, blossoms and fruits. This simile is frequently used, and excellently declared by Behmen; so that it doth not derogate from the honour and due unquestionable prerogative of the Apostles to say, that after their time such and such a one had the Word and light of God, in the same, or even in a greater measure; but their prerogative is asserted sufficiently by owning, that none had it to the same end. Like as it doth not derogate from the honour of great considerable boughs to say that they are not so adorned with variety of buds and blossoms, nor so richly laden with fruits as the lesser branches are which yet come forth out of them, are supported by them, and stand upon them as upon their foundation.

Q. 4. Great and sundry are the ends to which the Word and light of God was given, especially unto Behmen; and he certainly received it not for his own only, but also for a *general benefit* which is *yet to be expected*. Wherefore then I think that at least something thereof in the answer to this question might be mentioned. As for instance—It was given him, as he saith in the AURORA, for to declare to the world the morning redness of the instant day, and unto Babel its downfall, and to warn the children of God that are dispersed in all the streets thereof. Again, for an unfolding and explaining of those many deep mysteries that laid couched in the letter of the Scriptures, and were not understood, but must now in this latter age of the world be brought to light, according to the prophecy of Zech. xiv. 7.—*In the evening it shall be light*; and this (N.B.) in order to a *preperation for the coming in of the Jews, Turks, and Heathens*, etc.

Page 3. *Q*. 1. Between these two marks here expressed, I think this third could fitly be inserted,—by inquiring into their life and conversation, and especially their end or departing from this world.

Q. 2. This expression, *they may have erred in what they have delivered*, I think might be a little restrained or limited, by adding,—they may have erred as to this or that particular circumstance of what they have delivered.

Page 5. *Q. ult*. When here is declared, in or to whom the Word and light of God can become *a shining lamp* and a *living oracle*, all the qualifications, excellently here expressed, are indeed sufficient unto every one for to attain thereby unto that former, but as to this latter, something me-thinks is wanting: for such children of God, as, in whom his Word shall become a living oracle, are not only to have all those qualifications on their side, but something also from the side of God is further required thereto, viz. they must be *expressly chosen or preordained thereto by God*, intending to make use of them as of his *extraordinary messengers*.

Page 7. *Q. ult*. That the answer to this question might more directly satisfy the question, I would add to the words *to a more perfect regeneration*, these or the like-which (regeneration) itself carrieth along with it such a measure of knowledge of the deep things of God, as is proportionable to that degree thereof.

Page 19. *Q. ult. Knowing and loving* are here in the question, and in the answer knowing and delighting are combined, and both ascribed to the unity before the act of willing, which I think cannot stand so, because it giveth occasion to a confused apprehension and raiseth a great objection; for, if we consider in God a *loving* himself, we must needs imply (1.) a *lover*, (2.) a *beloved*, and (3.) a *ray of love*; and so our consideration represents to us a Trinity before the act of willing, which is inconsistent with the Unity. But a *knowing himself* may be owned before this act of willing in the Unity; for therein is the Divine intellect, called by Behmen an abyssal Eye. This cannot but know himself as one, and is therefore consistent with the Unity, and doth not at all import a Trinity, because it is not considered any further than as to a knowing only his central all-sufficiency for all what is in any sense posterior, or as it here in the answer expressed sufficiently, *as a knowing himself as one*, which is the same as all in one. It is true indeed that knowing and loving himself are inseparable from each other in God, but they cannot be so in our separate, gradual, imperfect consideration, wherein we cannot but look upon each in its own prior or posterior place. As then knowing precedeth loving in our reasonable conception, so our consideration placeth justly such a knowing in the eternal Unity; and as next to the Unity the Trinity cometh into consideration, so also next to this knowing, yet not as in the Unity, but in the Trinity, the loving himself can be considered.

Page 25. A. 2. When there is said of *spiritual fire and light*, and that our first parents were created in this image of God, I think it might be limited by adding—as to the invisible, spiritual man, or, as to soul and spirit. Not that it was not true and plainly enough expressed to him that hath understanding; but only that it may not be a stumbling-block to him that hath it not, who might presently cry out. It is contrary to Scripture, etc.

Page 37. What here is discoursed of the will, wants, to my thinking, more to be cleared up, for I see that there is spoken of another will, distinct from the will of the Unity, and subordinate to it. Whereas the generation of eternal nature begins with the desire, and presupposeth no other will but that self-same first Abyssal Will which is the will of the Unity, and cannot be distinct from itself, though it willeth two such things as are exceedingly distinct from one another. In the eternal generation in three, the first will is Father, and the second will is Son. Now this second will (in the first consideration of God as in himself, rightly considered as before nature, or as if nature were not yet generated,) is here in the second consideration of God as manifest in nature, rightly also laid aside, as if it were not yet generated, and there must be in our consideration as it were, a going back unto the first abyssal will, which is the only generator both of the second will, by its introducing itself into an eternal lubet, and of eternal nature also, by its introducing itself into an attracting desire. The first and second will therefore are distinct so as Father and Son. But this first will is no where represented by Behmen as generating another will distinct from itself, and antecedent to the desire, but only as introducing itself immediately into desire, like as on the other side immediately into a lubet.

Page 41. Q. 1. Darkness becometh an evil of punishment, as it exists separately from the light, not universally in every creature, but in such only as were created to the light, and left their habitation. For there are creatures in the darkness, unto which the darkness is good, and the light would be evil, pain, torment, and destruction.

Page 43. Q. 1. This description of the seven spirits is to my thinking not yet sufficient, nor distinct enough. For they are not all equally pure, simple, living, and active. The second, for instance, is in a spiritual sense and manner thicker and grosser than the first; the third is a composition or mixture of the first and second. The six only are living and active, when deadness, impotence, and passiveness belongeth unto the seventh. Wherefore then, this question might be answered in this or the like manner,—they conceive of the six first spirits as of living and acting beings, and of the seventh as of their passive, spiritual body; whereof the six are the life, and wherein they do, in a different respect, both work and rest.

And here after this first question, would be the proper place to add several things more, some of which are very necessary to the understanding Behmen's mind, viz.—that each of them is distinct from all the rest by its own peculiar essential character, which makes it to be precisely such a property, and not another. That notwithstanding this, they are not seven distinct things, but seven properties of one thing, wherefore also they are commonly called the seven properties of eternal nature. That they are not to be conceived as standing without or besides each other, according to the representation of seven distinct lamps in the vision of St. John, but as within each other, according to the fourfold wheel in that of Ezekiel. That they are in one respect but one, in another seven, and in another again but three, according to the Holy Trinity; the first and seventh, second and sixth, third and fifth being to be looked upon as one and the same, with only this distinction, that when they are called the first, second, and third, they are before the fire, and when the fifth, sixth, and seventh, they are after it, which fire maketh the most considerable distinction between the three and three. That none of them is properly the first or second etc., but that they are only called so according to our conception. That there is a reciprocal and perpetual generation between them, each of them requiring all the other six for its own generation, and being required again for the generation of each of them. That each of them receiveth the impression of all the other six, so that here also, in a sense it is true, *quidlibet est in quolibet*; from whence an infinite variety and multiplicity of wonders in the kingdom of glory ariseth etc.

Q. 2. The three last words, *light or glory, and joy,* I would place thus—light, joy, and glory, because of that correspondence which they have to the three last properties, joy being to be referred to the sixth, and glory to the seventh, as it is commonly so done by Behmen.

Q. 4. There must be a seventh, not only to unite the six, but also to make the distinction between the three distinct opposites manifest, which is done by the fire. And this distinguishing office is as much (if not more) needful to be observed and understood as that uniting one. For we should not be able to perceive darkness and light in their distinction, or rather opposition, if there were not fire, having the darkness before and the light after it.

Q. ult. In the answer is said, *the joy arising from it a sixth, and the kingdom of joy a seventh*. Here I would rather say,—the kingdom of glory, not as if the former expression were false, but only for a clearer relations sake to the properties, and because it is not plainly expressed how the Joy and the kingdom of joy do differ.

Page 45 *Q.* 1. Seeing that Behmen did not argue that four spirits are requisite to spiritual fire, from the like necessity to the production of material fire; but had the eternal nature sooner opened unto him than the temporal, and concluded rather from that unto this, nay knew also nothing of these new philosophical experiments, as afterwards is said, I am apt to think it would be better if this question were formed after such a manner—Have you anything for confirmation or illustration that four spirits are requisite? For otherwise the question seems to import, with respect to Behmen, a previous understanding of the generation of fire in outward nature, and a ratiocination from this–to the eternal. What is said in the answer, being all most proper, true, plain, and sufficient, might nevertheless be retained, *mutatis tantum mutandis, grammaticae constructionis gratia.*

Page 47. *Q.* 1. Here I cannot see why it is said *the fifth spirit, from which the light ariseth,* this light being itself the fifth spirit, or fifth spiritual property, arising not from the fifth but from the fourth, viz. from the fire, which is the fourth, as the answer also declareth.

Page 49. *Q.* 1. Instead of these words, *and no more intimate union of the Triune equally manifest in everything*, I would rather insert these or the like,—by an opening and essential union of the still eternity with it, which is to be conceived as all free, pure and clear, but without glance and lustre, before the first desire. This is more according to Behmens sense than that, and I think it is no less intelligible than that; and what in the answer is further added, for an illustration from outward nature, may illustrate this so well as that, if not better, as to my thinking.

Page 53. Q. 1. Grace and peace from the one divine essence, or threefold Spirit only, considered as in himself alone without the creature, cannot be profitable unto man. Man hath broken or disharmonised in himself the seven properties of the divine nature, is fallen thereby into misery, strife and restlessness, and wants now grace and peace. All the grace without him, cannot profit him, if there be not peace made within him; this peace therefore dependeth upon that grace, and from that grace this peace must be brought into man. But it cannot be brought into him except by an actual reconciling and reharmonising of the disordered properties of his human nature. And seeing this human nature is an offspring of the Divine nature, or of God as manifested in his eternal nature, unto this disharmonised nature therefore is rightly wished, not only grace, but also peace, and not only (1.) from God, as the only original of all grace and peace, but also (2.) from the seven Spirits before his throne, as the seven Divine open Fountains, out of which the human nature was flown forth, and unto which it must be brought back again, if man shall be partaker again of the Divine nature, as he was in the beginning. And (3.) also from Jesus Christ as the King and Head of men, in whom all this reconciliation was first effected, and by whom it is to be effected further in all his members. And in this consideration (as might be made out sufficiently), lyeth certainly the true ground of this Apostolical wish. But that it is not used so by any of the other Apostles, nay even not by St. John himself, except only in this mystical and prophetical book of his, doth shew us sufficiently, that it was not then the time for the opening and understanding this mystery, but that this book was written only for the future ages and generations then to come.

Page 53. *Q. ult.* Instead of the words *flowing out from them*, I would rather say—flowing out through them, or being unfolded, displayed, or manifested by them. For that former, as to my thinking, seems to make the seven properties an original of the Divine attributes, when their original (if we may so speak, for properly they have none) is in the abyssal Unity or central Allsufficiency before and without the properties of nature, and by them they are only unfolded out of their centre.

Page 55. Q. 1. Here I think it would be needful to say something, though never so little, concerning this expression, *before*. Not that an understanding reader should have need thereof, but only for to remove a stumbling-block from the sight of the ignorant.

Q. 2. A little more relation between this *Q.* and *A.* would there be, if in the answer to the words *to know and perceive*, were added, *distinctly*. And here might be considered also, what Behmen frequently objects himself, and answers also sufficiently, viz., Whether all the foregoing consideration of God in general, and this question of his distinct knowledge in particular, doth not import a beginning of the Divine Triune Being, or at least of the manifestation thereof. And whether Behmen's expression of an *eternal beginning* might not be so represented, that no man of sense could find a contradiction therein.

Page 57. *Q.* 3. This description cannot be said to be complete, for the light is not fed by the water directly or immediately, but the crater and oil (of which this latter is more spiritual, and that former more material, though they both are the light's materiality,) do feed rather the fire eternally, whereby as by its most noble food, it is enabled perpetually to give forth out of itself the most noble light. Like as we see in outward nature also, that the more pure, clear, and noble the fire's food is, the more clear, bright, and noble is also its light. And by this union of fire and light, water and oil is generated in the light; so that there is between These three, an eternal circling band without beginning and end.

And hereafter this question, I think it would be proper to ask also further. What is this water of eternal light, and how is it generated? which is indeed excellently and sufficiently declared by Behmen, and illustrated also from the generation of material water in outward nature. But I see not how it could be made intelligible, without declaring also many other things belonging thereto, and not easily to be represented to the understanding.

Page 59. *Q.* 1. For a more natural order's sake in our conceptions, the two last members in this answer, and in both of them several particular expressions, as to my thinking might be transposed and a little altered, that it might stand thus,—seeing in them, as in a twofold mirror, all the creatures which he would create out of the fire and light, as in ideas reflected from them; but in the latter especially, all the evils of sin and of punishment, which the creature was capable of, upon its dividing it from the light.

Q. ult. The words *remain in the fire* are right and true enough, if rightly understood, viz., of such a kind of fire as is vastly different from that which Behmen calleth the First Principle; yet because this is not by every one distinctly enough apprehended, I would rather say—fall through the fire into darkness, or only, remain in the darkness, which is more according to the Scripture's expression.

Page 61. *Q.* 1. When there is said, *powers and perfections of God, which are to be conceived to arise in his nature*, I think for a reason given above, it ought to be limited, by adding this or something the like,—to arise as to their distinction, or distinct activity in his nature.

Q. 4. Instead of the last words in this answer, *by the spirits of men*, I would say rather—by angels and men, because by mentioning the spirits only it seems as if the soul were to be more or less excluded, whereas this seeing and feeling is more directly and properly to be attributed to the soul than to the spirit, though the spirit is more immediately touched by this glance and power, and the soul not at all capable of this seeing and feeling, but by the spirit's being drawn up into that glance and power so essentially, as the soul, considered in its own soulish being, cannot be.

Q. 5. The answer to this question must needs be altered, for though it is good enough and true in its expressions, yet the construction thereof cannot be left so, because it cannot but cause a confused idea in the reader. It hath two parts: the first affirmeth the question as to God the triune being in himself, and the second as to his nature; and these two parts ought to be more distinctly represented. Concerning the first part, it is indeed lightly said, *God is in all things;* but unto this rather than unto the second, is to be referred that which is added, page 62, *of his containing all things, and being contained by none, and containing them even so as their infinite foundation or centre, from which they proceed, and in which they rest.* In which description, these two particular words, *centre* and *rest*, do require an addition, by which the former may be distinctly determined, and the latter more explained, so as to be made applicable unto all things. For seeing that eternal nature is also rightly to be called the *centre* of all things, from which they proceed, this centre must needs be distinguished from that. And though we cannot conceive in one circumference two centres, the one besides the other, yet we can conceive the one deeper than the other, so that from this deeper the whole circumference, together with its exterior centre, can proceed. Wherefore then, this deeper centre (God in himself) must needs he distinguished from that centre which is nature, by calling it the first, or the deepest and inmost. And further, seeing that in the denomination of *all things* the devil also is comprehended, this expression—in which they *rest*, (if understood in a sense relating to the Sabbath) belongs only to nature, and is not applicable to the devil. Wherefore then it must be so explained that nothing more than this may be understood thereby,—God is the first foundation-being, whereupon all things do stand and rest, so as that there is beyond it no farther progress to any deeper cause from which they could have proceeded. For so far is it true that God is in the devil also, as the deepest centre of that whole circumference, in which he also is one of its innumerable particular things. Concerning the second part, it is indeed rightly said, *his nature is in all things*; but the following description, *as the hidden inward ray, glance, or light, life, power, and virtue of them, imprinting etc.*, is (1.) not opposite to that general expression, his nature, because by his nature we cannot understand his light only, but must understand his whole manifestation, and even in that opposition wherein it now is manifest, viz., light and darkness, love and anger. Nor (2.) is it applicable unto *all things* in general, but only unto all things in this outward Third Principle, where, in all things is good and evil; for it is not applicable to the devil, who is contained again in this general expression of all things, though he cannot be considered as a creature belonging to, or created in this outward third principle. Wherefore then instead of his *nature*, might be said his *light*, or with the Scripture, his *unperishable spirit*, which is the superior part of nature; and the expression of *all things* must be restrained to this outward third principle. Which if done, another question will naturally flow forth, viz., Is then God essentially in the devil also? Which is distinctly to be affirmed again, (1.) as to his own eternal triune being in a sense mentioned before; and (2.) as to his eternal nature, one part which is manifest, and the other hid in him etc.

Page 65. In the definition of God it is said, *manifesting himself in a sevenfold spirit, in a kingdom of light etc.* And here I observe (1.) that by mentioning first a sevenfold spirit, and then a kingdom of light, occasion is given to apprehend this kingdom of light not to be included in this sevenfold spirit, but to be posterior to it; and might be supposed to be as it were an eighth number, when it is even the seventh spirit itself. And (2.) that the first in is more relating to the way or manner of this manifestation, and the second in more as it were to the place wherein he manifests himself. Wherefore then, that both the one and the other might be more distinctly expressed, I think it might be said—manifesting himself *by* six living and acting spirits, *in* a kingdom of light, exulting Joy and glory, which is the seventh.

Page 67. Q. 1. This very same cometh again, for there is said, *such a kingdom is eternally generated by the seven spirits of God's eternal nature*, when it is generated only by the six, and is itself the seventh.

Page 68. Q. ult. The answer to this question combineth two considerations, vastly different from each other, which makes the sense obscure, and must needs therefore be altered. Fire and light are indeed always and every where to be conceived as distinct, for the one can never be, nor become the other, each must keep eternally to its own peculiar essentiality; but in this kingdom, the distinction between their properties is not perceivable, for the fire is meekened and softened by water and light, and is not known in its own natural fiery properties, but is overpowered by the light, which ruleth in this kingdom, using indeed the fire's powers as its instrument, but qualifying every thing according to its own tender and well-doing qualities. And this is that, which makes fire and light to be unsevered in this kingdom, though they are separable in and by the creature. But what more is said in this answer, viz., *that they are to be conceived as two distinct, self-subsistent, and self-sufficient lives or spheres of activity, which they call principles*, can here have no place at all, for this is quite another consideration. And though the two principles may be conceived so (with a good explanation both as to their being self-subsistent and self-sufficient) now, after the fall and separation, yet they cannot be conceived so, as before his fall. And further, that they cannot be conceived so *in this substance* is evident of itself, because this substance, or this kingdom of light and glory, is itself the one of these two eternal principles, the other of which should never have been known or perceived, if Lucifer had not manifested it.

Page 69. Between *Q*. 1 and 2, could fitly be inserted, though it be not absolutely necessary, this Q.—Is there anything in temporal nature by which this might be illustrated? A. Yes; the night's darkness, hidden in the light of a shining candle and manifested immediately upon its being extinguished, is a proper representation thereof.

Page 69. *Q*. 3. *Ideas* are those transitory or changeable figures, Images, or representations that are formed in the seventh, by a perpetual play or love-wrestling of the six active spirits. Transitory they are, because each of the six spirits hath a hand in their formation; and as therefore now one and then another gets the upper hand, so each of them figureth or changeth them more or less, according to its own more or less then predominant qualification. And this perpetual play is that which Behmen calleth the *formed Wisdom*, and compareth to a looking-glass, wherein the Spirit of God seeth the powers and wonders of its central All-sufficiency, now displayed indeed and unfolded in a sense and manner, but not yet breathed out into created beings, and so therefore only for his own holy pleasure and delight. Hereof the Scripture hath an excellent place, Prov. viii. 22–31. Where, besides many other most considerable expressions, it is directly said (according to the German translation) that Wisdom was God's *oblectamentum* or *deliciae*, and that *she played delightfully before his throne;* which last words are the same which St. John hath of the seven spirits.

Page 69. *Q*. 4. *Essences* are the subordinate particulars, or lesser inferior properties of, or also necessary emanations from that generation or generated thing, which they are said to be essences of. So that this denomination cannot be determined or tied up to a fixed constant sense, which were applicable every where universally, but must be taken variously, according to the subject matter. Yet so much may be said in general, that it imports always a particularity of things stirring and moving, descended down from this or that, which considered as before this particularity, is to be looked upon not only as an universal, but also more or less as hidden and unknown, and manifested in distinction in and by its essences. *Powers* and *virtues* are in one respect one and the same thing, but in another distinct, by such a distinction as is answerable to that which there is between fire and light; so that powers have a nearer relation to the strong and mighty, lively, energetical, penetrating fire-source, and virtues to the soft, mild, lovely, refreshing, amiable tincturing light. *Colours* are not different from what we call so in this external world, except only by their being that heavenly, and as to our eyes, invisible original, which our colours are but an obscure, transitory, and shadowy resemblance of, viz., such a one as is suitable to the condition of this four-elementary world; when the colours in the holy light-world must needs be so much more noble than ours, as that eternal light is more noble than our perishable light of the sun. From hence now the difference betwixt ideas, essences, powers, virtues, and colours may appear sufficiently; and moreover can it be plain also, that one and the same particular thing can be capable of three or four, if not of all these denominations, if it be but considered in different respects.

Page 69. *Q. ult.* When there is said, The ideas, together with the fire-light substance, and *all its powers*, was breathed out: I observe, that this is true indeed, yet so, that in each particular angel *one power* is predominant, or chiefly manifest, and all the others hid. Or else, if all were manifest in every one, there could be no variety, no distinct offices, no different abilities, nor degrees of dignity, as it is unquestionable in the heavenly hosts such distinctions and differences are.

Page 71, line 7. *by the attracting desire in them.* Here will be objected. This being compacted is their being created, and then if the attracting desire *in them* hath compacted them, they must be conceived as to have created themselves. Now I know this manner of expression is good and right to such as have understanding, but it will be hard to satisfy them that are in want of it. Wherefore then, to prevent this objection, I think it might be thus expressed—by the first compacting property of eternal nature, which in conjunction with the eternal speaking Word, they call the Verbum Fiat, or the creating power.

Page 71. *Q.* 2. In the answer to this question, after the words, *to be a similitude of the eternal Word of God*, I think must needs be added this, or something the like—enabled to form and speak out again his powers and wonders, in a subordinate or secondary way, according to their several properties predominant in them. For even herein, their being a similitude of the eternal Word consists, and without this they cannot be conceived so.

Page 73. *Q.* 1. To these several ends of their creation belongeth also this—that they should form, or concur to the formation and multiplication of God's wonders in his formed Wisdom, viz. each of them in his station, and according to the different names and powers which they represented.

Q. 3. The *intellectuality* of angels ariseth *in* and *from* the sixth spirit, or from that mutual permeation of all the seven, whereby their distinct properties are represented and communicated to each other; yet this sixth spirit is not to be considered as by itself alone, but as in conjunction with the eternal speaking Word, willing them to be living and understanding creatures, able to dispose of the powers and ideas in his formed wisdom. For as the first compacting spirit, not by itself alone, but in conjunction with the eternal Word, was the Verbum Fiat; so now the sixth, not as alone, but as in the same conjunction, is that which giveth intellect to what by the first was compacted. And as the life and light of man, according to St. John, was in the Word (not in the seven spirits), so was the life and light or intellect of angels also. For by the seven spirits, before the creation of angels, only ideas were formed, which had no life and light in them, and the Word was that which spoke them forth with life and light. But as this Word could not bring forth this life and light, except by an instrumental concurrence of the seven spirits; so in the answer to this question not only the Word, but also the seven spirits, and the sixth especially, must be expressed. Nay, the sixth may be mentioned even before the Word, because of its being nearer to the creature, and as it were in the middle between the creature and the Word. And not only *in*, but also *from* this sixth spirit, the intellect is rightly said to arise, because of its being the proper seat of intellect in nature, wherein especially Wisdom's looking-glass is manifest; and further, because of its peculiar character, fitness for the raising up, and intimate correspondence with the created intellect. Like as if it were asked, From whence cometh the image, name, and arms of the king upon a golden piece of money? It might be rightly answered, From the stamp, but in conjunction with the coining master, who can stamp it with this instrument, but cannot do it without it. For as there is a likeness between the stamp and that image which is expressed thereby, so is there also such a congruity between the angelical intellect and the sixth spirit of eternal nature, which yet cannot imprint its character without the Eternal Word, whose instrument it is. The expression, *the eternal Word could not*, etc, cannot give offence, seeing that God himself said unto Lot, *I can do nothing till*, etc. And if this instrument is considered as it is of his own making, and made even in order to perform thereby all the purpose of his will, this expression is not derogating in the least from a full idea of omnipotence.

Page 73. Q. 4. *At to the manner of their knowledge*, I cannot find that it is or can be different from that of man, except by such a difference as is necessarily caused by the condition of their holy uniform world, without mixture of good and evil, their nobler objects without them, and their own greater purity in themselves, or in all their faculties. For as to that lower sort of knowledge, which more or less dependeth upon or is combined with the use of senses, they see, hear, speak, feel, taste, and smell, no less than men. And as to that which is more or most sublime, touching the Divine, Infinite Being, they are all clear, pure, and passive mirrors, wherein the Supremest Good may freely, and without hindrance, represent his infinite perfections, according to their several capacities; and may thus in what is formed in and reflected from them, contemplate his own powers and distinction, which is the same manner as the Mystics declare from their experience. Wherein this will be the chief difference, that man, because of his mysterious redemption from a lamentable fall, is such a subject of the Divine manifestation, as angels cannot be, and that he therefore finds also in God such other attributes and glorious perfections, for his peculiar objects, as angels cannot find in him, viz., so, as if they were or could be themselves concerned therewith, so much, or so deeply and directly as man.

Page 73. Q. ult. *Their souls consist of fire and light.* Here I must needs observe, that when Behmen considereth soul and spirit, each in its distinction from the other, and as to its own peculiar being, he attributes fire unto the soul, and light unto the spirit, and says expressly, that the soul considered strictly as to itself only, hath in its being nothing else but fire with its dark root, that is the four first properties before the light, which is the fifth. And if we say the soul of angels consists of fire and light, we must needs own, that Lucifer, by losing his light, lost something of his soul, which cannot be made out.

Page 75, line 1. *Their spirits of a heavenly power,* etc. This may stand, and is not contrary to what now was said of the soul, but may well be reconciled with Behmen, as it could be shewn sufficiently if there were a necessity for it. But concerning what now further is said of *their bodies*, this must be observed, that Adam before his fall had indeed a body, wherein he was equal unto the angels, but that besides this angelical body, he had also an exterior one, which was from this third principle, and which the angels have not. And therefore, in our full restoration we shall be equal indeed unto the angels; but we shall have also something more than they, in the consideration of which they shall not be equal unto us. For we shall keep eternally that body also from this third principle, and this is that unto which resurrection belongeth, not that angelical one; seeing that this, if once born again in the regeneration, dieth not in the dissolution of the four-elementary body, but passeth through death into life, or rather is passed already in Jesus Christ. If we say therefore only—their bodies are like that which Adam had, without any farther addition, limitation, or explanation, especially now in this beginning, when nothing has yet been said of Adam's body, we shall make way for a great objection to be raised from the Scripture saying, that Adam's body was taken from the earth. Which I think ought to be prevented, as it can be done easily, by giving but a hint at that distinction between body and body, which doubtless will be discoursed of hereafter.

Page 75. *Q. ult.* Concerning *their food*, Behmen saith it is all manner of true, real, substantial fruit, answering unto that variety which we have in our world, and that they take it with their hands like us, etc. Besides the testimonies of them that have seen it, this depends rationally hereupon, that this world was one of the three angelical kingdoms, as it shall be again after the end or time. Wherefore, then, by the creation, no new thing that had not been before was brought into it, but only that which was before was altered and brought into such a grosser materiality, as that its former prince may no more make any use thereof. And this, Behmen saith is intimated by the words of Moses, saying—that every thing came forth *after its kind*. That which is further said, page 77, of the fire-light and watery part of that fruit, and of their twofold effects, I do not remember indeed that I have found it so declared by Behmen, but for all that it may be consistent with him well enough, if there were only some few words added, which might declare—that this is not the only, nor the principal thing which softeneth their central fire, and causeth their humility. And then it might further be added—that our sound in prayers, praises, and thanksgivings, doth also something the like, because of its relation to the sixth property of eternal nature, which is one of the forming spirits.

Page 79. *Q. ult.* This expression, *ignorant of the time*, might give occasion to think, that they profess the angels were created in or after the days of the creation, seeing that the beginning of the first day is the beginning of time, and that before this there was no time. That therefore this might be prevented, I think this question, When were the angels created? might be thus answered.—They hold them to be created before the six days of the creation, but do not tell us how long before, rather professing themselves to be ignorant thereof.

Further, in this answer it would be most proper to declare a little plainer, and more significantly, the difference between their fire and light, for to lay thereby a foundation for what is to follow after, seeing that very much dependeth hereupon, viz.—fire was absolutely their propriety, which they could not lose, it was their own nature, which could not be taken from them without their ceasing to be creatures; but creatures they could not cease to be after they once were created. But light was not so their own propriety, it was but their inheritance, given them for a portion by their Father, who would have them to be creatures after his own image, and who would not have taken it from them if they had continued obedient sons. Which inheritance therefore, they could lose, without losing their created nature.

Page 81. *Q*. 1. I think this question ought to be formed a little otherwise. For (1.) they had not a law which could properly be said to be *given them*; seeing that this implieth their having been creatures before this law was given, when this law was rather natural unto them, inseparable from their being creatures, innate in them, or born with them in their becoming creatures. As soon as they can be conceived as intellectual creatures, their intellect must be conceived also as sufficient to tell them, that since they had not made themselves, they were not to alter their Maker's making. And this was all their law, and their whole duty was therein comprised.

(2.) This was not a *peculiar* or particular law, commanding them this or that particular thing, but it was that universal law, which may rightly be called so, because, (1.) it is extended to all and every kind of understanding creatures, none of which can be created without having this law imprinted, from its very first beginning, into its intellect. And, (2.) because it is the true, eternal root and ground of all the particular laws whatsoever in this inferior world.

Page 82. It is said, *God would not withstand them by anything, but by his wrath, which would have enkindled the fire in them, and then they would have fallen before they had sinned.* This seems to be somewhat obscure, and to my thinking could be plainer, if it were after this or the like manner expressed,—but by his wrath, which (if thereby he would have prevented their fail) would have enkindled the fire in them; and then they had been turned out of the light before their sin was consummated. Or thus,—and then they had fallen into darkness before they had themselves extinguished their light.

Page 83. *Q*. 2. This question and answer (in the sense which I can find therein) goeth too far; for I understand the meaning to be, that God offered his grace after their full consummated fall, and (according to the foregoing question) after they were actually turned out, which cannot be so conceived. For they had then already hardened and shut up themselves fully, so that they were no more capable of hearing the gracious voice of God. Though this cannot be denied, that the love and grace stood then as it stands to this day, over against them in its own principle, and would be ready to take them in, if they were to accept of it, by dying to their own fire-will, and turning into meekness and humility.

Q. 3. In the words, *over God's meek love and light, which they despised,* the words *and light* must needs be left out. For though it is rightly said *they would rule over love and light,* yet light cannot be connected with the following words, *which they despised,* seeing that they intended not to go out from the light, but rather to continue therein, and to make it greater, brighter, and more glorious than it was, that so their dominion might be the more exalted, and the majesty of their prince made more adorable, and so they did not (directly) despise it. But the love, meekness, humility, obedience, conformity with their brethren, and all that was not agreeing or conformable to the strength and might of fire in own will, they despised, thinking all this too low and contemptible for such mighty lords.

Page 85. *Q.* 2. § 1. Three things I may here observe, though but of small importance. (1.) The prince of it is now, since his fall called Lucifer, but before it he had another name, which is not known. (2.) He was absolutely the most glorious angel, because of his representing the Son, who is the *brightness of the Father's glory.* (3.) If by the fall is understood his being cast out from the light, we cannot well say, he fell first, for they were turned out altogether; but if the meaning be, that he began first to turn away from the meekness and obedience, it is true that he fell first away from it, for he was the centre and principle of this motion or insurrection in all his subjects, and none of them could have made such a beginning of apostacy.

Ibid. § 3. *Their fight consisted in their opposing each other.* This I think might be nearer and more significantly declared by saying—that it consisted in a magical operation, wherein they raised up the powers of eternal nature against each other. For the holy angels made use of the holy light-powers in a divine magia, and the devils contrariwise. This fight, saith Behmen, cannot be understood, but by the spirit (of a believer) in his own experience.

Page 87. *Q. ult.* A. Yes: they suppose according to Scripture, 1st, That God is love and light. 2ndly, That God's is also fire and might, together with its hidden root of darkness. And 3rdly, That darkness, fire, and light are all three requisite to make up a creature after the image and likeness of God. And now upon these premises they say—that which came out of God, viz., out of love and light, cannot be capable of such a state of damnation; but as it is his free gift, so it returneth unto the giver, when the creature severeth itself from it by turning its will and obedience away therefrom. But that which came out of God's fire and might remaineth in such a esse alone, and cannot be lost, because it is the creature's natural propriety, or that which makes it to be a creature. And this now, seeing it consists all of moving, stirring and active properties, cannot but work according to its own internal nature and essences. Which working is nothing else but a sensible manifestation of its own natural propriety, made in, and to, and by the creature itself. And this manifestation now, is that which we call such a state of damnation, and which this creature most naturally and of all necessity be capable of, because it cometh not upon it from without, but is raised by itself out of its own ground, and is only a discovery of itself, as of that which the Creator would have hidden from the creature, by his free gift of light, and would have glorified it in his love, as it is so in himself, or in his own eternal nature. To say therefore, that a substance which came out of God's fire and might, can be capable of such a state of damnation, is to say nothing more than this, that a rebellious creature is capable of losing the free gift of love and light, and of feeling what its own essential nature is, if separated therefrom, and living in and to itself. Which self-living and self-working is for all that, good in its kind and order, forasmuch as it must serve for the manifestation of God's honour, glory, truth, and justice, though it is the greatest evil, viz., of punishment, to the creature.

Page 89. *Q*. 3. Here, either in or after § 3, could most properly be added, according to Behmen—that the dark own-will of the devils, being entirely united to, co-essenced and con-substantiated with, and captivated by the dark world, *cannot* turn into God's light and the meekness of his love; because the dark world hath got such a mighty life, will and government, and no life can be for its own death, neither can any government desire or promote its own destruction.

And if then further another question should be formed, as an objection taken from man, who, notwithstanding his fall, can turn, and can ardently desire and pray that his own dark will in him may be slain and subdued, and utterly extirpated by the light and love of God; this could be answered sufficiently by shewing the differences between man's and the devil's fall, as also chiefly between this outward world's, and the dark world's condition, state, and properties.

Page 91. Line 3. This expression, *passing away of the new heavens and the new earth, after the end of this world*, depends, I suppose, upon a peculiar apprehension not understood by me. Wherefore then, I can indeed say nothing against it; but I can also not approve of it, finding it (as to that sense I can now see therein) inconsistent with Behmen's ground.

Page 91. Line 8. If these words, *actually force their wills*, were set in an answer, so that I could apprehend them to be your own words, I would humbly beg of you, Sir, to change them into these or the like,—Whether God will ever, in any space of eternity, find out, in his infinite wisdom, an expedient for their restoration into the light? Which expression would answer the purpose as much as that other can. But seeing those words stand in a question, and are, as I suppose, the proper expression of that person who said lately, *He may do so if he pleases, etc.*, they can perhaps not well be altered. Yet in the following answer, something might be said for a correction. For this is certain, that he who useth this expression of *forcing their wills*, whosoever he be, is altogether unacquainted with Behmen's ground, and cannot pretend to understand what a *Will* is, and especially what this will is, which here is spoken of.

Q. ult. This question and answer might give occasion to object, That if their office is to be Images of the eternal fire, there seems to be a predestinating will supposed, which would have had such officers and images. This now might be prevented, if in the answer were mentioned—That they must be images and officers by the same necessity by which they must be creatures, and as they could not lose in their fall their being creatures, so neither could they their being Images and having offices; but since they would not bear that holy image and office in God's love and light, they must now bear that in his wrath. And then I would not absolutely say, *an image of the eternal fire*, but rather *of the dark eternal fire;* that so it might not be understood of the first principle, from which they are cast out, though it is so also well enough expressed, for any one that hath understanding, and is acquainted with Behmen's style.

Page 93. Q. 1. To the words, *it is their work to transform themselves*, could be added, according to Behmen, into manifold terrible shapes, and the more monstrous they can make themselves, to ridicule thereby the holy, simple, angelical image, the more they take delight therein; as players, and indeed all kinds of mountebanks, in this third principle.

Q. 2. Seeing that only the two first lines of this answer, do relate to the question, and all the rest is a digression from it, and seeing also that this is a question of importance, I think there might be made some mention of—their considering the different properties and inclinations predominant in men, and then assaulting them accordingly, by raising up with their pernicious magical imaginations, such powers and properties of darkness as they find most fit, for to dart by them into their dark and astral minds, such thoughts, lusts and desires, as they know are most agreeable to their several natural constitutions.

Page 95. *A*. 1. Here it will be objected that the description of Moses, and the tradition of all nations, say something indeed of a dark, confused chaos, but do not tell us that the same came to be so by the fall of Lucifer, for Moses beginneth only with a work of God, saying expressly, In the beginning God created, etc. Wherefore then, that this might be prevented, and also that a more exact order might be observed, I think something could be inserted, and the construction a little altered, that it might be thus,—all the order, beauty, light, and glory of the seventh passive form in their kingdom, which all depended upon a harmonious love-wrestling of the six active spirits, must needs have been spoiled, wasted, extinguished, made desolate, and all turned into a dark, confused chaos, by their great disorder, strife, and opposition. Every war between two mighty potentates in this world, as it hath taken its original from hence, so it can be more or less a plain representation hereof. And that there was such a desolate state in the beginning of time, we see from the description of Moses, and the unanimous tradition of all nations, etc.

Page 97. *A*. 1. This description saith indeed something of the chaotic state, as to the invisible things of the angelical kingdom; but it saith nothing thereof as to the visible things, which yet are to come into the chiefest consideration. For therein were the sad effects of Lucifer's revolting (See AURORA, Chapt. xvi. and xvii.), and the disorder and strife of the invisible properties was but the cause thereof. The six active forms are the invisibles of this kingdom, which are perpetually generating; but that which properly by Behmen is called the kingdom itself, or the seventh passive form, and the innumerable multiplicity and variety of things generated therein by the six, are the risible things (viz., to the angelical eyes). And therein chiefly the chaotic state cometh into consideration, as in Moses's description also may be seen, who speaketh only of the visible material things; whereby yet the invisibles are not excluded, for their disorder and strife raised by Lucifer, was the only true cause thereof, which Moses mentioneth not.

And further, there are also in this description, several such expressions as cannot be maintained, for instance, may be this one only, *Darkness hath overspread the whole face of that dark or abyssal region*. When it should rather have been said—the whole face of the outmost generation, or of the holy, pure, and crystalline materiality. Wherefore then, I should think this description might be shorter as to the invisible things, and as to the visible something should be added, that it might stand in such or the like form:

A. They mean, that the invisible things of that kingdom were in a divided and confused state, nay, even quite turned upside down: the darkness being now predominant, manifest, and outermost, the fire more, and the light more deeply hidden in their several centres, so that none of these three could do its proper office; which was now directly contrary to that state wherein they stood before. And consequently also, that all the visible things, generated in this kingdom by the six invisible properties, were thereby utterly spoiled, ruined, wasted, deprived of all the former order, harmony, proportion, beauty, purity, and transparency, and were violently condensed, and made all gross, hard, and rough, by the sharp, harsh, astringent properties of nature, now prevalent and qualifying them, according to their own nature.

Page 97. *A*. 2. Instead of the last words, *This whole kingdom would have been soon to condensed, etc.* I think the two reasons which Behmen giveth, could properly be added, viz. (1.) This kingdom was not Lucifer's propriety, but only his inheritance, which he had under condition of obedience. Why then should it not have been taken away from him, by God, the only true proprietor? (2.) This kingdom, viz. the seventh form, had not committed any fault, but was only passive, according to its nature, and must have suffered all those violent acts of its robbers and murderers. Why then should it have been forsaken by God, so as not to be restored into its former state?

Page 99. *A*. 1. Seeing that this expression, *into a new order*, is ambiguous, and can be understood of another order different from the former, when it is rather the former order itself, only renewed, or restored at least in part: seeing further, that this renewing is so coherent with the breathing forth, that it cannot be conceived (at least, not wholly) as a peculiar act, done by itself, before this breathing forth; but as a thing done gradually and successively, during the days of the creation, though the first beginning thereof or disposition thereto, may be conceived as before it. And seeing, thirdly, that two or three things more in the following words might give rise to scruples, I think this answer would be less exposed to objections, if it were formed in this or in the like manner:

A. They say that God, restoring the invisibles of this kingdom into their order and union, (yet so that darkness and fire kept each of them its own awakened life and power, though under some restraint,) spoke or breathed forth out of them gradually, by his eternal Word and Spirit, in conjunction with them, an exterior and inferior degree of government; answering indeed, unto that former, but having now a twofold source, and being settled only for a certain time, which when fulfilled, this kingdom shall be fully delivered and restored into its former state. And that further, accordingly from hence all the visible things of it were generated, and fashioned indeed after their former kind, but in that mixture wherein we see them to this day. Which whole exterior, temporal government, they call therefore an outbirth, a mixed third principle, and, with a peculiar respect to the visibles, a coagulated breath or smoke from the eternal darkness, fire, and light, so that this whole macrocosm may be conceived as a kind of appurtenance or *accident* of the whole eternal nature, considered as in its manifested division into three.

Page 101. *Q.* 1. *How many mixtures, etc.* Seeing that every mixture implieth, or requireth at least two things, and that the four aftermentioned parts cannot be said to make four mixtures, but only one mixture made up of four things, I think it would be more proper if this question were formed thus—How many things, do they suppose, this mixture in the things of this world, consisteth of? Or also thus—How many different things, do they suppose, may be found in this mixture by chemical operation separating, or, as it were, anatomising the things of this world?

§ 20. *by the devil and man's sin.* Here it is to be observed, that man's sin did not introduce the wrath or root of evil into the things of this world, but only the *curse:* which is to say only, that he caused the blessing, viz. paradise's penetrating and greening forth through the earth, to cease and to withdraw; whereby then, that wrath and root of evil, which laid therein before, and was introduced thereinto by the devil only, but was hitherto kept under by the paradise, must needs have been enabled, or empowered to spring up and manifest itself again, etc. Wherefore then, the words, and man's sin, must either be left out wholly, or the whole sense must be thus expressed—introduced into them by the devil, and awakened again by the sin of man.

Page 101. *Q. ult.* Seeing that this question expressly asketh, From whence all mixed things arise, and adds further—as from their *first root,* I cannot see that a sufficient answer can be taken from the seven properties of temporal nature only. For the seven spirits of eternal nature are rather the *first,* or at least a deeper, though not yet the deepest root. And as to their being *mixed,* I think that this expression, also, might be more or less regarded in the answer. And further, when there is said, page 103, line 2, *Which are supposed, etc.,* it seems a little ambiguous what this which is to be referred unto, whether to the seven spirits of eternal, or to the seven of temporal same. To the former it is indeed rightly to be referred, yet so, that the latter may not be thereby excluded; for, during all the time of this world, they are inseparable from each other. And then also the last words, *according to the several kinds of things,* bring an obscurity along with them, and do not very well agree with what in the following question is declared, though I confess they might be reconciled therewith. For we cannot so properly say—the diverse predominancy is according to the several kinds of things; but rather to the contrary—the several kinds of things are according to the diverse predominancy, which is also in the following question plainly asserted. Wherefore then, these last mentioned words could be left out, without any hurt. Now, after this, I think it would be proper to insert this following:

Q. How do the seven properties of temporal nature differ from the seven spirits of eternal nature? A. They differ upon one particular account, as an accident differs from its substance, or as a shadow from its body; upon another, as an offspring of leaser dignity, from its nobler original; and upon a third one, as the darker, more impotent, and unactive productions, at the extremes of the fire's spherical activity, from the most luminous and active effects, at the nearest distance of a radiant flame. Which simile was mentioned above.

Page 102. *Q.* 1. In the answer to this question, I would say rather thus, and think it might be more distinct and plainer:

A. From the various combinations, and greater or lesser predominancy of some of these spirits, with their inferior subordinate properties, which did form ideas from eternity, in several kinds and species. And seeing they are now all in conjunction with the eternal Word and Spirit, they must needs bring forth those ideas, according to their in part restored and re-united state, which they were brought into by God in the creation. In which state, they are not only themselves still breathed forth, by the eternal Word, but are also enabled thereby to breathe forth again, to form and to compact. And this their secondary, or subordinate breathing forth, considered chiefly with respect to the first compacting property, is a temporal Fiat, still remaining in all things.

Page 102. *Q.* 2. From what now was declared in this foregoing answer, it appears, that this question will be plainer, if thus proposed. What is that *Word*, which still breathes forth the diverse kinds and species of things? For if there is said only—breathes them forth, it will be dubious whether these things, or whether the properties themselves of temporal nature are meant. And to this question now I would answer thus:

A. It is that same eternal Word which breathed them forth in the beginning, yet not considered as in that manifest and perceptible act which was done in the days of the creation, and entered into rest at the end thereof; but as in its secret continuing in and with all things, upholding, and still enabling them (by the powers, either of eternal or temporal nature, or by both of them together,) to increase and multiply, according to their kind.

Page 103. *A.* 1. I think it might be here very proper, if not necessary, to say—that as the seven planets and fixed stars are such representations above, so the seven metals and minerals are also the same below. For our earth, being made up of the grossest excrements, or most corrupted matter gathered from all the corners of this wasted kingdom, and compacted into one globe, must needs have in it something, answering to what is, besides it, finer, and more subtle or etherial, in the whole region. And this is certainly the ground (though some other reasons, no less considerable, might be given of that saying of Hermes, *Id quod est inferius est sicut id quod est superius.*

Concerning now, the following description of the three first properties, I have nothing to say of importance; but shall only gather from Behmen, what I may find here or there is attributed unto each of them. If it might serve, for to insert this or that particular thing, significant expression or circumstance, it would be well and profitable; and if not, no hurt can be done thereby. As to the first, then,

(Page 103. *A. ult.*) Behmen useth the words, *of a spiritual sharpness, harshness, grossness, darkness, etc.* and sayeth that of these three, (sal, sulphur, and mercury, commonly, by natural philosophers, called the three principles of things,) the first, viz. sal, is this same first property. Whereof he sayeth also, that it is the greatest and most potent, the beginning of strength and might, the Fiat (though never as by itself alone), and the keeper of all things; a drying and shutting up into death; a taking in unto self, and a true mother of selfishness; a cause of sound, noise, etc.; the beginning of every formation; a magnetism, or magnetical impression and coagulation of itself, filling and darkening itself, etc.

(Page 105. *Q*. 1.) This *second* quality is the motion of the magnetical drawing in; a cause of all creatural life, a trembling, stinging bitterness, or a stinger, stirrer, rager, and breaker; the cause of the essences; the beginning of enmity, and of all contrariety, and also of all qualification; the cause of distinction, speech, intellect, five senses, etc. This spirit (N.B.) is restless (or rather the restlessness itself), and is yet the seeker after rest, making its own unquietness by its very seeking. It is a ground of bitter woe, and yet the true root of life; and the vulcanus, striking the fire (viz. of or to the life). It is a cause of all sensibility and feeling; a ground of the air, in the outward world: it is the outflown moveable word; and in the creation this was the separator or divider in the powers.

(Page 105. Q. 2.) This *third* quality makes the triangle in nature, and is a whirling wheel, taken in, and as it were swallowing up into death the bitter essences, but giving forth out of it another life. A cause of death and life, and of the twofold fire, viz. of the first and second principle. Its proper name is anguish; its qualification, wrath and anger; and its materiality, sulphur. It hath a twofold fire in it, viz. a cold and a hot one, and is the devil's chiefest seat. Without the light it is the true foundation of hell: and in the light the cause of eternal joy, etc.

Considering, Sir, that this matter, concerning the *three first properties*, is of so great importance, so fundamental, and hath so much depending upon it, I cannot but recommend to your consideration, whether it would not be necessary, that several things thereof more distinctly and circumstantially, and even so might be declared, that always the things, belonging more properly and immediately to eternal nature, were placed first, and that then a descent were made to temporal nature, and farther to the grossest outbirth thereof; that so confusion might be the more avoided, and the connexion plainer might appear. I mean, that there might be declared—how strictly and inseparably these three are united, and make an indissoluble band, notwithstanding all their great contrarieties. That the second must necessarily be always and everywhere with the first; and that the first cannot be conceived without the second; as no attraction can be, nor be conceived, without conceiving a motion, etc. How the third ariseth from the first and second, and is a mixture of them both; and why it must necessarily whirl about, etc. That these three are always to be combined with the other three, if those particular effects or products, that are attributed by Behmen either unto the first, or second, or third, or also sometimes unto two, if not unto all three of them shall be understood. And that so therefore, the first belongeth to, and is accomplished in the seventh; the second in the sixth, and the third in the fifth, etc. Such, and the like particulars, I am sure, are absolutely necessary for an *understanding of the Seven properties*, according to Behmen's mind.

Page 107. *Q. ult. Where and how doth this water spirit arise?* A. It ariseth in the light, and is that same, which before the light was called harshness. The manner of its arising is this—when the fire in the three first dark properties is enkindled, it makes in them a (twofold) great crack, or terror, called so with respect to *sensible creatures*, which, if it were done so in them, could not but feel the greatest terror. This harshness then, being thus terrified, (in the second crack) loseth immediately, or, as it were, dieth to its former nature, and is made soft and thin, and qualified according to the meek and tender properties of the light; wherein it is now the water spirit, or that whose immediate production in the spiritual materiality is water.

Page 108. *Q. What do they mean by the sweetness of the water?* A. They mean, that tinctured and transmuted quality, with relation especially to the spiritual taste, which now the water hath in the light, in opposition to that, which it had before in the first harshness: and they distinguish thereby the water of light and life, from that of death and darkness.

Page 111. *A.* 1. The words, *arising from these seven spirits*, might be looked upon as inconsistent with what was declared above; and though it could indeed be reconciled, yet this would only make way for several other questions, and cause a digression. Wherefore, I think they might be left out, the more, because they are not absolutely necessary, and the sense is full enough without them.

A. 2. It is indeed rightly said, *this mercurial spirit*. But seeing that this denomination of this sixth spirit, depends chiefly upon an union with the second, before the light, which commonly by Behmen is called Mercury, when this sixth is Jupiter, unto some this expression will be obscure, and others might say that a mistake is committed. Wherefore, I am of opinion, that either this word mercurial might be left out, or something might be added, whereby this obscurity could be taken away, and needless objections prevented. And then, it will not be well enough to say only—those things sound most which have this spirit in them, seeing that it was owned just before, that all things have it in them. Wherefore, it must needs be more proper to say—most in them, or—which have it sufficiently stirring in them, etc.

Page 111. *A.* 3. *In which they work the work of God.* Nothing indeed can be said against this manner of expression; yet I am apt to think, it would be more expressive in this place, if there were said—in which they do, by their working, unfold and manifest in forms and figures, the hidden powers of God's central all-sufficiency.

Page 115. *A. in conjunction with his will (which they call the fiat).* This, I think, is not plainly enough expressed; for it might be apprehended so, as if the will (alone) were called by them the fiat, which it is not, as it was observed before. And then, instead of *will*, I would rather say, *eternal Word*. Because here is not spoken of a purpose, but of the execution thereof, or of a present act and deed, which the will may be conceived indeed as antecedent unto; but the Word is rightly conceived as nearer, and as actually engaged therein. And therefore the Word (in that conjunction) more properly than the *will*, was the fiat *in actu;* whereby yet the will is not excluded, but manifestly presupposed.

Ibid. (which they take to be the meaning of the word created.) This might justly be put in after the words, *compacting its earth*, for as it stands before them, it doth but misrepresent their meaning. Seeing that by the word *created*, they do not understand—he prepared the chaotic angelical world, which is a more general expression, but they understand precisely this compacting.

Ibid. And its heaven—into a state of purity. I cannot see that it is fit or proper to say—heaven was *compacted into a state of purity*.

For (1.) the word *compacted* is more fit for the earth, than for heaven, which might rather be said to have been *condensed*, (or if there is any such other more pertinent expression) for to show the difference between heaven and earth. Which two could not have been equally capable of the same degree of condensation or compaction. And (2.) heaven cannot be said to be—condensed into a state of purity. Because this purity doth not depend directly upon its creation or condensation (which selfsame word implieth already something of impurity, forasmuch as it is a changing from its former state into another, made upon such a sad account), but only upon its being, as it were, swept and cleansed from those gross impurities that were scattered up and down everywhere. Which when gathered and compacted in one place, the rest of this region was free from them, and became more fit for to receive another shape and condition, much inferior to its former. And this only is meant by Behmen, when he speaketh of that state, which the English interpreter hath expressed by *purity*.

Page 116. *A*. 1. To the last words, *which there was not before*, I think most pertinently could be added something of what over against p. 117, is blotted out, viz.—and that they might be a habitation, fitted and prepared for those innumerable kinds of creatures, that were to be in them.

Page 117. *A*. 2. All this is right and true, what herein is declared: only this may be observed. That not only the compaction into *palpable materiality* in particular, but also more generally, the whole condensation or outbreathing, coagulated into another inferior kind of grosser substance though never so fine in comparison to the earth, was that proper means, by which the devil's power was broken, his kingdom taken from him, and he disabled to exercise his wickedness any further therein, by his dark and false magia.

Page 118. *That it might be a principle, existing in itself.* Seeing that this denomination of a principle, in its full sense, wherein Behmen usually takes it, is not applicable to the earthly globe, but to the whole macrocosm,

I think it would be more tolerable, if it were a little limited, by saying—that it might be as a principle in some sense existing in itself; for in every sense it cannot be said that it exists in itself.

Page 119. Q. 1. This answer also is right and true enough, but only the two last lines thereof may be called obscure, and might easily be made plainer, and more freed from objections. For they do not say nor mean, that the earth was restored into a tolerable state, directly, or only by its revolutions; but by the different works, effects, and products of the six active spirits, which performed in and to the earth their several operations, and concurred successively to this restoration, during the time of these revolutions.

Q. 2. *Why the earth's revolution is made in a natural day*, cannot well be asked nor answered. Because, if we think to ask so, we must needs presuppose an idea of the length of a natural day, before the idea of the earth's revolution, which we cannot rationally do, seeing that the earth's revolution is only that, which made from the beginning, and still makes all the natural days, determining their constant length, and that without or before it no natural day can be conceived, nor any measure of its length can be imagined. And so, this question cannot be answered any more than this, Why hath a natural day precisely such a length as it hath? Which would be the same as if we did ask, Why doth not the earth move either more swiftly or more slowly than it doth? Which nobody will presume to answer sufficiently from natural reasons. And yet even so must this question be formed, with respect to the three first revolutions, which did not yet make a natural day; and were nevertheless performed in the same space of time, which is now the proper constant length thereof.

Page 123. A. 1. If to the last words, *by the motion of his Spirit*, were added, *upon the waters*, It would be more evident that this relates to the description of Moses.

A. 2. line 1. They say, *it is diffused:* here I would, for my part, rather say—It was diffused, for several reasons. And after the words, *became not bright and resplendent*, I would add, from Behmen, *but was of a blueish colour, like that of the clear firmament.*

Page 127. *A* 1. *A dark part, which is as a firmament.* Though this can stand so well enough, and could be maintained sufficiently; nay, though it may have been expressed so, by Behmen himself, which I do not exactly remember, yet I may justly observe, that it doth not represent sufficiently Behmen's sense. For, it is not properly and strictly that dark part itself, which is this firmament; but it is rather that, whereby this dark part, with all what belongeth thereto, and depended thereupon, is divided and excluded from the light. It is that which chiefly makes a principle, to be called so in Behmen's sense. In some places, I think the German word is translated,—a gulf, but not significantly enough. In a rude similitude it might be represented by that point, which is in the middle of these two semicircles, (two semicircles placed back to back, and joined, through the centre of which is a cross) But seeing that this is not fit for every one, I say again, that this expression, *of a dark part*, may stand so well enough.

Page 129. § 2. *ideas or essences*. Here I think it might be better to say, *ideas and essences*; that so these two might be left in a distinction, and not taken only for one and the same thing; though in a peculiar respect they may be so.

Pages 129 and 131. § 5. Concerning the description of the growing of vegetables; seeing that it is almost impossible to give in so few lines, a circumstantial and sufficient account thereof, according to Behmen's sense, I should be apt to think it better, if there were said only in general—that all the growth of vegetables cometh from the strife of the qualities of nature, raised up from without by the sun's heat, and carried on within by their own natural contrariety. And that therefore, no growth can be in the winter, when the sun is impotent, etc.

Pages 133 and 136. *They say therefore in short, etc.* In this description, I meet with several things which could be excepted against, and which, if they should be particularised, would but cause a prolixity, without any considerable benefit. I shall therefore, leave this alone, and set only down the order and chief circumstances of this generation; so as I think it might be best but not pretending to give that full satisfaction which might be expected:

They say, therefore, in short: (1.) That on this fourth day, the production of the planette orb, with all the fixed stars, being a visible outbirth and representation of the seven chief spirits, both of eternal and temporal nature, with all their inferior or subordinate qualities, was made in a manner, answering unto that which they were themselves from eternity, and still are generated in.

(2.) That the fourth spirit of eternal nature, the magic fire broke forth, and fixed its representative in the centre of our vortex, which is the sun.

(3.) That several particular circumstances, relating to the first astringent property, and this considered both as before, and as after that saying, Let there be light, (all which they are not wanting to declare sufficiently,) are most necessary to be well understood, and considered jointly; for to be informed and convinced thereby, that this first spirit of nature, the cause of cold, produced its representative (at this enkindling of the fire) in the remotest *orbit* from the centre, called *Saturn* which is, according to their doctrine (agreeing with that of the ancients), a cold planet.

(4.) That at the same enkindling of the fire in the sun, the fierce terrible crack, (always naturally preceding the fire's clear flame and light) was projected, or rather fled up itself from the centre, with a dreadful force, according to its own natural birth-right; and took along with it, for its substantial being, the fire's wrathfulness. And that so this ascended, until the sun's light, now rising and displaying itself, overpowered it, and stopped its raging fury. This now they say is *Mars*, the third anguishing and whirling spirit's representative, whose office is to stir and move all what is moveable in this whole macrocosm, and the planetary wheel especially.

(5.) That this light (considered not as to the shine or glance, but as to the power and virtue thereof) having thus stopped the course of Mars, left behind it its fierce wrathfulness, and ascended up still higher, as a soft rising life, according to its own natural right, until it came to Saturn's harsh, astringent sphere of activity, by whose compressive power it was resisted, and made impotent of rising higher. Where it therefore remained, and made, by taking possession of that place, the fifth spirit's representative, which is *Jupiter*, the meekness in outward nature, and rightly therefore situated between the astringent cold of Saturn, and the fierce fire of Mars, as a temperament betwixt them.

(6.) That when the light arose from this enkindled fire in the centre, and by this light the first harshness was broken, the same, but transmuted, and being now the mild water spirit, *sunk* humbly and softly *down*, and made a visible representative of the fifth spirit in *Venus*, which they say hath an inherent light of its own (which is asserted by some late astronomers), and tempereth the fierceness of the heat of Mars.

(7.) That this sinking went on from the property of Venus, so that the power of the first harshness, now softened in and by the light, sunk deeper down, and became a visible representative of the sixth spirit, which is *Mercury*.

(8.) That this sinking continued further from Mercury also, and attained its period in the *Moon*, which they say doth represent the seventh spirit of eternal nature, partaking of the qualities of all the others, and therefore the fitter to receive them, and transmit them to our sublunary world.

(9.) That the seven planets have a wonderful efficacy upon——, etc. Page 135.-§ 8. Concerning the difficulty, that the planets have so gross and obscure bodies, as cannot be imagined to have been projected from the sun, it can be plain enough from this short description, that Behmen saith nothing at all of such a gross material projection, but that he describeth a spiritual generation, or *displaying of the spiritual properties*, which needs must have been done in this macrocosm, at the enkindling of the fire in its centre, according to the manner of their eternal generation, wherein the fire's nature and office is to display all the properties, and to make them manifest in their distinction. Seeing then, that this was now done in a manner and degree inferior to that eternal generation, viz. in a temporal principle, in circumscriptive localities and measurable distances, etc., these planets, as to their several chief qualities predominant in them, and giving them their distinct names, may well enough be said to have been projected from the sun, for as much as the enkindling of the sun was their original, or the cause of their being thus made *visible* in this temporal world. It is not said that the sun hath generated them, this Behmen expressly denieth. And much less is it said, that so many vast, gross, and obscure bodies, were ejaculated from the sun. But only, that at this enkindling of the fire in the sun, such and such spiritual properties were raised and stirred up, so that they moved each of them according to its own nature, some mounting up from the centre on high, and others in opposition thereto sinking down: and this as to their predominant powers and virtues. But concerning now their corporeal being, it must be supposed, that each of them got it in its own place or sphere, wherein it standeth still at such or such a proportionable distance from the centre, according to Behmen's plain words, saying, sometimes of the one or other (which cannot but be applied unto all)—they were created in that place. For if we consider what he means by *created*, which was declared above, it will be self-evident that this saying cannot be reconciled with that other—they were projected, if we do not understand by this latter, a descent of their spiritual properties from the centre, and by that former a compaction of their vast material bodies. If there should be objected, that there was said above, (§ 4,) Mars took along with it from the centre, the wrathfulness, as its body, etc., it is easily and solidly answered, That in such a sense it may be said even of all of them, that they took along with them this or that from the centre, for a body. But that this was only such a body, as our thoughts are bodies of the spirit in them, mentioned above, p. 113. Which kind of body each of them must have had indeed, even in the first beginning of their departing from the centre. But that this body was as then, not yet that vast, gross, obscure globe, wherein they appear to this day, is evident enough. This spiritual body therefore, was afterwards immediately created or compacted, in their several places, and according to the difference of their spirituality. So that none of them can be reasonably imagined, to be altogether alike unto our earth. Nay also, none of them can be such a one as the moon's is, which is the nearest unto earthliness, and hath a mixture of them all, notwithstanding that they all may be equally obscure in themselves, etc.

And thus, I think, the chief difficulty is sufficiently removed, so that it can be tolerable to say, in such a sense as mentioned—the planets were projected from the sun, at the enkindling of the fire in the centre, though Behmen doth never use the word projection or ejaculation, but says rather of-their own free displaying and departing from the centre (though this was caused by the fire), either by flying up or sinking down, according to the manner of their generation in eternal nature.

Page 139. § 1. *manifested out of the fire of nature, etc.* This manner of expression, as to my thinking, is a little ambiguous, and though it can bear a good and true sense, yet it could easily also be taken in a wrong one. Wherefore, for my part, I would say rather thus—breathed forth out of the dark and light world, and manifested by the enkindling of the fire, in the sun, as in the centre of this our vortex, etc.

§ 2. Seeing that the fixed stars are not only a representation of energies, but also energies themselves, though in an inferior degree and order than those which they are a representation of, I am apt to think it would be fit and requisite, after the words, *energies of eternal nature*, to add this, or something the like—exercising in temporal nature, and after a temporal manner, the same powers and energies that are originally in eternal nature, out of which they were breathed, etc.

For though there followeth afterwards, (§ 3,) expressly enough, that they are of wonderful efficacy, yet there is not expressed—that this efficacy depends only upon this, their being representatives, of so many energies of eternal nature.

Page 139. § 3. *on all things here below.* Seeing that this efficacy cannot absolutely be restrained to things here below, though this may make the chiefest part thereof, with respect especially to man, I think it would be most proper to say—of wonderful efficacy in the whole extent of this temporal universe, and especially on all things here below.

To all the rest of the expressions of this paragraph, I must say, it is so obscure, that I cannot apprehend the proper meaning. The distinct particular expressions, looked upon each by itself are indeed plain and true enough, but the connexion of them makes a great obscurity, which yet may be so only to my sight, for want of a sufficient understanding of a good English style.

Betwixt § 3 and § 4, I think something could be most properly inserted, which might make plainer that which is said, § 4, and might also shew, at least impliedly, a ground and reason for it, viz. That good and evil, wrath, anger, and love, are manifest in the stars, and this because of their threefold original, which is the dark, fire, and light world, of whose powers and energies brought by Lucifer into contrariety, they are efficacious representatives.

And then, in any other convenient place, several things more could be added, according to Behmen, though they are but arbitrary, and may be left out also, as for instance,—That they have among them their orders and degrees, as of bigness or visible magnitude, so also of different, superior and inferior dignities and offices, in analogy to the angelical kingdoms, and also to the governments upon earth. That, in one sense and respect, they stand all in discord, disharmony, contrariety, and opposition, and yet in another, make up altogether but one great harmonious instrument: like as the many greater and lesser, thicker and thinner strings, of one or more musical instruments, can make a melodious concordant tune, as well as a dissonant, ungrateful noise, according to the skill or intent of that hand that moves them. That the whole nature, with all its powers and energies, is totally in every one of them, but one only power is principally predominant or manifest in each of them: wherefore then, there are not so many natures as stars, but all the stars together, are the whole nature, or the manifestation of all the powers of nature. That they are in a continual anxious turning, or rolling from the wrath-fire, kindled by Lucifer and his legions. That they are fixed, each in its own place, because this third principle is to stand in a constant abiding generation, unto the end of time; and all manner of life in the earth, shall be generated always by one and the same operation, and after the same manner. That they may draw, incline, or dispose man to good and evil, and many times to great wickednesses, but cannot constrain nor lay a necessity upon him, etc.

Between pages 140 and 141. *Q. 1. What do they say concerning the influences—with respect to the nativity?* Here I can produce nothing from Behmen, in particular. Behmen says only in general, that the hour of nativity can bring a great alteration upon that power which the constellation that was in the time of the conception, would have in man. Or that the constellation, in the hour of man's nativity, doth alter very much of that natural temper and inclination; doubtless also, very much of those accidents or chances, concerning temporal prosperity and misfortunes, which he would have, or which would befall him from the power of that constellation, which was in the time of his conception. As to the places alleged, viz. Mysterium Magnum, Chs. lxvii and lxviii, where, in the English translation, a scheme or figure of the twelve houses is added, the same is not only in the High Dutch original not to be found, but nothing also can be taken from the author's words, which did in particular refer to this influence, with respect to man's nativity. For in the first place, Chap, lxvii, he declareth only, that every man beareth in him an image of his own constellation, called by him a magic astrum, which must indeed needs be conformable to the figure of that firmamental constellation, that was both in his conception, and in his nativity, but cannot be restrained, or confinedly referred, either unto that former, or unto this latter only. Wherefore it must be referred to both of them in union together, viz. to the latter, as grounded upon the former, and to the former, as partly altered, and partly confirmed by the latter. And in the second place, ch. lviii, where nothing at all is said, neither as to man's conception, nor nativity, and even the word constellation is not so much as mentioned. Behmen declareth only, what a great difference there is between natural and supernatural figures, dreams, and visions; and sayeth that the dreams of Pharaoh were out of eternal nature, above the operation and figure of the stars and elements, and that even this was the true reason, why the Egyptian magi, which were but naturalists, could not give him an interpretation thereof. Now this indeed cannot be denied, that here also Pharaoh must have had, in his outward natural constellation of the stars, such a figure as stood in answerableness to that which came out of eternal nature, and whereby he was to be that person, under whose reign such a great and notable alteration of the Egyptian kingdom should come to pass. But whether this natural constellation was more to be referred to the hour of his conception, to that of his nativity, or also to both of them together, nobody I think can presume to determine.

Ibid. Q. 2. As to the influences of the planets and stars upon civil governments, Behmen says also nothing in particular, and nothing directly, but in general only and in many places he owneth, that civil governments, and the various chances, revolutions and alterations thereof do depend upon their influences, for as much as they are (in such a form and manner) but a natural order and constitution of the spirit of this world, though indeed, as to the substance thereof he granteth also freely, that they have a ground in eternal nature. And, moreover, all this dependance upon the starry influences, standeth but under the *inspection* and *direction* of the Most High, whose operating instrument all this temporal nature with *all its influences* is; which justly and significantly may be called an operating instrument, in a similitude taken from a watch, and frequently used by Behmen. For a watch, with all its parts and wheels, is but a dead, impotent, and unmoveable instrument of itself, and is nevertheless also operating by its own communicated sufficiency, if but once drawn up and directed by its master.

Concerning their influences upon the weather, Behmen says indeed expressly and distinctly, that the stars and planets cause fair weather, rain, hail, snow, excessive heat, frost, etc. But he goeth not further to any particular account, declaring which of the stars especially, or what manner of the planetary aspects do cause such or such a kind of weather, but he refers us to the skilful astrologers, saying that they found it out, at least for a great deal, by long and sedulous observations, etc.

Ibid. Q. 3. The meaning of the planetic wheel, in Behmen's threefold life, as to its turning, winding, or bending more and more towards within, is not to be understood with relation to the outward appearance of the planetic bodies; for it is notorious, that they stand all seven in an equal degree of outwardness, in one and the same outward or third principle, and have all seven an equal share in being visible objects of one and the same firmamental eye. But it is to be understood with relation to that which is in the planets invisible, but not incomprehensible, and which belongeth inseparably to the whole geniture of this third principle, considered in its union with, and dependence upon, the twofold inward world. For this, and thus considered, doth not stand with its seven different parts in the same degree of outwardness, and is not intelligible at once, or to an intellect that stands unmovable in one and the same station. For these seven different parts have not, nay, cannot have, an equal share in being intelligible objects of one and the same human intellect, if this be not as it were translocated seven times: seeing that they turn in deeper and deeper, according to Behmen's figure, as it were into a deep pit, wherein the centre must be conceived as at the bottom, and the windings all more and more upwards, until the outmost, which only may be visible to that eye that standeth at the mouth of that pit. Which eye therefore must be conceived as that it is itself to go down deeper and deeper, if it shall behold the one of these windings after the other. One and the same eye without being translocated from that place of the earth where it standeth, would be able indeed to see at once all the planets together, if they were but all elevated above its horizon. But one and the same human intellect cannot see all the windings of this planetic wheel, without its own being really translocated, that is, without its own being really deeper and deeper generated, or introduced into the one winding after the other. For that which is seen or understood is always a veiling or covering of that which followeth next. Which covering (N.B.) is not only in that planetic wheel, considered as without man in the macrocosm but is after the same manner in man himself also, who else could not be called a microcosm. In man himself therefore (N.B.) all these coverings must be removed, and so his intellect will be thereby as it were transplaced, and enabled to see what otherwise is but in vain for him to undertake. Plainer I cannot represent the meaning of this planetic wheel. Behmen saith expressly and intelligibly, not only that it cannot be delineated by figures, and not expressed by words, but also that it cannot be understood, except by the spirit, who may understand it in himself, viz. if he be made able to see and behold himself, what and how he is, for *as this planetic wheel is, to it the Spirit also*. And then also, he directs us to consider for an illustration hereof, the three different principles wherein we may find the same, or at least something very like. For all the three principles are in every man (like as all the seven windings of this planetic wheel are in every man also), and yet only that is seen and felt by him in which he standeth, or which is manifest in him, and by the same manifestation of itself it excludeth, covereth, or hideth always the other two. Which, if they shall be manifested or opened in his sensibility, he must be brought away from his former station, which is as it were a translocation, or a real transport from the one into another. A human soul, if in this natural earthly body only, can be sensible only of this third principle, and of things belonging thereto, and cannot all this while see or feel the first and second. If it be departed from the body, and entered into the dark world, it can no more be sensible of the third, and can have no perception of the second. But if it be in the second, the first is shut up from it, and of the third it can have no sensation. And though in this outward world one and the same soul may have, at different times, more or less a real sensibility of all three, yet there will always be required and presupposed something of a real translocation, in a spiritual sense. For no principle can be seen or felt, but by those creatures that are therein actually.

Page 141. No, 6. In this description concerning the *spirit of this world*, I meet with several things which I think do want some observation. When there is said, that the spirit of this world is also called the *archeus* and *separator*, etc. I observe justly, that the archeus or separator is expressly called by Behmen, the outflown word of God, an efflux out of the invisible world, the fiery mercury, that Creator which still createth, etc. Clavis, *v*.96. *Germ*. Wherefore then, (though perhaps upon this or that particular account, the spirit of this world may be called also the archeus or separator, which yet for my part I would not call so, when I intend to speak thereof distinctly,) I would here make no mention of an archeus, that I might not make the reader think these two expressions do always strictly denote with Behmen, one and the same thing. Considering especially that his fiery mercury is but a part of that spiritual habitation, wherein the spirit of this world worketh, as shall be said now by and by.

What farther here is added of—an *outward quintessence* of things, in which the spirit of this world opens itself and resides, out of which he hath power of effluxing, and which is his inward and more immediate body, etc.—cannot, to my thinking, in all particulars be reconciled to what Behmen says in that place, which the last lines direct me to, viz. CLAVIS, *v.* 96–105. *Germ.* Which only place can be sufficient to declare what he means by the spirit of this world, which, saith Behmen, is hidden in the four elements, like as the soul is in the body, and is nothing else but an efflux and actual power from the sun and stars. Its habitation, wherein it worketh, is spiritual, encompassed with the four elements. This spiritual habitation is (1.) A sharp magnetical power, from the first property of eternal nature. (2.) An efflux from the inward motion, or second property——*this I call the fiery mercury, in the spirit of this world*, for this is the mobility of all things, a *separator* of the powers, and a former of shapes or figures. (3.) A sensibility in this motion and sharpness, etc. from the third property of eternal nature. These three properties the ancient philosophers called sulphur, mercury, and sal, according to their matters which out of them are generated in the four elements, when this (threefold) spirit coagulates it makes itself substantial. In this ground the four elements also lie, and are not separated therefrom, nor something peculiar, but only they are the manifestation of this spiritual ground, like as a house or habitation of the spirit, wherein it worketh, etc.

The words, *which outward quint-essence, the inward and more immediate body of this spirit (for the four elements are its outward body), they call salniter, etc.* are, as to my sight, all obscure, and I do not think they can give to any a clear and distinct apprehension of the thing. For (1.) I cannot find that Behmen calleth the salniter a body of the spirit of this world. (2.) I cannot see what here is meant by salniter. That risible materiality, which is an ingredient of gunpowder, cannot be meant, seeing that this salniter is called an inward and more immediate body; when that is equally outward or distant, in the same degree from the spirit, as the outward salt, brimstone, and quicksilver. And that which is more inward in this outward salniter, is its being (in answerableness to eternal nature) that crack wherein all the properties are separated and displayed. But this also can here not be meant, because the crack, as a separator and displayer of all the properties, cannot be conceived as a body of the spirit of this world. (3.) This body or salniter is called a quint-essence of everything, which cannot be applicable any more to this salnitral crack, than to the palpable salnitral substance. (4.) It is called an outward quint-essence, and this makes all still more obscure. For every qnint-essence is the most inward of that thing whose quint-essence it is said to be. And though it might be understood as with respect to this outward world, and so thereby distinguished from a heavenly quint-essence of paradisical things, yet this will not be sufficient to make it out, as long as it is not declared, both as to this outward and to that inward world, that the salnitrous crack can be called the quint-essence of all things, which I see no possibility to do.

In the last lines, where there is said of three salnitrous substances, (1.) of a visible, (2.) of a heavenly, and (3.) of a divine one, a notorious mistake is committed. For the heavenly and the divine, if both called and conceived as substances, cannot be distinguished, but by referring the former unto God, considered as in, and the latter unto God as without nature. But now, in the Divine being without nature, is no such thing, but all must be referred only to the generation of nature. The salnitrous crack, in, or at the entrance of the fourth form, is that which may be called divine, but not yet divine substance. But in heaven, viz. in the seventh form, no doubt but there is such a substance, as the salnitral substance upon earth is a visible image of. Yet this heavenly substance is not a shadowy image of another divine salnitrous substance, but it is a body or chrystalline material being, expressed and made substantial by that salnitrous (not substance, but) crack, which is in the generation of eternal nature, caused by that conjunction between eternal liberty and the dark forms of nature, of both which, even our visible salniter in this world proves to partake, according to its low manner and degree.

Page 142. *No.* 7. Here I have to observe only this, that instead of these words, *this outflown word is not the pure Deity, but his outflown word, by which, etc.* the sense could be expressed with more grace, and with greater significancy, thus—this outflown word is not the pure Deity, but such an outflown power, as by which, etc.

Page 142. *No.* 8. Here, concerning *common salniter and its preparation, the philosophical mercury, oil of sulphur, oil of vitriol, spirit of nitre, the character* L *signifying gold, etc.*, I have nothing to say, neither pro nor con; the author may perhaps be able to make it out, but experience must confirm it. Only at the first expression I am a little stumbled, when there is said, *the matter of the philosophical work are the five vowels, which signify common salniter.* For I cannot see what relation these two can bear to one another. In all the description of this work (in SIGNATURUM RERUM) Behmen never useth the expression of five vowels. And though that very same which he doth understand thereby, viz. the divine life, power, virtue, the Spirit of God, the true spirit of understanding from the second principle of light, etc. is absolutely required to this work, yet upon what account the five vowels can be called the *matter*, I am not able to apprehend. But for all that there may be something therein above the reach of my capacity.

Page 143. *No. 9.* The *signal star*, mentioned not only in the Mysterium Magnum but also in several other books and places, hath a twofold signification, relating most evidently to the discovery both of the inward eternal, and of the outward temporal nature, according to his own words, saying, *Two suns are risen and shine unto us.* And again, *the signal star is so great as the whole world*, etc. With respect to the first, he understands chiefly this great manifestation, concerning the generation of eternal nature in its seven-fold wheel, with respect to which he called his first book Aurora, Day-break, Morning redness, etc. And so this signal star, in this first sense, is nothing else but that same, which, by some others now is called the *morning star of Wisdom*, relating especially to the mysteries of the kingdom of Christ, which cannot be fundamentally understood without an understanding of the generation of eternal nature in its seven properties, as from the Revelation of St. John is evident enough. And then with respect to the second signification, which is inferior unto that first, but necessarily depending upon and following after it, he reflects not only upon an understanding of temporal nature in general, but also in particular upon an understanding of the philosophical work, wherein the cursed nature is restored, from the strife of its seven disharmonised properties, into their paradisical union. For even herein lieth that provision laid up for the children of God, whereof he speaks in the Mysterium Magnum. And even this is that, by which according to his prophecy,—silver and gold shall be made as common as it was in the days of Solomon. And this is that same whereof he saith also, that—to the kingdom (of Christ) which is, and is not, and yet is, the ornament of gold and silver shall be added; for the Prince of the powers of the earth hath given it thereunto. And so now the signal star, in this second sense, is nothing else but this same manifestation, as it concerns the restoration of outward cursed nature. All this is fully agreeing with the construction of his writings, and could be made out sufficiently from a hundred places. But that he, by the signal star, should have directed us in particular to *antimony*, I cannot tell.

Page 143. *Nos.* 10 and 11. All what herein is declared, belongs to an outward chemical operation, which I know nothing of, and can be neither for nor against it. Thus much I observe only, that I could not say, *they say*, because it is not apparent to me, that Behmen says all these things, who in his writings hath quite another end, and so frequently and earnestly protesteth, that his intent was not to teach any man this art, etc.

Pages 143 and 145. *No.* 12. Several things are here expressed concerning salniter, which I can make nothing of at all; if they are of Mr. Pierce, he will doubtless be able to declare his sense more intelligibly. That salniter was *not created*, but only *made substantial* at the creation, is very strange in my apprehension; but seeing that I do not know what peculiar notion he may have of the word *created*, and what distinction he may make between *created* and *made substantial*, I can say nothing more against it. That salniter *brings the fire of God to man*, is no less strange than that former, though indeed I see obscurely, and as it were at a distance, something therein, if it be not understood of the outbirth, viz. of salniter, as created, or as made substantial at the creation, but of that which Behmen calleth the *salnitrous shrack*, wherein the two eternal kingdoms are severed, and in this world the four elements are displayed, etc. But if Mr. Pierce reflects, as I suppose by this expression, upon the philosophical work especially; meaning that salniter, even common salniter as before, is that matter which bringeth the philosophical fire into the artist's work, there may be something more in it, which I shall not presume to judge nor censure. That salniter is the *instrument of God* by which he worketh, is true indeed, if it be referred again to the salnitrous shrack, not to the dead outbirth; for as the whole nature, in all its properties, is God's instrument, so is that also especially, wherein all the properties of nature are brought into distinction and operation. That *the separator is in this substantial word*, and that *it is the spirit of this world, etc.*, something herein also is true, but indeed it is not pertinently expressed. For by saying, *in this substantial word*, the reader is caused to understand (in connexion with what went before) common salniter, created or made substantial at the creation; and though he may apprehend well enough that the separator is therein, yet that this *substantial word* is the spirit of this world, none I think can apprehend to satisfaction. What Behmen says concerning the spirit of this world, we had already above.—All the places quoted p. 145, I looked over, but cannot find that Behmen saith therein anything of salniter. Nay, in many other places also, which I consulted, I find very little of the outbirth or common salniter, but of the salnitrous crack, made in the kindling of the fire he speaketh very much.

In the SIGNATURA RERUM, xiv. 69, etc. *Germ*, (as in some other places) I cannot find that he treats concerning an *universal medicine*, that is a medicine resisting universally all manners and kinds of diseases, like as the universal tincture doth: but only concerning a medicine reaching deeper than the four elements, and resisting the evil of the astrum. Which every medicine should and would do, if rightly prepared, that is, if itself were first delivered from the four-elementary strife, and exalted according to his description; when yet for all that, it would not resist all sorts of evils from the astrum, but only such of them as it is in particular prepared for. For it would not yet be the blessed universal tincture.

Page 145. Q. 1. *What do they say, concerning the oil of life?* A. In order to understand what they say concerning the oil of life, it is absolutely required to understand also first, what they deliver, concerning in general the generation of eternal nature, and in particular, the generation of the water of life, in the second principle of light; from which water this oil is all inseparable, and of which it is the more spiritual part, fatness as it were, or unctuosity. The conjunction between the soft eternal liberty, and the harsh, strong desire, causeth in eternal nature the generation or kindling of the fire. From the latter of these two cometh a life to be, which standeth in, and is itself a fire; and from the former a water and oil, which is a pabulum of that fire and life. By the water it is refreshed and preserved; in the oil it burneth and flameth, and from this oil especially it getteth a shine or glance. If now this be transferred to the life of man, it may easily be understood what Behmen says, that—every sickness is more or less a spoiling, poisoning, or darting impurity or contrary properties into the oil of life, etc.

Q. 2. *What do they teach concerning the philosophical work?* A. They teach in substance that the process of the universal tincture, for transmuting metals, and healing the body (attainable, if all the requisites are truly in the artist found), is the very same, with the process of the holy spiritual tincture for the soul of man, attainable in the regeneration. That both in the one and in the other, this process in itself is very short. That the life of man, and so of metals as also of the whole nature, and all the things therein, standeth in seven properties. That these seven properties are now under the curse, and stand in mere strife and contrariety, each of them being in its own natural quality manifest, in opposition to all the rest; that is, each of them, according to Behmen's usual expression, hath its *own selfish will*. That this strife cannot be reconciled, except there come such a death into these seven properties, as may break and destroy their *own will*, viz. such a life as by its own essentiality may be first a death unto them, and then also able to raise them up again, into one harmonious life and will. That all this is done according to the constant unalterable generation of eternal nature, wherein there are the same seven properties indeed, but not seven contrary wills, all being harmonised and overpowered in, and by the fifth of love and light. That when this re-harmonising of the properties in the philosophical work is done, the universal tincture is prepared, the curse is removed, earth is turned in, and heaven out. And this, therefore, is able also to reharmonise all the seven disordered properties, both in the metals of the earth, and in the distempered bodies of men.

Q. ult. Why must gold be purified seven times? A. Because it must be brought through all the seven properties of nature, and in each of them a peculiar work must be done. For as they are all seven under the curse, so they are all seven impure, and want to pass the purifying fire seven times, if that gold or silver shall come to its perfection. In the first melting, the harsh quality, the gross, hard, stony dross is melted away. In the second, the harsh death in the water is separated; for in this second property the sweet water was killed or spoiled, and turned into the quality of a poisonous *aqua fortis*, which is the worst of all, and must now, in this second melting, be cast out. In the third, the bitter death must be melted down, viz. the stirring, raging, and breaking, stinging property, which makes the gold and silver brittle; so that it is not malleable before this be conquered also. In the fourth the fire-spirit must be destroyed; and then the matter begins to be like unto gold or silver, according to that property which is predominant therein; but it is not yet tough and pure enough. In the fifth melting the life, in the light and love's property, ariseth; and according to this, the matter which is left in the foregoing trials, gets again that virtue which from the first original hath been the propriety of that fountain-spirit, which is predominant therein. In the sixth, this life, risen in the fifth, stirreth, and from this stirring the metal gets its clear, tinkling sound, according to its kind. Here, says Behmen, the greatest care is to be taken, that the fire may not be too strong, or else this new life is easily kindled again, in the properties of wrath, and the whole matter burned to a hard, unprofitable dross. In the seventh melting it cometh (provided that the same care be taken about the fire, which must be more subtle or temperate, than in the sixth,) to that perfection which it is capable of in this third principle; and hath only this defect, that the spirit therein must leave its metallic body in a hard palpability, and cannot exalt it, so as he did, before the wrath-fire was kindled in the fall of Lucifer.

Page 147. *No.* 1. To prevent a certain needless objection, I think, when here is said, *The third principle being perfected on the fourth day*, there might be added this, or any other the like limitation—as to its own harmonious structure, essential constituent parts, order, government, or governing faculties, etc.

Nos. 2 and 3. *souls or spirits.* Here I observe, that in sensitive creatures, a difference between souls and spirits is not indeed by Behmen much regarded or insisted upon. But that, nevertheless, it is apparent enough, from his declaration, that in them also are both souls and spirits, or something answering, in its lower temporal kind and degree, unto that great considerable difference in man. Wherefore then, if a nice and curious distinction be not intended, there may be said well enough, *souls or spirits*. But if a more distinct enumeration shall be made, there might much rather be said, *souls and spirits;* with a short addition, declaring that the former is more particularly to be referred to the stars, and the latter to the sun. Whereof much could be said from Behmen's ground.

Page 147. No. 3. *Their bodies were made,* etc. Here I would, for my part, rather say, *brought forth;* not that the former were altogether unfit or impertinent, but only because it seems (at least to me) to represent the thing too grossly, as if there had been a certain maker from without, using his hands or instruments. Whereas, they came forth all freely out of the elements, when the eternal Word moved, and thereby enabled them to bring forth, in distinction and variety, those visible images or outbirths of their invisible powers.

No. 4. *from which the visible*, etc. Seeing that the elements and compounded bodies differ in degrees, and that from the former to the latter a descent is made, so that the elements are to be considered as joined to the invisible principles; when there is said, *from what compounded bodies do arise*, I think it would be proper to make the construction thus, or the like—*from which* (invisible principles) *the visible elements, and further* (or lower) *also, in conjunction with them, the compounded bodies arise.*

No. 5. *those are unclean, etc.* Seeing that this uncleanness cannot be restrained to terrestrial animals, because in the water also some are declared by Moses to be unclean, it would be better to say more generally— those are unclean, that had in their original a property of the dark world more or less predominant in their particular kind.

Between Nos. 5 and 6, these following particulars could be inserted; yet there is no necessity for it:

That living creatures are in all the four elements, and in each according to its constitution: and this, because of that indissoluble concatenation of all the elements, in one universal ground, by reason of which none of them is excluded from those powers and abilities, that were required for their bringing forth their own peculiar offspring. That from the food and habitation of every animal, its original may be more or less discerned. That the tame and friendly beasts, are, with respect to their original, nearer related to the one element; when the wild and not so tractable ones are nearer to the four elements. That the state and condition of the living creatures, before the fall of man, was much different from what it is now, after the fall and curse. That in all the living creatures, a character of the Holy Trinity may be found, though in none of them so plain and eminent, nor so glorious and efficacious as it is in man.

Page 149. *ad finem*. Two different things are here desired in one question, which yet must needs be parted in two. The first is concerning the two tinctures and their division, and the second concerning the *magia*, and the appearing of animals in it. (1.) As to the first, this I think may be a sufficient declaration thereof, and as short as I can make it. Fire and water are and must be in the generation of eternal nature, and so of temporal nature also. When and wheresoever eternal nature is in its right harmonious order, then and there these two cannot but be united, or stand in a most internal union. This union is consequently holy, pure, and heavenly, and so must also those creatures be wherein this union is. Now then, seeing that this third principle was spoiled, and all its properties disharmonised by the fall of Lucifer; seeing further, that it was not to be restored immediately unto its primeval glory and dignity, but that it should be settled for an appointed time in a lower and exterior condition, wherein it cannot be called holy, pure, and heavenly, but mixed, transitory, and elementary: and again, seeing that nevertheless in this mixed state it should have the whole nature, or all the properties of nature, working and generating therein; these two therefore which cannot be separated from nature, must needs in this third principle have been divided. Yet so (because of its being but one world) that a communion or mutual communication between them might be left both in the whole government, or whole generation of this temporal nature, and in the particular creatures also belonging thereunto, and governed thereby. Now this division was made accordingly on the second day of the creation, not in any particular place or thing, but generally throughout the whole extent of this region, that so a perpetual communication might be between that which is superior and that which is inferior. When therefore the living creatures now were produced, to be temporal, mixed, four-elementary, not eternal, holy, one-elementary creatures, they must needs have been formed in and according to this division also. For seeing that their original was only in, and their end only to this mixed world, they could not have been gifted with that holy union, which heavenly creatures only can be capable of. But man, having a higher original, came not out of this divided twofold source, but according to that end he was designed for, he had the whole eternal nature in its due harmonious order and union within his own single person. So therefore, as it was impossible that he should be a twofold male and female image in his first creation, so was it impossible also that animals should not be males and females, or should not have (which is the same thing) the two tinctures in their division. For the tincture here with respect to the living creatures, may be sufficiently described by saying that—it is that tender, loving inclination towards that which from the first original in eternal nature is its nearest and most internal part. Though I do freely grant that a deeper description thereof might be given by saying—that it is rather that ground which in animals is the root of that inclination, that which stirreth up the same, that which floweth out therein, and which is conveyed thereby from the one into the other. Yet seeing that this latter, abstracted from that former, is all imperceptible in man as well as in beasts, and that it is made perceptible only in and by that former, by a joint consideration of these two, the tincture may be sufficiently described, viz. in this peculiar place, and with reference to the living creatures. If then this be, as to the fiery part in males, and as to the watery in females, their longing desire from both sides after a conjunction, and in the conjunction, the impregnation, and propagation may be easily understood, (2.) As to the second; the *magia*, wherein all the living creatures shall appear eternally, is in short, that incessant operation of the six working properties of eternal nature in the seventh, whereby so infinite variety and multiplicity of figures, forms, and images, was produced, changed and altered from eternity. If there now had been intellectual creatures before the creation of angels, all these wonders of this eternal *magia* would certainly have appeared unto them; but since there were none, they could not be known except only to the Spirit of eternity. Considering then (1.) That after the time of this world there shall be innumerable hosts of intellectual creatures, men especially, that are more concerned with the wonders of this third principle than angels. (2.) That this principle with its wonders is not to be annihilated, but shall be exalted again into its primeval glory and dignity. (3.) That all these temporal creatures are but figures, representatives, and outbirths, of those eternal magical powers. And (4.) That it shall be kept eternally in man's remembrance, what God hath done with him in time; what wonders he hath brought forth by his eternal wisdom, and that nothing, neither great nor little, was done or made in vain, etc. Considering, I say, all these and the like things together, we may easily come to understand what Behmen meaneth when be saith that all the creatures of this world, and so the living creatures also, shall appear in the eternal magia to the praise and honour of the Creator, and rejoicing or delight of men and angels. Which yet is to be understood in a different way, according to the difference of the two eternal worlds. For the last day of judgment, and purification by fire, is a day of separation, dividing the good from the evil, and giving unto each its own proper place. So, therefore, of all the creatures of this mixed world, only the good part separated from the evil, belongeth and shall be gathered into the light; when contrariwise, the evil part, separated from the good, shall appear in the dark world, out of which it had its first original.

Page 151. Q. 1. Seeing that the greatest emphasis in this question lieth in the word *finishing* all his works; I think a little more might be reflected thereupon in the answer, by representing more distinctly, that the whole generation of nature, as to its working part, is finished in the six first properties; and that therefore, when these six had done what God would have them do, the creation-work could not have gone further, but must needs have been finished also.

Q. 2. Six days were employed in the work of creation, not only to *represent* (as here is said) which is as it were only *a posteriori*, but also and even chiefly to employ and set to work all the six operating spirits of eternal nature; which being just six, neither more days nor fewer, could have been employed.

Page 153. Line *ult*. More explicitly, I think, might here be declared, that man should have been translated into eternity, when the appointed time of this third principle had been expired, viz. if he had continued in rest from his own work.

Page 155. Line *ult*. I find something, which, if it shall represent the sense of Behmen, must needs be otherwise expressed; but if no regard is had to Behmen's ground, doctrine and declaration, it may be left as it is. For it concerns but an opinion, and such a one as he could not indeed himself approve of, but left it, nevertheless, to every one's own liberty to hold thereof what he thinks himself able to understand, viz. of the *seventh blessed time or age* (which, I suppose, is taken to be during this four-elementary world, before the period thereof is quite expired; that is, before the coming of Christ as judge of the dead and living,) two things are said here, which in such absolute terms Behmen would not have owned. (I.) *The creation shall be delivered from the bondage of corruption under which it groaneth.* For though, indeed, he owneth a seventh blessed age, which he calleth *the manifestation of Zion, the time of lilies and roses, the Enochian life, etc*, and whereof he foretells many great, wonderful and excellent things that shall be done therein to the church of God; yet he hath declared also himself, and shown his ground sufficiently, that the creation, during this time of the four elements and the starry heaven, cannot be fully, totally, and universally delivered from the bondage of corruption and vanity, though, it may, indeed, partake something of the immunities and advantages of this blessed *time of refreshment:* which expression of the scripture itself, denotes but such an imperfect state as cannot yet be applied to a total universal deliverance.

(2.) Of this blessed seventh age is said also, that *therein the paradisical, inward, invisible things, hid under the thick veil of this gross, earthly world, shall be manifested.* If this were so expessed that it could be understood of the mysteries of the kingdom of Christ, hid under the veil of Moses, and with a particular relation to the inward, regenerated part of man; or also, so that he might he understood of a nearer communication than what is now, between paradise and this corrupt four elementary world, nothing could be objected. But if the meaning shall be this—that paradise shall be re-opened in this world, and shall penetrate the earth and the four elements, as it did before the fall and curse; and that so, not only as to man and his regenerated part, but also as to all the creatures, the same state shall be again, which then was in this principle when man stood yet in entire perfection, without any apparent mixture of good and evil, very much could be said against it. But because it is not my intent to overthrow any man's harmless opinion, which Behmen himself hath left free unto every one, and hath only declared his ground and reasons why be could not embrace it; this only may suffice, viz. to recommend to a serious consideration, that a manifestation of the one pure eternal element, and a manifestation of the four temporal elements, cannot consist together in one time and place. For, when and where the four are manifest, then and there the one must needs be hid under and by this manifestation of the four. And so contrariwise,—when the one is manifest, the four are swallowed up in this one, and by this same manifestation thereof. Now, in the one is only good; and, in the four, is good and evil, mixed. Good and evil, therefore, cannot be separated (though this latter, in a great degree, may be suppressed and kept under by that former,) before the day of Christ's appearing unto judgment, who shall then find all still in a mixed state, which is apparent enough from that description he gave himself, concerning the day of his appearance. From hence, it is now plain that the following words, *which they think to be the opening of the seventh seal in the revelation,* cannot be understood with reference to Behmen; for he truly did not think that this which was so expressed, is the opening of the seventh seal, but only that which he did own thereof, and found a ground for it in his communicated gift, and which in part is here by me declared, and is answering also to his own declaration of the seventh seal's opening in the philosophical work; which doth not bring in an absolute paradisical or heavenly perfection, but only such a perfection as the creature can be capable of, during the time of this four-elementary world.

Page 157. Line *penult*. This matter would, I think, be plainer, and more significantly expressed, if it were shortly thus represented,—that Christ, as the eternal Word, belongeth not to the number of the seven, being beyond and above them; but that he came down into them, by taking upon him human nature: wherefore, then, he was truly and properly *as an eighth* unto them; and must have been so, because neither all the seven together in general, nor any of them in particular, was able to reharmonise the disordered state in human nature.

Page 161. *A*. 1. In this answer, nothing is said of that great, mysterious, principal point which Behmen delivered, by saying—man is created upon the cross: his body hath the figure of a cross, and because of that first creation, Christ must have redeemed him on the cross, etc., without which the creation of man cannot be fundamentally understood. But seeing that this is left out, because (as I suppose) of its being uncommon, and requiring a deep understanding of the generation of eternal nature and its cross, I shall say nothing more of it.

Page 161. *No*. 3 Here I meet with some obscurity. These two, *man's fallen estate*, and *the earthly property of his body*, seem to be set together as one only thing, without any distinction; when they must needs be distinguished. For the earthly property (according to what is said No. 4, and again Page 165. *A*. 1) was that which was in man of the earth before his fallen estate; when it was not manifest, but covered by paradise predominant in him. But his fallen estate is now the manifestation of that earthly property, made afterwards, when paradise was covered and veiled by his now predominant earthliness.

Page 162. Lines 4 and 5. *with a power of manifesting themselves*. Seeing that these words are indifferently applied to two different bodies, when only the one of them, viz. that which was interior and superior, can be said to have had such a power; I think the sense of these words might be rather thus expressed, or after any other the like manner-the one with a power of manifesting itself in its due time, and the other with an ability of being manifested by man's own wavering imagination. Or this latter part thus—and the other with a power of appearing and exerting itself immediately after a disappearing of that which then was still predominant, and kept it under. For that inferior, four-elementary body, while it was a body only potentially, had no power in it so to manifest itself, nor should ever have been able to do it, if man's own imagination had not impowered it, by turning itself away from its internal, pure and holy object.

Page 163. *A*. 2. The latter part of this answer I would alter a little, for several reasons, and to prevent a two-fold objection, saying thus, or something the like—but not so highly dignified, glorious, and heavenly, as it would have been at the changing of this third principle, if he had not fallen.

Q. ult. Seeing that the paradisical property was the middlemost, as having above it the heavenly, and under it the earthly, it is not very proper to ask (as here is done) *which was the next to it?* for though, in one particular respect, the earthly might be conceived as the next; yet in another, the heavenly may also be conceived so; and in a third, the one of them was as near as the other. Wherefore then, the question might be formed thus—which was the second property? or thus—which property may be supposed to be next, with respect to this exterior third principle?

Page 165. *A*. 1. *the corrupt property of the earth, which it had from the fall of Lucifer.* An understanding reader may find, indeed, in these words the intended, right, and true sense; yet to him that is not yet so well acquainted with these uncommon things, they may seem to be hard, and liable to several objections. To prevent which, I would express it thus, or after any other manner like unto this—the earthly property, which though pure in man,(as a quintessence is pure, in comparison to that grosser mass out of which it is extracted) was yet nearly related to the earth without him, which was infected from the fall of Lucifer. For though the whole third principle may well be said to have been corrupted by Lucifer, *viz.* when it is considered as his region or kingdom, and with respect to what he hath done and acted therein; yet, when it is considered as taken from him, and brought into another state in the creation by God, whose works are altogether good, we cannot well call it *corrupt*, without giving offence, more or less. But this we may say, that it had, as it were at the bottom, an infection from Lucifer, whose dwelling place in some sense it is; who still pretendeth to be the prince thereof, and who hath an access into the dark infected bottom thereof. For this is plain and demonstrable enough, from its having a certain period of time, appointed in the very creation, and a day of separation, in which it shall be entirely purified by fire, and delivered from that infection.

And so also the words, *with the corrupt property in it*, I would alter a little accordingly, that they might not be understood so as if the corrupt property, *as corrupt*, had also been formed into Adam's body. For this was extracted out of that, and by this same extraction made pure; but that which it was extracted from was infected: and this, therefore, by reason both of this extraction and of this infection, was able to bring the corruption into man's body, when he descended into this lower infected property, and stirred it up by his lustful imagination.

Page 165. A. *ult.* This answer cannot stand in these expressions, for the reasons following— (1.) The description here given of the heavenly property, is applicable unto the paradisical also. (2.) Between the paradisical and heavenly property, and so also body, I cannot find that Behmen makes any other considerable difference, but that of a higher and lower degree or dignity, relating to the two different stations of the first Adam. For the paradisical, as the lower, was manifest when he was in paradise upon earth, and should have continued so until this third principle had been recalled into eternity; and the heavenly, as the higher, should then have been manifested when he was to be translated and exalted from this paradise into heaven. Since, now, this first order is broken by his fall, and his blessed eternal station must now be re-obtained quite another way, viz. by a regeneration out of water and Spirit; Behmen, when declaring this way, and speaking of that body which he is to put on in the regeneration, takes no more great notice of a distinction between a heavenly and paradisical body, but useth these two denominations promiscuously, and calleth man's new-born body sometimes, indeed, paradisical, but frequently also heavenly; notwithstanding that we still do rightly own, with him, a difference of degree between paradise and heaven. All which could be further illustrated and confirmed from the forty days of Christ, between his resurrection and ascension; wherein he was but in a paradisical, not yet in a heavenly state, notwithstanding that he was always the Lord from heaven. And further also, from a consideration of the new Jerusalem, which, forasmuch as coming down is certainly paradisical, and is yet not said to come down out of paradise, but from God out of heaven. (3.) The simile of the gold in the ore, or the tincture in metals, is not applicable to the heavenly body in the paradisical: nor is it ever so used by Behmen; because there is no such difference between these two pure internal things, as there is between the other two external things; the one of them only being pure, and the other all impure. But with respect to man's fallen state and new regeneration, he useth this simile frequently, comparing the ore (or, as he commonly expresseth it, the hard, gross, rude stone) to man's corrupt four-elementary body, or flesh and blood, which cannot inherit the kingdom of God; and the gold or tincture to the regenerated body, born from above, of water and spirit; which he calleth sometimes heavenly, because it is from heaven; and sometimes also paradisical, because it cannot be had in man as heavenly, except it be first had as paradisical. Wherefore then this question, *What do they mean by this heavenly property?* I would answer after such a manner,—They mean the same paradisical property as to substance, they both being of the water and spirit of eternal life; but they consider it as higher and more inward, and with a particular relation to that exalted state which Adam, if he had not transgressed, was to have been taken up into, after the consummation of time, in the perfect restoration of this third principle. And then, for more distinction's sake, I would add farther this following question and answer:

Q. Is this paradisical and heavenly property still in all men? A. The paradisical and heavenly property lieth still in all, though in different degrees, as a possibility to their regeneration and exaltation. But the paradisical body lieth in them only that are actually born from above of water and spirit; and in them it lieth hid under their gross four-elementary flesh and blood, increasing more and more, as gold in the ore. And the heavenly body, or the paradisical considered as heavenly, cannot be said to be manifest in any, before the passing away of time.

Page 167. Q. & A. 1. From what was animadverted above, concerning the *corruption* and *infection* of this principle, it is here plain, that either this question cannot be so formed, if the asker thereof be supposed to have taken any notice of what was then given him in answer; or if, notwithstanding this, it shall be formed so that this answer must be altered. For (1.) barely as the words lie, and as they may be understood with a prejudice to the honour, goodness, and purity of the Creator (especially if the reader be apt to carp and dispute), *no corrupt property was in man;* but only it could be raised up in him by his lust, going forth without him into that which was by Lucifer infected. (2.) These words in the answer, *God permitted it to be so,* cannot well stand, because they are too popular, and in this place too insignificant. And though Behmen himself, in a popular sense and manner, may have used this expression, when he declareth this same reason which here is given of God's *forseeing the fall*; yet seeing that still a deeper ground is to be shown from Behmen, which this expression is not well consistent with, it will be needful to alter it. For (3.) It was not so much, or not so properly a permission of God, because of his foreseeing the fall; but it was rather an absolute necessity in the nature and in all the circumstances of the thing. Man was to be a prince and ruler of this third principle, instead of fallen Lucifer; out of the essences, therefore, of this principle he must have been made, and his own personal essences must have had some sort of communion and communication with the essences and things of this principle. And though he was not made out of the corrupted essences, as corrupted (which would have caused himself to have been corrupted also from his first creation), yet he was extracted out of those essences that were without him infected by Lucifer's corruption. And if so, these infected essences without him must needs have been in such a state and capacity as that they could have been stirred and awakened by their Lord and Ruler, and so have brought their infection and corruption into his own personal essences also. And (4.) This was the true deepest reason why man of all necessity must have been created in and out of this principle, which before was spoiled and corrupted by Lucifer; and that other, viz., that he might not fall immediately into the dark world, though also good and true, is yet as it were but posterior, and to be superadded or superstructed unto this. Wherefore, then, I think this question and answer could be fitly thus proposed.—

Q. Why was that earthly property which was infected from the fall of Lucifer permitted to be so in man as you mentioned above? A. We cannot properly speak of a permission, but may well of a necessity. For man was to be a prince and ruler of this principle instead of Lucifer; and therefore his essences must have been taken out of the essences and things thereof, and must have had a communion therewith, which he could have had without corrupting or infecting himself thereby. And then also God foresaw his fall, chose him in Christ Jesus from before the foundation of the world, and consequently showed even herein that he created him so, his endless wisdom, goodness, and mercy. For man being so created could not fall immediately into the dark, hellish principle, as the devils did, but into one which was capable of being changed and exalted again, together with its fallen prince, into its primeval station of purity and glory.

Page 167 to 169. Here are six different questions, all relating to soul and spirit; upon each of which several things, and some of great importance, were to be animadverted. And in some of the answers, also, this or that could be excepted against; but to particularize all this, I think, would be of greater prolixity than benefit. Wherefore, it may be the best and nearest way to set them only down so as they may be answered from Behmen's ground, with some alteration of their order, and augmentation of their number; when, nevertheless, you may, Sir, freely alter again what you please, and where you may find any more convenient expression. I represent, then, the sense as followeth:—

Q. What was breathed into this threefold body? A. A threefold breath of life, in relation to the threefold manifestation of God, made in the two eternal and in this third temporal principle which all three must have concurred and contributed to the creation and perfection of man, the true image and likeness of God.

Q. Which of them was breathed first? A. None was breathed first, and none last, but all three together in one single act: for they were all in a strict union; neither of them was without the other two, and all three made up but one life in one body, though both this and that is rightly also considered as threefold.

Q. But seeing that we cannot consider them, nor speak of them all three at once, is there not a certain reason to be had, by which they may be considered in order and distinction, as a first, second, and third?

A. Yes, there is a good reason why the fiery breath may be considered as the first, the light as the second, and the airy as the third. And this reason hath its ground, not only in the order of eternal and temporal nature, but also in that order wherein man's life was to continue in conformity to the eternal being and will of his Creator, who ordered his light to stand as in the midst, and to rule both on the right hand and on the left; as it is so with himself in his threefold manifestation through eternal and temporal nature.

Q. What was then that first breath? A. A spiritual fire out of the first principle of eternal nature; which had, therefore, the four first properties thereof in their own reciprocal generation, so knit together that they nevermore can be dissolved.

Q. How is this properly called in man? A. When so considered as separately and to itself alone, it is peculiarly and eminently called the soul, and described as a dry, hungry, anxious fire, or fire eye, having the centre of its birth in itself, and being the proper root and only original of life, though also life itself.

Q. What is the meaning of its having the centre of its life, or birth in itself? A. This is so much as to say, that its life, or whole living being is perpetually generated in and by itself, without concurrence of anything without itself; the four essential properties thereof being all of that active nature that each of them is generated by the other three, and must concur again with all the rest, to the generation of each of them: which is also the nearest and most internal essential reason of its being an immortal life.

Q. If it be thus an immortal life itself, why then is it said also to be the proper root and only original of life? A. When life is taken for that eternal glorious and blessed life, man was created and is redeemed unto, this soulish being is nothing else but the root and original thereof; having, as in itself alone, no glory nor blessedness, but only restlessness and mere anxiety. But when by life is understood a never-ceasing continuance in its will, desire and sensibility; it is for itself also an immortal living being, which never can desist from being what it is, and doing what it doth, according to its own peculiar fiery nature.

Q. What was the second breath? A. A spiritual light out of the second principle of eternal nature, called strictly and peculiarly the spirit, or the spirit of the soul; and described as a glorious flaming breath of light and love, illuminating, tincturing and harmonising all the fiery properties of the soul, and making it to be an holy angel of God, endued with Divine wisdom, and fit to stand and worship before his throne.

Q. Is not the soul then perfect without the spirit? A. No; for though it is perfect as to its own peculiar nature, requiring nothing else but its own four eternal properties, for to make it a living soul: yet it is not perfect as to that life which God had introduced it into; for it is not that entire image of God which he created.

Q. How doth the spirit chiefly differ from the soul? A. So as the second principle in eternal nature differs from the first; and as in temporal nature the light doth from the fire. For as the light is a product of the fire, upon which notwithstanding its own quite contrary constitution, it so dependeth as to have no being of itself without it, so also is and doth the spirit in relation to the soul.

Page 169. This question concerning the *pre-existence of souls*, I think would be answered sufficiently by the four first lines, if they were put in such a construction, viz.—that they did not pre-exist as creaturely formed beings, but only as to their ideas in the divine intellect, and as to their unformed essences which were from eternity in eternal nature. Souls may be conceived to have pre-existed from eternity, in such or the like sense as in which our souls that live to this day in the temporal world, may be said to have pre-existed from the creation of the first Adam's soul; when we all were in his loins. Concerning which some considerable places might be produced from Behmen; with the whole analogy of whose writings this sense is moreover all consistent, and firmly supported by the generation of eternal and temporal nature, considered as both concurring in the creation of man.

Page 169. *Q. 2. What was the third life breathed into Adam?* This question belonging still to the former, and requiring, as I think, several things more to be added, might be answered thus with the following additions.

A. An astral and elemental life out of this outward world; which life especially made him to be a living creature in this created temporal principle, and to have communion in his essences with all the things therein. Like as the former two, and especially the second made him to rule over them, as a mighty, glorious prince; and not to have their own twofold qualities manifest and qualifying in his pure paradisical life and body.

Q. Which of these three was that breath of life which Moses saith was breathed into man's nostrils? A. Seeing that all three were but one life, and were all three breathed together by one only act, standing in such a connexion as the three principles are connected in one only, though a gradual manifestation of God; they were all three that breath of life (or according to the Hebrew text of *lives*) which made man to be a living soul. Notwithstanding that this particular expression of breathing into his nostrils, is properly applicable unto this third only. For the former two being much deeper and interior, could not have been breathed from without into his nostrils, but were rather raised and breathed from within, each out of its own internal world.

Q. Can there any ground be shewn for a confirmation hereof? A. Yes, several ways could it be confirmed, but this only can do it sufficiently; in the dying of man this third astral and elemental breath is only that mortal life which goeth out of his nostrils again, into that same outward receptacle, whereout it had its original; and therein it can be perceptible, like as a smoke arising from a candle as soon as extinguished. When the soul and spirit are much deeper and interior, and do not go through his nostrils from within into this outward world; but go rather out of this world into their own spiritual eternal ground.

Q. How doth this third life differ from the other two? A. So as time differs from eternity, out of which it is, and into which it is to be reduced again. Or so as this third mixed world differs from the two eternal principles. Or so as air differs from fire and light: which all three are notoriously different enough, and yet also all three so firmly combined that none of them can be without the other two.

Q. How do your authors call this third life in man? A. They call it the *astral spirit*, the exterior spirit, the outward part of the soul, the transitory, mortal soul, etc. Not that it was mortal from its beginning; but because it is now mortal since man's transgression, and cannot but be mortal, because of the earthliness manifested in his body.

Page 171. *In what do they place the image of God, after which Adam was created?* God created man after his image, not as he is in himself unmanifest, but as manifest, not only in eternal, but also now in temporal nature; after (and not before) the creation of which man was created. If then this manifestation of God was now threefold; viz. according to the two inward, and to this third outward world; man also, who was to be an entire image of God manifested, and a prince of this outward world, must have had all these three as so many essential parts of his created human being. Not therefore only in the soul's fire illustrated with its light, the entire image of God consisted, (which might be said indeed of the holy angels, created before the creation of this world,) but in all these three considered in their due order and relation to each other, wherein they stand also in God, manifested in eternal and temporal nature. Wherefore, then, this question might be thus answered.— A. They place it in his having all the three principles in his created being which God hath likewise himself, as manifested in eternal and temporal nature; but especially do they place it in that due order according to which the first and third were to be subject and ministering unto the second, which only was to be predominant. And unto this I think could well and properly be added that which here followeth:

Q. Do not they exclude hereby all those perfections of holiness, wisdom, dominion, etc., wherein the image of God in man is commonly said to have consisted? A. No; but they consider all such glorious attributes as posterior consequential things, which of necessity must have resulted from the union of these three, and none of which could have failed or been prevented from proceeding forth thereout freely, so long as he stood without alteration in the order of this threefold life: which therefore, they look upon as the very basis of all his perfections, and think, therefore, they have sufficient reason to say, that in this order, chiefly and fundamentally, the image of God is to be placed.

Page 171 *Q*. 1, and 2. *Concerning paradise, and the paradisical state.* In the first question no mention is made of that notable distinction, between paradise and the garden Eden. And in the second, nothing is said but what is common and general, when Behmen hath declared thereof so many particular and most considerable things. Wherefore then, if his sense as to these two questions should be represented, it might be done in the following manner:

Q. What was the paradise, or garden Eden, In which this glorious person was placed? A. The garden Eden is not to be confounded with paradise; seeing that into paradise no beast can enter, when into the garden Eden all the beasts were brought before Adam; though these two are also not to be divorced, but owned in their union: nay, if but a due distinction between them is understood, the garden Eden may well enough be called paradise in some sense and respect.

Q. What distinctions do your authors make between these two, which are commonly understood to be but one and the same? A. They say, with a good ground, that paradise was a holy spiritual qualification in Adam's mind, or in all the essences of his spirit, soul and body. But the garden Eden was a certain circumscriptive place upon earth, or a part of the earthly globe, which remained still a part thereof, though paradise was lost and gone in Adam's fall.

Q. In what respect and tense can then this garden be called paradise? A. It can be called so (and for distinction's sake it may be called the local paradise), because it had a paradisical property manifest and predominant in it, which was not so in any other place of the earth.

Q. What was this paradisical property, and what were the effects thereof in this garden?

A. It was a quint-essential or one-elementary principle of vegetation, producing the most excellent, incorruptible vegetables of all sorts, wherein the four elements were not manifest in their contrariety; which fruits, therefore, were fit for man, when no beast was capable of eating thereof.

Q. This principle our philosophers assert to be a nitrous salt, which giveth fecundity to all things: to which not only vegetables, but minerals owe their original, and which is the spirit of life in all animals; and is not this that very same? A. A paradisical property lieth still, indeed, in all things, yet no more manifest and predominant therein, but all surrounded and infected with a four-elementary corruption: and upon his account, therefore, it cannot be said absolutely to be the very same. For if it were, all things would still be paradisical and incorruptible, as they were then. Man, also, would still be in paradise, and enjoy a paradisical state, both within and without, as he did then, when he was in this garden in paradise.

Q. What do your authors say of this paradisical state? A. Many great, glorious, and most considerable things. For instance, concerning this paradisical state within, they say that it consisted in an entire subjection of all his exterior faculties to his immortal fire-light-soul, and of both to the holy Will, Word, and Spirit of God; in a child-like, innocent mind; in a continual holy communion with God and Angels; in his being filled with angelical joys, delights, and praises; in being endued with divine wisdom, and understanding all the creatures of this world: in an ability to look into all their essences, and to have dominion over all, etc. And as to his paradisical state without, they describe, particularly, (1.) the glorious condition of his body, which could freely pass through earth and stones, without being withheld, resisted, or hurt by anything. (2.) His living indeed in a temporal principle, but standing not so much in time as in eternity; having no night, no weariness, nor sleep in him, and not wanting to take in his breath from the outward air, so as he must do now. (3.) The manner of his eating and drinking, which was done in his mouth only, without filling a belly and emptying it again; but almost like as the sun swalloweth up water, and is yet never filled, nor made gross and thick thereby. (4.) The manner of his generation, or multiplication, which should have been pure and undefiled, without concurrence of a woman, and answering, in a sense, unto that in which he was himself brought forth by the Creator—from not being, into being. (5.) His clothing, which was no other but his own interior brightness and lustre, breaking forth, penetrating, and covering his outward body, so that its nakedness could not appear. Like as the obscurity of an iron may be entirely covered by the brightness of that fire by which it is possessed and penetrated through and through. (6.) His work or business, which was a childlike play, but full of wisdom, and freely left unto his own pleasure; all was pure unto him, for he was pure himself. He might have planted trees and flowers, and searched out all the wonders of this third principle, especially in the noble metallic tincture, etc.

Q. But what evidence can be given for the belief of all these things, which seem to be impossible for man to know? A. Paradise is not annihilated nor destroyed, but is still that same now in itself which it was then, though it be veiled by the curse, and fallen man be not therein. If, then, there is a possibility that man can be raised up from the fall and curse, and as to his renewed, inward part can be admitted again into paradise, and this even still during his outward life, there must needs be also a possibility for such a one to know what paradise is; what the first Adam, and what his paradisical state was. And as that former cannot be doubted of, so this latter, also, cannot be questioned.

Page 173. *Q. 1. What command was given to Adam in paradise?* According to Behmen's ground, this question is more deeply and distinctly to be answered. Adam, in paradise, must be considered as in a twofold different state. (1.) As he was, before the first beginning of his wandering imagination, only and purely a workmanship of God, having his threefold life out of the mouth of his Creator, and being an entire image of him, made in purity, without any defilement, or disposition thereto. In which state he had in him all the characters expressed of the perfections of him whose image he was: viz. so far as they could have been expressed in, or be communicable in the creature. And (2.) as he was in the first beginning, and further carrying on more and more his own work of a lustful imagination, taking delight gradually more and more in things inferior unto himself. In which state that holy image of God was not yet indeed wholly destroyed, but, nevertheless, already more or less polluted; and began with the beginning of his own work to decrease, decreasing still further always as much as that did increase. Now, in this latter state, viz., in the first beginning thereof, not in that former, the command was given him. The command is to be considered as posterior, and presupposing a previous beginning, or a ready disposition to the transgression: when the transgression is to be looked upon as prior, and as that which had given occasion to the command. For the command, *Thou shalt not eat,* presupposeth the tree of knowledge. Now, this tree was not before, but was brought forth by the concurrence of Adam's lusting imagination, and presupposeth therefore a beginning of the transgression, or a moving, active disposition thereto; and so the command is posterior both unto this and that. All this is conformable to that order which the apostle observed, saying, *Because of the transgression the law came in;* but not the transgression came in because of a foregoing command, or law. Nay, with that first state of man in paradise, before the beginning of his transgression, it is all inconsistent to speak or think of a command or law. This was formerly represented more particularly, and, as I think, sufficiently. But seeing that in this answer no notice is taken thereof, because, as I suppose, it is thought to be of little or no importance, I say here nothing more thereof but this,—that as to me, it is of great consideration, and hath very much in it, and depending upon it, in this present matter of man's perfection, temptation, and fall.

Page 173. *Q*. 2. *How long was Adam in Paradise?* This question, according to Behmen's declaration, is to be answered thus: *A*. They say, that Adam alone, before his Eve, was in paradise forty days, until his sleep; and then with his Eve forty days again (?) until they both saw that they were naked. And that (besides many other types or figures of the Scripture) first our Saviour's resisting the temptation in the wilderness for that space of time; and, secondly, his forty days between his resurrection and ascension, are a sufficient proof of it: the second Adam being to continue under the temptation so long as the first had done.

Page 173. *Q*. 3. *How and by whom was Adam tempted?* A. By his sensitive soul, etc. Here the question is twofold: How and by whom, but the answer only single; for to that former nothing at all is replied, though the manner of the temptation, as to my thinking, is well worth to be declared. And then, further, there is nothing at all said of a necessity, viz. that he needs must have been tempted. Which, if something shall be said thereof, as I think it needful, would have here its proper place. Wherefore, then, for my part, I would represent this matter by several distinct questions and answers, after this or the like manner:—

Q. *Do they give any reason why the first Adam was tempted?* A. Yes, they give several reasons, all concentrated in this point,—that there was an absolute necessity for it. For they say, that as there was a necessity, by which Adam must needs have had a threefold life in him, if he should have been an entire image and likeness of God, and a prince in this created world; so there was the same necessity, also, that he must needs have been tempted, if he should have possessed the throne of fallen Lucifer. And this necessity they demonstrate chiefly from the very nature, combination, and internal constitution of that threefold life.

Q. *But his threefold life stood, as you said before, in a good and excellent combination, order, agreement, and harmony, as only one, because only one was manifest and predominant in him, which was the paradisical; how then could this have caused or necessitated a temptation?* A. His threefold life stood so, indeed, in him; and even this made him to be an entire image of God. But it stood not so without him in the three great worlds which he was an epitome of, and each of which had a natural communion, answerableness, or sympathy with that part in man which was extracted out of it: for in them it was disordered and disharmonised by the false magia of Lucifer. And from hence the cause of the temptation can be seen sufficiently.

Q. *How, then, or in what manner was this temptation done?* A. The third life without him, viz., the spirit of this world, represented unto him its manifold powers and wonders, which he must needs here been affected or touched with, so as to be made sensible thereof; because the third part (if I may so say) of his life was extracted out of it, and he was a lord and ruler thereof. And the devil, being full of malice and envy against him, pretending still to be the prince of this world, and having also an entrance into the dark root thereof, stirred by his false magia that which he had infected before, and darted so by this means his malicious imagination into that third life of man, in whom he raised up and increased thereby successively and gradually, first an attention, then a delight, further a lust, and, at length, a consent and desire.

Q. *Here you set chiefly the spirit of this world and the devil together; but which of them was properly that by which Adam was tempted?* A. Whether you say he was tempted by the devil, or by the spirit of this world, or by his own lust, or by his sensitive soul, all will be right and true, each in its sense and order. For the devil was, indeed, the chief agent, and more secret; but the spirit of this world was his active instrument, and more appearing. And as they both were without man, so there was also within him his own lust and his sensitive soul, answering unto, and concurring with the two without him.

Page 173. Q. *Why did the sensitive soul, etc.* From what was said in several places above, it is apparent that this question might now be reasonably looked upon as superfluous, because it is answered, as to substance, several times. But, notwithstanding this, if it shall stand so, and be answered again more explicitly, it is well to be observed, that the words, *The knowledge of the wonders of this world depends upon the knowledge of the forms of things, etc.*, cannot so be brought in as a cause why the sensitive soul tempted Adam. For although they are now all true, in a sense, yet they were not so in the same sense before the fall; or, at least, the full sense as it is applicable unto Adam in paradise, is not thereby expressed. For Adam, giving names unto all the beasts, and being able to look deeply into all their essences, originals, constitutions, properties, etc., *knew certainly the internal forms of all things*. In a word, the whole nature, with all its powers and wonders, stood open before him, and he had knowledge thereof. Which, if it had not been so, he could not have been so tempted as he was: but then he could also not have been a prince and ruler of this principle. His temptation and fall, therefore, was not because he desired a knowledge of the wonders and forms of things, but because he had such a knowledge of all the wonders and powers without him, he desired to know them within himself also, in a *sensible manifestation of their contrarieties*. And this was the knowledge of good and evil, which, as then, he had not yet, and could not have had it, without falling down himself from his eminent station in and under the same twofold government of good and evil. That former knowledge was well consistent with his paradisical state, nay, it was a precious jewel of his crown, when this latter was his utter destruction. Not knowing whether I have expressed my sense and intent intelligibly enough, I cannot but declare it again, by saying, that Adam knew, well enough, there were contrary qualities and qualifications without him, in all the things of outward nature; and this knowledge was an eminent perfection of his, without which he could not have been what he was ordained to be in this world: and this, therefore, was not that which he lusted after. But because of this he came to lust after an experimental knowledge, or own sensation of these contrary qualities within himself. His sensitive soul would prove actually by feeling and tasting how it would be with itself, when these contrary qualities were manifest, each in its own operation. And this was the thing which was agreeable to the nature of the sensitive soul.

In the next following Q. (Page 175,) something the like is said, indeed, as to the words, but not as to this sense, viz., *which experimental practical knowledge, I suppose, was the thing chiefly desired by the sensitive soul*. This, I say, hath almost indeed the same expressions; but is, for all that, greatly different in sense. For I cannot understand it otherwise but that there is meant thereby only a *setting of forms on work in things without him*; because I see it is said afterwards to be *now so useful and praiseworthy*. And this is so indeed now, and was also so before; for it was an eminent piece of Adam's dominion over all things; but for this same reason it was not that which the sensitive soul so blindly desired. For it was never useful nor praiseworthy, but always hurtful and accursed, that Adam set on work the forms of nature within himself; because of which he must now bear in soul and body all the disharmonised properties in their contrary operations, and is fallen into sin, anxiety, vexation of spirit, trouble, misery, all manner of sickness, and death.

Page 175. *Q. ult.* In the first part of the answer to this question, if I should form it, I would leave out those things that are brought in only as probable, and would rather put this No. 1 into such a construction:

Q. Did not Adam resist the temptation? A. Not faithfully, and therefore also not successfully, for he was wearied and overcome by it. As appears,

1. By his desiring a help meet, or a female associate, as he saw all the rest of the living creatures to have. When God said, *It is not good that the man should be alone*, it doth declare sufficiently, that an alteration or change, more or less, from good into not good, was made already in man; and by man himself, because not by God. If, then, by man, it must needs have been from his not resisting faithfully the appetite of his sensitive soul. And that this appetite was not only in general after a sensual knowledge of good and evil, but also in particular after *such a help-meet*, can be manifest from the event, wherein that same was given him which he desired.

2. His falling asleep argues, etc.

3. The divulsion, etc. Here, instead of saying, as in uncertainty he *seems to have been overcome*, I, for my part, would rather say positively,—he was overcome; or, at least, as hitherto frequently,—they say he was overcome by the temptation.

Page 177. *Q. ult.* and 178. What is here objected concerning the honourableness of the matrimonial state, could have been objected also (*mutatis tantum circumstantialibus*) against the doctrine of our Saviour, concerning polygamy. Which doctrine seemed to the Jews no less offensive, and reflecting upon Moses and the law, than this may seem to reflect upon the words of the apostle. If I were asked, Was there somewhat not good in Adam, and what was it when he desired a female help meet? I would answer, it was *that same* which the Lord called the *hardness of the heart*, because of which Moses had permitted polygamy. Not that it was so gross in Adam .. and in such an outbirth as it was in the Jews; but yet it was the same internal root out of which this hardness came forth afterwards. If, then, this hardness was not good in the Jews, when outborn in this world, its root also could not have been good in Adam, when first conceived by his sensitive soul in the paradisical state. From the beginning it was not so, saith the Lord, that man should be married unto more than one wife; and yet he would not say absolutely the law and Moses's permission was not good. So also we may say justly, From that first beginning which is to answer unto that ultimate end, wherein, according to the Lord's own words, *there shall be neither worrying nor being given in marriage*, it was not so. And yet we do not say thereby that the permission and institution of God was not good; but we say only that it was made by God, because man was departed already, in his imagination and desire, from the first, most pure, and best paradisical state; which departing of man was certainly not good. In the creation of this world, God saws all his works, that they were all good; and yet all this goodness is hardly comparable to that goodness which Lucifer had destroyed, and unto which this world shall be brought back again. So then there is goodness and goodness, not indeed lighting against each other, as good and evil, but nevertheless distinct and different in degree and order; so that when both compared, the one is better, but when considered separately, each is good by itself. What then can this objection signify against the apostle's word? He says, indeed, the matrimonial state is honourable, and shall be accounted and kept so; but truly, honourableness in a state of this world is not an absolute holiness and purity in the paradisical world. Marriage, therefore, as it is an association from without of male and female, is justly to be accounted honourable here in this world, but will not be honourable in that which is to come, where the Lord said himself it shall not be at all, and where, nevertheless, nothing that is pure and holy shall be wanting.

Page 183. *A*. 1. *By the rib they mean somewhat taken out of all the essences, etc.* Though it is true, that they say somewhat was taken out of all the essences, yet it cannot be said that *they mean* or understand this *by the rib*, as if this rib did signify all that which was taken. More members besides the rib were not taken out of Adam, saith Behmen, expressly. And by this rib, which as then was not yet so hard and gross, he understands nothing else but that which then, in Adam's body, answered unto what we now call rib, and which also came to be the rib as a particular member, when the body came to have such gross earthly flesh and bones as it hath now.

Page 185. Line 3. Here I think it is not well said, *that text seems to say, etc.*, as if there were only a probability of this text's saying so, when it is clear and plain unto every one, that this excellent text saith positively, and by so many express words, that *God created but one, because he sought a godly seed*.

Page 185. *A* 2. Here, the description of Adam is well and right enough; but that of Eve, calling her a *gross elementary creature*, is not applicable to that state wherein she stood before her eating of the tree. For she was indeed flesh of Adam's flesh, and bone of his bone, but not yet grosser nor more elementary than Adam was. She was indeed made for to be his wife afterwards, in the elementary state of this world; but as then the elements were not yet manifest nor predominant, neither in her nor in him. But they were both alike in glory, happiness, holiness, and purity, and were both in paradise, though they had none of these things in that eminent degree in which Adam had them all, when he was a single person.

Page 187. Line 1. *A perfect virgin, with fire and light in union.* This must here needs be expressed with an addition of these or the like words—with fire and light, and with the two tinctures thereof in union: or shorter, thus—with the two tinctures of fire and light in union. For the union of the tinctures in one person presupposeth and implieth also an union of fire and light, and is therefore enough to describe Adam as a perfect paradisical virgin; but the union of fire and light only, without an union of the two tinctures, is here, in this place, not enough, where Adam is considered not only as a single person, but also immediately as divided into two: so that an account is to be given of what was divided, and what was given unto each divided part. Not fire and light, but only the two tinctures thereof were divided. For Eve had a fiery soul, or soulish fire, as well as Adam, and had also a shining light, as well as he; and had therefore fire and light in union, neither more nor less than he. But for all that neither he nor she was any more such a perfect paradisical virgin as Adam had been before his sleep.

Page 187. *Q. What do they mean by the two tinctures?* A. I know not how to express it better than by what I have expressed it already, saying that they mean the two generating powers in man, out of the two eternal principles; neither of which can be complete by itself, nor acquiesce with itself alone; but each must embrace the other, find its accomplishment therein, and be enabled thereby to produce a living image after its likeness.

Q. Which of these two was left to Adam? and is there a reason to be had, why that which was given to Eve could not as well have been reserved to him, so that Eve might have had that which now Adam hath? A. The temptation before Adam's sleep was chiefly about propagation, and even especially was it in his fiery soul; for therein the lust was conceived, and the desire arose after a female associate. That part, therefore, of the propagating power which was inseparable from his soulish fire, must needs have been reserved to him; and that was the strong, fiery, masculine tincture. And so then that other part which he was not willing to have had further within himself in a paradisical integrity, but without or besides himself, after the manner of all the beasts, must needs have been taken out of him and given unto Eve. And this was the weaker watery female tincture, not able (for want of fire) to raise up a life by itself.

Page 187. *Q. 4. Could not a paradisical birth or godly seed, etc.* Here are two reasons given for a negative answer, which are both indeed right and true; but that which might be the most considerable, at least upon some certain particular account is not mentioned, which I think should be set in the first place, and thus expressed:

A. No; because (1.) in the womb of Eve no union of the two tinctures, according to the right of eternal nature, was, nor could have been made; but only an outward familiar conjunction, which soon after must have been turned into disagreement and strife. And moreover (2.) both tinctures were defiled, etc. Concerning the next following words, I observe this, that Eve did not expect *such a birth*, or such a *paradisical virgin*; because after her being turned out of paradise, she knew paradise no more, and much less what a paradisical virgin was. But she expected (according to her understanding the promise of the serpent treader) a valiant champion against the devil, who should conquer him after an outward earthly manner, etc. And this she called *a man from the Lord*. But as she was disappointed in this her blind opinion, so she must have been disappointed much more, if she had or could have expected a paradisical virgin.

Page 189. *Q.* 2 and 3. These two questions belong together; and seeing that several things could be expressed and represented plainer and more distinctly; and also, that this and that expression could be excepted against, I think therefore that this matter might be declared in such a manner:

Q. What do they say concerning the formation of Eve's body? A. They say, with the scripture, that the Lord God made of the rib a woman. And more particularly do they declare their sense by saying:

(1.) That the chief work-master was the eternal speaking Word, in conjunction with the first attracting, binding, or compacting spirit; not only of eternal, but also now especially of temporal nature, which latter they call the exterior fiat, under whose power man was fallen in his sleep.

(2.) That this exterior fiat gave in this act unto Adam, as well as Eve, those distinct marks of male and female, now required for their propagation; and those other parts and members, also, that are now necessary for their living an earthly life; though nothing thereof was as yet manifest unto them, until their eyes were opened, when they had actually eaten of the earthly fruit, and seen that they were naked.

(3.) That therefore Eve was made to be a woman of this world only, and for the use of this transitory life; and not to continue a woman for ever, but to be restored into a perfect virgin image in the world to come, such as the first Adam was before she was taken out of him.

(4.) That all this was done with Eve from the sixth hour to the ninth; whereunto, they say, do answer the three hours of our Lord's being nailed to the cross, until his dying to the male and female of this world.

(5.) That in this space of time her body, as then yet not so gross and earthly as it is now, arose into a full stature; and this by the power of the tincture (the principle of growth and increase), which then was still very lively, though not so powerful as it had been before the heavenly virgin was withdrawn from Adam.

Q. What do they say concerning her soul and spirit? A. They say, (1.) That her soul was not created anew, or infused into her body by a repeated act of creation, but generated out of Adam's soulish essences, as all souls now still are, viz. according to the process of the generation of eternal nature, in its four first properties.

(2.) That her soul was neither higher nor lower graduated than Adam's soul was in that state, which having been defiled already with his lust, could not but have infected with the same lust the soul of Eve also, as it showed forth itself soon after.

(3.) That her spirit arose out of her soul, as the light out of the fire, and as all the soulish spirits do to this day; which will be made more clear hereafter.

Q. But was not something of the substance of Adam's soul taken from him, and given unto Eve? A. No; only the watery tincture, as the one-half part of the propagating power, was taken from him, and given unto Eve; but this doth not belong to the substance of the soul, of which he lost, and could have lost nothing; like as the flame of a candle may communicate its fiery essences to another candle, and can for all that lose nothing of its substance.

Page 191. *Q.* 1. *What do they mean by the eternal Virgin Wisdom?* A. They mean that breath and mirror of the power of God, that image of his goodness, that ray of the Almighty, and that treasure of man, which is called so by the author of the book of Wisdom; and which, in the Proverbs of Solomon, viii. 30. 31, saith of herself,—*I was set up from everlasting: I was by him as one brought up with him: I was daily his delight, rejoicing always before him: my delight was with the children of man*, etc. And this, they say, is that same which the prophet Malachi, ii. 14, 15, calleth *the wife of thy youth, thy companion, and the wife of thy covenant, against whom thou hast dealt treacherously.* This Adam should have cleaved unto faithfully, but dealing treacherously against her, he got, instead of her, the woman of this world, called a strange woman, and described emphatically, Prov. v. 3, etc.

Page 193. In this matter, concerning the temptation of Eve by the serpent, I see it would cause too great a prolixity, if all the observations that might be made should be particularised. I will, therefore, only set down the sense of Behmen, so and in such an order as I am apt to think it might best be represented.

(1.) They say, that Eve was tempted by the devil, who envied man, because he was to have possessed that third angelical throne from which he fell.

(2.) That the devil did not tempt Adam directly, but Eve; because he had tried it already with Adam before, and could not prevail against him, so far as for him to condescend to this degree of transgression, though he was prevented chiefly by an intervention of the great mercy of God, who caused a deep sleep to fall upon him, and divided him. But after this division, he saw his own evil seed, which he had sown into Adam, spring up in Eve, whom he knew to be made for a woman of this world; and whose watery tincture, as the weaker, he might well suppose, would not prove so strong as to resist effectually the poisonous darts of his dark magic fire.

(3.) That he did not tempt her immediately by himself, because, having nothing of this third outward principle in him, he could not have wrought so effectually upon her sensitive part; and wanted, therefore, a medium, fit to procure a familiar communication, and then an union of will between himself and her.

(4.) That this medium was the serpent, which in its own living substance was of the same qualities as the tree of knowledge was of in a lifeless figure. And that, therefore, unto this tree, as its own most agreeable likeness, not only the serpent could and did apply itself, but also through the serpent the devil could and did act his parts most properly, to persuade Eve that she might freely eat of the fruits thereof.

(5.) That he therefore entered into the serpent's properties and tincture, and especially into the subtlety in this tincture; for this was the most suitable for his end, viz. to insinuate himself after the most advantageous manner into the tinctures and properties of Eve.

(6.) That the deepest ground why he made use of the serpent, rather than of any other living creature, is to be found in the serpent's originality. Concerning which they say,—That ens which in the creation became the serpent, was nearly related unto Lucifer before his fall. For as he was a most eminent prince, both as to fire and light, so that also was a fire-light image of great powers and virtues. No wonder, then, that in and after his fall, also, it was nearly related unto him, when, by his false magia, he had infected and impregnated it more than anything else with the properties of the dark world. These properties, say they further, not being able to exalt that kind of intellect which is therein to a degree of holy wisdom, and true understanding of truth, do sharpen it only in subtlety, guile, deceit and lies, fairly coloured with the glistering astral light of outward nature. Now all this being so in the serpent, he was for this reason more fit than any beast of the field to be made use of by the devil in his present purpose of transforming himself into a creature of light.

(7.) That he spoke through the serpent, and by that speech transfused his infecting subtle tincture into her, which eclipsed her light and weakened her will more and more, till at length her former secret lust came to be an open resolution to try whether she might find out that hidden treasure which the serpent told her God had kept back from her; and laid it up within the good and pleasant fruit of this desirable tree.

(8.) That this the devil's transfusing his poisoning tincture into Eve, was done after such a manner as still to this day his wicked instruments are able by incantation to convey poison, pain, sickness and all manner of evil into another's mind and body, if he be capable thereof, by not being armed or provided against it.

Q. I do not well know what you mean by the tincture of the serpent, nor what the subtlety in this tincture is: pray, Sir, therefore satisfy me in these doubts? Here I am to show the reason for which I left out the word *twofold*, together with this whole question, *Why do you assert this creature alone to have this tincture?* And then also why I say the *subtlety* in the tincture, instead of the *property of subtlety*.

(1.) It is plain enough that one and the same thing, and under the same name, may be considered and spoken of differently with respect to different qualities, powers, operations and effects. Now then the tincture is here not considered any more as that propagating power which upon its division came to be twofold, as it was so spoken of above; but as a power operating upon another thing without it, influencing it, and communicating or conveying unto it this or that. The tincture is a powerful thing, whose true name, says Behmen, is wonderful, and none can name it but he to whom it is given; and he can name it only in himself, but not without him to another. It is not the spirit itself, but the spirit's and soul's habitation and instrument. Through the tincture the soul can overthrow mountains, and do all those wonderful things that the Lord and his apostles did. It is indeed in all things whatsoever, yet not in one as in another, but in every thing according to its nature and condition. All the communication between intellectual creatures is done by the tincture; all the thoughts and senses arise in it, and without it there could be no seeing, hearing, feeling, etc. This therefore in the serpent the devil made use of to transfuse his poison into Eve, which he could not have done so by his own tincture only. Now then it is apparent that it is one thing when Behmen speaketh of *two tinctures*, and another when of a *twofold tincture*. For that former hath a particular relation to the two divided propagating powers in male and female; but this latter to the twofold means of communication between intellectual creatures: which here in this case of the serpent was the outward and inward tincture. The outward from the astral light of this outward principle was that which Eve could immediately be sensible and capable of, and which the devil could not have entered into immediately. But the inward from the inward dark world's properties, was that which the devil had a free entrance into, and by which he could direct that outward also; and so through this outward, convey and transfuse his hidden poison into Eve's tincture, if she would hearken to the serpent's speech. So then, it is evident, that this question, *why the serpent alone had this twofold tincture*, if the twofold tincture be understood as now declared, hath no sense in it: for it is nowhere said, that the serpent had it *alone*, but only that the serpent had it in a manner and degree more fit for the devil's use than any other beast of the field. But if it be understood of the two divided tinctures in male and female, it doth not belong to this place at all, and is therefore justly left out. And though I might well have said *twofold tincture* in a sense as mentioned, instead of *tincture* only, yet I left out the word *twofold*, also, to give no occasion for this prolixity, and because the matter can be, and is, as I think, represented intelligibly enough, though this word is not made use of.

(2.) Instead of the *property of subtlety*, I say only the *subtlety in the tincture;* because that former expression is a pure Germanism, and the translator might rather have said, the *subtle property* in the tincture: for, as to my thinking, that former represents, as it were, three different things, viz. (1.) a tincture, (2.) a subtlety in this tincture, and (3.) a property causing this subtlety; when there are but two. What *subtlety* is, I think, is seen and known in this world sufficiently, wherein yet it is but an outbirth from the dark-world, and must be described from the properties of them both together in conjunction. That which is in the holy light-world wisdom, is in this astral light-world subtlety; and in the dark we have *no proper peculiar name for it*, but call it subtlety also, though certainly a distinction ought always to be observed. When, therefore, Moses saith that *the serpent was more subtle than any beast of the field*, he says in the ground and substance nothing else but that the serpent (1.) with respect to the dark-world, was, more than any other beast, infected possessed, and filled with its properties; and (2.) that it was with respect to the outward light-world, more than any other, of a friendly, fallacious, false loving, penetrating, and insinuating temper; those inward dark and wrathful properties being thus, in a sense, corrected and tinctured, or exalted to a specious appearance. And so in these two together in conjunction, this subtlety consisted; wherefore, then, the serpent was the fittest for the devil's use, who wanted such an instrument. Now, this subtlety is not the tincture itself, but in the tincture; and by the tincture, as by a proper vehicle, it was conveyed to, and transfused into the tincture of Eve. For it is not essential to, nor inseparable from, the tincture, but shall be separated from it again, and came to be therein only by the devil's false magia. Wherefore then, the sense is rightly expressed by saying, *the subtlety in the tincture*.

Q. What is now further their doctrine concerning the tree of knowledge of good and evil? A. They say,

(1.) That like as the serpent was a fit medium to convey the devil's poison from the dark-world chiefly into the mind of Eve, so this tree was such a medium also to convey the same, by her eating thereof, especially into her body, for to make it beast-like and mortal.

(2) That this tree was such a one, and neither better nor worse, than our fruit trees are, which we now eat of, after the curse.

(3.) That the difference between this forbidden tree and all the other trees in the garden Eden, was just such a one as there is between the now earthly body, and that paradisical body which man had then; the quintessential property being then in all the other trees predominant, when in this only the four elements in their strife and contrariety were manifest.

(4.) That it was called the tree of knowledge of good and evil, because man, not having had before an experimental knowledge of these two in their contrarieties, could only, by eating of this tree, come to have a knowledge and feeling thereof in his soul and body.

(5.) That no creature can live without food, but every creature, according to its kind, must eat of the fruits of that world wherein it is to live. And that, therefore, in this tree an infinite mercy of God appears, who, foreseeing the fall of man, and not willing him to fall into the dark-world, ordered all things so, that, by eating of a four-elementary fruit, he might fall into this outward mixed world; whose four elements being but so many issues of the pure quint-essential element, may be brought back again into their root, and so therefore man also to his primeval state.

(6.) That this tree came not forth with the rest of vegetables, on the third day of the creation, but that it was afterwards brought forth out of the earth by the strong magical imagination and desire of Adam, when he was already deviated from the first paradisical perfection.

Page 199. *A.* 1. Seeing that this objection hath a fine outward appearance, I think it would be needful to answer it more particularly; and for this reason there might be added to the last words of the question. *What reason can they give for this assertion?*

A. They think they have a solid ground firmly to believe that they do not contradict Moses, any more than he seems to contradict himself, when he saith, Gen. i. *Male and female created he them;* and in the second chapter, *He took a rib and made a woman.* But some of their plainest and most obvious reasons for this assertion, may be these:

(1.) This tree was not altogether good, much less very good, and therefore we cannot say that it was made by God on the third day, with all the rest of vegetables. For on the fifth day God saw everything which he had made, and behold it was very good.

(2.) It brings with it great prejudice to the honour of God, to say that he made such a tree to grow out of the ground, when man stood yet in his entire integrity; for this would be as much as to say directly, God himself gave the first occasion to the fall, or God tempted him, and laid a snare at his feet, by setting desirable fruit before him, and yet commanding him not to desire nor touch it. When God is not a tempter to the evil, and when we can show the right and true ground of this temptation.

(3.) This assertion is all consistent with Adam's princely state and mighty power; and if this be joined to a consideration of his threefold life, it is to them that can understand the constitution thereof, a strong, convincing proof, that this tree came not forth before, but after the beginning of his deviation; and that he brought it forth himself, though God is not absolutely in all and every sense excluded. And though Moses makes mention of this tree before he says that God brought man into the garden, seeing that it is evident enough that Moses, in all this relation, is not so nice and accurate as to put everything in an exact order.

(4.) As it is greatly prejudicial to the honour of God to put any appearance of evil upon him, which cannot but be done by saying, He, without any concurrence of man, and before he could concur to it, made this tree to grow; so it is, contrariwise, highly exalting his honour, goodness, and tenderness to man, to ascribe all evil, in the greatest latitude, unto the devil and man; which is done by saying, when man, through the instigation of the devil, lusted and longed after such a food, then only, but not before, God gave it him, or let him have it so; and yet declared withal his displeasure sufficiently, by commanding him, Thou shalt not eat thereof; and telling him of his eminent danger.

(5.) Like as he that says, *God gave, or raised up a king to the house of Israel,* is not contradicted by him that declareth orderly the manner of this raising up, and says, *The tribes of Israel find departed with their hearts from the Lord their God, and rejected him, that he should not be their king;* and then they desired importunately, not of God, but of the prophet, that he should set a king over them, after the manner of all the nations; and so by this desire they were themselves the immediate cause of this kingdom, and of all their following calamities: so also Moses, in what he says of God's doing about this tree, is not contradicted by him that makes the strong desire of Adam, after his imagination was departed from the Lord, his Father and Tutor, to be the proper immediate cause of this tree's coming forth out of the ground.

Q. How could such an evil, infecting tree grow in paradise? A. Thinking still, Sir, on your last question, I might well ask reciprocally,—How could such a tree as you describe have been brought forth by God, the only good, without an immediate operation of man himself, and even before he was infected by the devil? But to resolve this new scruple, also, I must needs say, there is no difficulty in the matter at all. For this tree grew not in paradise, but in the garden Eden, and even in the midst thereof where Adam and Eve were tempted. We discoursed before, concerning the difference between paradise and the garden Eden; and from thence you may easily apprehend that this tree was as little in paradise as the devil or the serpent was: but in the garden, in which all the other trees were paradisical, it could be; for only the pre-dominion, either of the quintessential or four-elementary property does make the difference.

Q. Why is this tree of knowledge said to have stood in the midst of the garden? A. As all outward things are figures or signatures of the inward, so was this also. Adam and Eve were tried as in the midst, between the three principles, having them, indeed, all three in them, but being not yet fixed in any of them: and in answerableness to this, the tempting tree stood also outwardly in the midst of the garden. But another and deeper reason can be given, which is this: This standing in the midst is chiefly and in the first place attributed to the *tree of life*, representing the second principle of pure eternal life, which standeth in the midst, between the first and third; but to the tree of knowledge it is attributed but secondarily and consequentially. For it was not two trees in number, standing the one besides the other, but only one manifest in two principles, which as to its outward figure in this world, could not but stand in the midst of the garden, because it stood, as to its inward representation, in that midst; and this in conformity to the second principle's standing in the midst, between the first eternal and the third temporal world.

Q. How can this assertion, of one tree, be consistent with the description of Moses, who tells us expressly of two? A. The tree of knowledge, forasmuch as it had corruptibility and death in it, was not indeed the tree of life; like as also this four-elementary world is not paradise. But like as paradise is only without the qualification of this world, but not without the place of it, so also was this tree of life with relation to the tree of knowledge. As then, upon that former account, Moses rightly speaks of two trees, so upon this latter, there is also rightly spoken but of one, yet such a one as is twofold, or manifest in two different principles; and Moses is not contradicted at all.

Q. This distinction and difference between these two trees, which you say were but one, wants yet better to be illustrated. A. There was such a distinction and difference between them, as there was between man's outward astral and inward soulish spirit. When his imagination wandered out, he found in the midst of the garden an object was represented to his astral spirit by the spirit of this world, which invited him to eat, that he might get an experimental knowledge of good and evil. And when he withdrew his imagination from this, and turned in, he found in the midst of the garden (though it might now more properly be said, in the midst of paradise) an object was represented to his superior soulish spirit by the spirit of God, which invited him to eat, that he might be strengthened, and enabled to go forward unto his being confirmed to that higher eternal life, which he was to have been translated into at the end of this temporal world. And so there was the greatest difference, even to a contrariety, between these two objects. And yet they were not two such trees as stood besides or without one another, each upon a peculiar spot of ground, so as that they could have been seen at once in one station of man, and by the self same seeing faculty. And though they both were always before him, yet each of them affected only that part of him which it was conformable to, and he was sensible of that only which his imagination applied itself unto. And as he was but one man, or one soul with an interior and exterior spirit, so was this but one tree, with an interior and exterior appearance, answering unto his twofold spirit.

Q. How did this tree of life differ from the other paradisical trees? and to what end was it set before him, in the midst, as you say, of paradise? A. The very name thereof showeth us that it was more dignified, or higher graduated than the rest of the paradisical trees. For though they also had nothing of death in them, yet they brought only fruits for man's then present paradisical life, when this offered him fruits from that higher heavenly life, which upon his having held out his trial faithfully, he was to have been confirmed unto eternally. Wherefore, also, it was set before him in the midst of paradise, for to show him that this paradise, then upon earth, was still but, as it were, a circumferential state, from which he was to enter into a higher or deeper central rest. But especially was it set before him because of this temptation, that he might have the highest antidote against the devil's poison, hid under the veil of the spirit of this world; that he might be altogether inexcusable, and find afterwards no fault with his loving Father and Creator; but that God, as he is just, might be justified also in all his works by man, who must needs own that he would not have had him fall, but that he did for him all that be could do, consistently with that free will which he had given him. When, therefore, Eve neglected this, and applied herself to the tree of knowledge, and gave Adam also of the fruit thereof, they both could not but fall, by their own fault, into death, and lose not only the tree of life, but all the rest of the paradisical fruits also.

Page 205. No. 4. For the sake of a clearer distinction, and better agreement with what was declared above, might here be said,—They had lost paradise, and were driven out of the garden also. For paradise, as to their own persons and paradisical state, they had lost before, and saw that they had lost it when their eyes were opened; but in the garden they were still, till they were driven out of it afterwards.

Ibid. Q. 1. Concerning *the cherubim and flaming sword*, might thus be answered:

(1.) That the words of Moses are indeed to be understood, according to the letter, of a dreadful appearance, to Adam and Eve, of a mighty angel, having a flaming two-edged sword, and driving them away from that place. But that, nevertheless, this was but an outward figure or representation of an inward reality, which is of a very large signification, and full of mysteries. Whereof they say further:

(2.) That but an obscure external notion can be had thereof, without a self-experience in the process of regeneration; seeing that it is not only without, but much rather within man.

(3.) That this sword is the spiritual fire of eternal nature, considered as divorced from the light in man; and so that it is that only passage which he must go through, if to be restored to his entire primeval perfection.

(4.) That the whole dispensation under the law, with all its types and figures, is to be referred hereunto: this fire being all that time advancing forward to a re-union with its light in the humanity, until in the fulness thereof this re-union was accomplished in the human person of Jesus Christ.

(5.) That from this Adam and Eve's being driven out of paradise, no soul of their posterity was able to pass through this fiery sword into paradise again, because no male nor female can be admitted into it, but only that perfect virgin-image which was therein created in the beginning; and such a virgin-image was not among all living, until the Lord from heaven came down and took upon him human nature.

(6.) That He, though outwardly a male, being internally a perfect virgin, broke this fiery sword in his death, by passing through it into paradise, and carrying along with him the holy patriarchs, prophets, etc., and that in this entering into, and passing through this sword, that article of our Christian religion, concerning his *descending into hell*, is understood.

(7.) That this breaking the fiery sword doth not yet import a total abolishing or removing of the same, but only a having weakened and made it impotent; so that though everyone is to follow that same way after him, yet this angel is no more able to keep out any soul that is endued with his Spirit, and much less any that has put on his new humanity.

(8.) That the office of this angel is to cut off from the soul (N.B.) all what it is infected and polluted with from the devil, the serpent, and the tree of knowledge of good and evil.

Page 207. No. 4. *that he implanted in their souls.* For certain considerable reasons I would here much rather say,—in them, or in their mind, or, in their ground. Because it was not implanted in their souls, if the soul is taken strictly for that fiery being which in itself is distinct, and was moreover now separated from the spirit: but it was inspoken into them, or in their ground, without their having any power to do or act with it according to their pleasure. Nay, it is even more properly to be attributed to Eve than to Adam, seeing that Eve, not Adam, was to bring forth that holy seed which was to bruise the serpent's head. When the fiery soul in Adam, chiefly (for Eve's soul is not thereby excluded) was that same serpent in man, whose head, or fiery predominant power was to be bruised by that seed of the woman, not of the man. In Adam the soulish fire began to be raised up, and in Eve the light thereof was first extinguished. Into this, therefore, not into that immediately, this seed was implanted, for to stand in opposition against that first beginning made in Adam.

Ibid. Q. 1. *The same in substance with what divines commonly call universal grace,* etc.

Though I do not *exactly* know what they understand by *universal grace,* yet I think this supposition, which here in the answer is passed by in silence, and as if it were all granted, should be answered in a sense inclining more or less to the negative, by showing a difference between them, consisting herein,—that the universal grace is that ability in all men, which is freely given them after the fall, to turn their will, desire, and imagination unto God again, who offers them a gift, and to receive the same from him; when this *ingrafted word* is that divine gift itself, though still but considered as a little seed. For though even this also may verily be called an universal grace, yet there is also something lower than this, and in a sense prior, and more as on the side of man, by which he is to procure the manifestation and increase of this gift in him, which else will never be manifest in him, nor do him any good. In a word, that first, all men have absolutely; and this second, all men can have, by means of a right use of that first.

Ibid. A. 1. *propagated, but in a hidden manner.* Here, I think, might well be added.—in its own inward principle, and not as by the soul's own propagating power. For the soul was not sufficient for it; and therein also chiefly, according to Behmen's plain declaration, that hidden manner did consist. And, that the last words, viz., *the first-born commonly the figure or type of the sinful image*, might not seem so dry and useless, I think these words could conveniently be added,—which they say is very mysterious. For Behmen's declaration testifieth sufficiently, the great mysteries contained therein, and showeth also plainly the deep mysterious cause thereof; even from the generation of eternal nature, wherein the fiery, wrathful properties are, and must be, prior to the light, as the soul also in man is and must be prior to the spirit.

Pages 211–218. Here is a compendious description of the beginning of the *natural generation*, represented first, as to the sense of Behmen, and then also as to that of several other philosophers and physicians, which are apprehended to be not only different from, but also contrary to him. I cannot but say hereupon in general (1.) That same which I find is said afterwards (page 229. *A. ult.*) is absolutely true; viz. that internal eyes, looking into the inward ground, are more to be valued than external ones, beholding only the superficies of things, though never to well instructed with microscopes. (2.) That these latter are to be censured, judged, and rectified by those former, but not the former by the latter; according to the apostle's word, which herein also is true in a sense and manner, *the spiritual man judgeth all things, and is judged by none.* (3.) That notwithstanding this, if, by the outward eye something is plainly discovered contrary to, and inconsistent with what internal eyes have delivered; in such a case it may be granted, that in this or that particular thing a mistake is committed, either by the author himself in his delivery, or by the reader in the apprehension thereof. For this could have been done upon several accounts, both on the reader's side and on the author's, who not only never pretended to an infallibility in all and every punctilio, but also owned plainly himself, that he had not declared all particular things; whereto, he saith, in this matter only, concerning the natural propagation of man, many great volumes would be required. And (4.) That in all what here in these seven pages is related from the physicians, I cannot yet meet with anything which I could say is plainly and directly contrary to what Behmen hath delivered. Nay, as to those particulars wherein they differ among themselves, and are contrary to one another, I dare say it is apparent, from Behmen, that in both their contrary opinions some glimmerings appear of a deeper truth, which in its brightness was not risen unto any of them, and could not therefore by them have been discerned. So that they are not only not so contrary to Behmen as they may seem to be from without, but also not so contrary to one another as they think themselves to be. This, I shall, in the first place, endeavour to show by going through all their eight positions (from page 213 to 218,) and then I shall also say what I think is needful to be observed upon the six positions (page 211), declaring the same thing according to the sense of Behmen:

(1.) *The physicians say, the semen of the male consists,* etc. In this whole first position, I am not able to discover any the least contrariety between Behmen and them; nay, as to some particulars, not so much as a difference, but what may be in the construction of words. Behmen speaks of a *blood of the heart*, and they of an *arterial blood conveyed from the heart:* and is not both this and that one and the same thing? Behmnen considers chiefly the first, the principal and the more insensible original of the seed, in that place whereout, as the Scripture witnesseth, are the issues of life; not minding so directly that which is secondary, which yet, in several other places, he also plainly expresses and asserts. And the physicians consider chiefly that which is nearer to apprehension and sensibility; not minding so directly that which is first and principal, which yet they also do not deny, but assert and express it plainly, by their saying it is conveyed from the heart. Behmen doth not say, that *the semen is elaborated in the heart;* but that in the heart the beginning is made of its generation, not in the spermatic arteries. For to the brain, which is the astral spirit's residence, the heart, as the chief residence of life, is nearer and more immediately related than those arteries. Upon the heart, therefore, the first operation is done, from the agent in the brain, and then from the heart it is conveyed down: which I am sure the physicians will not deny nor contradict. Further: I see they disagree here, more or less among themselves; for some add *to the animal spirits*, the *nervous juice*, the *succus nutritius*, or *succus genitalis*. But Behmen will disagree with none, having asserted, that in the greatest latitude all the powers and virtues of the whole body are comprised in the seed. And to their last particular in this position, viz., that the gross parts of the semen are as a vehicle to the spirituous parts, etc., he will be found not only to stand in an entire conformity, but also to be able more than any or all of them to declare, from his internal sight, what and from whence those grosser and these more spirituous parts are, what it was that made such a difference between them, and how the former came to be so gross and beastlike as they are.

(2.) *Physicians say, the females have no semen: their testiculi are ovaria;* and from hence it is concluded that Behmen, saying much of the female semen, cannot but contradict their ocular experiences. But I think this contradiction will be but seeming, and lying in different apprehension of the word semen. The females, they grant, have something in them requisite to the generation: even such a thing as *hath the lineaments of the foetus in it, before the knowledge of man*, and which is to *drop into the fundus uteri*, as a seed into the ground. Now why this may not pertinently be called a seed or semen, I cannot see, when the Scripture itself speaks of the *woman's seed*. When, therefore, the physicians say the females have no semen, I cannot think that they intend to set up their ocular experience as a witness against the Scripture, but only that their meaning is this: that which the woman hath is not like to the semen of the man, and hath not those requisites which they conceive to be needful in the man's semen. And if this or the like be their sense, it is not contrary to Behmen. For he nowhere saith that the female semen is thoroughly such a one, or that it is generated entirely in the same form as the males; though he doth also say nothing of that form of an ovum, which whether he knew or not I cannot determine. It is at least apparent, from his saying—that hands and feet have their signatures in the centre, before they come to an outward appearance, that he knew more than he delivered. But let this also be taken notice of: Seeing that the physicians say little of that which needs must precede every generation, viz., will, imagination, lust, and desire, which yet is not of little moment; and seeing that these things are and operate in the females as well as in the males; why should they be in them quite without effect, when they are so efficacious in men? May we not reasonably think, that their astral spirit in the brain, acting upon the same object as in males, must also have the same effect in them, according to their peculiar kind or female constitution? And could not therefore a *massa* (or however else it might be called), chiefly of more spirituous parts, be raised up thereby from the blood of the heart, and then conveyed into their *ova*, for to stir and influence the same with a concupiscence after the male semen? Truly, if they have, as the physicians own, their *spermatick arteries* and vessels, as well as men, they must have them in vain and to no purpose, or at least the physicians must give them this name in vain, if they do not at all minister to the generation of the seed. But I will herein not be positive, not pretending to be a natural philosopher. I say only, that what I have now offered to consideration is not inconsistent with Behmen, and that I can as yet, in all what the physicians say in this second position, see nothing directly contrary to him.

(3.) The things said in this third position are partly belonging to the foregoing second, and are considered already. Partly they will be repeated in the following positions, and shall be then considered; and partly also they are depending only upon the females having *ovaria*. Wherefore it is plain, that if this can be consistent with Behmen, that also which depends thereupon can have nothing in it directly contrary to him.

(4.) Here is also, at least on one side, a harmony to be perceived; and though on the other something of discord may be observed, yet seeing that this discord is only about a thing delivered by the physicians from their ratiocination, and not from an ocular experience, nothing thereof can beset in opposition to Behmen, as able in any wise to detract from his authority. *The seed of the male*, they say, *is no part of the conception, but only the active principle or efficient cause of the foetus*. Above (position 1st), they have owned the masculine seed hath both gross and spirituous parts. Now then, let them make these spirituous parts the active principle of the foetus, Behmen shall well enough agree with them. But as to the gross parts, which they themselves call but a vehicle of the spirituous, none I think will deny but that they are in the coition mixed with the limpid liquor in the female ovum, or else how could this be impregnated thereby? And if so, it might well be asked by what sort of microscopes they could have discovered that this limpid liquor only, and not also that which is so mixed with it, is the matter or the passive principle of the foetus? Male and female are one flesh, saith the Scripture; now this one flesh in two persons jointly generates a third flesh. What ground then can be shown why the female only should generate the flesh, and the male should contribute nothing to the substance of the flesh, but only be an active principle thereof when it is so plain that the masculine seed is more fleshly, or nearer unto flesh, than that limpid water of the female.

(5.) That all what here is said in this fifth position, if it be really so in the outward appearance, as some of the physicians declare, can be consistent with Behmen, appears sufficiently from the foregoing observations. I shall add only this, as to the two different words, *fecundated* and *impregnated*, that they seem thereby themselves tacitly or implicitly to grant, that the male semen is not only an active principle, viz., as to its spirituous parts, but also as to the gross, a part of the matter or passive principle of the foetus; for unto this the *impregnation*, and unto that the *fecundation*, is proper, which two cannot be attributed unto both promiscuously. If the masculine seed doth fecundate the female ovum, it works thereupon and enables its faculties to bring forth that which they cannot bring forth as of themselves alone; but if it doth impregnate the same, it makes it only thick and swelling, not by working thereupon, but by adding or infusing something into it which is agreeable thereunto. The gross parts as to themselves cannot fecundate it, or else they would be the active principle themselves, and not a gross vehicle thereof. And so the spirituous parts cannot impregnate it, viz., directly and immediately by themselves, or else they would be but a gross vehicle without activity. And if these two should be attributed to each of them promiscuously, the distinction (which yet is real enough) between grossness and spirituosity in one and the same seed, would signify nothing at all.

(6.) In this sixth position is nothing that wants any reconciliation with Behmen. *Those that profess they do not know*, etc., might learn something thereof from him; and others, *who think their opinion to be very probable*, might be more by him confirmed, and get a clearer sight, seeing it is undeniable that he hath declared this matter deeper than they were able to do.

(7.) This position of some, though it be exploded by others, hath certainly something in it which is not absolutely to be rejected. Of the *animalcula* in the male semen I will say nothing, though I think something might be said for it, though not perhaps in their sense. I will say only, that it is most agreeable with Behmen that the *lineaments of the foetus are therein*, no less than in the female ovum; though, I am sure, so deeply hid and secretly, that they shall not be discerned by any microscope, but found only by such an eye as Behmen had, whose words we heard above. And though perhaps these lineaments may be nearer to appearance in the female ovum, yet this cannot be a sufficient ground to assert that they are not at all in the male seed. The second part of this position, saying that *the conception is in that animated male semen, and not in the ova of the females, which they take to be only the receptacles of the semen virile*, though it is likewise exploded by others, hath nevertheless some part of truth in it, and is so far consistent also with Behmen, which hereafter more and more will evidence itself. So, therefore, this exploding one another among the learned physicians themselves, cannot be derogating from Behmen's authority, but from their own; and must rather exalt him the more, because by his principles many assertions of theirs can be reconciled, and their sparkles of truth, scattered among them here and there, can be discerned from what is false.

(8.) *The heart is not the seat of our affections, etc.* What is here asserted is so exceeding well consistent with Behmen, that this whole position (if but one small and inconsiderable particular be excepted) is more than any of the former to be excluded from the sentence in the first words of this question, saying, *our philosophers and physicians teach us otherwise.* If by the *seat of our of affections* is understood that particular place wherein they reside, act, and play their parts, it is true that it is not the heart, but the phantastic or astral mind. But if there be understood the ground from which they came first into the astral mind, and out of which they may still by the fancy be raised up, some more and others less, it is true again that it is the heart. For our Lord says himself, *Out of the heart come evil thoughts;* and Solomon warneth, *Watch over thy heart with all diligence, for out of it are the issues of life.* Both this and that did Behmen well understand, and hath asserted distinctly. He hath not asserted that this *love,* which indeed is *one of our affections,* ariseth, resideth, and playeth in the heart; but rather that by this love's playing in the phantastic mind, the *first conceptions* (as it is in this position well expressed) *or rude draughts of the sperm are begun.* But as this is in the brain but an active spiritual play, so it must have a certain passive and material object or instrument, which is the blood of the heart, from which it is further conveyed to the testicles. Brain and heart must both concur; for that which is active in the brain raiseth up that which else would be quiet in the heart. What the author of this position adds further of something particular, that seems to him very probable, needs not to be examined, because his probability can be no argument against Behmen. But what he says at last, of the *fancy's assisting in the business of generation,* always in order to coition, etc.; and of its *stigmatising the foetus,* etc.; is as well and true as anything could be from him expected. Wherefore, then, I cannot see how this position can be brought in as an instruction of the physicians contrary to Behmen.

This now being so far made out, that the pretended differences and contrarieties are not so many and great, nor so considerable and deep, as first they were believed to be; and that nothing hitherto was shown from the ocular experiences of the physicians, which could give a demonstration of Behmen's being in the wrong, it can now from hence appear sufficiently what is to be replied to those two questions that are proposed in the conclusion, page 217, section *ult.,* viz. :—

(1.) That *the conception is in both male and female.* For as every child is generated from the sinful will and lust both of father and mother, so every one bears also both his father's and mother's flesh and blood. If the masculine semen is not a part in the conception, as to its fleshly grossness, as well as it is an active principle of the foetus as to its spirituosity, what can the words of the scripture signify, when it saith, *Adam begat a son after his own likeness?* A chief part of his own likeness was certainly his gross, earthly, mortal body, out of which his fleshly seed proceeded forth. And again, what can it signify, when the Scripture says, that the children of this world are *born of the flesh, and of the will of man?* If the whole being of man and woman did consist only in soul and body, a greater outward appearance of probability for that other opinion might be found. But since there are in the whole human being not these two only, but three distinct things, body, soul, and spirit, and all three both in the man and woman; yet so that the soul, as to the stronger, fiery, active power, is more in the man; and the spirit, as to the weaker, passive, watery part, more in the woman; but both, and both in the man and woman, equally clothed with the flesh, or body; which flesh, in the man especially and chiefly, is to do the outward work in the generation; it is apparent, from a due consideration of all these things, that all these three parts do and must concur in this business, each in its kind and order, and according to its ability. And that the male semen is not only an active principle of the foetus in its spirituosity, but also a passive part in the conception, as to its grosser and exterior being of fleshliness.

(2.) *That the spirituous part of the semen of the male, or that semen considered* κατὰ δύναηιν, *and the limpid, prolific liquor in the ova of the female, are not to be accounted the two tinctures themselves;* but only two things coming very near thereunto. The tinctures themselves are prior and higher, more spiritual and of far larger extent than to be concerned only about this particular generating business; when these two things are notoriously posterior and lower, more material, and appointed only for this peculiar work, in the consideration of which they may be accounted the two chief and most immediate instruments of the tinctures. As to the males, indeed, much of this account will depend upon the different considerations of their semen: for this κατὰ δύναηιν, might be so far extended, that but little of a discernable difference between the spirituosity thereof and the tincture, would be left; though it can never be so far extended that the tincture in itself should not always have a pre-eminence of priority and universality. But as to the females and their ovum, wherein the limpid liquor cannot be considered in such a great, active spirituosity, the distinction or difference between this and the tincture, is much plainer. For the limpid liquor, with the lineaments of the foetus, is in them, not only before the knowledge of man, but also before the maturity of their tincture; during all which time this ovum is not fit for generation, nor can by the male semen be fecundated, though it might, perhaps (for I am not positive in it), be impregnated thereby. But the female's own tincture, after it is come to its maturity, must first fit, and prepare, and make it capable of being by the male seed impregnated and fecundated, which none, of any reasonable sense, can deny. And so now is it in the males also, *mutatis tantum mutandis*. For the tinctures in them both, playing first in their astral minds, stir up the seed, and raise the lust and desire after the carnal conjunction; which is the consequence and effect thereof, like as that is the first active principle.

And now I am to go back to the six first positions, page 211, which are to represent this same matter, according to the sense of Behmen; for in them also, I meet with several things, which I think must needs be altered. Yet I shall not enlarge, by making particular observations upon them, but think it may be enough to set down only the positions so as the sense of Behmen, according to my meet apprehension, might be expressed; which accordingly will be in the following manner:—

(1.) That the only true ground of this natural generation or propagation, is to be found in the two divided tinctures, which, when come to their maturity in male and female, cannot but press forward naturally for their re-union.

(2.) That this their pressing forward is first done in the astral spirit, whose residence is the brain, and whose open gates are the eyes, wherein the tinctures of male and female mutually do meet, lay hold on, and unite with one another.

(3.) That this their kind of union in the astral spirit is that natural love, which is one of the chief agents in this business.

(4.) That this love-union, as long as in the spirit only, is indeed much purer than afterwards, when the flesh comes to concur with it; but that it cannot fully satisfy that natural inclination of the tinctures, nor stop their further pressing forwards, because they are generating powers, which cannot generate, because of their being divided, without concurrence of that flesh or body wherein they live and act.

(5.) That because of this still pressing forward, which is turned into a fervent desire after a fleshly copulation, this flesh is mightily stirred, and according to the different conditions of the several instruments and vessels thereof, proper and requisite for that business, severally affected and acted upon.

(6.) That this affecting and acting toucheth in the first place, and as to our chiefest, consideration, the heart.

(7.) That from the sweet water or oil which is in the blood of the heart, a mass is drawn together or coagulated, and that this is filled, not only with the animal spirits, but also with all the powers and virtues of the whole human body.

(8.) That this coagulation is the generation of that semen which is now fit for propagation, when it was not so before. And that this hath a fiery tincture in the man, but a watery in the woman.

(9.) That these two masses and tinctures, or generating powers, united in the womb, are the causes of the conception and foetus; the male semen being both a part in the conception, and an active principle of the foetus.

(10.) That each of these two masses is a one-threefold substance, being not only fleshly and producing the mortal body, but having also in it, though in different degrees, the two eternal principles. And that none of these three is manifest or comprehensible to the other, but each in it's own sphere only; and yet all three in such a combination, as the two inward worlds are with this outward third.

This, now, as to my best apprehension, is Behmen's sense, and from hence it may appear that several of the other positions of the physicians, and also that sentiment which is given thereof in general, cannot be left so as it is expressed in this conference, because the contrariety is not so great as at first imagined. But one thing more I must here mention, which I did not so exactly observe before: The physicians, if I do not misapprehend their meaning, declare from ocular experience, that the conception is done in the female ovarium, above what they call *tubae fallopianae*, and before the *vesicula*, impregnated with the masculine seed, drops through them into the *fundus uteri*. Now Behmen, saying nothing of this, but only and simply of an union in the womb, cannot but be looked upon as contrary to them, and as one that is quite out. But I must answer hereupon, not questioning, but supposing their relation, as here represented, to be true, the following things may well be considered:— (1.) A sufficient assurance must be had, not only that their ocular experience is taken from the inspection of a woman, not of a beast; but also, chiefly that the dropping of the vesicula into the fundus uteri is done after its being impregnated by the masculine seed; and not after its being impregnated or influenced only with its own female tincture, or propagating power, after this is come in her to its maturity. For that the ovarium with its vesiculae, was in being before the female tincture was ripe and fit for propagation, is granted; and that the vesiculae, during all the time of infancy, was not so qualified as it cometh to be in the time of the tincture's maturity, by the astral spirit's playing in the brain, and stirring the blood and water of the heart, cannot be denied. But let all this be supposed to be true, viz., that the dropping of the vesicula into the fundus uteri, is done in a woman, after its being impregnated with the masculine seed; it may be considered, (2.) That all the words, *ovarium, vesicula, tubae fallopianae, uterus, fundus uteri*, and if there be any more belonging hereunto, are denominations but of so many particular places, parts, vessels, instruments, etc., all comprised sufficiently in that general expression of *matrix*, which Bemnen useth, who had no intention, as he pretended not to have ability, to instruct us in anatomy. (3.) That the Spirit of God, which also hath not such an intention, though he wants no ability, useth the like general expression in the Scripture, saying the conception is done in the womb, and calling children the fruit or blessing of the womb: *Thou shall conceive in thy womb*, said the angel unto Mary, etc. (4.) That the whole work of propagation from the conjunction of male and female, is done in the lower region, under the heart; and that he who calls this region so generally either by the name of womb, or belly (which is not unusual nor improper in the German language), or *matrix*, doth not fight thereby against another that gives a distinct enumeration of more particular places or things contained therein. Like as this latter also doth not, by his enumeration, contradict that former, who may have left such a particularity, either by reason that he had not a sufficient understanding thereof, or also, that he could declare without it all that he intended. From all which, now, (5.) This conclusion, doing justice unto each party, may be drawn: First, in general physicians and anatomists are more able to show the superficial appearance of these lower visible things, that are of their profession, and which only they bestow their time and labour upon, to little further purpose than to satisfy their natural curiosity, which yet remaineth always in the dark, as they must own themselves; and Behmen is more able to show the spiritual inward ground from the two internal worlds, which no microscope can reach into; and this is to a far greater use and benefit, tending to man's regeneration, which is always attended, more or less, with light. And then, in particular, as the physicians in this present matter may be in the right, so Behmen is not in the wrong, any more than the Scripture is. And so therefore, between these two parties there is no more contrariety than between A and B, when A says the meeting was in such a house, and B the congregation was in such a particular chamber of that house.

Page 219.–221. Here the further process in the natural generation is represented in five positions, according to the sense of Behmen. And here I must observe—as to the first, That when it is said, *the two tinctures in union are much delighted with each other, and there is somewhat paradisical in that delight;* this is expressed too generally, and not so as to represent the sense of Behmen faithfully. For that which is called by him *paradisical* is not in the mutual delight of the tinctures, so long as they are, or can be said in a sense to be in union, nor also so long as they are *delighted with each other*, but only in their very first meeting and receiving one another, when the seed is sown by the male into the female; where it is, he saith, but for a moment, and vanisheth away immediately, being but a small obscure glimpse, and not to be referred at all to what the beast-like flesh is sensible of.

At No. 3. That when there is mentioned a following *strife to produce the paradisical image which Adam lost*, this strife is not sufficiently represented by referring it to the two tinctures only, but it must be referred and declared also (though not so properly here, where this strife is as yet all but in love and friendliness, yet soon after, when there is spoken, No. 5, of their *being oppressed and polluted*) as to the spirit of this world, and the four elements, and that which Behmen calleth the *fiat;* all which distinct things are mightily (each in its order and degree) for the bringing forth a paradisical image. And if it were not so with them, nothing else but a beast (though in an outward human form of body) and beast-like senses could be produced. So also

No. 4. This *incapableness* to produce that paradisical image belongeth not only to the two divided tinctures, but also to all these things now mentioned, that all have the same natural inclinations.

At No 5. Concerning the *blood's being taken into the matrix*, I am apt to think that this also might be more circumstantially expressed. Chiefly when it is said *the tinctures retire*, it will be needful to be more distinct, and to say in what sense this is a retiring. For it is not an absolute and total departure, but only as to that clearness and purity, which in that state they are capable of. Whereby it would shew forth itself, that it might better and more properly be said (*in singulari*)— the tincture retireth. Again, here is nothing said of that great alteration, which is made in the blood, which yet is the chiefest thing in this consideration, that makes, nay constrains the tincture to withdraw, as to its former clearness and purity. And from this defect, it is now further, that a stranger to Behmen's writings about this matter, will hardly be satisfied by that short and imperfect account, that here is given from whence the longings and pains of women arise; telling indeed something of what he asserts, but not declaring his true ground or reason for which he doth assert it.

Now all these things might be represented indeed more fully, and without any great difficulty: yet seeing that in what now followeth from the modern physicians and philosophers, nothing is mentioned in particular, but only in general, that they give quite another account; I am doubtful what to do, and think it enough to have now observed only these things, and that it may be best to let them rest at present, until a revision can be made, because in the meantime, this or that might be more cleared up in the following discourse, so that unnecessary repetitions may be avoided. I have only to say a little more about what is replied upon these five positions.

The physicians, it is said, deny that anything of the mother's blood is taken in the matrix. But the ground they think they have for it not being expressed, I cannot say more to it, but that their denying this seems to come forth from not knowing, What the blood and tincture are, not having found that anything is mentioned by them concerning the tincture, which yet is in this matter of the greatest importance. And if it were so with them, their denying would signify nothing at all.

But concerning especially the *menstrua's being poisonous*, which they also deny, at least in part, if I do not misunderstand what here is said thereof; it is to be observed, that Behmen, asserting them to be poisonous, doth not take so much the word poison, as they seem to do, with relation to this outward world, wherein adders and toads, arsenicum, mercury, aquafortis, etc., are called poison and poisonous; but in a more mysterious sense, relating to the lost paradisical world, which he explains by adding, that in the menstruum lieth the greatest antipathy and contrariety to holiness and purity. In which sense, if the physicians did deny the menstrua to be poisonous, I could not but have a very low opinion of them, and little value for their understanding the fall of man from the one paradisical into the other four elementary world. And, moreover, it is remarkable that Behmen had a familiar conversation with many physicians and graduated doctors; nay that he had written the same thing of the menstruum to an eminent one among them, and that yet it was never heard that he was by any of them contradicted, or less valued afterwards than he was before.

Page 223. Q. *What do they mean by the essences death to paradise?* This question not being answered, and I not being able to answer it in two or three lines, I shall declare the meaning, and leave, Sir, to you the finding out of better expressions, and of a shorter construction thereof. It is easily intelligible, that this death in every individual generation is not such a one as that was, which all the first Adam's essences died in his transgression, but only an effect, and an indispensable consequence thereof. For he having lived before to paradise, could have died to it, or could have lost this life. But here in this natural propagation, the essences had no foregoing life to paradise, and cannot therefore properly and directly be said to die to it, or to lose that which they have not. But this is the meaning thereof: In every generation of man's life is a process tending to the production of the paradisical life and image. The two tinctures in their meeting and receiving each other, are in that way and process, in a sense comformable to their now divided state; and, therefore, as declared above, they are in an endeavour to produce it, and in an expectation thereof. This process would always have been effectual, if Adam had not fallen; so that in all and every one of his offspring that life and image would have been generated. But now in this natural propagation after the fall, a stop is put to that process, making it always ineffectual. And this even in that same point in which the paradisical life and image is to arise. This stop is partly that which is done in the blood, and partly also that which the spirit of this world doth in the essences, who insinuates himself into them, captivates them, exalts himself in them, obstructs the rising of a paradisical life, and forces them to bring forth in his service instead thereof an astral life and light, and a beastlike image. And this is their death to paradise, different from the first Adam's death herein, that as his death was an extinguishing of his paradisical life and light, so this is a violent hindering, because of which the same cannot be kindled again.

Page 223. Q. 1 & 2., together with their answers. The things following (immediately and primarily) *from or upon the former disorder and death*, are here not mentioned at all. For here is nothing said of the crack (or schrack) terror and trembling, great alteration in the tincture, and consternation in the fiat, spirit of this world, and all the essences. All which are spiritual things, and even such as upon which all that is done in the seminal mass dependeth, and from which it is by Behmen deduced and declared, according to the generation, constantly the same both in eternal and temporal nature. By answering therefore, *A motion of the whole coagulated seminal mass*, etc., the question is answered but half, and only as to the lower and posterior part, which without the higher and prior, cannot be understood according to Behmen's mind, much less can it represent his sense to another that is unacquainted with him. And when thereupon is asked again, *What followeth from this motion*, and answered, *A distinction of the mass*, it cannot but cause a misapprehension several ways. For the single word motion, will not declare that which is to be said. A motion, in what sense and respect soever, was before also, even from the beginning of the conception; how therefore, this is different from that should be declared. And which is more, I cannot see how this *motion*, and the *distinction* of the mass could be represented as two so evidently different things, the one following upon the other. Seeing that there is not first a motion made in the mass, and then as a thing following thereupon, as it were at a perceptible distance, a distinction of the parts. But in this motion is the distinction made, and this very motion is different from that which was before herein, that it is the distinction of the parts itself. And though there might still be imagined something of difference between them, yet it will never be such a one, as that they should be so distinctly represented as two things following the one upon the other; and this so much the less, because the chiefest thing, which is a great tumultuous motion in the spiritual properties, is not mentioned at all. And from this a transition should immediately be made to the distinction and formation of the parts; which so then would evidently imply already a motion in the seminal mass, seeing that without a motion therein, it cannot be distinguished and formed into parts. But when a motion of the mass is placed so distinctly by itself alone, before the distinction and formation of the parts, (and that is said to be preceding, and this following thereupon), the formation of the parts is ascribed only to a thing done in the seminal mass, when it should be ascribed primarily to a thing done in the spiritual properties. Wherefore, then, I think the shortest way would be to contract these two questions and answers into one.

Page 223. Q. *ult*. No. 1. Here I cannot but observe as by the way, that by these, here styled *the most experienced philosophers and physicians*, all that is utterly overthrown which before by others so positively, and from ocular experience, was asserted, concerning the lineaments in the ovum. Which contrariety I know not what to make of; for I thought they had found it so by the help of microscopes, and had reason to believe that every one making use of the same means could not but see the same thing, so that none could further contradict. But when they now assure us that the lineaments are in the ovum after an insensible manner, and that nothing appears but a limpid crystaline liquor, they are directly contrary to each other; but none of them can be to to Behmen, because the one assertion of—an insensible manner, is plainly his own, and the other he hath not meddled with at all, and so not contradicted it. But it could be consistent with him, if it were really true, so as it was expressed and represented above.

Page 225. No. 5. This confession of *much obscurity* is not only for exalting Behmen the more, but also for confirming what he hath said; viz., that without an understanding of the generation of eternal nature, and of the spiritual properties and essences (which the physicians commonly know little of), these things cannot be understood; and that no anatomist can be able to find out, and to show the true ground, though he should dissect many thousands of men and beasts.

Page 227. A. 1. *They do not, I think, pretend to this, or at least not to any great exactness in it.* Though Behmen hath not made an exact description of the order of the formation of the parts, yet that he was not able to do it cannot be asserted, seeing that he says plainly,—to describe especially the order would require many great volumes. And it is easily to be apprehended, that he who had such a deep understanding of eternal and temporal nature, as to the manner of the generation thereof, and could show, so far as permitted, the internal ground of every external thing in this natural propagation of man, could not have been ignorant of the order wherein every thing is done; because this order depends upon an order in eternal nature chiefly, and then also upon an order in those spiritual properties and essences that are posterior to eternal nature, but prior to this formation of the parts and members.

Page 231. Line 4. *the tough property of the first astringent spirit*, etc. This tough property is not indeed by Behmen referred directly to the first astringent spirit, but to the first schrack or terror, because 'tis this which makes it moveable. Yet, seeing that of this terror nothing was said before, and that this first astringent spirit cannot be separated therefrom, having certainly this property also in it as a lesser branch; I think, in such a short and imperfect description, it may stand well enough so as it is expressed, though I could not but mention this for some peculiar reason.

Ibid. A. 1. Line 3. *formeth the brain.* Here, I think, instead of *brain* should be said *head*; for Behmen declareth, that by this flying up of the tincture, with all its essences, and also with the spirit of this world, here especially insinuating himself, the *head is formed*, which he described as the superior part of the body, distinct from it, and yet communicating therewith, like as heaven in relation to the earth. All which would not be appropriable to the brain in particular, but to the head in general, though he had not named the head expressly.

Ibid, in the same *A.* 1. *the hard property puts a stop to its ascent, and forms the skull.* This is not so expressed as to represent the sense of Behmen faithfully. For to the hard property only and directly, that is ascribed which it never would be able to do, of or by itself, if there were not something superior to it, by which it is directed and forced to do what it doth; viz., the fiat, by griping and binding down the hard property (which itself also is flying up with all the rest), puts a stop to its ascent; and so the fiat, by this hard property (which now being griped and bound cannot rise any further), forms the skull.

So also accordingly, ibid., *by the same compacting astringent spirit.* If to these words were added, *which in conjunction with the eternal Word, is the fiat*, the sense of Behmen would be completely expressed; when it is not so, if this be left out.

Ibid, again. The nerves only are called the conduit-pipes of the tincture, and of the powers of the stars; but the *veins* seem to be excluded therefrom, because they are set afterwards alone, without this title; when this description belongeth no less to the veins than to the nerves, nay, as to my apprehension, to the veins more especially.

Page 235. A. 2. Concerning this *water of the heart*, Behmen says—that it is answering to the water of the soul, like as this is to the water in the generation of eternal nature: that the soul also hath its own water and blood, which are not indeed a perceptible substance in this world, but are nevertheless in this perceptible water and blood of the heart: that this blood and water are answering to the water above and the water under the firmament; the water above the firmament (viz., in the creature, and in a sense relating to the creature) is blood, and the water under it is this water of the heart: that in these two, two kingdoms are understood, and that in the blood the soul resideth, and in this water the outward spirit.

Page 236. Q. 2. What they say concerning *blood*, appears from the next preceding answer, where the reason also is manifest, why the creatures having blood are more noble than such as have it not. And concerning its colour, they say that it cometh from the tincture, and is the tincture's proper compounded or mixed colour, which tincture itself also is a compounded or mixed virtue of fire and light.

Page 239. Q.1. *It is altogether unaccountable why the lungs should be the seat of the earth, and the bladder of air*, etc. Here I cannot but answer in short: Balthasar Tilken made four principles, and it was altogether unaccountable in his sight that Behmen made but three. But Behmen replied, Let him freely make ten; the wisdom of God hath no bounds; but let him declare what he understands by a principle, and show that he has a true sense therein. In my understanding, which I have declared, and according to that sense wherein I take a principle I cannot own more than three, etc. Now to the same purpose, I am sure, if Behmen were living, and should hear how unaccountable his doing is in the eyes of the physicians, he would reply, Let every one freely place the four elements in never so different parts of the body; none can do altogether amiss, for the whole body is four-elementary; but let every one declare his reason, according to his peculiar understanding and degree thereof. Let the one say, The air's residence is the nostrils, because the Scripture says that in the nostrils is the breath of man; another, It is the lungs, because they draw in the air, and breathe it out again; a third, It is the whole concavity of the body, because no vacuum can be granted to be therein: they all do say something, each according to his measure of understanding, and all three may well enough agree, if they do but compare their different reasons, and take each of them in its proper sense and place. And I also do disagree with none of them, though according to my gift or understanding, and to that sense and respect wherein I look upon the four elements, I cannot say otherwise but that the air's residence is the bladder, and the spirit of the earth's, the lungs. Many things could be said for Behmen, to show, not only that his saying is not unaccountable, but also that he himself hath given a good account thereof; though not directly, because such a thing was not objected to him. But to make no prolixity, without which it could not be done, I pass it by, saying that if desired it can be done at another time.

Page 239. *A. ult. The essences stretched forth for nourishment are compacted and formed into hands.* This is expressed indeed intelligibly enough to such as truly do understand anything of Behmen in this matter; but seeing that it is much subject to a rude and gross apprehension, because of its too great shortness, it must needs be more fully represented. For I see it is understood and gathered from hence, as if the hands were griping after such or such a nourishment, to be taken by the foetus, and put into its mouth, when there is no such thing. That such a gross apprehension thereof is easily made, appears from what is hereunto replied (page 241.), where it is said that *it cannot be accounted for, because the foetus lieth with its hands lifted up to the head*, etc., and *seeks nourishment with its mouth*, etc.; all which cannot so much as shake, much less overthrow, what Behmen says, who hath a deeper ground for his words than what can be reached from without. He doth not say, the hands are stretched forth for any nourishment; but as he declareth all this matter from an invisible spiritual root, so it is here also to be understood accordingly. Let the hands of the foetus lie which way they will, their chief office, after they are hands in this world, is to stretch out and gripe earthly food for nourishment. And before they were formed and visible hands, such a disposition thereto was in the spirit of the soul, because of its being infected and possessed by the four-elementary qualities. And let the foetus in the womb be nourished which way it will, Behmen doth not say that it is nourished by taking this or that food with its hands, but that the four-elementary spirit, according to its own internal essentiality, is even then already, as it is always, for elementary fruit or food, even such as Adam had eaten in the garden Eden; and that this spirit, having got predominion over the spirit of the soul, showeth now in this natural generation his power over him, so that this latter must, in obedience to him, stretch forth his essences towards that which he as ruler, lusted after; and that from this stretching forth, which as then is still but a thing done in the spirit, such fleshly hands come to be as are no more able to stretch forth after the fruits of the tree of life.   etc.

Page 241. A. 2. What they mean by *the spirit of the soul's fetching the essences of the earth to feed upon*, can be understood, I think, sufficiently from what was just now declared, viz., That it is not an outward actual work or doing, but a mere preludium in the spirit of the soul, who is captivated, ruled, and drawn away by the spirit of this world. The essences of the earth, considered in their outbirth, are indeed all that the natural body feeds upon, or is nourished by, as well while it is still in the mother's womb, as afterwards, when in this outward world; for even in the womb also, all the nourishment of the foetus, whatsoever it be, is earthly, not paradisical, but of the essences of the earth, making such an earthly flesh as must needs return into earth. But Behmen doth not go down so low, nor make it his business to tell us, after the physicians' manner, what, in particular, the foetus in the womb is nourished by; but hath enough to declare this preludium in the spirit, and to show the ground of man's earthliness as to his body, and earthlimindedness as to his spirit. And to his whole most excellent dialogue between the four elements and the spirit of the soul, in the THREE PRINCIPLES, is to be understood accordingly.

Page 241. *A*. 3. Concerning the *stomach* and the *guts* they say (all in a sense relating to and depending upon the former), that the stomach hath its original from the same ground of the four-elementary food desired, and of necessity required, by the spirit of this world in the foetus, according to his own nature, which the spirit of the soul must submit unto; though as yet it is still, as said above, but a preludium in the spirit of things that unavoidably must come so to pass. For if there be in the spirit such a previous disposition and natural tendency to earthly food, a receptacle fit for the same must be prepared in this natural generation, which receptacle is the stomach. And because the grossness of the earth is not fit for nourishment, is also not desired, but seriously excepted against in the spiritual dialogue of the four elements, and resolved that it shall be cast out; like as it was also cast out, or in a sense precipitated down, in the creation of the macrocosm; an opening of the body, therefore, must be made, and a passage must be provided for from the stomach downwards, through which this grossness may be carried out, and this is the guts.

Page 241. *A*. 4. No. 1. And 243. No. 2. What here is said concerning the *tongue* and *eyes*, cannot stand so as here expressed; but I see not what I could do more, beyond what I did formerly. To declare this matter but so much as tolerably, without a great prolixity, is impossible; and to make here a large digression to a thing which is to be supposed long before, would not be proper. Wherefore, I should think it best if this question were answered in this or the like manner:—

A. They say that the formation of the tongue and eyes belong together, as done by one and the same process, but in two distinct parts thereof. Which process they deeply declare from what they suppose is done in the generation of eternal nature, and in man's regeneration also.

Page 247. *A. ult.* No. 1. *The language of nature in general*, must here more generally be described. For it is not only (as here is said) each thing's manifesting *its inward predominant power and property;* but also, its whole inward constitution, showing the whole mixture and combination of *all its powers and properties*, whether more or less predominant, or more or less subject and subservient. So that, indeed, the predominant power and property is the chief that can be discerned from the outward signature, but is not all; seeing that all the properties, and their different degrees (which is the chiefest thing), may be discerned. And this is done, not by some outward sign (*in singulari*), but by the whole outward form, figure, shape, colour, smell, taste, etc., and all what is therein or can be an object of our outward senses; though the name signature hath more especially a relation to the visible appearance of things.

No. 2. *the one language*, etc. This one language, before the division of tongues, as to the outward formation and sound of words (for something beyond this is implied in that name), was not different from any of the now divided languages or dialects thereof, except only by having been the mother or root of them, which in the division was lost or swallowed up. It was not therefore any of those languages that were used afterwards, though a great affinity therewith may have remained in the Hebrew, Chaldee, or any other such as was afterwards spoken in the oriental countries. And Behmen doth not tell us what language it was, and how this or that thing was called therein, but only that the nearest to it is the Hebrew.

No. 3. The *division* was, not chiefly and primarily in the language, as to the outward sound and formation of words, but in the mind and understanding, (wherein what Behmen calls the sensual tongue and the mental tongue is to be placed); and this now being in different families divided and confounded, their outward language consequently must needs have been confounded also. So that, as they were barbarians to each other in their intellect, they must needs also become such as to their words, each of them calling one and the same thing by different names, not proper to the true internal signature of that thing, and this was the division.

Page 249. Line 3. *a whole treatise.* By this I suppose Behmen's SIGNATURA RERUM is meant; but if this be the meaning, I cannot see how it could be said, *they have written a whole treatise concerning the signatures of men;* seeing that this book is but in general concerning the signatures of all things; and that which is mentioned therein concerning men especially is very little, and all but in general also; so that hardly anything particular of the different signatures of men can be learned thereout.

As to all the following *ten positions*, I must observe in general, that whereas both the inward and outward signatures are therein mentioned, and yet no distinction between them went before, nor any declaration what by each of them is meant; this cannot but bring in an obscurity upon all the matter, and a disorder also in placing before or behind the particulars thereof; which obscurity could for a great deal be done away, by altering something in the order of these positions; but chiefly by declaring, in the first place, not only that there is a distinction between the inward and outward signature to be observed, but also what so well by the one as by the other is to be understood: viz., That the outward signatures are but the visible, or by other senses also perceptible signs, marks, and express characters of the inward invisible, and (by themselves without the outward,) all imperceptible signatures. And that these latter are not the spirits of men themselves, but as it were, their vessels or receptacles, by which the spirits of men are set in innumerable distinctions and differences, which differences further are manifested unto others by the outward signatures, derived down from the inward, and representing them exactly; so that the imperceptible form and figure of the outward must be the very same which the imperceptible of the inward is, which inward imperceptible signature Behmen compares to a lute standing still, that is, not played upon. For as a lute, furnished with strings, must have a certain signature, form, or something either of harmony or discordance in its strings, by which it is distinguished from all other lutes; further, as this signature cannot be by any means perceived, except the strings be touched and moved; again, as the perceptible sound of these strings, caused by this touching and moving them, is but a discovery and outward manifestation of that interior signature, from which, as to the form, it cannot differ at all; and lastly, as this inward signature would not be the spirit of the lute itself, but only its instrument, if the lute were, like man, an understanding creature; so also is it, in a sense and manner, as to all these four particulars with man: which I think is intelligibly enough declared by Behmen, in the first chapter of his SIGNATURA RERUM.

Page 249. No. 1. *and have divers beastial properties*. Here I must needs observe: (1.) That these words, joined with them that go immediately before, may seem to pervert the natural order of these things; seeing that we can rightly and properly say,—the beastial properties have their signatures, being themselves prior, deeper or more inward, and therefore naturally showing forth more outwardly their characters. But the signatures, and even the outward signatures (for that these especially are here meant, appears by No. 2, where it is said, *they arise—from the internal forms*) cannot be said, *vice-versa*, to have beastial properties, but only to be the perceptible signs of the invisible beastial properties, and these even tame, friendly, and good or harmless, as well as wild, cruel, venomous and evil ones. And (2.) That it is not applicable (as it here in this position is applied) to the signatures in general, nay, not to all the outward signatures, to have or to be the characters of beastial properties; seeing that besides them, not only those properties that are in man divine or heavenly, but also those that are devilish or hellish, have their divers signatures.

Ibid. No. 4. Here I cannot see why these words, *under the Spirit of God*, should be inserted; seeing that by this freedom is not to be understood a free liberty, indifferent to good and evil, so as if man were not to give an account, and to be punished with justice, if he moveth from the former to the latter; but only an ability to take in, or to raise up, or to move towards the one, as well as the other. And if now here is said, *he hath such an ability under the Spirit of God*, it would almost be as much as to say, or at least it might easily be so understood, as if the Spirit of God assisted him in moving to the evil as well as to the good, which would be quite intolerable. This same is clearly and rightly expressed thus,—under the Spirit of God, or the spirit of Satan and of this world.

Page 259. Q. 2. is asked especially, *What do they mean by the sowing and seed of the soul?* But in the following positions, though I find something is said hereunto, yet I find not an answer directly given, concerning these two expressions. Wherefore I shall but observe in short, that by the sowing Behmen means the natural work of begetting, and calls it a sowing (like as in another respect the apostle, speaking of our natural body's being buried after death, saith *it is sown*), because it is a putting only, as it were, the first rudiments of the soul into that natural place where they are to be orderly disposed, and then to be brought forth again no more as rudiments, but as a perfect living soul. And concerning the seed of the soul, it is plain, that if there is a reason why this work may be compared to a sowing, there will be a reason also why there may be spoken of a seed. And this reason can be the more plain, if we do but consider that the soul, viz. that which truly and really is and may be called a living soul, is not sown, but only those spiritual properties that by their own due process come to be the soul, lie in the seed of the man; and these are sown in and with this seed. If, then, they are that of which afterwards the soul is made up and doth consist, they may significantly be called the seed of the soul, while they are not yet so far advanced in their process, as actually to be made a living and immortal soul.

Page 261. No. 6. *These propagated essences were not actually living (but only* in potentia), *until the conception of the foetus.* And again. No. 7. *At the conception, an actual life, or living soul, was generated out of them.* These assertions are not at all consistent with Behmen; nay, I do not see how they can be conceived as consistent with themselves. (1.) Not with Behmen, for he expressly says, that the soul is not generated at the conception of the foetus, but at the formation of the parts and members thereof, or after the formation of some of them; and that before this time there is no immortal life in the foetus. All life in general before this time is not denied: the propagating essences could not but be living actually, each in and for itself; but they could not be an actually living soul until their process was absolved: the end of which is their being in this foetus indissolvably knit together, and then only they are and can be called an immortal soul. (2.) With themselves also these two assertions are not well consistent; for the conception of the foetus is in and with the propagation of the essences; or if there be any distinction between them, it must be very small and nice, seeing that the conception implieth propagated essences, and essences cannot be called propagated before the conception be done. If, then, the living soul is generated at the conception, according to No. 7, what time could there have been before this generation and conception, in which (time) the essences might be called propagated, and asserted, according to No. 6, not to have been actually living until the conception of the foetus? seeing that this conception cannot be separated from the propagation of the essences.

Page 265. No. 17. Instead of saying only, *the stars*, it will be needful to say, *the stars and planets have the dominion.* And the rest of this position will require also a considerable alteration; for it is not yet enough to say, that *the life breaketh off when the stars and planets come to their limit;* nor also that this breaking off is inevitable when Saturn cometh to his limit: but something more besides this limit is required for the life's breaking off; which will appear from what now followeth:

Page 264. Q. *What is the limit of a star?* To this question Behmen hath plainly and directly answered, that the same place or point wherein a planet stood in the creation, is his limit and his seculum; and whenever he cometh to that place again, all that is broken which he hath been a sovereign master of. But, says he further, this must be rightly understood—this limit of the planet must agree with the crown of the stars—and here it lieth why we cannot find out the time of our death, because we do not exactly know the limit of our leader: for we must not only know the number of that, but also the number of the sign, if we will know the limit of our life. THREEFOLD LIFE, xviii. 11, 12, 13. What now this agreeing with the crown of the stars, and what this number is, I cannot give a sufficient account of; but this I can observe, as every one can easily, that the thing which inevitably breaketh off our life, is not only Saturn's coming to the place or point wherein he was created, but that something more is required thereto. If that only were the thing, we might reasonably conclude, that nobody could live above so many years as Saturn requireth for absolving his whole circuit, and coming to the place of his creation again; which yet is utterly false. Witness our own experience.

Page 266. *Q.* 1. *How could the outward kingdom be taken from Enoch and Elijah without dying, and this painful death?* This question hath two parts or members, distinctly to be answered. Viz. 1. How could it be without dying? and 2. How without this painful death? As to the first, it may be answered: (1.) Behmen says it is not yet absolutely or totally taken from them; they have still the body of the turba, the outward kingdom, and Adam's flesh: but having also the inward, they are in the inward and outward mysterium, with a twofold body; and this outward mysterium must give forth again that outward body, which is to appear before the great tribunal of Christ, no less than that of all other men (2.) The apostle says, *We shall not all die, but be transmuted.* If, then, in this transmutation, the outward kingdom can be taken from many thousands without dying, and without prejudice to the first universal sentence of death, it could also have been taken from these two persons, in whom it was done for such peculiar and eminent ends: whereof see the 35th. of the FORTY QUESTIONS of the Soul. But (3.) How it was or could have been done, Behmen says, the inward kingdom swallowed up in them (in Enoch especially) the outward, and kept it under, or excluded it from its own manifestation.

As to the second, it may be said, (1.) Behmen says, The spirit of the soul feeleth no pain, but only the soulish fire-life, from which its matter is broken off. Now, whether or no these two persons felt any pain in their soulish fire life, and how much or how little thereof, we cannot tell. Truly, the feeling of pain must be greater or less according as there is either more or less of such matter surrounding the soul, and as the same is either more or less held fast, beloved, and cleaved unto by the fire-life. That now this matter, in Enoch especially, was very little, and at length minded no more at all, his foregoing walk with God for the space of three hundred years may witness. (2.) Painfulness, in every sense, is not always, nor in every person, nor in every kind of death, an inseparable companion thereof. Several sorts of death may be found, both natural and violent, which do not deserve to be called, with any considerable significancy, a painful death. (3.) If we can believe and conceive that, and how, many holy martyrs, even in the greatest outward torments, could go from this outward principle into paradise without feeling any pain, nay, with exulting joy, singing, and praising God, we can here also be satisfied easily. But (4.) As to the manner how it was or could have been so, nothing but self-experience can teach us fully; though a true understanding may tell us so much, that the inward kingdom of peace, joy, love, light and glory, fulfilling all the sensible faculties, could have left no place at all for feeling any pain.

Page 266. Q. 2. *How is the soul united to the body, and kept in its due union?* A. The soul, if regenerated, is united to the inward paradisical body, and they both together to the outward Adamical flesh; so as the first principle is united to the second, and both of them to this outward third, which without this union could not consist, and hath nevertheless no union with them as to their true internal essentiality. If, then, thus the soul between these two standeth, as it were in the midst, it can be kept in union with both, if it but always minds its own station and duty therein; for during this time they must all three, in their order, be subservient to the manifestation of the wonders of God. In which respect to the now fallen and restoring state only, this may be called a due union, when it may not be called so with respect to that which the first Adam was departed from.

Ibid. Q. 3. *How was it breathed into man?* This has been declared already several times, and nothing more could I say now than what was said formerly. The *breathing into man* is not properly applicable to that soul whereof here is discoursed, but to the third life, which was breathed from without into his nostrils; when the true immortal soul was raised from the deep within, brought forth, and introduced into his heart.

Page 266. Q. 4. *What is the food of the soul?* A. If the soul is considered only as in a natural unregenerate state, the outward complexion, viz., that same which she hath predominant in her, the astral spirit, the carnal pleasures and sensual delights, the works of her own hands, the manifold objects of this third principle, etc., are her food, which she draws in by her lust, longing, and desire, and feeds upon by her imagination. But as to regenerated souls, what answer could here be expected, but that same which the Lord from heaven gave himself, when saying, *My flesh is meat indeed, and my blood is drink indeed?*

Ibid. Q. 5. *What do they mean by the fire-spirit of understanding, and the council-house of the seven spirits?* A. To say, the fire-spirit of understanding, is nothing else but to say simply, the spirit of understanding; and the word fire is added to the spirit, only to give to the reader of Behmen a deeper sense, and to this denomination a greater weight of emphasis; viz., to show and to recall into his mind what he so many times insisted upon; which is, that the true spirit must have passed through the fire, and that before the fire there is no true understanding. As to that other expression, *the council house of the seven spirits*, I see not what difficulty can be therein. The seven spirits are in man, and in him they may be variously considered. If they are considered with a peculiar respect to man's contriving or designing this or that, wherein they all must be employed, they may be compared to so many counselors; and if so, that place, sphere, or region, wherein they are so considered, be it in the outward principle, either the head or heart, may be fitly called their council-house. Like as the very same again may be called their work-house, if they are therein considered with a peculiar respect to their mutual and never ceasing activity.

Page 267. No. 2. *The soul taken generally, or for the whole inward man.* Seeing that by *the whole inward man*, always the new-born body, also and sometimes the same even chiefly is understood; which yet in the denomination of the soul is not contained, nor implied, in this present consideration; I think it would be more proper to say-the soul taken generally, or for the whole spiritual being, as far as the same is distinct from what is bodily.

Ibid. Q. 1. *What are ideas and images of things in the mind?* A. Such like representations of intelligible objects as the images in a mirror are of visible ones; arising also in the mind by the same necessity by which these do in a mirror, if an object is set before it. Because the mind of man, being in itself most quiet, empty, and undetermined to any sort of act or motion, stands in the same relation, and bears the same indifferent disposition, to things conceivable in all the worlds out of which it is brought forth, which a mirror bears to things visible in this particular world, wherein and whereout it is made. Yet with this difference, that whereas a material mirror is capable only to receive passively, and to keep unmoveably an image in it, as long as the object standeth so before it; this spiritual mirror is capable also to admit from its own side something of activity, whereby its images and ideas may be altered, compounded, divided, displaced, and transfigured into innumerous shapes: though, indeed, as then, it is no more strictly called the mind, but cometh as under another consideration, so under another denomination also.

Ibid. Q. 2. *Do we see all things in God? A.* In some sense, generally answering unto that wherein we are said in the Scripture to live, and move, and have our being in God, we may be said also to see all things in God. But as true as this is in one sense, so true is this also in another,— that the greatest part of mankind do not live in God, but in themselves, or in their selfishness; and that their very light, the only proper means of seeing, is darkness. How, then, can such a one be said to see all things or anything in God? To answer, therefore, this general question by a simple and general yea or no, is absolutely impossible. But let the eyes, the things, the worlds, and above all, those senses also wherein the name God may be differently taken, be duly distinguished, and then of some it may be affirmed more or less, and of others it must be either totally or more or less denied.

Page 269. No. 6. All what is here said concerning *subtility* is true indeed, but might be plainer, if it were thus, or in a manner like to this, expressed:

Subtility is considered (1.) as it is in the first principle only, wherein it ariseth chiefly from the tincture of the same, and is devilish, or if it might be so expressed, the devil's intellect, having in its generation the three first forms of nature only. And (2.) as in this our third principle, wherein it is indeed tinctured, softened, made glittering, and in some measure transmuted by the outward astral light; but nevertheless, still earthly, sensual, devilish, and always evil, from its own proper root, which is so in the dark world, and which all the tincturing with astral light is not able to turn truly into good.

Page 269. No. 7. *Reason hath for its object only,* etc. Here it may be objected, that reason is able, in a sense and manner, to make all things, without exception, the objects of her speculation, be they either transitory or eternal, and in what principle soever. And this objection would be prevented, if some words were inserted, *e. gr. : reason hath for its proper and adequate object only the transitory things of this world, and even them also, since the fall, but in part, and great obscurity.*

Page 271. Line 6. *but not the primitive faculty.* Here I see not how this particular assertion could be saved. As the spirit of this world, the elements, and all the things of this principle, are now still the same which they were before the curse was pronounced upon them, though they are not altogether in the same condition; so reason, also, which came not by the fall into man from without, but was in him before the fall, must needs be the same faculty, though it hath no more now, in its usurped dominion, the same qualities which it had then, in its ministry and subordination to the superior faculties.

Ibid. Line 6, 7. *nor doth it distinguish men from brutes.* Though this is certainly true, yet I think it might be expressed with a little more moderation, that it might not be so offensive as justly may be feared it will. For, that eminent degree which reason hath in man, and which no brutes can reach unto, brings in at least so much in favour of him, that it makes him more noble than any of them, nay, than all of them taken jointly together. Though, indeed, that which doth wholly exempt him from their order is not to be found in reason, but in understanding.

Page 273. No. 22. *The soul, by its will, turns itself from darkness into light.* This is true, indeed, if rightly understood; but it might be more circumspectly expressed, that nobody might take occasion to say, that Behmen makes the will the saviour of its soul; which, under a specious appearance, might be drawn from hence. True it is, that Behmen speaketh so sometimes in short, presupposing his reader has read and understood his plain and sufficient exposition thereof, and is able to take these, his compendious words, in a sense conformable thereunto. *The soul*, says he expressly, *cannot enter or turn itself into the light, which is extinguished in the fall; but it can turn into that deep or ground wherein it is extinguished; and therein is he also who is the light of the world, able and ready to kindle the light in that soul again.* This turning now of the soul is done by the will, and cannot be done without it; the soul, therefore, (which thus can never meet with disappointment,) turning into that ground, and being taken into the light by him who hath surely promised he will in no wise cast out such a one, may well enough be said, in a compendious way of speaking, *to turn by its wits from darkness into light;* so to be understood, that there is only named that lesser medium, sine quo non, which is on the soul's side; and yet that greater one, which is only effectual on the side of the light's principle, be not thereby excluded.

Page 273. No. 23 *The will may be broken, but it is better,* etc. This is a little obscure, for it may be taken in two different senses, and which of them is here intended I cannot enough discern. For (1.) the will, as to itself, before an evil act is performed, is said to be made substantial, if it is but come forth into a perceptible determination, design, or purpose. And (2.) the will is also said to be made substantial in and by its act and deed, really performed and executed. This latter, not that former sense, seems here to be intended; and therefore it might be more clearly thus expressed—The will may be broken, and even much more easily when it is only a will, than when this will, by the fiat which is in it, hath wrought out itself into such or such a substance; for in the former case, the will only, and in this latter, both will and substance, must be broken (in which the desire of the will is very powerful and its effect very great) if the soul shall be made free.

Page 274. *Q. What do they say of dreams?* A. They say that natural dreams are magic images, represented by the firmamental constellation, and seen by man's astral spirit in his own peculiar magic astrum; which astrum, they say, is nothing else but an epitomised figure, expressing, as it were, in a little compass, the vast extent of his great firmamental constellation. That is, the whole scheme of the astral heaven in the macrocosm, with all its energies and possible contingencies, lieth in every man, according to that peculiar form or posture, wherein it stood at the time of his conception and birth. And this in the superior astral heavens, being like a watch, and unfolding itself successively, represents also successively its operations, by such like images in these inferior heavens, which in man are answering unto them. And so of supernatural dreams, also, they speak almost after the same manner, mentioning only, instead of an exterior firmamental constellation, an interior eternal one, which all men have in the greatest variety in their deeper ground of soul and spirit, out of eternal nature.

Page 275. No. 25. *the astral and sensitive soul.* Here I would say rather, *astral* or *sensitive*, because they are not two, but one; though these two expressions are both fit, and may represent to us something of a distinction, consisting herein, that the former showeth more its original, and the latter more its quality. But this being of no great importance, I would not have mentioned it, if occasion had not been given by what is said, page *eadem*,—

No. 3. *the sensitive soul is a glass of the third principle.* For here it would be much more proper to say, instead of *sensitive*, the *astral soul*, or *astral spirit;* seeing that the third life, soul, or spirit in man, not as it is a sensitive light, but as it is an astral spirit, is a glass of this third principle. The reason whereof is by Behmen, in the fifth of the Forty Questions, so plainly laid down, that I cannot see what difficulty can be found therein. All what is in the whole third principle, and all the properties thereof, lie herein, and represent themselves as in a glass; and this is even that same, for the sake of which, man is rightly called a microcosm. It was that same glass wherein the powers and wonders of this principle were represented unto Adam; wherein he delighted to see them, and which he turned his imagination and will into, till it was fixed and captivated therein.

Page 275. Line *ult. that it cannot be regenerated.* This is too absolute and general. Behmen says only that it is not regenerated during the time of this outward third principle, like as also the earthly mortal body, during all this time, is not regenerated. And the reasons, whereof many and great may be given, are sufficient for the astral spirit, as well as for the earthly body; because they both are equally under the spirit of this third principle.

Page 278. *A.* 2. and *Q.* 3, etc. Concerning the words, *fallen man was from all eternity chosen in Christ,* I observe (1.) that because they are not the formal words of the Scripture (which never and nowhere says so), instead of *from all eternity,* might be said, *from before the foundation of the world.* Not as if there were indeed a great important weight in this alteration; but only because several reflections could be made upon it from Behmen's ground; and then, also, because there is no reason why the proper words of the Apostle should be thus altered.

(2.) The interpretation of these words is so represented, that occasion is given thereby to call it *uncommon*: and to think that it delivers more, if not quite another and different thing from what divines generally take these words to mean; nay, also to suspect it of having some conformity with what the Gnosticks and Valentinians asserted. But seeing it can be made out sufficiently, that Behmen's interpretation of that Scripture expression contains nothing else nor more than what divines generally will be ready to grant, and what of their plain sense is expressed in Q. 3; I justly conceive that it would be much better, nay, even necessary, to represent this answer in some other terms; and then to make no mention of those *early heretics* and their *eternal AEons*. For certainly, *nodus est hic in scirpo quaesitus;* and without any necessity, Behmen is aspersed, at least, with a suspicion of having communion with those ancient fables. The plain words both of the Scripture and of divines in general, *fallen man was chosen,* etc., must needs presuppose, that the fall of man was seen by God before man was a creature; and this must needs import, that it was not seen as a thing done actually without God, but as an image or idea in God's eternal wisdom, which expression, I think, none can be offended at. If this be so, the restorer also of this fallen image must have been seen, and must have been appointed in that wisdom; for all this the word chosen doth import. If, then, thus they both were seen, they were not seen as at a distance, the one from the other, but as in conjunction and union with one another. The second Adam must have been seen as entering into the first Adam's nature, and restoring the same; and the first as restored in the second. But now, all this having had no being without God, before the foundation of the world, but having been only in the wisdom of God, a foresight of what was to have a future being in time, hath and can have no other sense but that selfsame which our divines generally express, by saying-man was chosen in Christ, *considered as to be incarnate, or as already incarnate in the divine decrees.* And that this is Behmen's sense, containing neither more nor less, could be shown from twenty places of his writings. But now, contrary to this sense, or at least very much different from it, these words in this *A. 2, the second person entered into the image or idea of man, represented,* etc., seem to be so understood, as if there was made, before the foundation of the world, a strange kind of incarnation and conjunction; or as if the eternal Word had taken upon him then already the nature of that fallen image or idea: when Behmen plainly declareth, that by *entering into that image,* he meaneth nothing else, but that there was seen in the eternal wisdom not only the fall of man, but also the fallen man restored in and by the eternal Word; or that foresight of the eternal Word's future entering into the fallen human nature. If, therefore, only these words were expressed otherwise, or at least a little explained, it could not be replied, *This interpretation is uncommon, and the Gnosticks and Valentinians have asserted some such thing,* etc.

Page 280. *A.* 2. No. 2. Here to the last words most properly might be added something declaring that all, and even the meanest of those circumstances, as well as the greatest, had their significant relation to him. For this hath Behmen not only asserted, but hath also explained many of those (from without inconsiderable) circumstances, rites, and ceremonies, so that they all and each of them do most significantly represent, as it were, a shadow of that substance, which is to be found in the only real and expiatory sacrifice of Christ. So that this also is conformable to his own words, saying, *There is not one* ιῶτα *in the law which shall not be fulfilled.* Wherefore, then, such an addition would still more emphatically represent Behmen's doctrine as agreeable to Scripture.

Page 280. *A. ult. Jesus—did in time take unto himself the Christ.* Against these words I have nothing to say; they are Behmen's, and have their true significant sense in their place, viz., when he was about to rectify Stiefel's confusion, made by him concerning the names of *Jesus* and *Christ.* But whether they can be in this place (where, in answer to the question is to be said what Behmen means, not by names, but by the work of incarnation,) so fit and proper; or whether they have so much substance in them as to declare sufficiently Behmen's meaning, I think, could much be doubted of. Chiefly, because Behmen's sense is thus, in the very beginning of this matter, represented as containing strange and questionable things, and making, as it were, two distinct persons; whereby, it seems, occasion is given to slight it, and to think strangely thereof. Which occasion (given at least to such as love and like to take it) might well be avoided by giving another short declaration of what he means by the incarnation of the eternal Word. And then these two names, and their different signification, could nevertheless be mentioned also. But I tell only here my simple thoughts, and leave it, Sir, to your good pleasure.

Page 282. A. 1. *They say that it* (the name *Jesus*) *belongs to intimate his person only with respect to his divinity,* etc. In the next following question, I see it is said of this assertion. *I do fear it is not true;* and I think it may well be said so, with this addition—that there is nothing to support it. But Behmen's assertion it is not, for he saith quite another thing; and the words following immediately in this same *A.* 1, do themselves also manifestly overthrow this assertion, by saying that which cannot be consistent with it. For if (as here is said) *they say further, the name Jesus signifieth the Son of God's humiliation of himself, and his exaltation of the human nature,* they cannot say, that *it intimates his person only with respect to his divinity;* seeing that here a respect to the humanity is manifestly implied in the signification of this *name.* Now, it is certain that they say this latter, so therefore they do not, nor can they say that former. Behmen expressly declareth that in the first syllable, JE—he understandeth his humiliation, and taking upon him a human soul and body; and in the second, — SUS, his exhaltation of the human soul, etc. And moreover he owneth that the name JESUS *signifieth* a Saviour, according to the words of the angel to Mary; and that she was commanded to call him so, because he was to save his people from their sins. And though it was the name of the eternal Word before the foundation of the world, yet even then also was it not without a respect to the fallen humanity: for even then already was he appointed to be that Saviour in the fulness of time. And how can we conceive of this name otherwise, but by conceiving also and presupposing something that wants to be saved? This name therefore signifieth indeed his person, yet not with respect to the divinity only, but rather chiefly, as to which it chiefly belongs to be the Saviour; seeing that without Jesus, Christ (or the humanity only) could not have been a Saviour of mankind. And so there will be no need of any fear that this assertion is not true; for by many places of the Scripture, and of Behmen, also, can it be supported.

Page 282. *A.* 2. The great emphasis in the signification of the name *Christ,* or *Christus,* is in this answer not expressed. For Behmen understandeth in the first syllable—his entering into death, and in the second—his almighty power, breaking forth through death and hell into paradise.

Page 286. *A.* 2. No. 1. To the words, *she became a perfect virgin as Adam was*, I think might well be added—as to her inward man: for that the outward was never perfect as Adam was, her death to the outward female image declareth sufficiently.

Page 285. *Q.* 1. *What is the meaning of his heavenly humanity's coming down from heaven; is it not everywhere altogether and undivided?* A. Yes, it is so, everywhere, but in its own inward heaven of the second principle, unmanifest unto this third. The *coming down* therefore from heaven doth not mean a local transportation, or descending from above the firmamental heaven unto this earth; but an opening or manifestation upon earth, in a personal union with an elementary mortal body, which truly is a coming down; because the second principle cannot but be conceived as higher, and this third as lower. That God is everywhere altogether and undivided, no man can question; and yet he says himself unto Abraham, *The cry of Sodom is come up unto me, and I came down to see*, etc.

Page 285. *Q.* 2. *Why and how would sin have been propagated, if he had been begotten by such a concurrence?* A. For the same reason and in the same manner, for which and in which it is propagated in the begetting of every child that is generated by the concurrence of a male and female. For if the male's seed is an active principle in the generation, and is sinful in itself, what else can be propagated by its concurrence but sin and guilt? And if the soul of a male cannot propagate another soul higher graduated than itself is since the fall, but only such a one as hath a natural disposition to sin, like as itself hath; how could this sinful disposition have been avoided in Mary's son, if he had been begotten in a natural way, by the concurrence of a male?

Page 288. *A.* 1. Instead of saying, *from the essences of his mother*, I think it will be needful to say—of his mother's soul: for it is not the essences in general, but in particular the soulish essences which generate the soul.

Page 293. *A.* 3. All the reasons here mentioned, why he had an inward heavenly body, are good and true indeed; but nevertheless something, which is even the chief and most convincing, might well be added, viz.—because he was to be the second Adam, whose office was to reintroduce the children of the first into paradise, and to be for ever their head and king in that paradisical body which the first Adam had lost. This therefore he must have had himself, that by him it might be communicated to his members, like as the first Adam should have propagated it unto all his offspring.

Page 295. *A.* 1. All what is here said is indeed right and true, but methinks it is not a direct answer to the question, which was this, *If Christ had a spirit—what need was there then of his going through the process of regeneration in his life, and at his death?* p. 294. Which question I think would be answered more directly, if there were made three parts in this answer, by saying, (1.) That there was no need of his going through all this process for his own sake: for although he had need indeed of putting off again that which was mortal and earthly, after he had voluntarily taken it upon him, yet he could have done it without such a severe suffering of pain and death. (2.) That there was the greatest need of his going as a public person, as the second Adam, and head of the whole human race, through all this process for our sake; not only for to do for us what we were not able to do, but also to show us, and chiefly to make us a way, in which he might draw us, and we might be enabled by him to follow after him. (3.) That he was not therefore regenerated in his life, and at his death, as we are, by putting on, etc.

Page 294. As to these *general ends* of Christ's coming into the world, and suffering for us, I observe these several things following: (1.) That it would be proper to place in the beginning that which he himself declared, saying, *therefore the Son of God came into the world that he might destroy the works of the devil.* (2.) No. 3. as it is here expressed, cannot be called an end, because it was but a medium. If, therefore, it were expressed thus, or in another manner like to this—to become the regenerator of nature by going through the process of regeneration, both end and middle would be expressed. (3.) I cannot see how that which is said No. 4. can be called a general end of Christ's coming and suffering for us; for he came not to put off, (which seemingly doth presuppose a having it already upon him before he came,) but rather he came to put on our imperfect corrupt image, that so by putting it off afterwards again, he might deliver us from it. (4.) *No. 5 to manifest the primitive glorious image in himself*, can also not well be called a general end; but much more general would it be, if it were said—to restore the primitive lost image, and to manifest himself in his glory as the head, and all his members with him, as partaking of his glory. For the manifestation of the glorious image in himself only, was not the ultimate end which was intended, but the manifestation thereof in the whole disharmonised human nature. (5.) It would not be impertinent to mention out of the Scripture something of those excellent expressions which speak of an universal reconciliation, ἀνακεφαλαίωσις etc. Ephes. 1.; because it is plain that the Apostle gives us this as a general and ultimate end of Christ's coming and suffering for us. Though it is not of an exigent necessity; seeing that all what is said above is in this ἀνακεφαλαίωσις summarily contained, and this is displayed in all the mentioned particulars, like as a tree is in so many branches.

Page 295. Q. 1. Do they describe this process, and show the particular reasons and ends of Christ's actions and sufferings for us? If they do, pray give us them in short. A. Yes, they do; and even so that but a short running through all the particulars would easily fill several sheets; wherefore I shall give you but some of them. They say then—

1. That his circumcision on the eighth day was to heal or purify our impure natural generation and birth, effected by that member on which the circumcision was to be performed, according to the law.

2. That his baptism was to make our soul capable of having the holy fire, light and love kindled in her again. That this was to be done by an outward elementary medium, because man was fallen into the four elements: and that this medium must have been water, because the water of life above the firmament is that without which the fire in eternal nature cannot burn, nor the light shine.

3. That being circumcised as a Jew, and also baptised as a Christian, he united these two churches or dispensations of the law and gospel in and to himself, into one body, under him, the head.

4. That his forty days' temptation in the wilderness, was to answer and to rectify the forty days of Adam and Eve at the tempting tree: and that he must needs have gone through this temptation after he was baptized, that he might overcome all which the first Adam was then conquered by.

5. That all his miraculous deeds were the true effects and consequences of his overcoming in this temptation: like as all those calamities, sickness, death, etc. which he delivered so many distressed souls from, restoring them to life and health, were the proper effects and consequences of the first Adam's being overcome in the temptation.

6. That all his miracles are distinctly to be referred to the seven properties of nature; to that for instance, his raising up of the dead belongeth to the first; his making the dumb to speak, the deaf to hear, the the cleansing of lepers, to the second; his casting out devils, to the third; his turning water into wine, and feeding thousands of people with a few loaves, to the seventh, etc.

7. That his doctrine was delivered to the people most in parables, to fulfill the Scripture: but that it was so prophesied of him in the Scripture, because the Spirit, teaching then before his death and resurrection, was not yet that which the people should be tinctured by. That it was indeed a spirit of love, but of love not yet having conquered fully, but still being much in the Father's property, which only the apostles, that were to work miracles in the Father's power, should be capable of; unto whom therefore he expounded privately his parables.

8. That all the particular circumstances of his sufferings have a relation and answerableness unto something which happened in the first Adam's fall; for that this second Adam, if the first should be restored, must have entered wholly into the state and woful condition of the first, not only to suffer for him, but also to call it all back, and to rectify what he had misdone.

9. That the punishment of our sins came to be substantial in his sufferings, for to set before us a dreadful example, to show us that all that our own will takes in and burthens our soul withal, cometh to be a substance, and must appear before the judgment of God.

10. That he was taken and bound in a dark night, and even in a garden, because the first Adam, by his transgression in a garden, was fallen out of the paradisical day into eternal darkness.

11. That he was mocked, derided, spit upon, etc., because the first Adam was also deservedly so treated by the devils, when they had persuaded him to put on the serpents image: and that all his posterity with him must have continued subject to all their insults, if the second Adam had not taken all this upon himself, as it was inflicted on him by the devil's ministers and officers.

12. That he was crowned with a crown of thorns, because the first Adam suffered himself to be persuaded by the tempter, to take upon him, as a king of his own making, and in his own will and pleasure, the crown of this world, which yet proved to be unto him, not a crown of honour, but of contempt and pricking thorns.

13. That he was sentenced and delivered up to death by his own people, but that this sentence was executed by a heathen magistrate, because by man's doing, contrary to the will of God, sin was brought into the world; and by man's doing also, but without his knowing and contrary to his expectation, sin was to be cast out again, and the sinner reconciled. And therefore the two chief branches of the human tree, Jews and heathen, must both have a hand in this doing; that the blessing which was to be brought forth thereout might be extended over all, and both might be forgiven, because they both knew not what they did.

14. That in the properties of eternal nature, there is the generation of a cross, immediately before the coming forth of the light; that this cross, by the light, is illuminated and glorified; that man's eternal soul had here its original; and that his fall was in effect nothing else but a departing from this glorification of his cross within, and a turning his paradisical body without, into hard, rough, and gross flesh and bones, retaining still the figure of a cross, which now his soul must bear as a heavy burden.

And that this is the true reason why the Lord must bear himself his cross, and must be nailed to it, and die on it, and why no other kind of death could have done that which by his death was to be effected.

15. That he was hanged on the cross between two murderers, because the first Adam, by manifesting in himself this cross, fell into two such different regions or kingdoms, as proved both to he murderers of his paradisical life; and if he be upon the way returning home, he liveth verily as in the middle between them. And that the one of them, viz., this outward world, hath a promise of being delivered from the curse and vanity, like as also the one of the two murderers received a gracious promise, that he should be with Christ in paradise.

16. That all his words spoken on the cross, *Father, forgive them—I thirst—Into thy hands I commend thy spirit*, etc., and all the other circumstances also; the title written above the cross, the casting lots for his vesture, the giving him vinegar mixed with gall, the praeternatural darkness, the earth's quaking, and the rending of the rocks, and of the veil in the temple, etc., are all full of deep mysterious wonders, and all relating or answering to the first Adam's fall and restoration.

17. That his side was opened, and gave forth blood and water, after he was departed the life of this world; and that this was done to heal, or to make up that breach which then was made when the first Adam's side was opened, after he was departed his primitive paradisical life, and fallen into sleep, the true forerunner of his following death; where his Eve was taken out of him, and the two tinctures in his holy blood and water were divorced.

18. That his body lay forty hours in the grave, because, not only this was a space of time sufficient, on the one side, to convince all men that he was really dead, and, on the other, to fulfil on him the promise that hit flesh should not see corruption, but also, and even chiefly, because this was the time which the first Adam lay in his sleep.

19. That an angel rolled away the stone from his sepulchre, not that this stone otherwise could have hindered his arising out of the grave (for he came out with a paradisical body, to which no wall nor stone could be in the way), but only in condescension to the infirmity of his disciples; for so they could go and look themselves into the sepulchre, and see with their own eyes what they had laid therein was no more there.

20. That Mary in the garden (though she saw him) knew him not before he spoke to her; and the two disciples in the way to Emmaus (though he spoke to them, and opened to them the Scriptures) knew him not until he had broken bread with them: which is to show us not only in general, that he cannot be known without his own manifesting himself

by his living word; but also more particularly, that all what he speaks to us outwardly, in and from the Scripture, as he did in the days of his flesh, or through his servants, as he doth still, cannot make us to know him internally and sufficiently unto salvation, if his own internal manifesting himself in and to the hearer be not concurrent with that speaking: and that is the true breaking onto them that bread of life, without the eating of which, as he said himself, we have no life, and so also no real living knowledge of him.

21. That the first person he saw after his being raised from the dead was a woman, and even such a one as formerly had been possessed with seven devils; in answerableness to the first Adam's process, who, immediately after his being awakened from the sleep, saw a woman besides him, even her that soon after, by her lust and the fulfilling thereof, opened a door for entrance to these seven devils into the humanity.

22. That in the last forty days of the second Adam, between his resurrection and ascension, during which time he showed himself alive, and spoke with his disciples concerning the things appertaining to the kingdom of God, the Turba, born or conceived in the first forty days of the first Adam, was wholly overcome, and the work of his redemption consummated.

Page 297. *A. ult.* This whole No. 1., concerning *the hell in Christ's imperfect outward nature*, I think might nearer and more properly be expressed thus—the hell in the human soul, which he took upon him for our sake, was its own fiery disharmonised nature, which he entered into (and it was a descent, because the light is of a superior nature to it), tinctured and harmonised in his agony, and by shedding into it his inward immortal blood upon the cross. For by speaking only of *Christ's imperfect outward nature*, nothing more is denoted but what he had of this outward third principle; whereas not this third, but the first broken off from the second, was the hell awakened in the human soul, which, by shedding his inward blood into it, was to be re-harmonised and turned again into paradise.

Page 301. *A.* 1. Concerning that difficult place, 1 Pet. iii. 19., Behmen says nothing in particular; but so much may be gathered from him in general, that the benefits of the work of redemption through Christ, being extended universally to the whole fallen humanity, he must needs have gone in spirit through all the regions, centres, mansions, prisons, or however else those many different places or states might be called, wherein any departed souls were detained. That his preaching to them was done after the manner and in the language, (if this may be called so,) in which the spirits do speak and communicate their mind to one another. And because, without doubt, there was a great diversity of those spirits that had been unbelievers in the days of Noah, this conquest of Satan, death, and hell, must needs have reached unto them also; so that all of them that were but any way capable of grace and mercy (though all captivated under the powers of darkness), were made partakers thereof, each according to his own particular capacity.

Page 301. *Q*. 1. *What do they say concerning Christ's resurrection, ascension, glorified body, and intercession in heaven?* Here, *his sitting at the right hand of the Father*, could fitly be inserted; and then the question might be answered thus:

A. Of these five points they may say many great and weighty things, whereof in short the chiefest may be these following:—

1. That his resurrection was a springing up again of the paradisical life out of death, as that all the properties thereof were perfectly chrystalised and harmonised, as they were in themselves and in the humanity before the fall.

2. That as his incarnation was an appearing in this four-elementary world, according to the fallen Adam's state and figure, so his resurrection was an appearing again in the paradisical world according to the first Adam's primitive state, wherein he stood before his Eve.

3. That his resurrection was done in or by the power of his Father, and nevertheless also in or by his own power; according to the Scripture affirming this so well as that. *The Father raised him up*, is said in one place; and in another he saith himself, *No man taketh my life away from me; I have power to lay it down, and to take it up again*. Both which sayings are true, and easily reconcileable by his own words, saying, *All what the Father hath is mine*.

4. That his ascension after the last forty days, was a taking possession of that third angelical throne which Lucifer had lost; though as to this outward world, all his enemies are not yet put in subjection under him.

5. That he ascended into the central place of this principle, which is the place of the sun, from which Lucifer also was cast out; yet not to be considered as in this four-elementary world, but as in the inward world of pure light and glory, hid under the veil of this mixed out-birth.

6. That his sitting at the right hand of the Father is the exaltation of the humanity in his love above the wrath and anger of God, which before was kindled and predominant therein, and is now kept under. And that that place, or rather state, where the love subdueth the anger and generateth the paradise, is rightly called the right hand of God.

7. That by his sitting on this right hand, his now obtained rest, peace and establishment in the principle of light is to be understood, and that we are not to think of what we call a sitting in distinction from a standing; but that he sitteth in himself and standeth in himself, wanting no chair nor benches. His power is his seat.

8. That his glorified personal body, considered as to itself only, is still a creature, and continueth so for ever and ever; and that it hath a finite, visible, and measurable stature and figure, even that same which it had upon earth.

9. That the prints of the nails shall appear in this body to all eternity, and be more glorious than morning stars.

10. That he is in this body no more a man, that is, hath no more the marks of a male, but a perfect virgin image, as Adam was before his sleep, and as we all shall be after the general resurrection.

11. That this glorified body is in a far higher state of glory than ever the first Adam had in paradise, though the whole throne, or his whole mystical body of the Church is not yet brought unto perfection, nor yet capable of glorification.

12. That his intercession in heaven is not a particular actor doing, interrupted sometimes, and then begun again, as we might think that our various occasions upon earth would require; but a constant prevailing over and keeping under the powers of God's wrath; and always effectual, if we do not hinder it ourselves, by siding with the powers of the dark world, and making ourselves unworthy and uncapable of his prevailing for us in the love and light.

Page 301. *Q. 2. How do they conceive of the union of the Godhead to the humanity?* A. As of an union between the soul and spirit. Not that they would compare the Godhead in Christ to the spirit of man, and his humanity to the soul; but only to say thereby so much, that as the union of these two makes up one only perfect intellectual being, which by neither of them alone can be made up, so the union of the Godhead to the humanity makes up one only personal second Adam and mediator between God and man, which cannot be made up by either of them alone. Man was wandered out from the love of God, and there was a real separation made between them: a real reconciliation and reunion, therefore, was needful, if man should not be lost for ever. But seeing that in man there was no power to reconcile and unite himself to God again, God therefore, not as Father (because men belonged unto the Father already, and were fallen moreover into the Father's Fiery centre), but as Son (because he is the Father's light and love, which man stood in great need of after his fall), must unite himself to the humanity, not only to reconcile his children to the light world by his sufferings and death, but also for to be himself their head and king, etc. : all which required such a personal union of the Godhead to the humanity, as we may conceive between the spirit, soul, and body.

Page 301. *Q. 3. Seeing the Divine essence is everywhere alike, wherein lies the difference of its union with Christ, from its union with any other man or creature?* A. It is true that the Divine essence is everywhere alike, but only in itself, without a respect to man or other creatures; for with respect to them, it is notorious that it is not everywhere alike, that is, not in all of them equally manifest, nor communicating itself unto all of them in the same manner and degree: or else all men should be alike in knowledge, sanctification, glory, etc., and no different degrees between them could be found. That therefore there is and must be a difference, cannot but be plain; and that this difference lieth chiefly herein, that this union is a personal union, is evident also: for the God-man, Jesus Christ, is one individual person, and a person in the Holy Trinity, nay, the only person, seeing that without him we cannot conceive of another person in the Trinity, according to the common notion we have of this name. But such a thing cannot be said of any other man, though never so highly united unto God. Another difference the Scripture showeth us, by saying that *in him the fullness of the Godhead dwelleth*, and that *in him all the treasures of wisdom lie:* which cannot be said of any other, angel or man, but all have only their particular gifts, according to the measure of their capacities, and as their different offices and stations do require.

In the places quoted out of the Mysterium Magnum, Behmen sets forth, not only man's being made, in and by the regeneration, one with God and Christ, according to the Scripture, *He that cleaves unto the Lord is made one spirit with him;* but also man's being nevertheless eternally distinct from God and under Christ, and that the union of the Godhead to the humanity of Christ is much higher for ever than the union thereof to any other man. So for instance, Ch. xlvii. 18., he says indeed, that in the perfect resignation Christ and man are wholly one (which he explains intelligibly enough, and truly, so that no true Christian can stumble at his expressions); but he adds also, that nevertheless no man can say, *I am Christ, but only, I am his member, his branch, his dwelling-home*, etc.; because the union of the Godhead to his humanity imports that the seven properties of rectified and reharmonised nature (which in that discourse of his are the fountain of eternal living water, that was stopped in the humanity, by the fallen souls' essences, but digged again by Christ's suffering and death) are his, as his natural due and right, he having bought and paid a great price for them; as Behmen in the following figure of

Abraham's buying the twofold pit for a burying place for Sarah excellently declareth. When contrariwise, the union of the Godhead to the humanity of any other man, imports only so much that these reharmonised properties are his by free gift and grace of the giver. Chapter li. 7, the author doth not declare directly the difference between the union of the Godhead with Christ and with a Christian, but rather only the difference between our human soul and the Deity, showing that notwithstanding they come to be united, yet that is never changed into this: which he doth by several similitudes, but chiefly and most intelligibly by that of a piece of iron, made all fiery by its union with the fire, and yet never changed into fire, but keeping always its own iron nature, dark, gross, and obscure in itself, as soon as it is taken out of the fire. Chapter lxx. 60, he says something of the union of Christ with a Christian, to the same purpose as he did before; and then also of a difference which is for ever between Christ and all his members, whereby, also, the difference of the union of the Godhead with Christ, from its union with a Christian, doth manifestly though but in part appear. The occasion of this discourse is the figure of Joseph's eating a part, and his brethren eating a part, and the Egyptians eating a part also. And this figure he declareth by showing, that the God-man, Jesus Christ, hath a food which no other man can feed upon, according to his own words to his disciples, *I have food which you know nothing of.* And here he says the heathen woman's faith was his food. Truly, there is in this expression no difficulty at all; for he understandeth his delightful taking in, and being well pleased with man's faith, prayers, and praises; explaining himself in another place, that it is like as when a lover of music entertains himself delightfully with a melodious tune, feeding as it were his mind and senses upon the outward harmony which is so agreeable to his own inward harmonious constitution. Certain it is, that such a lover of music may be as much delighted in hearing a harmonious song, as another in eating and drinking the most delicious things; and as these do satisfy his fast and belly, so that doth the ear and mind. It is not therefore so quite impertinent to say he feeds upon it, especially here in such deep spiritual matters, where we cannot but take our expressions from sensible things. That our faith, prayers, and praises are due to Jesus Christ, is unquestionable; that they are not arbitrarily offered unto him, but necessarily, so that it is impossible by an internal impossibility, that his redeemed ones should not believe and trust in him during this time, and praise and give him thanks to all eternity, is unquestionable also; and that he is well pleased and delighted to receive and take in these offerings, nay, caused also thereby to show forth more of grace and mercy in this time, and of the wonders and riches of his lore, wisdom and glory in eternity, is no less unquestionable also. Well, then, may we say, in a human manner of expression, he feedeth upon these things, no less than we feed upon his grace and mercy. And this even the more, because we can say, that as our feeding upon his grace and mercy preserveth our being his redeemed people, so his feeding upon our prayers and praises preserveth his being our merciful Father, Head, and King. For he cannot continue so to us, if we do not continue so to him; and if he had not a redeemed people that praised and owned him to be their head and king, he could not have the being of a redeemer, nor the character of a king over a restored humanity. So also says Behmen rightly in another place, that the praises, songs, and voices of angels and men, are a food of the holy fire; where certainly he doth not mean, that this fire wants such a food for the preservation of its own being in itself, or that it was not a holy burning fire before the creation of angels; but only, that it is preserved in its being unto them, that which it was unto them from their creation. For if they all did fall away from their obedience and attendance to that holy fire, this would indeed not cease to be in itself what it is, but it would cease to be to them, what it is to them as long as they continue in their duty. And what shall we say of the Jewish meat and drink offerings? We know God has declared, he doth not eat the flesh of bulls, nor drink the blood of goats; but nevertheless may we not say with the Scripture, (1.) that there was in those meat and drink offerings something which God expressly required of them that offered them. (2.) That this was faith, prayers, praises, thanksgivings, etc. PSALM 1. (3.) That God delighted *to eat* these offerings, in that same sense in which the Scripture saith, the Lord *smelled* a sweet savour in Noah's sacrifice. This certainly was not the smoke of the burned beasts, but that which arose from Noah's soul and spirit; for the Lord took it in, was delighted therein, and so moved thereby, that he said in his heart, I will not again curse the ground. What reason then can be given for which the expression of *eating* should be more offensive than that of smelling, when both are referred to the same thing, and taken in the same sense? If then now faith, prayers, praises, etc., are not to be offered unto any man, but only unto God and Jesus Christ, as he is God and man (which that new song in the Revelation demonstrated sufficiently), it is self-evident that the union of the Godhead to Christ imports much more, and is much higher than the union of the same to any of his members; and that all will be found concentrated in what was said above, viz., that the difference lieth chiefly herein, that this union is a personal union.

Page 301. *Q. ult. How is the second person in the Trinity more united to the human nature, than the Father and the Holy Ghost?* A. So as the light is more united to the light-world than the fire; for though we are not to think of any division or separation, yet from the light immediately, not from the fire, the light-world hath its name and properties. The Father is a consuming fire, and the Son his light and love. Now Adam was not fallen away from the Father's property, and wanted in his fallen state no fire, having awakened in himself the Father's firey property. But from the Son's property of light and love he fell away, and this he wanted. The Son, therefore, not the Father, must have united himself personally to the humanity, that so the same, through the Son, might be reconciled to the Father. But that the Father is here not excluded, is evident sufficiently in that he sent the Son. If we then have no access to the Father but through the Son, whom he hath sent; he that is sent, and through whom, as through a way, medium, or mediator, we come to the Father, must be more or nearer united to us, than he that sent him, and whom we come onto through the Son. That which was disappeared and lost in Adam's fall, was that life and light which he had out of the light-world. Now, this life and light of man was in the Son, or, as Saint John saith, in the Word; that is, in him from whom the light-world hath its name and being. Unto this life and light therefore, he must have united in whom it was, so as to make up by his union with it, such a perfect, substantial human person as that first was, which had lost its life and light, that so this life and light might be brought into the human nature again, and the humanity might be restored into the light-world. As, therefore, the light is more united to the light-world than the fire; so the Son also is more united to the life and light in the humanity, and so to the human nature, than the Father. Concerning the Holy Ghost, the same could be shewn also in like manner; and all may be found contained in the words of our Lord, saying, *Father, the men were thine, and thou gavest them me, and I give unto them eternal life.*

Page 303. No. 3. *God hath no consultation within himself,* etc. Though this may be sufficient for such as do understand Behmen's ground, yet it is not so for others; for it is only an assertion without a reason or demonstration thereof. Wherefore, then, I think the reason which Behmen giveth might well be added, viz. *If God* (here considered as in himself only, without any will towards nature and creature), *had a consultation within himself, there must be something before, behind, or besides him, about which he consulted; there must be a cause moving him to this consultation, and a beginning thereof; there must also be thoughts and a variety of different conceptions in him, making such, or such images and representations of things, and comparisons of this method with that, until such a one were found out, as in which this or that could best be performed, etc.* But now, he being in himself alone an universal all, will, power, sufficiency, ground, beginning, and end of all things, without any alteration, no such thing hath any place in him. This reason, I think, is the more needful to be added, and as significantly as possible to be expressed, because it is certain that if this be not well understood and minded, there can never be a true apprehension of Behmen's sense.

Page 303. No. 4. *God, as manifested, eternally willed or purposed, and eternally generated a root of evil.* This position is not consistent with Behmen, and though there is added immediately, *which being good in itself,* etc. yet this cannot rectify what is amiss therein. For God, not as manifested, but as manifesting himself, or in the very beginning of his manifesting himself through nature, generated, indeed, that which afterwards became the evil of punishment, but he never willed nor purposed that it should be so. In this eternal manifestation through nature, something was generated, wherein and whereby he shewed himself afterwards, in the creation, a loving God and father to the works of his hands. Why, then, not also something wherein and whereby he might shew himself an angry, just, and zealous God upon their wilful disobedience? Doth not justice become him so well as mercy? (When yet we do not say that this latter was generated from such a purpose, or directly to that end; but we can give another substantial reason why it must have been generated so as it was.) But now he willed indeed, or purposed, that all his intellectual creatures should love and praise him, and to that end he created them all into the light-world, wherein his love and glory are manifest. But he never willed nor purposed that any of them should leave his habitation in the light, and fall into that deep pit or ground of his manifestation, wherein his wrath in justice must needs be manifest in and to such a fallen creature. How then can we say or think that he willed or purposed, and eternally generated a root of evil? He generated that inferior part of nature, without which the superior part thereof could not consist; and these two he united, so that the former was hid under the latter, but never willed that the creature should break this union. Wherefore, then, I think that this position might be thus expressed—God in his eternal manifestation through nature, generated such properties as became accidentally the evil of punishment to the creature, upon its own, etc.

Page 302. This other question is proposed, belonging hereunto. *But how will you avoid the consequences charged upon the reprobatists, if you assert that God*, etc. A. If Behmen asserts that *God as manifested, or God's eternal nature, or his formed word in eternal nature, did will and generate evil*, it will be true that the consequences charged upon the reprobatists cannot be avoided. But if it can be made out, that no such thing is asserted by Behmen, then no such question can be proposed. And seeing this question thus proposed, depends only upon the next preceding erroneous, position. No. 4. viz., *God as manifested, eternally willed or purposed, and eternally generated a root of evil*, which position is justly denied and rectified; this question, therefore, would not want any further answer, if Behmen's ELECTION, Ch. vi. 82, etc., were not quoted, and the expression of a *formed word* were not to be cleared up: so that it may be evidenced demonstratively, that by Behmen no such thing as this question mentioneth is asserted. Let us see then what he says, Ch. vi. 82,etc. I cannot find (and I am sure it cannot be found in any other place throughout all his writings) that he says, *God as manifested, or God's eternal nature, or his formed word in eternal nature, did will and generate evil*. This latter, it is true, he says in almost such words, but in no such sense as could give forth those consequences that are charged upon the reprobatists, which shall be evidenced by and bye. His own words relating to this matter are these—*In whatsoever hath severed itself into the good, therein he willeth the good; and in whatsoever hath separated itself into the evil, therein he willeth the evil; as the Scripture says, Such as the people is, such a god they have*. These words he explaineth according to his gift in these positions and expressions following—*All beginnings, decrees, and predeterminate purposes arise in the formed word through nature. All evil proceeds from and out of nature and creature. The hardening in nature and creature originated in the science or root of the creaturely self, so that if it turn itself into the wrath of nature, then it is laid hold on and hardened therein. All that where it is written, He hardened their hearts, etc., is performed and effected in the formed word of the eternal and temporary nature.* Now let us in the first place inquire, what is that which he calleth the *formed word*. He answers himself, in this same paragraph 85, that it is the *creation* and *creature*. And so sometimes he understandeth thereby the whole creation in general; sometimes the angels in particular; and sometimes also man, according to the subject matter of his discourse. Here it is man; as he says expressly, vi. 104, *Adam is the outspoken, formed, creaturely word, and in thi*s (not without, but in this) *formed word, evil is willed and generated*. But how, by whose instinct or direction, and by what means? Hath God, as manifested, willed evil, and that he might execute his will, put such a will to evil into this formed word? or hath he generated evil through the same, as through or by his instrument? No; God forbid. Hath God's eternal nature willed, and hath this generated evil in this formed word? No; far be this also. Hath then this formed word itself willed and generated evil? Yes; but not in that sense wherein this expression might be taken and is taken in this question, and which could bring forth such consequences as are charged upon the reprobatists. Well, what is then the meaning of this expression? A. This is the meaning: this formed word, viz., Adam, not as it was formed by God, in, as here is said, or out of, as it might be said better, but as it departed from that formation, or in its departing from the order of eternal nature, willed and generated evil. Out of what root, and by what means? A. Out of the root of his own free will, and by means of his own misusing the same. And that this is the only original of evil, and the efficient cause thereof, is Behmen's constant doctrine, and was rightly asserted so in the last words of the fourth position. If then not God, nor eternal nature, but only man, misusing his free will (which in the science or root of the creaturely self is prior or antecedent to the acts and deeds of his own formed human nature,) hath willed and generated evil, contrary to the will of God, and contrary to the order of nature, what consequence can be drawn forth from hence, and charged either upon God or his eternal nature? Truly, the sun cannot be clearer nor more blameless than this assertion is. If any would object, and say, If God had not given man a free will, he could not have misused it; and therefore, the giver is the cause of that mischief which is done by this misuse, I think he would not be worthy of being answered any further (though Behmen hath answered sufficiently), than by telling him the words of the Scripture, *Woe unto him that says unto his Maker, Why hast thou made me so?* But here will now be asked, Why then saith Behmen so expressly, *All evil proceeds from and out of nature and creature?* Is not this to charge nature as well as creature? and what nature, if not God's eternal nature, out of which man was created? A. No such thing; Behmen says right and well, and doth not contradict by this saying, that which was said above, viz., that all evil proceeds out of man's misusing his free will. An hundred places of his can plainly show, his meaning is, not that evil lay in eternal nature, much less that God hath laid it therein, and willed or purposed that man should bring it forth thereout, as he may bring forth the poison out of an adder, wherein it lay before; but rather, that man brought the evil into his own nature, out of his own will. God's eternal nature is all order, regularity, and harmony; and so was man's formed nature also: no evil lay neither in this nor in that. But in man's free will lay the possibility of misusing it; which also was not evil, and would never have been evil (for it was essential to the will's freedom) if it had not went out into an act of misusing. This free will, in its deepest root is naturally antecedent (as mentioned above) to the acts or workings of man's nature. When therefore this got the first insensible disposition to turn away from the regularity and harmony of God's eternal, and his own formed nature, the evil was conceived in the womb of that free will. This turning consequently broke the order of nature, and made it all irregular; and then in this now broken nature, the evil was generated, and went forth in act and deed. And so it was introduced into nature, and nevertheless proceedeth also now out of nature. Not therefore can man's formed nature (and much less God's eternal nature) be charged with being the original of evil; but only man, or the creature Lucifer before man, must be charged with having misused his free will, and disturbed the order of nature: which disturbance is itself the chief evil, and lay not before in nature, which never would have broken nor disturbed itself. And therefore, to show that no evil proceeds from God, Behmen joineth nature and creature together, and saith it proceeds from them. Not from nature, as it is regular and harmonious in God and holy angels, and as it was in man; as if this had any evil in it, and were or could be an original of evil (for the free will is deeper and prior than all the acts of nature), but from nature, as it is now turned upside down, by man's misusing his free will, if, then, man's own nature, before its being disordered, cannot be charged with an evil intent or purpose, how much less can God's eternal nature be charged with such an evil thing?

This, I think, is clear enough to answer the question, concerning the consequences charged upon the Reprobatists. But there is yet something behind, viz. these words of Behmen, *In whatsoever hath separated itself into the evil, therein he willeth the evil:* which will still be a stumbling-block to them that do not understand, according to Behmen's gift and declaration, what God is; but always imagine and frame, as he saith, some strange thing and afar off, when they will speak of God. To represent, therefore, his sense intelligibly unto such, will be the most difficult, if not an impossible thing. Yet I will, in the name of God, endeavour to do something, for brevity's sake in these following positions: I conceive with Behmen, and know it is his mind,

1. That *God is love:* and that this definition, given us by the Spirit of love in St. JOHN, is the most beneficial, and the only sufficient one to a true Christian; who, in all his way homeward to his Father, whereupon he shall meet with many trials, is to own, to adore, and to worship in spirit and in truth, no other God but *love.*

2. That, notwithstanding this definition, there are many things not attributable to love, and yet attributed unto God, in plain expressions of the Scripture.

3. That therefore, only for our own better apprehension's sake, we may use the name, *God*, when we speak of our only adorable good, which is *love*. And when we meet with anything different from, inconsistent with, or contrary to the properties of love and light, we may use either that of *universal being*, or also that of *wrath* and *fire*, according to the exigency and different conditions of the subject matter.

4. That this distinction, between God and universal Being, or between light and fire, love and wrath, as it was not before, nor also in the creation of angels, but came in only by their fall; so it doth not make a division in God the universal Being, but is only to be referred to the division made in the creatures: but is nevertheless attributable to God so far, as the creature's being necessarily dependeth upon God's being, as further shall appear. Attributable, I say, because it is actually attributed unto him in the Scripture, calling him in plain words, not only *light* and *love*, but also a *consuming fire*.

5. That in God, as he is love, all his obedient creatures do live, and move, and have their being: but that a creature may rebel against God, that is against love, and may cease to live and move, and have its being in God, that is, in love.

6. That no creature, though rebellious, may cease to live, and move, and have its being in God, that is, in the universal Being.

7. That if the creature ceaseth to live, and move, and have its being in love, which is its heaven, it must needs at the same instant begin to live, and move, and have its being in wrath, which is its hell.

8. That God is in hell as well as in heaven, which the Scripture tells us expressly; and that from this expression it is evident, that the name, God, it taken in different significations in the Scripture. For God, according to St. John's definition, is not in hell, because love cannot be in hell, as wrath cannot be in heaven. If, then, nevertheless, the words of the scripture, Psalm cxxxix. 8, are true, telling us God is in hell, he must be there as he is an universal Being, or as Behmen declares it, He is manifest in hell as well as in heaven, yet not in the same manner of manifestation, but in each according to its state; to that in heaven is his love, and in hell his wrath.

9. That all the evil spirits have forsaken God, are departed and broken off from God, and have left their first habitation in God, that is, in the love and light.

10. That the evil spirits are not departed, nor can be broken off from God, that is, from the universal Being; and can never leave their habitation, or their living, moving, and having their being therein. But that they are still in God, though not in his love and light, and he is still in them, but not so as he was in them at their first creation.

11. That therefore, there is still a band between God and the evil spirits; yet not that band of perfection which is love, but an indissoluble band, tying and keeping them together, and consisting herein, that their created being so depends upon God's universal Being, that it could not be a being, even not for one moment, if God's being should or could withdraw from them.

12. That this band is that which keepeth them still in subjection, so that they must be obedient even against their will, and without their knowledge; and must do by constraint his will according to that world which they are fallen into, even that will of his which is manifest in the wrath: which wrathful will they have made themselves subjects and slaves unto, by departing from the freedom of the sons of God.

13. That this band imports a manifestation of God, the universal Being in them, and an influencing them with what they have made themselves capable of. So that it is a principle-truth, in what intellectual creature soever God is not manifest, and not influencing it according to his love, in the same he must be manifest and influencing it according to his wrath. Because they cannot be broken off from his universal being, but must live, and move, and have their Being, either in his love, or in his wrath.

14. That love and wrath were not both manifest before, nor also in the creation of angels; but only love. And that therefore, the wrath had then no will nor power, except in potentia, and upon the supposition of being stirred up by the creature; for it never would nor could have raised up itself. But that now, after its being raised up in and by the creature, it hath a will as well as love, and a power of influencing into whatsoever it can reach.

15. That this raising up the wrath, and making it have a will and power, did not rend the will of love into two, nor make two contrary wills in God, the only good; but did only in the formed word of God, or in the creature, open as it were a twofold door and way, in which that only will of God which he had in the creation, viz., that he will be glorified in his creatures, is now in a tenfold manner, and in two contrary worlds performed: he being now glorified not only in the salniter of his children, but also in the destruction of his enemies, according to plain expressions of the Scripture.

16. That this twofold opened door, not having been so opened by God, nor decreed and predetermined by him that it should be opened by the creature, doth evidence sufficiently, That God was not manifest, and had no will in the wrath, before and in the creation of angels; nor ever willed and purposed to be manifest, and to have a will therein: for so he would have willed or purposed that his own will should be broken, which would be in deed and truth to make two contrary will in God.

17. That Behmen therefore instructs us rightly, by saying. That all the decrees and purposes, reprobations, hardenings of heart, etc., do not originate in God before and without the creature, but in the *formed word*, or in the creature, upon its having misused its free will, and separated itself into the evil.

18. That, now this door of wrath is opened, God is manifest, and hath a will therein. For, though the act of manifestation, and the effects thereof are the creatures, and in the creature, yet the wrath is his, and is not without, but within the compass of his universal Being, from which the creature cannot be broken off, and without which it can have no being. The wrath, indeed, is not in him, as he is our God, according to St. John's definition: for so the hell would be heaven, and the heaven hell; but it is in his universal Being, which containeth all, and without which can be nothing. For the properties of nature, kindled in the creature, are his, and so the wrath is his, according to the plain word's of the Scripture. He is therein, though his love is not therein, and he is the ruler, disposer, and pourer forth thereof. *A fire is kindled*, saith he (viz., by the creature; or he saith not, I have kindled it), *and shall burn unto the lowest hell*. And again. *See now that I, even I, am he, and there is no God with me; I kill, and I make alive*, etc. Pray who is this *I*? Truly it is not God in love, as he was only so before and in the creation of angels: for love killeth not; nor is it God in wrath, for wrath maketh not alive; and yet it is God, even he with whom there is no other God. It is God, therefore, in his universal Being: for he containeth and speaketh both of love and wrath, and both of life and death, or heaven and hell; in both of which He is now manifest, and hath a will and power, after and because the creature, by misusing its free will, hath separated itself into the evil.

19. That now of this wrath and wrathful will rightly can be said, In what creature soever God is manifest in wrath, in that creature he cannot will nor do, what he can and will do in such another creature, as wherein he is manifest in love: because the wrath cannot will and do what love willeth and doth, else it were not wrath, but love; and so vice versa.

20.—That this willing and doing in the wrath, is indeed in the creature only, and not without it, and is the creature's originally; because not only the wrath was impotent before and in the creation of angels, but is also still impotent in itself, and hath no will nor power but in the creature, and in the creature also not further, than as it is enlivened and empowered by the creature's own will and self-doing. But,

21. That nevertheless, this willing and doing in the wrath is also attributable unto God, as he is an universal Being: (1.) because of that band and dependence of the creature's being upon his being, spoken of above. (2.) Because the wrath is his, and was his from eternity, before it was wrath, and when it was sealed up among his secret treasures. (3.) Because many things are said in Scripture of the wrath, and expressly attributed unto God.

22. That, as in the kingdom of love and light, the inhabitants thereof cannot work without cooperation of the Holy Spirit of God, raised in them by their own humbling themselves, so that all their works (as also all our good works in this mixed world) are the works of God, though they are also verily the works of them that are his active instruments; so also in the kingdom of wrath and darkness, the prisoners thereof cannot work without concurrence of the spirit of wrath, raised and empowered in them by their own exalting themselves, so that all their works are indeed verily and properly their own, nay, much more their own than in the kingdom of light: and yet are also in some sense and respect, the works of the wrathful Spirit of God, and of those dark properties of nature which they have made themselves subject unto. And this, because there is no living, nor moving, neither in this kingdom nor in that, without the spirit of this kingdom, or of that.

23. That, these words of the apostle, *To whom ye yield yourselves servants to obey, his servants ye are*, etc., though spoken by him with reference to another matter, are here also rightly applicable to this; and as they are now true in a particular sense, relating to the mixed multitude of Adam's children, so they were also true as to their substance from the beginning, in a more general sense: nay, even from this beginning of Lucifer's fall, the truth of these words is derived down to all the children of man.

24. That therefore, as a servant doth either freely, or must do by constraint, the will of his master, so in both these kingdoms the will of that spirit is done which is the master therein; yet with this great difference, that in the kingdom of light the will of the holy Spirit of God is done freely, willingly and joyfully, by that innate principle of love, which the holy angels kept unto from their creation, in full obedience and resignation. And in the kingdom of wrath, the will of the wrathful spirit

of God is done in trembling, and, in a sense, by constraint. For, though verily and most properly it is their own will which the devils do, because it is not the will of God, in and to which they were created, but in and of themselves, and from their own ground, they raised it up, and endeavoured to put it in execution, as they do still; yet this expression of-their own will, doth not make them absolute or sovereign lords and masters of the kingdom of wrath, but only servants thereof, and prisoners therein: for by their own will they have manifested and empowered the wrathful spirit of God; to him they have yielded up themselves in obedience, and his will they must do, and do continually, even in and by the doing of their own will.

25. That accordingly, God, as love, willeth and worketh nothing in the devil, and the devil nothing in God, because he hath separated himself from God, and is dead to love; and so that band or communion of willing and working in the light, that was between them in their creation, is broken. But that the devil, who is a living and active creature, willeth and worketh in the wrath of God, and the wrath or wrathful Spirit willeth and worketh in the devil, because it liveth and is manifest in him, and ruleth over him, as a master over his servants, and as a prison-keeper over his prisoners. And that there is now a band or communion of willing and working between them, because when that first band in the light was broken, this other in the darkness must needs have been made manifest, wherein he cannot be without willing and working: for by this band he is kept in being within the universal Being of God, and is not annihilated; which also cannot be, because it is contrary to the fundamental rules, laws, and principles of eternity.

26. That this willing and working in the wrath, considered as on the creature's side, consisteth chiefly herein, that the creature, being departed from the will and work of love, having rejected the influence and co-operation of the holy Spirit of God, and having turned itself into the dark wrathful properties of nature, doth still move and act in them, and formeth innumerable strange, false, monstrous, and lying forms or images, in thoughts, words, and deeds, which are all evil, absolutely, without any limitation, and mere abominations to the holy will and Spirit of God, in the kingdom of love and light.

27. That this willing and working in the wrath, as far as it is attributable unto God, as manifest therein, and whose wrath it is, consisteth not only herein, that the active and restless properties of wrath, which are, and must be subservient to his manifestation in light and love, exert their own natural powers in the creatures fallen into them, and give them continually food, and quasi materials to their forming and imaging; but also herein,

that the Spirit of this wrathful kingdom (which is the Spirit of God, even he who in the kingdom of love is the Holy Spirit, but in this kingdom manifest as a Spirit of the fiery anger of God) delighteth, strengtheneth, and exalteth himself therein, and willeth that it shall be so, that he may manifest and show forth in and by them, the wonders of this kingdom. Like as we might think in an earthly similitude, that a kindled fire delighteth in a dry wood, strengtheneth and elevateth itself therein, and willeth, or naturally inclineth to have such food continually, that it may have something to consume, and to show forth therein its power; all in a direct contrariety to the kingdom of light and love.

28. That all this, on the side of God, as manifested in the wrath, is good, and no evil maybe found therein; though it is the highest evil of punishment to the creature. For herein his justice is manifest, giving unto each creature, in due measure and right proportion, not only what it deserveth, but also what it willeth, and what it still maketh for itself; for the works of their hands are their food. And this justice is in and to him as good as his mercy, though not so to the creature; nay, so essential to him, and so inseparable from him on this side of the evil creature's own will, as his love and mercy on the other side of the creature's good resigned will. Herein also the wonders of the deep beneath are brought forth into manifestation, and thereby the great and holy name of God, though the creatures as much as in them lie think to revile and blaspheme it, is even hereby also magnified and exalted, contrary to their will, and without their understanding it. Wherefore Behmen rightly says, That as the holy angels praise God freely in his love and light, so the devils must praise him in his wrath, though not intending it.

29. That the dark properties of wrath, and so also the Spirit of this wrathful kingdom, which is God as manifested in the wrath, will indeed now (after having got a predominance in the creatures by the creatures own willing and empowering them in themselves) that their subjects and prisoners shall be what they are, and do what they do. And that because this their doing is absolutely evil in them, we may say well and soundly enough, The dark properties and the spirit of wrath in them, not without them, will the evil in them. Yet they will it not directly as it is evil, but as it is naturally the proper food, nourishment, and increase of their qualifications, and the only medium to the manifestation of their powers and wonders, which are all good in themselves. And this we may say, because (1.) the good cannot be willed in them by the Spirit of love, they having separated themselves into the evil: and (2.) because without either the Spirit of love, or the Spirit or wrath, upon which all their being and willing must depend, they can be and will nothing at all. The dark

properties, and so also the Spirit of this wrathful kingdom, are themselves (according to Behmen's plain expression) enemies to the devil, and hate his perfidiousness, treachery, pride, and folly, wherein he still thinks to be their lord, when he is but their slave and prisoner, etc. : which is in them a good and sure mark of justice and equity, nay, of their subjection also to the love and light of God. Which latter especially doth more plainly appear from what this author asserts expressly, viz. That the devil is as it were abominable even to the kingdom of wrath, which accuseth and blameth him continually, because he hath spoiled and lost his own kingdom in the light, and dareth now still be so impudent, as to pretend to be a king in a kingdom which never was his own. All which plainly showeth, That the dark properties and the Spirit of wrath will no evil as it is evil, but only as it is subservient to the manifestation of their great powers and wonders.

30. That therefore, when Behmen says, *In whatsoever hath separated itself* (by misusing his free will) *into the evil, therein he willeth the evil,* these words do not contain nonsense, nor a contradiction to the plain words of the Scripture, repeated by himself an hundred times, *God willeth no evil;* but a deep, substantial solid truth, worthy to be understood by a lover of the mysteries of God and of his kingdom, *though not fit to be proclaimed to a promiscuous multitude of ignorant people:* for certainly, the meaning of these words is not so gross and superficial as either malicious or short-sighted eyes might take it to be. Which now I think may appear sufficiently from the coherence of these *thirty positions*, though several more could have been added not impertinently.

Page 302. Q. 2. *How shall we know when the word God in Scripture, signifies God only, and when it signifies (his) nature?* A. If Behmen is understood concerning these two different considerations of God, it can be known without a great difficulty, at least for the greatest part, (yet only according to the measure of that understanding,) what of the words of the Scripture is to be referred unto the former, and what of them unto the latter. For though God as in himself only, without all nature and creature, is not an object of our understanding; and though, therefore, the Scripture doth not instruct us directly in this point, by telling and declaring what he is, yet it tells us that he is; and there are places in the Scripture, in which one thing or expression may belong to the former, another to the latter, and a third unto both, in a different sense. But I do not think that any place may be found, which only and altogether may be referred to the former; though there are many that only and altogether belong to the latter. For this is certain, and may be a sure and constant rule, That all the places and expressions wherein God is spoken of with relation to creatures, especially to men, so that either he be represented to them as their loving God and Father, as their King and Lawgiver, as their dreadful Judge, etc., or they be instructed concerning his Divine attributes of righteousness, justice, mercy, omniscience, long-suffering, fatherly care and providence, etc.; and all those places, also, wherein there is spoken of his will, counsel, decrees, purposes, election, and reprobation, etc.; and further, all those places which declare anything of his love and anger, of his great works and wonders, of his kingdom in the light and calling to it, of the Father's drawing, the Son's reconciling the Father, and the Holy Ghost's being poured out upon the children of men, etc. : they all are to be referred to the latter consideration. But in those places chiefly wherein his unity, greatness, infiniteness, omnipresence, unchangeableness, etc., are declared, there maybe found this or that, which not only belongeth to the latter, but to the former also.

Page 302. *Q. ult. How can you avoid the texts in Scripture, which attribute reprobation to God himself?* How is the word, God, to be taken in those places? A. No text in Scripture attributes reprobation to God as in himself only, without nature and creature; and though the Scripture doth not determine this so expressly, by saying—God as in nature and creature, yet (1.) the whole series and concatenate harmony of the truth in its particulars, and (2.) also the divers senses in which we cannot deny but that the word God is taken in Scripture, do evince this assertion sufficiently. Let us not stick to words and notions, but consider only and even but simply, without subtleties, What *reprobation* is. We shall find it is an essential shutting up the kingdom of light and love, and an excluding the creature out of it; implying that the creature hath been therein, and presupposing that the same is no more capable thereof, or no more fit to dwell therein any longer. Now where is that text in Scripture that asserts, either that God willed or purposed in himself from eternity, before the creature was, that the same should be excluded from having communion with him, in his kingdom of light, love, and glory? or that he himself by his own doing, hath cast the creature out, and shut the door upon it? Doth not the Scripture plainly tell us, That angels and man wen created to have communion with God, and to praise him in his light and glory? That the devil stood not or abode not in the truth, but left his habitation in the light; and that man lost his paradisical state, by the devil's cunning craft and his own sinful lust? Truly, we must take this to be the first doing on the creature's side; and then we may take that other to be the consequence thereof, which the Scripture tells us was done by God, viz., the devil was cast out, and his place was no more found in heaven, and Adam was driven out of the garden. As no man of any sound sense can make this latter the foundation, and that former the superstructure; so also no man can separate these two from one another; but both together in conjunction are or make up what we call *reprobation*. Which in substance and reality is nothing else, but that God, who before was manifest in the creature, in his love, becometh now manifest therein in wrath; because (1.) the creature in its own will is no more capable of his manifestation in love, and (2.) because without him, as manifested either in love or wrath, there is for the creature no living, moving, nor having any being. From all this it is evident, that much more unto the creature than unto God, and unto God as without the creature not at all, *reprobation* is to be attributed. If we would consider man especially, whom both election and reprobation concerns, the matter would still be much more evident. But not to run out into this wide, open field, I shall say only this in short, according to Behmen's declaration,—Adam, with all his posterity, was to be as a harmonious instrument, which the Spirit of love manifest in him would play upon: and as to his own person, he was actually made and prepared so. But the spirit of this world creeping in, disordered the strings thereof (the properties of nature in him), and tuned them so, that they made up an instrument fit for himself. Now therefore, it was no more fit for the Spirit of God; but this departed from him, or ceased to be manifest in him, according to his former manifestation in love, and came to be manifest in him according partly to the first, and partly to this third principle, which both are his. And here man was reprobated, that is, excluded from paradise and heaven, wherein he could be no more, because he had it no more manifest in him. But now the Scripture no where tells us, that it was decreed or purposed by God, before man was a creature, that he should transgress and fall, and should be reprobated; but on the contrary, this the Scripture tells us, that *man was chosen in Christ Jesus before the foundation of the world:* which doth not presuppose (but rather contradict) that the fall was decreed by God, but only that it was seen and known in his wisdom; for an efficacious remedy was found out against it. And what was this else, but that afterwards in time, the same primitive manifestation of love in the humanity (though quite in another and much higher way) returned again, and called unto all men to give way to it, and to receive the same into themselves, as it still doth so. If they do, they are elected; that is, separated from the world, and taken in into this new or second manifestation of love, not without but in the humanity, and even in themselves. If they do not, they are not reprobated by a new, peculiar act or deed of God, as without them, or far from them above the stars; but only they continue in their, being already excluded from having his love manifest in them, and from the communion with God in the light.

And there is nothing that did or could exclude them, but their own having yielded themselves servants to the devil and the spirit of this world, and their wilful continuing to love this service more than the freedom of the sons of God, and the manifestation of his love in them, etc.

Page 303. No. 5. The reason of what is asserted in this position, declared in these last words, *because the evil would have been from him*, cannot give us a right idea of the thing; for it supposeth, as it were, that God could have willed or fore-ordained all things which have come to pass, but did leave it freely, upon consideration, that if he had done so, the evil would have been from him: which hath but a very superficial sense, and doth not represent rightly, what God is, according to Behmen's gift and declaration. It is true indeed, that if it could be lawful for us to say, God willed or fore-ordained all what came to pass, it would be lawful also to say, The evil is from him, and he hath willed it. But as this latter is the devil's lying assertion, so that former also is not much better; seeing that this dependeth upon that, and that is the ground of this. As we therefore rightly say, God cannot will the evil, no more than he can lie or die, so we must say also positively, and hold it firmly, That God not only did not will and fore-ordain, but also *could not* have willed and fore-ordained all things which have come to pass, viz., those that relate to the manifestation of his wrath; because God is love, and was manifest in light and love only, before and in the creation of angels, but in his wrath he was never manifest before the fall. Now God, as love, could not have willed or foreordained that the wrath should be made manifest, and get a predominion in his creatures, whom he purposed to create in and to his light, love, and glory (if we think he could, we do not yet understand with Behmen what a principle is): and in his wrath he could never have been manifested, nor could his wrath have manifested itself, if the creature had not manifested it; no more than the fire in a flint can manifest itself. Nay, his *love* cannot be concerned with anything, nor take any notice of what is in and belongeth to the wrath; except only so far, that it hath *an eternal will, most essential to itself, to overcome the same, and to exalt itself over it, where it pleaseth, and where it is not resisted, by the creatures own wilful continuing in the misusing its free will.* And therefore, when God foresaw that the creature would misuse its free will, fall into his wrath, and manifest the same in itself, he, according to this eternal essential will in his love, willed, purposed, or fore-ordained, that the wrath manifested in man should be broken and overcome by love. In and through the humanity of Jesus Christ; and that so the first manifestation of love in man should return unto him again, to the end that love might exalt itself, and triumph over the wrath, and show forth for ever, what it is. And therefore also this is the only purpose or fore-ordaining, whereof the Scripture tells us, that *it was made before the foundation of the world*. But no such will or purpose concerning the wrath, viz., that this should be made manifest, can be found in any place of all the Scripture. So then, the manifestation of the wrath is only and wholly to be attributed to the creature's misusing its free will. And so it is not enough to say—God *did not*, but we must say, He *could not* will or fore-ordain all things which come to pass.

Page 305. No. 6. *God foresaw in his anger*. This expression is right and good, frequently used by Behmen, and well enough to be understood by them that are acquainted with his style. But all this notwithstanding, the more to condescend to the capacity of such as do easily find scruples in words, and might here think or ask, Had God an anger before the creatures were made and fallen; he must then have been angry with himself, etc.? I think it might be thus expressed—God foresaw in the natural qualification of the three first properties of nature. For, in God was no anger before the fall, nor is in him even now; but in the first properties of nature, if divorced from the rest (which may be done in a creature, but not in God), there is such a qualification, as is and must be wrath and anger in that creature that hath made this divorce in itself. And this is called his anger, because these properties, and their natural, necessary qualifications, all good and harmonious in his eternal nature, are his. So therefore, when Behmen calleth it, *his anger before the fall*, he doth it only because it is that which, after the fall, is called so in Scripture; explaining himself sufficiently, That it had not, nor could have had this name before the fall, which it hath now after it, because it was then in God not such a thing as it is now in the creature: nay, that *it is not anger in God properly*, but only in the creature, and attributable unto God no further, than as he is manifest in the creature, and as the creature's being dependeth upon his being.

Ibid. Line 3. *if it had been infused into them*. This expression doth not declare the thing consistently with Behmen, though he may have used the same words in another construction, and with other circumstances. For in one sense, the *love was infused* into the devils; that is, given, offered, presented, so that it shone upon them, drawing, calling, and inviting them, no less than all the rest of the holy angels. Which was an infusion in such a sense, as Behmen declareth in the simile of a thistle, into which the sun continually infuseth its light, warmth and tincture, having no other will nor inclination in itself, but to do the same good to the thistle which it doth to the rose; when the thistle, for all this loving-kindness of the sun, doth still but remain a stinging thistle. But in another sense we must say also, that the *love could not have been infused into the devils;* for how can wine be infused into a vessel full already of stinking water? The wine may be poured out indeed over the vessel, and so was the love over the devils; but the vessel cannot take it in, so neither could they, because their own will, which they were full of, could not receive it. In short, God did all the good which he could do to them, he being unchangeable, and having no other will but to do them good; but they did nothing, nor would do anything, of what was their duty to do.

Page 305. No. 6, *permitted both for good ends*. I say nothing directly against this expression, knowing not only that it is most common, but also that we cannot well avoid it. But I must say, nevertheless, that it is not sufficient to declare the depth; because God's permitting the fall for good ends, seems to presuppose that he could and would have hindered it, if he had not seen good ends therein. Which cannot be said by any that understands with Behmen, what God is. For such a one will grant indeed, that the fall must serve for good ends; but he will say also, that God could not have hindered it, and will be able to understand, that by so saying, he doth not make him impotent, nor derogate anything from his omnipotence, any more than by saying, God cannot save him that will not be saved, or, which is the same, that will not leave off his own will: which is a good and true assertion. No ill consequences, therefore, do follow from saying, God could not, but rather in abundance might they follow from saying, God could have hindered the fall, and did not, and says nevertheless still of himself, *As I live, I will not the death of the sinner*.

Page 305. No. 7. To the last words might well and pertinently be added—or a predestinate purpose of the free gift of grace. Because Behmen calleth it so also, and it is of a good consequence to express that all this is owned to be free grace; that when afterwards something is said of the human will, and its required turning, it may not be so easily mistaken, as if salvation were by Behmnen ascribed unto man's will.

Ibid. No. 8. I see no reason why here, after these first words, *God purposed or willed by an eternal will in himself*, these words are added, *which they call election*, ROMANS, vi. 16. For (1.) It is certain that Behmen doth not call this will, election. (2.) That which is expressed in the four first lines of this position, might rather be called—God's universal call; which is so different from election, that the Scripture attributes that former unto many, and this latter unto few. And (3.) In the quotation of the Scripture there must be a mistake, so that one place is set for another; seeing that in ROM. vi 16. nothing may be found which could here be referred to. But I think that which St. Paul saith is here meant, viz., that *man was chosen in Christ from before the foundation of the world*. And if this be meant, it is true indeed, that it is the first ground of election, nay, in a sense election itself, so for as it could be in God before man was a creature: but it is not yet that which Behmen calleth so, when he declareth what election is in its full sense, from which it is greatly different. For, that which was done in God from before the foundation of the world, reacheth all men; as in this position is said, that God willed to put his grace into all mens' hearts, without any condition required of them: but this which properly is called election, reacheth not all, but only a few; because not all, but only a few do fulfil the condition that here is required, viz., to turn their wills into that grace.

Page 306. No. 9. Here I would not say, *which they call God's clock-work*, but rather—and they compare it to a clock-work. Because, though Behmen sometimes calleth it so, when he discourseth thereof, yet it is not an appropriate name, whereby this outward mysterium could be distinguished from the inward. But as the word *mysterium* is common unto both, and is distinguished by outward and inward, so also can this name of *clock-work* be, etc.

Ibid. No. 10. In general, I must observe, concerning this whole tenth position, that so many different things, expressed therein so shortly, do make the sense very obscure, as to my sight: but maybe it is not so in the sight of others. In particular I have to observe (1.) The words, which *God for wise and good ends permitted to remain in him*, are tolerable indeed; but much nearer to the bottom would it reach, if it were said—that this principle of evil cannot but remain in him until the day of judgment, appointed for a separation of good and evil. (2.) The words, page 307 *which is reprobation*, are true, but do not give the whole or full sense of what reprobation is, according to Behmen's depth, and that sense wherein he frequently taketh this word. For, when a man, not having turned out of the principle of evil, is rejected by God to all eternity, this is his reprobation indeed, in its accomplishment and irrevocability. But, Behmen calleth that also reprobation, (and so election,) which is done in and with man in time, wherein it maybe revoked and altered. For instance: as long as a man remaineth voluntarily under the power of the principle of evil, he is actually reprobated and rejected, became he is actually excluded from communion with God in his love and light. But such a man may, during this life, turn his will, and elect the principle of grace in him; and then he is by that re-elected actually, because he cometh to have actually communion with God in love and light. Though this also is not yet unalterable; for he may turn out of the grace again, and if he doth, he is reprobated again, etc. And still deeper, Behmen declareth also, how of all these alterations man maketh in time, may be conceived and said—such a man was elected or reprobated from eternity, notwithstanding that he changeth his will several times. (3.) The words, page 306, *with his will, or at least a desire*, may be taken in a right sense indeed, but may also easily give an occasion to object something, which might be prevented by saying—if he turneth not out of it effectually, or at least in an earnest desire to do so.

Page 307. No. 11. *is called—God's manifestation in anger, awakened by man's sins, and his formed word in man, which is the fire, etc.* Here the sense is very ambiguous; for, as for my part, I can hardly discern whether the meaning be this, that the principle of the evil of punishment in man is called God's formed word in man; or whether it be this, that anger is awakened by man's sins and by his formed word. And though I have reason to believe it shall be that former, yet I see not how the following definition can be applicable to this formed word, when it is said, *it is the fire* in man *separated from the light, upon a misuse of its free will;* though it is applicable to the principle of the evil of punishment in man. From whence then it appears, that this principle is not called by Behmen, God's *formed word* in man. But so is the thing to be conceived: Behmen calleth the whole man a formed word of God, from his very creation, before the fire in him was separated from the light, upon a misuse of his free will. And now, after it is separated, like as man retaineth, notwithstanding this separation, the name of a creature, so he may retain also that of a formed word and may be called so: not as if this denomination were now so proper unto him, and did exactly declare what he is (which rather might be declared by calling him deformed): but only, because he is still the same creature in substance, which was formed by God, notwithstanding that he hath deformed himself. But to give the name of a formed word, directly to the fire in man separated from the light, is not excusable. And though it may be that Behmen hath such words, yet they will certainly stand with him quite in another construction. Wherefore, then, I think this particular of the *formed word* might be left out, and then the rest could be coherent, thus, *anger, awakened in his fire in man, separated from the light, upon a misuse, etc.*

Page 307. No.12. If here shall be said, how they call *the principle of grace*, the nearest and most usual name with Behmen will be this—that they call it the second purpose of God in the blessed name Jesus; as they call the first purpose, according to which Adam was created, the first predestinate will or purpose of righteousness, out of the Father's property. That Behmen calleth that former *God's temporary will of grace is the creature*, I could not find, though much inquiring after it. If he doth, it will be very seldom, and the circumstances, or whole construction of his discourse, must declare why he calleth it *temporary*. But this name mentioned, is much in use with him.

Ibid. Line *ult. the actual as well as original sins of parents are propagated.* Though this is right and true in its right sense, yet I fear it will meet with opposition, and be thought contrary to the Scripture, where it says, *The son shall not die for the sins of the father, but each shall die for his own sins.* And therefore I think it might be a little explained to this purpose—that by the propagation of actual sins no more is meant, but that the actual sins of the parents infect and pollute their natural seed, and make thereby the turning of the will in their children more difficult for them, than it would be if their essences were not thus infected.

Ibid. (Page 309.) The words, *from Adam as out of one lump*, might either be left out, or put into another construction; because as they stand now, they make the sense, at least as to me, obscure. That this propagation is derived from Adam down to this day, is understood of itself; and that it was true in Cain, the first-born of a woman, as well as in all other children born after him, is no less evident. And a plain instance thereof we may see (according to Behmen's declaration) in that foolish persuasion of Eve, who thought in a carnal way, she had got the man of the Lord who would be the treader on the serpent. For this principle was so predominant in her first child, that instead of braising the serpents head in himself, he bruised the head of his brother, even of him who was a type of the serpent treader.

Ibid. To the last words, *heavenly bodies concur*, I think could be pertinently added—either aggravating this infection, if their aspects are bad, or lessening the same, by putting a stop to the effects thereof, if they are favourable.

Ibid. No. 13. *although a turba enters into the seed.* Instead of this I would rather say—although a turba may enter into the seed even of good parents. Because there is a turba already originally, more or less, in every seed of good and evil parents: of which turba is not here spoken, but of a turba which may enter; not which enters necessarily and always into every seed of good parents, but only which may enter from exterior accidents, or actions, or also from evil influences of the stars, etc.

Ibid. they reach not God, is right and true, and if I well remember, it is Behmen's own verbal expression; but plainer and less exposed to objections would it be, if there were said with a nearer termination, as Behmen useth sometimes to determine this expression,—they reach not God in his light, love, and glory.

Page 309. No. 14. The sense contained in the first two lines I would rather thus express—Jesus Christ undertook from eternity to redeem fallen mankind, which was elected or chosen in him from before the foundation of the world. And this alteration I would make, only because Behmen says, in a place where he declareth this text, *When Lucifer fell, the foundation of the world was not yet laid;* and gives thereby, as it seems, to understand, that the choosing of man in Christ Jesus is to be conceived of, as following in order upon the fall of Lucifer. For so he says also in another place, *If Lucifer were not fallen, man would not have been created.* Because now Lucifer is fallen indeed before time, (seeing that time began only with the creation of heaven and earth,) but not from all eternity, we may say better—man was chosen from eternity, than from all eternity. And then also the following expression, *from before the foundation of the world*, is the Scripture's own, which therefore may be kept more safely than that, *from all eternity*.

Page 309 (also 311). *to give up the will into God's righteousness, or anger-fire-will, to be slain, and suffer, and rule over sin.* These words must needs be put into another and plainer construction; for they may be taken in a twofold sense, which yet on both sides will be obscure, and not intelligibly enough coherent with the last words. Though the meaning which is intended, may be understood by them that are acquainted with Behmen's style, viz. this,—the first predestinate purpose of righteousness requireth of man, that he shall give up his own anger-fire-will into God's righteousness, to be slain thereby, and subdued under his love-will: which subduing of his own anger-fire-will he is to suffer, and in the power of his renewed love-will to rule over sin.

Page 310. *Q. But can they will this?* A. Yes: for (1.) this willing is not a work or doing, but rather a resting or ceasing from the works of their own will. If they can work in their own will, why not also rest from this their own work? when there is no constraining force from without, compelling them irresistibly to work, but only that force which is the nature of their own-will itself, and which cannot be called irresistible, as further shall appear. (2.) This resting is not to be done by a power of their own, but by use of the power of that first grace freely given them for that end; which must be no grace, and can signify nothing to man, if it doth not enable him so far, that he can will this. (3.) This willing is required by God, as the first ground or beginning of their restoration on their side; and God can require nothing of man, but what he hath enabled him to do. (4.) Man's own will excludes God, and shuts the door upon him: and to say—God shall open this door, not man, is to say—God shall open the eyes of a man that shuts them wilfully, that he may see the sun; and man is not required to do it, though he can open them, by that moving faculty which God hath placed in his eyelids. (5.) A wheel running the contrary way to what it shall run according to its master's will, must first be stopped, before it can be set by him to run that way which he pleaseth. And that this first stopping, as to the human own-will, cannot be done by God, but must be done by man, is evident from the difference between a wheel, which is but dead and passive, and a human will, which is a living active thing. But especially and chiefly is it evident from the nature of a will. And that this doth not make God impotent, is evident also from hence, that notwithstanding it is rightly said in one respect—God cannot, but man must do it; it is also rightly said in another—God doth it, and hath done it, because it is he alone of whom man hath this stopping grace. (6.) If we say, Man cannot will, we must needs say, God doth hinder him; for the devil cannot force the human will, *Voluntas cogi non potest*, and there is no power superior to man but God. But now this latter, that God should hinder him, is false; that former, therefore, that man can will, must needs be true. (7.) If by this assertion, Man can will, were meant, that this willing is so efficacious, as that he can thereby take unto himself strength, salvation, life, and light, it would be false, indeed; because it would rob God of what is due to him only, and attribute to man what no creature can be capable of. But because there is no more meant by it, but that he can stand still from his head-strong course in own-will, and so be emptied of himself, and consequently able to receive into him that salvation, life, and light, which then will be given him by God, it must needs be true: because, as on the one hand it is consistent with the honour of God, unto whom all and every good gift is ascribed, so on the other, it agrees with the nature of a rational, living and moving creature; which cannot but justly be required to stand first still from taking in his own evil things, before he do receive the good gifts of God. (8.) The testimonies of such, as had not only a real experience in the work of regeneration, but also illuminated eyes especially, to see deeply what man is, what is in man, and what man's will is, all tending to the destruction of his own-will, are transcendently more firm and valuable, than all that reason can suggest in own-will's defence. (9.) The testimonies of the Scripture plainly confirm, that man can will, and even these alone should convince us of this truth, and keep under all that would make an insurrection against it. Moses, the mediator of the old covenant, says expressly, *I call heaven and earth to record this day against you, that I have set before you life and death, blessing and cursing; therefore choose life, etc.* Pray, what signifieth this saying, and this command, if man cannot choose life by standing still and hearkening to the voice of God? And Jesus, the great Mediator of the New Testament, says: *O Jerusalem—how often would I have gathered thy children together—and ye would not*. Pray, how could he have laid to their charge their not willing, and their resisting thereby his will, if they could not have willed, and concurred with his will?

Page 311. No. 16. *fulfilled God's righteousness, in the love and in the anger, turning it into divine joy*. These words have indeed a sense in them, but more expressive and nearer to Behmen's ground would it be, if the construction were made thus—fulfilled God's righteousness, transmuted (or also filled) the Father's anger with his love and humility, and turned it, in the human soul, into divine joy.

Ibid. No. 17. Here I think it might be most proper to say what this *redemption wrought in us* is, and more explicitly, how it is wrought in us. Viz., that it is, according to the Scripture, a deliverance from the old Adam's life predominant in us: and is wrought out in us by means of his leading us by his Spirit, and our following after him, in a daily increasing conformity to his life and death. For what here is said in the last words, viz., *through a gracious concurring efficacy of his divinity and humanity*, is true indeed, but is not all; seeing that it relates only to what is on his side, but makes no mention of what is on ours.

Page 313. No. 18. *had not been substantial in any of the faithful; that is, the six spirits in the soul had not been harmonised into one seventh substance*. This explication of the word *substantial*, is indeed right and good, and intelligible to them that have read Behmen; but unto others it might be plainer, and not meet so easily with opposition, if there were said—that is, none of them had nor could have put on the new-born humanity, or Christ's new paradisical body, because this was not yet come down from heaven. And their putting on Christ only spiritually, in faith and hope, could be declared, if needful, by showing the difference between their eating manna and drinking water out of the rock, and a Christian's eating and drinking the flesh and blood of Christ. But if that former explication shall be left as it is, there might be made only this little alteration, viz., instead of saying, *in the soul*, might be said better—in the human nature. Because this harmonising the six spirits is not only to be referred to the soul, but to the whole human nature, and even to the body of man especially.

Ibid. No. 19. *opening itself in the very womb*. Pertinently could be here added—when the soul gets its life in the child; for so this opening would be more determined: and hereby would be intimated, that when the child cometh to be a living soul out of the first principle's properties of fire, the second principle of light also is opened; and this because of the incarnation of Christ, who dwelleth therein, and from that instant is ready to protect, to be united to, and to have the soul in his love, and with him where he is.

Ibid. No. 20. *whose strong persevering act they call, faith.* This is indeed true enough; yet so, that from this denomination of faith, even that also be not excluded which is but weak, and only to be compared, as the prophet doth, to a *bruised reed*, or to a *smoking flax*. For Behmen expressly calleth faith even that little also, which of this nature is in many at their departing this life; and whereof he saith, *that they hang, as it were, but on a thread* (of faith).

Ibid. he gives himself (that is, his Divine spirit, and spiritual body, and all the heavenly things and benefits accompanying both,) into the willing mind. All this is true also; but so that I think it should be a little limited, by an addition of some few words. For in this *beginning*, God gives not these things (especially the spiritual body) distinctly and manifestly, but implicitly and secretly, without the soul's knowledge or perception. But the soul is in this state, like unto Joseph's brethren, who knew not what a great gift of grace they had, when not only their money for the corn, but also their brother's silver cup, was laid into their sacks. See Behmen's explication in the Mysterium Magnum.

Page 315. Line 5. *in which fire in man they remain, even after they are forgiven; which forgiveness is the first justification or forgiveness.* All this is also true and plain enough to him that understandeth Behmen's ground; but unto others that know not what or how the forgiveness is, it cannot but be obscure; and there might be objected, that the Scripture says nothing of a *first* and *second justification*, etc. Wherefore, then, I think it might be made plainer, so that the meaning might appear distinctly to be this,—in the central fire the sins remain, not only so as to appear no more, if the soul goes forward directly and constantly; but also so as to appear, and to lay hold on the soul immediately again, if the same turns back. And therefore, with respect to them that go directly forward, this justification needs not to be called the *first*, because there is not following upon it such another as could be called the *second*. But with respect to such as fall back, and yet rise afterwards and return again, it may be called the *first*, because in them the same process is then repeated again a second time. But if we understand by the word first, nothing more than a beginning or *first* degree of justification, which henceforward increaseth more and more, there is no difficulty in the matter, nor do I see that any such objection against it can be made.

Page 315. No. 21. *Christ's dying in them.* This, I think, might either wholly be left out, or explained by adding this, or something the like or *Christ's dying* made in them their own. Because an ignorant one might easily misunderstand the meaning, and think the words of the Scripture to be a strong objection against it, where it is said, *Christ risen from the dead dieth no more.*

Ibid. *We are to fulfil all the law of righteousness by the Divine substance in us.* This also might easily be misapprehended, and wants therefore to be expressed a little plainer. For one might think the meaning thereof is, that the Lord Christ's fulfilling is defective and insufficient, if we do not complete it by our fulfilling the same with our works or sufferings. Whereas the meaning is no more than this—that it is defective in us, or unprofitable unto us, if we have not in us that Divine substance which hath all sufficiently fulfilled all the law. And that, by having the same in us, and by our being conformable thereto, our own great emptiness of the Divine righteousness is really filled. Wherefore, then, we are rightly said to fulfil it, though not we do it, but he in us; like as the apostle says, *I live, yet not I, but Christ liveth in me.*

Page 316. *Q. How do they distinguish regeneration-pardon of sins, justification, sanctification, purification, and redemption?* A. They are not so nice as to give a distinct definition of each of these names; but from their declaration of the whole redeeming work, it appears sufficiently that they conceive them to be but so many different denominations of one and the same principal thing, expressing only several respects and different circumstances thereof, all so connected, that none of them is superfluous, and none can be separated from the rest. That principal thing is this, according to the Gospel, whereof it is the whole sum and substance in short, (viz.) The sinner is saved in and by Jesus Christ, whom the Father hath sent, to bring him back, upon his narrow way, from under the powers of darkness, into his kingdom of light. Now herein, they will say, all these names are contained, and do declare this only truth, but so, that each of them hath its own peculiar relation, either unto this or unto that particular thereof. And so, *redemption* expresseth in general this whole work, but with a chief respect to the Saviour himself, through whom man is redeemed, and to that great price he paid for him. *Pardon of sins* represents the same redemption, but as in its beginning, or as to its first effect on the side of man. *Justification* the same again, but with a relation to the Father, by and before whom, he whose sins are pardoned, is justified as one that hath fulfilled all the law; and thus also owned to have now a free access unto himself, through him who is himself his justification in him. *Purification* declareth of this redeeming and justifying work, that though it be wrought out and completed by Jesus Christ at once, yet it is not so in man, who wants continually and gradually more and more to be redeemed from his daily sins, failings, and infirmities, as long as he is upon the way; and even this is nothing else but a gradual purification, which intimates also something of the condition of this way, viz., that it is narrow, full of crosses, trials, temptations, etc., as so many proper means by which this purification is effected. *Sanctification* represents that same again, but so as to express more especially, in opposition to man's former sinful state, what by this redemption, justification, and purification is effected in him, both as to himself, and as in the sight of God, viz., holiness, without which he cannot see the kingdom of light. And *regeneration* expresseth in general again this whole saving work, but so that it declareth as on the side of man, what it is in and to him; how that which the Saviour hath done for him cometh to be done also in him, and so also by what means it is made profitable unto him: intimating also, moreover, not only his having been degenerated, but also his being redeemed effectually, in such a process as is directly opposite to his first natural generation.

Page 317. No. 23. *He leads a new life from a new principle, as Christ did after his resurrection.* These last words, *as Christ did after his resurrection*, I find might better be left out, because they cannot be applicable, without a great limitation to this new life of man. And in the places quoted out of the Mysterium Magnum, xxxix. 8, 9.; and Election, x. 99, 100, I can see nothing to support such a construction. For though this is true, that in such a regenerated man Christ is really risen; and this also, that such a man leads a new life from a new principle, yet this new life cannot be compared to the life of Christ after his resurrection, but might rather be compared to his life in this world, before his death. Seeing that the soul of such a man is not yet, as his soul was, separated from the mortal body, and so not yet entered into that paradisical state which he entered into at his death and resurrection; and that this expression, *of leading a new life from a new principle*, implieth only a ruling over and keeping under sin in the flesh, in opposition to the old Adam's life, which he lived before his regeneration, when sin was predominant therein: in which sense we cannot say at all, that Christ led such a life after his resurrection. And though this new life of a regenerated man, considered as to itself only, and as abstracted from what it is still joined to, may be truly said to be in and with Christ, according to St. Paul's word. *Our conversation is in heaven*, so that, in some sense, it may be said to be comparable to the life of Christ; yet this sense belongeth not at all to this outward principle, and is not in this world, but in its own heaven: nay, this life is not yet manifest, but, according to the Scripture, *hid with Christ in God*, and therefore not yet such a life as Christ lived after his resurrection, who wholly lived in paradise, and was able to show forth the glory thereof unto others. And moreover, I cannot see that it would be a fit expression to say, Christ after his resurrection led a new life from a new principle: for one might presently reply, that this were as much as to say, He led, before his death, an old life, from another or old principle; whereas, all his life was from the same principle, and he was the new or second Adam, not only after his resurrection, but also before his death.

Page 317. No. 25. *all is from Christ working in us.* This is well enough, indeed; but only for to prevent a needless and insignificant objection there might be said,—all is from God the Father, and Christ, working in us through the Holy Spirit. For then the words of our Saviour, *No man cometh unto me unless the Father draw him* (from the which something, with some appearance, might be objected), cannot serve unto any for such an objection.

Page 319. line 12. *God hath chosen none but Christ in his members.* This, I think, is one, and perhaps the chief of those expressions, of which in the next following question it is said, *they seem to be less accurate than they should be.* And it is true, that such as take more notice of the literal construction in the Scripture words, than of the coherence of truth in the interior scripture sense, and of this or that peculiar aim or intent in such or such a place of the Scripture, may have a good reason to say so of this expression; because the Scripture doth not say, God hath chosen Christ in man, but man in Christ; which is, as to the grammatical construction, quite the contrary. But as the Scripture words express that rightly, which the apostle in that place intended to express, relating to what was done before the foundation of the world, in that general election spoken of above; so also Behmen's words express rightly and significantly that which he would have expressed, relating to that particular election of which our Saviour saith, *many are called, but few are chosen.* For in that former, man was chosen in Christ; and in this latter, the same sense is not indeed nullified, nor contradicted: but more significantly, and much more subserviently to Behmen's discourse and proper intent, instead of saying, Man is chosen in Christ, the apostle could have said, Christ is chosen in man; because he was to declare, that in this election nothing is regarded nor looked upon by God but Christ, and that all what is not Christ, and Christ's in man, is reprobated. If, then, out of the numberless number of men, none is chosen but he that hath Christ in him, and none chosen for any other reason but for this only, that he hath Christ in him, and that he is a living member of that head, which alone hath a right to the kingdom of heaven, may we not as well say, in one sense, Christ only is chosen in man, as we may say in another, Man is chosen is Christ only? Nay, if all whatever is in such a man, besides his being a living member of Christ, is to be reprobated, what then, can we think, is there left in man, which could be said to be chosen, but only Christ? Just such another sense, running exactly parallel with this, we may find in the words of our Saviour, saying, *None ascendeth up into heaven, but he that came down from heaven, even the Son of man which is in heaven.* In the which words, he attributes unto himself alone that which he makes all his living members partakers of; for they also ascend up with him by no other reason, but by this same, that they are his living members, and have in them, nay also are in him, that which came down from heaven. This he knew and affirmed, and yet, notwithstanding this, he speaketh so plainly in these words of himself only, excluding all what he is not himself. If we, then, can say soundly, truly, and exactly enough, upon our Saviour's own words, that none ascendeth up into heaven but Christ, why may we not say also in the same sense, that none is chosen by God (to ascend up into heaven) but Christ, even Christ in his living members?

Page 319. *Q. ult.* A fourth important reason could here be added, viz. this,—because it is formed by concurrence of his personal body, wherein he hath redeemed us. So that upon this particular account, we are not only spirit of his spirit, but also flesh of his flesh; and hear, therefore, justly his name, as children ought to bear the name of their Father.

Page 320. *they say, that this omnipresent body is the New Jerusalem etc.* Here, I think, the sense of Behmen could be represented more distinctly thus,—The universal body of Christ is that tabernacle of God with men, and that New Jerusalem spoken of in the Revelation; and that him also, but considered especially as formed in many thousands of heavenly human bodies, as so many living stones combined together, is that glorious temple prophesied of by Ezekiel, which shall be seen before the corruptibility puts wholly on incorruptibility. For though Behmen, in the places quoted out of the THREE PRINCIPLES, doth not himself make such a distinction, yet from a collation of other places of his, it appears sufficiently that this is his sense.

Page 321. *Q. 2. But if it be omnipresent it will then be God. A. No; because it hath only a circumferential,* etc. I had formerly used that expression of a central omnipresence, with relation to God, but not that other of a circumferential one. And though that former might seem to carry along with it this latter, which also would be well enough, and not hurtful at all, if but taken in a deeper sense than I see it is taken, when there is replied, *If it be only circumferentially everywhere, it is not omnipresent, because it is not centrally present:* for then it would evidence itself that this objection signifieth nothing, and that the one element is verily also centrally present in one sense, viz. in that which is required to its own kind of omnipresence, but not in in other, viz. not in that which is attributable unto God alone,—though, I say, that former expression of *centrally*, might seem to carry along with it this latter also of *circumferentially*, yet here it doth not so in this matter; because I had declared what I mean by centrally, and that I do not take this word as in opposition to a circumference, from which its centre is distinct as a small point standing in the midst thereof, and being nowhere present but in its own narrow central place; but that I take it as in opposition to an out-birth or superficies, of which this so-called centre is the internal ground or bottom as great as, nay greater also than the whole outbirth, or all the circumference (if we will call it so) is. From whence I further showed a great and even a twofold difference, between omnipresence, as attributed unto God alone, and omnipresence (though I wished we might here have another word) as attributable unto the *one element*. And all this was declared to my thinking (as I said also in the conclusion thereof) so, as to be not only intelligible enough, but even palpable as it were, and obvious unto common sense. Seeing then, now, that if I should explain this distinction, as in the next following question is desired, I could not do it without another prolixity, nor hope to be plainer than I was in that former declaration, I think, therefore, these expressions of *central* and *circumferential* might be wholly laid aside, and the question here proposed, *If the one element be omnipresent it will then be God;* might be answered thus: A. No; because there is the greatest difference between what we mean by the omnipresence of God, and the omnipresence of the one eternal element. For when we say God is omnipresent, we understand that he is everywhere without any kind of extension or dilatation of his being; and even so as to fulfil all things, to dwell in all, and both to give and uphold by his presence every exterior being, remaining, nevertheless, himself free from them all, and comprehended by none of them: all which is attributable unto his omnipresence alone. But when we say (for want of another expression) the one element is omnipresent, we mean but thus much, that in this outward world (whereof as on one part it is the ground) there is no place to be imagined of which we could not say, The one element is there, but in its own interior principle: for if the spiritual ground, root, or bottom were not there, the out-birth thereof could not be there neither. This answer, I think, might suffice: but if it were thought needful, it could be declared further, by representing, That though we can say in a good and deep sense, God was omnipresent from all eternity; yet it would be great nonsense to say, He was everywhere before the creation. Because, before the creation, as there was no time, so was there also no where nor there, nor any place, but himself only, who wants no place for his being, but is much deeper than any place, etc. That only with the outbirth, place and locality began to be; and that therefore this outbirth, being neither greater nor less, but just so great as place and locality is, cannot but be said to be omnipresent, that is, in every place; because there is no place without or beyond its own extent; when there is nevertheless God without or beyond it, who is not confined thereto, nor comprehended thereby, and wants no place at all, etc. That this outward world is not God, nor suspected of being made god-like, by saying of it in such a sense, that it is omnipresent to itself: which can well be said, because there is no place therein in which it is not manifest, more or less, according to its own four-elementary qualification, etc. That so also the spirit of the world is not God, and yet is omnipresent to the whole extent of all his region; for there is not the smallest point therein, whereof we could say, he is not there, etc. That heaven and all the heavens of heavens are not God, because the Scripture says of them, *they comprehend him not*; and yet they must be omnipresent unto him, because wherever he is, either within or without the world, he is in heaven: and we cannot say that he is in heaven only with a part of his being, and the other part is extended beyond all heavens; but we must say, he is whole in heaven and whole also beyond all heavens: so that the Scripture expression, *they comprehend him not*, doth not mean that he is extended without or beyond them, but that he is deeper or more inward than all the heavens, etc. That the same is to be said also of the one eternal element; and that this omnipresence thereof, now declared and limited, I hope sufficiently, cannot make it to be God, nor equal unto God, because it is not thereby exalted from or beyond its being a spiritual corporality, into that much deeper and only spiritual Being which is God, of whom, by whom, and to whom it is and hath that inferior holy being, which it is and hath, etc.

Page 327. *A. 4. life and strength from the death of the outward old man.* Seeing that the inward man, being quite of another nature, can have nothing from the outward; and this can only by his own death make him way, or open him a free place for to display his life and strength from his own internal principle, I think it might be said more properly *by* than *from* the death; if this *from* imports what I conceive it doth, wherein I may be mistaken.

Page 329. *A. 2. as a descent into its own hell.* Here I apprehend that the particle *as*, might well be left out; because this sensibility of the soul's own anguishing properties, is really a descent into its own hell.

Page 331. No. 3. *Upon this death*, etc. This particular (upon several considerations, of which an account can be given, if desired) I would rather express thus, or after any other manner like unto this,—Into this death the soul must give itself up, as quite forlorn; and through this death it must sink down into that ground wherein Christ dwelleth, and whereout he is to raise anew life in it.

Page 331. Line ult. *doubt-ariseth from the weakness of the fire of the spirit*. Though this may have a good and true sense, yet more directly and particularly I think might be said—from the division in the fire of the soul, which partly tends unto God, and partly cleaves to the spirit of the world. For so the true ground of this weakness would be expressed.

Page 333. In the answer to question *ult.* that which to me seems to be the chief particular, is omitted, viz.—that God's pardoning sins is inseparable from a real going out from sin, and leaving it behind, or, as it were, beneath, and an entering into such another region as whereinto sin cannot follow after us, but must be drowned in the blood of Christ.

Page 335. No. 3. *his former sins and guilt remain.* That they remain was said in the foregoing particular. No. 2; and more expressive would it be if here were said,—his former sins and guilt lay hold on him again, for then he returns back into their own region.

Page 337. *Q. ult. How then doth it attain rest?* This question might very well be answered more circumstantially after this or the like manner. A. By sinking down into that ground wherein light can be enkindled by Christ: for every standing still is a continuing in this miserable state, and every rising up is an increasing of the same; but sinking down is the only way for coming out from it.

Page 343. *Q. 1. What is that principle, and why do they call it, liberty?* A. It is (with respect to souls, which are but creatures,) that internal supernatural state of rest and peace, which Christ promised to them that would come to him, and take upon them his yoke, and follow after him. And they call it *liberty*, because it is free from, and superior to all those violent commotions that are and act in the inferior restless part of nature.

Page 343. *A. 3. united in one will, viz. the will of the soul and the will of God.* This explication of the words, *in one will*, referring them to an union of God's will with the will of the soul, cannot stand. For they mean, in this description of the tincture, no other wills, but the will of fire and the will of light, which two are to be united into one, so that the fire may have no more its own fiery will, that is, its own destroying and consuming nature, or natural inclination, according to its fiery properties, but may have them subdued to the light, to act in concurrence with it, etc. The union of the soul's will with the will of God, and their becoming one, is not here denied; but only said, what is meant by one will in this definition of the tincture.

Page 343. *Q. What do they mean by the virtue of fire, and the virtue of light?* A. They mean that wonderful efficacy which ariseth from the union of fire and light, which cannot be expected either from this or that alone; and which is chiefly an uniting and harmonising virtue, able and sufficient to restore into their due order and concordance, all the disharmonised properties of eternal nature in the soul, and so of temporal nature also, in all things.

Page 345. *Q. 2. Are there not several other lights besides the true one, and how shall we distinguish them from it?* A. If you ask with relation to others, how to distinguish the true light from the false ones, in other persons without you, that make a noise and show thereof, that you may not follow them, and be misled or deluded by any of them? they will tell you (1.) that as no man in this outward world followeth a light which only another seeth, or pretendeth to see, except he do thereby plainly own himself to be blind; so also, and even much more (according to our Saviour's plain doctrine) must it be in the inward world, and upon our way to salvation. (2.) Then they will ask you again, What rules or directions you can give to such a blind man in this world, how to distinguish the light of the sun from that of the moon, and these two from that of a burning candle; whether all your endeavours would not be in vain, because the light is an object of a seeing eye only, and where this is not, there a discerning eye cannot be? But, nevertheless, (3.) they will tell you also, that no man is so blind as not to have something of the true light, though never so little, shining in his own conscience; for Christ is the light *illuminating every man that cometh into this world:* which, therefore, if he will take heed unto, to follow it always, and never to run before it, and though he hear never so many pretenders to great and high things, to take nothing of them in, but what he sees agreeing and conformable to what this light plainly shows and directs him to, his walk will always be sure: and so doing, he shall never follow another light without him, but only that which shineth in himself, and is given him to be his leader.

But if you ask, how one may distinguish in himself the true light from the false ones; you must take this true light either as in its fulness, or as in a lesser degree. If you take it as in its fulness, they will answer, That it cannot be discerned but by him that hath really seen it so: and if any one hath seen it in its fulness, that he wants no direction from without how to discern it from a false light, or from a true lesser one; because it bears and carries along with it, in its own essentiality, such a mark or character as cannot be doubted of. Christ, according to his promise manifesting himself to a soul, wants no testimony, either from angels or men, to prove him to be the Sun of Righteousness: and such a soul needs not to see any other evidence but his own light, to distinguish him from a devil transformed into an angel of light; but with its own seeing eyes it shall see, according to his plain words, that *he is in the Father, and the Father is in him*. But if you take this true light in a certain inferior, and beginning or increasing degree, shining whilst the soul is still but upon the way to the full regeneration, or manifestation of Christ; they will give you several marks of discerning, whereof this one only may be sufficient for every one, viz. the true light hath always three inseparable concomitants, the *cross, love,* and *humility*. Every light that shows a way how to avoid, escape, or refuse the cross; how to favour selfishness, and to maintain the soul's life, according to its fiery properties, that its own essential cross may not be made known, etc.; every light that is not accompanied really with love, (according to the plain doctrine of St. John) light and love being not only of one and the same Second Principle, but also of one and the same first property thereof; and every light that leads not downwards into our own nothingness, and into that deep ground within ourselves, wherein the light was extinguished in Adam, and wherein only it can be kindled again, is absolutely false.

Page 345. A. *ult. from the collision of the first four,* etc. Instead of this, I would much rather say,—from the inkindling of the fire, which, by its flying up, displayeth, or, as it were, disperseth the soulish properties and essences, and makes them to stand in such a spiritual figure as is like a cross, etc.

Page 349. *Q. ult. How do they conceive the light to arise in the soul?* The answer to this question says, that *the light is water rarefied, made thin and clear;* and so places the water before the light, as a material cause before its product: when I cannot conceive it so, but must with Behmen say, that the light is prior. For, though in eternal nature, light and water are inseparable and co-eternal, yet I cannot but understand with him, that materiality cometh forth from spirituality, not *vice versa;* and that the light, as a pure spirituality, ariseth in the fifth form; but the water, as a spiritual materiality, in the seventh, etc. The conjunction of the eternal liberty with the restless part of nature, enkindles the fire; the separation of these two again, or the distinct exerting of each one's peculiar quality, is the breaking forth of the light. So that, according to Behmen, the light is not water rarified, but the free liberty sharpened by the harshness of nature. For which I refer to what was said thereof in the discourse on the seven forms of eternal nature. For as the light ariseth in eternal nature, so it doth, *mutatis tantum mutandis,* in the soul also. Water may be the air or aether condensed, and so it will be true that air or aether must be water raerfied; but air or aether is not yet light, but only that expansum which is made so thin and clear as that the light can shine through it. Wherefore, then, I would answer to this question thus. A. They conceive that when the sharp properties of the soulish nature reach the liberty, they break out in a clear and open flame; and thereby this liberty, which before was nothing to the soul, comes to be its something, stands in union with it, gives unto it its own meekness, and receives from the sharp fiery properties again that glance or lustre which disappeared in Adam's fall, and which it cannot have without the fire; like as the soulish fire cannot have a clear flame without this liberty. And as therefore now fire and light are in love and union, so must needs also all the properties of the fiery nature burn in love.

Page 353. *What are these inward senses of the new body?* I have indeed nothing against the answer to this question; but yet I think there might well and pertinently be mentioned therein, that they are the same which they were in the first Adam's paradisical body.

Page 356. Q. 1. *What is inward Divine hearing?* The place quoted out of the Prayer-Book, page 10, I hardly know by what words to make plainer. The meaning is in substance this—It is a power opened again, and restored to the fallen humanity, by free grace, in Jesus Christ; by which the human soul is enabled to approach confidently to the mercy-seat erected in its own ground, and there to hear God speaking in it, according to David's words, saying, *I will hear what the Lord will speak in me.* Which speaking is a real word, not only sounding according to the light world's condition, but also operating, effecting, and giving forth something of what it speaketh; which in substance is nothing else but his mercifulness bestowed on us in and through Jesus Christ. But this I can add further,— it bears a true analogy to the outward sense of hearing, and is a perception of something answering to a plain and express or articulate human speech, though not comparable to any kind of earthly languages; and the soul, though it may never have perceived the like before, needs no instruction, but understandeth what is said immediately, the very first time, without any doubt, plainer and clearer than ever it can understand anything spoken in this world.

As to the other two senses, viz. smelling and feeling, whereof the next following question, page 335, asketh, *whether they say anything?* I cannot but answer, that Behmen says indeed nothing thereof, (especially not of the former,) in particular; but it is nevertheless evident enough, that they bear also such an analogy to what in our outward life is called so, and that they are different powers of the new regenerated life, restored to the humanity in and by Jesus Christ.

Page 357. Line 1. *But inward motions and visitations are very dangerous, and the power of melancholy, etc.* All this is true enough; but for my part, as all this cannot make me to deny, that there are such communications between God and his children, even during this their outward life; so neither can all this make me to see, that these things are more dangerous than the temptations from the devil, flesh, and world, which every one is subject unto. For, like as on the one side, all what any other soul in reality and truth enjoys, of the like heavenly motions and visitations, cannot help me in the salvation of my own soul, if it remains without me; so also on the other, all what he falsely pretends to enjoy, or what he (in a delusion, or as it were, in a drunkenness from the astral spirit) believeth himself to enjoy, and to be directly from heaven, cannot hurt me. If I leave it without me, neither approving nor condemning it, till there is given me a clear, sufficient evidence.

Rules, for distinguishing false inspirations and enthusiasms from true ones, many others, I suppose, have prescribed, much better than ever I could do; and so, therefore, I beg to be excused, but will nevertheless, not to be wholly wanting, set down only this threefold one from my own practice, wherewith, for my part, I can be well contented. One thing I know is absolutely necessary, as the only great fundamental point or work, to be done in my own soul no less than in any other; viz., in short, the *slaying of the fiery soulish dragon*, and the *raising again that new life that is captivated under him*. All now what of inward motions points at this, or leads and directs thereto plainly, sensibly, and more or less effectually, cannot but be good and true. All what plainly, sensibly, and more or less effectually tends to the contrary, must of necessity be false. And all what hath not such a plainness and sensibility in and with it, under what shape soever it may appear, is not to be curiously searched into, and is of itself neither profitable nor hurtful; though it can be made to be both this and that, according to my own different behaviour about it.

Page 360. *Q. What is death to sin, and resurrection from it?* A. Death to sin is the soul's continual putting it off, going out from it, and leaving it behind; and its resurrection from sin is its continual entering into and laying hold on that opposite degree of a new life of righteousness, seeking the things that are above, which degree of life, every particular degree of dying is immediately followed by, and joined with.

Page 361. No. 8. *The pearl may be lost and regained, but with difficulty, when it hath disappeared.* This is true indeed, yet not so universally as it is here expressed, but only in its place, or kind and degree of disappearing. For there is also a total loss or disappearing, after which Behmen expressly saith it cannot be regained; viz. when it was once obtained, and is so lost as the epistle to the Hebrews declareth it. For then another sacrifice for sin would be required; whereas there neither is nor can be had any other but that which once was made in the Lord's death on the cross.

Page 363. After these twelve particulars, still another I think might pertinently be added, containing in substance—that all this order and method now propounded is not exactly and punctually to be applied universally to every individual person; but that everyone is led to the same end indeed, and through the same principal ways, yet not exactly in this order through all the little by-paths, but as the Spirit of God is pleased, and sees it most expedient for every one, according to his peculiar constitution.

Page 363. Q. ult. *What do they mean by union to Christ? and is the soul united to his personality or natural body, soul and spirit; or only to his Divinity and universal body?* First I observe, that I see not, why Christ's personality, as to the most outward part thereof, here in this place, where it is especially distinguished from his universal body, is called *natural*: for though it be natural indeed, yet it cannot by this denomination be distinguished from his universal body, which is natural also. And therefore, I think it would be better to say—to his personality in body, soul, etc. And then I answer to this question thus. A. By union to Christ they mean nothing else but what he meant himself, in his last sermon to his disciples, and in his simile of the vine and branches, which are and must be in union with the vine, if they shall be able to bear fruit. And as now his personality in body, soul, and spirit, cannot be separated from his divinity and universal body, so also none of these distinct things can be separated or excluded from his union to the soul, but all must be implied therein, though not all in a full equality of sense, because not all can be equally capable of this union; which will therefore differ so, as an union between a branch and tree differs from an union between a father and his children, and as both these kinds of union differ again from the union in a red hot iron, between iron and fire.

Page 365. Q. 1. *In what sense are they said to put on Christ's righteousness, who put on Christ, or Christ's universal body?* A. In the same sense in which we can rightly say, we put on the first Adam's unrighteousness, by putting on in our natural generation, his universal body whereinto he fell. For, in his first paradisical body he was righteous before God: now that body never sinned, nor put on any unrighteousness, but it disappeared only in his transgression. If then Christ hath brought, and formed it again into paradisical flesh and blood, and if he is in this body the righteousness before God, in opposition to the first Adam's unrighteousness; we, by putting on him, or his universal body, by concurrence and efficacy of his personal body, must needs put on not only righteousness, but also his righteousness; and cannot in this body be looked upon otherwise than as if we had never sinned, that, and all that which hath sinned, being put to death.

Page 365. No. 3. *They bid them be very temperate, etc.* The places here quoted say in substance plainly and shortly this—The soul is a kindled fire; kindled not in the light and love of God, as it was in its first creation, but in the astral spirit and love of this world, and the things that are good and pleasant therein, but especially of its own elementary body. This kindled fire now desireth food from that principle wherewith it is joined in love; and this food (be it taken and considered either as only spiritual, such as the soul feeds upon by false imagination or lust, or also corporeal, such as the outward body feeds upon) is no more paradisical, but earthly. And so therefore, even upon this only account, sin is not only very nearly related unto, but also quite inseparable from it. And though it is now not sin directly and absolutely, to eat and drink earthly meat and drink, which our mortal body wants for its subsistence; yet it is originated from sin, belongeth not to paradise, and must perish together with the mortal body; nay, it worketh also and causeth sin, if taken in superfluity, because the soul's kindled fire is more thereby enkindled in that kindling of its own, which is an enmity to God, and is thereby hindered also from pressing forward to a being new kindled in his light and love.

Page 366. No. 4. *They advise fasting, etc.* In the THREEFOLD LIFE, Chap. xvi. 31., where Behmen says something of fasting, I can find nothing but what is very plain, and conformable to what just now was said. He means by fasting nothing else but (besides a continual temperate sober life) sometimes an abstinence from all eating and drinking, yet without appointing certain days, times, and seasons for it, but leaving that to every one's discretion, according to his circumstances; and says, that as the earthly food fills the belly, and the superfluity thereof makes it thick and unable to work, so the earthly spirit fills and impregnates the soul, and makes it unfit for spiritual things; and that then the Spirit of God departs from such a soul, at least for that time, finding no open place to dwell and work therein.

Page 367. No. 7. *That prayers are to be made with respect to the eternal internal powers of the days, etc.* I find nowhere that Behmen says such a thing; but so the matter lieth,—In all the printed prayer-books of his nation, divers and peculiar morning and evening prayers are prescribed for every day, some of which are made with a respect to the seven days of the creation. Accordingly, then, Behmen, knowing the mystery thereof deeper than those common books, which mention only the creatures brought forth on such or such a day, wrote his prayers with a deeper respect to the eternal powers thereof; yet never said that the prayers were to be made, or must be made so by every one. As he himself had no necessity incumbent upon him for to do so, so he hath not laid it upon any other; but he that can and will, and understandeth what he doth, may do so freely.

Page 367. No. 7. *That prayers are to be made with respect to the eternal internal powers of the week, or seven spirits.* The more I look it over and consider, the less can I find of such a thing. No such expression may be found in the German original: and in those few prayers the author hath set down, he makes only sometimes an allusion or accommodation to those planets after which the day is called, and raiseth the mind above them into that which is their deeper ground; and this very sparingly too, not as if he had designed everywhere an equal exactness, but only so as this or that was obvious to his mind. So for instance, in the first prayer of this kind, on Monday noon, he says nothing at all in a peculiar or proper reference to this day and hour, but only a general contemplation of his state, both as to the creation, fall, and restoration thereof; which, as he saith also himself in the title, may be used whenever one finds himself in his devotion thus touched. In the second, for the same day and hour, he considereth (as the title says), the day's quality, and raiseth the mind into the inward moon, which is the heavenly substantiality. But in the words of the prayer itself, every one may see that there is nothing peculiarly expressed, which did or could belong unto this day more than unto every other. In the third, on Monday evening, which the title says is concerning a descent of the mind, like as the former was an ascent thereof, nothing more can be discerned but an allusion to the outward moon's changeableness, increase, and decrease, and this but obscurely too. The substance thereof is a contemplation of our misery, both spiritual and bodily, and an earnest groaning for deliverance; all which is not in a peculiar manner more fit and proper on a Monday noon, than on any other day and hour. On Tuesday, no footstep more of such an allusion or accommodation appears at all; for he presently begins to consider the ten commandments, without giving a reason for it. And though it might be said, that he chose this matter for this day, because of that communion or relation between the fiery Mars and this fiery law, yet it is as fit and proper, and as needful also, for any other day, as it is for this. And so, if he had not been prevented by death, he might easily have found matters, fit more or less for every day, or capable of such or such an accommodation, but not altogether appropriable unto one only, with exclusion of the rest.

Page 367. No. 8. Concerning the *Lord's prayer*, Behmen says that it expresses the eternal generation, the three principles, the fall of man, and his regeneration. What he observeth, according to his peculiar gift in the language of nature, as to every syllable, and sometimes as to single letters, cannot be expressed by a paraphrase. But the whole substance in general he hath set down himself in these or the like words,—Every true prayer is not only a desiring, longing, and asking, but also an obtaining, taking in, and possessing. In the first words of the Lord's prayer the soul's will raiseth itself and enters into God; in the seven petitions it declareth and asketh what it wants; and in the Amen it compriseth and taketh altogether, and dwelleth therein, or eateth thereof; and strengtheneth itself thereby.

Page 369. Concerning Behmen's *sense of the ten commandments*. His interpretation, as to the *first* goes not so directly nor principally upon what is common, viz. a plurality of gods, a making and having idols, a loving and applying his heart to this or that creature, etc., though all these things be included as particular lesser branches; but the chief thing is, that he says, a full relying or depending upon and cleaving unto God only, an acting and working of the soul's will with and under God only, a ruling with him over all creatures, without appropriating unto itself anything, a casting the soul's desire into his love only, and in a word, a leaving and going out from selfhood in the very deepest sense, ground, and bottom, is in this commandment required: and even selfhood is that principal other god, which man set up in his first transgression, and which is still the maker of all the other gods or idols, numberless in variety, which every one sets up according to the peculiar constitution of his corrupted nature.

Of the *second* Behmen hath nothing, because it is not in the Lutheran church. Dr. Luther hath left it out, saying that it is but an explication of the first words.

Of the *third* (which in the Lutheran church is the second), he saith that it reacheth much further and deeper than generally is apprehended; and that the name of God is taken in vain not only in cursing and swearing, and where the name *God* is directly and expressly named vainly, but also in a more general sense in all our speech, and every word thereof, though there is no express mention made of God, if the same be not according to simplicity and truth, but formed more or less by the serpent's seed or ens in us. And his ground hereof is shortly this: Adam had his speaking faculty out of eternal nature, wherein all the names or powers of God are manifest, moving and working; and his giving names unto everything was an imitation of their being spoken or brought forth into being and substance by God. Though now this be lost in the fall, as to man's paradisical speech, yet something answering thereto, according to this third principle, lieth still in the human speech, and in all the languages. And whereas now before the fall, all the words were formed in conformity to and by concurrence, nay, predominancy of the holy names and powers of God in the light world, they are now formed more or less in conformity and by concurrence, nay, many times in a full predominion of the serpent's ens. Whereby then all manner of false abominable images are figured, and so the powers of eternal nature and the names of God are abused after the same manner as the devils do, though it be in another principle, wherein there is a mixture of good and evil. Concerning all which, Behmen hath a large, plain, and well intelligible discourse in the Mysterium Magnum, Chap. xxii.

In the *fourth* (which Dr. Luther hath only in these words—*Thou shall hallow the Sabbath*, leaving out all the rest), Behmen leaves indeed the seventh day of the week, as an outward symbol in its place, and owneth that the hallowing thereof is here commanded; but he insists also chiefly upon that internal Sabbath which Adam was set into in paradise, and which we are to come into again in Jesus Christ, viz. a ceasing from our own will and work, and resting in the love of God, that he may work in us. For if this be the true inward ground of that outward, the law, being spiritual, understands certainly the inward in the first place, and the outward in the second, as in subordination to that. And so also,

In the *fifth* he owneth indeed that we are commanded to honour our outward natural parents; but he maketh also a deeper application thereof, saying that God is our Father, and his outspoken word in eternal nature our mother, in whose womb we are conceived and nourished, and into which we are to return again from the strange mother of this world. *If I am your Father* (as the Lord saith by the prophet), *where is my honour given me by you?* etc.

Here now Behmen's prayers upon the ten commandments are at an end; but what he would have said in substance upon some or the rest, may easily be gathered from several other places, viz.

In the *sixth* he would not only have reflected upon killing our neighbour with the hand, or with the tongue, which is commonly understood therein; but also chiefly upon that spiritual killing, stifling and keeping under (in the Scripture called crucifying) Christ and his spirit in ourselves.

In the *seventh* he would certainly have spoken of that marriage-band the first Adam was tied with to the heavenly virgin, the wife of his youth, against which we all do still deal treacherously, more or less.

In the *eighth* he would not only have said that all manner of deceit, used in the world, to cheat our neighbour of his goods, is forbidden; but also chiefly all appropriating unto himself anything either of spiritual gifts, or of worldly possessions. For though even these latter may be had by a right and lawful title, yet the soul directly commits a robbery with respect to God, if it doth not attribute all unto him alone, and owns not deeply and really that all is his, etc.

As to the *ninth* and *tenth*, I find nothing but what would be conformable to what is ordinarily understood therein.

Page 369. Q. 3. The particular sentiments concerning those three or four requisites may be these following, viz. They say,

(1.) That the *narrow way*, as to its inside, is the *inward process of regeneration;* and as to its outside, a course or *manner of life contrary to that of the wicked world*.

(2.) That as to the former, or inside, it is called the narrow way, chiefly because every one shall meet upon it with manifold temptations, and as it were, many narrow holes, through which the will-spirit of the soul must creep, and everywhere be stripped of something which his natural will is not willing to be deprived of.

(3.) That these are those manifold particular deaths mentioned above, every one of which is followed immediately by such a degree of life, as is always answering proportionably to the foregoing degree of death.

(4.) That it is called also the narrow way upon this account especially, because they that walk upon it shall find a great opposition from the anger of God, kindled in the whole fallen humanity, which if they fight against it with his love, will many times press the soul so down, as if whole mountains laid upon it, and bring it into such a straitness, that as to all its sensibility in that state, the whole world is too narrow for the same.

(5.) That as to the latter, or outside, it is also justly called the narrow way, because of the great oppositions and difficulties from the world and our own corrupt flesh, which both inviting and drawing the soul one way, and laying innumerable impediments in the other, cannot but make the same to be as it were a small foot-path, in comparison to that broader way that leads into perdition.

(6.) That both in this and that, viz. both inwardly and outwardly, the cross, and the yoke of Christ is to be taken up and carried after him.

(7.) That by so doing the wickedness of the mixed world must needs be avoided; for he that bears the cross of Christ can certainly not *walk in the counsel of the ungodly, nor stand in the way of sinners, nor sit in the seat of the scornful.*

(8.) That this wickedness is in general expressed by the apostle's *lust of the eye, lust of the flesh and pride of life:* and that which each of them is more particularly, every one will be told in his own conscience, if he be but willing to hear the voice thereof.

(9.) That all this, *thus practised*, is nothing else in the very ground and bottom, but a continual SELF-RESIGNATION; for it is always a leaving behind its own will, and giving up itself into the will of God.   And

(10.) That all this in its order and progress, is also nothing else but the WAY FROM DARKNESS TO TRUE ILLUMINATION; for the soul, say they, is not capable of true illumination as long as it is filled and darkened by all manner of impurities in its *own will*; like as a water is not capable of receiving the sun's light and representing its image, as long as it is thick and muddy: but when the soul, putting off all what is of that nature and kind, resigns itself to God, his light is ready to illuminate the soul, and the soul, like as a purified water, is able to receive that illumination.

Page 368. *Q. What are God's calls to repentance?* A. Here is not asked, I suppose, with respect to anything that is without man, as for instance, the word preached, public and private calamities, pestilence, earthquake, and the like, which all may well be called so; but only with respect to what is done by God in man himself: and thereupon they will answer, That these calls are the secret motions and dictates of every one's conscience; for this doth tell him that he is to *depart from evil, and do good.* In the conscience God meets the sinner, and none living can say, that he never heard such a call in his life.

Page 370. *Q. What do they mean by this shape?* A. They mean that spiritual figure or image which is opposite to the soul's former divine image, and which, the beastly properties and qualities it is infected withal, must needs represent to the intellectual eye, considering them and finding a conformity between the soul and such or such a brutish creature. For as every thing hath its outward form or figure according to the various compositions of its parts and dimensions, so it must have also, answering thereunto, its inward shape or figure, arising from the various combinations of its spiritual properties. And if the soul had once the image of God, when all its properties were harmonised, it must now needs have that of a beast, when they all stand in disharmony, and exert such operations as are conformable to those of a beast, either tame and harmless, or wild and hurtful.

Page 375. *Q. 2. This seems to be a strange doctrine; pray what do they mean by it?* A. It is certain that neither this doctrine, nor this manner of expression is strange to the mystics: with whom in their declaration of this state, nothing is more frequent, than to speak of a *transcending surpassing, leaving behind or beneath, being up above and transported beyond all creatures, holy angels, and even themselves also;* and an *entering, sinking down, melting away in an uncreated abyss,* etc. And they do not mean thereby, that ever a soul puts off its nature and creature, and hath no more other creatures standing besides itself in the same degree of being; but only that it cometh into such a state of holy silence, as wherein no creature is perceived, and the soul hath no other object but what is uncreated. And that they mean nothing else but this, you may clearly perceive from these words of the famous mystic, M. Eckhard, saying, Oriebatur in me Diapsalma, hoc est silentium sacrum omnium rerum exteriorum, et quiescebant etiam omnia interiora met, cum suavissimo cordis coelestia quaerentis jubilo, cum oblivione omnium rerum, cum plenaria abnegatione mei ipsius, ita ut sola, tui, O Deus remaneret notitia.... Tunc rapiebar in obliviounem mei ipsius, in Te.... a Spiritu S. ducebar in abyssum, etc.

Page 375. *A.* 3. No. 1. So as this first position is here expressed, it cannot stand conformable to Behmen's mind; but I think it might well be thus expressed,—that God's essence of love and meekness (or the divine virtue—*virtue* belonging more properly to the second, and power more properly to the first principle,—the fire of love, the holy light's virtue, the heavenly ens or substance) was before the fall, in and to the soul a spiritual oil and water, whereby its fire was refreshed, fed, and strengthened, and its shining light kept and preserved.

Page 377. *Q. 1. Why is a medium necessary; cannot God forgive sins without it?* A. If by forgiveness of sins, is understood only such a pardoning, as whereby an earthly prince may clear or pardon a malefactor, God not only can, but hath also actually done so with our first parents. But now the soul wanted not only such a forgiveness, but a new birth; and this new birth could not be brought forth in him, without a foregoing undoing, drowning, or washing away the sin in the old man, which, without a medium, cannot be done. And as then there is a necessity for a mediator, so also for a medium, as an instrument of that mediator. This medium is blood and water: *without bloodshedding, is no remission of sins;* and the Mediator came not *with blood only, but with water and blood.* In the baptism, though the Mediator's blood is not excluded, yet the water chiefly (as the beginning, ground, or if it might be said so, the first rudiments of blood,) is considered; because this is, or makes also the beginning, or lays in a sense, the ground of that new birth. And the reason why it must be water, not any other thing, depends upon the inward ground of man's paradisical body, which he had lost and wanted. If then, there was, and is the same analogy between the inward and outward water, which is between the paradisical and elementary body of man, the reason is plain, why elementary water must be used in the outward baptism. Moreover, man is to lay hold by his will, faith, and imagination on God, through the Mediator, and, consequently, also on that medium which the Mediator useth; for it is plain, that he cannot lay hold on God, nor come to God immediately. His will, faith, imagination, are, by his fall, departed at such a distance from God, and so corrupted, that they cannot, especially in this beginning of regeneration, lay hold directly and immediately on God's pure spiritual being; like as also God in his holiness cannot lay hold on, nor be united immediately to the soul in this state: a medium, therefore, fit for both, is necessarily required, in which they both may meet. And this medium can be no other but on God's side the inward water of eternal life, because this is the same light's materiality, wherein God had created man; and on the outward man's or body's side, the earthly or elementary water, because man's body is also become earthly or elementary, etc.

Page 377. *Q. 4. Why was elementary water made use of as an outward medium?* The chief reason hereof was given just now; and that which here is desired to be made plainer (from the Two TESTAMENTS, iv. 9.) can have no obscurity, if man's falling away from that principle of meekness wherein God dwelleth, and which was shut unto man, as to his spirit, soul and body, is but considered. For if there is in baptism such an infusing of the water of eternal life into the soul, the soul hath thereby, as it were, a little gate reopened unto her, which, in its progress, may be made wider and wider, and through which it may go out from its own natural fiery properties into the light, love, and meekness of God; for which end, also, this gate is opened in baptism. In the other place (THREE PRINCIPLES, xxiii, 28.) this same is also said, though with other and deeper words, and more circumstantially, to show that as the beginning of the life is, so must also the order in the regeneration be, etc.

Page 379. *trembling.* I remember that but lately was asked, why trembling was necessary to repentance? Now in the places quoted, viz. pages 20, 21, I find in the High Dutch no such word as could be rightly expressed by *trembling*; but that word signifieth properly and directly a *violent breaking.* And why this is necessary he gives a plain reason, which may be illustrated by the simile of a hard stone, not able to receive any impression until first the hardness thereof be broken, or of a lump of ice, which must first become melted into water, etc.

Page 383. *Q.2. How did John's baptism differ from our Saviour's?* A. (1.) John baptised only with a spirit of anointing to repentance, in order to the forgiveness of sins; but Christ with fire and the Holy Ghost. (2.) John's baptism was to prepare the way for the baptism of the spirit of Christ. And, therefore, also (3.) John's baptism had not yet those glorious effects, which our Savour's baptism had after his resurrection, because, in John's baptism, the Holy Ghost, in a certain true sense was not yet; the blood of atonement was not yet shed, and the anointing tincture not yet prepared. But, nevertheless, John's baptism belonged, not to the types of the Old Testament, but stood, as it were in the midst, between those types of the old and the real substance of the New Testament, partaking something both of this and that, and being, therefore, different also both from this and that.

Page 383. Q. 3. *Why was John of the lineage of the priests?* A. Because, as the types were now to be brought out of their shadow into the substance, or out of the law covenant into the covenant of grace; so also that agent, which in this beginning was made use of, must first have been endued with the spirit of the law-covenant, as the priests were especially, that handled the circumcision and bloody sacrifices; that so with this spirit a beginning, and from this a progress might be made into the covenant of grace, and in this progress the former might be overtaken and fulfilled by the latter: which could not have been so, if John had not been of the lineage of the priests; but the order, coherence, and harmony of the whole, would have been broken in this part.

Page 383. Q. 4. *What was Christ's baptism by John? or why was Christ himself baptised?* A. Christ, as a public person and representative of the whole human race, and as one that was to go through the whole process of regeneration, must needs have made also this beginning thereof with being baptised by John: *for thus* (saith he himself), *it becometh us to fulfill all righteousness.*

Ibid. Q. ult. *What is the true order of administering baptism?* Here, I think, the practice of the primitive Christians enquired for in the church history, might give the best answer. In the place quoted from the THREE PRINCIPLES, xxiii. 30, Behmen represents it very simply, and without any ceremonies, minding only the sprinkling of the water in the name or the holy Trinity, as the only needful and principal transaction.

Page 385. Q. I, *Why doth baptism precede the Eucharist, or Lord's Supper?* A. Because the beginning or generation of the new life (which is made in the baptism) must needs precede the feeding or nourishing the same, which is done in the Lord's Supper.

Ibid. Q. 4. *How, or in what sense, were these types of it?* A. As in the Lord's Supper, an union is made between man and what man feeds upon; so, also, was such an union (but only in its kind and degree, according to the nature of that dispensation of the covenant) made in the paschal lamb, in the sacrifices, and add also in the shew bread. But as these things had not in them the real heavenly substance manifested, but were only like as shadows thereof, pointing thereat, directing thereto, and showing what there was to be expected, believed, and hoped for; so, also, they could not fill nor satisfy the partakers thereof with that heavenly substance itself, whose types they were; but, nevertheless, were they such medium, as by the right use of which men approached in faith unto God, and God drew near in mercy unto men. So, therefore, not only (1.) a bare likeness which there was between these shadows of the Old, and the real substance of the New Testament, but also (2.) that benefit which the church of God received by them; and, more especially, (3.) that ordinance, whereby they were so instituted with a reference to the substance to be manifested in Christ, made them to be called holy things and types thereof.

Ibid. Q. 5. *How were they brought into substance by Christ?* A. Successively and gradually in his incarnation and whole process of suffering and death, resurrection, and ascension. For the real substance of the New Testament, in opposition to the shadows of the Old, is nothing else but the perfect image of God, the heavenly humanity, the holy tincture of light and love, the bread and water of life, etc. : all which in and to the first Adam was disappeared and withdrawn into its own principle or heaven. When, therefore, in the second Adam all this came down from heaven again, and when he had fulfilled all righteousness, and was gone through death and hell, and had led captivity captive and communicated these things or heavenly gifts to believers, both dead and living, then the types thereof must needs have ended; for there was no more need of a feeding on things, that only represented as in a picture what was to come, but a taking in (as to the inward man), and being really fed and clothed with and by the heavenly things themselves, that were typified before.

Page 387. *Q.* 1. *Is Christ's particular soul given to believers?* A. Yes, in such a sense as the spiritual being of a soul can bear; not importing that the individual soul of his human person is out of him transported into the persons of believers, and makes them to be Christ, but only that between his soul and the souls of believers such an union is made, as there was before between the first Adam's soul and the souls of all his children, which makes him to be the root and them the branches. For if his light, inseparable from his soul, enkindles and tinctures their fiery souls, they owe indeed the original of their soulish being, as to itself, to the first

Adam, their natural father; but the original of their renewed soulish image, or the reunion of soul and spirit, they owe to the second Adam, their spiritual father, or to his soul and spirit.

Page 387. *Q. 2. Is his particular glorified body given to believers, or only his universal spiritual body?* A. Both together in conjunction; for neither of them can be given without the other. And though the former chiefly may be considered as the giver, and the latter as the gift, yet it is not so in this case, as our reason tells us it is with other gifts and givers; as from the nature of the thing is plain, and by that simile of the sun's particular glorious light-body standing in a circumscribed place, and the sun's universal unformed body extended throughout all this principle, may be illustrated.

Ibid. Q. 8. If this were true, would not his particular body be omnipresent as well as his universal? A. No, no more than the sun's particular body is required to be omnipresent, as well as the universal body thereof; when, nevertheless, without a concurrence of its particular body, nothing could be formed in or of its universal body in all the world. For, if there be given a power and virtue of Christ's spiritual formed body, this power and virtue is certainly in and of his particular body, and proceeds from the same and stirs his universal body; and, without this proceeding from his particular body, or flesh and blood (which he saith is meat and drink indeed), no paradisical bodies and mystical members of him could be generated in and of his universal body.

Page 387. *Q. 5. What it the true meaning of these words of Christ, Take, eat, this is my flesh?* A. The words of Christ must, according to St. Paul's doctrine, by a spiritual man be spiritually discerned, for they are, as the Lord himself said, *spirit and life*; and, therefore, they must be distinguished, but not separated from that outward act which he then performed, when he spoke these words. He took in his hands the bread and broke it, and gave it unto them: this was an outward visible act in this elementary world, wherein they saw with their firmamental eyes nothing more than what everyone of us would have seen, if we had been then present, viz. that he had natural bread in his hands, not flesh; and so, also, not blood in the cup, but wine. But now, if he had given them no more but what they thus saw and took, he would have fed only their earthly stomach, and natural life in this world, which would have profited them nothing to the kingdom of heaven. His words, therefore, cannot be principally referred unto that elementary bread which they saw and took; for truly that bread was not his body, which was to be broken for them to the remission of sins, though it was according to St. Paul's explication, a communion of, or had communion with his body. He gave them, therefore, at the same time, together with this bread and wine, as to the inward heavenly world, his real flesh and blood, to be taken by their inward man, and unto this his words, being spirit and life, must be principally referred; and, though they are not to be separated from the outward elements, yet unto each must be attributed only that which it can be capable of: and always in this act the two principles, viz. the outward and inward, must be joined and minded together, so, that the outward visible act be referred unto this world, and unto the outward man, but the words of Christ, which he saith are *spirit and life*, unto the inward; and the connection between them be understood in that communion which the bread hath with his body, and the wine with his blood, consisting not only in that assimilation which is in the breaking and pouring out, attributed both unto this and that, but also, and even chiefly, in the interior quickening and strengthening tincture, which is the highest, as to this outward principle, in bread and wine. So far therefore the Calvinists say well enough, that bread and wine are a *symbol* or *sign*, for indeed they are so; but when they add *only a sign*, and a sign of an *absent* or *far distant thing*, this is false. The place quoted from Behmen's THREEFOLD LIFE, which is said to be not rightly translated, is in substance this,—The outward mouth of Christ's disciples took and gave to the belly that bread which Christ gave unto them; but that word, when Christ said, *Eat, this is my body, was*, or came forth from Christ's eternal or inward body, and was surrounded with heavenly flesh and blood: this the soul took, and put it on as a new body. Thus there were together at once in the hand of Christ two kingdoms, or two principles, viz. a heavenly one, and an earthly one; but you must know, that the heavenly cannot be comprehended and carried about from place to place by the earthly, etc. Now, from hence it can be plain enough, that all what was said hereof above is conformable unto this, and that the true meaning of these words of Christ, *Take, eat, this is my body*, cannot be apprehended, found out, or understood, in one principle only, nor by a man that liveth and is immersed only in this outward principle: further, that from hence all the disputes arise, and needs must arise, between the divided parties of Christendom: and lastly, that the true meaning of these words of Christ (when in each principle that is understood which is therein, and belongeth thereto, and when they both are taken jointly, and unto each is attributed what it can be capable of) will be this,—(1.) With reference to the inward world, Take and eat with your inward man, will, faith, desire, etc.—this (not this visible bread, for this is not in the inward world, but this) which I give you here with my word spoken unto your inward man, is my body. And (2.) With reference to the outward principle, Take and eat with your outward hands and mouth—this bread, which you see I break and give unto your outward man, is the communion of my body. So hath St. Paul explained and paraphrased it; nothing therefore can be excepted against it. But nevertheless, without any contradicting him, the words may be left also in their own construction, and can be rightly understood (if the principles are but rightly discerned) so as they sound, viz. *Take, eat, this* (bread, not as to its perishable substance, but as to its pure, inward ground of the heavenly tincture which is therein) *is my* (universal) *body.*

Page 387 *A. ult. No, but it is under them, etc.* Although this answer is sufficient, if it be rightly understood, so that I have nothing to say against it, yet it may easily also be misunderstood, seeing that the words in and *under* are a little ambiguous, and bring therefore along with them something of an obscurity. For as there is indeed a true sense wherein we can say, This invisible body is not in but *under* the outward elements, so there is another also, no less true, wherein we can say again, it is in the outward elements, viz. so as paradise is in this world, and it is not under, but above them. It is then indeed in the outward elements, yet not as in their sphere of being, or as belonging to their kind; but it is under them, or hid as it were behind their veil.

Page 390. *Q.* 1. *Is Christ's body only participated of in the use of bread and wine?* A. No: for Christ hath not confined himself to this use of bread and wine, but to the faith of man: which faith, if it be always living and operating, may always eat and drink of Christ's flesh and blood, whensoever it turneth itself thereunto, and maketh it to be its object; which it can do as well without, as in this use of bread and wine.

Ibid. *Q.* 2. *Why then is that outward medium made use of?* A. (1.) Because of reasons like unto those, that in the baptism required an outward elementary medium: for man also was become outward and elementary, and having disordered himself in all the principles, he wanted a restoration in all of them; and in order thereunto, each principle in him was to be fed by its own likeness. (2.) Because of the communion of saints in this outward principle: for there is in the use of this bread and wine a holy band of union tied, even outwardly also between the members of Christ, participating of this common food; which union cannot be made in this outward principle without an outward medium.

Page 390. *Q.* 3. *To what end is the tincture of the elements conveyed to the soul?* A. Although the tincture of the elements is not properly or directly conveyed to the soul, but to its own likeness in man, yet it may be said also to be conveyed to the soul, as the chief agent in man; and though this tincture is made use of but as a medium, so that no ultimate end may be fixed upon it, yet it may be said also, that it is done to this end, that the soul might have again, in due order and purity, what she had, as to every principle, before the fall.

Ibid. Q. 4. To these two particulars, this third one might reasonably be added,—to complete the image of God in man, which doth not consist in soul and spirit only, but in spirit, soul, and body.

Ibid. Q. 5. *Why hath the soul need of food?* A. Because it is not a self-existent nor independent being. This makes even the holy angels also to have need of something for their food: and from the intrinsical essentiality of the two eternal principles, the reason is yet more plain and evident. The first cannot consist without being continually fed, softened, and sustained by the second, and so thereby kept in union with it. But if that first be rent asunder in the creature from the second, it can be nothing else but a perpetual hunger and dryness, never filled nor satiated, etc. And for such a state the soul was not, nay, could not have been created.

Ibid. Q. 6. *Why hath the soul need of a body?* A. The soul, considered as after and with respect to the fall, must of necessity, and according to plain reason, have need of what she lost in the fall, which was her glorious body: and considered absolutely in its creation, and as to its own soulish being, it had need of a body also, because it was to be a full image of God, as manifested in and through eternal nature, wherein there are not only the fiery, but also the light's properties, and the heavenly corporality as well as pure spirituality.

Page 392. After the two particulars here mentioned, I think could well be added,—(3.) because it hath continual need of keeping faithfully to that fraternal band or association, and therefore also of renewing frequently that covenant or confederation, which in this sacrament is made between the members of Christ, in opposition to Satan, the world, and their sinful flesh.

Ibid. Q. 3. No. 2. That same which here is said of *a man in a state of renewal*, Behmen saith expressly of the beastial man, or earthly flesh and blood, wherein dwelleth no good thing, and which is so, as to itself, in every one living, more or less. But notwithstanding Behmen's words, it is very rightly said, as by an explanation of Behmen, *The man, in a state of renewal, receiveth, as to his outward earthly flesh, the judgment of God, for the breaking and killing the lusts of the gross body:* and there is no difficulty in the matter at all. Every property in man receiveth what it is capable of. The lusts of the gross body are condemned by God, and his judgment and curse lieth upon them, as well when a man eats this bread and wine, as when he abstaineth from the same: this every one will grant. Now then, when a man receiveth this mysterious bread and wine, the testament or covenant of grace, and all what on God's side belongeth thereto, or dependeth thereupon, or is necessarily consequential to it, is stirred in or upon that man, and so therefore that judgment also upon the lustful outward flesh. If, then, the receiver of this bread and wine is in a state of renewal, and able to receive Christ's body, he receiveth the same as to his inward man, but he receiveth also, as to his outward, that judgment of his sinful flesh, nay, thereby his inward man is strengthened to judge down, to break, and kill himself his own lusts in the flesh. But if he be not in a state of renewal, he receiveth indeed that judgment under the elements, yet he cannot be sensible thereof, but rather a greater enlivening and strengthening of his own lusts is made, and Satan gets a wider gate of entrance into him. So, therefore, only the man that is in a *state of renewal* can receive it thus profitably, for a destruction of his outward sinful, and an increase of his inward holy man.

Page 392. *Q. penult. Why may not infants receive this sacrament?* A. Because they cannot try themselves, nor discern the Lord's body; nor have they a will, faith, desire, or hunger after it, nor any sensibility of their wanting it, but only that ground wherein these things may be raised in their time. But especially also, because they know yet nothing of that brotherly band of union and communion of saints, which everyone freely, willingly, with a due understanding thereof, and earnest purpose suitable to it, is to enter into; which is the chief end of this outward sacrament, and which of infants cannot be required.

Ibid. Q. ult. What was the true apostolical way of celebrating the Lord's supper? A. The records of antiquity may give the best account hereof. What Behmen says thereof is very short, and making no reflection upon any ceremonies, but mentioning only that which is declared by St. Paul.

Page 394. *Q. 4. May it not be called a commemorative or representative sacrifice?* A. That there is in this supper not only a commemoration, but also a representation of the Lord's sacrifice, is true and plain, both from the words of our Saviour, and from his breaking the bread. But upon what account it should be called such a sacrifice, I cannot see. Christ is not offered up to God in this supper, but only a remembrance is made of his having been offered up once on the cross, and he rather offers and presents himself with all his benefits onto man, which man, if yielding himself up to obedience, is himself a living sacrifice, and ought to be so not in this celebrating the Lord's supper only, but also in all his life.

Page 394. *How do we eat of the sacrifice of Christ, by eating of the Lord's supper?* A. Not only by a thankful commemoration of his sacrifice, made once for us, and without us, on the cross, but also and even chiefly, by taking into ourselves and strengthening our inward life with the effectual power thereof, which is to crucify and kill the lusts and love of this world, and of ourselves in our mortal bodies and astral mind; and so to be made ourselves also, in different respects, a living sacrifice, both as to every communicant in particular, and the whole fraternity in general.

Ibid. Q. ult. What do they mean by the inward word? A. The living of itself, and therefore also quickening, enlivening, comforting, raising, and upholding Spirit, power, and virtue, which is contained in, and so hid under the outward word, that not every one, and no man always according to his own will, can be sensible thereof, when he looks upon the outward letter killing, and killing only, if it be separated from that Spirit. Which inward hidden word is in such a manner different from the outward letter, as for instance an almond kernel is from the almond shell, or as the pure sweet honey from that wax frame wherein it is contained.

Page 396. *A.* 3. These differences between the calls of the inward word are obscure, and have something of confusion in them; and I, not knowing from what places they are taken and expressed so, can say but this thereof in general, viz. That all men are called, and the differences of these calls are rather on the side of them that are called, than of the Word or Spirit calling them: for every one hears these calls only according to his state, or progress made in his way, or also disposition for an entering into the way. In some the Word is unformed indeed, and in them very little or no disposition at all to obey their call, that it might be formed; in others, it is in a beginning of formation, more or less, but not yet fixed; and in others again it is really born, and hath made its abode in them, etc.

Page 396. *Q.* 4. *How shall we discern the speaking and calls of the true Word in us from those of the Father; or how may we discern the true word from the false?* A. The speaking and calls of the Father are always (viz. in the beginning of the actual conversion of sinners) preceding these of the Son, and, according to his fiery nature, and the dispensation of the law, they are dreadful, and accompanied with terror and trembling, more or less, according to the sinner's state and complexion: when contrariwise the following ones of the Son are healing, comforting, refreshing, according to the nature of light and love, and the Son's dispensation of the gospel. But as to a discerning of the true Word from the false, the chief if not the only thing requisite and sufficient, (as I am for my part apt to think) in all cases, is in short, a deep, sincere, and attentive *minding of our own selfishness*, with an impartial examination whether the same, by such or such a word, be set forward or *turned backward*; for this cannot but be true and really beneficial, when that other must needs be false and hurtful. But if this setting forward or turning backward by no examination be discernable, then also no regard is to be had to such calls, words, or speakings, no obedience is to be paid unto them, and neither hurt nor benefit is to be expected or feared from them.

Page 398. *A.* 2. *No; none but such are true members.* Seeing that here is spoken only of the invisible church, or of them (as it was explained, page 396, A. *ult.*,) that are in Christ, I cannot understand, why here is said, that *none but such are true members*, whereby it is plainly granted that they who are not in Christ are false or dead members, whereas they are no members at all of the Church (which can have no dead members), but only of the outward mixed congregation.

Page 399. *Q.* 1. *What do they mean by Antichrist?* A. That mystery of iniquity (common unto all the divided parties of Christendom, and exerting itself in the one of them more, and in the other less, according to their different circumstances) which professeth indeed the name of Christ, but liveth and acteth contrary to the spirit, will, and pattern of Christ; not suffering itself to be taught, led, and guided by him, but setting up itself, and suppressing all the rest, according to its own will, for its own selfish ends, and upon the principles of its own corrupt reason, all tending to greatness, splendour, and love of this world.

Ibid. Q. 3. *Which do they account the chief error with the Antichristian papacy?* A. The departure from the leading of the Spirit of Christ, according to the pattern of his love and humility, and the exalting itself into a worldly state, and then also persecuting those that resist or witness against it, cannot but be the chief, because it is the ground and deep foundation of all the rest. But if this question means the chief error in opinions or articles of confession, I could not say, in particular, which is the chief; but think that for several of them something might be produced, which could make it the chief in this or that particular respect.

Ibid. Q. 4. *In what consisteth the Antichristianism of the Reformation?* A. Though this be answered already, at least in part, in the above question, *What do they mean by Antichrist*, yet this may be said here in particular, That it consisteth in not leaving to the Spirit of Christ his right and due, viz. his inward dominion over the souls of men; but presuming to be themselves their leaders and teachers, and directing them, not to Christ *in everyone's own ground*, but to their particular parties, and the outward rites, ordinances, words, doctrines, and ceremonies thereof, all crying, Lo here is Christ! And then again in hating, persecuting, and killing one another, at least with the tongue, if not with an outward sword.

Page 400. *A.* 1. *soon after the time of the apostles.* Seeing that the preceding particular of a false church in the true one is universal, and extends to the whole course of time, from the beginning of the generation of men, this particular also might be represented more universally, and its beginning be placed in the time of Cain, rather than after that of the apostles. And this even the more, because in the beginning of this answer was said, *They give an account of the state of the church, from the beginning to the end of the world.*

Page 400. No. 5. *The golden candlesticks were withdrawn, etc.* Behmen's meaning in these expressions, is in plain words this.—The glorious light of the gospel, and the extraordinary gifts of the holy Spirit of God, which the Lamb of God, after he had satisfied the Father's fiery anger and justice, and broken in the humanity the seven seals of the book of life, had bestowed on the church, were, when the church would walk no more in that light, taken away and sealed up again, or hid to the church under the same seven seals of the Father's wrath: wherefore then, instead thereof, the seven vials of his anger and indignation were poured out from his throne, etc.

Ibid. No. 8. *not wholly free from wickedness, strife, and contention, etc.* In that state of the church which Behmen calleth Zion, no such thing will be; nor hath he anywhere declared his mind after such a manner, but said only that Zion will not be so universal, as that there shall be left no wicked man more upon earth. If strife and contention should still be in that state, what prerogative could it have above the beginning or infant state of the apostolical churches? And, moreover, many places of the Scripture speak expressly and directly to the contrary.

Page 401. *Q. Do they admit of a supreme pastor or pope?* A. They admit of none now in being; and as to the future, I can say nothing positively. The words of Behmen alleged from the FORTY QUESTIONS, ANSWER xxxix, make not plainly enough for this purpose; but rather, if they are compared to some other of his places and expressions, it is plain that he understands them of Christ, the only head of the church, and only true shepherd and bishop of souls.

Page 402. *Q. 3. Will not their errors and superstitions be imputed to them as sinful by God?* A. They will be burnt up in the last fire, as straw and stubble; and so they shall suffer loss of these things, which were, if not directly sins and sinful, yet at least so many effects and products of sin, and not able to abide the fire.

Ibid Q. 4. *What is an honest, simple, Christian to do amidst variety of sects and contentions?* A. He is to meddle with no contentions, but to keep his heart peaceable in himself, and in love with all men, of what persuasion soever they may be; and to mind nothing but the inward work of the

Spirit of God upon his soul, in all his outward performances, as knowing that nothing can avail him nor make him acceptable unto God, but his own being made a new creature in Jesus Christ.

Page 404. *Q. 2. Pray what do they mean by these two last assertions?* A. They do not mean that the civil magistrate is the head of the church, that is of them that are in Christ, but only of the outward congregation, as the same is in this world, wherein the magistrate is ordained, authorised, and commissioned by God to have an inspection over, and care for the welfare of his subjects. And that the priests have no such outward power, commission, and authority given unto them by God, or Jesus Christ, but that their power and authority is only spiritual. Wherefore then, with respect to the outward congregation, they are not rulers nor governors, but rather servants of the same, as to the outward functions; when, nevertheless, with respect to the spiritual kingdom of Christ, they are not servants, but are or ought to be fathers or elders, excelling their flock in age (of the inward new man), and in experience of things belonging to the kingdom of heaven. And this makes them to be worthy of double honour, which is nowhere applicable unto any servant.

Page 403. *Q. Do they say that a lay-man may administer the sacraments, and perform the other parts of the ministerial function?* A. In Christ is no distinction between a priest and lay-man, but all that are anointed with his Spirit are priests: all, therefore, by virtue of this anointing may, without any doubt or question, administer the sacraments, and perform all the other parts of the ministerial function; that is, they are in themselves, by the Spirit of Christ, qualified for it sufficiently. But, on the other hand, seeing that in the outward congregation there is such a distinction, and that God is a God of order, no layman may attempt to do such a thing, except in cases of necessity where no priest may be had.

Page 405. *Q. Is not confession to a priest, and absolution by him, although he hath only ordinary gifts, of great use?* A. To such as have only an ordinary understanding of things belonging to the kingdom of Christ, it may be of great edification; but as an universal rule for all it cannot be set up.

Page 410. *Q. 2. What do they say of tithes?* A. No more but that Abraham's giving tithes unto Melchisedec, denotes in the inward mystery, or is a figure of the full restoration of man, or of the completing in him the image of God again. Man is to give the tenth property of the human properties of his soulish fire unto Christ; and Christ giveth thereinto his blessing, his love-fire, light's tincture, and heavenly substantiality (as Melchisedec, the type of Christ, gave with his blessing bread and wine), by which conjunction of these two, the image of God in man is completed. If it should be asked, What is meant by the tenth property of the human properties of the soulish fire? I must confess that I cannot sufficiently penetrate Behmen's sense; but think, nevertheless, that it may be enough to understand in simplicity the whole fiery soul, without dividing the same between Christ and the spirit of this world. For as, in the tenth number, there is a fullness of numeration (which is so also in, and hath even its original from, the ten forms or eternal properties of fire), and a falling back into the first; so the whole soul must first fall back into its ground, and be first given up wholly (which it cannot, if it be not at the end of its own numeration in selfishness), before it can receive this blessing, and be reunited to the heavenly substantiality in Christ.

Page 416. *Q.* 1. *What do they particularly deliver concerning the Revelation of St. John?* A. Besides the several particulars of the whore, beast, dragon, etc. mentioned above, they say,

(1.) That the time was not yet, wherein the mysteries or this book could be unfolded and plainly understood; but that it draweth nigh, and that this gift will be a key to them.

(2.) That, therefore, they who have endeavoured to explain that book, are not to be insulted nor contemned, though they mistook frequently.

(3.) That the mysteries contained therein are to be understood, not only with respect to the whole body of the church, both as pure and as apostatised from her purity, but also with respect to every individual person that is a member of either this or that.

(4.) That all the numbers seven, occurring therein so frequently, and applied now unto good, holy, and heavenly, and then also unto evil, impure, and hellish things, have their certain respect and relation to the seven properties of eternal nature, considered either as in their union and harmony in the light world, or as disharmonised in and by the creatures of this and of the dark world.

(5.) That in the representation of Christ, standing in the midst of seven golden candlesticks, and holding seven stars in his right hand, etc., not only the humanity, but also the Deity, or the eternal Word is expressed, as having conquered the fiery anger, and keeping it in his power.

(6.) That the seven churches in Asia, and their angels or bishops, are typical of so many periods of the church, from the beginning of Christianity to the end of the world.

(7.) That the book of life, sealed with seven seals, denoteth that human paradisical life, which in the first Adam disappeared, when he disordered its seven harmonised properties, which thereby came to be so many seals, not to be broken but by the Lamb, etc.

(8.) That the vials of wrath are first poured out in the courts of kings and princes, and in their councils.

(9.) That the seven thunders, or rather their voices, which John was prohibited to write down, came from the fiery first principle, which man is not to know, nor to inquire into, but to rest in the meekness, light, and love of the Lamb.

(10.) That the eminent vision of the woman clothed with the son, having the moon under her feet, and being in travail with a male child, and the dragon casting after her a flood etc., is not only a figure of the whole church, fulfilled in a measure always, and still to be fulfilled eminently in the time approaching, but also a circumstantial figure of the whole work of regeneration in every particular soul, attaining unto its accomplishment during this temporal life.

(11.) That the figure of the strong angel's coming down from heaven with a great chain and key of the abyss, and binding the dragon, was not fulfilled in the time of Constantine, nor ever since, but belongeth to the time of *Zion*, or of *the Lily*.

(12.) That the new Jerusalem coming down from heaven (as also the mystical temple of Ezekiel) is to be referred to a state of the church upon earth, or in this third principle before the end of time. etc.

Page 416. *Q. 2. What do they say concerning death?* This question is particularly answered afterwards, page 422. and this only may be added,—that death is a shutting up or suffocating of the tincture, and that the most terrible thing therein is the dissolution of the four elements, which is a breaking off of the third principle from the first: and because now this third principle was so nearly consubstantiated with man, had captivated him, and taken possession of his will, this breaking off cannot but be dreadful to him, and accompanied with pains, more or less, according to the inward and outward condition of his soul and body.

Ibid. Q. 4. *What do they say concerning the resurrection, and the day of judgment?* A. Concerning the resurrection is spoken afterwards, page 430, but this might be added more particularly.—that the dead shall hear the voice or call of God from within, viz. in the depth of their own souls, whether they be in happiness in the second, or in misery in the first principle. And that every particular receptacle, viz. that of the earth, water, air, etc., when the universal mysterium is moved, must give forth again all that it hath taken in of man. Concerning the day of Judgment something also is said, page 430, and this might be added,—that in a manner contrary to that, or going as it were backward to that order, in which the world was created, its dissolution shall be. That the *fire of nature* (not an elementary fire, which would not consume earth and stones) shall kindle itself. That in this kindling the separation of good and evil in all things is to be done, everything entering into its own principle; and that this strictly is the last day, time being then no more.

Ibid. *Q. 5. Do they tell us what will be the state of things after the day of judgment?* A. As to this, I think, they say nothing but what in general may be expressed, as commonly is done, by an eternal happiness in the vision and fruition of God, and an endless misery in the separation from his light and love.

Page 418. No. 2. This particular would be more plain, if the other part of the reason were added, thus,—which (wrath of nature) they are all subject and liable unto, at least as to their outward man.

Ibid. No. 8. *saints war not as Christians, but as heathen.* These words are universally, without limitation or exception, true. But if this limitation here mentioned be added, viz. *when they war unlawfully and seek self*, this position is inconsistent with No. 4. And the matter is plain. If any war unlawfully, and seek self, they war not as saints; this is self evident. But if the saints (as in this instance Abraham was) war lawfully, and seek no self, they war not indeed as those heathens, but also not as saints; for all this lawfulness is only in and belongeth merely to this outward principle, wherein there is a mixture of good and evil, of right and unright, and whereof even the saints also are children, that is, natural men or heathens, as to their outward man. This therefore (not their inward sanctified ground) is the property which wars in them; and the only difference between the wars of these heathens and heathens, so vastly different from each other, (the former being merely heathens and nothing else, and the latter heathens only as to their outward man, but saints within.) consisteth herein, that the merely heathens seek self, war for ambition and covetousness, raise up themselves their heathenish property, and manage their war in their own will, all which is unlawful. But in such a case (as Abraham's was) of the saints warring, they war not for such ends, nor from their own drift; but God makes use in his anger and Justice of the heathenish property of the saints, and thereby opposes them that are mere heathens, as he did here with Abraham. And this, therefore, makes it so far lawful, as that it can be tolerated in this outward principle; but, nevertheless, into the holy light-world this heathenish property cannot enter, neither in Abraham, nor in any other saint, for it is not holy: which by the figure of Melchisedec, and what he did to Abraham, is represented plainly enough. And if it now was so with Abraham, David, and other warlike saints, under the Father's fiery dispensation in the Old Testament, it will certainly be much more strict with Christians, under the Son's meek dispensation of love, in the New. etc.

Page 420. No. 9. I see not how this *spiritual subtlety* from the *Mysterium Magnum*, lviii. 24, etc., can be referred to this place; for it hath a quite spiritual sense, not relating at all to outward possessions in this world, but to the wonders of outward nature, showing how they may be taken along with us through death, and brought into the kingdom of Christ, in the holy light-world.

Ibid. No. 10. If governors are verily in the inward process of regeneration, as Joseph was, they cannot but mind, how God carries on his work in them, after a spiritual manner, in the spirit of love and tenderness, and for their good: and, in conformity thereunto, they also cannot but manage all things about their subjects in a creaturely manner, in the same spirit, and to the same end. But if they are not, no wonder that they do not govern so as Joseph did, but so as we see they generally do.

Page 422. No. 7. *near and far off are all one.* The meaning of this expression is plain and simple. If there were in the light and love of God, a distinction between *near* and *far off*, God were not everywhere in the light or angelical world equally. They that are therein, are not nearer to him when they are in the kingdom of Christ, nor further from him when they are in that of Michael. *Near* and *far off* are things belonging to this outward principle, like as also time, which if dissolved, must be dissolved also: when, nevertheless, even in this principle, also something the like may be observed in our mind, spirit, thoughts, etc., with respect to which, it is not further to the West Indies than to Westminster; our thoughts being able to be as swiftly in the one place as in the other. John Engelbrecht, in his *Vision of Heaven and Hell,* saith, I remember, that which might be accounted as a thousand miles from him, he could see and discern as plainly and distinctly as that which was next to him. So that, indeed, not all manner of distance is utterly excluded from the creatures in the light-world; but that, nevertheless, all near and all far off from God, have lost in that world all their distinction, etc.

Page 426. No. 13, *bad wishes or curses hurt them.* Here, I think, this caution might be added,—that it is not fit for the children of God, nor lawful, to curse or wish bad wishes to damned souls: because they thus sow their seed into hell, and will certainly reap the fruits thereof, if a revocation is not made by repentance.

Page 426. No. 14. To the first part of this position might be added,—chiefly if this be done at their departure from this body; which is also expressly added by Behmen. For afterwards indeed, though it be not denied as utterly impossible, yet it is not a thing so easily done. And in the latter part of this position, Behmen's sense is not expressed, which is this,—The soulish spirit of a living saint may go along with his departing brother, to assist him in his way through darkness and fire; but when he is in the light, he can help him no more to have a greater glorification, but that spirit returneth unto its own soul: and the glorification of his brother is not from the assistance, prayers, or help of any other, but only from and according to his own essence, will, and works.

Ibid. No. 17. This *raising and disturbing* cannot be extended universally to all the departed blessed souls. But those that have put on their new body must be excepted: none living can raise nor disturb them, but they can appear of themselves if they will, and find it agreeable to the will of God.

Page 426. No. 18. The sense of this assertion is plain and easy: and the meaning of the words of Behmen is not this, that we are in the deceased blessed souls, as a soul is in a body, or one vessel in another; nor that we are one individual substance with them, and have their own personal knowledge and senses. But that we, if renewed with them by one and the same spirit of Christ, and to one and the same light-world, are able to see in that one light, into the blessed souls, as into our own members; and to understand, by virtue of that one spirit, which is in them and in us, what, where, and how they are, etc. As in this world we see not all by one individual eye, hear not by one and the same ear, and feel not in one and the same personal body; and yet we see, hear, and feel by one and the same light, air, and living faculty of feeling, which is in all, and which enables us to understand what by others also may be seen, heard, and felt: so is it in the light-world also, after its kind and manner. As it is, therefore, rightly said, We are all in one land of the living, so it is also rightly, We see all of one spirit, to wit, that of Christ, become man in all of us.

Page 428. No. 21. *Abraham's bosom is the Christian church, etc.* Seeing that this definition of Abraham's bosom might be so understood, as if thereby were meant the Christian church militant upon earth, which, though in a sense true enough, is yet not so used in the Scripture, nor by Behmen, there might only be added some or other word, declaring that it is the Christian church as in the second principle of light.

Page 430. No. 23. *The perfectly regenerate have their new body and soul, but in different principles, etc.* Behmen saith no such thing: what the English translation says, I cannot tell, nor can I see what sense there could be in these words. He saith expressly, Betwixt those souls that have not yet put on their new body, and those that have put it on, is still a gulph indeed, but not a principle; for they are both in one principle. If, then, different souls, and in so different states, are nevertheless in one principle, how can one and the same individual person have his soul in one principle, and his body in another, different from that? And again, Behmen doth not say, They have their body in paradise, and they have their souls upon the cross; but *they shall have it so*, or *they shall be brought into paradise again, etc.* But this is Behmen's sense, and the plain construction of his discourse is this, viz. Those souls that in this life have put on the body of Christ, must, nevertheless, still wait for the resurrection of their paradisical body: for, though they are indeed in paradise, or in the paradisical world, yet they are not as yet in paradise so, as they were at first (in Adam) created and introduced into paradise; this third principle being not yet turned into paradise, and the paradisical joy being not yet manifest in them, as to its completed fullness, because their good and holy works were all done or wrought by them in this world, and in their inward and outward body, which works, therefore, cannot be enjoyed by them before the resurrection of their body, and their being introduced again into paradise, as manifested in this restored third principle. And upon this ground he declareth, That as this doth not make two paradises, but only two degrees or different manifestations of paradise, so, also, not two bodies of the saints, but only two degrees or manifestations of their paradisical body; and that, from hence it is plain that they bear indeed Christ's body in God, in that state wherein they are now with Christ; and that, nevertheless, they still expect their first Adamical holy body with its wonders, which they shall put on with a paradisical qualification. (And now he adds,) *For the purpose of God must stand. He created the first body into paradise, to remain therein for ever; it shall, therefore, be brought thereinto again, and the soul upon the cross of the ternary in the mouth of God, from whence it came, etc.* Here is no separation of soul and body to be thought upon; but, as in the first creation, the whole man was formed and spoken or breathed forth by God into paradise, so in the full restoration it shall be done again. Soul and body are now indeed in God and in paradise; and the soul especially is upon (not in, nor under the cross, as it was in this life time, but upon) the cross, in the majesty, surrounded with light; but, with respect to the future state, it is still as it were in his mouth, or power of breathing it forth into its lost primeval state, and by that mouth of God it is not yet breathed forth, or introduced into paradise as restored and manifested in this third principle: which also cannot be done before the resurrection of the body, and the separation of good and evil in this mixed world."

With the omission of a few immaterial paragraphs, such are Freher's corrections and completions of the Rev. Mr. Waple's synopsis of the scope and contents of Behmen's philosophy, undertaken at his own request, and for his own satisfaction. Which, however, was not the only instance wherein a similar service was rendered to him; for amongst Freher's MSS., we find one entitled, "Three Conferences between a German Theosopher, and an English Divine," consisting of a series of queries upon points of recondite truth, put forth by the latter, and answered at large by the former, who were the parties here in question.

And now, after the preceding extracts (without reference to other of Freher's works), it is for the reader to consider, as before stated, how far Lee, the learned, the accomplished and gifted Lee, whom Professor Ockley, in a letter to Dr. Haywood, published in the first edition of Lee's 'Dissertation on Esdras,' and dated Swavosey, March 16th, 1710, designates "the greatest writer of the age, *by far*." was justified, in his 'Poem,' (after apostrophising Behmen as the "fountain of science, art and mystery", before whom, "all past sages veil and disappear" and "alone by eminence the *Divine*") in describing Freher as a philosopher, the 'second to Behmen.' up to his day. [POSTSCRIPT.—It is but proper to state that since the above was in the press, the writer has found a slip, in the handwriting of Leuchter, attached to one of Freher's books, which runs thus: "The author of these writings was Mr. Dionysius Andreas Freher, from Norimberg; they were written (in London) in the years 1717, 1718, and 1720," (he being then 68–71 years of age.) What is inserted on p. 206 and 258, is however perfectly consistent herewith, on many accounts. For either one or other of these worthies, GICHTEL and FREHER, was meant by Lee; who were intimate with each other, and about the same age and theosophic genius, the former being born in 1738 [1638? —Ed], the latter in 1740 [1640? —Ed], though not commencing authorship till he had long passed his fiftieth year.]

The first reflection which naturally suggests itself, after a careful perusal of the above 'Observations,' is this: What a noble popular compendium of theology, and classic text-book of Christian doctrine, would Mr. Waple's work have formed, with the above corrections and alterations introduced into it! As also, would doubtless immediately follow, a hope that the MSS. in question—indicative, as the nature and profundity of the subjects therein treated of attest, of no mean attainments on the part of the author—may have been preserved, as an honourable contribution by him to the establishment of Christian truth and doctrine, and to the facilitation of the attainment of theosophical knowledge, for the benefit of posterity. The writer of these lines regrets, however, to state, that a considerable doubt may be entertained of their being now in existence, inasmuch as, after some research, it has been impossible to obtain any tidings respecting them. In the preface to 'Waple's Sermons' 3 vols., 8vo.

which were published after his decease, there is inserted a brief memorial of the author, wherein the following passages occur, which may perchance lead to some further light being thrown upon the subject:—

"As for the author [of these Sermons] of whom some account might be here expected, as he was careful that his life should be indeed hidden from the world; and as certain private memoirs of his own life written by himself (wherewith he acquainted an intimate friend in confidence some years before his death,) were *probably* destroyed by him together with *some other valuable papers*, when he began to apprehend the approach of his dissolution, *lest it might happen that some or other might make a bad use of them*, since they are not now to be found after the strictest search made for them; the reader must be contented (without having the veil drawn from that which was hid with Christ in God) with that most authentic testimony which he hath left of himself in his last will and testament, wherein is to be seen the true picture of his mind." In another place is mentioned, that "he gave a very large and curious collection of books, which at great expense he had been for several years amassing, to the library of Sion College, in this city." In another it is observed concerning him, that "his great reservedness may indeed be esteemed by some a fault; and I deny not, (continues the editor,) but by it we have lost some *excellent productions* of his, of *various kinds*. But he was a person who had so studied human nature, and was so well acquainted with the springs thereof, that he found but too great reason for his general diffidence, both of himself and of the *rest of mankind*."

From these passages it would appear that his papers were destroyed, and amongst them the MSS. in question; nevertheless, may we not venture to hope that the results of so much study and labour, as they undoubtedly were, which had been corrected with so much pains and exactness, as we have seen, and which were in themselves of such intrinsic value and excellence, conducing to the best interests of mankind, in the diffusion of Divine light and truth, and the promotion of practical piety—that, by the providence of God, they have been preserved, and will yet be brought to light, in due time.

It was proposed, p. 328, to have closed the extracts from Freher, in this POSTCRIPT, with the above 'Observations upon Mr. Waples' writings,' as being from their nature, a suitable termination to them. Upon further consideration, however, it had been more complete,—as affording a particular insight into the highest science, and showing how it does and must, when true, naturally issue in simple practical piety of the gospel form and mode and spirit, (according to the unvarying experience of all the sons of wisdom, from the conclusions of 'the Preacher,' down to those of Mr. Law's 'Way to Divine Knowledge,')—to have presented in this place, Freher's Treatise of 'Microcosmos,' or the theosophical and evangelical science of MAN; being a compendious enlargement of a German publication, which is thus entitled: "Eine kurtze Erollnung und Anweisung der Dryen Principien und Welten Im Menschen, In unterschiedlichen Figuren vorgestellet: Wie und wo eigentlich ihre Centra im innern Menschen stehen; gleich sie der Autor selbst im Göttlichen Schauen in sich gefunden, und gegenuertig in sich empfindet, schmeclet und fuhlet. Samteiner Beschreibung der dreyerley Menschen, nach art des in ihme herrschenden Principii oder Geistes. Worinnen sich ein ied erals in einem Spiegel besehen kan, unter welchem Regiment er in seiner Lebens-Gestalt stehe und lebe. Nebst einer Anweisung, Was der Streit Michaels und des Drachen, auch was das wahre Beten im Geist und Wahrheit sey: Abgemablet und vorgestellet, Durch Johan Georg Gräbern von Ringehausen, und Johan Georg Gichteln von Regensburg; Im Jahr Christi 1696. Auf vieler Berlangen aufs neue dem Druckubergeben im Jahr 1736." But, as the insertion of the treatise would have extended this publication to a much greater and perhaps inconvenient length, it may suffice simply to refer to the work, as worthy of perusal in this place, and to express a hope that it may be published for delivery herewith.

Selection Thirteen.

[Freher's 'Confession', from the Commentary on the First of the "Three Tables"]

[Freher's work is prefaced by a long section by Walton discussing the work itself and related issues. —Ed.]

Mr. Law, in his writings (alluding to the abuse that is made of spiritual science by *strivingless prayerless, ideal* transcendentalists), speaks upon the folly of attempting to understand divine mysteries (which only mean the manifestations of the divine nature in the soul), before the proper time. This he does in the "Spirit of Prayer," but more emphatically in the "Way to Divine Knowledge," and lastly in the third dialogue of the "Spirit of Love." In reference to this *practical point*, and by way of relief to our narrative, we here insert the following 'Confession' made by the theosophical *savant*, Freher, who, occasionally (1715,) frequenting a society (a revival of the early Philadelphian Society, see Roach), which met together for the plausible purpose of spiritual edification and conversation upon the mysteries of Behmen, in whose theory and language they were well versed, commonly there held his peace. Being reproached for his general taciturnity, as "hiding his talents under a bushel," and told that it was his duty to edify the church by his high wisdom and understanding, and to make converts to the truth, he in reply, promised to give his reasons for the conduct he had pursued, which are contained in this confession. The opportunity which he most judiciously avails himself of for so doing, is at that stage of his theosophical discourse, upon the First of his "THREEE TABLES," where, treating "of man in his primeval state," he is shown his original relations to the abyssal Deity, and consequently the steps that he must take in the regeneration to regain his native place. He has brought the demonstration to that point which is designated *fire*, in strict and proper spiritual language, and so termed by Mr. Law, p. 75, supra; which means that particular *state* in the spiral, introcircumvolutions of the life of nature, through which the soul has to travel, in its journey of regeneration or purification; in other words, the gate of the full birth of the spirit of love the further and more sublimated degrees or interior stages of which, described by one who intellectually had had experience of the same in himself; namely Behmen, are justly and philosophically designated, *Tincture, Majesty, Ternary,* and lastly, "in the deepest depth, the ineffable Holy Name," JEHOVAH; (though not all *living* souls are philosophers, or have their senses exercised to understand the terms of philosophy.)—The following quotation, then, is Freher's 'Confession,' which we urgently recommend for perusal in this place, for its practical value, and for the suggestions it offers to the *wise in heart.* Though writing all his voluminous, and indeed invaluable (in their way) interpretations, justifications and demonstrations of Behmen, as the original truths of God, at the earnest request and instigation of others, he, Freher, though thus purposely performing a duty to society, and to the praise and glory of God, yet finds, that the application of his thoughts and mind to the subject, and to the labour of writing, detrimental to that *robust* and *lively* growth in grace, purity and perfection, which is and should be *the sole end of all knowledge,* by withdrawing the efforts of his body, spirit, soul, from devotion. For though many things may keep the soul alive in God, prayer—*Bramwell-like* prayer is the most powerful stimulant and nourishment, or means to educe the divine life in the soul. In the proper Christ-like freedom and purity of development.—We most heartily recommend this long quotation to the meditation of the reader and to the notice of the candidate, as the substance of it must be made to preface, and to close *all* that shall be ever set forth in *any* book or books, in recommendation of the study of theosophical verities. We would only add one remark, if needful after what we have given, p. 527, concerning the two ways of learning goodness and virtue, which is this, that we are justified in recommending the study of Behmen, Law, &c., theoretically, to those who are called to education in divine knowledge, until they apprehend their ground; for it is by such apprehension and knowledge that they can become *true, divine workmen* themselves, as to their own souls, and with regard to the world at large. Without further observation, then, we present the extract :—

"Having now done with the *Fire*, in the first circumvolution of our spiral line, on the fore side of the figure of man, looking *into* eternity; I should, according to my first intent and promise, go farther on to the second, third, and fourth, where *Tincture, Majesty,* and *Ternary,* where their different characters, and lastly in the deepest depth, the ineffable name JEHOVAH, do appear. But I must needs declare, that I cannot go farther; for, being weary within and without, I must here stop, and apply from henceforth my mind wholly to another more necessary business, which will be of much greater importance to my own soul.—Accordingly, I here part with the prosecution of my first intent, and ask pardon for having inconsiderately promised something which, because of some deeper emergent occasion, I cannot perform; observing daily more and more, that *an inward progress in the only necessary work, is hindered and retarded in my own soul, by applying so continually all my faculties to write with pen and ink.* Yet will I not part with it so hastily, as not to lay down first, more explicitly, & solid substantial ground and reason for my doing so, even such a one as cannot but be acknowledged good and firm, and standing upon a solid bottom, both with respect to *all of us in general*, and also with respect to *myself in particular.*

With respect to all of us in general it is undeniably true, that we *know already much more than we need to know*, of things requisite and necessary to *that end, which all our knowledge is to lead us to;* and that we are also convinced in ourselves of the truth thereof. For we do all know and own, that the *Fire* (and the fundamental doctrine of *conformity to Jesus Christ*, so eminently implied therein,) is the *only gate* through which we can be let in deeper; and before or without which none can see, much less possess and enjoy, what is behind or within that veil. And that it is that *great point*, wherein all our duties from this side, and all our happiness from the other side, do meet and concentre themselves; and which, as long as *not attained* and passed through, must needs hinder and retard the attainment of all really great and solid matters, in every soul—seeing that on this side of this great point, there is nothing really great, solid and weighty. If we then strive in *sincerity, earnestness,* and *constancy,* to enter through this gate, and to reach this great *central point*, we shall find, every one in himself, according to the measure and degree, what *Tincture* is, what *Majesty* is, &c.; whereas without so finding it in ourselves, no angel from heaven can make us understand it from without. Why then should words be multiplied any further, about such things as are not relating at all to *what we shall do*, but only to what we may expect in mercy, when we have done, or rather *in doing* that which we know we are to do. And

With respect to myself in particular, I must needs declare openly, that all that I could say or write further concerning *Tincture, Majesty*, etc., would be said and written only as on *this side* at that *great gate* and *point*. But pray, what can be said thereof on this side? To what end, intent, and purpose, can any thing be said thereof; and what benefit could be expected either to myself or to any other, from such sayings and writings? Should not I swerve about in empty notions, and fill my own brain as well as the brain of others with *shadows*, having no life, reality and substance? How can I declare to any other what I have not seen myself, but only heard and read thereof? If I did say, I have seen these things, and know them in the ground of my own soul, I should be an impudent liar before God and men. If I did say that I have read in J. B., and have heard of these things (or the *Light of Majesty* especially,) both here and beyond sea, and never without perplexity and amazement, I should say the truth. And if I did say, I can repeat the words or at least the substance thereof, written or spoken by others, I should say the truth likewise. But if I did undertake to bring forth words of my own concerning the Tincture, Majesty, &c., though they were never so true, pertinent and consistent with the ground of my friend J. B., I might justly be called presumptuous. And though I might not be called so by others, yet mine own conscience would tell me that I am so, and that I intend to set up a fine shew, and to make myself a name and reputation &c., but no manner of benefit could arise from it, neither to myself nor to any other; but hurt rather, and detriment might be expected both on my side, and on the side of them that might think my words are what they are not.—But from this my *plain declaration*, and from the instance of my breaking off, whereby I declare both to myself and others, That there is the highest necessity for us to do what we know we ought to do, but none at all to speculate, and search curiously after things not to be found out in any reality, but only as in a shadow, before we have done what our own heart tells us we are obliged to do; from this declaration and instance, I say, more benefit may reasonably be expected.

True it is, that I have formerly written something of these matters also, though very shortly, because I knew then as well as I know now, that I could do it but *historically*, not experimentally: but at this time, the case is quite altered by many other circumstances, and therefore I cannot do that same now again, which I could do then, but must break off before I come to the end of this "First Table." And of the other two Tables I must say, that not only there are many things in them which are already touched upon, and at least implicitly declared in this "First Table;" but also, that *there is nothing in them which will not open and declare itself in reality and substance, when this gate is opened, and this point attained*. If this be not a fully convincing argument, I will be willingly informed better; and if it be, this consequence is plain and evident, That it is much better both for myself and others to go forward within, than to run any further without, although perhaps I may be blamed by the one or other for so doing; which I may expect the rather, because such a thing was done already several times of late. For,

One friend found fault with my living so much retired or in secret, and advised me to make myself known, to seek more of conversation, to go abroad, and to do with my talent some good in the present generation, by instructing others, and making proselytes to the truth: for, said he, I should find myself obliged to do so, if I had that knowledge that you have,

&c. This friend I answered but very shortly then; and now think it not worth my while to take any farther notice thereof, for reasons best known to myself. But,

Another good friend of mine, soon after this, found fault with my keeping, even among friends, so close to myself that they could hardly get anything from me, and told me, that others with whom we more conversed formerly had found the same fault, and the conclusion of all was this, that I was not fit for conversation. And to this friend I then made a serious promise that I would answer him, and lay open before him my inward ground and whole heart, without equivocations and mental reservations. This promise therefore I will now perform, according to my best ability, without regard to this or that which might arise in my own mind to dissuade me from such a freedom, and without fear of his taking anything amiss, or putting a wrong construction upon my words; and I will do it (1.), with a more general respect to those other friends whose testimony he brought in, and then also (2.), with a more particular respect to the conversation between himself and me.

IN THE FIRST PLACE, this is undeniably true, that this fault you find with me in outward conversation, hath its deep ground in an internal secret constitution, or essential signature of my own mind. Further, this is true also, that if this signature be entirely of my own making, a much worse name than that of a fault may be justly given unto it. But again it is no less true, that so man knoweth the things of a man, save the spirit of man which is in him. Seeing then my friend, that according to this general rule, you can as little know the things of mine, as I can the things of yours, you can judge no further than as this or that doth outwardly appear to you, and you can understand it. Therefore to settle your judgment upon a deeper bottom, I will open to you the things of mine, as much as words of this world can be able to open secret spiritual depths. If you find a self-justifying spirit therein, you may justly reject it and condemn it, as much as I have formerly condemned and rejected such a spirit, in another friend. But if you meet with a spirit of sincerity, that speaks the naked truth, and speaks it for good ends, and speaks it as in the presence of God, without self-justification, then *have a care to judge*, and do not trust to your own deep-piercing and penetrating spirit, but say rather, *I understand it not*.

This internal signature of my own mind, and so consequently this fault you find with me, is indeed, in some great sense, of *my own making*, and was made by myself before I could well discern my own right hand from my left, or when I was most terribly blind and ignorant. So far therefore it is evil, and falls under the indicature of the Almighty. But he who brings forth good out *of evil*, hath made use of this mine own evil for my own good, and for the preservation of my own soul. For by this disposition and signature of my mind, changed and improved by Him, I avoided many nets and snares, was kept from self-exaltation, restrained from rashly judging others, and was led through many strange things and dangerous passages, without receiving hurt. Even by your self, my friend, I should have been led away and involved in one labyrinth after another, if it had not been for this internal disposition of my mind. So for therefore it is *not of my own making*, but God, in his infinite *love, free grace* and *mercy*, shall be praised and glorified by it for ever and ever.

Now to give you a short verbal delineation of that inward invisible figure of my mind, considered as changed and improved by free grace, I tell you, that after my dreadful sudden [spiritual] *shock*, (though indeed long before it also, I had something much like it, but it never came up to that pitch,) I could never acquiesce in, or be much pleased with anything *inferior* to what, I then perceived, was attainable only, by attaining that *great point* and entering through that *gate*. And besides this, I had from that time a deeper sense in my mind, than the astral spirit can give to any living in this world, and a stronger impression of that sense in my soul, than any words in this world can declare, concerning a vast, or rather an immense difference or distance between knowledge and understanding. And therefore when I was afterwards quite unexpectedly called, entreated, and mightily desired to write about J. B., I was often strangely amused, how it could come to pass that I could be so pressed to write of things, which my own heart told me *I did not yet understand*. This now was the true ground and reason, why I never could nor did put any real value upon my own writings, squeezed as it were out of me; and why (I dare say) I could have seen them all burnt without any *inward concern*. And when I perceived afterwards, that they were read, valued, and enquired after, I was thereby put into such a state of mind that I knew not what to think, or say thereof. I own freely that I thought within myself, not once and not superficially, Surely all those that make so much of what I make so little of, must needs be *altogether blind and deplorably ignorant?* Yet at the same time, as I had always before mine eyes, against me, that commandment, *Judge not;* so I had always also for me, this plain reason, viz., If they could see with their own eyes, and if they had a spirit able to discern between *knowledge and understanding*, and between things really valuable and things of no great value, they would presently perceive, that all these books of mine were written before that *gate* was opened in me, and that *great point* attained; and would therefore not value them any more, than I can and do value them, myself.

Every one that could speak of great things consistently with J.B., I thought must needs know something of this *gate* and *point*, and must have such a discerning spirit; and thoughts to the contrary I durst not freely entertain of any one, being restrained by a superior power, which I cannot account for. And yet such their doings and proceedings I could never reconcile with what I bore in my own mind. And this, if I had run into it too far with mine imagination, might have made me distracted. My words I know are much confused, yet I cannot help it, the invisible figure of my mind was much more so; and the internal sensation thereof which I had, as also that deep impression which these things made in my soul, I cannot give you. But,

To come nearer to the matter, let me tell you that, upon this ground, at that time when you were eager and busy to bring me over, (not knowing then yourself, what you were about to do, nor what you were to do next year quite to the contrary,) to that assembly which I came into afterwards by some other means; that at that time, I say, I had a greater opinion of those friends than of myself, and thought myself *not fit for their conversation*, long before you heard them say so. Yet when I was come among them, this great opinion of them was soon mixed with a great confusion in myself. For something in me would secretly suggest to my mind, that this gate was still shut up in them, and this *great point* not yet attained. And some other thing in me would reprove me for thinking so, and would not let such thoughts settle in my mind, as a certain truth.

Reasons for that former were these: (1.) because I never heard any mention made thereof; (2.) because they valued so much, what I could value so little; and (3.) because I could never see any real good effects, which I was sure could not have failed to follow the *opening* of that gate, and the *attainment* of that point. And a reason for the latter was, that I heard so many excellent words, fluent discourses, and *confident declarations* of great, high, and *glorious* things.

Between these two I sat in great doubtfulness, and hesitation, for of them I durst not say positively, they are under delusions; and of myself I durst not utter any such glorious things. And so I came so far and so deep into confusion, that I knew not at all what to think or to say, either of them or of myself. Of its effects, which it had in me, I say now only this, that it made me on one side more and more sensible of my being not fit for their conversation, and on the other side more and more weary of every thing, and almost of every body too; because I never knew what to say to the one, nor what to take in from the other. But a while after, these private disputes, frequent fallings out, continual discords, heats and animosities always agitated in that assembly, gave me some relief, and extricated me more and more out of my confusion; for they shewed me, and convinced me of the truth of what I before was so slow, backward and cautious to let settle in my mind. What was done on my side to compose all those differences, and to keep up peace and union, you know; and what the effects and consequences of my so doing were, you know as well as I. Could you find at that time, that I kept so close to myself amongst those known friends, whose testimonies you now allege that they could hardly get out anything from me? If you then did find me so, tell me now though you did not tell me then. And if you did not find me so then, but must rather own that they got from me ten times more than ever they would or could digest, then give me leave to tell you, that in all those matters I was not understood, neither by yourself nor by others. For if you had understood me you would have taken other measures, according to your own free and voluntary promise, yea you would take such as I should shew you; which yet you never did, for want of understanding me.

You most needs allow, that there is a vast difference between understanding the words of another *grammatically*, and understanding him *essentially*. Grammatically, though my words were not ordered according to the rules of an English grammar, I was always understood well enough: for what I said or wrote was approved of, the truth thereof was owned, and whenever I said, I am not understood, I was always answered, We understand you very well.

Who shall here be judge, whether I was understood or not understood? I say mine own internal *essences* (and to also the essences of every one that proposes any *spiritual matter*) can be the best, and ought to be the *only* judges. For they only can be sensible in themselves, whether or no they have really reached and stirred the internal essences of the hearer, and whether or no they have raised in his essences a full harmony with themselves, and an equal disposition of mind towards that, which the speaker verbally owneth to be truth. If they have, the good effects intended must of necessity follow. And if they have not, those internal essences in the speaker want no other testimony from without, but are clearly convinced in themselves of this plain truth. That they are *not understood essentially*, but only outwardly, grammatically, and superficially; neither can they be blinded nor made senseless by any of those confident replies, saying, We understand you very well; for their feeling cannot be beaten down by words.

If then (1.) in the state of that confusion I spoke of in the foregoing paragraph, the internal invisible figure of my mind was such as I declared, it is no wonder that I could with more pleasure and readiness, 'take a pipe' with those friends, and talk of the Sultan and the great Mogul, rather than of things which I had no great relish in; which I could not perceive to flow forth out of a solid ground, and out of which I had no prospect of any real good effects that could be produced;—having experienced how I had fared with my first declaration made to them, concerning matters of practice. If now this was a *fault in me*, let it be one without my contradicting it, and let it be as great or as little as they please to make it, I for my part shall neither be the better nor the worse for it. (2.) In that following state, when I was come out of the inward confusion, and had occasion afforded to utter many things, all for good ends, and allowed to be good and true; if this was my condition, that I could not be understood essentially, that we continued strangers in our inward ground, that discord and division increased so much amongst them, as much as I endeavoured to promote peace and union—and that I durst not say, *I am not understood*, without being contradicted immediately, what should I have done then? Be you judge. Of my grand secret, which I may call my *philosopher's stone*, which the preservation of my temporal life without being burdensome to any, depends upon, I durst not utter one word, for twenty good substantial reasons. To you my friend, I gave several hints thereof, but found you in the ground, bottom, practice, and *serious endeavor* after practice, as much a stranger to it as I am a stranger to your *stone*.

Of mysteries and *high speculations* I durst not speak, because I did not value those things half so much, as I valued things on the other side of the great gate and point. Of this *gate* and *point* I durst not make any mention, except I would have wilfully raised a new dispute. Of *matters* relating to the *practice* of Godliness, to the doctrine of *confonmity with Jesus Christ*—to the reading of our own book, to the judging of none but ourselves first, to the looking first into our own dark root and ground before we look into that of another, to our being all but one both with respect to the one side and to the other, &c., you know that I have uttered much more than could be taken in by them, for it was neglected (though not contradicted) for want of practice and of understanding it.

Nothing therefore was left for me, which I might have employed my tongue or rather my pen about, but such things as the greeter part of them, delighted to be entertained with, viz. *enjoyments, triumphing joys* and *exultations, openings of the second principle*, &c. If I had but praised, exalted, and admired these things, and had shewed a desire to get the same in their way and manner, I should have been an excellent fellow in their opinion. But of these things I had nothing to say at all, because, as they themselves rightly and truly said, (and I thank them for having said this truth,) *I was not acquainted with such and the like things*. If then I was not only unacquainted with those things, but did also declare openly that I did not desire them, and could nevertheless lay before them many good and necessary things which they truly wanted, and were not acquainted with, it is plain, that my essences had embraced something which theirs had no acquaintance with, that their essences valued something which mine made not much of; that therefore we were strangers to each other in our internal essences, and consequently, that they were *as little fit for my conversation, as I was for theirs*.

But now my Friend, with a more particular respect to *yourself and me*, give me leave to ask you this lawful question, *What was our conversation?* You know that some of our acquaintances, whose testimonies you alleged, knew nothing of this *gate* and *great point*; and that some others did not deny nor contradict what they heard thereof, but owned the truth, some of them more and others less coldly, indifferently and superficially. But this my question shall not be extended to any one of them; but only between you and me, I ask, *What was our conversation all the time of our acquaintance?* I will not answer it by a definition or description thereof, made by myself, because such an one of my own might be liable to various different exceptions; but Moses, the mediator of the old covenant shall answer it both to you and me. *We spend our years*, (says he,) *as a tale that is told*. These words, I own on my side, are a plain, full, and true description of our conversation, which you are as well to take good notice of as I am, and I as you. For I lay no more from these words to your charge, than I lay to my own; yet not one grain less. Pray remember, in a serious recollection and introversion of your mind and in the fear of God, *how many fine tales were told* between us, concerning this *gate* and this *great point;* and do not misapprehend me, as if I did now condemn and reject all what was spoken about this matter. No, No, God forbid! But I say only these three things, and you may know that I say the truth. (1.) All these *tales wherein we spent these years*, came never yet to any solid fixation, much less to any true internal reality; and that *spark of an omnipotent will* which lieth in our souls, was never yet so essentially touched by those tales, as to produce any good, great or considerable effect without. What good you may have got by them within, I can as little judge of you, as you can of me. (2.) I say, that like as it is much better and more profitable to *go on slowly and moderately*, but *steadily and constantly*, in our own way we are in-maintaining that ground we stand upon, although there be but little or nothing known and said of this *gate* and *point*—provided our way be right and straight, not wrong and crooked; so it is much worse and more hurtful, to *tell tales* thereof, and to shew, in those tales, great earnestness and fervency one day, and be cool again and remiss the next. (3.) I say to you my friend, do you judge and decide yourself, whose mind at the two is more harmless, and whose years are more innocently spent? His, that *tells more tales*, and is on that account more *fit for conversation?* Or his that *tells less tales*, and is less or not at all fit for it? I for my part, do hereby freely end openly declare, that I am in my mind and spirit, as weary of *telling* and of *hearing tales* concerning this *point* and *gate*, as I am weary of anything in this world.

On your side my good friend, and of your person, you have shown and proved more then sufficiently, that *you are fit for conversation* even with the greatest princes and courtiers in the world. But give me leave to tell you, that you are more fit for conversation with such, than with simple, mean and despicable people; although I own that you can condescend, and in a manner force yourself to it sometimes. To prove this, besides my own observation, I could allege against you such testimonies of my familiar friends, as you have alleged against me. But it would be great folly in me to do so, and would give you a just occasion to think, that I was angry with you, that I took your words as an affront and would be revenged of you. No such thing. How could I take them so in anger when you said no more than what I said many times of myself; not from affectation of a proudish humility, but from a deep sense and feeling of my own constitution. And if I never took any notice without, and was not moved within, when you once before called me a *fool*—distinguishing that fool without, from my ground within; how should I now take this so ill, which is not so harsh and rough as that? Besides I know, and own before God, that your words, declaring me not *fit for conversation*, have no such extensive, injurious and malignant sense, which might be resented so much, as I may seem, but only seem, to do. For I take them with a better distinction than you are aware of, and my intent in writing these things, looks quite another way. I thank you sincerely for this expression of yours, because it hath taken off from me a greater burden, and hath made me more light and easy than I ever was before. And hath moreover afforded opportunity to discover something, which else might have lain hid to the end of my life. *Evil* will not come out of it, at least not on my side; but good may be produced on both sides, if we make ourselves, assisted by the grace of God, capable of his blessing. Therefore my friend, do you take nothing amiss of me, but remember that I told you before, I would be plain and open; and consider, that *sincerity* as much as *justice* is no respecter of persons.

On my side, and of my own person, I acknowledge again and again, that I am *not fit for conversation*, and that I was made unfit for it, partly by the spirit of this world, and partly by that dreadful sudden *shock* I hinted at before. For this gave me such a strong sense, and made such a lively deep impression in my soul, of my own *being nothing* and *having nothing*, that I never shall be able in this world, to make any other soul by any words of mine, as sensible thereof as I was made; or to make myself to be understood as *essentially*, as I was made to understand myself essentially within. Neither can I always represent it to myself so deeply, as to have the same sensation and impression thereof which I had then; but I must acquiesce with this, that the same good effects thereof and the same wholesome disposition of mind, do continue and remain with me; and through the grace of God they shall remain, as long as I live in this world. That you also yourself have a deep sense and impression in your soul, of your *being nothing* and *having nothing*, I do not question, but say only, that your sensation and impression thereof, is not mine, and mine is not yours, for if it were, you would have been as little fit for conversation as I am; and it would have been an eternal impossibility for you (I know what I say,) to have done those things you did.

Therefore my kind request of you is this, that you would be pleased hereafter to find no more fault with my unfitness; for though you would do no hurt to me, yet you might perhaps hurt yourself, which I would not have you do. What we call in this world, *conversation*, is rightly called with respect to another world, *communion of saints*. Conversation includeth a two-legged beast, which will be devoured by worms, and be turned into dust and ashes; but this communion excludeth that beast, although during this mortal life, it cannot be entirely in every sense excluded. This *communion* must be the inward ground and bottom of conversation, if conversation shall not perish together with the beast and with this world. If conversation stands upon this ground and bottom and is animated by this communion, it is then blessed and sanctified and able to bring forth good fruits; but if not, it is a certain truth, that the more one is fit for conversation in this world, and the more he cultivates and keeps it up, though in the best way, sense and manner thereof, the greater damage, and loss he must expect to meet with, in the world to come; because this *conversation* and all his fitness for it, having no eternal root, and being not animated by this *communion*, cannot go with him through death, but must sink down in the grave together with his beast. I for my part, have reason to thank my God and Father in heaven, that *I am not fit for it*. Neither can I pray to him to be made fit for it in this world and in this sense. But my prayer is rather to this purpose, that I may be made *unfit* for it more and more, and that all the world, and all its conversation (not standing upon this bottom, and not being influenced and animated by this communion,) may be crucified to me, and I to the same. May God our Father in his infinite love and mercy make us altogether fit (as he is willing and ready to do, if we do not hinder him, and do not think *we are fit already*) for a *conversation*, not made up by *telling and hearing tales*, but by *finding, feeling, touching, embracing*, and *keeping* each other, in our inward renewed or *renewing ground;* for thereby and thereby only, *our conversation* may be in heaven within, even in this time already, whilst it is and must be still in flesh without.

HAVING THUS BY THIS ANSWER, discharged myself of that obligation I was under, by reason of a promise to a friend, and having said before, that I cannot go any farther in the explanation of these TABLES, but that I would henceforth employ my mind wholly in another necessary business; I shall here for a conclusion of all, declare explicitly what business I mean. Not only that the truth of my words may appear the plainer, to my friends (it is of much greater importance to my soul) but also and even chiefly, that this my declaration written by my own hand, may stand as a testimony against myself. If I should not perform or not continue in the performance of what I intend and promise through his grace, to do in secret before my Father in heaven, which seeth in secret.

My whole intent and purpose is to seek by earnest unceasing application to God my Saviour, for his perfect manifestation in my soul, and in respect to my studies to read and meditate only upon the Scripture, and my worthy friend J. B., to be, by these two, always excited and stirred up to recollect and introvert my mind, whether I be at home or abroad—to let it not wander out in things unnecessary; to remember always that saying of my Lord to Martha, One thing is needful; to keep my heart with all diligence because out of it are the issues of life; to seek for no conversation with children of this world; to refrain my tongue from telling tales; to keep mine ears open, that I may be ready to hear what God will speak in my own conscience; and to have mine eye always intent and fixed upon Him, and *him alone*, as if no creature were in the world besides myself—yet so, as never to exclude from my mind that inward ground in any of my *fellow members*, in whom but so much as the smallest grain of grace is sowed by his Spirit; but whatever I may desire for my own soul, I will desire for them also, and nothing for myself alone. For although these two things may seem, as to some of my outward expressions, to be more or less inconsistent with each other; yet do I know sufficiently, that they are in substance and internal reality so coherent, and so firmly linked together, that they are inseparable; and that the one relating to my own soul in particular, cannot be pursued with any good success without the other, relating to all my fellow members in general. And this through the grace of God and by his assistance, I intend to do without any outward hypocritical shew, peculiar affectation, or ostentation, as if I were not as other men are; and in one word, without alteration from what I have appeared outwardly hitherto. Because, I do not intend to make my outward, *two-legged beast* holy and fit for heaven; but only to have a bridle put into his mouth and a hook into his nostrils, that it may not kick and trample me under its feet, and turn again and rend me.

My ultimate end in doing so, shall not be the salvation and happiness of my own soul: no. For if I should make this my ultimate end, and reach no deeper in the spirit of my mind, I knew that I should act from a very subtle, secret and almost imperceptible root of *selfishness*. Mine ultimate end therefore shall be this, (beyond which I know not any farther nor deeper, and which is not invented by the subtlety of reason,) that my whole created being in body soul and spirit, with all the essences and faculties thereof without any exception, may be possessed by Him who is the right and sole proprietor and purchaser thereof; and that He may receive the reward due to his bloody labours, according to the promise made unto him by the Father, saying, *Ask of me, and I will give thee the heathen for thine inheritance*, &c.: which as it is said in general with respect to all the nations upon earth, so it is applicable also in particular to every individual person, and therefore to *myself* also. And this only I shall constantly desire to be fulfilled and performed in me. "For the labourer is worthy of his reward;" and *for my soul he hath laboured and travailed*, and ought not therefore to be served so by me as to have occasion to complain, and to say, *I have, laboured in vain, I have spent my strength for nought*.

But seeing that I know, the Father cannot give, and he cannot receive any soul, but what is made conformable unto him by his Spirit, therefore his fundamental doctrine of *conformity to Him*, according to that sense he hath given me thereof, shall be my principal rule; which if I follow, taking his yoke upon me, which is easy, and his burden which is light, and learning of him, I shall have no need of casuists and commentators: because he hath promised, that he who followeth him, "shall not walk in darkness, but have the light of life and have for a guide his Spirit, that leads into all truth, necessary to salvation. But I shall have need only of *simplicity, sincerity, humility and love*. These four I take peculiar notice of, and enumerate them particularly for my own sake, and for reasons best known to my self. Although I know very well, that in each of them all the other three are implied; so that if I have one of them, I have them all in that one, because they are all inseparable companions, and none of them can really be had without having all the rest. And these four, I am sure enough, will be the best and fittest casuists and commentators—sufficient also for my necessary instruction in all cases and matters whatever.

And to this fundamental doctrine of *conformity with Him* I shall apply my mind and spirit, neither out of fear of hell nor out of hope for heaven; but only because it is imprinted on my soul and spirit, and I can read it therein as plainly as I can read what I do now write thereof, That so it *ought to be*, without asking or answering any *Why*; without a foregoing examination of any argument pro or con; without deliberation and consultation with flesh and blood; without sour looking, murmuring or repining, but with gladness of heart, willingness of spirit and cheerfulness of mind. Knowing and always remembering, not only that my Lord and master says of himself, "Lo I come, in the volume of the book, it is written of me, *I delight to do thy will, O my God?*" but also that in the same volume of the book it is written of me likewise, if I will be in the number of that people of whom it is said, "Thy people shall be willing in the day of thy power," or, according to the German translation, "*After thy conquest, thy people shall serve thee willingly*"—not with uneasiness and reluctance, as being compelled by force; nor in a mercenary manner, as hired by wages; bet freely, willingly and with delight, having received from his own free grace, this spirit of willingness.

This Spirit of willingness in the soul, not only implieth and strongly confirmeth what I said before, that my ultimate end in the spirit of my mind ought not to be the salvation of my own soul; and not only resolveth this question, Whether a man can love God and do willingly his will, without fixing his eye upon the reward promised to them that love him: but it answers also sufficiently an objection made from the words of the apostle, saying of our Lord and Saviour, that "he for the joy that was set before him, endured the cross" Which silly question cannot be asked, and which senseless objection—senseless in the internal ground, though specious enough in the superficiality or the sight of reason,—cannot be made, by any but such as know nothing in their own ground, of the life and motions of this spirit of willingness, and very little of what our future salvation and happiness will be.

I for my part, and to my own full satisfaction know, that my Lord and Saviour having said, "Lo I come, I delight to do thy will, O my God," declareth immediately the deepest ground and the only foundation of this delight, in the next following words, "Yea thy law is within my heart" I know that here no other why is to be asked, and no deeper ground or reason to be enquired for. I know nevertheless that in an inferior and exterior sense and respect, more accommodate to my own weak capacity, and to excite in me the spirit of willingness, or to raise it when clouded or suppressed, it is rightly said of him, that "for the joy that was set before him he endured the cross." But I know also, that it is a false conclusion to say, He made this joy his ultimate end in the spirit of his mind, or that he would not have delighted to do the will of his God, if it had not been for this joy, or for this necessary consequence of his delight. This I say, is injurious to him, and to that spirit of willingness, which he had in the highest perfection; because he had also the law of his God in the highest perfection within his heart.

And of mine own future happiness I know, that it will be a necessary consequence, or an appendix inseparable from that *ultimate end*, which I named above, and which, relating to my Saviour, is greater and more dignified than anything relating to myself can be; and that therefore it would be perverse doings, if I should make that which is less and inferior, to be my ultimate end. Aad further I know also, that this salvation and happiness will consist in two things, united into one, viz. on one side, in the greatest riches, fulness, life and glory, that I can be capable of; and on the other side in the utmost poverty, emptiness, death and nothingness of my *self*, and of all that is my own. Or rather, that it will consist in an everlasting harmonious union of these two–in this world contrary things. Even such an union as will bind and cement them so together, that they shall be for ever and ever inseparable from each other. Such an union, that they shall make as one *perfect circle* wherein the beginning shall not be discerned from the end nor the end from the beginning; nay, such an union, that I may freely and truly say of each of these two things, This is that, and that is this. For dying to myself perpetually, is living unto my Saviour eternally, in happiness and glory,:—and this living is that dying; emptying myself continually of an mine own being, is my being filled with his riches for ever,—and this my being filled is that emptying myself; losing my soul for ever and ever, is finding my soul to all eternity,—and this my finding is my losing it, world without end.

If then my merciful God and Father in heaven giveth me a *simple, sincere, humble* and *loving* heart; not according to my notions which I can have of these words, but according to the sense in which his Spirit taketh those words in the Scrtpture, which sense I cannot yet have a right, true and adequate idea of. If he *giveth me*, I say ——— (though indeed this is a very silly expression, fit only for this world and for earthly senses, but altogether nonsensical in the internal ground; and a very signal instance, shewing what all our words are in this world, when we will express thereby spiritual matters, belonging to another world. For it implieth something of an uncertainty, hesitation or doubtfulness, whether our merciful God and Father in heaven be willing to give it; whereas I know, not only that he on his side is *always ready and willing* to give it, nay *giving it continually*, but also, that in those *earnest desires* and longings for it, which were his gifts, he hath given us also the thing desired and longed for. Notwithstanding, at the same time I must own to my own shame, that I have it not; that so "he may be justified when he speaketh and be clear when he judgeth." But let me go on with my nonsensical expression, because it is so common in this world, and I can have no better; and let it suffice me, that his Spirit understandeth the internal sense of my mind.)

———— if, I say, he giveth me such a heart, I shall be (according to my friend Jacob's words) *one of the richest and noblest men on earth;* because they are such riches and such a nobility, as will continue and be perpetuated, and go along with mo through death into life. Yet, so as I know I shall do in another world to all eternity, (N.B.) so I must begin to do in this world; I must lay them down entirely and continually at the feet of that merciful Giver, denying them to be my own, and owning myself to be *one of the basest, vilest and poorest creatures among mankind*—And this, (N.B.) I must not do in affectation, and imitation of such words as I may have heard from another, and may own to be good and true; for this would be very superficial if not quite hypocritical. Neither must I do it only in a sincere assent and consent of my refined reason, for although this be good and necessary, yet must I not rest therein, nor think to have attained thereby the highest pitch. But I am to know, that there is still something much deeper or higher and more solid, viz. a profound, substantial, unutterable sense or sensation of the truth thereof. Which sensation, my refined *reason* can give as little as it can give me a spirit of willingness; although it can apprehend, and convince me both of the truth and of the necessity thereof. But this sensation can be given only by that Spirit from above, which can give also a spirit of willingness; and without His giving it, no living soul can ever have it, let her reason be ever so much refined. Yet this refined reason may safely go on in this *practice;* for her sincere going on therein will not be in vain, but have a good and blessed success.—And this my laying them down and denying them perpetually, I know will be my constant keeping, preserving and securing them. *Poverty* therefore and *riches, baseness* and *nobility,* am in this harmonious union, not two, but only one thing—one everlasting life, happiness and glory."

Selection Fourteen.

Walton's Summary of the Contents of "Serial Elucidations A–E"

THE CONTENTS of the A. B. C. D. and E. Volumes, of FREHER'S JUSTIFICATIONS and DEMONSTRATIONS of the PRINCIPLES of TEUTONICUS, are these:—

(I.)—OF GOD CONSIDERED WITHOUT NATURE AND CREATURE.—See pages 258, 259.

(II.)—OF GOD, CONSIDERED AS MANIFESTING HIMSELF THROUGH ETERNAL NATURE. [Of the two eternal principles. Of the seven properties of nature. Of darkness, fire, and light.]

We are an image of God. Many books without us are hindrances. We are to read our own book. Will *in potentia;* and will *in actu.* Desire. God and nature not confounded. References to the places in Behmen's writings, where the *forms* of eternal nature are particularly treated of.—References in like manner for the *cross* in eternal nature. Demonstration of the *number seven* in the forms of eternal nature, *a posteriori* and *a priori.*—References for what Behmen means by a *principle.* References for the two eternal principles. And references for several other things relating hereunto.—The manifestation, of GOD; the FATHER, the SON, the HOLY GHOST, in TRINITY, and VIRGIN WISDOM. With references for each.

The *three first forms on the left hand,* the most abstruse. The nearer they are to the temperature, the nearer to oneness. Difference betwixt, and oneness of, the first and second. The first represented by Saturn the planet; and the second by Mercury the metal. The first and second, without a further progress can by no means be reconciled.

The third form's necessity shown from natural motion. A caution relating to the expressions of anguish, rage, fury, &c. *Madness* in a man; and in a watch. This third form really whirls about; and that it must be so, is plain from the case of the first and second. Which, themselves, in their war and fighting are this third.—A *character* of the three first forms explained. Some expressions of Behmen concerning these three first forms.

The *fifth* and third but one. What it was before, and what it is now, explained by a simile of a wicked raging man, renewed; and of the air, turbulent and appeased. Related to the Holy Ghost.

The *sixth* and second one. The difference betwixt what it was before, and what it is now: declared by the words of St. James concerning *the tongue*. Why this sixth is called *sound, intellect,* etc. And what communion these expressions can have with *mobility*, explained from our speech and thoughts. Related to the Son, who is but one, and yet another Word, when etc.

The *seventh* and first one, the seventh (notwithstanding the manifold denominations thereof) shows by its own deadnesss, that it is the first in perfection; as the first was the seventh in beginning. Related to the Father, who is the first, and the last.

The generation of the *fourth* (the *fire*) must be most of all enlarged upon. The condition of the three first forms is recalled to mind. If this had been so of itself only, there could be no possibility for etc. But there is something with them secretly, and unto them incomprehensibly; the *lubet*. The difference between these two, declared by similies, taken from our mind, and stomach; and further by their own different essentiality. From these two, a twofold desire within each other, neither of which can satisfy itself.

Some preperatories to the kindling of the *fire*, explained by a simile of rubbing two pieces of hard wood. Note (1.) the free lust, or lubet, is the mystical cause of the desire after rest: (2.) this desire (or hellish hunger) is false, arising from own will and self-love. The manner, by which the three first raise a *transient conjunction;* and so, a fire indeed, but only to be compared to that of a swift lightning; though with a great difference. Upon account of which it is rather to be compared to that of a flint, when fire is struck out indeed, but without light, or at least etc. The simile of striking fire and kindling a candle, much recommended. The lubet's twofold resolution, viz., for a nearer conjunction, and further separation.

The great difficulty, and yet necessity of this *conjunction;* and the great work (neither easy nor pleasant) to be done thereby. Here, and here only God is called a *consuming fire*. Here Lucifer etc. found him so. In the generation of this fourth form lieth the contradiction.

The contradiction lying here in this single word of a *conjunction* is reconciled. That this conjunction must needs be made by nature and by something without nature is proved. Further the necessity of this *conjunction* is demonstrated by four arguments. Note especially, what here is discoursed, of omnipotence, and omnipotence. Of the transmutation of metals. And of the process of our *regeneration*.

The great stumbling block in *transmution* is mentioned; but the reconciling and vindication of Behmen is delayed till the conjunction itself, and what belongs thereto, be declared. The name *conjunction* improper, quite relating unto time. It is an eternal conjunction without beginning. Principle what. What is meant by an *eternal conjunction*.

This *conjunction* a most dreadful thing. Now all is a fire. The abyssal will is manifested. Must be understood from the process in our regeneration. Terror is on both sides. Why on side of the wrath, and why on the side of eternal liberty. Our Lord Jesus hath felt it etc. and all his etc. This *fire* is the first born of this conjunction, illustrated by our element fire; what it hath from nature and what from liberty; is still in contrariety; which is the cause of its destruction. In eternal nature the fire not only consumes but also generates again its food, the water. This fire properly the *first principle*, though Behmen gives this denomination to the dark world also, either by itself alone, or in union with the fire, upon different accounts.

The effects of this conjunction. Made by a *crack* (1.) *on the left hand*, as to the first form. Illustrated by a simile of a great piece of ice. As to the second and third forms. And further as to the *triangle*; now a *cross*. (2.) *On the right hand*; the second birth of this conjunction, the *light*; declared by paraphrasing THREE PRINCIPLES ii. 9–13. And further, the glorious transmutation of the three first, declared in the same paraphrase.

The lubet's returning home triumphantly; and setting the first temperature all in another condition. Temperature in substantiality. Saturn married unto Luna; Mercury confederate with Jupiter; Mars embracing Venus; Sol with its fire and light. All in one individual will.

The most considerable point now to be considered and demonstrated. The glorious *transmutation* of the three first, and their impotent *flying away*, two things, as different as day and night; or right and left; or as the first and second crack. The latter explained by *heaven and earth's flying away before* &c. in the Apocalypse.

Of *transmutation* and *annihilation* with respect to this third principle. Our common concept hereof exceeding how, and why. Illustrated only by day and night. Shadows, chimeras, etc. cannot be annihilated, and why. Nor changed into each other. What *place* is; and what to *dwell in itself*.

Of *annihilation* with respect to eternal nature. What is annihilation? None can be, and why? In Adam's fall was no annihilation, but only, etc.: so also in his restoration. Nay, in this, the three first cannot be so deeply annihilated or swallowed up, as etc. Even all our *evil works* shall follow us. Even much more the three eternal roots thereof. If man could fall again, whither should he fall? etc.

Of *transmutation* with respect to eternal nature. None can be, and why. *Distinction* and *oneness* must be together, the former looking forward, the latter backward. Each is to keep to its own peculiar office. They are not only three in the temperature, but also seven in the temperature, and in nature, and in the midst between temperature and nature. This is further explained by showing how *nature* is taken differently. Upon this difference, the different enumeration of the forms depends. Why no passage from darkness into light, but through the fire. Hence is evident the three forms on the left hand *cannot be transmuted* into the three on the right hand, so as etc. And what further follows, is for this demonstration also.

Here we find the *two eternal principles*. By an eternal opposition is meant quite another thing than etc. (1.) Not as day and night by turns. (2.) Not as black and white in one superfices. God knew not the fall of Lucifer. (3.) Not as *good* and *evil*. In eternity but one good thing. Friendship and harmony between darkness, fire, and light, declared by root, stock, and branches. Darkness, fire, and light, all three good, not good and evil with respect to themselves; nay to creatures also etc. Where the opposition of good and evil is. Behmen could not so much as have dreamed of an eternal opposition of good and evil. The question, How could he write hereof so positive, and with such an assurance? answered.

What this *eternal opposition* is, is declared by looking on the first step, made out of the eternal unity or oneness. There is really opposition, but all good, not good and evil. *Will and desire*, how one; and how two. And differences between them. All good. Eternal will, neither darkness nor light. Desire necessarily dark, but (N.B.) not without itself. The will, not desire. The difference exceeding subtle; but remember this is the first step. *God* and *nature* by Behmen not confounded. Will and desire as light and darkness. Who can pick up here such an opposition as of good and evil? To whom could darkness have been evil? What reason to call it evil? But here lies the knot etc. Adam's nakedness. The light not properly good from eternity. Darkness would never have done any hurt, if etc. After all this, what shall we say of God? etc. A state may be attained, wherein all this opposition is vanished away. Behmen, justly called Philosophus Centralis.

The consequences of this consideration. An *objection* that the three forms are thus transmuted only by halves, is answered. John, i. 5, *the light shineth into darkness, but the darkness comprehendeth it not.* Why can it not, or will it not? is answered. Why not, when it is a desire after light? is answered.

How *darkness was; not was* and *yet was*. So the glorious transmutation was done, not done, and yet done. Lucifer could not have been the cause of darkness being what it is now, if it had not been something in and to itself before. This is demonstrated (1.) because God hath not created it so; and Lucifer is but a destroyer. Beginning and end in a broken ring appears. (2.) Because, if darkness was by the light quite annihilated, Lucifer must have annulled this annihilation. And is thus set upon the great white throne. (3.) Because, if the three interior forms were transmuted into the three superior forms, so as etc., Lucifer was stronger than this omnipotent transmuting tincture, and went directly forward etc.

Darkness had no beginning, and darkness *had a beginning*; both true. The higher, and more intellectual truth of that former, is demonstrated. (1.) Upon supposition that darkness was in Lucifer's fall created by God: by showing what *nothing* is; and that darkness must have been something to the abyssal eye, before it was something to itself. Eternal without beginning. (2.) Upon supposition that darkness was not created, but only manifested: by showing that then it must have been something hid before this manifestation. Eternally something without beginning.

A strong objection, that darkness is but a *privation of the light*, answered. Chiefly by considering this *privation* in ourselves, or in our fallen and regenerate condition. A foundation axiom is, *God dwelt in the light from eternity*.

Epitome of all what was declared hitherto. No way, neither on the right hand nor on the left, but what will lead us to this truth, that *darkness had no beginning*. For whether we say, (1.) darkness had a beginning, or (2.) light had no beginning, or (3.) light had a beginning; all turns to the selfsame end. The sense of this expression is limited, by saying *an eternal beginning*, or a *beginning without beginning*. These two positions, darkness *had no beginning*, and darkness *had a beginning*, compared: both owned, as without contradiction; but the former much preferred, as much deeper, more solid, really central, and therefore not obvious unto everyone.

The conclusion. A symbolical figure or plate, showing *temperature—nature—*and *temperature*.

(III.)—A Discourse in answer to an objection, Concerning the Desire's attracting itself.

Pregnant reasons for this discourse. Light will not be laid hold on by force in deep speculation. The position, and the consequences said to follow from the same. The next immediate consequence, flowing forth freely. The will is not a desire, and the desire not a will. Differences betwixt them. Desire hath nothing to attract without it. What the meaning is of *attracts itself*. Here no distinction yet, between *attracting* and *attracted*.

A proper simile, from our mind and senses, runneth from hence through all the discourse. The next immediate consequence. Difference betwixt mind and senses; and so God, and nature. There is a *self* in the latter.

Desire attracting itself, a good significant expression. Explained from our simile, and applied to eternal nature. This *itself* is the only thing reason is deluded by. By sharp inquisition after what is attracted, nothing can be found, neither within nor without. *Objection.*—Such a state is attracted, as the desire will raise itself into. Answer.—This is true on the left hand, but false on the right, etc. And all what followeth further is in answer to this objection:

That (1.) a state of *rest* is not attracted by the desire, is demonstrated from the nature of attraction, which is an approaching unto union; when contrariwise, etc. That (2.) this state of rest in our senses and the light in eternal nature are not that which the desire is filled and impregnated with. (3.) What it properly is wherewith the desire filled itself, and which is attracted by it. Full of light, to be understood according to the left hand. Light of the moon, and of astral reason, near related to, etc. Self or selfishness. *Covetousness*, as the second element of hell, almost the same; devouring heaven and paradise, and yet, nothing but itself. Conclusion.

(IV.)—An Explanation of that Scheme or Figure or Teutonicus, (being the first of the Three Tables, *v.* page 27.) wherein God is considered in the Unity and Trinity, without all Nature and Creature. Which Discourse shortly after its commencement was interrupted in order to an Explanation, which is here given, of the Table of the Divine Revelation (*v.* p. 32.) appended to the Book of the Election of Grace.

God ⅄ unintelligible; undeclarable; and why? Poiret's *Eruditio Superficiaria et Solida. Thou canst not see my face.* From his (even affirmative) expressions we are to learn rather, what God is not, than what he is. *Nothing* an affirmative expression; and Behmen's affirmative expressions lead us only to a negative apprehension: *e.g. meekness* and *softness*. Paraphrase upon Theos. Q. i. 1, 2. Introductory observations. The Scheme. Every letter, word and syllable of which is set down significantly and exactly, in its proper place and relation, and must be so regarded, or the greatest confusion will be caused.... [Here the discourse interrupted, and the other Table desired to be explained.]

Behmen's scheme of God ⅄. *Manifestation*, a progress from internal or central, to circumferential. Abyssal *nothing and all*, most abstruse; and yet a key. *Abyss* and *byss* explained from a resemblance we bear thereof within ourselves. And references, for abyss and byss. *Nothing*, i.e. none of all particular some-things. *All* rectifies *nothing*. Nothing here with respect chiefly to its own something. *Hath a will and is a will*, (God here not distinct from his habitation,) both well consistent. Hitherto the Unity.

The *Father*. Behmen vindicated in saying, the Father an *obscure valley* without the Son. *Delight*. Reason thereof in *impression of the will*. Which is explained largely; from infinite latitude, without etc.; not such a one as the bottomless pit, etc. *Cannot love itself.* Abyss and Byss, Father and Son *one*, in the highest sense. *Who seeth me, seeth the Father. The Father greater than I*. What the Father were, if he were without the Son. *Motion*. Spirit how distinct from Father and Son, and yet also *one*. *Sc–i–ence*. Je–ho–va; and references to Behmen.

God in Trinity. How the three distinct names, viz. Father, Son, Spirit, are to be taken here. They are rectified by this repeated expression. *Word in God*, and *Wisdom;* why to be taken together. Wisdom here, not properly in, but under God; and nearest to nature and creature.

(V.)—Of the furthermore exterior Manifestation of God, through the Creation of Angels. Wherein is treated of *material causes*.

The first motion of God to the *creation of angels*, shall not be inquired after. Demonstration that the Angels are *out of God*. They are *children of God;* who is fire and light having darkness under his feet, which was first manifested in their fall, when they did like Ham; which is proved by Paul, *If we are the offspring of God, the Godhead is not like etc.* If Angels *out of nothing* their fall must have been a relapse into nothing, not a downfall into darkness. Reason thinks to honour God more etc., but he is not more honoured by an image of gold, than by one of clay. Speculation the mother of all our inventions. Consider what this *nothing* is, and the impossibility will shew forth itself. God cannot send forth his word beyond the infinite sphere of his all-filling existence.

If angels not out of God, what is the meaning of their *bearing his name written upon them?* What is that *spark of divine being*, in all the mystics? What is that *breath of life*, breathed into man? If the life, which was the light of man, was in God, and was God, before man was made, how come it into man, but *out of God?* and what is the *seed of God, remaining etc.* From whence are the wonderful *magic powers* of angels, and stupendous effects of *faith* in men? Our *regeneration* gives an all sufficient testimony. *We must be born again, from above.* If not so, what can the mysterious communion signify, typified by the first *Adam* and his *wife?* What are the names, *Christ's; God's; Saviour's?* What is *be like unto him; sitting upon his throne; become one spirit with him; ascend with him into heaven?* What is the distinction betwixt a *son* and *servant? Go to my brethren. I ascend to my father and your father.* The devil's cunning craft. The foundation of Christianity dangerously undermined, and deprived of etc., if this truth be denied: acknowledged by many that *shall come from the east and from the west* etc.

The consequences examined, by similies:— *If out of God, they are God*, is shown to be false. The true consequences are, (1.) They are distinct and different persons. (2.) They bear his name. Females rel. to regeneration. (3.) They are alike him, men and whole persons. (4.) They are under his direction and government. All this follows exactly as to God and his children, and the reason why. But (5.) for an addition is granted freely, If out of God, they are Gods. Reasons, both from before, and from after eternal nature, why this consequence, *they are God* is false; and this, *they are Gods; and if Gods out of God, they are not God*, is true.

II. *If out of God they must be part of God.* This is shown in our simile (1.) to be false, as to soul and spirit, but (2.) it is granted to come a little nearer as to body. Wherefore we should look into the *magical generation*. But to give greater satisfaction we will keep to our simile. Wherein is shown again, the consequence is false in the common grossest sense; and the Scripture *partaking of the divine nature* is the only true immediate consequence, as in this world, so in that superior world also.

If this *partaking of the divine nature* such a stumbling-block also, who laid it in our way? Our saying *out of nothing* is a far greater, and a real one. Strange consequences of this *out of nothing* are touched. The *in him* (which might more easily) does not confound God and creature, and there is no offence taken. Why then at the *out of him?* They are equally gross in their utmost sense looking towards materiality. Both the *in him*, and the *out of him* are infinitely surpassed by our *being one, as he is one with the Father.* Here the proper argument for reason's saying, We are confounded with God. But that we are not is plainly proved. What hurt (if; if; if) would be done, to say, *we are part of God.* So hath Behmen said of Lucifer; regarding not enticing words which human wisdom teacheth. So our Lord Jesus also, *I am the true vine* etc.; not solicitous what his disciples could have inferred. The *branch* wants no demonstration how near it be related to the vine. Our *out of God* so established that the gates of hell shall never prevail against it, how then the philosophy of this world, by its material cause? Transition to the IIId. alleged conseq. viz., *material cause;* and why the anatomising thereof is undertaken.

What is meant by *materiality*. *Material* and *visible*, *spiritual* and *invisible*, not the same; showed from, *if our earthly house etc.* Materiality and *material cause* in this temporal world, what. Great difference between matter and spirit in general; and a far greater between our gross matter and the pure matter of the eternal world. Yet, we say, (1.) of material things, (2.) of spiritual, and (3.) of material and spiritual, the same *out of;* who then sees not the great difference in sense? What is implied in the *out of*, when said in the grossest sense. What shadow of answerableness hereunto, when the same *out of* is said of spiritual things out of spiritual, or, of material things out of spiritual properties. (N.B.) *A discourse with the six forms of nature*, concerning the material cause of their material eternal house. Oneness united with distinction. Descent from spirit to materiality. What combineth the two extremities. The *six*, no material cause, nor answering to a material cause of the *seventh*. Whether the *nothing* be a material cause of things, or no.

Material cause considered again. Carved image out of wood. A plant out of the earth; smell, colours. Spark of fire out of a steel and flint. Flame out of wood etc. Innumerable great flames out of a little one. Heat, light, air, out of the fire. Four elements out of each other. All four out of one ground. Elementary spirit and body out of the four elements.

The seven metals out of no material cause. That spiritual properties are sufficient for the bringing forth materiality out of themselves without a material cause, is demonstrated, from the *philosophical work*, where is shewn that the first cursed matter is not the material cause of the blessed stone. This is indeed out of that, and so that out of this, but this *out of* makes no material cause; the consequences follow not. Further is this demonstrated from Scripture, *Thou fool.. God giveth it a body*. And further again from our *regeneration*, where is largely shown, that our earthly body cannot be called a material cause of our glorious body; but rather this must be called a material cause of that; if the doctrine of material causes a rule for every thing; and reasons why so. *Out of* and *out of* different. That the dark spirituality is much nearer than the light's materiality, to what we understand by material cause. Proved from the gulph between three and three: and from St. John's out *of the will of man*, and out *of God*.

The former position (commencement of last §) is (after some hints at the rainbow, tempest, hail, thunderbolts, etc.) further demonstrated from the prodigious quantity of *waters in the deluge;* out of *the fountains of the great deep*, and the *windows of heaven. Storehouses of wrath. Treasures a sealed up.* So, *storehouse of mercy.* Hitherto as in opposition to what is brought forth out of material causes by *nature*. Now, as in opposition to what is out of material causes by *art*, it was intended to have considered, man. The effects of divine and of dark magia. That nothing impossible *to him that believeth.* Joshua. Elias. Jesus and Apostles. Dark magic glasses. Man's speech. The omnipotent *fiat.* Natural propagation. Regeneration only with respect to Paul's saying. *Ye have not many fathers…I have begotten you:* and, *faith* out *of hearing.* After all, that man was the *image and likeness of God. Signatura omnium rerum.* All this would have shown the sufficiency of spiritual properties for producing; altering; and swallowing up. But etc.

These two, *out of themselves and without a material cause*, must be joined together. Reasons why. The former implies not out of nothing, because they act forward. The latter implieth, (1.) they have not and want not a material cause; proved from their acting forward. Material causes not *in infinitum.* Gulph. Orderly coherence without interruption in the Divine manifestation. Secondly and chiefly, they answer not to a material cause; proved from their needful unalterableness. By saying this or that we break etc., but by joining the former two we keep up *union* and *distinction*. If ye say *out of nothing*, what prerogative leave ye to God? He is *Alpha* and *Omega.* So, he is not confounded with creatures, but rather etc. The *out of nothing* not utterly rejected. If eternal nature out of him (as is plain from the desire), all what out of eternal nature out of him also. The will of God the only cause of all things; true, but taken in the wrong. *Band of union; the eternal character* ☉. This is the ground why we cannot say, *out of nothing.* And why no possibility for reducing anything into nothing. *Objection.*— Such a band empties the fulness of, and lays a constraint upon God. *Answered*, by rectifying this, and utterly denying that. This discussion of material causes closed.

[Note: Selection Nine, "Of the Furthermore Manifestation of God", was inserted by Walton here.—Ed]

They were the first creatures. They had a beginning, though not their essences. To what end created. Their personal being their own propriety.

SECONDLY. As to their *order* and *distinction*. A resemblance of the Holy Trinity. Three kingdoms. Seven princely courts, etc., etc. THIRDLY. As to other circumstances of their blessed, glorious condition. The same figure and members as man in his creation. Spirit, soul, body, five senses. Breathing love and humility. All one harmonious instrument, etc., etc. FOURTHLY. As with relation to man. Ministering spirits. Lovers of children. Guardians to cities, nations and kingdoms. References for all these particulars, with a foregoing kind of apology for the imperfection of his AURORA.

(VI.)—Of the Fall of Lucifer, and all his Angels.

Lucifer's fall. Reasons, why so shortly here discoursed of. References, for the ground, why he excelled in glory all the rest of holy angels. References, as to his kingdom being the room of this now third principle. His fall, and the cause thereof, in a great variety of Behmen's expressions; and references for the same. Why still called a *prince of this world;* and references for it. His fall, the occasion of the *creation* of this temporal universe; and references to places in Behmen for this position also.

(VII.)—Of the Creation of this outward Third Principle, wherein we live and move and have our outward being.

What the *creation* is; and why made. Beginning of time implies an end. The vulgar opinion (though in a sense not hurtful) exploded. And a twofold objection, that Behmen makes Lucifer either a creator of earth and stones, or a binder of the sovereign will of God; answered. As to the first, the whole matter is largely represented. As to the second, it is shown that it stands upon a false hypothesis, and the whole matter is further circumstantially declared. According to the description given by Moses, Gen. i. 1, In the beginning, etc.

[Note: Selection 6, "Considerations on Lucifer and the Third Principle" was inserted here by Walton.—Ed]

(1.) Abyss without all beginning. (2.) Abyss itself the beginning of all posterior things. (3.) Abyssal Nothing and All is God himself, though not yet to be considered as Father. Abyssal condition. Trinity. Father Son and Spirit had a beginning; reconciled with Behmen saying, the Father is beginning-less. That the distinction between the Father and the Abyssal Will is *cum fundamento in re*, is plain from Scripture. This *beginning not* related to the abyssal will, but to its actual moving.

The *word was* (if we say) generated in this beginning, we say true enough, but not yet all. This was implieth also its having been in the Father before this beginning: shown from the Scripture, *I am in the Father, and the Father is in me.* Why the Son is called the *word of the Father*, is largely declared by the generation of our word.

To declare that, and how, Father and Son are one and not two; and yet also *two*, and not one, is first shown what Teutonicus understands by *Unity*, by *Abyss*, by *God*, by *Father*, and by *Son*, *Word* or *Byss*. The real ground of the Father and Son being *one*, is this, that not only the Son is in the Father, but also the Father in the Son. How the Father can be in the Son when the Son is in the Father, explained. That Father and Son *are one*, not *two*, is demonstrated. (1.) In the Father is all, and in the Son is all what is in the Godhead. (2.) The glory is the Fathers, and the glory is the Son's. (3.) The Father's is all power, and the Son's is all power. (4.)

I am the first and the last. (5.) *No man has seen God;* and *we have seen with our eyes. The pure in heart shall see God*, reconciled declared and demonstrated, by showing, how *God* here is taken. An objection that the Jews were the peculiar people of the Father, answered. *Objection*, This makes two eternal Gods, a visible and invisible one. Answer, No. Philip's request, and the Lord's answer. Not we the makers of the trinity.

Again that Father and Son are also *two*, not *one*, is declared and demonstrated, from the Abyss being not a Byss, and the Byss being not an Abyss; (and hereafter, further in the words, *with God.*) God, not always taken in the same sense and respect. The many strong holds of antitrinitarians. Reason cannot be pulled down by another reason; but only by etc.

And the word was *with God*. Difference between in, and *with* him. The *father's bosom;* and why called the *father's*. Son *with the Father, upon the Father's throne. And God was the word.* Complaint against the English translation. The apostle goeth directly forward, explained and proved. Distinction and unity must be together. God his own beginning, and his own end. *Two*, and *one. God was the word* in which was life. In the following words, the Apostle descends down unto *things*; and so unto eternal nature, which is the first of things.

As to the *second beginning*, these words of Saint John are explained in some positions. Lubet with desire; why and how. How it goeth along with it, explained by a simile. The first original will was itself that lubet, and itself that strong desire; declared and proved. *All things*, (all the forms of eternal nature) *made* (or caused to be what they are) *by him;* declared particularly as to all the seven forms.

As to the *third* and *fourth* beginning, *without him was not any* etc., became all in eternal nature was made by him. *In him was life;* must be understood with respect to the fall. In the Father without the Son no life for men and angels. *Father, men were thine . . . I give unto them eternal life. And the life was the light of men.* Life and light, not so distinguished before the fall of man; both *one*, and yet also *two. And the light shineth into the darkness.* Especially in men and angels, before they extinguished it. Eternal darkness and death not absolutely nothing etc. *Darkness comprehended it not.* If light shall be light, darkness must be darkness. [End of the DISCOURSE on Saint John's words. *In the beginning, &c.*]

In the beginning God created etc. Herein, in one sense, a work *preparatory* for the creation; and, in another, *a complete account thereof*, containing all etc. The *first* is declared by a simile; to stop a misapprehension (as if there had been already stones, rocks, etc.). Behmen's sense is plainly represented, and he vindicated, by showing it is rightly said that, if this fire not quenched, a black soot will not cease to be generated. That this kingdom must needs have been taken away from Lucifer, and he be cast out. Why; and by what means? By creation; which implieth chiefly a compacting and bringing down lower. Declared by *light* and *water* which exclude him. All this more evident from, *In the beginning:* for this not the beginning of Lucifer's revolting, but of God stopping him. Beginning of time; *place; palpability*. Denomination of a *third* principle. From hence plain, (1.) the earth of the vilest excrements. (2.) Why it consists of an innumerable multiplicity of materialities. (3.) Why in all a mixture of good and evil. (4. That, and how everything may be changed. (5.) That, and how this mixture (as before the curse) consistent with, *God saw all. . . very good*. (6.) That the earth *belongeth unto the centre of Sol*. (7.) That this work was preparatory. Which last expression could still be made plainer, (1.) by *earth was void;* (2.) by *darkness upon the face* etc., (3.) *by spirit of God moved* etc.

The *second* begins by an earnest declaration against our own learning, labouring, running, making, and expolishing images etc., which it was necessary to say thus plainly and chiefly for the writer's own security; having in all a twofold end. The thing itself proposed but in one page, by the example of Teutonicus, and referring to his declaration. Concluded with some instances of his mockers being dreadfully punished. And with references to Behmen.

The *seven days jointly considered*, in fourteen positions. (1.) The literal sense true, but a deeper hid therein. (2.) Seven days, seven properties of eternal nature. References. (3.) Seven days so linked together that every following day flowed etc. (4.) After the method in eternal nature, the whole temporal nature in these seven days produced. And why so. (5.) All what is in eternal nature, and its eternal seven, is in temporal nature and in its temporal seven also. (6.) Temporal nature must needs have been brought forth in seven, (7.) and just in seven days, or seven circumvolutions of the earthly globe. (8.) In these seven days all things restored, not only, after the same process; but also in the same fashion of order, state and government; but not the same degree etc. (9.) Therefore this world a *principle*. This description reconciled with some other sayings of Behmen. (10.) Five reasons for the truth of Behmen's words, that the process in the creation is more easily to be understood in the regeneration, than any outward etc.; and a sixth reason at the end. (11.) We see this world but half, and how we may see it whole. (12.) The seven days may well be called after the seven planets. (13.) The three first days, without sun and stars, reunited by Christ's three days in the earth to the perfect number seven. (14.) The eighth day therefore in the Christian church justly substituted in the place of the seventh.

The *first day* (1.) The impure materiality gathered together. (2.) Darkness upon the face of the deep, better upon the *superficies of the abyss*. What Behmen means by *three births* must here be understood. (3.) These three births explained. What Lucifer hath done; and where the effects of his doing. (4.) Behmen vindicated, about Lucifer extinguishing the light. Darkness but upon the *superficies* of the abyss. (5.) If these two could have been totally divorced, no light could be produced. (6.) *God said, let there be light*. Behmen's declaration of God's speaking, unintelligible, but useful, if etc. References. (7.) This light not bright shining etc. (8.) The reason, why. (9.) *Query*, the first property being predominant, from whence then, and how came this light? Answer, It is intelligible, if etc.; but not expressible so, as etc. Something said thereof as to the Microcosm in the third of the Three Tables. (10.) The production of this light plainly to be understood in the compaction of this day; largely explained, and references.

(11.) This light to be considered also as diffused through all things, even earth and stones; declared. (12.) Here the ground, first, of *signatura rerum*; secondly, of things subservient to dark magic; thirdly, of things quite contrary; fourthly, of transmuting herbs or flowers; fifthly, of every thing having somewhat of goodness in it. (13.) *God saw all-good*. Darkness in one sense, not among the things which God made; but in another, he so made it, as he made earth and stones. Not therefore here called *good*, when yet, in a sense, it is good also. (14.) *God divided* etc.: in eternal nature they divide themselves. This expression therefore relates first, to Lucifer's disorder; secondly, to their compaction; thirdly, to their being both together everywhere. To what end divided. Lucifer a *prince of this world*; may from hence conclude etc. This division of great importance. (15.) *God called . . day . . night*. Not arbitrarily; proved from Adam's nominating everything; and from Behmen's excellent declaration of these two names.

The *second day*. (1.) The first and second properties of eternal nature. (2.) The first and second day of the creation. (3.) *Firmament* to be considered in a twofold sense. (4.) Firmament, in the first sense, the *gulf* betwixt time and eternity. *Schluss*. An outward representation thereof in the visible firmament. Gulf not proper, and why. No benefit to have a distinct notion thereof, if but a notion. If we are at the borders of time . . . impossibility of breaking . . . will open in our sensibility with such an astonishing etc. (5.) *Water* under, and *water* above the firmament: what, where, etc. And references to Behmen.

(6.) *Firmament* in second sense what; *Schamaim. Two tinctures* divided, not divorced. Correspondence between heaven and earth. (7.) Here the ground of the two sexes. Man was above etc. (8.) Chief benefit of this dividing; as to the macrocosm the stopping of Lucifer, and as to the microcosm the breaking his fall. References, for word *him-mel.* References, for the second day. Conclusion; firmament will bring forth another age. Not all to be rejected promiscuously, because not understood.

The *third day.* (1.) Connexion of this third with the second. (2) This dividing of *waters* and *earth* the last footsteps of the second property, and but as an appendix of that former. (3.) *Meer,* what, in the language of nature. (4.) Behmen cleared, and largely explained, concerning the water's quenching the devil's fiery wrath; chiefly with respect to Sodom etc. (5.) The three first properties considered; and so the three first days. Compacting. Dividing the tincture. Their combination. *Each after its kind.* References for the third day. (6.) How the earth came to bring forth, a whole day before heaven etc., answered. See Behmen.

The *fourth day.* (1.) This of the greatest consideration, and why. (2.) The Sun's production largely declared in analogy to the fire in eternal nature. Travailing of the whole outbirth, double then. *Liberty,* here the inmost generation etc. References. (3.) Generation of the planets cannot herefrom be separated; and why. (4.) They are considered in general, as to *up* and *down.* (5.) In particular. First crack or shrack. *Mars.* Second crack, *Jupiter.* Pearls not to be ridiculed. References to Behmen for generation of the planets.

(6.) *Sol,* tincture of fire. Number *eight* opened. Sun's light one light with God, if etc.; explained. Compared to the light in man's eye. Sun's supernatural eclipse, at Christ's death. References for this. (7.) Sun's several denominations. (8.) Reference to Behmen's THREEFOLD LIFE, ix. 105, 106. explained; and afterwards, he vindicated. What the Sun is. Upon three postulata is largely demonstrated that *Sol* is the *centre.* And farther the same is demonstrated from the kindling or opening of the Number viii. Earth immoveable. Objection from Scripture, answered. Absurdities of the sun's moving. Now Behmen vindicated in saying, *It was reserved unto opening of the seventh seal.* (9.) Sun's office. References to Behmen. (10.) Heathens had reason to worship the sun, rather than etc. (11.) Sun's *metal,* why so beloved. References. (12) Gold purified seven times. (13.) To collect places for philosophical tincture not profitable. (14.) Gold and silver shall be given to kingdom of Christ upon earth, as an ornament.

(15.) The *six planets* and their *metals* in what order to be considered. *Up* and *down,* relating to their properties and centre; and references. (16.) Mars first (not Saturn, Luna) and why. (17.) Mars' nature and office;

various denominations. Behmen gives unto *eternal* the names of temporal things, because etc. (18.) Mars' distance from Sun. (19.) Mars ruleth the first hour of the third day. (20.) Behmen vindicated concerning the time of Mars' revolution. (21.) Relation of Mars to Sun, and to Venus: so crack, fire, and light; so also iron, gold, and copper. Mars hath no body of his own; Saturn compacteth it for him; therefore devours etc. If this relation were not so, Iron could have no toughness: Venus also could have no body without Mars, who showeth his redness in copper. Because of this relation, these two more easily transmuted. References for Mars and *iron*.

(22.) Jupiter the causer of *meekness in every life*, minded and understood by very few; yet, much more therein, than we can think of: this *meekness* quite another thing than etc. References for what a life is. If Jupiter not in the midst, Saturn would unite with Mars, breaking through etc. (22.) Jupiter's residence in the brain; and he *the brain of the Macrocosm*. (23.) *Tin*, Jupiter's metal. The third degree given forth by the lubet. References, for Jupiter's nature and office.

(24.) Saturn's nature. Saturn with Sol ruler and former of all this third principle. (25.) Saturn's station, where; and why. (26.) Saturn's residence the brainpan. (27.) Saturn's *metal* more profitably considered with relation to ourselves. References for it; and references for the original and nature of Saturn, compared to references for Saturn's property in eternal nature.

(28.) Venus only hath a proper light; why. (29.) Venus a *true daughter* of the Sun, explained by similitudes, and defended against men of learning, sincerity, and sense, (saying *planetas evolasse a Sole*) qui si tacuissent philosophi mansissent. (30.) Venus considered with relation to Jupiter. Jupiter causer of meekness, and Venus meekness herself. As she appeaseth Mars, so she makes Jupiter humble. Immense riches here; shown from Lucifer's fall. Order of the seven properties in the Aurora, altered in following books; and alteration in this third principle as to Jupiter and Mercury. An important consideration that Jupiter is not able to . . . but that he must be empowered, first, by another; secondly, standing on the other side; thirdly, having a proper light; and fourthly, being a female power. Jupiter a causer of, and Venus meekness itself, reconciled, Venus wants, besides Mars such another confederate as hath those five requisites, that are nowhere but in Jupiter. Mercury and Jupiter make a square; shown. All these things but little fragments. Behmen wrote in the divine light, and not to be read by spectacles of our own making. References for Venus and her metal, *copper*.

(31.) First of Mercury (not the planet) must be said something, and why. (32.) What *mer*-or *mar-curius*, in the language of nature. (33.) Behmen reconciled and vindicated in calling the sixth property, *mercurius*.

References for *sound* in the sixth property. (34.) A twofold word; in the Fathers centre, *mercurius*. *Mercurius* in every principle. Behmen's several expressions. (35.) An objection that Behmen confounds God and nature; answered. (36.) References to Behmen for *sal, sulphur,* and *mercurius.*

(37.) Mercury's *original*; and why his place exchanged with Jupiter. (38.) In Mercury the knowledge of what is in the centre of nature. (39.) Mercury causeth in Jupiter, understanding. (40.) Mercury, hath from Jupiter his good temper and inclination. (41.) Mercury's proper office. (42.) Mercury hermaphrodite. (43.) He ruleth the first hour of the fourth day; and this fourth day of the creation proper to him. (44.) Mercury's metal, *quicksilver*. References for Mercury and his metal.

(45.) Luna the last and lowest, why. Heaven and earth come into conjunction. (46.) Luna's office, a mediator. (47.) Luna, wife to all, but chiefly to Sol. (48.) Luna more desirous after Sol than any other, and why. (49.) Why this so peculiarly offered to our consideration. (60.) Luna half dark, half light; why, and Behmen vindicated. (51.) Luna draweth in the shine of Sol; receiveth only the pale colour. Declaration of Behmen, vindicated. *Greater light*, and *lesser light*, though no light, can well be justified, according to Behmen's ground. (52.) Luna false; fugitive; Behmen vindicated. (53.) Luna ruleth first hour of second day. (54.) Luna's metal, *silver*. Man's body before the fall compared to pure silver. References for Luna and her metal. Metals in general; a water and oil kept under by wrathful properties. The first creation discovered therein.

(55.) *Fixed stars* came forth with the planets, and why. (56.) Must be conceived both as prior, and as posterior to the sun, and why. (57.) Stated, what. All, the whole nature. The manifold powers of eternity; looking-glass. An outspoken word, enabled to speak out again. A quintessential spiritual substance. That which is superior, in dignity more than locality. A *quintessence* of the four elements. Inferior to the planets, as a body to the soul; shown from, *essences*. Not a material palpable thing. Fire and water, explained from water's matrix, and water compacted. Not consumed, nor extinguished, because this water, like oil, &c. (58.) In their creation great things, but the world's wickedness, etc. (59.) Stated, just so many, as many essences stood open when the sun kindled. (60.) This number infinite; not to the Creator. Argument for immortality of souls. (61.) Why *fixed*.

(62.) All but one harmonious instrument or kingdom. Like a watch. (63.) Each hath the properties of all, but, etc. (64.) Each its proper office. (65.) Each inclined to bring forth its wonders. (66.) Many stars not seen. Why. (67.) Wrath, the original of their wheeling about (68.) Their effects. For a general idea of the connexion . . . may be added, what Behmen means, by *astrum*. (69.) Mysterium Magnum, xiii. 7–17, of astrum and astrums, and paraphrased. References for the fixed stars. (70.) The roost profitable consideration of the stars, with respect to fallen man. And references for the same.

Concerning the *spirit of this world*, generation of the four elements, and *sal, sulphur,* and *mercurius*. Now the spirit of this world arose from the union of all the moving powers. Simile of an instrument, its strings, sounds, and harmony. Another of a watch. *Spiritus mundi* considered: first, with respect to what is immediately above him; secondly, with respect to himself only, where he is largely and plainly declared. True way to get understanding. Thirdly, with respect to what is immediately under him; where, *sal, sulphur,* and *mercurius*, his spiritual object, and the four elements, his exterior habitation, must be considered. (1.) The three common principles: harshness, *sal;* stinging motion, *mercurius;* anguish, *sulphur*. Understood by the wise heathens, Character of the Trinity in all things. Here should be added *oil*, and *sulphur*, if . . . but, etc. (2.) The so called *four elements*. Their generation declared, from the one pure element; from the four first properties of eternal and temporal nature; from the sal-nitral crack and kindling of the fire: it is not meant thereby the eruption of the fire in the centre, on the fourth day, but, etc. References for the *spirit of this world;* for *sal, sulphur,* and *mercurius;* for the eternal *one element;* and for the so called *four elements*.

The *fifth day*. (1.) From the fourth day, the springing up of this third property properly to be reckoned. (2.) Opening of this fifth jovial motion out of the fourth. (3.) Behmen considers all the *living creatures* here on this day, and why. (4.) They are not out of so many pieces of clay. Concerning their original, Behmen's expressions different, and yet concordant, why. Largely explained, and Behmen vindicated, as not contradicting, but giving the true sense of Moses. Variety, the astrum. Aftersound.

(5.) *Four kinds of living creatures,* and in each of these varieties a subordinate numberless variety; why. A difficulty concerning the fire's astrum, resolved. (6.) Distinction in two sexes. Cause of their propagation is seeking the love. Only the serpent excepted, in the division of sexes. (7.) Several creatures have a mixed original, out of two mothers. (8.) Some have blood, others not; these through the devil's will. (9.) Some clean, others unclean, and reason thereof.

(10.) The *final cause* of their creation, declared in a connexion of what is to be considered both before and after. (11.) Necessity of this appearing in the eternal magia. (13.) The condition of the living creatures before the fall, as to their food, clothing, and cruel, wrathful properties. (15.)

None is able to speak; yet the fowls understand the language of nature, in their kind. Tower of Babel. (14.) In all a character of the Trinity; but in none so as in man. They are but for food and propagation. References for the *living creatures*.

The sixth day. All what Behmen saith of the *creation of man* depends upon the *seven properties*, the *two principles*, and the *fall of Lucifer*. (1.) Original and formation of his body. *Haadamah, Haarez,* Behmen's different denominations. Two-fold, also three-fold body, etc.; must be left to him that *hath the true pearl*, in the regeneration. References for man's body.

(2.) The breathing in was *one life*, but also three, or three-fold. Fire; light; air. *Spiraculum vitarum*. This triplicity demonstrated. First, *airy breath*, outward part of the soul; exterior spirit; mortal soul, explained. Secondly, *fiery breath;* properly the soul; worm that dieth not; why. Dry, magic-fire. Cross. Fire-eye: root, and original of life; yet also life itself. Thirdly, flaming breath of light and love; properly, spirit of the soul; properly, that noble creature because of which the eternal Word was made flesh. Hence plain, first, that like as in eternity; so also here the fiery soul stands in the midst. Secondly, their different degrees of nobility. Thirdly, that the soul is only an inseparable propriety of man. References to Behmen for this threefold breathing.

(3.) The *image of God* commonly so described, that it be not erroneous, but *imperfect*. No man is blamed thereby, and why. It consisted chiefly and fundamentally in this threefold life, and in the union and order of these three. Both as to this, and that declaration, *man had no law*, but an ingrafted principle, *truth*, as an excellent character of uniformity with his Creator; till this, because of his wavering, was turned into a law. References to Behmen for what has been said of the image of God.

The *seventh day*. From the *work*, and *rest of God*, is plain, these seven days signify quite another thing than etc. (1.) In outward nature was an order and succession of these seven days. But (2.) with respect to eternity, work and rest equally co-eternal, and perpetually together. (3.) In what sense the seventh is prior to the sixth. Declared as a *key* to several obscure places. (4.) *e. g.* Out of the seventh day the first took its beginning. (5.) The seventh day in eternal nature always combined with the first. (6.) *God rested on the seventh day*, in the *substantial temperature*, or *end* of nature, etc. (7.) Behmen's *several denominations* of this seventh day in eternal nature. (8.) This seventh day considered with a particular respect to man: and first, as in his creation; (9.) further, as in his fallen state; (10.) and lastly, as in his restoration. The seventh day the paradise, reopened through Jesus Christ. The true image of God, new restored in Jesus Christ, who therefore both the eighth day and the seventh. With respect to the whole creation, this seventh day that *seventh blessed age,* wherein the mystery of the kingdom of God shall be finished. References for the seventh day.

(VIII.)——Of the Fall or Man, from his primeval glory and perfection, down into and under the dominion of the Spirit of this world.

Man's primitive state of glory and perfection, in the strictest sense always taken for what he stood in, when but one single person. This state considered. (1.) As to the foundation-pillar. Interior body penetrated the exterior. Red hot iron. (2.) As to the manner of his *eating* and *drinking.* One element's greening [pa-ra-dis-ing] through the earth, the outward local paradise. (3.) As to his magical generation. Eternal nature not rent asunder when he was *formed upon the cross,* and brought away from it into another world, etc. (4.) As to his clothing. Naked. Iron and fire. (5.) As to his labour. Why the tincture so much searched after; and why found by so very few. References for these subjects.

The *first forty days.* Behmen contradicts not Moses. Every number *forty* in Scripture related hereunto. The five instances .. . relating to the five degrees of nature. The first and second Adam's process, parallel. References for these forty days. The great mystery of iniquity conceived. Adam began by little and little, etc. Tree of knowledge arose; law came in, etc. But we will consider in these first forty days, only in general the following three things:—

First, That, and why Adam must have been *tempted.* This both lieth indeed in understanding (1.) what he was, and (2.) to what end he was created. But much deeper it lieth in our own internal ground. The word *temptation,* here not yet proper. Temptation here a representation of each principle in man's three-fold looking-glass. Explained. Let none blame God. Necessity of such a temptation, and more arguments for the same. References to Behmen.

Secondly, How, and by whom, man was *tempted.* Might now seem, but is not superfluous. *Spiritus mundi* comes here chiefly into consideration, and why. No such evil design as to *kill,* etc. in any but the devil. *His* twofold design, (1.) To manifest his wonders; (2.) to get the Eternal Virgin, who manifest only in man. He the original of all delusions. References.

Thirdly, The *end* and *consequence* of this temptation. Sleep, death. Simile of oil in a burning lamp. As Adam's eating, so his death in sleep. References for Adam's sleep. *Production of the woman,* in eighteen positions. (1.) Generation of eternal nature and man's original in the first creation must be understood. (2.) Man fallen home to the holy name Jesus, who was now the second Creator. (8.) This not contrary to what before of the *spiritus mundi* or exterior *fiat*. (4.) Neither this nor that without man. (5.) Adam's sleep, and being divided, the first token of God's love and mercy. Proved. (6.) The scope of Eve's creation; so much lower than that of his, as etc. (7.) She never stood in virgin purity. (8.) Was infected with Adam's twofold lust. (9.) All this reflects rather upon him than her. (10.) Rib, and the half cross in the brain-pan. (11.) Adam's body really broken. (12.) Rib showeth her the weaker part. (13.) Something also out of all his essences was extracted; which now a loss to him; but not so if he had brought forth, etc. (14.) Adam's *paradisical rose-garden*. Out of which the woman, what; and why she cannot pretend to any superiority. (15) What left to Adam. What given to Eve. Christ of the woman only; yet a man, and why. (16.) Not meant that Adam had a soul only, and Eve a spirit only. Why cannot these two bring forth the whole image again; and why must every child partake of this division? The first is considered and answered largely. The second, especially from the *fiat's* incorporation into all the essences, being authorised so by God. Hermaphrodites. (17.) How the soul came into the woman's body. (18.) Formation of her body; in three hours. References to Behmen for all this matter.

The *second forty days*. Adam and Eve, their state in paradise. The *tree of knowledge*, etc. (1.) Its *original* in a seeming contradiction described by Behmen. But (2.) reconciled, and shown that both is true. (3.) What tree it was: not in paradise, but in the garden. (4.) Why called so, and how distinct from the *tree of life;* declared by a paraphrase of MYSTERIUM MAGNUM, xvii 10–16. References.

The *serpent*, its original, subtlety, and near relation to the devil, after a threefold previous observation declared: and references. All the rest in twenty-three positions.

(1.) Adam awakened by the spirit of this world. (2.) Knew presently, and wanted not to be told what Eve was. (3.) *Therefore shall a man leave*, etc., seem not to be Adam's words. (4.) God's command declared by Adam unto Eve; and reasons for it. (5.) Eve had also from Adam the lust against that command. (6.) These two showed forth themselves in Eve. (7.) This lust the devil knew; and so he knew the serpent fit for his design. (8.) This design could not be executed without a conjunction of these two. (9.) Such a conjunction could not be made without a third convenient thing. (10) This third must have been so, and so. (11.) And this was the tree of knowledge.

(12.) The whole order of this magical operation. (13.) Eve could not be sensible immediately of the great alteration. (14.) Both died, and what a dreadful thing this eating, and dying to the one holy paradisical element, see at the death of Christ. (15.) This dying not understood with respect to paradise; explained by similies. (16.) This dying imported an educing into predominion a latent earthly life and body. (17.) And this further, a gross compaction, opening of eyes, feeling of cold, &c. Slavery, bestial properties, etc. (18.) Devil's triumph.

(19.) They *heard a twofold voice*, according to the twofold word in eternal nature. (20.) *Where art thou?* The true eternal helpmeet called, and here Eve must be excluded. (21.) They heard also the angry, dreadful voice or the Father; plain from etc.

(22.) The *gracious promise*. Now Eve concerned; and Adam must be excluded. Declared circumstantially. The *inspoken word*, what. A little gate re-opened. An obscure prophesy; and why. (23.) Of their being *driven out*, by etc., nothing need be said here more, because etc. This driving out after the promise, a solid argument for universality of grace. References for the whole process. And references for man's miserable condition under curse.

IX.—OF THE NATURAL PROPAGATION OF MAN, IN THIS NOW CURSED FOUR ELEMENTARY WORLD.

Title ambiguous. *Bivium*, in THESE PRINCIPLES AND MYSTERIUM MAGNUM, thus:—"Our author, having hitherto at large treated of the fall and curse, and of man's being driven out of the garden Eden, stands now as it were at the parting of a way, the two different paths whereof do bear the same name indeed, but are nevertheless so much distinguished from each other, as that they cannot be walked in or looked over at once, when yet they may at different times, which he also himself hath done, going through the one in his MYSTERIUM MAGNUM, and through the other in the THREE PRINCIPLES.

In the MYSTERIUM MAGNUM he declareth now further, how this Adamical Tree (forso he styleth the first progenitor of all the earthly generations) hath set forth and displayed himself in branches great and little, both into a numberless multitude as to individual particulars, and multiplicity also, as to differences and varieties of tribes, nations, people and languages. In him the mixture of good and evil began, and by eating of the tree of knowledge he was now become himself a living tree of good and evil properties. This mixture therefore, unfolded and showed forth itself in the first beginning of human propagation by Cain and Habel: of whom the firstborn (like as commonly, if not always in the following generations also) was a figure of Adam's own outward, sinful image; and the younger, in whom the woman's seed began to bruise the serpent's head, a figure of that inward, holy, virgin image, which should be restored in the fulness of time, and so a type of Christ, who therefore in conformity unto his antitype, must depart this four-elementary life without having issue therein, and another seed, namely Seth, must have been appointed to Eve instead of Abel. So that now further from these two the propagation of mankind went on. For as to the rest of Adam's sons and daughters not particularised by Moses, they come not into consideration with our author, who says that Moses named only them that in a direct line descended from Adam, and were the *chief representatives of times to come*, with respect on one side to the kingdom of nature, and on the other to that of *grace*. From Cain then, who minded nothing but this world, and the natural wonders thereof, a peculiar line or race came forth in seven generations, unto Lamech, which our author calleth the *line of wonders;* and from Seth another in seven generations also unto Enoch, which he calleth the *line of the covenant*. And then he declareth also further, how after the flood, by the three sons of Noah, this same Adamical tree spread forth itself again in a threefold kind of men, distinguished chiefly as to their internal threefold signature, wherein they stood in the sight of God; saying generally that, in all the names expressed by Moses, and chiefly of the patriarchs before the flood, both in the line of Cain and of Seth; in the number of the years of their age, wherein they begat that particular son, who is mentioned by name; and further in the years of their following, and of their whole life; and, as to them that lived after the flood, in the number of their sons, called then especially by name, *exceeding great mysteries lay hid*. And that the whole course of this world, the propagation and alteration of nations and kingdoms, their several conditions, their appointed time of rising and falling etc. until the end of time, shall be found and seen plainly therein, in its own due time; when the great branches of this Adamical tree shall no more say they are trees by themselves, but see they are branches of one only tree, all partaking of one and the same sap." *Curse*, what; explained by declaring two places of Behmen, the latter by a simile of the sun and earth. References, for the curse.

Here a wonderful explanation of Psalm cxxxix., is intended. What Behmen saith of the *seed*, AURORA xxvi. What in APOLOGY STIEFEL, Text IV. Point ii. 87–135; declared in more short positions. References for some general reflections relating to this matter.

The first thing after conjunction of the tinctures is *strife* and *fighting*; between what. For what they wrestle, viz. the heavenly Virgin; declared from the tincture. Why no Virgin can be brought forth. Premonition, (1.) concerning the outward character of male and female. (2.) Concerning the order of all these things.

Female tincture *takes the blood, to hold fast*, etc.; declared from the generation of water in eternal nature, which, as the water of life, hath all powers.

As in the two tinctures, a *delusion*; so in the *spiritus mundi* (even more than in the tincture.) And so in the *fiat* also; but in both, needful and beneficial. Declared from the sweetness of the blood. Expression of *thinking, delighting*, etc., explained and vindicated by similies.

All delight turned into anxiety; (1.) by the *spiritus mundi* bringing in the four elements. Longing. Tincture's withdrawing: and yet remaining. *Spiritus mundi* more confined in his delusion. (2.) By the blood's being stifled; from whence tumult and uproar. In these two, the first essential *death to paradise*. A twofold sense and respect. Perpetual continuation of the first Adamical death.

Tincture made false, and full of anguish. *Fiat* also struck with terror and made to tremble. Signature imprinted in this terror or crack, into all the parties (viz. to disperse) and effects thereof; declared from eternal nature.

Crack or shrack the proper uproar-maker with its *tough* and *hard* property. Skin. Tincture and *spiritus mundi*, flying up also. Head. Brainpan. Neck. Veins.

According to Behmen, we go here to the *generation of life;* declared in continual answerableness to eternal nature. *Death*, the worm to the generation of life. The only difference between the process in eternal nature and this generation of life, from the astral spirit. In the second joyful crack, the beginning of life. The soul thus introduced into the perishable life of this principle; after the same manner, as in eternal nature into the light of the second, but not to the same end. *Generation of the tincture*. (N.B.) In the *light of the Virgin* all mysteries may be found: and how this is done in a conjunction of the Virgin's light with the astral.

The rest in forty positions. (1.) In the *heart* the life is generated; and the life generates the heart again. (2.) In the rising of the life, the three first properties indissolubly knit together. And the tincture is their etc. Why this repeated. (3.) Before the kindling of astral light, no soul. (4.) Soul's dreadful fall, here known. Its light is borrowed; not generated directly forward. (5.) Soul, cause of all the members, viz. Internal and principal. The two cracks characterised in the *gall*. Behmen defended in part, concerning *gall above the heart*.

(7.) Sum of Behmen's dialogues between the four elements. Fire, heart; water, liver; earth, lungs; air, bladder. (8.) Difficulty in the order, wherein Behmen placeth these four habitations of the elements; resolved in part.

(9.) A plain evidence of the soul's most lamentable fall. (10.) Original of hands. Stretching forth, explained and illustrated by a simile. (11.) Stomach; guts. Behind; beneath.

(12.) Establishing of the astral kingdom. Gate, *where the children of this world wiser than* etc. (13.) The deepest ground of the *spiritus mundi's* seeking and longing after the eternal Virgin. (14.) A query, how could sun, stars, and elements have known the Virgin in Adam, when they never were in the second principle? is answered. The greatest comfort for a wandering soul. (15.) Most all hitherto, common unto men and beasts; we must rise up higher to see the image of God. Freedom of will. And here Behmen invites all that are hungry and thirsty, etc. (16.) Contents of Behmen's large and excellent discourse.

(17.) *Free will* considered, but as in an exterior court. Two principles, as two semi-circles, back to back. Flash. Regeneration in a general sense. Original of the will showeth it to be free. Proved; objections answered etc. Three sayings explained, reconciled, and found agreeing. No constraining power, neither in darkness nor in light. A prevailing power common unto both; transferred from the one to the other by the will. If this in man, it is in vain to seek after it in God. The whole sum and conclusion of all.

(18.) *Speech, senses* and mind take their original after the same etc. (19.) Before the light of life, the body but a beastial figure etc. (20.) Original of the *tongue* and *eyes*. First, and second will. Flash or crack. Rejoicing power (71.) This latter paradisical; not so in beasts. Here an irrefutable argument for free will. (22.) Here, the eternal Virgin espoused to the spirit of the soul. Her throne both in the head and heart. (23.) Star in the eyes. (24.) A precious and profitable observation in the near connexion with, and in the great difference of the *tongue's* original from that of the *eyes*.

(25.) With the rising of the life, each of the three principles taketh its own light; explained as to each in particular. (26.) Here the tincture also of all the three principles ariseth. Second principle admitteth no light from nature. First and third nearly related. (27.) Tincture is the spirit's habitation, and is three-fold. The first principle's tincture, the *terrible light* of the sun: an expression here proper and significative, and not contrary to etc. (28.) Tincture of the first principle, compared to the strong might of God; and what its offices and effects are in man. (29.) This tincture of the first principle is that wherein the devil tempteth man, explained particularly as to the fiery bitter and harsh essence. (30.) This now is the first principle with its tincture; but in the light it is another thing. Out of this eternal depth (of first principle) the worm of the soul is originated.

(31.) This is now further demonstrated from the *five senses*. From whence is thy *seeing?* (32.) What is that which maketh thy *hearing?* The sounding of the tincture in man much nobler than that in beasts. (33.) The same of *smelling, tasting,* and *feeling*.

(34.) The turn of Behmen's Sixteenth Chapter, and his considerable preface. (35.) Wisdom's speech: *mine is the light.. thy desire after my virtue, is my own drawing* etc. (36.) *Mind* is the desiring will. The sharp power not immediately in the will, but in its piercing sight. (37.) Original and generation of *blood*. Why eating of blood forbidden unto man.

(38.) Five sense considered as five counsellors. In the generation of our words all three principles concerned. (38.) Original of the great difference of men, chiefly as to mind, will, tincture, etc. (40.) The contents of the rest of the Sixteenth Chapter; all plain, in eleven short positions.

X.——Of Man's Regeneration, through the Blood and Death of Christ

This Behmen's only aim. The meanest need not complain of obscurity; the strongest will find strong meat enough etc. Excuse of this writer, who only writes according to the measure of his experience. Behmen's places in great abundance.

Some *general observations*. (1.) Regeneration, what it presupposes; and what it implies; and what it is. (2.) Name *regeneration*, ambiguous: as to the whole man, better *restoration*. As to the body and exterior soul, better *conquering*, and *keeping under*. As to the soul, better *renovation*. Only the spirit's glorious body, properly *regenerated*. An *objection*. If the soul cannot etc., because its process cannot be repeated; how can the spirit, whose generation wholly dependeth upon that process? is answered. These differences not made in imagination by a nice and superficial curiosity, but etc.

(3.) *Regeneration* taken variously. One transaction, the regeneration properly; and this again in a two-fold sense. Behmen's saying, *None regenerated, who do not understand* etc., explained and defended.

(4.) The whole work winding, and turning inwards. (5.) *Beginning*, placed differently in various respects. *Progress*, putting on Jesus Christ more and more, as to his death and life. *Consummation*, though expressed by great variety, a re-union of the tinctures. (6.) *Perfection*, how far attainable in this life, and how far not. *King's daughter all glorious, within*. (7.) The most considerable *agent* on man's side, declared as in opposition to his generation.   *Vine and branches*.

The great and principal *transaction*, which was properly the *fall*, at the end of forty days. And what here this great and principal *transaction* is, expressed variously. Conformity to the *life*, and to the *death* of Christ.

From hence is plain, what was said above of soul and spirit Soul but *renewed*. The sensibility of the soul's generation can be repeated. How the soul nevertheless also rightly said to be *regenerated*, explained from its connexion with the will.

Of *what is Christ to us?* in eighteen positions. Like as. What is regeneration? so this also is generally answered but by halves. (1.) By saying, we know not what Christ is in us, we lay down a testimony against ourselves. (2.) He that hath ... need not be told ... but cannot declare it so, etc. Behmen's intent in writing.

(3.) Not only the Spirit of Christ, and not only the light, but also the new light's body must be mentioned in the answer. Before the conformity to Christ's *death*, we are not *actually* his members; though we may be his. (4.) When this brought forth we may say, *this is Christ in us*. A passage of Behmen, where both taken together.

(5.) If we will say how that which is in us can bear the name of Christ? we must first consider Christ's glorified body, and the first and second Adam, both as to distinction and union. (6.) Christ had a four elementary, and a one elementary body, proved. Is opposite unto the first Adam, yet also the first Adam himself; explained. (7) Why he must have had them both, at once. (8.) His now glorified body of the same figure and stature etc. (9.) Not so vast as to fulfil etc; and one element not so shut up etc.

(10.) One element, and four elements considered as *unformed*, and as *formed*. (11.) This doth not make two bodies; yet must be considered distinctly, and why.

(12.) From hence the dispute, concerning the *omnipresence of Christ's body*, can easily be decided. (18.) This omnipresence, maketh not the one element to be God, nor equal unto God. (14.) Presence and omnipresence, relative expressions. As attributed to God, it is (1.) a *central omnipresence;* explained. (2.) An omnipresence without extension. Explained, and shown that neither this nor that applies to the one element.

(15.) This *one element* put on, makes none to be Christ, but only his member. So would it have been aa to the first Adam, etc.: and so it is still with the four elements. (16.) Difference between Christ's glorified body, and bodies of the saints: also between themselves.

(17.) A question. Whether this new body be natural to the soul, etc., answered distinctly. Such a body was natural to her, in one sense; but not a propriety in every sense. It is not natural now; explained and proved. The *twenty-four elders* own it so. Simile of fire and iron. (18.) For a conclusion; the first and second Adam both within us, in war and opposition. A good and sure way, to find out what Christ is in us, by considering not only what the first Adam was, as to himself, before the fall, but also what he now is in us. Like as the first Adam could do us no hurt, if he were not within us; so the Second cannot do us any profit, if he be only without us.

XI.—Of the Eternal Word's becoming Flesh; or of the pure immaculate conception and Incarnation of our Lord Jesus Christ, in the womb of the blessed Virgin Mary.

A fundamental position, That the restoration of the first Adam could not be effected, but by *the eternal Word incarnate;* and that the understanding of the second Adam is inseparable from understanding of the first: demonstrated.

Of the *blessed Virgin. Mary* signifies, a deliverance out of the valley of miseries and calamities; explained. And that such a thing must have been done with her, before the incarnation etc., demonstrated.

(1.) Against θεοτόκος, in the Greek church; and what he called her the mother of. (2.) Against the Roman *idolatry;* and that he (Behmen) exalted her much higher than either, etc. No mediatrix, and why.

(3.) Against *Stiefel, Meths,* and *Tilkin,* concerning Mary's perfection. *Perfection* differs from perfection, so far as the one element from the four elements. Explained and considered in the person of Christ, whose perfection and imperfection is shown. Not a vain curiosity. Further demonstration by considering what the *curse* is; and that the four elements are in a sense the *curse*, etc. Stiefel's *perfection* rejected; Behmen's, in union of two tinctures, asserted. But what is this to the husk, the residence of sin, the tomb of sin. Difference between the second Adam and all the saints. *I counsel thee to buy of me* etc. Mary's *perfection by faith,* rejected. Tilken's dream of Mary's high descent, refilled.

(4.) Against (the learned) *Weigel, Schwenckfeld,* and *Felgenhauer,* of Mary's *virginity*. Their opinion greatly different from Tilken's; wherein, and how. No virgin in this world; and no male or female in the paradisical world; and why. They may be joined in one person, but without mixture. This *without mixture* takes all Weigel's scruple away. A re-union of *Sophia* and Adam must have been made; but how, and by what means? Answered and explained. From the beginning of the promise to *Eve,* till *Mary;* all without *mixture*. The same more evidenced by considering what person the second Adam was to be. *Sophia* without Mary could not: and Mary without *Sophia* could not etc. What virgin Mary was, before the blessing. Yet in greater purity than Eve, before known by Adam. What virgin Sophia is, declared in Behmen's simile of the *macrocosm*. Conjunction between Mary and *Sophia* and the manner thereof; not from without, not with her outward essences in flesh and blood, but etc. References for all these things.

What JE-SUS, and what *Chris-tus* each by itself, and what both together signify in Behmen's *natural language*. In each the Deity and humanity individually connected; and Behmen owns, all what can be said of the one, may of the other also, but etc. Reason and occasion of Behmen's large discourse, and manifold distinction between *Jesus* and *Christ*. And he defended in his nicety and superfluity. All reduced to three heads: (1.) distinction between Deity and humanity. (2.) Humanity, taken from man, and that brought from heaven. (3.) Christ as promised, and as incarnated. And explained, with application to *five errors* of Stiefel. References.

Behmen's Treatise of the INCARNATION, Part I, Chapter x, translated, in a construction of things, rather than of words.

The chiefest thing for understanding the *incarnation* lies in due distinction between that body, or flesh and blood he took from Mary, and that he brought down etc. That former known too much: this latter cannot be known, except, etc., nor be declared to, as that etc. Order of consideration: (1.) Of the outward body. (2.) Of his soul and spirit. (3.) Of this heavenly immortal body.

Of Christ's *outward body*. Behmen's saying, *Christ never had a quite earthly body, altogether alike unto ours*, explained, reconciled with Scripture, and he vindicated. Why Christ must have been a male, three reasons; a plain, a deeper, and deepest.

Of Christ's *soul* and *spirit*. They that say, Christ had no soul, but his body was animated by the Deity, pitied rather than refitted. Tilken's opinion, of *a soul from heaven*, convinced of absurdity. And some sayings of Behmen explained; and shown, that they favour not Tilken's opinion. As the soul of Christ a human soul; so his spirit, a human spirit.

Soul and spirit commonly not distinguished; or if, the spirit of the soul confounded with the outward spirit. Consideration what they are in us, from the two eternal principles. Soul, what: and spirit, what. Spirit only can dwell *essentially* in the second principle; explained. The soul introduced into the light-world, significant enough in a popular sense: but better— shall be brought in union with the light-world. Soul as spirit not capable of etc., but all its capacity dependeth wholly upon its union with the spirit.

The soul, a true representative of the Father; the spirit of the Son. The soul's figure, a sphere or globe with a cross through it. A *fiery eye;* explained. A *tree*. A human figure. But the first only, without relation to this or that, says what the soul is in itself. Explained, both as to *cross* and *globe*. *Historical relation of N. S.* [This most extraordinary narrative is recounted after a somewhat diversified manner in the biography of Gichtel, a work published many years after this account was penned.

Freher, however, being a correct man, this account might serve to modify that; and both be of profit, to the rightly qualified reader.] The *spirit's* proper figure, a human figure; and why.

Differences between soul and spirit considered, in the simile of a *flower out of the earth*: and in that of *fire* and *light*. Further in ten short positions. (1.) The simile of fire and light, defective. (2.) Because in the consideration of this, our object but one principle, whereas in considering soul and spirit must be two. (3.) In the spirit (not soul) the *image of God*. (4) Spirit, an image of the soul. Soul not an image, but a central fire. (5.) Spirit the only living image, both with respect to God and to the soul. (6.) Soul cannot feel itself, and why. (7.) Spirit preserved by the soul's standing steadfast in etc., and preserveth the soul again. (8.) Spirit dependeth wholly upon the soul's free flame; but not reciprocally. (9.) Spirit cannot be spirit without the soul, but soul etc. (10.) Soul loseth only its flame. Simile in outward fire; and instance of Lucifer banished out from the fire, the great city of the Almighty Father. Elucidation of what easily might be misapprehended, concerning the spirit of this world's dethronising the spirit of the soul. The soul's losing its burning flame, with respect to the second principle explained, by simile of the oil of a lamp. The unregenerated soul's spirit. The regenerated soul's two-fold spirit. From hence the soul's warfare.

A *large digression,* in forty-four positions. (1–6.) *Mind,* in general; and etc. (7–8.) *Senses* and *thoughts,* in, from etc.—(9–15.) *Will,* and its generation. (16–18.) *Will-spirit.* Two now. (19–20.) *Science of the groundless will.* Declared by a simile.—(21–23.) *Imagination,* between will and will. (24–25.) *Desire* and *imagination,* two collateral branches. (26.) *Hunger.*— (27–51.) *Understanding, reason, subtlety.* (54–35.) *Understanding,* its original, and residence. (36–57.) *Reason's* original and residence. (38.) *Reason* distinguishes not man from beasts. (39.) Behmen. no despiser of reason. (40.) Consequences of this axiom. Reason cannot know itself.— (41–44.) *Phantasy,* which captivated Lucifer.

Generation of the spirit, in a twofold description. (1.) Faith is originally but a will, this will is a seed etc. (2.) The spiritual generation is done in nothing, or by a real progress from something into nothing. Explanation. Losing and keeping of the soul. The spirit is nothing, when the soul its own something. This *nothing* here more significant, than all the somethings that could be named; its pregnant signification on both sides. Herein the only key to the understanding Behmen: from this ground he hath written etc. These two descriptions are of one thing; but so, that in the first the whole process is declared; and in the second, reflected especially upon this great transaction etc.

Analogy between the generation of eternal nature, and generation of the spirit in the soul. Flame. Liberty. Conjunction. Two-fold crack. No annihilation. Falling back; into nothing; into the hands of God—*of the living God.* All this expressed in the language of Teutonicus. First crack the basis of everlastingness. *Woman in travail hath sorrow,* etc., here eminently applicable.

This *generation of the spirit,* not so applicable to the spirit of Christ, though he went through the same process. May be called rather—an entrance of his spirit into the light world. Further explained from. His disciples followed after him in *regeneration.*

Father, into thy hands I commend my spirit. (1.) What spirit this is spoken of. (Leah, Rachel.) Plain, from saying *my spirit.* (2.) What this commending signifies. Christ's death, directly opposite to the first Adam's death; declared as to several considerable particulars. This *commending,* not chiefly a petition to be protected against infernal powers; but a delivering the whole image etc. Spirit himself *protector* to the soul.

(3.) Why not, *my soul,* nor my soul and spirit, but *spirit only?* The reason given by saying, The spirit went up into heaven, the soul down into hell, and the body in the grave; is exploded, and shown, what here was separated. That the soul alone could not have been a *plague* unto *hell:* and for want etc. And the true reason is declared. To say. The spirit had soul and body under his wings, is much, but not yet all. The soul was in the Father's hands already. Hell more properly in the soul, than soul in hell Soul in hell so properly, as before hell in soul. By taking in the spirit, hell could no more be in soul, much less the soul in hell. Why no mention of *body;* could be made out, chiefly from the first forty days in paradise, and the forty after the resurrection; but etc.

Of Christ's *heavenly immortal body.* Christ's glorified personal body. Universal body of the Eternal Word. When Christ considered relatively, as head of the church, both must be taken together; demonstrated. Christ's personal body, and bodies of the saints, must be one, and yet distinct. Distinction, wherein; oneness, wherein. Explained largely from what the first Adam should have propagated, if he had not wandered out; and what he hath instead thereof actually propagated.

What body the Lord gave in his last supper. Not the outward visible; proved. Not only his universal, but also personal body, implied in this giving; proved. The manner of this giving illustrated by simile, of the sun's giving substance, growth, life, etc., to plants and trees. But, because of a defect in this, another simile must be joined, of the sun's producing its own visible image in a glass.

The former simile unfolded, in twelve positions. The sun's generation, and manner thereof and the generation of eternal nature, must be understood; for upon both this and that, all weight and emphasis depends. (1.) The visible sun, an emblem of Christ's glorified personal body. (2.) That which without the sun's central place, answers to the universal body of the eternal Word. (3.) Upon what account called universal body of *spiritus mundi*, and of *eternal Word*, rather than of sun, and of Christ. (4.) Upon what account rightly also, universal body of the sun, and of Christ. (5.) In every place without the sun, that very same which in the central place; so etc. (6.) If it were not so, there would be no reciprocal communication, neither in this third, nor in the second principle. (7.) Sun, the only *glorified place*, though all partakes of that glory; so also, etc. (8.) Without the sun, nothing but death in this principle. Sun only hath the *key*; so also etc. (9) Sun raiseth life, in a process answering its own production on the fourth day; so also, etc. (10.) In this process, sun raises its own image in the tincture; so also etc. (11.) Sun communicates not its personal body, yet without this nothing can be effected in the universal body; so also etc. (12.) A concurrence of the plants and trees with the sun is required; so also etc.

Query, Whether Christ as to the humanity, a creature, or uncreated? Answered, (1.) with respect to them that own him a Son of man. (2.) With respect to them that insist only upon his being the Lord from heaven, (as Weigel, Schwenckfeld, and others,) is answered, by this distinction between his personal and universal body. In *from heaven*, the universal body tacitly implied. As to that, he is a creature; but as to this, uncreated; and reason, why."

Selection Fifteen.

William Law's Discourse, Made from Extracts of Freher's Works.

[Prefaced by a Note from Walton —Ed.]

[Note.—This and the subsequent discourses are to be understood rather as *abstracts* from Freher, made by Law for his own use, than verbatim copies of the originals: from which they differ in the form of the paragraphs, and in omitting here and there whatever *Law* considered not deserving *his* copying, or as unnecessary to the discourse. But the omissions (of which there are large portions in this and other places, antecedently and subsequently, which are not always distinguished by asterisks) may be of great value to such as are not so far advanced in theosophical science as he was: and therefore in case of publication of Freher's works, it would be proper to print from the original, however voluminously expressed for clearness and perfect conviction, and as a foreigner, than from any abbreviations thereof by a master of logical composition, and native of this country.]

In the MYSTERIUM MAGNUM, iv. 3. in an explication of the following characters [See 1, 2, 3, and 4 of Note.] he says.

The superior cross signifyeth (N.B.) *the unformed Word in Trinity, without all nature: and this character* [Note 3.]* *signifyeth the formed word, viz. the angelical world.* First,

The *unformed Word* here, is the same as *unmanifest*, both to be taken with reference to nature, declaring there is a Trinity unformed and unmanifest in nature, fitly represented by this character ⅄ an emblem of the Unity as unfolded in Three.

Secondly, in this character [Note 3.] both the first and the second world, both the eternal generation and the eternal manifestation of the Trinity he represents together. For he says expressly, that this *superior* ✢ is an emblem of the *Trinity without all nature*, and the [Note 5.] a character of the angelical world, that is, of nature in fire and light.

---

*Note:— ⅄¹   ⊕²   ⌀³   T⁴   ⊖⁵

I know indeed, that in the SIGNATURA RERUM, ch. xiv. 29, he declareth this same character [Note 3.] after a manner quite different from this explication made in the fourth chapter of MYSTERIUM MAGNUM. For there he says, the *superior cross above the circle is the kingdom of glory*, which plainly implyeth the generation of eternal nature.

But what wonder is it, if upon a different account one and the same word, and so also one and the same character be used to represent different things, or also one and the same thing differently considered?

In the MYSTERIUM MAGNUM he considered directly the Trinity without all nature, but in SIGNATURA RERUM he says not one word of the Trinity either as before or after nature, but considered only the generation of the principles, and especially the production of the fire, which in the Mysterium Magnum is not mentioned at all.

In the SIGNATURA RERUM therefore he placeth justly the kingdom of glory, or the angelical world (as the highest in nature, which nature only he then considered) in the highest place immediately above the principle of fire.

And in the MYSTERIUM MAGNUM he placeth justly also the Trinity without all nature (as the highest of all that can be named) even above the angelical world itself. Representing both that former and this latter, by one only character, but by such a one as is fit for both.

It appears also in this same chapter xiv. 8. of the Signatura Rerum, that Behmen had not forgotten what he had said thereof in the Mysterium Magnum.

For he says, *This impression is the only mother of the Mysterium's manifestation* (N.B. not of the Mysterium but of the Mysterium's manifestation) *and is called nature and substance, for it manifesteth what from eternity hath been in the eternal will.*

We are to understand, that in the eternity hath been a nature in the eternal will, as an eternal mind, but in the will it was but a spirit, And the substance of its powerfulness (sufficiency or ability) *was* (N.B.) *not manifest, except only in the playing of the will, which is the eternal wisdiom.* (N.B. 1.) That here expressly a manifestation is asserted, so well as denied: denied with respect to nature as nature generated, but asserted with respect to the eternal will; yet (N.B.) not with respect to this will, considered strictly as an abyssal will in itself, but considered as *playing* with itself, that is, with its byss, which byss itself is a manifestation of the first abyssal will. In this consideration then, nature was manifest in and to that will, before it is to be conceived as nature generated and manifested in and to itself.

(N.B. 2.) That in this playing of the will, the Three, or Trinity is understood, as our author expressly declareth.

For this *playing* is a *moving* even that *moving life* of the Deity, Mysterium Magnum, i. 7. And this playing of the abyss in or with its own byss supposeth a generation of this byss, even this eternal generation, wherein we are to understand three things, before and without the eternal manifestation thereof in and through nature. (N.B. 3.) That this playing is the *eternal wisdom*. If there is Wisdom (in what sense soever) before and without the manifestation in nature, there is also a Trinity before and without it; for that implyeth this, and this is inseparable from that. So then our author says here in the Signatura Rerum, that self-same which he saith in Mysterium Magnum.

But let us go now a little farther.

In the Aurora, which was our Author's first book, written as he thought only for himself, and, according to his own words, like as by a stammering child, we shall not find so much as one word of the first world, or of the first consideration of God, as generating himself in himself in trinity, without and above all nature. Not the least mention of an eternal nothing, temperature, liberty, chaos, mysterium magnum, abyssal eye, mirror of wonders, eternal generation wherein we are to understand three things, etc. :

But his deepest consideration is only the generation of eternal nature, in its seven distinct properties; from whence he proceeds immediately to the creation and fall of Lucifer, and further to the creation of this third principle. His account of the seven properties of eternal nature is here and there different from what he declared thereof in his following writings; especially concerning the generation of the fire, which is not so distinctly and circumstantially declared as afterwards. But the true reason thereof, is this: The understanding of the seven-fold generation, and chiefly of the fourth property thereof, depends a great deal upon an understanding of that eternal liberty, lubet, chaos, temperature, which is before and without nature. He then, as yet having no understanding of what is without nature, could not have declared the generation of the fire from an eternal conjunction of the liberty, with the dark properties of nature; but could and did declare it only so far as then his eye could reach, so therefore accordingly in the Aurora, he says very much of the most holy Trinity, but only as manifested in and through nature. Though he doth not yet use this word of manifestation, as distinct from his eternal generation in himself, for the reason mentioned above. All therefore that he says of the Trinity throughout the whole Aurora, is to be referred only to the second consideration of God, implying and presupposing the generation of eternal nature.

So also in the THREE PRINCIPLES, his second book, written seven years after the first, when the day-light, as he says, had overtaken the first dawning of the day, we may find indeed a clearer and more distinct explanation and continuation of what he had begun in the AURORA, concerning especially the generation of this our third principle; but we shall not find anything of this eternal generation of God in himself, without all nature, wherein *we are to understand three things*.

If now that former declaration of the Trinity, which implyeth and pre-supposeth the generation of nature, is the deepest and the only declaration thereof, why hath not our author in his following writings kept unto this only? Why hath he, or how could he have given us quite another and as he says, a deeper consideration thereof, under such an express title: *so*, or *so far* is God considered as in himself only without all nature.

May not this show us sufficiently that when he wrote these two books, he had not yet that great opening of the first abyssal world in his spirit; but only an opening of the second world, or of the generation of eternal nature in its two principles? And that his description of the Trinity in this beginning is good and true, and solid indeed, but not yet the deepest; and that he hath given us a deeper one in his following books, after he had a deeper opening in his spirit. In which deeper description therefore he speaketh, like as from another world, so also of another thing, for though he speaks but of one Trinity, and not of two, yet this one may be called in a sense and manner, another thing when it is looked upon in the first world and another again when in the second. Wherefore it doth evidence itself, that we ought not to confound the one description with the other, nor to take the one only, and to reject the other, much less to fight with the one against the other, but to leave each of them in its own place: the first, which afterwards was given, above nature, is of no benefit to us who are in nature, and yet of necessity to be known, *if we will understand the deepest original of all what is posterior:* and the second, which was given in the beginning, in nature, as that which we are only concerned with, and which our regeneration and eternal happiness depends upon. So doing we shall lose nothing of his writings, but find all the parts thereof in union and concordance.

Now this latter description of the Divine Being in Trinity, before and without nature, we find also not to be so full and plain, when he began to have an opening thereof, as it was afterwards, when it came to be wider and wider, but as this opening in his spirit went on gradually, so also his understanding and description did by degrees.

For in the THREEFOLD LIFE, his third book, which might be called with respect to this particular point, his Aurora; we cannot yet find a distinct consideration of God in Trinity, before and without nature, when yet we may find a plain disposition thereto, and as it were a mixture of these two considerations. Ch. iv. 86, 87, 88 he saith, *In the number Three are three centres, which are understood in eternal nature, but* (N.B.) *without nature, they are not understood. For without nature* (N.B.) *the name of God is Majesty, but in nature he is called Father, Son, and Holy Ghost.—That which is without nature profits me nothing, I could to all eternity neither see, nor feel, nor fathom it —— but since the Majesty* (N.B.) *hath generated nature, and hath thus opened or manifested itself therein in three persons, I do rejoice in that opening or manifestation, as a creature living therein eternally.*

Let us here observe, (1.) that in this third book of his, our author owns that, which in the first and second he was silent and doubtless quite ignorant of; viz. that *there is something without eternal nature.*

(2.) That he says of a *number three* and of *three centres*, both without and in eternal nature, with this distinction, that in nature they are understood, and without nature not understood.

(3.) That he useth before and without eternal nature, that relative expression of three centres, in answerableness to the three things In the Mysterium Magnum, and in opposition to the three persons manifested in nature. Whereby he placeth expressly before nature, not only One, as generating itself in Three, but also Three, as generated out of One, in the eternal generation without nature, and manifesting themselves also to be Three in nature.

(4.) That he says positively, Without nature, the name of God is *Majesty*; and giveth us this (N.B.) as a reason, why the three centres, or things without nature cannot be understood. Which must be further considered by and by.

(5.) That he placeth the three distinct names of Father, Son and Holy Ghost in nature; and without nature, that only single name of *Majesty*, which yet is such a one as by no means can be attributed unto the Unity, considered as abstracted from and antecedent to that eternal generation, whereby God in himself generates himself in Trinity, but is a name common unto all three, and must needs be attributed to the Tri-unity.

Whereby therefore he combineth the Unity with the Trinity before and without nature.

(6.) *The Majesty hath generated nature*, therefore not the Unity, but the Tri-unity hath generated nature.

(7.) That he distinctly says, *the Majesty hath opened or manifested itself in nature in Three persons.* If the Majesty hath opened, or manifested itself in nature, it hath not generated through nature a Trinity, but hath only manifested that which before was generated. Or else the distinction between generation and manifestation could signify nothing.

But a question will here arise, What sense can there be in the words, *without nature the name of God is Majesty?* Since Behmen says, that without nature is no light, lustre, glory, etc.

I know it may be said, for to reconcile this, The first abyssal will is before and without nature, and hath if so considered, as in and to itself, no majesty. This first will generated nature, and through nature it generated the second will, which is the first will's co-eternal son, called by Behmen nature's end, because it is free from nature, it is above nature, and is not belonging to nature, as one of the properties thereof, though it is generated in and through nature. Now in this eternal only begotten Son the Father's majesty appears, for He is, according to the Scripture, the brightness of his glory. Rightly therefore upon such an account, could Behmen have said, That without nature the name of God is Majesty. For in all the four chapters of the THREEFOLD LIFE, he placeth the generation of eternal nature between the first will, which is Father, and the second, which is the Father's co-eternal Son. Setting thus the Father before, and the Son after nature, but free from nature, and above or without it, as well as the Father.

This explication now, I grant is plausible, if looked upon from without, and superficially: for Behmen's own words do plainly say all these things; and if there were but that due and true distinction observed, between the *eternal generation without nature,* and the eternal manifestation in nature, and through nature, nothing more could be desired. But seeing that in this representation, and the application thereof to the majesty without nature, a confusion is made between these two, a great mistake is committed.

Yet none can be blamed for this mistake, because Behmen himself, in this book of the THREE-FOLD LIFE, (for reasons mentioned above) maketh as it were a mixture of the two considerations of the Divine Being, and doth use many times the word *generation,* when he speaks of the eternal manifestation. For which also neither can he be blamed, (1.) because not only in this beginning of the daybreak, as to this particular point he could not yet (as it is probable enough) discern sufficiently the one from the other. But also, (2.) because upon a good account, and with a particular respect, he could well have used the word generation, even in discoursing of the eternal manifestation through nature.

But yet from his following descriptions, when he was more especially upon this point, of the eternal generation in Trinity before nature, it is clear enough that such a distinction must be observed, and by them also this may be understood sufficiently, which of itself alone, would not be intelligible enough.

But the mistake in this account or explication of the word MAJESTY, is plain enough from hence, viz:

If Behmen by saying, *without nature the name of God is Majesty*, doth understand that majesty which is after nature, and is rightly called without nature, in a sense, and upon an account given thereof above; it must needs be a wrong and preposterous saying, when he adds, *the Majesty hath generated nature*, for this is absolutely false, and much rather must he have said, *nature hath generated the Majesty*, for this is true in its sense and place, but cannot be applied here. Where he, by saying the pure contrary, *the Majesty hath generated* nature, doth show sufficiently, that by this majesty he understands not that. Wherefore then, we must needs look out for such another sense as may be consistent with himself.

It is certain that the majesty of the Second Principle of light and glory is not here understood. And it is certain also, that we cannot compare this place with any other parallel one, in which he might have the same, or the like expression of a Majesty without nature.

Wherefore having observed, (1.) that this is the only place, in which he says, *without nature the name of God is Majesty*. And (2.) that this is the first place, in which he makes any mention of the Divine Being without nature, in distinction from an eternal manifestation thereof in nature, I say now upon this ground further, that here he had, the first time, upon his spirit that opening of the first abyssal world, with such an effect, as that his sight was instantly confounded and consumed, so that in a different sense, as mentioned above, he had seen and not seen.

That same now which he here in this first opening had seen or observed *without nature*, he calleth *Majesty*. Not that he had perceived or seen something distinctly, which could have given him a proper idea of what we use to call so, but because he could not find a more convenient expression than to call that *Majesty*, which his spirit could not bear, and was not able to look upon, and which must needs have been transcendency more terrible and awful to its eye, than the visible majesty of a great Ahasuerus was to queen Esther, etc.

And that he meant here by *Majesty* nothing else but this, may appear from this plain construction of his words. Without nature the three centres are not understood. For, says he, *without nature* the name of God is *Majesty*, giving us this name, as a proper reason, why the Three before nature cannot be understood. This *Majesty* therefore must needs denote something which is confounding man's understanding, not only by its own being so far above it that it cannot be looked upon, but also and even chiefly, by its working upon it so strongly, that all its natural powers must be overcome thereby. All which he asserts plainly of the chaos, or Eye full of wonders which is before nature.

However it be with this expression, it is undeniable, that since this majesty, hath generated nature, which nature in its first appearance showeth us the spiritual figure of a triangle, △, the three centres or things without nature, must needs be those three, which this triangle in nature is generated from, etc.

His fourth book of the Forty Questions we shall pass by, though a considerable place relating to the Majesty without nature might be observed.

In the fifth book then of the Incarnation he begins to distinguish expressly the two considerations of God in Trinity. Part II. i. 8–12, he showeth us the eternity without nature and its eternal stillness, the Eye of eternity, and looking-glass of wonders; the first Abyssal Will with its magia, which we are not to search into, because it hath no original, but compriseth or maketh itself in itself and is without all nature. (*Ergo*, there is (N.B.) a magia in the eternal generation, which is distinct and different from that magia that is in and belongs to eternal nature,) *Vid*. Six Points i.17.

Further he speaks of an eternal beginning, and an eternal end; of an eternal wisdom, or mirror of wonders distinct from the seeing and from the eternal Spirit; and which is of the greatest consideration, he says also of a *desire* of the first abyssal will, and that this desire is drawing of itself, which he explains by saying, this desire is the will's outgoing *lubet, or pleasure, ergo*, not that desire to nature, which is the beginning and first property thereof.

Chapter ii. he begins with the eternal byss, which the abyss, says he, *maketh in itself*, and maketh it by the desire, which in the chapter before was called Lubet, and here is expressly explained by *imagination*, and so distinguished again from the desire in nature. See of this distinction Signatura Rerum, vi. 1, 2, where he plainly says, The desire is a *hungry will, and is the natural spirit in his properties, but the lubet is out of the liberty, for God is desireless, as to his own being* (or in himself) *seeing that he wants nothing, all is his, and he himself is All. But a Lubet*, it hath, and is himself that will, to manifest himself,* etc. He will manifest himself in nature, which manifestation cannot be done without the desire. But having in himself a lubet, wherein the eternal generation of the Trinity is implied, he is manifest in and to himself, before and without the manifestation in nature, and cannot but know, etc. himself. [* a *lust-will* in the German.]

This eternal generation now our author further declareth, by an impregnation of the abyssal will, which makes in the abyss a byss. And by a *motion*, as distinct and different from that which is the second property of nature, as the lubet is distinct and different from the desire. *And thus, says he, we know an eternal abyssal Divine Being, and therein Three persons, none of which is the other, viz. the eternal Will, which is the cause of all beings, is the first*————In this will originateth the eternal beginning through imagination, wherein the Will impregnateth itself out of the Eye of wisdom, which is with the will in an equal eternity, without ground and beginning. This impregnation is the ground, or byss, of the will, the Son, heart, word, sound, or (N.B.) manifestation of the Abyss.—The third is the Spirit.

And that no one may fancy that eternal Nature is here implied, because there is spoken therein of a desire, moving, life, etc. he prevents that misapprehension by expressly adding, *This now is a short declaration of the Deity in the Abyss, showing how God dwelleth in himself, and is himself the centre of generation. But the human mind doth not acquiesce with this, but it enquireth after Nature, viz. after that whereout this world is generated, and all things created, etc.*

In his sixth book, called the SIX POINTS, i. 1–22. He first speaks of an *unessential will*, which is *dumb, mute*, and without knowledge of itself, until the fiery essences are raised therein, which cannot be raised up without *desire*, etc. Now this causeth the misapprehension of such an absolute necessity, as that the generation of nature, from the desire unto the production of Art, must be implied and pre-supposed in every consideration of the Trinity.

But let this here be taken notice of, that after he had spoken of such an unessential will, and applied it to the first abyssal will, he goeth on immediately to a consideration of a God in Trinity, without all nature, and showeth us, that the first abyssal will, (which is unessential indeed, and therefore dumb and mute, if considered strictly as to itself alone) is not alone before and without nature, and therefore also not unessential, and not dumb, and mute, but becometh essential in and by its own co-eternal byss, generated by the desire, viz. by that which before he had called lubet, pleasure, imagination, etc. and not by that *desire*, which is the beginning and first property of nature. For this byss is the only essence or essentiality of the abyss. And so is nature with all its properties from this consideration utterly excluded, and to be conceived as posterior.

Thus he saith directly, when he had spoken of the eternal Eye, mirror, etc., *Here we understand the eternal being of the Divine Trinity, together with the abyssal Wisdom. For the eternal will comprehending the eye, is the Father, That which is comprehended in the wisdom, wherein the comprehending makes a ground, byss, or centre in itself, is the Son or heart; for it is the word of Life, or (NB.) his essence wherein the will with its glance appears.*

And that we may have no apprehension of nature herein implied, he excludes it thus, *This we understand, that the Divine Being in Trinity in the abyss, dwelleth in itself, and generateth a byss in itself.*

Again, *Thus we understand, what the Divine Being is in itself without a principle and what the eternal beginning is in the abyss, and the eternal end in its own byss generated in itself.*

Again, *In that wisdom,* (wherein the eternal generation of the word, in the will was done, and is still doing from eternity to eternity) *the eternal principle, as a hidden fire, was known in the figure from eternity, and is known so in that wisdom to all eternity.*

Here (N.B. 1) that there is something before and without nature, which, upon a good account, may be called an eternal end, distinct from an eternal beginning, and that this eternal end is that same, which, in the eternal manifestation thereof, made in and through nature, is called nature's end. And that nevertheless there is a distinction between them running parallel with that, which there is between generation and manifestation, lubet and desire, three things or centres and three persons, etc.

(N.B. 2.) That here expressly is asserted, the principle of fire, that is nature, not only was known, but also, is still known, in that wisdom, which in the eternal generation of God in himself, is implied, and is even known in the figure only, as a hidden fire, that is, as not yet generated or brought forth actually.

If we then are to understand a Trinity without a principle, and if in the wisdom of this Trinity, the principle is known as a thing still hid, how can we think that the manifestation of this principle, or the generation of nature, must be implied or pre-supposed in, or is required as needful to the eternal generation of this Trinity? And how can knowing, perceiving, etc. in this Trinity be denied?

It is not only said, It was known so, as if this knowing had ceased in and by the manifestation of the principle, but it is also expressly said, It is still known so. This Trinity therefore, and this wisdom must still be a Trinity and a knowing wisdom in itself, and must still be considered as before, without and above nature, notwithstanding that nature is actually generated. *Quod erat demonstrandum.*

The next in order is the little treatise of the *Earthly and Heavenly Mystery*, comprehended in *Nine Texts*.

Thus then he begins: *The abyss is an eternal nothing, but maketh an eternal beginning, as a seeking. For the nothing is a seeking after something; and yet there is nothing which could give anything; but the seeking itself is the giving of that, which itself also is nothing but a desiring seeking. If then there is thus a seeking in the nothing, this seeking maketh in itself the will to be something, and this will is a spirit, like as a thought, this goeth out from the seeking, and is the seeking's seeker, for it findeth its mother which is the seeking.—And herein we understand, that the will is a spirit, and is another thing than the desiring seeking.—For the will is an imperceptible and unknowable life; but the seeking is found by the will, and is a being in the will. Now it is understood, that the seeking is a magia, and the will a magus, and that the will is greater than his mother.—*

Thus we give you in short to understand Nature and the Spirit of nature.—If then thus the eternal will is free from the seeking, but the seeking not free from the will, seeing the will ruleth over the seeking, we own therefore the will to be an eternal omnipotence, for he hath nothing equal unto itself. And the seeking is indeed a moving from the attraction or desire, but without understanding, and hath indeed a life, but without science. Now the will ruleth the life of the seeking, and doth with it what he pleaseth; and though he doth something, yet it is not known, until that being with the will doth manifest itself.—And thus we own the eternal will-spirit to be God, and the moving life of the seeking to be nature. For there is nothing sooner, both is without beginning; each is a cause of the other, and it is an eternal band.—And thus the will-spirit is an eternal knowing, or understanding of the abyss, and the life of the seeking is an eternal being of the will.

These are the words of our author, wherein he represents God and Nature. And from hence is now inferred and said, We see here, that he begins with the first abyssal will, and placeth nature in an equal eternity with the abyss; that he not only says, the abyss is an eternal nothing, but also, that the seeking (or nature) makes in itself this nothing to be something, and this even so, that he calleth this seeking the mother of the will, and the will an imperceptible, unknowable life. And again he says expressly, There is nothing sooner than these two, they are both without beginning, and each of them is a cause of the other.

Wherefore then, we cannot conceive a Trinity in any sense, nor any knowing, perceiving, or understanding, before and without nature; but we must conceive such an eternal Nothing, or such an Unity only, as afterwards is made Something, and is unfolded into Three, not only in nature, but also by the help and concurrence of nature. This is the argument drawn from this treatise against the Trinity before nature.

Trusting on the Divine help, I thus endeavour to answer it.

(1.) Then I say justly, that in this whole treatise, he hath no intent to show us directly the Trinity, neither as considered before, nor as in and after nature; but his purpose is only in general, to show the deepest and most internal original of this our third principle, and especially of things done and existent therein in *contrarieties*. This he deduceth rightly from the first abyssal will; and from that seeking, whereby afterwards he understandeth nature, saying, That there is nothing sooner than these two. All which is obvious and evident of itself, unto every attentive reader of this treatise, from the beginning to the end. Wherefore then

(2.) In all these words alleged concerning God, he speaks not of God considered as the whole Divine Being, and hath no occasion, much less necessity to tell us, in this place and for this purpose, what this Divine Being is in itself, or in its own eternal generation;

But he speaks of the abyss, only considered strictly by itself, and as abstracted from the byss. Which abyss, so considered, is God indeed, and may be called so; because it cannot be separated from its byss any further, than as to our separate consideration, but is not fully God, because not all what the name of God imports; and what we are to understand in God, is in this separate consideration implied. And

(3.) In all these words concerning *Nature*, he speaks not of nature, as nature actually generating or generated, but as considered before its generation and before it can properly be called nature. This is undeniable from v. 8 in the *Fourth Text*, and v. 3 in the *Fifth*, where he calleth these two, viz. God and nature, not only two *mysteries*, but also two *principles*.

By calling them two *mysteries*, he gives us to understand, that neither this nor that is as yet unfolded; but that each of them is looked upon as still concentrated in itself; for this is, in his style, the signification of a *mysterium*.

And by calling them two principles, he showeth us plainly enough, that here he takes not the name of principles in that sense, in which he takes it when he speaketh of the three principles throughout all his writings. For in this sense, he says himself that God is not a principle. And in this sense Nature also is not a principle in the singular number, but if considered as nature generated, is itself the two principles of fire and light, which the third is a visible outbirth of. But he calleth them two principles in that notorious common sense, in which the originals or the most radical beginnings of things, are called the principles thereof. And this latter sense is applicable both to God and nature, but not that former.

If then nature is called a principle in the singular number, and this even so, that it is joined in conjunction with God, called in the same sense a principle; nature must needs be considered as yet before the generation of fire and light, and as lying still in the first abyssal will, as a hidden fire, which burneth, and burneth not, according to his own expression above.

In which state, or rather in the consideration of which state, it must nevertheless be looked upon as distinct from the first abyssal will, without making any kind of mixture or confusion between them. And this distinction of the one principle from the other, or of nature from the first abyssal will, he showeth here as in the deepest root, and saith nothing at all of its properties; nay he doth not call it directly nature, but a seeking, and the will a seeker, and saith afterwards only, that by this seeking (viz. in its progress and unfolding itself,) nature is understood. So therefore it is plain, that here in this place he considereth nature, as not yet nature generated, but nevertheless as distinct from the first abyssal will, and (according to his own words) a mysterium in itself, distinct from that other mysterium, which is God, or that of God which Behmen calleth the abyss, and considereth as not yet unfolded in a byss. All which concerning nature, is punctually agreeing not only with this whole treatise, but with the rest of Behmen's writings. Now then

(4.) Our author not intending in this place, to declare what God is in himself, viz. what the whole Divine Being is in its own eternal generation in Three; nor also what Nature is, in its unfolding and displaying itself into seven; but only to declare what God and nature are in the deepest root with a mutual respect to each other, before they are to be considered, as three and seven, he could well have said, The Abyss is an eternal nothing, but maketh an eternal beginning, which is a seeking, etc. But if he had had an occasion and a mind in this place, as he had in others, to declare what the whole Divine Being is in itself, without nature, without a principle, in its own eternal generation only, he would have turned these words quite another way, and would have said, certainly to this effect, The Abyss is an eternal nothing, but maketh an eternal beginning, which is its co-eternal byss, heart, Son, or word, etc: for so we find he hath said in many places, especially in the MYSTERIUM MAGNUM. Where he not only saith of the abyss, that it is the will towards something, and the father of the beginning to the byss; but also of the byss, that this is the first will's eternal *finding*, and the perceptibility *thereof*, the ens (or something) of that abyss, which in comparison to the byss, is nothing, notwithstanding that it is also all in itself. And further calleth he that byss, the *seat* or *habitation* of the abyssal will, the eternal mind, the ground, and (N.B.) the *beginning of all beings*.

So then we see manifestly, that in two different considerations, in a twofold sense, and upon a twofold account, he speaketh of a twofold *finding*, and of a twofold *beginning*. Now we cannot take the one only, and reject the other, nor can we oppose the one to the other; but we must take each in its own place, and no contrariety can then appear.

The Abyss, which, if strictly and abstractedly considered as in and to itself only, is an imperceptible, unknowing, and unmoving being, or nothing, in comparison to all what is posterior, doth on the one hand find and perceive himself in himself; and this in and by his byss, which is his only begotten Son, in whom he is well pleased, and which is one with the Father. And on the other hand, the same abyss doth find and perceive himself without himself; and this in and by nature, as yet called here but a seeking: which Nature or seeking is not one with the Father, and is never called by Behmen the Son, heart, word, seat, etc. of God; though he be called the father of nature.

And so also concerning the beginning; the byss is the beginning of something in the eternal generation, when God, viz. the whole Divine Being is considered as in himself only:

And this seeking is the beginning of something in nature. The two beginnings are well consistent with each other, and none can destroy nor deny the other.

This I could demonstrate from more than twenty places, but one from this treatise will suffice. See then *Text* iv. 3, 4, 5, and *Text* v. 1. Where you shall find, that he says not only of an *impregnation* and *generation* in the spiritual life, or in God, according to what we heard thereof above, from many other places, but also (N.B.) that this generation goeth inwards (*introrsum*) into itself, and dwelleth in itself; when contrariwise the nature-life, or the generation of nature, from this seeking goeth outwards, (*extrosum*) towards without, or straightway forward.

And though he says also, That these two are not without one another, yet he explains himself by adding immediately, *So that there were a separation between them*. Without one another therefore they are so far, and upon this account, that without mixture each of them is in itself that which it is, and neither of them doth or can comprehend and contain the other, in its own essentiality;

When there is nevertheless an eternal band, and union between them.

If then this be so, no argument can be brought forth from this saying, The Abyss makes an eternal beginning, which is a seeking; as if this position must needs exclude, or could overthrow all what he says, in twenty places, or an eternal generation of God in himself, and of an eternal beginning in this generation. For, if we shall conceive, according to the words of this treatise just now quoted, that in the Divine Being, from the first abyssal will one progress is made towards within, and another towards without; we must needs conceive also, that each of them must have its own beginning.

For the beginning of the one, which needs must be considered as it were an essential part thereof, cannot be a beginning and part of the other; though these two beginnings may be both together at once, and even inseparable from each other.

And if thus in this treatise is inserted an impregnation of the first abyssal will, and such a generation as tendeth towards within, and dwelleth in itself; with a notorious distinction from nature, which tendeth towards without, and dwelleth in itself also; it is plain and clear, that in this treatise is asserted, though not declared particularly, the selfsame eternal generation, before, without, and above all nature, whereof we have heard so much hitherto, and wherein we are to understand three things. But,

(5.) There will be still replied, That Behmen says expressly, *that there is nothing sooner than these two,* viz. the abyss, and the seeking. If then these two are the soonest, we cannot conceive three to be sooner than these two.

Answer. In this consideration of God and nature, both looked upon as tending towards without, he says rightly, there is nothing sooner than these two.

For in our inquiry, made backwards, from the most outward things, towards the most internal root thereof, where always the remoter cause is conceived as sooner, prior or deeper, than that which is nearer, we cannot proceed any further, and can therefore find nothing sooner than these two. But in that other consideration, wherein we say with Behmen, That there is an eternal generation, whereby God generates himself in himself in Trinity, and this from eternity to eternity, without a principle, and without all nature; we may freely say the same words, There is nothing sooner than these three, viz. the abyss, the byss, and the band of union between them.

For seeing that the same abyss, is the first of these three, and the first also of these two, and this even so, that neither here nor there, this abyss can be separated, from what, so well here as there, is joined with it in union;

There is an equal beginning of numeration on both sides, and nothing can here be sooner than the three, like as there also nothing can be sooner than the two; and the three must needs be so deep and so central, and radical in this latter consideration, as the two are in that former. Nay, we may say also more, upon a good account, and without contradicting Behmen, that the three are sooner than the two.

For it is plain enough, that by saying so we do not mean, that there was a time, or instant, wherein the three were and the two were not; which would be most ridiculously said, that the abyss was sooner than the abyss, because the abyss was, when the abyss was not.

But we own with Behmen that the two are co-eternal to the three, and by saying, The three were sooner, we mean only, that in our regular conception they are to be conceived as if they were sooner, and that it would be a preposterous doing to conceive them otherwise.

Because we cannot say in any sense, that the abyss is descended from nature, or from this seeking, but we must say, that nature, with all that belongs to it, is descended from the abyss. For the abyss makes the *seeking*, says Behmen, but not the seeking makes the abyss. Wherefore then, we conceive this abyss as the very deepest and most internal, central root, driving forth as it were, in the same instant, two collateral branches, the one towards within, and the other towards without; and so far we say, Neither this nor that is sooner, but the abyss itself is sooner than both its branches. But further, upon another and deeper account, seeing that this same abyss is incomparably nearer related, and infinitely more familiar to that branch which is driven forth within, than to that which is without. For that which is within is one with itself, and equal unto itself, generated in its own bosom, and dwelling in it for ever;

When that which is without is different from itself, inferior in dignity, and used but as an instrument in its hand, etc. we can by no means therefore think or say, That which is within, is descended caused or originated from or by that which is without. But we must say, That which is without is from that which is within; and that which is within must needs therefore be sooner than that which is without.

Now, that which is without showeth us presently, in its first unfolding, the spiritual figure of a triangle; and that which is within, is nothing else but those three, that are to be understood in the generation of God himself in himself. If then these three within are not from the three without, but these latter from the former; the three within are rightly conceived and said to be sooner than the three without.

And to show that this is not a construction of my own, see Six Points, chapter i. *v.* 9 where having declared what the abyss is, not as here, with respect and relation to nature, but as considered absolutely in itself; and having told us, that it is an eternal seeing Eye, wherein nature lieth hid, and is nevertheless seen and known, etc. he says expressly the same words, which he says here, *There is nothing sooner than this eye, nothing is before it, which were deeper*, etc.

From hence now it is evident, that if nature itself in general, and so also all what belongs unto nature in particular, was seen and known, nay, which is much more significant, is still seen and known in the figure, as a hidden fire before, or sooner than it is nature generated or unfolded: Farther, if this seeing and knowing nature, doth imply (as hath been proved) the eternal generation in Trinity: and again, if there is nothing deeper or sooner than this seeing Eye; the Three in the eternal generation within, must needs be conceived as sooner or deeper than nature, with all its three and seven without.

Nay, from the plain words of this same treatise, it may be proved sufficiently. For he makes an express plain distinction, between within and without, saying not only Text v. 1, that the one of these two mysteriums tends towards within, and the other towards without; but he says also more explicitly Text iv. 4, that *since the abyss is impregnated, the generation goeth towards within, and dwelleth in itself, for the essence of the other life (viz. of nature) cannot comprehend this impregnation, and cannot be a receiver, (or a receptacle) thereof. So therefore the impregnation must go into itself, and must be its own receptacle, which is a son in the eternal Spirit*, etc.

Now it is evident to every one, that always that which is within must be conceived as deeper than that which is without; and seeing that always that which is within, is a source, cause, ground, original, root, etc. of that which is without; that therefore which is within must in one sense needs be conceived as sooner than that which is without, notwithstanding that in another sense, the one is so soon as the other.

If then here in this treatise, such an impregnation and generation of a Son is asserted, as tendeth towards within, with an express exclusion of nature, which is said that it goeth towards without, and that it cannot comprehend this generation, then there is in this book as well as in any other of our author, an eternal generation, without and above all nature, asserted, though not declared particularly. But,

(6.) It is objected also, That Behmen placeth nature next or immediately to the abyss, and that therefore nature must be conceived as standing in the midst, between the abyss and byss, and consequently no Trinity at all can be imagined, before and without nature.

Answer. Rightly doth he place nature next or immediately to the abyss, as to that which is the first of all, the deepest and most central: but doth it follow from hence, that nature must be conceived as standing between abyss and byss? By no means; it would follow indeed, if there could be shown, that Behmen placeth the byss at a further distance from the abyss, behind or after nature. But no such thing may be found in any of all his writings.

He placeth the byss not only so near, but also, in a sense even nearer and more immediately to the abyss, than nature; so that abyss, nature and byss are not to be conceived as three things following the one upon the other in a direct forward line, but, the byss and nature are to be conceived as two collateral branches, the former tending from the abyss towards within, and the latter from the same abyss towards without. Of this see MYSTERIUM MAGNUM, vii. 6. *The Father*, says he, *is the will of the abyss: he is without all nature or beginning; the will towards something: this (father) sets himself into a lubet for his own manifestation, and this lubet is the will's or Father's power comprehended; and is his son, heart, and seat; the first eternal beginning in the will*, etc.

Pray what can be plainer, and more for our position? If the byss or Son is the first eternal beginning in the will, how can that beginning, which is, in a sense, without the will, and which the abyss maketh with the seeking, be before it, and stand between the abyss and the byss? And if this beginning is rightly called the first, so well as that, so that there is nothing sooner than this, and nothing also sooner than that, must not they both be conceived as two collateral branches?

And must we not say, The seeking is the first in that progress, which tendeth towards without; and the byss the first in that generation which is within? If we then will not turn out of doors, or make it an insignificant nugatory prattling, what he says of such a distinction, between within and without, we cannot but freely see and own, that from his placing nature next and immediately to the abyss, no argument can be taken against an eternal generation in Trinity without all nature.

(7.) Concerning that part of this argument, where there is said, Behmen calleth the abyss an eternal nothing, and says, the seeking, that is, nature maketh this nothing to be something in itself, which seeking therefore he calleth expressly the mother and the cause thereof; so then we are not to think of any other something, but what is made in and by nature.

Concerning this, I say, little more wants to be added, for what we declared hitherto doth answer all these things sufficiently. It is demonstrated above, that the abyss is not absolutely nothing in and to itself, though it is rightly called nothing, with respect and in comparison to nature. For the abyss in itself, is an eternal seeing Eye, which seeth and knoweth nature, in the figure, as a hidden fire, before it is nature generated. Nature therefore doth not make the abyss to be something to itself, and Behmen tells us no such thing, but the pure contrary: he tells us, viz. that nature makes this nothing (which before was nothing in and to nature) to be now something in and to itself, that is, in and to nature, not in and to the abyss. How can nature make something in the abyss, when it is not only without it, and tendeth altogether towards without, but also, when it is itself made by the abyss to be an eternal beginning, and when this abyss is in itself beginningless, nay, when it is an abyssal seeing Eye, which seeth nature before it can be called nature? Nowhere shall we find in Behmen, that nature makes the abyss to be an abyss, neither that it is called the mother and the cause of the abyss, but only (N.B.) of the will.

There will be replied. The abyss and the will are but one, if then nature is the cause of the will, it is the cause of the abyss also. Answer. It is true, they are but one; but it is true also, that in this consideration, they are nicely to be distinguished, and you may find this distinction plainly enough throughout the three or four first texts of this treatise.

The abyss is in this consideration prior to the will, and is an absolute name, bearing no relation to nature; but the will is a relative name, and implieth a notorious tending towards without. The abyss as abyss is nothing to nature, for there is not yet any concern between them; but this abyss as a will towards nature, is now concerned with nature, and is upon this account something to nature, and no more something only to itself. The abyss, considered as abyss only and strictly in itself, is not the father of nature, but an eye, seeing nature before it is nature generated; but this same abyss considered as a will towards nature, is the father of nature. Nature therefore is not the cause of the abyss's being an abyss, but may be called the cause of the abyss's having a will to nature, and further of being a father of nature; because from nature's being seen in the abyss before it was nature, this will is to be conceived, as raising itself and tending towards without, like as almost in such a manner, a son may be called a cause of his father's being a father, but not of his having been a man, fit and sufficient for his generation. So now this something, in the progress from the abyss towards without, cannot make us to fix our eyes upon itself only, and to deny that there is any other something, but what is made in and by nature. But rather it directs us to look up higher, for that something which we find in the eternal generation, which turneth as it were away from nature, and tendeth towards within.

For it is plain and obvious everywhere in all the books of Behmen, that the byss in this eternal generation is constantly called the father's or abyss's ens, essence or something, his eternal perception, his heart, word or son, wherein the father is well pleased, etc.

Having now, as I hope, sufficiently answered all the parts of this great objection, we are to proceed further—

[Note.—Not finished in because the objector (one Mr. Pierce) owned himself mistaken, and satisfied by thus much, as expressed in the following letter:]

Selection Sixteen.

List of Freher's Works

[Compiled by Walton, possibly based on a list by James Pierrepont Grieves.—Ed.]

[…] It remains then, in this Postscript, to give the particulars respecting Freher's writings; which are only known, and only can be known to ourselves. These intimations may therefore serve as a direction for their future publication, should it not please the Divine Providence to honor us as the immediate instruments of so great a benefaction to the world.

The following then, is a correct account of Freher's Writings, and in the order in which they were composed. After which statement, we shall present our annotations respecting the editions to be followed in case of their publication. The Titles and Contents are these following :—

(1.) SERIAL ELUCIDATIONS of the PRINCIPLES of PHILOSOPHY and THEOLOGY of BOHEMIUS, surnamed the Teutonic Theosopher. In NINE VOLUMES.

VOL. A.—(1.) Of GOD considered WITHOUT all NATURE and CREATURE. (2.) Of GOD, considered as MANIFESTING HIMSELF through Eternal NATURE. Of the Two co-Eternal Principles—Of the Seven Properties—And, of the Three Constituent Parts of Nature. With a SYMBOL in illustration of the subject.

VOL. B.—AN EXPLANATION of that SCHEME, or Table of BOHEMIUS, wherein GOD is CONSIDERED in the UNITY and TRINITY, WITHOUT all NATURE and CREATURE.— (3.) An ANSWER to an OBJECTION, concerning the DESIRE'S ATTRACTING ITSELF.— (4.) Of the further MORE EXTERIOR MANIFESTATION of GOD, through the CREATION of ANGELS. Of Material Causes.—(5.) Of the FALL of LUCIFER and ALL his ANGELS.

VOL. C.—(6.) Of the CREATION of this our OUTWARD THIRD PRINCIPLE, wherein we Live, and Move, and have our Outward Being. With a Discourse on the Scope of St. John's Words, 'In the beginning.'

VOL. D.—(7.) Of the FALL of MAN from his primeval GLORY and PERFECTION, down INTO the SPIRIT of this WORLD.—(8.) Of the NATURAL PROPAGATION of MAN, in this now CURSED four-elementary WORLD.—(9.) Of MAN'S REGENERATION, through the BLOOD and DEATH of CHRIST.

VOL. E.—(10.) Of the ETERNAL WORD'S BECOMING FLESH. Or of the PURE, IMMACULATE CONCEPTION and INCARNATION of our LORD JESUS CHRIST, in the WOMB of the blessed VIRGIN MARY.

NOTE.—The above systematic discourses are presumed to have been written between a.d. 1699 and 1703. The references therein made to J. B.'s Works, it may be proper to mention, are to the German edition of 1682, the numbers of the paragraphs or verses of which, do not always correspond with those of the English translation. The next treatise to which the author applied himself, was that which we have hereafter denominated MICROCOSMOS: the idea of which was originally taken by him from a German publication of a.d. 1696, by *Johan Georg Graber* and *Johan Georg Gichtel*, entitled, '*A brief Manifestation of the Three Worlds or Principles in Man.*' The original title of this treatise, was THREE DIFFERENT TABLES WITH THEIR EXPLANATIONS. In the year 1717, the author made considerable enlargements in the 'Explanation' of the First Table; and in the the year 1727, an alteration was made in the Second and Third Tables, by the substitution of a *Peacock* for a *Hunting Dog*, according to J. B.'s metaphor in his 'Mysterium Magnum,' xxi. 12. We shall therefore present this work as if composed a.d. 1717.

[The preceding treatises in elucidation of the scope and principles of philosophy and theology of BOHEMIUS, were written at the request of esteemed friends of the author, and lent to them for perusal; amongst whom may be mentioned the learned Francis Lee, and the Rev. K. Waple, of St. Sepulchre's, Skinner Street. Indeed, it would appear from observations interspersed by the author throughout his writings, that what he undertook of this nature up to the year 1712, was altogether done at the entreaties of his friends, on emergent occasions. About the close of the Seventeenth and the early part of the Eighteenth Century, the writings of Bohemius (such of them as could be obtained, for they were then as now rare to be met with,) were earnestly looked into by many learned persons; some of whom (as might well be imagined,) formed misconceptions of their very profound yet exact and true sense, and so raised objections to such points and averments in them, as seemed to them in disaccordance with sound philosophy. Among the latter parties, it appears was one Mr. P., a friend of the Rev. Mr. Waple above-mentioned, who therefore requested our author to clear up the true sense of J. B.'s ground which had seemed to his friend uncertain; whereupon he wrote the following Treatise, as on similar occasions, the remaining pieces of this series. These latter, we conjecture, were composed between the years 1705–12.]

VOL. F.—NOTHING and SOMETHING. Being a DISCOURSE concerning the true significant sense of BOHEMIUS's DEEPEST, ETERNAL or ABYSSAL NOTHING. HOW this NOTHING (according to his Gift and Declaration) BRINGS FORTH ITSELF into SOMETHING, in and through the PROCESS of Eternal NATURE. HOW this SOMETHING is DISTINGUISHED FROM, (or WHETHER, and in WHAT SENSE it may be called OPPOSITE TO,) that former NOTHING. BUT more especially, HOW ALL his different DESCRIPTIONS of the DIVINE BEING, in UNITY and TRINITY, now as BEFORE or WITHOUT, and then as IN or AFTER Eternal NATURE, (only by means of UNDERSTANDING distinctly the PROPER MEANING of his ETERNAL NOTHING and SOMETHING.) may be found standing, without all Contradiction, in a MOST HARMONIOUS CONCORDANCE. Written in EXPLICATION of FOUR EMBLEMATICAL FIGURES, in which what is herein stated in Words, is for more distinct Apprehension, represented by several Signs and Characters.

NOTE.—The Four emblematic Figures mentioned in this title, (or as they might have been very properly termed—a Four-fold spiritual Figure,) constitute the first four of the 'Thirteen Theosophic Emblems' which were afterwards engraved and inserted at the end of the Second Volume of J. B.'s Works, large 4to., published a.d. 1764. These four Figures, containing the basis of the divine revelation, the author enlarged into the Scheme in question, we judge about the year 1710. They were, probably, composed in elucidation of the single Symbol invented and inserted by the author at the end of VOL. A, *supra*, which figure might not have been clear to the readers of that discourse; whereupon on further reflection, the author was enabled to present his conception in this more lucid and felicitous manner. Query, Were the four circularly inclosed figures on p. 4 of our 4to. collection of fair copies of all the Author's symbolic illustrations to his writings, also originally intended for, or belonging to this figure at the end of VOL. A., or to the treatise here in question : which are thus respectively headed, *Without all Nature—An Eternal Nothing—Why the Eternal Nothing introduces itself into Nature and Creature—*And, *How the Eternal Nothing introduces itself into Nature?* We think whether so or not, in case of publication they should go with the latter.—[This treatise was not finished, because the objector owned himself mistaken, and satisfied by what the author had so far given. The first Nine pieces of the next following Volume (G.), however, supply what is wanting to it.]

VOL. G —(1.) NINETY SEVEN POSITIONS concerning GOD in UNITY and TRINITY, CONSIDERED both BEFORE and AFTER Eternal NATURE, according to BOHEMIUS'S CENTRAL PHILOSOPHY.—(2.) GENERAL POSITIONS concerning the DIVINE BEING in UNITY and TRINITY, and especially the GENERATION of ETERNAL NATURE, gathered from our FORMER WRITINGS, according to the mind of BOHEMIUS, and all taken either immediately FROM his own plain unquestionable WORDS, or by means of an EVIDENT CONSEQUENCE flowing forth freely out of them. *An unfinished treatise.* [At the end of some thirty pages of this Discourse, we find the following remark made by the author, *Here the matter was interrupted, nay broken off with violence.*]—(3.) HOW the PROPERTIES of Eternal NATURE are to be considered IN GOD.—(4.) HOW that the TWO SIMILIES made use of in a FORMER DISCOURSE, do NOT IMPLY that there are TWO TRINITIES:——(5.) FIVE QUESTIONS, raised OUT OF the FORMER DISCOURSES, ANSWERED.—(6.) CONCERNING the Expression, DARKNESS in GOD.—(7.) ANSWERS to the following TWO QUESTIONS, first, *Whether Bohemius asserts, that there was a motion of the central fire with its own self-desire, whereby the Will of God was stirred in both fires, and the wrath fire broke forth, before the Fall of Angels? Secondly, What is the true notion of own self-desire as it relates to fire and forms, and such like things of themselves inanimate; will and desire, in propriety of speech, belonging only to intellectual and rational beings?*—— (8.) A CONFERENCE (between A and B.) concerning ETERNAL NATURE, whether OUT OF GOD, or only EFFECTED BY his WILL.—(9.) REPRESENTATIONS of BOHEMIUS'S ETERNAL LIBERTY and ABYSSAL UNITY, *pari passu ambulant.*

NOTE.—Here at this place, of this collection or arrangement of the author's earlier writings, might not inappropriately have been inserted, the Fragment entitled, 'The SUBSTANCE of THREE CONFERENCES between a GERMAN THEOSOPHIST and an ENGLISH DIVINE,' written it is supposed about a.d. 1710.—We also take this opportunity of stating our conjecture, that the Fragment of this author, (of the exact character of writing of this last mentioned, and doubtless of the same date of composition,) headed IMMANUEL, and treating expressly of the 'SEVEN PROPERTIES of NATURE, with its TWO co-eternal PRINCIPLES, and THREE constituent PARTS,' was designed as a sequence to the Discourse of NOTHING and SOMETHING heretofore mentioned. Whether the author ever finished this piece, or whether he abandoned it, with a view to present its purposed contents in the projected *Conferences on Predestination*, cannot now be ascertained; but it is certain that the last mentioned 'CONFERENCE' Fragment, was left by the author in the state in which it is now found.—Further, there might have been also introduced in this place and relation, the remaining Fragment, in the author's handwriting, (as indeed are all these Fragments here mentioned,) which we have denominated A THEOSOPHIC CONFESSION of FAITH,' written in German and English, face to face, which commences at PROPOSITION XCV, and ends at Proposition CXXIV. There is every reason to conclude, this last inestimable piece was really completed, and that it was written by the author, *immediately after* the treatise of the 'BECOMING MAN, etc.' described Vol. E, *supra*; but no traces now exist either of the antecedent or subsequent portions of it, to those above described. To resume.

(10.) The PROCESS of the PHILOSOPHICAL WORK, considered as thoroughly ANALOGICAL with THAT in MAN'S REDEMPTION through JESUS CHRIST; and REPRESENTED by POSITIONS, as to its PRINCIPAL CIRCUMSTANCES. According to the DESCRIPTION given thereof, in J. B.'s SIGNATURA RERUM, Chaps, vii, x, xi, xii.—(11.) The GROWING of VEGETABLES (with RESPECT to their YEARLY RENEWING in the SPRING-TIME) as DESCRIBED by BOHEMIUS.

VOL. H.—CRITICAL OBSERVATIONS upon the REV. EDWARD WAPLE's EXERCITATIONS upon the PHILOSOPHY and THEOLOGY of BOHEMIUS, as elucidated in the PRECEDING DISCOURSES, and as set forth In J. B.'s WRITINGS, made at his own request.

VOL. I.—The PARTICULAR CONTENTS of all the Former Treatises, (v. pp. 461–91 *sup*.)—[The above series of Writings were composed, as we have stated, between a.d. 1699 and 1712, when Mr. Waple died; at which time, it would appear, our Author resided in his house.]

(2.) HIEROGLYPHICS SACRA, or DIVINE EMBLEMS, in THIRTEEN FIGURES, with their EXPLANATIONS. In elucidation of the BIRTH and BEGINNING of Nature, and of the MORAL PROGRESS and END of THINGS.

(3.) SIXTEEN CONFERENCES, CONCERNING the modern DOCTRINE of PREDESTINATION. Illustrated with SYMBOLS and DIAGRAMS. Wherein the Subject is fundamentally Resolved from the Ground of Nature, as well as from Scripture. In Eight Vols.

VOL. I.—THE FIRST CONFERENCE. A Dissuasive from searching into the doctrine of Predestination.—The Second Conference Proving that the Scriptures do not always understand the selfsame by the words, God, and Lord.—THE THIRD CONFERENCE. Of the Deity considered as in himself only, *extra naturam*. Point, Centre, Circumference.—THE FOURTH CONFERENCE. Of the Deity as manifested in and through the Properties of Eternal Nature, which are and must be Seven.—THE FIFTH CONFERENCE. Concerning the Three Radical, or Inferior Properties, and of each of them in particular.

VOL. II.—THE SIXTH CONFERENCE. Concerning the Fourth Property of Eternal Nature, standing between the Three Inferior, and the Three Superior properties. With Three large Digressions. The First, against Socinus; the Second, proving that this Nature is justly called Eternal; and the Third, against that New (*Bourignon Poiret*) Doctrine, which denies an Absolute Necessity for the Death of Christ upon the Cross. [The subject of this latter digression was made the foundation of a large special discourse; which immediately succeeded the present work.] THE SEVENTH CONFERENCE. Concerning the Three Superior Properties of eternal Nature. The production of the Fourth Property, or united Power of Fire and Light. A parable of *All-mine* etc. God, and our God. J. B.'s Word, *Scientz*, not rightly expressed by the English word, Science. A true Fable of *Will-mine*. Riches and Poverty of Eternity.

VOL. III.—THE EIGHTH CONFERENCE. Concerning the Two co-eternal Principles of Nature. Of Annihilation and Transmutation.—THE NINTH CONFERENCE. Being a Particular Consideration of that Noble Simile, so much recommended to our Consideration by Bohemius.

NOTE.—Hitherto, the Author has only been preparing the way for a fundamental resolution of the doctrine, according to the central philosophy of Bohemius. In the remaining Conferences, it is settled first according to the Scripture, and then according to the previously opened ground of Nature, being represented according to J. B.'s deep and full sense thereof. The chief importance of this work consists in the comprehensive and perspicuous elucidation of the seven properties of Nature, with its two co-eternal principles, and three constituent parts, of darkness, fire and light; which is contained in the Third to the Ninth Conferences, above described. This most essential knowledge, of the *seven properties* of Nature, is in no other of this author's works, so clearly, copiously, and demonstratively exhibited as in the present treatises.—No one can have any solid pretensions to a knowledge of theosophical truth, until he shall have mastered in understanding and experience, this most fundamental subject, of the constituent ground of Nature.

VOL. IV.—THE TENTH CONFERENCE. [Wherein the Doctrine is settled, as yet, only according to the Scripture.] Predestination cleared up by Seven Particulars in the Simile of a Wise Man. Five Kinds of Predestination cut off from this Discourse. Proofs that God neglected no Soul, neither before, nor under, nor after the Law.

VOL. V.—THE ELEVENTH CONFERENCE. Three Preliminaries; first, What Truth is in the Scriptures; secondly, Of the Letter and the Spirit; and thirdly, Of rightly Dividing the Word of Truth. *Voluntas Signi et Beneplaciti*. Of the Turning of Man's Will. Of God showing Mercy to whom he will. Of Pharaoh hardened. Of Jacob and Esau. Of the Father's giving men to the Son. Objections raised from Romans ix, and other places in Scripture. Of St. Paul and St. James about Justification.

VOL. VI.—THE TWELFTH CONFERENCE. St. Paul and St. James reconciled about Justification. The Strongest Predestinarian Argument, Answered. A Dream about the Doctor. Of Pharaoh again, as also of Jacob and Esau. Election and Reprobation not two collateral Branches of Predestination.

VOL. VII.—THE THIRTEENTH CONFERENCE. Concerning Pelagianism, or, the Grace of God and the Free Will of Man.—THE FOURTEENTH CONFERENCE. Concerning Semi-Pelagianism. Of Jeremiah, Ebedmelech, etc. An English Simile. A Wise and Foolish Son. The Preventing Grace—and the Engrafted Word are one, and yet also distinct. Saul and St. Paul. With a Translation of *Gottfried Arnold's Impartial Account of the Pelagians and Semi-Pelagians* in his 'History of the Church and of Heretics,' in the German Language.

[In the author's Original the following remarks are prefaced by him to this discourse:—"To this Fourteenth Conference belongeth my translation of a treatise of one who calls himself *Hilar. Theomilus*. But here is only the half part thereof, because the other half is not restored, but kept back from me wrongfully, by one, who certainly would have charged me with injustice, if I had served him so," etc.]

VOL. VIII.—THE FIFTEENTH CONFERENCE. Concerning a MS. of Bishop Sanderson, so far as his Ninth Position, upon the modern doctrine of Predestination, the Series of the Decrees of God, and the Causes and Means of Men's Salvation: as also many Questions which are now most in agitation, not only in the Church of England, but in many foreign Churches also, popish and reformed. Written by him, part in Latin and part in English, but now (upon a certain emergent occasion.) translated and transcribed all in English by one, who heartily wisheth that Babel might be pulled down, and that the Spirit of God might be built up in Jerusalem.—THE SIXTEENTH CONFERENCE. Concerning the same MS. from the Bishop's Ninth Position to the End. Also further considering several Distinctions between Grace and Grace, which are used by Predestinarians.

NOTE.—These sixteen conferences are considered to have been written by the author, chiefly in the year 1715; who, it is presumed, adopted the dialogue mode of representation, as being best calculated to elucidate his very profound subjects, without too much wearying the attention and patience of the reader. Still it were to be wished that the substance of the *Third to the Ninth Conferences* had been presented in a more condensed form, as indeed the worthy author would appear to have proposed to himself to do, in and by the *'Immanuel'* Fragment, referred to in the notices of the contents of VOL. G, *supra*, but which whether completed or not, does not now appear. The theosophical student may very profitably go through these intermediate Six Conferences, and extract out of than that which is purely of solid instruction. This work is duly illustrated with symbols.

(4.) FIVE CONFERENCES, concerning the ABSOLUTE NECESSITY of all the HOLY SUFFERINGS and DEATH of JESUS CHRIST upon the CROSS. With a large HIEROGLYPHICAL FIGURE, representing the PROCESS of CHRIST, in effecting the REDEMPTION.—THE FIRST CONFERENCE. Being Preliminary to the Arguments against the position—'That the Mediation of Christ Implies no Necessity of his Death;' and giving an Account of the Origin of the said Opinion.—THE SECOND, THIRD and FOURTH CONFERENCES. Proving the Necessity of the Death of Christ, from the Ground of Scripture. The FIFTH CONFERENCE. Wherein is demonstrated the Necessity thereof, under some Emblematical Figures.

NOTE.—This work is supposed not to have been completed by the author, though the special mention of *two more conferences*, made at the end of the Fifth Conference, and also of the *large hieroglyphic figure* which was to be the subject of these remaining portions of it, would seem to imply the contrary. If the two deficient conferences were really written, they were not with the Author's other MSS., at the time of his decease, nor have they been in the possession of his intimate friends, and admirers of his writings since, up to the present moment. The original copy of this work, which is supposed to have been written a. d. 1716, is likewise no longer known to be in existence.—The portion of it which will be of most esteem with the theosophical Student, is the Fifth Conference. And we are not sure that, in case of a republication of the 'Third to the Ninth Conferences' of the 'Predestination' work, in a severed form, this last or fifth Conference of this Work might not very Judiciously be placed before them, though an "unfinished" piece.

(5.) MICROCOSMOS, or the Formal IMAGE of DEITY and all NATURE, MAN. Considered in his PRIMEVAL STATE, his FALLEN STATE, and his STATE of REGENERATION. In THREE TABLES or SYMBOLS, with their EXPLANATIONS.

NOTE.—As may have been perceived by the annotation made on VOL. E. of the *Elucidations*, etc., these Tables with their Explanations were originally composed immediately after that said treatise; but that the author's improved knowledge in subsequent years of his reflections, led him to make a great enlargement of the Explication of the First Table; though for want of convenience, leaving the other two in their original state. This First Table with its Explanation, would appear to have been regarded, either by the author himself, (on account of its universality of comprehension and completeness, and its practical Christian scope,) or by his particular friend, copier and illustrator, *Leuchter*, as one of the best of his performances, for in the portraits afterwards made of him by the latter, this Table is generally represented as being held in his hand, and the subject of his immediate contemplation. As we have observed, the finishing stroke was put to this Explanation of the First Table, in year 1717: and some time afterwards, after the author had finished his two last pieces, which were written in his *native German language*, the translation of this Table and its Explanation, was also made into the same language, whether by the author himself or by Leuchter, does not now appear. The writer however is inclined to think only by the latter; whose German copy is that in the British Museum; and which was made to match his copies of the author's last two pieces, in the German language and character, which are in our possession. The author's first *rough drafts in German* of the 'Tables' themselves, with English Explanations, were then made, it is conjectured, about a.d. 1703; the final ones, from which the colored copy in the B.M. was afterwards made, About a.d. 1727.—We should observe, that the German translation of the Explanation of this First Table, is more illustrated with Diagrams and Emblems than the English original; wherefore in case of publication, our English copy should be compared with that, as to where the Emblems and Diagrams (of all of which we hold separate copies,) should be inserted. The Tables themselves were subsequently engraved for insertion in VOL. III. of J. B.'s Works, 4to., pub. a.d. 1772, with a purported Explanation of them annexed; but this we must state, is a sad mutilation of the original, and should no longer be tolerated. The drawings of the Tables are also not done justice to, by the engraver of those plates; these being much deficient in expression and spirit, to the said original fair copy drawn by Leuchter, now in our possession.—The real origin of these Tables and their Explanations, we must not fail to add, was to elucidate the plate (or truth couched in it) by J. B. himself, in Chapter ix of his THREEFOLD LIFE.

(6.) EPISTLES. WRITTEN in London, during the YEARS 1713–1717.

THE FIRST LETTER To the Church or Religious Meeting, in Bow Lane. Wrote in the early part of the year 1713. (2.) THE SECOND LETTER. To the Same. With also, PART OF A LETTER read by the Author at the Conference held according to the Proposal in this Second Letter. (3.) THE THIRD LETTER. Read and delivered by the Author to the Church in Bow Lane, November 1st. 1713. (4.) THE FOURTH LETTER. Wrote probably 1714, or early in 1715. This Meeting was not, as has been stated incorrectly in a letter of Mr. Law of April 8th. 1747, the celebrated Philadelphian Society, (which arose about a. d. 1697 and continued until a. d. 1703 or 4, and the spirit of which, as appears from Roach's writings, was somewhat maintained up to the date of his two publications,) but was a Society formed about a. d. 1706 of a number of persons who were also well versed in the terms and phraseology of the writings of Bohemius, but some of whom it would appear, made a lamentable abuse or perversion of them. These Letters, as the observations at the end of the 'Explanation' of the First Table of 'Microcosmos,' show, how their Author was induced to visit and assemble with that Society, about 1712, and what he thought of its proceedings; and containing his views how to render the company a truly spiritual Church. (5.) THE FIFTH LETTER, addressed to one Mr. Inglis in Scotland, dated September 20th. 1715. This Mr. Inglis had addressed a Letter to this Society in November 1712, (which is attached to our collection of these Epistles,) in answer to one from it; also another in, it is presumed, the following year, both of a deeply pious practical character: and it appears that a correspondence was kept up between them, also that Mr. Inglis was privately made a referee, by one of the members, whose spiritual conduct had subjected him to the suspicion and censure of his brethren; whereupon ensued the Letter of this author last mentioned. (6.) THE SIXTH LETTER, which is found in the Copies of his Letters, next following the *Letter to the Bishop of Bangor*, but which we think might judiciously be inserted in this place, was probably addressed by the author to the members of this Society generally, or to his own particular friends amongst them, at what date does not now appear, but probably previous to the above mentioned Letter to Mr. Inglis. (7.) A LETTER of 15 sheets, to a Mr. Gildersleve, wrote immediately after the Tenth of the Sixteen Conferences, a. d. 1715. (8.) A LETTER TO THE BISHOP OR BANGOR, dated August 8th. 1717, on the subject of the Bangorian controversy, in support of his Lordship. (9.) A LETTER, in the German language, to a Mr. *Leuthecher* (residing across the sea,) dated February 5th. 1723, wherein the author mentioneth his particular friends, viz. *Berry, Leppington, Leuchter, Lorentz* (Laurence) and *Carlshoff.*

NOTE.—These letters to the Church in Bow Lane, beam with the sublimest piety, and most enlightened and profound Christian science. Also the 'Letter to Gildersleve,' which relates chiefly to predestination, the subject of the Conferences in which he recently had been and was then employed, contains here and there some beautiful elucidations of recondite truth. In this work is found the Symbol of the Eye of Eternity, seeing at one view, in itself, all that is past, present and future.

(7.) A TREATISE AGAINST the DOCTRINE of the RESTORATION of ALL the DEVILS and LOST SPIRITS. Herein is SHOWN, FIRST, THE GREAT DIFFERENCE BETWEEN THE FALL OF LUCIFER AND THAT OF ADAM. NEXT, THE NOTION OF THE 'EVERLASTING GOSPELLORS,' together with their EIGHT CHIEF ARGUMENTS. FURTHER, THE AUTHOR'S IDEA on the SUBJECT, accompanied with EXPLANATIONS AND ILLUSTRATIVE SYMBOLS. And LASTLY, the METHODICAL ANSWER to the said EIGHT ARGUMENTS of the 'EVERLASTING GOSPELLORS.' Written in the German Language, in London, a.d. 1718.

NOTE.—This treatise is one of the most elaborately illustrated of all the author's writings, and perhaps the deepest metaphysical or logical treatise that was ever presented to the world upon such subjects of recondite truth, as those upon which it treats.

(8.) A TREATISE of GOOD and EVIL. Wherein Good and Evil are considered, FIRST, as in this OUTWARD THIRD PRINCIPLE. SECONDLY, as in the TWO INTERIOR WORLDS, yet as BEFORE the DAY of SEPARATION. And LASTLY, as AFTER the DAY of SEPARATION. In a Conference between A and B. Written in the German Language, in London, A.D. 1720.

NOTE.—In the author's Original of this work, now before us, the Fourth or last Conference is no longer to be found; nevertheless it is contained in the Copy of it, which we also hold, made by Leuchter.

This treatise commences at "page 561," in face of which is an 'Antiscript,' by the author, calling attention to this circumstance; which is to intimate, that this treatise implies an antecedent one, and the due understanding of it, in order to apprehend the present work. From a Note at the head of it, it appears to have been drawn up to clear a Scruple. On looking over the author's own writings, we can find no work to which this remark may be supposed to refer, except it be the 'Sixteen Conferences on Predestination,' the pages of which are double pages. Page 560 therein, we find to be in the Eleventh Conference, the subject of it (see Title above given) being *Voluntas signi et bene placiti*. This page begins with the words, 'ever any other man'—and the bottom of the said double page, ends with these words, 'which the triune God.'—Were the original of the work "against the restoration of devils" numbered with this extent of pages, then we should conclude this treatise to have been an appendix to that work.

(9.) PARADOXA, EMBLEMATA, AENIGMATA, HIEROGLYPHICA, de UNO, TOTO, PUNCTO, CENTRO. Being ONE HUNDRED and FIFTY THREE THEOSOPHIC DIAGRAMS and EMBLEMS, with LATIN CIRCUMSCRIPTIONS, and an ENGLISH TRANSLATION thereof affixed. Composed in London, a.d. 1717, 1718 and 1720.

(10.) A large, elaborate Symbolical Figure, Table, or Emblem, upon stout papier-maché or cardboard; whereon is represented at one view, the Mystery of All Things, in their mutual and reciprocal relations. The different Considerations of the Abyss of Deity (in which the great sphere of all Natural Being floats,) being distinguished according to their respective characteristics, by different depths or indentations, and the relations of Nature and its principles thereto, and these to each other, by more exdented, or outward and raised superficies and colours. An Engraving of this large symbolic model was inserted in Vol. IV. of J. B.'s Works, published a.d. 1781, headed, THE TRUE PRINCIPLES OF ALL THINGS; also, a plate made from the colored drawing, we hold, of the 'Tree of the Soul.' Whether invented by Freher, or only by Leuchter, does not now appear; but this Figure might very well preface J. B.'s great work, the MYSTERIUM MAGNUM.

Part Two:
Francis Lee

Selection One.

Lee's Letter to Henry Dodwell.

[This is prefaced by Walton's introduction to Lee's section, and followed by two letters from contemporaries of Lee's included by Walton, critical of the Philadelphian Society. Several of the letters having to do with more mundane Church matters have been excluded. —Ed.]

POSTSCRIPT.

We have already, in the previous pages, alluded to the Philadelphian Society, and to the correspondence which took place between the celebrated 'Mr. Henry Dodwell,' and Francis Lee, (Fellow of St. John's College, Oxford,) by reason of the latter's connection with that society, and his reputed secession from the communion of the established church. As Lee was not only an enlightened practical Christian, but profoundly versed in the Jewish, Philosophic, and Christian Mystic science of all ages, which he brought to bear in that controversy, in defence of Mrs. Lead's pretensions and writings, and of his own conduct in relation to the Philadelphian Society,—a society, by the way, which might in a sense be considered a prelude to, or budding of that universal evangelical spirit which broke forth in the next generation, as referred to in the Note of p. 176; and as the subjects of that controversy belong to the considerations of the present treatise, particularly as exhibiting the character of the spiritual theology and transcendental science of this country at the close of the seventeenth century; it may not be inappropriate to insert the most interesting portions of that correspondence, as a sequel or Appendix to the present Section; which we now propose to do.

The controversy was begun by Dodwell, (who, as the world knows, was not himself orthodox in certain points of Christian doctrine,) in a long and learned discourse, (addressed to Lee in the most respectful and affectionate remonstrant terms,) in support of ecclesiastical rights, proving the necessity of adhering to the visible communion of the Church, and to a strict dependence on the lawfully constituted governors of it. It began as follows:— [...]

The reply to the above letter having been deferred, Dodwell addressed to Lee a further communication, which, as it may be supposed to represent the natural sentiments of scholastic theology and sober scripture piety of all times upon the subjects in question, we give at length, with the categorical reply of Dr. Lee, and some subsequent letters. Dodwell's additional communication proceeds thus:—

Dear Sir,—I never received any answer to my second Letter, relating to your new unhappy schism from your old brethren. Since my writing that I have been at Oxford, and seen many books of your mother-in-law, [Mrs. Lead,] who is the only person of your sect that has her prophecies published, that I know of. And her being so, I look on as the best security you have against schisms among yourselves, whilst you do so manifestly favour enthusiastical pretences for withdrawing your dependence on your lawful ecclesiastical superiors. So long this security may hold, and no longer, than whilst the rest of you are more modest, and dare not rival your own pretended revelations with hers. But since I have looked into what has been published in her name, I have a worse opinion of your cause than formerly. I find her plainly to decry the trial of her cause by reasoning. This alone would make a wise man suspicious, that her cause was not thought defensible by that way of decision, and that they who manage her cause were conscious that it is not that way defensible. Yea, even you yourself interpose such cautions in admitting reason, as if you were distrustful of that way of determination. You might have some pretence for this, if your credentials were stronger reasons than any that could be drawn from the nature of the things themselves. But I find no credentials so much as pretended by you yet; no Schechinas, no signs of the prophets, no miracles, no fulfillings of predictions by answering events. Yet she pretends to equal her own prophecies with the confessedly inspired Scriptures, which had all these testimonials of the Divine authority of those that wrote them. She presumes to warn us not to admit them in the trial of her own pretences to inspiration, contrary to St. Paul, who pronounces an anathema even against an angel from heaven, that should presume to teach us any doctrine besides that which we have received. Yet pretending to no external credentials, the enthusiasm itself is far from being an evidence of its own Divine original. Imagination alone is sufficient to represent golden groves, and golden cities. Complexion, and fevers, and many other diseases affecting the brain, make such things appear as plainly as if they were really present. Much more the influence of evil spirits, permitted by Providence in such who break the unity of the good Spirit, which is the bond of the political society of the Church. So far is your discourse (if that discourse be yours) from proving yourself as certain of heaven, in your way of enthusiastical sensation, as you are of London. It is certain, that the representing of sensible ideas to the imagination is in the power of the devil, where God is pleased to permit him to exercise that which the Apostle calls ἐνέργειαν τῆς πλάνης in his Energumeni. And I find nothing in your mother-in-law's case that doth immediately relate to the purely spiritual faculties, which are the proper subject of the true spirit of prophecy.

Thus every way her case is suspicious, in her distrust of much stronger topics than any she can insist on in favour of her own pretences, both of reason and authority; in her being destitute of any external evidences of the Divine original of her pretended familiar conversation with God; in the suspiciousness of the faculty here employed, where there is no security against the interposition of evil spirits, the faculty being the very same wherein they are permitted to act by the ordinary rules of Providence. And so far is her case from giving you any security against the interposition of evil spirits, as that indeed evil spirits are the most likely to be expected in the ways made use of by you for attaining the Spirit you pretend to. God's Spirit cannot warrantably be expected, but by those means which God has instituted for conveying it. And those are all of them, such as are externals, in the power of those persons whom he has authorised for governing the spiritual society. His way of giving it was by imposition of the hands of the Apostles, and of their lawful successors in deriving that authority, to the age we live in. Your pretence for reconciling the present differences of Christendom is to draw men from all these externals, even of Christ's own institution, under pretence of a greater perfection than can be consistent with your needing them. Christ's design was even to oblige the spiritual gifted persons to a due subordination to their governors. This is the principal design of St. Paul and St. Clement in their epistles to the Corinthians, to prove this obligation. Your design is quite contrary, to break off such persons from their dependence on their superiors in the spiritual society, on this very pretence of their being spiritual. The apostolical age distinguished the Gospel state from the Legal, even as to the externals of both of them: that the legal dispensation was to be succeeded by the evangelical, as a more perfect state in this world; but that the gospel state was everlasting, at least as to this world, to cut off all pretences of enthusiasts for breaking the positive institutions of the Gospel. You, on the contrary, pretend to abrogate all obligations, even to the true communion, on pretence of a more perfect dispensation even in this world. The Scripture, therefore, supposes all other spirits that move oppositely to that subordination, for that very reason, to be other spirits from that which is the bond of the Church's unity; and that all divided spirits are also, for that very reason, to be taken for spirits of error and delusion. It highly concerns you to secure yourselves against the consequence. I hope, dear Sir, you will prefer your soul before your affinity, and excuse my freedom in the case of a person so nearly allied to you; the rather, because it is so necessary on account of considerations much more important than that of your alliance. I desire to exercise my freedom no further than the cause shall require, and with all the candour which I value as the best ingredient in your sect.

I know not how your mother-in-law is qualified to write the style in which her books are penned. But this I have observed, that there are many things ingredient in that style, which are quite out of the way of the education, or conversation, or even reading of women. It consists of many Latin terms, of terms of art, of the old Platonic mystical divinity, of all the modern enthusiasts, of JACOB BEHME, of the judicial astrologers, of the magic oracles, of the alchymists, of which too many are in English, but not ordinarily to be met with. I very much doubt whether she would be able to give an account of the terms used in the writings which go under her name, if she were critically examined concerning them. But I think i have discovered footsteps of another, and a more likely author of them, I mean Dr. Pordage. I find she has been very intimate with him ever since the time that she has set up for prophetic visions. She calls him her fellow-traveller; she generally pretends to have her revelations when he was praying by her. She pretends a divine revelation that he was to recover out of a very dangerous ailing, and shows a very great concern for him. And at the end of her first vol. of the "Fountain of Gardena," either she or the editor [LEE, himself,] has subjoined an attestation of the Doctor's, penned in the same enthusiastic style with the revelations themselves, only more accurately and correctly, but full as luscious. And that lusciousness is a particular, that I find none of you besides able to imitate in that perfection as he doth, as far as I can judge by the prefaces and postscripts, and the tracts in the "Theosophical Transactions." I observed, withal, that it is given as a reason why several revelations are wanting, that they were wanting in the Doctor's copy, and that they were received in the Doctor's absence. Why so, if she herself had been able, and used to pen her own visions? These things make it very suspicious to me, that the words and style of all her books are that Doctor's, and none of hers. How the matter of fact is, you can have better information than I can, and I earnestly recommend it to you for your own satisfaction.

There was really a Dr. John Pordage ejected out of the living of Bradfield in Berkshire, by the Commissioners in Cromwell's time, in the year 1654, for doctrines and practices of the same nature with those, of which I suspect your mother-in-law's friend; whether this be the same, you can better know than I, and you are greatly concerned to inform yourself as accurately as you are able: but so many circumstances are alike, and yet so singular, as will make it very difficult to have been otherwise. That Dr. Pordage was then accused for unwarrantable conversation with spirits, some of them certainly ill ones. Nor did he deny his being for some considerable time molested with ill spirits. For such favours as your mother-in-law pretends to, in conversing with God and good spirits, he is so far from denying them, that he glories in them. He pretends to have *tasted much of that tree of life, which groweth in the midst of the paradise of God, to have seen through the veil of the sensitive nature into the spiritual glory of eternity;* to have had *the rising of Christ's image in him;* to have had *the secret, hidden treasure of eternity, the outgoings of divine goodness; discoveries of celestial glory, instillations of the heavenly dew, and secret touches of the Holy Ghost, bright irradiations of eternal light, strong motions of divine life, pleasant streams of eternal love.* I give you his sense in his own words, that you may thereby see a specimen of his style, and judge how like it is to that of your mother-in-law. He disowned not his being taken up into heaven, like your mother-in-law, but parallels it with that of St. Paul. He was then charged with pretending that the *New Jerusalem had been seen in his house come down from heaven;* and that *in it was a globe, which globe was eternity, and in that eternity all the saints.* He then mentioned a *virgin essence*, in all likelihood, the same whom you call now the *virgin Wisdom*, with whom your mother-in-law pretends chiefly to converse. He was then charged with proselyting women, and the women so proselyted were said to exercise themselves, as yours are said to do now, in singing hymns.[!] He then also pretended to a power of *bestowing the gifts and graces of the Spirit on whom he pleased.* Why then should it be wondered at, that your mother-in-law might from him derive these visions she pretended to? Mrs. Pendar, upon the like or less familiarity with him, is said to have had such sights, that made her think herself bewitched by them; they came on her so unaccountably, and with so manifest tendencies to wicked and unlawful practices. And the case was frequent with the old heretics, to make their women disciples believe themselves prophetesses; so Simon Magus with his Helena, so Appelles with his Philumena, so Montanus with his Prisca and Maximilla. I could wish you would particularly look in Irenaeus, lib. i. c. 9., where you will find what arts were made use of to this purpose by Marcus, the father of the Marcosian heretics, with good judicious remarks of the father himself on the philosophy of it. The same Doctor then pretended that he had *seen the world of devils, evil spirits innumerable, their order and government;* that he had *heard, felt, tasted, and smelt hell in salt and sulphur, and that by a magical tincturation.* Magical and tincturation are, as I remember, terms also used by your mother-in-law. His *salt* and *sulphur* shows how he also affected terms of chemistry. He pretended also to have seen *the world of angels, and of them without number, bright as the rays, sparkling like diamonds; that he had tasted and heard the dews of paradise and harmonious music,* etc.; and speaks as favourably of magic as your mother-in-law, and with as much caution, to distinguish it from that of a notoriously bad signification. In a word, you will find the notions charged on him then, as exactly agreeing with those of your mother-in-law, and the style too, as could have been expected, after forty years refining and improving upon them. My authority for what was then charged against the Doctor is Mr. Fowler, of Reading's *Damonium Meridianum,* in the year 1655, where several things are transcribed from the Doctor's defence of himself in his own words. You may possibly get the Doctor's own book, intituled: *Innocency appearing,* etc., which I have not seen; and there you may find more instances of his own style and notions, which may make his agreement with your mother yet more clear and indubitable. If you shall upon examination find that I have guessed right, and that the Doctor is indeed the true author of your mother-in-law's revelations, and that he was indeed guilty of the wickednesses then deposed against him, I believe you will not easily believe them divine, nor really so pure as they pretend.

Yet though you could prove your mother-in-law's cause separate from his, I cannot see how you can avoid very just exceptions against her writings, though they were entirely her own. The primitive Christians never used to speak so honourably of magic as she doth, but condemn all sorts of it, the white as well as the black, to speak in your own language concerning it. The Chaldee or magic Oracles are the ancientest monuments, I think, of that kind, from whence any terms have been borrowed into the mystical theology. They are certainly elder than Porphyry, who grounded his philosophy ἐκ λογίων upon them. Yet even the name of magic was of so ill report among Christiana, that Simon and his heretical followers, the Gnostics, were then upbraided with ascribing any authority to them. Indeed, how could they do otherwise, who universally condemned all the heathen demons of what sort soever—who condemned all such curious familiarities even with good angels themselves. Col. ii. 18. They were later ages, and very degenerate, that forged a book of magic under our Saviour's name, inscribed to St. Peter and St. Paul; that forged so many magical offices, under the names of great saints, still extant in MSS.; that are supposed to have admitted professed magicians into the prime sees of Rome and Constantinople ; that leavened so many of the later writings of the later Rabbis, and occasioned so great a loss of them. In those first and purest times it was sufficient to brand the reputation of even any heretic, that pretended to it. Nor is there any reason to have any better opinion of even this white magic, because of its so great pretensions to purity. The devil has, even in these particulars, also transformed himself into an angel of light. Cornelius Agrippa pretends also to great purity and prayers; and so do the chemists, also, in their inquiries after the philosopher's stone, who are another original for forming your mother-in-law's style. But God doth not promise the rewards of piety to such worldly designs, however speciously pretended. And there are no books of the chemists extant, that I know of, even in MS., beyond the 4th century; so far are they from being agreeable to the best and purest ages of our Christian religion. Yet even these pretensions of piety in enthusiasts who cast off duty, do seldom answer expectation after the first heats of enthusiasm are evaporated. It were easy to show it in very many instances, but hardly in any more remarkably than in the case of Dr. Pordage. However, there is no reason to believe the style divine and sacred that is borrowed from the customs of such unjustifiable curiosities.

But this affected innovation in words might have been more tolerable, if it had gone no further than words. And indeed I expected, when I first looked into your mother-in-law's writings, that it had gone no farther. But I was surprised to find her stumble on several antiquated heresies, condemned for such in the first and most infallible ages of our Christian religion. She calls her Virgin Wisdom a goddess, directly contrary to all that those purest ages have declared against the difference of sex in the Divinity. She agrees herein with no Christians of these times, but the gnostic heretics, who made their Aeons $\alpha\dot{\rho}\rho\varepsilon\nu o\theta\acute{\eta}\lambda\varepsilon\iota\varsigma$, and allowed of a Sophia of that sex in the $\pi\lambda\acute{\eta}\rho\omega\mu\alpha$ no doubt by her meaning the Heavenly Wisdom; besides whom they invented a daughter of hers of an inferior rank, by them called, Achamoth, if the word were Hebrew, Chochmoth, an inferior terrestrial wisdom also, such as was admitted also in the philosophy of that age. But perhaps the word being of a singular signification, was rather Egyptian. This same Virgin wisdom your mother makes the mother of the Son of God, as to his eternal generation, directly contrary to St. Paul (Heb. vii. 3.), who makes the Son of God as $\dot{\alpha}\pi\bar{\alpha}\tau o\rho\alpha$ in relation to his humanity, so $\dot{\alpha}\mu\acute{\eta}\tau o\rho\alpha$ as to his Divinity. Yet your mother makes her Virgin Wisdom born under Sol and Venus; with what possible congruity? when her son is supposed to have created those planets. But thus it is likely that it should fall out, when an ungoverned fancy has the management of terms taken from arts not understood by the person who uses them. And I am apt to think that the Doctor, though he has made his jargon the study of his life, yet is not much more-skilled in these things than she is. I have elsewhere observed her giving an account of the original of Good and Evil, by two co-eternal principles in the Deity, the one good the other evil, exactly agreeing with the condemned doctrine of Manes, and several other heretics of those first ages. But in this age of licentiousness, there is hardly any doctrine of hers of more pernicious consequence than that of her pretending Divine revelation for her doctrine concerning *the finiteness of hell torments*. I hope these heresies will oblige you to bethink yourself seriously, whither this favour to enthusiasm is like to lead you. For my part, I think what I insisted on formerly, both in my book of Schism, and my first letter, a just prejudice against your venturing your soul on so dangerous a course; that it cuts you off from your dependence on the governors of our church and our communion, from which even spiritual persons were not intended to be exempted; and that it overthrows the establishments of our Lord for settling and establishing the true communion, as well as the inventions of men for settling and establishing false communions in opposition to the true one. But I did not then so well know, as I do now, that this was avowedly your design, to restore peace by destroying obligations to all communions, allowing no prerogative to the true communion, but reckoning it on equal terms with all heretical and schismatical rivals of it. This being your case will oblige you to pitch upon the proposition, where you think the proof insisted on in my book will fail me. And I should be suspicious of it, if I had any private concernment in it any otherwise than as to the personal weakness of the management of it.

Our good God extricate you out of the snares of enthusiasm and seducing spirits, wherein you are engaged. May he not suffer so many good works, and so much good meaning, as you have shown on other occasions, to fail of their reward. May he reduce you to the true fold, from whence you have thus long strayed, that you may be saved in the true Israelites. So prays he who most heartily desires that you will be pleased to qualify yourself, that he may be able to subscribe himself as formerly,—
Your most affectionate brother and fellow-sufferer,
Shottisbrook, Aug. 23, 1698.   Henry Dodwell.

We now come to Lee's long Apologetical Letter, in reply to all the unanswered points of the former correspondence of 'Mr. Henry Dodwell' which was written about the latter end of the year 1698, but having then been laid aside, was afterwards revived upon fresh instigations, and the conclusion added, upon April 9th, 1699:—

Dear Sir,—You need not excuse yourself for any freedom taken by you in a case of so great importance: you have a right to command the same on several accounts. And though I did forbear to answer your second Letter, on consideration that you were not then so rightly informed in the state of the cause you undertook to oppugn, as you might be now; yet did I it not with the least disrespect to a person, that has deserved so much from the Christian world, as well as from the learned: from whom to dissent, would be very difficult, had I not other grounds than what seem yet to be apprehended by you. For I have considered your strictures upon my mother's books, and have some reason to doubt, whether you did not rather content yourself with a cursory view of them, than accurately to examine their whole scope and contents. Which if you had thought worth your while to have done, some of the more principal objections perhaps would have fallen off. And a plain representation of the matter of fact will best determine of what weight those general prejudices ought to be, which are brought to render her case suspicious.

II. —The design then of her writings [see Note p.46, pp. 141, 148] is to *lead up the soul, as by various degrees, and through several purgations, lustrations, baptisms, and deaths into the Divine life.* This is most, distinctly laid down in her first treatise, called the *Heavenly Cloud*, which is the foundation to the rest of her works. Now in order to the attainment of this, she shows how it is necessary in the first place, to be mortified to the sensitive and brutal life, wherein we are all born.

And for this end, reason is very useful, she distrusts it not here, but freely makes use of it herself. But then this is but as one end of the ladder, one step heaven-ward, or according to her own style, one death. And betwixt the sensitive and Divine life, there may yet remain a great chasm. And it is certain that many stick here, who pretend to be great masters of reasoning. And many who have first reasoned themselves out of a spiritual principle and life in religion, have afterwards reasoned themselves out of the very subsistence of the eternal Word or reason, which is God, and last of all out of the very being of a God, by confounding him with the world. It is very true, that right reason could never persuade either the one or the other of this; but it is sufficient that the ratiocinative faculty in man may be so depraved, as to give its assent to that which it ought not.

Whence there did appear to this inquisitive spirit, as absolute a necessity for the mortification and resignation of this faculty also, as to its corrupt and unbounded activity, as even of the sensitive and brutal part in men. Nor is there any injury done hereby to the light of reason, nor any just prejudice given against that cause which is here maintained, but rather a great advantage doth thereby accrue to reason, when regulated from a superior principle, and irradiated by a greater Light, as in this case is pretended, at least. And since there is professedly an intention to superinduce a principle superior to reason, as much as reason is superior to sense, and to make use of a Light more highly originated, as flowing more immediately from the Father of Lights into his reflected image, when made pure and clear; hitherto I do not see why this should be any just matter of prejudice against what is offered, unless it can be evidently made out: (1.) That there is no such superior principle, life, or light. Or (2.) that it is not now communicable longer, nor to be expected in the regenerated image of God. Or (3.) that the process here taken in order to its communication, is not right. Or lastly, that an error is committed in this process, or in the admission of the Divine principle into the soul, and in its application, specification, and determination to particular objects. Besides, I must premise this one thing once for all, that you must not expect all the accuracy of expression from a person of no letters, as from one that is skilled in the true definitions of terms.

You well know, Sir, that the Spirit of God doth accommodate himself to the capacity of the subject into which it flows. Neither the prophets nor the apostles have the same style, or indeed so much as the same turn of thought. And all the world knows how differently *faith* is taken by the brother of our Lord, and the doctor of the Gentiles.

Confident I am, that the word *reason*, as used by my mother, is taken in quite as different a sense, from that you and others may take it in; and that she has as good reasons to depreciate it in her sense, as you can have to magnify it in yours.

Of this I could give many clear evidences from her writings. And I doubt not but you yourself will find these upon a more narrow and strict examination of them, if you shall think it worth your while. I have never heard of any whom inspiration has made to be critics. It is enough if the scope and intent of an author be understood. If more than this were required, the Holy Ghost would never have spoken by fishermen, or would have made them orators and philosophers.

III. —Another prejudice brought by you against her writings is, that *she pretends to equal her own prophecies with the confessedly inspired Scriptures.*

But, dear Sir, what is her pretension, I pray? Is it any more than this, that she believes herself fully inspired by God? What grounds she has for believing so, are in their proper place to be considered. It is very true, that she does think herself to be conducted and taught by the Holy Spirit, as really as the prophets under the old, or the apostles under the New Testament did themselves. And consequently her own Divine inspirations must to her be of equal authority with theirs, i.e. according to the *degree* and *nature* of them. Yea possibly farther yet, hers may (and ought to be) of no less authority to herself, than theirs were to themselves, who were thus confessedly inspired.

For if I have a truly Divine inspiration, it is certain, that it is not in my power to give a less credit to it, than to the Divine inspiration of another; both being supposed an inspiration of the same degree. And there are some grounds I think, to allow, (if possible) a greater credit to that which is immediately communicated to myself, than to that which is only communicated immediately through others, how well soever attested.

Thus far, then, is certain, that it ought not to be any prejudice against the truth of her prophecies, that she herself doth firmly believe their truth, and wait for their completion; and that not without an equal assurance to that, which is by the universality of Christians given to the ancient prophecies, and confessedly inspired writings, which do testify of the glorious coming of our Lord and blessed Saviour.

But notwithstanding this firm and solid assurance in herself, I do not find, (either from her writings, or from her conversation) that she does pretend to oblige others to give an equal authority to her writings, as to the sacred Scriptures, or even any at all to them, which a sober inquirer after truth, will not be obliged to of his own accord, after the best scrutiny.

She hath, indeed, published them for the sake of others, upon a particular admonition given to that purpose, and various concurring providences strongly inciting her, very contrary to her expectations, as from manifest signs can be made to appear. But hereby she doth not impose any new articles of faith, or bring any new gospel; she only declares the lights which she says, were communicated to her, and leaves every one free to receive or reject them, since the damage or advantage will be to themselves.

But she doubts not at the same time, but that many good souls will be stirred up by the Spirit of God to acknowledge and embrace them, even before the Divine wisdom shall see it expedient or necessary to consign them by some external and public mark which may in its time be given, though not presently.

IV.—A farther prejudice against her writings is this, that *she arrogates an authority to them equal to the Scriptures, without any or all of those testimonials of Divine authority which they had who wrote those, such as schechinas, signs of the prophets, miracles, and fulfilling of predictions.*

As for the first of these, it is true, she pretends not to any visible Schechinah, such as was accommodated to the infant state of the Jews; but she pretends to that which is a higher and nobler, to a Schechinah that is substantial and permanent, even to the real inhabitation of the Holy Ghost as in his temple.

And if this her pretension be well founded, and the truth of it made manifest to her, as it cannot well be supposed otherwise, I cannot see why she may not depend safely upon the Divine authority of what is thus revealed from the inhabitation of the ever-blessed Spirit, as a vital principle of light and love, or why also others who are, or shall be, after the same manner convinced, may not securely trust themselves to this superior way of administration, as to a more certain word of prophecy.

V.—As for the signs of the prophets, they were generally required and given upon particular messages, whether of judgment or mercy, as by Moses, in that of the famous Exodus of Israel, by Samuel, in that of the kingdom conferred on Saul, by the man of God, in that of the birth of Josiah, by Isaiah in several cases, by Jeremiah also in several, but which were all particular.

But it doth not appear, that these were given by all the prophets, or even by the greatest, or most eminent of them, in prophecies in a more universal nature, or indeterminate as to persons and times.

Of these last, instances are frequent in Isaiah alone. Of the former there are two witnesses at once,—the prophets Haggai and Zechariah, of whom it doth not appear that either of them showed a sign, or wrought any miracle, though both standing together in the same commission. And the reason of this may be the difference of the commission of these prophets, from that of some others who went forth with a sign.

For the spirit of prophecy fell upon these, to promote the building of the second temple, which had no need of a new sign, this falling in so punctually with the expiration of the seventy years, according to the precise prophecy of Jeremiah, which had been already confirmed with a sign, and being corroborated with several extraordinary providencies concurring.

Another instance may be that of Daniel, a man highly favoured with the revelation of hidden secrets, with a most singular gift of interpretation, and which great angelical communications, who yet brought no external sign but the verification of what was declared, or the event of the interpretation. And whether it might not be thus also with Amos and some others, for the first years of their public prophecying, may not unreasonably be doubted.

But moreover in the most particular and extraordinary messages, and of how public and universal a concern soever, it doth not appear that a sign was always required, or given by God through his prophets. Of this there are two signal instances, and more eminent than these there cannot be.

The one is Noah, who is believed to have prophesied to the old world concerning the approaching deluge, no less than one hundred and twenty years before it came to pass; and during all this while, there is not the least probability of a sign being given to that wicked generation, but that of his own strict righteousness, and of his building of a strange machine, or house, apparently very extravagant, for the saving of himself and family.

Here was an express command from God, to declare that his Spirit would not strive with man beyond such a limited season. The prophet that was to declare this, was to expect no better than scorn or pity at least from the whole world at that time. There was no faith then upon the earth, and to humour such with a sign from heaven would have been of little effect, if of any. God was not obliged to give it, and it might not have suited with the methods of his wisdom to do so. But this righteous man, though laughed at by all, being moved with fear, would not tempt God to demand a sign in his own vindication; but he believed and obeyed, and thereby condemned the incredulous world, and became heir of the righteousness which is by faith, and the father of a new world.

The second instance of this kind is Jonah, whose commission according to the modern hypothesis of prophecy, would be very unaccountable. Certainly if Ninevah had been as London, or Assyria as England, they would not have so easily repented, but would have called aloud for signs, before they would have hearkened to the word of the prophet. Therefore shall Ninevah rise up against London, and thou Assyria against England.

To this case when fully and clearly stated, I cannot see anything that can be opposed with any solidity, supposing that matter of fact to be just as it is related. And to suppose the matter to be otherwise, and that there was a sign given when none is mentioned, is altogether precarious, and a begging of the question.

I am not ignorant that in both these cases, there are good reasons producible, why a sign was withheld, but the very same reasons will hold as good in the present case, as would not be difficult to make out particularly.

One instance more I cannot omit, of a prophet without a sign, and that is the precursor of our blessed Lord, who though he was a second Elias, yet neither wrought miracles, nor showed a sign, whom all men nevertheless owned for a prophet.

Wherefore he is called only a voice, and a voice of one crying in the wilderness, to prepare the way of Messiah. And though he was afterwards publicly owned by the Messiah himself, yet this was but as a succedent ministration to ratify a former, not to give any authoritative sign or seal of its truth; he having in a manner already finished his office, being in all places wherever he went, and by some of all ranks of persons, taken for a true prophet.

And whether his case may not be peculiarly applicable to some in this day, or sometime before the end of the world, as the precursors of the second glorious coming of our Lord and Saviour, I leave you. Sir, to consider with as much accuracy as you please.

VI. —As for miracles more may be said perhaps for them, than for signs. A sign must be a miracle, but neither every miracle, nor every great miracle can properly be said to be a sign. And notwithstanding those great miracles which our blessed Saviour did, he refused to give a public and determinative sign, which could not have promoted, but rather would have served to frustrate the design which he came into the world for.

Wherefore he roundly told his unbelieving countrymen, that no other sign should be given them, but that of Jonah the prophet; which could not be without their first putting of him to death.

So that there was no proper and public sign during the whole course of his ministration, notwithstanding all his miracles, whereby he could be discriminated from Moses and Elias, or any other great prophet, who had wrought miracles, even abating from the signs which they gave, as more immediately declarative of their Divine mission.

Indeed at the beginning of his ministration there was a sign given, but it was not public, being determined, (for aught that appears) to one single person, who was to bear witness of it, by crying, Behold the Lamb of God.

The next sign that he also gave, was private, in the presence but of three witnesses: and it was not till he was finishing the last scene of his commission, and was only precursory to the great promised sign, the sign of Jonah.

A third sign may be what happened in the consummating point itself of his ministration, or the threefold sign of his crucifixion. (1) The rending of the veil of the Jewish temple. (2.) The earthquake. (3.) The darkness. This also was not so properly a sign, as a *wonder*, being too indefinite for the former strictly taken. And all this together did but make up the beginning of that grand, adequate sign, which had been twice in the most solemn and public manner promised though not understood by any.

This was presently preached up as the true and proper sign of the Messiah, and everywhere throughout the New Testament joined with him, even so far as by some to have been taken for the Goddess of Jesus. That it had all the marks of a true and adequate sign is indubitable, except that it was not exhibited in the open view of his crucifiers, which (yet remains to be done); not but that this was sufficiently compensated by their sealing of his sepulchre, and by many other corroborating evidences.

Now if it shall please Him who is exalted above every name, to send forth his prophets and messengers in his name, to prepare a way for Him against his glorious return, I cannot indeed but conclude, that many miracles must be wrought through them, and many concurrent wonders also both in the heights and in the depths, equivalent to a sign, openly demonstrated. That these then may be expected, is not denied. Notwithstanding which I doubt very much whether any sign (that is properly so) ought to be expected, or called for, before the sign of the Son of Man shall appear.

And what that is can be understood from the foregoing grand sign.

But let this be what it will, or the miracles preceding never so many, or great, yet to the inquirers after a sign, what they seek after may be refused as heretofore, and that without any impeachment to the Divine glory or truth. And as the sign only of Jonah the prophet was given by the great Son of man to those of his own generation, so verily shall the sign only of the Son of man be given by his Holy Spirit to them of the last generations of the world. With which most aptly doth concur, according to my sentiments, the plain and literal meaning of Apoc. xi. 2. For the fulfilling of whose place I do not look either in this or the next age, clearly discerning that it must be the last great event immediately preceding the sound of the last trumpet. In which interval, as I do expect the apostolical spirit to revive, so with it the apostolical powers or miracles: whereto these very writings, though not attested themselves at first by miracles, will most mainly contribute, whensoever and by whomsoever they are rightly digested.

This is visibly throughout a principal design of them. And I think no deeper foundation can be laid for the resuscitation of the miraculous powers by the spirit of faith, than what in them is to be found.

If these do not break out immediately, or all at once, but seasonably and gradually, I do not see why this should be any disadvantage to these writings of my mother, or any just exception against her pretensions. It is what she herself hath declared again and again, and doth still declare. Her pretensions may be firm and valid, without external and public miracles to guard them, if infinite Wisdom shall see fit, to begin weakly and contemptibly for a greater manifestation of his glory. But besides, though she may not *so much as pretend* to miracles, possibly God may sometimes honour his handmaid beyond what she pretends to; and I have not, therefore, a worse opinion concerning her, but a better.

I love not to make a mountain of a mole-hill; but what I have seen and known within these few years has certainly been too much to confirm either an imposture, or a delusion.

VII. —As for fulfilling of predictions by answering events, which you make another credential of true prophecy, I do not find that this could be pretended to by several of the ancient undoubted prophets in their life times, their prophesies, you know, for the most part being for a considerable time after their decease: and by this, alone considered, Jonah might have passed for a false prophet; as possibly several of the true prophets did, when they were stoned, or otherwise put to death, by the public judicature, for their testimony; till after their deaths, their predictions coming to be fulfilled, they who had before rejected, did now come to receive their prophesies, and build their sepulchres. And yet, even upon this head, there may perhaps be more of reality, than what is pretended as to the present case. Some things of a private nature may be evidences, in this kind to particular persons, which cannot be made so to others. And some things also there may be of a more public nature, predicted or visionally represented, which have happened to be confirmed many years after, by corresponding events, even when the prediction, or vision, hath been utterly forgotten. An instance of this may be a visional dream in the beginning of 1678, concerning the public exercise of the Roman worship tolerated in several parts of this kingdom, wherein is mention made of the pope's vicars, which seems to have been fulfilled seven years after, though taken no notice of, and not found till this very year, upon the occasion of the importunity of some persons from abroad requiring what yet remains unpublished. And one more instance there is, which I cannot but hint, being a vision in December, 1688, apparently relating to the peace last year at Reswick concluded.

Nor would it be difficult to find some other parallel instances of predictions, that have either been answered by events, or at least have been very applicable to them. But on these I do not lay any very great stress; the conviction that I have from other grounds, is incomparably greater as to me.

VIII. —Another prejudice against her writings is, that she *presumes to warn us not to admit even the Scriptures in trial of her own pretences to inspiration.*

How far this is true, or is understood, may easily be decided. It is then true that she makes her pretension to an immediate revelation of God's mind, in some matters not before revealed in the Scriptures, and in which by consequence no Scripture ground may appear. But if this be any just prejudice against her, and if even an angel from heaven may be anathematised, who teacheth any other doctrine but what is clearly expressed in the Scripture; then will it be also, if I mistake not, against Catholic tradition for the same reason. And I am much afraid that the anathema will rebound upon the holy fathers themselves of the ancient church, and upon its most renowned councils in many cases that are well known. The doctrines of infant baptism, of the translation or defection of the Jewish sabbath, of unity of baptism in opposition to the rebaptisation of heretics, of prayers for the dead, with some others, are certainly ancient doctrines, for which it will be very hard to find a satisfactory ground in Scripture; but it would be no less hard to condemn therefore all those who have believed and practised according to these.

For by the same parity of reason, I do not see at present why the whole Church may not fall under an anathema, as well as any single person, if they should receive any other doctrine, than what is evidently grounded in Scripture, however consonant it may otherwise be to universal tradition, or any other medium of the knowledge of the truth. This is, indeed, agreeable enough to the principles of some, but because it is not so to yours, I cannot, Sir, but promise myself a more generous treatment than if I had fallen amongst them who will narrow up the evidences of truth to public written inspiration, and that too taken according to their own glosses.

Besides, she doth not pretend to say, that there is not Scripture-ground for the doctrine which she brings, but only ingenuously confesseth that she has not found it. But it may be there, I suppose, notwithstanding she could not find it. If she could not find it there *at all*, or could not find there so *plain*, as to satisfy herself or convince others, this may be brought as an example of her ingenuity, not of her presumption. For it can be no presumption to declare what God has revealed and hath commanded to be declared, but a duty.

And if she doth really believe that God did by his Spirit reveal this doctrine to her, and command her to declare the same publicly, against all kind of disadvantages, whatever the doctrine may be in itself, and though she may be mistaken as to the revelation, her only crime will be to have acted according to the best of her light, after the most earnest search made into this matter, by praying and waiting upon God. However, this is not imposed on any as an article of faith, and they that cannot digest it, may pass it over. Though I think there may be as good grounds even from Scripture itself to make it so, as the supralapsarian doctrines which so many confessions have raised up to that rank, if not far better.

Again it is also true, that she doth declare, that we are not bound to stint ourselves to any foregoing dispensation or revelation, nor to be so taken up in the Scripture itself, or to rest on it, as if nothing more were to be revealed, for the benefit and instruction of mankind. And the inference which she thence draweth is, that whatever shall be thus revealed, so far as this shall be made to appear to the person receiving a revelation, or to any other, ought to be no less credited and esteemed, than a revelation from the same Spirit of a more ancient date; the truth of which is most evident from the very nature of the thing. And this can be thought no superseding of the authority of the Scripture, no derogation to any precedent Divine revelation, nor any arbitrarious introduction of new pretended revelation, since what is asserted upon this infallible maxim,—that God cannot lie, and consequently that whatsoever was, is, or shall be communicated from Him, either for a more particular, or more public benefit, ought to be received with the same veneration.

This is the substance of what she says, so far as I understand her; and is no more than what every one doth believe, i.e. if the matter-of-fact were but supposed to be true. I do not find that she any where evades the confessedly Divine authority of former divine revelations, to set up her own, or refuteth but so much as in one particular, that is this way determinable, to bring what she hath had communicated, to the holy Scriptures as the standard of true inspiration. On the contrary, I find she is taught by that Spirit which guideth her, to put a most high esteem upon them, to appeal to them in all that they contain, to meditate in them almost continually, and to search into their most hidden depths, and concealed truths, by and with the assistances of the Holy Inspirer who dictated them. It is the general method of the Spirit by which she is acted, after a revelation or manifestation is given, to apply and confirm the same to and by some text of Scripture, then brought to her remembrance and most emphatically unfolded, for the proper occasion; which certainly can be no sign of an evil spirit. And I do not think this would excite her to call daily for the Scriptures to be read to her, as is her custom. But let it be even supposed, that she had in express terms warned us not to admit even the Scriptures themselves in the trial of her inspirations, how harsh soever this may sound, it is no worse than the greatest part of Christians, and even the learned and wise, as well as pious, do in effect, with regard to many of those doctrines and practices which they maintain. Not that they do hereby seek to put any difference upon the Sacred Writ, but only to avoid all contention about its interpretation, which is so manifold according to the different education and various habitual prejudices of the readers. This may be in them a prudential caution, upon good and weighty considerations: and if so, it may be the same here also.

But there is no need of it. And I know she is so far from distrusting the authority of the Scripture in her present case, as the greatest pretenders to it can be: who thinks she has a better claim from it, to the teachings of the Spirit, than any man can bring for his estate, or than all the world can produce to oppose it.

Now I will not (yet) say, that this is any more than a warm imagination. Let it pass for such, it will however sufficiently vindicate her from this main charge.

IX.—It is then a further prejudice against her writings, that *imagination alone is able to represent and transact all that is here reported.*

But to this I cannot yield myself, upon the following grounds: It is not enough that imagination can represent golden ladies and golden cities; doubtless it may do this, with all that is in the book of Revelations.

It can represent all that Daniel or Ezekiel saw, all that Zachary typified, or that Christ himself spake in parables. But notwithstanding that the sacred representation by them exhibited, were expressed to the Imaginative faculty, St. John, Ezekiel, and Daniel are not less esteemed to be true prophets with Zachary and others. Nor is it any derogation from the authority of our blessed Master, that he made choice of a method so agreeing with human imagination.

Complexion and fevers may do very much, and the power of imagination I dispute not. But there is no greater sign of a strong imagination, than to implead realities, or to conclude what it can do it doth.

There are some things in my mother's writings that do undoubtedly relate to the purely spiritual faculties. Some indeed mediately and others immediately. A particular enumeration of which with respect to those superior faculties of the intellect and will, would be too tedious. There are some passages, I think, that visibly tend to illuminate the former; and others strongly to touch the latter. And it is impossible that I should think otherwise, or that you yourself should, if but the contents were allowed, or supposed to be true. For certainly the doctrine of the Spiritual kingdom of Christ, and the unity and sanctity of the church, of the order and discipline of the apostolical fraternity, of the communion of saints, of the ministration of angels, of the original of simple spirits, of the various mansions allotted to beatified souls, of the consubstantiality with the glorified humanity of the Lord, of the nature of a spiritual body, of the different steps of transfiguration, transformation, and transubstantiation, of the Divine Virgin principle through which the Deity is manifested in nature, of real and spiritual manducation of the spiritual internal senses imaged by the natural and external, of the first paradisical state of man, of the gradual defection and lapse, of the scale of the regeneration, of elementary spirits and their receptacles, of the various states of purification in other regions, of the general restitution of the creation, and some other coincident with these, are doctrines that do as peculiarly according to their degree, tend to illustrate the understanding, as any other that in the Christian religion can be named. And supposing this at present to be both equally true, I cannot think that the least question would be made of it. Neither would it be any easy task to transcribe all those passages that do properly affect the superior will of man, and strongly impel the same, as soon as they are rightly understood. Of this nature are such as lead to a pure and naked dependence upon God, to the incomprehensible peace of God, to that perfect thing which is described by the Apostle, to an high and masculine faith, that can be called truly apostolical, and to the holy and undefiled magia which doth thence proceed, and is the greatest of all wonders in purified and resigned wills, as being therefore frequently called the great mystery.

How many cautions, counsels, exhortations, and encouragements are here to be found, for the retrieving the evangelical spirit amongst Christians, and for the waiting for the promise of the Father? All which I cannot but conceive do relate more immediately to the spiritual faculties of the soul, unless the imagination be the seat of the evangelical spirit.

There are also judgments and blessings pronounced, the one on the obstinate refusers of this Spirit, and the other upon all such as shall yield themselves to the call of it, as it shall grow louder and louder. This also bears a relation to the will; and it is so correspondent with the methods of divine providence, and to the manner of all ancient, undoubtedly inspired prophets, as I know not what can be reasonably objected against it, after what hath been already considered under the foregoing prejudices: by the evidence of which, I am forced to conclude that there are some, yea many things in these writings that do relate to the faculties which are the proper subject of the true spirit of prophecy.

Not only so, but the very scope and drift of all these writings is to set the mind free from images, to purify all the avenues of the imaginative faculties, and to drive the soul into a Super-sensual and Super-imaginative state. And however sensible mediums and images are made use of in the process to this attainment, and, to make the same known to others, are taken up instead of words, for their great significancy and expressiveness;

yet all this is but an artificial way of denudating the imagination with the greatest familiarity and ease to itself, in order to that blessed state of seeing God from, in, and through a simplified and pure heart.

There may be, and really is a great distinction betwixt imagination and the work of God upon imagination. The greatest part, if not all of the angelical ministration doth herein consist. Thence is it not of force to say, that the imagination itself is sufficient to represent such objects as really as if they were present. Unless it be likewise evident that there could be no operation of God upon it, or co-operation with it, by the interposition of angels, to presentiate the objects to that faculty.

The imagination is properly Speculum Anima, which in its lapsed, depraved state, is filled with innumerable broken images, very inadequate and preposterous; but in its restored and pure state, all these images being cast out, it becomes a bright mirror, to reflect the immaculate and entire image of God, as it is in the Virgin nature of the Lamb (then seen upon mount Sion); and so through this one image, hereupon reflected, the spirit of the soul, as in a glass, may be said to behold God, and the Divine world (all whose figures are adequate and regular), not indeed nakedly and manifestly, but somewhat obscurely and enigmatically.

And thus proportionably as the imagination is more or less evacuated, all the Imaginations of the heart of man being evil, and evil altogether, there is (or may be) an admission into it of that vision for which it was originally formed, either in a higher or lower degree. Whether it may be so in this case, or how far it may be, may not be perhaps unworthy of a wise man's search.

But sixthly, you yourself, dear Sir, seem sensible enough, that all could not be the mere effect of imagination, since you are so willing to admit the influence of evil spirits upon it.

Wherefore, this prejudice of imagination being insufficient, even according to your own method of reasoning, I shall consider the next prejudice, which instead of corroborating seems to overthrow the former; unless the obsession and influx of an evil spirit should be confounded with a constitutional or accidental infirmity, and the same thing might be said at once to be both natural and preter-natural.

X.—Another heavier prejudice then remains against her writings, even no less than this : that *it is in the power of the devil to represent sensible ideas to the imagination, where God is pleased to permit him; that there is no security against the interposition of evil spirits in a faculty, wherein they are permitted to act by the ordinary rules of providence; and that evil spirits are most likely to be expected in the ways made use of by us for attaining the Spirit we pretend to.*

Now if there can be a security against the interposition of evil spirits, even in this faculty, and we actually have this security, then will this prejudice that is levelled against these writings in special, and against the society in general, fall to the ground.

Now, that there may be a security even in the imagination itself from evil spirits interposing themselves, I think may be made good, not only *a posteriori,* from undeniable instances, but also *a priori*, from the nature of the subject. Now it is firm, that every faculty in its original constitution must have its proper certainty, otherwise God would deceive his creature, i.e., be no God. And as certain as truth cannot be the fountain either of a verbal or essential lie, or as two contradictories are incompossible, so certain it is that every faculty, power, or might which proceedeth from God, the essential Truth, must attain to its proper object for which it was formed or procreated; conditionally, that all that which would debilitate, darken, or impede the same, be removed out of the way : and when it hath attained its object, it must of necessity be certain of this its attainment. Intellectual truth is the proper object of human understanding, and though it be possible for the understanding to be mistaken with respect to truth, in almost infinite cases, yet it is absolutely impossible for it to be mistaken in some, as particularly in those common notions wherein all mankind do most unanimously agree. Nay, it is impossible to be mistaken in any, where but the objective truth is fairly and fully presented, and the faculty sound and naked of all prejudices.

Besides, there are some few general rules for finding out and discerning of truth, which being strictly observed in the application of them to particulars, no error can be admitted into the understanding. All which is in like manner applicable to the imaginative faculty, that has its common images, wherein can be no mistake; that has its soundness as well as its infirmity, and its true position as well as its false. And that is to be regulated by such plain, easy rules of discretion as will exclude all illusions.

This is universally so in the several faculties and gifts of God to men, without any exception, natural or super-natural, purely spiritual or mixed, internal or external.

Good is the proper object of the Will, to which, according to its true original constitution, it may attain. And Infinite Good, or the supreme Good, is the only true object of the will of man, for which it was formed and capacitated; and to which it may therefore, according to its original formation and native capacity, attain, and having attained, rest satisfied in the possession of its object, with an infallible certainty. And though we daily and hourly experience how possible it is for the human will to be misled with respect to good, yea, how very difficult (and almost impossible) it is not to be mistaken or biassed in this pursuit; yet where the objective good is perspicuously and sensibly presented, and the will unfettered, and in the full liberty of the spirit, it is perfectly impossible for it to be here misled, or not to have a sufficient security against the deception of apparent good.

Material beings are the proper objects of the external senses, and though it be notorious what innumerable errors have sprung up through these, and what gross and even ridiculous mistakes are hence made by the unlearned, yet is it altogether impossible for these to be when the organ is sound and perfect, the object proportioned to it, and the distance neither too remote nor too near. There are common sensations in which mankind do all mutually concur; and there are also certain natural rules of addition and subtraction of sensible ideas, of their division and multiplication, and of their negation or abstraction, and comparison, which do afford many solid and substantial truths, and cannot anywise lead into error when attended to.

Nay, it is an impossibility for the senses of themselves to deceive any one, since the error is not in them, but in the judgment that is made upon them. And all that has been said with respect to these, and the superior and purely spiritual faculties of the mind, are likewise applicable to the imagination, as might be distinctly showed, if I were writing to a person of less penetration.

Thus, then, even the Imaginative faculty is capable of its proper evidence, as well as the intellect, or as the will, or any of the senses are of theirs; and indeed as capable as any faculties or powers whatever, angelical or human, since all alike do so equally depend upon the nature of the Divine truth. Nor is it enough to urge that this is only a natural evidence, and therefore to be suspected for fear of a supernatural deception by the subtile insinuation of evil spirits transformed; for were it but in their power but to null or supersede this evidence, where there is a due disposition of subject and object, they would be more powerful than God himself, who hath willed such as evidence to arise from this or that disposition or combination, according to certain immutable and eternal laws of truth. And though so long as this faculty or fountain is impure, and not regenerated from above, there may be no security against the intrusion of each kind of spirits, yet certainly, as this is purified and renovated by the spirit of JESUS, the greatest security is possible to be obtained. In comparison whereof, that of external signs and miracles, can be but of an inferior degree. Since no evidence from without, (how great soever,) is any, but so for only as it is apprehended by, and doth correspond with, the internal principle of sensation, and perception, by what name soever called.

An instance whereof I take to be the famous ecstacy of the great Pythagoras, when he ran about as an Energumen, or possessed person, with his Eureka, for having found out that noted theorem, which is as the basis of all Trigonometry. He was thus transported out of himself by the energy of truth, so as to forget that he had a body; this transport was caused by the inaction of the truth upon his mind, whereby his animal spirits being so actuated, through the surprising clarity of what before was very obscure, his imagination was filled with the ideas relating to such a sort of a triangle, during the suspension of his outward senses.

This inaction or energy of truth was so powerful only from the conformity of certain imaginary ideas one with another, and the combination of them according to such and such laws, that are necessary and self-evident. This conformity even of imaginary ideas, was of itself a proof vastly superior to any other that could be given. For I believe that no man will think he could have been half so certain of the truth of that proposition, if he had spent all his days in measuring of triangles by rule and compass, or if the whole body of mathematicians at that time had declared it unto him, or if any wonderful operation of magic had been wrought by any of these for confirmation of the same.

All external proofs, all mechanical figurations, and miracles themselves, even to the raising of the dead, would have been given as an inferior evidence to that which he had, and which every one may have also, when the first elements and terms of geometry are clearly understood.

Thus it is, every faculty of the soul hath its proper evidence and its proper energy, which all things can never be able to balance or arrive to.

And here I cannot but observe, that the Divine energy upon the soul is not without good reason so often mentioned by the great Apostle; I should think with some particular regard to those degenerated times, if he may be allowed to have had the spirit of prophecy, as he doubtless had, when he prophesied of the son of Belial (ὁ ανομος), to be manifested in the energy of Satan, with apparent miracles, signs, and prodigies. But without pretending to uncypher this prophecy, I dare be confident, upon as good grounds as we can have for the interpretation of any one text in the whole Scripture, that the application, neither in part nor in whole, ought to be made to the present case.

Nor can I but take notice, that in seven places where this word Ενεργεια is used by St. Paul alone, in his Epistles, there are no fewer than six of them where it is certainly taken in a good tense. And in this *one* place by you referred to, where it is taken in an ill sense, it is only incidentally, and upon an extraordinary occasion, though for the deeper emphasis and impression this be indeed repeated. Wherefore I cannot yet see a ground, either in reason or in Scripture, to conclude, that even in this very faculty of the imagination itself, there can be no security against the interposition of evil demons, or that there may not be a natural as supernatural evidence in this so decried subject, when it is rightly disposed, through the holy energy of God in the soul; which may be in any or every part or power of the soul, as the soul hath its energy in any and every part of the body. Whence ariseth that great diversity of $\dot{\varepsilon}\nu\varepsilon\rho\gamma\acute{\eta}\mu\alpha\tau\alpha$ (which I take liberty to call Seminal Operations) of the Holy Spirit, mentioned in a very accurate diatribe upon this matter by this very Apostle, for the use (as I suppose at least) not of one age of the Church, any more than of that one particular church alone whereto it was immediately addressed, but of all ages of the Church: some of which are more internal, others more external, and all have a peculiar energy, manifestation, and ministration, different from all the rest.

And for farther confirmation of this considerable position, that every faculty hath its proper evidence, as well as its proper object, and that consequently, there may be a security obtained from all fallacy of any kind whatever, there are not lacking arguments *a posteriori* that I could produce, if it were necessary, and instances in the imaginative faculty of unsuspected truth, $\kappa\alpha\tau\ \varepsilon\nu\varepsilon\rho\gamma\varepsilon\iota\alpha\nu\ \varepsilon\nu\ \mu\varepsilon\tau\rho\omega$, as the Divine powerful energy is commensurate with it. This faulty was very predominant, or rather exalted in the prophet Ezekiel, more than in Daniel himself; i.e. more masculine and vivid. And it will not be more difficult to answer how he could be secured against the interposition of the spirits of delusion, than it will be how some others may also have been secured from them, and especially upon the consideration of those three grand visions, that of the wheels, that of the dead bones, and that of the temple. He and many others have had this security, notwithstanding that the ordinary rules of providence do permit evil spirits to act in the imagination, wherein Divine visions are also exhibited.

Now that there may not only be such a security, but that we actually have this security, may be made out from several grounds, not easily to be shaken. But, to omit others, I shall here insist on two, that are taken from that very passage in the second epistle to the Thessalonians, to which you have been pleased to refer me, as which, I think, do necessarily flow from the design of the Apostle. For if I know the cause or causes that do expose me to the interposition of evil angels transforming themselves, and to their energy of delusion, I know also certainly, that my security doth consist in removing the said cause or causes. And if a contrary cause must produce a contrary effect, I cannot but know, that if there be the sign of this contrary cause, it would be absurd to expect the same effect.

Now the causes of the Divine permission of evil angels to interpose themselves, are expressed to be two, (1.) an opposition to the gospel of Christ, and not only so, but even a fixed hatred against it; the opposition being expressed in these words, $μη\ πιστευσαντες\ αληθεια$ discrediting the gospel, and the hatred by these, $την\ αλαπην\ της\ αληθειας,\ ουκ\ εδεξαντο,$ they admitted not the love of the gospel. (2.) An obdurate impiety expressed by these words, $ευδοκησαντες\ εν\ τη\ αδηκιο$ taking pleasure in unrighteousness, as we translate them, entirely approving, acquiescing, and being possessed by it, resting in it, as in their nature, never, or rarely at least, moving out of it, or beyond it, but still carried towards it by a strong self-propension, with the greatest affection and contentation of mind. This was the case of Pharaoh, and of Ahab, in the Old, and of Simon Magus, in the New Testament, for their *infidelity* and *impiety*, being given up by the just judgment of God to believe a delusion, after that they had wilfully resisted the truth.

On the contrary, the causes of Divine protection against the interposition of evil spirits, for to work after this kind, in the *deceivableness of unrighteousness*, are, (1.) faith, (2.) holiness, as they both are taken here in a lax sense, and in the lowest degree that they can properly be predicated of any subject. Otherwise, the argumentation of this Apostle hereupon would be infirm, the inference that he draws for the support of his beloved charge, would halt in a great measure, and his sacrifice of thanksgiving which he offers unto God for them, would be extremely maimed, (v. 13.) Whence I must conclude, that the very lowest degree of faith, or belief of the truth, and the very least measure of holiness, or sanctification of the spirit, are real, proper, and sufficient preservatives against all fear of diabolical enthusiasm. And that wherever the signs of these are found, but in any degree or measure whatever, there to lay such a charge as this, or even but to insinuate it, is not only most unsafe, but also most unreasonable.

Nay, farther yet, if there be but a possibility of doubt in this matter, through the insensibility of the signs, there may be greater danger to pronounce so severe a sentence, than you, dear Sir, with many others are aware of at present.

Another corollary that I hence deduce, is, that the more intricate points of schism and heresy, are not the proper criterions of such an enthusiasm as this, though they may be the effects of it, and so may, indeed, be made use of as subsequent proofs, where the evidence is plain. For this is the most terrible judgment of God that ever can be inflicted against the most obstinate, and refractory opposers of the Gospel, as in its full latitude, and after the knowledge of it; and therefore cannot be justly declarable against those, who are mistaken in the profession of it, how gross and unhappy soever their mistakes may happen to be. Since also this delivery up to Satan is not for their reformation, but for their destruction, it is upon a full and decisive judgment against them for their former crimes perpetrated. And it would be very hard on the part of a most righteous God, if this were only for points of a disputable nature, that have been and are continually agitated on both sides by men of good will, and wherein it is not impossible for men of learning and probity to be deceived.

And as on the part of God it would be hard, so on the part of man it will be much more so, to set himself up a judge in this critical case; since even he himself can never be so catholic and orthodox in his own sentiment, but that a much greater body of Christians will be against him, than any one that can be for him, (the Church of Rome itself not being excepted,) and cannot be safe so much as one moment from falling under this very judgment, with sorcerers and witches, if he should be so unhappy as through inadvertence to mistake in a matter which very few can agree about. For the majority will certainly agree in this, let him take what side he please to, that he is a schismatic, or heretic, if not both. And let him depend upon the infallibility of his own reason, or the infallibility of another's, by what name soever this or that is called, whatever sincerity and love of the truth he may truly pretend to, I do not see how any one can have but a tolerable security of not suffering even in this life, according to the sentence pronounced against the first born of the devil; if either schism alone, or schism with heresy be allowed of, as a true criterion of enthusiasm, when diabolical and when not. Unless the irresistibility of Divine truth (in its strictest sense) be maintained, and likewise the particular application of it, infallibly and irresistibly demonstrated. No other passible security can be invented, and to assert either of these, is, I confess, an enthusiasm that I have not yet reached to. Now God forbid, that I should make myself by this a patron either of schism or of heresy. I know very well the evil and the danger of them; and I bow my knees continually before the God and Father of my Lord Jesus Christ, that he may preserve me from them both, and keep me evermore in the unity of his Holy Spirit, with all the true Israel. This only, I beg leave to any, that all the topics of reasoning that not only are, but can be drawn from either of these, are much too short to infer in any one a diabolical energy.

And that how many and how great soever the arguments may appear, that hence are raised, they cannot amount to a proper criterion of such an enthusiasm as is pretended, nor be accepted as such, without running expressly counter to the design of this Apostle, who maketh it to consist in infidelity and impiety, and in these two when arrived to their crisis. And that these only can be relied on as the inseparable and characteristic notes of all anti-christian delusions, I take to be further manifest from sufficient matter of fact, proving the invalidity of any other: since it is not only possible for such sort of delusions and obsessions of evil spirits to be found there, where there be not the least appearance either of schism or of heresy, but examples or them have likewise actually been that can hardly be disputed. Among which I place Simon Magus and his companions in the first place, while they yet continued visibly in the communion of the Church, and in the fellowship of the Apostles. Whence the Christian Religion fell under the odium of the times for their sakes. And all Christians being thought to be involved in the same crimes with these, were by some good and wise heathens condemned, as well as by the wicked and ignorant.

In the Apostolical Church of Thyatira, as also in that of Pergamus, it is highly probable that they did not separate themselves from the external communion of the saints, or publicly maintain any heretical doctrine against the catholic faith. And it seems that the faithful Thyatirans were therefore reprehended by Christ because they tolerated in their communion persons guilty of such enormous impieties and idolatrous practices; which they were not wanting to cover with some specious pretexts from the false and evil spirit of prophecy, which did strongly move in them. Apoc. ii. 20. Thus it was even in the first and most pure age of the Church. And how it was in the succeeding and more degenerate ages of the Church, you know, Sir, very well. You know what sort of persons were sometimes raised to the chief patriarchal sees, and how Satan (in a more real sense than is ordinarily understood) might be said to have his throne in the temple of God.

I will not now ask what communion there can be betwixt God and Baal? Or how can such as these be the instruments of conveying the Holy Spirit to any? Or why the two mentioned Asiatic Churches should be utterly exterminated for permitting the evil leaven of Balaam and of Jezebel to creep in among their prophets and teachers, and others who have trodden in the same steps should not also be laid in the same bed with them, according to the equal and righteous Judgment of God?

These and many questions more would naturally fall in; but I am not willing to be burthen-some to you, and do leave them only to your consideration, and your free disposition to take notice of them or not.

XIII. —Now the sum is this: there is a security to be had against the interposition of evil spirits, and that in the imaginative faculty itself. This security is not hard and perplexed, but easy to be obtained, and to be judged of by all Christians. It consisteth in knowing the grounds of God's permission of such evil spirits to interpose and act after this manner, and the preservatives against them. The grounds why God permits evil spirits thus to interpose, are malice against Christ and an abandoned life. The preservatives against their interposition are faith and holiness, though but in an inferior degree and measure. Schism and heresy do not of themselves expose to this danger: they cannot be justly or safely made the presumptive marks of a diabolical energy or enthusiasm. This is no less possible, and no less frequent also (if not more), in the external unity of the true Church, than without it. Wherefore, if the visible unity maintained with the undoubted catholic Church, and the external profession of orthodoxy, can be no manner of security against the greatest of all evils; and some may fall into one or both of those two evils, before mentioned, and yet have still a sufficient security (if they please) of not falling into this last, so long as there is but any sincerity remaining in them; I cannot see how it can be denied, that we may, or actually have a security of this kind that is sufficient for us to rest on, without running into such consequences as you yourself will not be willing to allow of. For it will not be difficult to find out, now there are many living witnesses, whether it has been a life of infidelity or a life of faith, which this person has led: and especially for these thirty years past, wherein she lays claim to the more immediate familiarities with the true Spirit, whether it has been a life of impiety or a life of angelical sanctity; whether she has had pleasure in unrighteousness, or rather in righteousness. If the former be found true, then is there no security; but if the latter be true, then is there all the security that can justly be demanded or expected. This security is stronger than miracles themselves. It is all that God is pleased to give, even for the discernment of pretended miracles, in that most perilous case instanced in by the Apostle. And though it may be indeed possible for some persons that are neither wicked, nor unbelieving the Gospel, to be hurried beyond themselves by the efforts of a natural enthusiasm, innate or accidental; yet it is as impossible for any but the maliciously wicked, and the perversely unbelieving, to be delivered up to that which is diabolical, as it is impossible for God to deceive.

Nay, should they be sometimes even exposed to this, by the course of Divine justice, for some wilful misdemeanour against the truth and holiness of God, it would yet be impossible for his good Spirit to leave them to the ravage of the Evil one, before they shall have filled up the measure of their iniquities, and not to set bounds to the incursions of the disguised enemy.

Such a security then there is in this present matter, as great as the justice and truth of God himself.

Since if we have received not the love of the truth, or if we have rather believed it, when and so far as it is made manifest, our consciences must answerably condemn or acquit us. And it cannot but be known to the persons concerned, if they have rejected obstinately the sanctification, or sanctifying energy of the Divine Spirit, or if they have embraced it, in order to the attainment of the glory *of the Lord Jesus Christ*, whereof such frequent mention is by them made. And if this may be known to the persons themselves, (as it is known to them infallibly,) so may it be known likewise to others, according as the external demonstrations are given of either.

As for my own part, I stand before the judgment seat of Christ. But it is well known what my exterior life has been, and my interior is known where it ought to be, I dare not justify myself: for if I do, my justification is not true. Only give me leave to observe, dear Sir, that you herein so unawares justify me, while you most condemn me. Since if I were truly under the energy of Satan, it must have been in vain that you have taken so much pains to recover me; and all endeavours of this kind must of necessity be frustraneous, being directly opposite to the expressed will of the Sovereign Judge.

XIV. —Another general prejudice there is against these writings, that they were not penned by the person under whose name they are published, but by another, and by one also that was censured publicly for doctrines and practices of an evil nature.

And here I must confess, that so much is said, and so well laid together, that had it been a matter of fact some hundreds of years ago, I could never have resisted the force of so many probabilities amassed together, but must have surrendered myself to your sentiment. Which I cannot now do, because the matter is fresh, and because the most plausible conjecture will avail nothing against real experience, and sensible demonstration.

For the plain truth is this. I find it was the constant course of my mother to write down with her own hand day by day, all her own experiences and discoveries, with several memorandums also relating to her external as well as internal life. This was observed by her so long as it pleased God to permit her the use of her eyes, which was for almost a year after I was brought to be acquainted with her. In which time she described in secrecy with her own pen, the Treatise of the "Eight Worlds" (the original of which so written I do keep by me), with some other things not yet published. But since the loss of her sight, (occasioned by the intense exercise of her head in meditation and recollection and by much writing) she has been constrained to dictate to another, and not always to the same, but to several persons. In which her great expediteness in all subjects and upon all difficulties before her, is not a little remarkable.

She had indeed for some years the assistance of a man of letters, who accidentally (if a Christian may use this word) contributed much to the preservation of the greatest part of her Diary.

For whereas what she wrote was in loose slips of paper, like the Slbilline leaves, he transcribed them for his own private use, without any thoughts of their publication: whence in haste he frequently copied the very grammatical errors, and false orthography, leaving void spaces for the words he could not read, some of which were filled up by her own hand, but others not. And upon comparing the originals that remain with the copies, I do not find any interpolation of words to make them look more pompous, any variation of the style, or of the sense, (except through mistakes in the punctuation,) this being only to be confessed as to the former, that he sometimes transposes the verb to the former part of the sentence, with which my mother useth to close it.

Whereby while he renders the style a little more familiar and natural to the ear, It is indeed broken and made more languid. Of which I could bring instances not a few, if it were worth the while to stand upon such little niceties.

There sure also omissions in the copy of a word, of a line, and even, though rarely, of an entire sentence. Yea, some of the loose cartels were forgot to be written by him (where some whose dates are omitted), and others are verbatim twice written over.

The very first book which she published, being the *Heavenly Cloud*, (printed 1681, that very year when her friend died,) was printed off from her own hand, and never transcribed by him, nor indeed so much as revised as to the prose. And I dare appeal to you, Sir, whether the style be not the same in this book, with that which is in her late printed Diary, and even in the very parts of it which being lost in the original, could be found only in the copy.

For some parts of it are printed from the original itself, where the copy happened to be lost; for the evidence of which you may see June 20th, 1676, p. 253, vol. i.; and June 30th, 76, p. 256, with the note at end of the former, to omit others.

But had there been no such evidence to be brought that my mother is indeed the author, next to that spirit (whatever) by which she is conducted, of what has been published under her name; yet have I daily undoubted proofs of her capacity to write in such a style, and that upon all sorts of cases and subjects, that have been presented to her from abroad, by persons of several nations, ranks, and qualities.

XV.—But notwithstanding this, a considerable doubt will still remain, if her friend were truly such a one as some would have him to be. But I have made the most narrow search into his life that I am able to do, without the least partiality or favour, and I cannot find him guilty of that black charge, most barbarously laid against him. As he was not exempted from human passions and infirmities, so he showed himself not an indiligent combatant in the Christian warfare. And from all that I can possibly learn, I most believe him to have been a person of much integrity, of very deep experience in spiritual matters, and of most worthy and holy aims. Such an one was this Dr. John Pordage, that was ejected out of the living of Bradfield, by Cromwell's commissioners, in a most arbitrary and illegal manner.

But whatever he might have been in 1654, and before that, it is possible that in the space of twenty years, and those too under the Cross, he might become a new man. For it is not till about that time, as I perceive, that his familiar friendship began with my mother.

It being in August, 1673 or 74, (the date differently through mistake entered in two places) that they first agreed to wait together in prayer and pure dedication. And from this time till his death, his conversation was such as malice itself can hardly except against, he pressing forward to the most perfect state that is attainable, though not without the sense of his imperfections, and of the manifold temptations of Satan. And in the year 1675 I find remarked under his own hand, how many years he had been earnestly striving after the heavenly pattern contained in the Gospel, complaining how he had fallen short of it, and giving the reason whence this defect proceeded. I find several other private remarks relating to his internal state, by him made, which do invincibly (as to me) demonstrate that he could be no hypocrite; that he was not one fit to manage clandestine designs, that he was not imposed on by lying spirits, and that he was guilty neither of those doctrines nor practices, with which some have charged him.

He has written a Treatise against the errors of the Quakers, and has fundamentally overthrown the principles of Rantism in another of his unpublished books. From which, and his other remains, it doth appear, that he was an impartial seeker, and hearty lover of truth. Yet as he was one that desired, as he says himself, to hold the *just balance with the even weights*, so it will be evident to every one that examines his case, that he indeed met with from others false weights and measures. This you cannot but discover yourself, if you consult but his very accusers: there is such a confusion amongst them, such a disordinate passion, such a plain wresting of words, such a ridiculous report of matters, and throughout such an unchristian demeanour, as doth recoil upon their own heads, and so do hurt these more than his.

Instances whereof are evidently to be found in the author of *Famalism arising out of the bottomless pit*, in the *Demonium Meridionum* of Mr. Fowler, and even in Mr. Baxter himself, though with far greater moderation, than either of the others, and but at the second hand. If you read his Apology, called *Innocency appearing*, to which the second pretends to be an answer, you will find a distinct relation of the matter of fact, that is principally disputed, concerning the apparitions both of evil and good spirits, and the manner of the openings of the two contrary kingdoms or worlds, as it came to pass by the will of God in the Autumn of 1649; which was also lately reprinted by Mr. Edward Stephens in a Treatise concerning witches, etc. [Son-in-law of Judge Hale, and author of "Ancient Ascetics."]

And truly having considered not superficially both the printed accounts, and what other corroborating evidence I have met with from several persons, that could be exactly acquainted with it, one of whom was then of All Souls College, and went with another Fellow of the same college to Bradfield, to make on purpose an inquiry into the truth of this matter, they being both of them persons of an unblemished piety, and also of a good understanding.

I must freely say, I see as much reason to confound Simon Magus and Simon Peter, as to confound Everard the sorcerer, and Pordage the divine, together. St. Peter resisted and overcame his adversary, who had hypocritically insinuated himself to be a visible member of the church; so did Dr. Pordage also by virtue of that promise, (not appropriated to the Apostles alone, but to every true Christian,) *resist the devil and he will fly from you*. This, and no other, was the case of Bradfield.

But it was not an easy combat; there was required to it, continual watching and praying, without any interruption, for whole weeks together: while one slept, others watched and prayed in their turns, and whensoever there was but the least flagging, the enemy as I have heard presently prevailed, and recruited his force. But though by the grace of God, and name of Jesus, he was constrained to fly with his wicked instrument, yet did not his malice here expire, but lay a new plot, which took effect five years after, by the intemperate zeal of those times, and some personal piques (which it has been always ordinary to cover with the cause of religion), that must not be raked up afresh.

But herein I except Mr. Fowler, in whom I believe it might be pure zeal, for the most part. Of which he (or any one) could not give a more signal instance, than in the present case, all matters duly weighed. However had the Doctor been never so guilty, it would, I think, have been of far better report, if any other had undertaken the cause, than one that is said on many accounts to be obliged to him, and to have been raised through his means from an indigent state to what he then was, so as even to sit as a judge on his quondam friend, while he also made himself both a party and witness, for the surer dispatch.

Thus an ungoverned zeal transcends all limits, and especially when it flows from rigid principles. For it is no wonder if one that took pleasure in denouncing of hell and damnation not only as infinite, but as inevitable also, and that even according to principles, condemned them who knew not their right hand from their left to an irreversible destruction, so as in the flight of an enthusiasm, to fancy the very place of everlasting terrors to be paved with the souls of little children; it is no wonder, I say, if such a one (if it be true what is reported generally concerning this *Durus Pater*) should be transported into a paroxism of zeal, upon hearing of matters so extraordinary, so little understood, so misrepresented, and lastly so loaded with other criminal charges.

But notwithstanding what this severe justiciary hath brought to invalidate the *solemn appeal* to God, made by the Doctor, when there was no redress to be expected on the earth, and a re-hearing of his cause which was sued for, had been denied to him; since he would never afterwards withdraw this appeal, by appealing again to man, or returning an answer to the accusations of the *Demonium*, I dare not offer to put in my plea against it, but must let it rest there where it is. And therefore also I shall omit many things that might pertinently enough be urged on this behalf, for the setting right so distorted a case.

This one thine only I cannot but mention, which in other cases is constantly allowed of as a certain evidence of credibility in the person, and which the special Providence of God hath here favoured me with, beyond what I could ever have expected or desired to have found. I find there among the papers of his which are fallen into my hands, (some of which were never designed to be seen by any,) several unquestionable marks of an undesigning honesty. And I must needs observe, that he is so far from concealing his own faults and imperfections, (as a cunning impostor would have done,) as that he has in sundry places taken shame to himself, and given glory thereby to God, by the act of his own hand. And this he hath done when there could be no invitation (so much as presumed) for so doing, unless from a generous and open principle that moved in him, and the holy conduct of the Spirit of Truth. Hence he did transcribe several admonitions, reprehensions, and even some prophetical threatenings, that were expressly levelled against himself. And were the cases never so secret, to which these did respect, he was never less faithful, or less diligent to preserve them, doubtless for caution and instruction.

Neither could he indeed hide his infirmities, as far as I can learn, would he never so fain. He confesseth ingenuously the dulness of his soul to comprehend or express what was revealed to him in the Spirit. He cautioneth against confounding the ratiocinations of his mind, with the illuminations of the Spirit. He complaineth of his inadvertence, of the irregularity of his natural fire, of his elevation for some time, and of his too great activity at another. He reporteth of himself in his Treatise of the *Dark World*, how that not many years after his ejectment out of the living of Bradfield, a most terrible voice came to him and said, *Take this unprofitable servant, and cast him into outer darkness.* And how that immediately hereupon, he was snatched away thither in spirit, and made to feel there the heavy strokes of Divine justice, so as to be able thence to describe that world in the manner that he hath done.

Where he owns, even after all the Divine enjoyments and communications, which he had had, that he was still but an unworthy servant in the eye of God, and had strictly merited to be cast alive into hell, according to that dreadful sentence, which was sounded in his ear, as from the Sovereign Judge. And if this be the mark of an impostor or of a wizard, I must confess, that such a one was this known (or rather unknown) person.

But neither is this all, there are many other corroborating circumstances of his veracity, in this particularly, which can be produced, if need require. And I must say, if he were not innocent of these charges against him, it may behove us perhaps to consider well how to dear holy Job, and David; of whom it is probable that they were made in like manner to undergo the pains of hell in their souls for a season.

This lasted upon him, by fits, for some years: during which times the heavens were shut to him, and he continually exposed to the buffeting and scourgings of Satan, so that he was enabled to write as he solemnly saith, what he had in those dismal regions heard, and seen, and felt, and tasted. And in this very Treatise he taketh sufficient notice in a few lines of the injustice of the *Demonium*.

Upon all which considerations, and many others that might be instanced, were I to write an Apology, I am (after the most exact enquiry that it is possible to make) fully convinced that this very Dr. John Pordage, who is so much blackened, though he was like other men not quite free from human passions and frailties, yet was a man truly fearing God, and hating a lie: yea, that he was a laborious searcher after truth, and utterly incapable to be the father of such a grand imposture as is surmised.

XVI. —But there remains still a nearer prejudice against these writings, that is, supposing them not to have been contrived by another head, nor forged upon another's anvil, yet there is ground enough to suspect their original, from the style itself wherein they are composed, and principally from the honourable mention there is made in them of *magic*, against the practice of the primitive Christians, who condemned all sorts of it, as well the white, as the black.

This is indeed a very considerable exception; if you have taken here this word in that proper and most determinate sense, according to which it is used in these writings throughout. But give me leave to say, that I very much doubt whether you have done so: and it is no wonder if upon a cursory view, we frequently mistake an author's sense, and find there our own meaning, where there is it may be just the contrary. I have done so myself, (and even in this very case too,) and therefore can pardon it in another.

And let it not seem strange to you, Sir, if my mother do no less condemn, the white magic, so called, than the primitive Christians did themselves. Sure I am that she doth in that sense, which it is commonly taken in. For the whole scope of her writings is clearly against all manner of intercourse even with good demons and angels, by the means of certain religious rites and invocations; and against every degree of communion, confederacy, and familiarity with these (could it be obtained *without* such rites), but in and through the Spirit of Jesus; whereby she agrees exactly with the sense of the primitive Christians, and is no less distant from the Porphyrian magic, than they were, when both are rightly understood. But more peculiarly this is the design of the Treatise of the *Enochian Walks with God*, where this very subject of the communion of saints and of angels, is expressly delivered, and the method of attaining to this communion is proposed according to her own experience.

Whence if there were any of this evil science in her, it would certainly be found here, if anywhere.

Whereas the quite contrary is found, and no society is recommended with them, otherwise than as in the body of Jesus Christ, and no way to arrive to this blessed society declared but the life of Christ.

So that consequently she condemneth all demonalatry of the Paganising Christians, ancient and modern, and all that $εθηλοθρησκια$, and all that pomp of worshipping of angels, which was condemned by the Apostle in those of Colosse, by her making the body of Christ the sole medium, and vehicle (if I may so say) of communication with beatified spirits, and assigning no other mediational natures for the recalling up the soul to the Deity, than this one in him, wherein the pleroma of it (and of nature also) did corporally reside.

And that false humility, which is the foundation of this sort of magic, is so diametrically opposite to the very character and spirit of these writings, that were all the libraries of Europe to be searched, it would be hard to find any, (since the days of the Apostles) that have less of it, or that do more directly press into the very bosom and heart of Jesus.

For this counterfeit humility doth variously transform itself, and is more or less to be discovered in most writers, even in them of the very best fame, as being the mother of a twin-offspring that at one time or other do govern all mankind (viz. superstition and infidelity) under several disguises or mazes, by the fair names of piety and prudence. By which it is most evident, that it could never be the intent of these writings to honour this magic, which is called white, whose very foundation they do entirely overturn, or the meaning of the author to introduce into Christianity a cult of demons, which is so contrary to what she everywhere drives at, of doing all things in the name and power of the Lord Jesus.

Which alone is to me a sufficient characteristic of the truth of her spirit, and of her estrangedness from whatever savours of the pretended angelical art, the *Ars Paulina,* or the Key of Solomon.

My curiosity, I confess, has led me heretofore to look into these, and by this I am the better able to Judge in a matter of this nature. For indeed among all the prayers I have seen in such sort of curious books, printed or manuscript, which are many, some of which prayers are also very excellent, as to their substance, I do not remember so much as one that was offered up to the Father, in the name of the Son, explicitly or implicitly. This is the fundamental error of the magic which the ancient Christians so much condemned, and which to this day, (as I am well informed,) is really practised by many nominal Christians, even of great rank. And for this very cause, I cannot but place an exceeding value upon the greatest part of the Collects of the English Liturgy, as which seem most directly levelled against this practical error, and so likewise on these or any other writings, that tend so much to the exaltation of the mediational dignity of our blessed Saviour, as might be demonstrated.

Therefore the word magic, in these writings, is not to be taken in any sense contrary to the practice or the belief of the first Christians.

But if you would know in what sense it ought to be taken, you need do no more than admit the author's own explication of it. The word, Magia, saith she, in a marginal note to a book, the most obnoxious of any, *is the created power of the Holy Ghost, so to be understood as often as named.* — Rev. Rev. p. 51. And again, in another marginal note, she saith, Magia is the faith of the operation [energy] of the Holy Ghost. From which it is clear, she means such a Divine faith as was in the Apostolical Church, being begotten in the soul by the inhabitation of the Holy Ghost, as the gift of Christ, to give a demonstration (both internally and externally) of his kingdom, and of the subjection of all nature and creature to his all-powerful will. And however this may have been degraded, or condemned by the after and corrupter ages of Christianity, I humbly conceive that it was not so by the first and purest. [See Freher's Treatises, and Law's "Way to Divine Knowledge" for the full justification of Behmen's word *Magic*.]

XVII. —The other exceptions that are brought against the style of this author, are of far less moment, and might be enervated without any difficulty, by a bare explication of the terms that give offence. And though they should appear to be borrowed many of them from the customs of unjustifiable curiosities, there is no reason that I know, why it should be a more just prejudice against these, than against some others that are to be found in the Old Testament, and also in the New.

Both Judicial Astrologers and Alchymists do find in these, what is very consonant to their style. The Chaldee Oracles I understand not: but when they were made use of by the enemies of Christianity, who knew how to counterfeit and interpolate them for their turn, it was then very reasonable to censure them. In the old Platonic divinity there may be as much truth, I am apt to think, as either in the old Aristotelic, or modern Cartesian divinity. I am sure the style of the first is more agreeable to the primitive antiquity of our Christian religion, than either of the last. And if this be any objection at all against my mother's style, it will be as good against Justin Martyr, Athenagoras, etc. Whether it be so or no against St. John, I do not say.

As for the style of the modern enthusiasts, and all that you bring under that denomination, let them speak for themselves. But, however, a true and a false prophet may have the same manner of speaking; and the same character of style, may be exactly imitated by persons of a quite contrary design. You instance only in JACOB BEHME, who is *little understood by any;* for whom there is much to be said, to prove him to have been no enthusiast at all, in your sense of the word. I am told that the learned Zimmermanus has written a very judicious Apology for him, against a certain professor at Frankfort. And I know a *person of great accuracy of thought, and coolness of mind, as well as of a most holy and primitive life, who is undertaking to render him intelligible, by a true and genuine representation of his Principles, both of Divinity and Philosophy, after having read all his books in the original more than ten times, though not without the greatest disgust imaginable in the beginning.*

And yet I do not mind that J. B. doth any where attribute a sacredness to his style; but on the contrary supposeth it to be full of faults of his own, which he was willing to correct, by the advice of learned men, his friends. Whence, living in a place and age wherein Paracelsian chemistry was greatly favoured by many, it is no wonder if he was persuaded to make use of its terms, when they were proper.

XVIII.—And indeed there is not a greater, and perhaps more grievous mistake, than to imagine, that *every person inspired by God, is infallibly directed in the use of the phrases and words that do express this inspiration.* For from this, once allowed, many bad consequences will naturally flow, which you can see into without my particularising them. So that should these which are objected be real faults in the style, and not only these, but several others unmentioned, yet it is still possible for the substance of the inspiration itself that is here laid claim to, to be true.

That this is really so, and that God doth actually accommodate himself to the infirmities, (yea, and prejudices) of the instrument which he takes up, is not difficult I think to be made out from the histories of Moses, of Joshua, the Prophets, yea from that of the Apostles themselves. Now this is all that is pretended to, that the matter of the Revelation, where it is delivered as a revelation, be true: and that the manner of expressing it has been sufficiently taken care for, yet not superfluously. Had the latter been more accurate, I should not the less, but more have suspected it. The Alcoran of Mahomet is said to have been written in a far better style, than the Gospel of Jesus Christ: and you know there are some who tax his Apostles for writing like barbarians, who do not hereby think that they lessen their authority, or deny that they were guided by the Holy Spirit; and consequently maintain the *matter* which they deliver to be no less worthy of regard, than if all the syllables were externally dictated as by a local voice, wherefore I proceed to your exceptions against the matter.

XIX. —But as the imperfections of style are no justifiable prejudice against the sacred authority of the matter revealed, so *neither is every mistake in the matter itself derogatory to the principal design of the author, though truly inspired.* Justice requires of me, that I should distinguish betwixt matters less principal and accessory, and them that are fundamental and essential; betwixt what is delivered as an express word of revelation, and that which may be only a deduction made from it, by that soul to whom the revelation came; and lastly betwixt what may be conditional and what positive in a revelation, what mutable and what immutable, what in nature and what above nature. And if the foundation be but true, though some errors should be found in the superstructure, I shall not be much concerned at them. For if that be Divine, it must abide when whatever is of human production superstructed upon it, shall be burned up, notwithstanding it might come from a very innocent and good meaning. Instances whereof are to be found among such, whom the catholic Church hath ever accounted for saints, and lights in their generation.

So if what is essential and given as a clear express word of revelation fail not, and if what is positive, immutable, and above nature declared by this word, can stand the test, we are not obliged I think, thence to invalidate this that is so in any writer, though what is accessory and matter of deduction only, should indeed fail, and what is conditional, mutable, and in nature, should seem to suffer loss. St. Cyprian may have been truly illuminated, and have had many of the more extraordinary Divine favours, visions, and voices, yet is it possible for him to have been mistaken in the point of rebaptization, and in his revelation about the elements to be consecrated in the eucharist. Yet do I not positively say, that he was so, much less dare I be so bold with this holy martyr as some Protestant writers are, being satisfied that he was far from being either a dreamer or a cheat.

St. Chrysostome was a burning light in the catholic Church, and had, for certain, true inspirations himself, and excited others also to believe and wait for the same. Yet was he certainly mistaken in the prophecy of his return from his exile. Of St. Austin I doubt not in the least, but that he was converted by a revelation, and that he was also afterwards followed by sensible Divine teachings and intellectual openings, if what he has written of these (in his book, de Magistro especially) can be credited, there is no question to be made. But I do not therefore think that he was guided at all times without error, or that there was no need for him to write a book of retractations.

Besides these three instances, there are others no less obvious in antiquity; whence I cannot but greatly admire at the vulgar apprehension of inerrability to accompany all them who at certain times have been inspired by the Holy Ghost, for a private or public good, no less than at that of some others, of thinking impeccability to be a consequent of regeneration, or an effect of the ordinary Divine grace, since there appears to be one and the same bottom for both of these. And therefore I do not see but that there is as much need of a spiritual as of a natural discernment, according to the diversity of the object, whether from revelation or reason.

Nor would it be more unreasonable to reject the many excellent natural truths that are to be found in the most rational writers, which they have learnt from the common light of mankind, by a due application thereof, for the sake only of some errors with which they may be mixed, through either an inapplication or misapplication to the said standard; than to cast away (or but under-value) those Supernatural Truths which are to be found in the best spiritual writers, which they have learnt from the Divine light, the true Light of the world, by the means of a right conversion to it, and application of it, for the cause only of some mistake committed in the use of this superior standard.

And if in the former the error may be discerned by its proper light, which is reason; so likewise in the latter may it be discovered by its proper light, which is the Spirit of God, when lightly attended to.

Nor is this any greater disparagement to the true Spirit than it is to true reason.

In some sense it may be said, every man is, or may be infallible; but in another none is, and perhaps cannot be while we are in these bodies.

And truly I am so far from easily attributing infallibility to any one, howsoever highly illuminated and favoured, that I do indeed doubt whether in its strict sense it can be applicable to any but Christ himself.

That the Apostles themselves might be mistaken, both in understanding of the Scriptures, and of their own revelations also, sometimes (without derogating from the foundation of the Christian faith), there are two notorious instances which I think render it more than probable. The one is of St. James, the brother of our Lord, the most stiff asserter of the perpetual obligation of the Mosaical law, grounded upon some expressions in it, and confirmed by the catholic interpretation thereof.

The other is of the great St. Paul, who having had a particular revelation of the glorious return of our blessed Lord, seems to suppose it to have been then very near, and by consequent hereof, to confound as it were the impendent fate of Jerusalem with that of the whole world, a private with an universal judgement, and a temporal deliverance of the Church with the general resurrection of the saints. Whence I conclude, that it is possible for them who are at some times extraordinarily assisted by the Holy Ghost, and even *filled* with it, to err nevertheless, in matters both of faith and practice, where they suffer themselves to be guided either by tradition (oral or written) or by particular inductions of their own, drawn from that which is of revelation.

And thus it is not so extremely to be wondered at, that Nicholas the Deacon, a person *full of the Holy Ghost*, was misled himself, or at least was the occasion of misleading others into a pernicious error, by a mistake by him (or them) committed in the latter. This to keep all humble, and that every one take heed not to exceed the measure of the Spirit given to them, or to frustrate it by succedaneous sentiments, either of others or of themselves, which has been often done.

XX. —But how it is in the present case, I shall leave you to determine, when I shall have represented the matter as it is, and not as it may at first seem to be.

There are three points which you take notice of, and call *antiquated heresies*, which I shall say nothing to vindicate in this place, but only set them in their true light; whether it be heresy or truth, new or old. The first charge is of Gnostocism, from the seeming to introduce a female personality into the Deity. The truth is this: she useth to speak of Wisdom in the same manner as doth Solomon in his Proverbs, and the author of the Book of Wisdom: yea, as Christ himself doth. Matt. xi. 19. Upon the reading of the first, she had her first vision; and this was the representation of her under a female figure, presenting the book of the Holy Trinity, and promising to unseal the same.

This she supposeth to be as an Effluence or Glance from the whole Deity, but principally from the Father, or αυτοθεος, the original source of existence and power, and it may be called agreeably to her sense by these several names, Speculum Trinitatis, the Tabernacle of God, the Eternal Schecinah, the Heavenly Bethel, the φως απροσιτον, the Throne of God, the Mundus Divinus, the Vehicle or Chariot of the Divine nature, the Chasmal of Ezekiel, the Hand of God, and more expressly still, the Right Hand of God where Christ sitteth. In the famous prayer of Solomon, it is called Shamaim, and addressed to by him, 1 Kings, viii. 32. And in the prodigal's confession, ο θυρανος Luke, xv. 18., many other names are given to it by the sacred writers, by philosophers, and by the illuminati, in the confessedly purest and most infallible ages of the Church. Some expressing one character or property, and some another, of this holy Divine principle, through which God is conceived by them to descend into Nature, and to clothe himself as it were with Nature. This is believed by my mother to be as the matrix of all immortal spirits; and more eminently with a particular regard to man, the true mother church, the matricula and fountain της παλιγγενεσιας, that must be entered or rather re-entered into by all, and the womb of the morning of the resurrection, which was seen in an allegory by one Apostle, Gal. iv. 26., and in a vision by another. Rev. xxi. 2.

She calleth this by an harsh expression, the Spouse or Bride of God; yet not without the warrant of the ancient Prophets and Apostles.

She distinguisheth as to this, the inexistence in God from eternity, and the figurative manifestation in time. Of the former she says, that it *lay hid in the Triune Deity* (tanquam in semine planta); of the latter, *it was taken into God's bosom*. I do not know that she anywhere expressly calls it a *Goddess*; but amidst some hundreds of places in her writings where this Eternal Virgin nature is mentioned, in only one I find it said, she may be termed so (φυσις θεια, 2 Pet. i. 14.), by reason of her near relation to the Godhead. But neither is this there said simply, without any restriction: for to prevent all manner of suspicion of an evil meaning, or of transformed paganism in the word, this very limitation is added, in *a high and sober sense*. And it is directly opposed to the attributing Divine honours to the blessed virgin Mary, whom yet none will strictly call by this name, or Queen of heaven, but only derivatively. Yet, however, had such a limitation of the word been omitted, if the reason of the Apostle be just, 1 Cor. viii. 9., as also of Christ himself, John, x. 34, 33, 36., it might not have been so altogether indefensible as it doth at first, appear. This Virgin Divine nature she maketh to be the true mother or manifestatrix of Christ before he was born of the blessed virgin Mary. But as she distinguishes betwixt the hidden inexistence and the figurative manifestation of this Divine nature, so consequently of the Divine Word also, by it manifested. And therefore, as she clearly supposeth not only an eternal co-existence and inexistence of the Word, with and in the majesty of the Father, while yet unmanifested in the creature, as Λογος ενδιαθετος, or the MIND, but also a visible figuration of this very Word before time and creature, in eternity indeed, but yet not from all eternity properly, in-order to a manifestation thereof in the creature and time, as the Λογος προφορομηνος or IMAGE of this mind.

Hence according to this latter, she asserts Christ to be born, or manifested in a glorious figure, out of the Virgin nature of the unmanifested Σοφια. And this manifestation or birth is called the beginning of the works of God, the first born of the creatures, the Divine image, the eternal Adam, the Heavenly Humanity, and the Son of Man which came down from heaven.

By means whereof she believes that Christ did really appear to Adam, to Enoch, to Noah, to Abraham, to Moses, and to most of the patriarchs and prophets. So that her meaning is, that as Christ was born of the Virgin Mary in the frail figure of our sinful flesh, so he was also actually before brought forth in another more glorious figure by another Virgin, not of the earth, earthly, but of the heaven, heavenly, containing in it the primogenial matter and life, out of which all created beings were afterwards to proceed. And that this was the Similitude after which Adam was created in his original purity and beauty, which is called by Moses the similitude (or form) of God, and expressly the God of Israel, Exod. xxiv. 10, and by Ezekiel several times, the glory of Jehovah, and perhaps by the apostle $\mu o \rho \varphi \eta\ \tau o v\ \theta \varepsilon o v$, Phil. il. 6. And was the Goel [or kinsman] of Job, that was seen and believed in by him, chaps. 19, 25, chaps. 41, 11, 5. And the proper medium of communication betwixt God and man in all ages. The glory that appeared in the Jewish temple sitting betwixt the cherubims, and the tree of life in the superior paradise, on which Adam ought to have fed had he not sinned, thence called the bread that came down from heaven, (i.e. that of Paradise,) the bread of God, the hidden manna, as being most emphatically the $Z\omega\eta$, and the $\Lambda o \gamma o \varsigma\ Z \omega \eta \varsigma$ upon which the whole system $\Lambda o \gamma o \iota$, that is angels and men must live, is very often clearly insinuated in these writings.

Her meaning is, that Christ had a celestial form before he had a terrestrial, both generated from a Virgin nature, by the omnipotent Father. In the former of which he gave forth his laws and rules to Moses and the prophets. As also Justine, M. Theophilus Antioch. Tertull. Cyprian, Euseb. Caesar, (besides Origen,) do:

And in the fulness of time was superinvested by the terrestrial, for the transformation and glorification of our vile forms. She denies not any where Christ to be the Wisdom of God, as well as the offspring of Wisdom: that is, according to this manifestation. But as the Nicene Fathers themselves thought it no robbery to style Christ, Light of Light, though he be called the *Light*. So also she thinks it none to call him the Wisdom of Wisdom, or to say that he is generated out of the Wisdom (and Light) of the Father, though he be also rightly called the Wisdom.

She means not to assert any diversity of sex in the Deity, as the Gentiles and Gnostics did, who is so far from it, as to think that it did not even appertain to the created Humanity in its first and best state, which was paradisiacal, and that it shall again cease to be in the state of the resurrection.

Whether her sentiment be true, or no, I am not concerned, but thus much at least it proves, that she can never be guilty of such a gross imagination as she is charged with; and by consequence that there ought to be a presumption rather for, than against her, where some metaphorical and symbolical expressions are made use of, that are capable of more senses than one. This would be allowed in another case, therefore, I hope it will not be denied here. Since then it will not be unreasonable to interpret these expressions, or the like according to the analogy of the rest of the sentiments of an Author; since the sacred writers themselves, do (under a veil) frequently attribute human passions and members to the Deity, which are interpreted in a high and sober sense; since the appellation of male and female, when appropriated to the Divine Being are equally Improper. Since, that the affections of both are attributed to it in holy Scripture, according to a sound meaning, and that not only in the prophetical writings, but in the very epistles of the Apostles. Since the common name of God in the book of Job, seems to be of a feminine termination, and no less, also, possibly that most high and lofty name of JAH, so frequent in the book of Psalms; and since the female doth constitute part of the Divine character in pure and undefiled nature, as well as the male, she being designed as the *glory* and crown of the *head*; and lastly, since the *glory of God* may be considered distinct from God himself, (though in him and out of him.) Heb. i. 3, it doth not appear why her words should be interpreted in a low and gross sense, when they are capable of an higher, which is neither dissonant from Scripture, or antiquity, nor derogatory to the simplicity and spirituality of the Divine Being.

And in this high sense, she supposeth the *glory of God* to have pre-existed in God, as Eve did in Adam, before the Απαυγασμα thereof did break forth in the visible person of the Λογος, and was produced as out of the womb of this *glory*, being no other than the Eternal Wisdom itself, (called by her both a Virgin and a Mother,) going forth into manifestation in the said glorious Person, by whom all things were made, and without whom nothing was made, that was made. He being properly

Χαρακτηρ της   του θεου, in his laying the foundation of all things and still upholding the same, as her writings do elsewhere declare. And whether this may not be the meaning of Tertullian, to whom you refer me in another case, may, perhaps, deserve to be a little considered. Who in his book against Hermogenes, as if either he had conversed with my mother, or my mother with him, writes thus:—

Prophetiae et Apostoli tradunt primo SOPIAM conditam initia viarum in opera ipsius. Dehine et SERMONEM prolatum, perquem omnia facta sunt, et sine quo factum est nihil, c. 18.23.49.

Whether he delivers this as his own private sense, or whether as an apostolical tradition; and whether what he has written in other books concerning the Divine body, ought to be understood so grossly, as it is generally, and not rather soberly, and in the same, (or near the same) with the former, according to catholic prescription, I leave to be considered. But if this Father's meaning in his controversial writings against the heretics of his age, as to this be either defensible or excusable, then is not my mother's cause so bad as you might imagine, even there where it has been the the weakest.

Indeed his and her meaning are so akin, that I cannot distinguish them asunder: and I have not been wanting in diligence to find out what is truly hers, or in sincerity to represent the same, that so judgment may pass on it accordingly.

XXI. —But there is another block of stumbling, which is (and unless this block can be removed, all that was said besides will be to no purpose,) that *she is inconsistent with herself.* Now whatever foundation there may be for such a charge against her, in any other particular, I dispute not: but in this I can see none. Well, doth she not make the Virgin Wisdom born under the planets Sol and Venus, the planets created by her own son? If she *doth* so, I will confess all that you would have me to do. And if she doth *not,* I confide that the great generosity and integrity of your soul will not let you be ashamed to acknowledge that you have misunderstood her, and also that it will incline you more strongly than ever to forgive another when mistaken.

It is true that she doth make use of these terms, which did indeed shock me for some considerable time; but withal she premonisheth to take them in a *sober sense,* and expressly declares but a few lines before, that she intended not by the planetary names what the astrologers did, or the inferior and visible planets, which they make to have the dominion over man, so long as he is in subjection to the curse. But the superior and invisible ones, which are so many Divine powers, properties, attributes, modes, energies, etc., which do deliver from the curse. Moreover it is evident, that she speaks not of the nativity of wisdom, as in eternity, but only as in time; not of her origination before the world, but of her manifestation in the world; not of her first manifestation in this our orb, but of her descent again into it, after that she had been constrained (by the fall) to forsake it; not of the process of the Divine form (or beauty) through the universal system of beings, which was in the beginning, but of that in one particular order of them, and which is yet to be in the *end*.

She speaks of its renovation, restitution, reproduction, and regeneration, evidently supposing an antecedent rise and formation, as is clear, both from the main drift of that very book whence this objection is started, and the passage itself to which I suppose it may refer. The words are these: *Wherefore it is all-worthy to be enquired, in what planet the nativity of the Virgin may be again RENEWED? which must be by bright Venus, which must bring forth the mighty birth under Sol; in conjunction with the rest of the SUPERIOR planets, which are all harmonized in one*, etc. Rev. Rev. p. 24. And in the MS., with some little variation, I read thus: *Which must be by serene Venus, that must bring forth the mighty birth under bright Sol*, etc.

Again, presently after, these words also do occur: *The Divine mould for her SHAPE is again found according to what was BEFORE either angels or men were formed, which is not to be pourtrayed till she come to be essentially manifested within it.*

From which it is evident, I think, that she can mean nothing but a certain manifestation to the soul of man, not superficial, but essential, of some preexistent substance that is spiritu-corporeal. But to express what is her mind hereby (depending upon a thorough understanding of that whole book, and of the nature and progress of the Divine kingdom which she expects), cannot be done in a few words.

The terms of Sol and Venus which are not taken up at random, ought for this end to be well understood, in a sense that is both physical and metaphysical. And how harsh soever these may seem, or unwarrantable, yet are they not also without a ground even in Scripture, the one in Psalm xix. 4, 5, 6.; the other in 2 Pet. i. 19.; Apoc. xi. 28.

We may call one of them *Light*, and the other *Love*, or *passive Love*. Or we may regard one as the energy of the Son of God, and the other as that of the Divine Spirit. But whatever other names we shall substitute in their room, there will still somewhat in these hieroglyphics remain unexpressed.

The mystery of the Divine numbers, if there be any such, doth here lie couched. And the seven spirits before the Father's throne, from whom the greatest of mystics wisheth grace and peace (Rev. iv.) are these *superior planets*, those *high and exalted powers*, which must all concur, in the most perfect harmony, to the formation and production of this mighty birth, so frequently spoken of in these writings, and to which all the powers and wonders of the kingdom of Christ are appropriated.

This she supposeth always to be the way of natural causality, and correspondent to outward and fallen nature, and not by such a rushing, transient influx as descended on most (if not all), in the first promulgation of this kingdom after the ascension of our Lord.

And this according to the spirit of these writings, is the establishment of the Melchisedechian priesthood in his members. Upon whom He doth not barely reflect his image, as the visible sun reflects his on the waters; but in whom he doth represent himself really and vitally, and beget in them his express similitude, as the same sun doth also in a low degree bring forth his in all the subjects of temporal nature. He standing properly as the tree of life, in the midst of this our vortex, without whom, all that is therein contained of visibles would presently be dead.

So this royal manifestation, or birth of these holy, priestly Magi, is said to be *under Sol*, i.e., under the direct rays and immediate communication of the Divine and invisible Sun, who is become to them the tree of life and immortality, on which they continually feed, without danger from the cherub of Moses or the chariot of Elias.

And such a continued participation of His light and life, may in a sober sense not unfitly be called an eternal and substantial generation. According to which, every one that is called of God, as Melchisedec was, must be both $απατωρ$ and $αμητωρ$, with regard to his eternal generation, according to the express appointment of Christ, Mark, x. 29, 80; Luke, xlv. 26 ; and also his example, Matt xii. 46–50. Whence he will be likewise $αγενεαλογητος$, without any genealogy, whether paternal or maternal, in this mortal world; calling no man father on earth, and not hanging upon any mother, though even the universal mother of all flesh, as having one Father in heaven, and one mother, which is the new Jerusalem: being therefore said to be *redeemed* or separated, *from among men, and out of the earth*, said to be a *virgin, i.e.*, without succession or *end of days*, and figuratively represented to us, standing out of this gross atmosphere, upon an high and glorious mountain.

Now, to arrive to this eminent state and honour of the everlasting priesthood, belonging to the first fruits, according to the present theory, it is required there be an antecedent state of revelation, and Divine vision opened in the soul; and that all the spiritual faculties, senses, and powers, which will in the future life come to be manifested, be so in this (p. 43, 44.), which state is by the author continually appropriated to Wisdom, and in this place named her *renewed nativity*, as it is distinguished from the succedent state, which is by her appropriated to the WORD, according to the former distinction of the African father. And this state is much more noble than the former. For though that be here represented as exceeding glorious, and is really so in itself; yet falls it vastly short of the glory that is revealed in this other, which is no less than the very brightness and refulgent character of the glorified person of Christ, as the firstborn from the dead. And therefore to this state, as derivatively through Him, is applicable that most eminent decree of God, Psalm xi. 7., upon which the order of this priesthood (there at large treated of, p. 92.) is founded, and may as well be called a *birth*, she thinks, as that which is but the beginning of a low and mortal life. The one is a state that is *all glorious within*, but vile and contemptible without; the other is glorious outwardly also, and makes the vile to become honourable. The one is as the exemplar of the other, and which contains the other in its womb. But to both there is required the exact harmonization of the powers of the world to come, and of the seven principal emanations from the throne of the Divine Majesty, that so nothing be redundant or defective, nothing disproportionate or discordant.

Wherefore it is said they *agree to bring forth* (or manifest) the Mother and then the Son, in the Virgin humanity. And as the foetus receives figure and form in the womb of its mother, and her earthly matter, so does this from the *heavenly matter* of undefiled Virgin nature receive both in the sense of this author.

They are called by almost as many different names in these writings as the most cabalistical authors have been able to invent, either for the prima materia, or the summum bonum in nature. But the most ordinary are the *birth of Wisdom*, and the *birth of Power*.

In the last consists that which is the new creation; and in the first the idea of it. In which idea, the generative or prolific virtue (expressed here by the term of Magia) being included, it is called therefore the Divine Venus, in a sense well understood by many of the ancients. And as all generations in the fallen state of Adam's transgression, do proceed forth from the earthly and impure Venus (who truly sits as a queen upon the beast of nature, and can be said to be the Goddess or idol of all flesh); that is, as they come out of the same polluted mass and seminal corruption, so do all the heavenly generations, and the children of God that are brought forth in the regeneration and resurrection, according to the restored state of Christ's righteousness, proceed from this heavenly and pure Venus (that is, as the virgin clothed with the sun) out of the same one undefiled substance and seed of incorruption, which some have significantly named the *One Element*.

And also as the planet Venus, when a morning star, doth arise before the sun, and yet doth not shine from any other light, but what proceeds from the sun; so in like manner, the morning star of Wisdom, allowing the present hypothesis, may be properly said to arise in the soul, before the sun of the intellectual world come forth out of his Chuppah, and yet it may shine in the soul by no other light but what is reflected by this sun, while he remains in the Chuppah; which is an antecedent, internal ministration of familiar Divine converse, preparatory to the more public and glorious manifestation which is to succeed in the coming out together of the bridegroom and the bride.

Now, should we suppose the outward sun to be the creator of that outward, planetary body, the star of Venus, and that because the light of this star is produced from the light of this sun, and is inferior to it; yet notwithstanding. I do not see any inconsistence, or even inconvenience, in mentioning the said star, either as before the sun, or as after the sun, according to different respects. And thus will it be with the superior star of Venus, according to the same hypothesis.

For if there be any such star, or power in the intellectual or angelical world, corresponding to that which appears to us in the visible heavens, though it be inferior to the light of the intellectual and angelical sun, and have no more than a derivative light from its light, yet with respect to manifestation may be conveniently and truly said to be before it.

Nor is that which is manifested, in the order of science, known after that by which it is manifested, imaged, generated, or even created; but on the contrary: which different respects are sufficiently distinguished by this author.

XXII. —But moreover, that which appears so very confused at the first reading, and the mere product of imagination, is perfectly agreeable to the principles of the *most acute and deep Philosophy* that I have ever met with.

And as the most regular system of the universe doth favour the same, so likewise many passages in the holy Scripture are not (as far as I can apprehend) otherwise intelligible.

This hath been very surprising to me; but I cannot here expatiate into particulars, neither stay to lay down those principles, according to their due light, or to produce those passages, and apply them as would be necessary. Only, in *transitu*, I observe, as the astronomers do now make the Sun the centre of our vortex or world, so do these philosophers make their Sun (as distinguished from both the unoriginated sun, and from the first begotten image of it,) the centre of every vortex and world, both visible and invisible.

And this sun, in the Septenary System of spirits, they place the fourth or middlemost; calling it the fourth form, the fourth power, fountain or spirit of Nature; the Fire, the Holy Fire, Ignis Magorum, the Cross, and

Tree of Life, universal and eternal. So that the birth of Wisdom in the soul, by opening therein the secrets of the invisible worlds, the soul becoming as a clear, unspotted mirror, to receive their reflections, cannot be, according to the principles of the *true central philosophy*, but under the fourth form and fountain of nature. i.e., under Sol. And they show, consequently, how this magical birth, originated under the fourth, cannot be brought forth but by the help of the fifth form of nature, called the fountain of Love and Venus, in conjunction with the rest of the superior forms, fountains, powers, and spirits, constituting the *wheel of Nature*, which St. James is thought by some to allude to, iii. 6. Particularly they make the harmonisation of the Seven Spirits of God, and the conjunction of the seven forms of incorruptible nature to be after this manner, viz.: the fifth with the third, the sixth with the second, and the seventh with the first; so that out of each conjunction there ariseth an eternal harmony in the perfect octave, an eternal circulation of love and joy in the soul. All the said Spirits and forms being thus *harmonised in One*, which is the fourth, standing in the midst of the rest, they make the fifth to contain in its womb the sixth, and the first combination of forms to flow into the second; which second is the reproduction in the soul of the image of the *Word*, as the first was the image of the *Wisdom*. And the seventh they make to finish the whole mystery of God in nature, by the third and last combination receiving the other two into itself, which is the Sabbath of nature, beyond which it cannot go. —All this perfectly agrees with what has been the occasion of so much scandal in the writings of an illiterate woman.

XXIII. —And this may suffice to let you see, that she is not inconsistent with self, or with principles, in the present account that you were pleased to urge. And that there must be somewhat more than *ungoverned fancy* to speak so consistently with what she has delivered in other places, and so consonantly to the principles of a *certain Philosophy*, which doth require *more than ordinary penetration* of spirit to understand *but in part*. The truth of these Principles there are much abler persons ready to vindicate. However, let these be disputed ever so much, it can hardly be denied that she has written according to them, with an agreeable harmony that is indeed wonderful. And it is plain, that the terms taken from arts not understood by her, have yet been managed by her as if she understood them perfectly. These two births some also do understand as well outwardly in nature, as inwardly in the soul. And in the former interpretation they say doth lie couched the process of the renovation of all things, by a new virgin earth, and new virgin heaven, according to the famous prophecy of St. Peter hereunto applied. Also, besides this universal regeneration, which is two-fold, there are grounds in nature to believe a particular regeneration, in like manner two-fold. And this regeneration of certain individual subjects, as plants, etc., which some chemists do speak so much of, would, according to the description that is given thereof, much elucidate this matter, were it proper here to enlarge. Whence, some persons even of a mechanical head, and busied in the examination of nature, I have heard greatly to admire at some passages in her writings, which they said they had found to be exactly conformable to the truth of experimental philosophy, whereof she herself could not yet be supposed to have any knowledge at all. —Wherefore I conclude that she cannot be justly charged with introducing a difference of sex in the divinity, or with inconsistencies and unintelligible jargon in this point; but that she must have had the assistance of some superior intelligence in her account of wisdom.

XXIV. —The next charge against her writings is the Manichean heresy of *two co-eternal principles in the Deity*. But here also I doubt much whether she has been fully understood. I do not see anything that may seem to favour this but the private resolution of a question that was put to her, the answer to which she doth not say she did receive from any voice or vision, as it is frequent for her to do; whence it might as well be from reason, as from a principle more disputable. And if she doth here reason amiss, in a point which the wisest heads have not been able to unravel, yet what is said to be, elsewhere, from express revelation, may be nevertheless true.

But whether what she declares in the *Postcript* to *the Enochian Walks*, (which is the only passage of this nature) be from her own reasoning, or from revelation, her meaning may perhaps not be so heretical, as is at first easy to apprehend; yea, may be as far wide from the doctrine of Manes, as that which is most common at this day. This may be made to appear from what she elsewhere delivers, speaking again to this very question: she says, *hell, death, destruction, and the lake, are of themselves*. And if they are of themselves they are not of God, or in God; and there can be no coeternal principle of evil in or *with* the Deity, from whence they could be originated, she opposes the imperfect act of a created being, to the perfect act of the Creator: and the confusion and disorder of evil arising from the one, to the unity and harmony of good, existing in and flowing forth from the other. She makes good to be natural, and evil to be preternatural: good to be eternal, without beginning, or end, and evil temporary, as having both a beginning and an end. All which seems to me directly opposite to the condemned doctrine of Manes, and

Valentinian, making the evil to be no leas natural and eternal, than the good, and to owe its original, not to the creature, but to the Creator himself.

Nor is it simply asserted by her, that hell and death, etc., are not of God, but of themselves; For it is a conclusion drawn by her from the premises which she had laid down; which premises are exactly conformable to the principles she before went upon in the *Post-script*.

Which do turn upon the manifestation of God in nature, and the breach of the original band of nature by him constituted. Now as all variety is comprehended in this *band*, and doth branch forth from it, so as soon as this is broken, there must needs arise disorder and confusion, instead of order and beauty, by the will of the creature being separated from the Divine will, to act independently, and of itself.

This will appear to be the origination of evil according to her meaning. The only difficulty will be, how this variety in the band, could proceed at first out of the eternal Unity. But whatever way may be taken to account for the creation, this difficulty will alike recur.

That which is most easy, and according to that chain of principles upon which all this turns, is this. The UNITY is the beginning and the centre of the variety, which variety was comprehended in the unity. The variety is generated from the unity, and is the end of the unity, and must return back into the unity: the harmony proceeds both from the unity and variety together, in the unity without the variety there could be no harmony; and in the variety without the unity there could spring up nothing but contrariety. This UNITY, VARIETY, and HARMONY, was before the angelical creation: it was in the angelical creation, and it was after it.

It was before, in, and after, all creations whatever in the Deity: and after all creations, and revolutions, that are to be, it will still be in the Deity; throughout all the circles of eternity, when shall be all in all, Deity in nature, and nature in Deity.

This unity, variety, and harmony, was in all the angels at their creation, when they sang together for joy: and it would have forever continued in them all, had not some of them adventured to make a trial of the *might of their own wills*, whereby the harmony was perfectly broken, by their not returning back into the unity, by, and in, an humble resignation of their wills. And so through the variety brake forth the contrariety. In this contrariety is evil, and it springs up out of the separation of the perfect band of nature. In this band while unbroken, was every created being to have existed eternally; and therefore was it called an Eternal Band, and this nature, Eternal Nature, that is, immortal and incorruptible nature. There would have been an eternal circulation of life, light and love, in the unity, through the variety, by the harmony; if this eternal band had not been violated, as to some, in the angelical nature. And there is such an eternal circulation of life, light and love in all, where it hath not been violated, or where, having been once violated, it is again renewed.

On the contrary, in this band while it remains broken, or dislocated, no created being can exist eternally, but is made subject to vanity, there can be no circulation of life in the creature thus made subject. There may, indeed, be a temporal circulation of life in this state, but the vanity which is in the creature, and which flows from the contrariety, cannot live for ever. The vanity of the creature is not eternal, but as it stands in the contrariety, it must pass away with the contrariety sooner or later: for it cannot subsist out of the contrariety. And the contrariety must be at last conquered, unless there be two contrary co-eternal and co-equal principles, that is, two Gods; and being conquered it must pass away into the harmony. And thus entering again into the harmony of Divine Love, through the most beautiful variety of the heavenly light, centres in the original unity, which is the very life of God. Whence, where there is an eternal circulation of life, there must be also an eternal circulation of light and love, in the band of perfect nature, without all contrariety, and all disharmony.

And if the creature, through the contrariety, and through the disharmony, be made subject to vanity for a long duration of ages, the better to display the wonders, both of time and eternity, this contrariety must, in the end, be made itself subject to Him, who is the head of the whole creation, the Alpha and beginning thereof, in and by whom the variety of all things created, were manifested in perfect harmony; and who alone is able to subdue everything unto himself. Whereupon, all disharmony in the creature must vanish away, all things being again put under his feet, as it was in the beginning; through the all-powerful harmony of love, prevailing over that which has stood in the greatest opposition to it.

In the contrariety stands all evil, death, darkness, and wrath: in the harmony stands all good, life, light, and love. When the harmony subdues the contrariety of nature, then is death swallowed up in life, darkness in light, and the wrath of God in his love; and all the evil in the creature, whether of sin or of punishment, vanisheth away, as if it had never been. This is the victory of the Divine Harmony in the spirit of CHRIST.

But when the contrariety breaks the harmony of nature, whether in angels or in men, (which during the times of their probation can only be,) violating the natural subordination of their wills to the Divine will, and not centering in the supreme unity, from whence they primarily were originated: all manner of evil must be expected to proceed out of this breach and violation of eternal Nature; according to the degrees of the contrariety, and proportion of the disorder, multiplicity, and confusion thence arising in the creature, that has departed from the fountain of its unity.

Thus death, say they, entered into the world, through the transgression (or deviation from the unity) of one head angel, or angelical patriarch, and then of one man, or patriarchal head of the human race: whereby both the angelical and human natures in those hierarchies of Lucifer and Adam were as totally separated and divorced from the original source of their life, and from the unity and harmony of the Divine Being, which had before comprehended the variety in them, and kept all in its proper place and station, unviolated. And thus, through this disharmony and separation, did life disappear in death, the light vanish in darkness, and the love cloud itself in wrath. Yet the life was in death, the light in darkness, and the love, in wrath. But the death could not comprehend the life, neither the darkness the light, nor the wrath the love. So that the life, the light, and the love, were now unmanifested, and incomprehended: as death, darkness, and wrath, were before unmanifested, and incomprehended, which stood but as a faint shadow in the creature; and could never have been manifested, or comprehended by the creature, but through the contrariety of feeding on the knowledge of good and evil, life and death, etc.; and these should never have been manifested to all eternity, but for the better display of the wonders, the glories, and the triumphs of the eternal Life, the eternal Light, and the eternal Love.

But being manifested, they have not yet a positive existence, thereby in themselves, as everything derived from God hath. They have not their existence in the band of Nature, for that is good, yea very good, but they have it out of this band; and therefore the existence of them, and consequently of all evil, is more relative than real, more negative than positive.

For their existence is formally nothing else, but the separation and disunion of this sacred band, which was derived from God entire. And their manifestation in nature (as it is now lapsed and broken,) is but the hiding of the Divine love, light, and life in the creature, or from the creature: so that God becomes to it, as a hidden God, an angry God, a God inhabiting thick darkness, and a consuming fire. And yet, by this, here is not the least variation in God, the Spirit of eternity. Nor is there any new existence, or new degree of existence given hence to the spirits in time. Nor anything new produced (notwithstanding this change in the creature,) which was not already before in the band of nature, actually or potentially. But only a loss, and breach effected in the same.

Notwithstanding which, as God, so also Nature abideth invariable, according to its eternal order that was given it in the beginning; which is good, and eternally good. So that the good which is in nature hath an existence most real and positive, and also eternal: but the evil which is introduced into nature, or manifested by the separation of nature's eternal band and law, not existing after this manner doth stand as a dark shadow in opposition to the Divine Light and Truth; and hence death is called a shadow, and hell outward darkness, and sin blindness.

For this blindness and darkness have only a shadowy existence, from the violation of original nature, as angelical in one order of beings, and paradisiacal in another.

And yet had there not been the potentiality and root of darkness in nature, neither the outward darkness, nor the inward blindness could ever have sprung up, or in either of these two orders of beings have been made to exist after any sort.

And had there not also been something in the Deity to be manifested or glorified through this potentiality and root, it could never have been in nature after any manner: or even supposing it to be in nature, it never could thence have been brought forth; but must have remained for ever hid in a mere empty and impotent possibility, as it is in the blessed angels and perfect spirits.

Now what that is in the Deity which was to be manifested through this dark root of nature, is not difficult to be seen. It must be good in itself, because in the Deity: but it may not be good to the creature, because all that is in the Deity is not communicable, or manifestable to any created being, but according to its proportion of aptitude.

It cannot be positively evil: but it may be relatively evil, where it meets with disproportion and disharmony. Nay it must be positively and essentially good, but it may not be good to be tasted by the creature.

This is no other than the severe Justice of God, which could not be manifested before the birth of the contrariety. This Divine justice is both darkness and light, both death and life, yea both good and evil, according to different respects in the creature. But before the contrariety of the creature arises, it is unmanifested; it being in the Unity, and not in the divided root of good and evil, wherein the knowledge of it can only be had. And this is no less glorious and excellent in itself, than the Divine Mercy; which also could not but remain unmanifested without the contrariety.

But being terrible and unsupportable to the creature, it bears the relation of evil, and comprehends under it the manifold scenes of misery, all which do serve to a fuller unfolding of the mystery of the kingdom of Christ, of the beatitudes of the saints in light, and of the exceeding riches of the Divine Goodness; and to an higher manifestation of the wisdom, power, and holiness of the infinite Creator: which will be *eternally surprising*. Wherefore, if that be terrible which is glorious, and that evil in the creature, divided from his root, which is good in the Creator; then that which is glorious and good *in Him*, may yet in the creature, and with respect to the creature, be termed dreadful and evil, without any design to advance the condemned heresy of Manes, or to deny the unity and simplicity of the Godhead. And this is no more than what the infallibly inspired Divine writers both of the Old and New Testament have done, whereof frequent instances cannot but be observed by you, which having not been understood by many, for want of a very easy distinction of *GOD in Nature, and GOD above Nature*, has occasioned them foolishly to make God the author of evil; the most, indeed, consequentially, but some also directly. Which had been impossible to have been done, if they had known how the Divine justice, or the Divine mercy though they be two in nature, yet are but one in God; or how God in nature as the supreme universal cause, acts in the divided root of nature, remaining yet in his own eternal unity. In which eternal unity all things, according to this writer, are comprehended; and were in the beginning comprehended, as they were created, and did flow forth out of it, through the variety, into the harmony of nature. Thus she constitutes one undivided principle in the Deity, containing all principles, elements, and seeds, in an eternal temperature. And she considers the Deity in a transcendental sense, above all that is called material or spiritual, dark or light, mortal or immortal, terrestrial or celestial; and above all names, specifical, or general: so that matter and spirit, darkness and light, life and death, earth and heaven, may be said to be in God, or not to be in God, according to different relations; and both without injury to the eternal unity, and the eternal harmony of God. Now how far this is from making two co-eternal Gods, or two co-eternal principles in one God, the one good, the other evil; how far this is, both from the Chaldaean doctrine, as to their Oromasdes, and Arimanius, or from the Valentinian, as to their Achamoth, and Ananche, I leave you, Sir, to determine.

XXV. —The third charge of heresy against her writings, is that called the Origenian, for maintaining *the finiteness of hell torments*.

But if this be an heresy, it is absolutely inconsistent with the original of good and evil from two co-eternal principles, in the Deity. For if they are co-eternal a *parte ante*, they must necessarily be co-eternal, a *parte post*, and consequently the torments of hell must be as infinite as the joys of heaven: which consequence is so natural and easy, that every one must see it. And therefore if the torments are to be believed so infinite in their duration, as not to cease before God ceaseth to be, it is impossible for me, (I must confess) not to fall in with the Manichean doctrine, or to refuse to believe an eternal principle of evil, as well as of good, that is an eternal root and cause of hell in the Deity. But while I believe the torments of hell, and consequently all evil to be finite, it is impossible for me to believe the principle and root of evil to have been co-eternal with the good *a parte ante*. And therefore, if by such an easy train of thought I am driven to embrace one of these two doctrines, I had much rather incline to that which makes only the principle of good to be eternal both *a parte ante*, and *a parte post*, than to that which makes the principles both of good and evil to be in like manner so. Since it appears equally absurd to believe two universal principles (the one good and the other evil) eternal *a parte ante*, and but one of them eternal *a parte post;* and to believe one universal principle eternal *a parte ante*, and two co-eternal principles *a parte post*, standing immutably in the contrariety to each other.

Wherefore it being impossible for any one to hold at once the finite duration of evil, with Origen, and the infinite duration of it in both respects with Manes; and my mother having so professedly expressed herself in favour of the former, and never professedly in favour of the latter, she ought not to be taxed with the belief of this which is so inconsistent and incompossible with the other position, and is also absurd, pernicious, and blasphemous.

XXVI.—But that position of the finite duration of evil, and the infinite duration of good, however it may seem at first, in this age of licentiousness to be hurtful; yet certainly it is not against the light of reason, or against the honour of the Divine Majesty. There is neither absurdity, nor blasphemy in it. And if it be pernicious, it must be so to them that understand it not. And thus the most undeniable truths of the Christian religion may be, by accident, pernicious to many. Nay, it is uncontrovertedly true, that the vulgar doctrine itself, hath not been without its pernicious consequences.

And if this doctrine of the universal restitution or final annihilation of evil, be reconcilable with the Scriptures (as some men of no small learning and piety do aver), then will there not be the least shadow of difficulty remaining, why it should not be embraced. For I esteem it none at all, that the books of that great and holy man, whose name is famous for it, were publicly prohibited about three hundred years after his death, by a counsel that gave the fairest lift to the establishing the papal supremacy; or that it was privately condemned by some persons of name in the church, but notoriously partial, an hundred and fifty years before, but about as many after his death. It doth not appear from this that it might not be a doctrine of the catholic Church, or at least held piously probable in the second and third centuries; or if it were not then publicly known as a general doctrine, but reserved only, among some few that were initiated into the mysteries, it doth not thence appear that it ought not to be published now; or that it is unsound, because *unfit for every age.*

A clear view of the matter of fact and right will be here the best evidence that can be desired.

XXVII. —The substance of her doctrine as to this point, is plainly this, viz. angels and men were created by God, to be eternally happy, by loving and enjoying Him. That they might eternally love, and eternally enjoy God, they were in their creation made partakers of the Divine nature. This participation of the Divine nature, consisted in the communication to them of the Divine Life, Divine Light, and Divine Love; whereby they were, as it were, branched forth out of the Deity; and were to have lived for ever in the Deity, as their root and fountain. God communicated himself to angels and to men in the unity of his life, in the variety of lights, and in the harmony of love. This He did, that they might love him, and loving him, behold him, and beholding him, be transformed into the express image of his life, which is life eternal, both to the angelical and human creation. By this communication of Himself, he did not design, that any angel, or man, should hate him for ever, should turn away from him for ever, or should be transformed for ever into a shadow of death. It was in the power of angels and men to interrupt this Divine communication in themselves, but it was not in their power totally to cut it off, any more than it was to create themselves, or to annihilate themselves; since it entered into their original constitution.

The original root of all spirits, is the Divine Being, and their beginning or root, must not be different from their end. Their author and finisher is God, their beginning and end is Christ, their first and last life is the divine Spirit in harmonious concord and blessed unity.

One great angel was permitted to go out from the face (i.e. the light) of God, and so leaving his first place and station, he was not only distinct, but separated and turned away from his original source. And thus not keeping his *beginning* and native principality (Jud. v. 6.) but running from it in the power of his will, he entered into the contrariety against God, and against his *beginning*, which was the eternal Light of life. And hereby was first broken by him that heavenly harmony, which was in the band of angelical nature; and instead thereof, a sinful disorder brake forth. This being broken by one angel, other angels finding the same liberty in their wills to abide in the unity (with God), or to go out in the contrariety (from God), they immediately consented with him to the latter, which appeared of the two more noble, potent, and great.

They found where their might and strength was, and so they awakened what they could not fathom the nature of. Now their strength was their fire, the fire of nature, spiritual and eternal fire.

This fire while it was in union with the spiritual and eternal light was good, but as soon as it was separated from it, it became evil and the root of all evil. Thus sin was conceived, and evil brought forth in the angelical heavens, by the fiery strength of the Luciferian spirits; not kept within its bounds, in a meek humility, and parted from the Divine Light; being parted from which they could no longer remain in their angelical principle.

Therefore man was created by God in their room, and essenced a little lower than they. And hereby it was provided that his fall should not be so great as theirs, if he likewise should not keep his first estate and beginning. He was created upright; but he stood in a free liberty either as to the good, or to the evil. Both angels and men were created good: but before the end of their probation they were to be *immutably* good.

Immutability of good is in God alone, and therefore every creature, intellectual and rational before their fixation in him, must be mutable to good and evil. But after their fixation in him, as in the fountain of their being, they become immutable to evil, and are unchangeably good, as he is eternally good.

The image of the Eternal Goodness is also eternal. The *eternal image* of God, *in which* man was created, could not be destroyed by man; for that he stood essenced in it, as to his superior part. Yet it might *disappear* to man, by the superinducing another image: which was accordingly done. For the fallen angels envying this new and heavenly image in man, conspired how they might involve him in the same state with themselves, and make him to bear their likeness.

And as he was essenced, as to his inferior part, in that very matter which they knew how to defile, and had actually defiled in themselves, so they more easily effected their conspiracy.

This was the poison and seed of the serpent cast into the human nature: and the fountain being poisoned, hence came the infection of all mankind. The universal human nature being infected, an universal antidote was hereupon prepared to expel out all the poison. This must have its effect sooner or later; and cannot be resisted by any particular, inferior, or subordinate causes. In some it has its effects in this life, and they are the first born, and the first fruits, in others it has effects, not till after this life, and they are the after born, and latter fruits.

The principle, or seed of sin and defilement in the fall of angels did extend to the curse of that heaven, whereof Lucifer was king: and so an hell was there prepared for him and his angels.

The principle and seed of sin and corruption, and sin in the fall of men, did extend only to the curse of that earth (with its atmosphere) whereof Adam was king. And so the earth was corrupted and defiled. And death was prepared for him and his progeny. This death is passed through in soul and in body by every man; every man being under the same condemnation. And the great degeneration of the soul from the Divine life, and of the body from the paradisiacal life, was a real proper death, when man was cast out into this accursed earth.

And answerable to this twofold death, there is a twofold resurrection, to be attained by every man, but by every one in his order: the principle and seed of holiness and incorruption, extending itself, no less universally to all.

The seed and principle of corruption, conveyed to all mankind, has a greater place in some persons, originally, than in others; yet in none doth it extend so far of itself as that any shall be condemned for it to the flames of hell, which was not prepared for fallen man, but for the devil and his angels. Whence none of mankind can be cast into hell, strictly so called, to suffer the second death, but such as shall have by unbelief and disobedience wrought together with the devil and his angels, and loved darkness rather than light.

So that all who die in a state of minority, as under the age of about twelve years, have a certain world or kingdom allotted them (called by her the children's kingdom), where they neither know the torments of hell, nor the joys of heaven, for the present, but are there trained up in all that is needful to perfect them for the latter, according to the variety of their previous dispositions, and of their being found within or without the covenant.

Also the holy seed has originally a greater place in some than in others, as in Isaac than in Ishmael, and yet it doth not reach so far, as that any shall simply for it be admitted into the kingdom. But it must be perfected in them, first by the obedience of faith, in co-operation with Christ, till they be redeemed fully from the defilement of the earth.

From this holy seed of Divine Light, there is a common illumination, whereof Heathens, Mahometans, and Jews, do partake with Christians, as the law which is written in the hearts of all men. And there is besides a special illumination, which none but *true Christians* can partake of;

which is the *internal revelation* of Christ's *death, resurrection, ascension,* and *descension* in the *powers of the Holy Ghost*, operatively and effectively, whereby the regeneration is perfected.

They who have only had the former, however faithful they have been to it, cannot yet thereby be admitted into the kingdom of God. But being not far from it, they are reserved in custody, where their souls are kept from evil, and they have the gospel of Christ crucified preached unto them, and inwardly opened in the mystery, that so they may ascend where he is.

Moreover, of professed Christians who depart out of this world, besides those that go to heaven or hell, there is a great number who are imprisoned for a season in certain elementary regions, or middle places, till the contrariety of the evil shall be at last wrought out in them.

And even of them that have had a good degree of knowledge and belief in God and Christ, and have seriously laboured after the new birth, being truly convinced of their depravity and lost estate, and of the necessity of their redemption through Christ, and having come off in part but not clearly from the world, there is none that can enter presently into the kingdom of heaven. But they have a higher degree in the elementary regions, near to Paradise; where as they feel not much pain, agony, or sorrow, so but little pleasure or joy, because they cannot reach the vision of God so long as *any impurity* remains. And that impurity may be done away after the separation of this body from the soul, she thinks none ought to withstand, who deny perfection of purity to be attainable during this conjunction : for that otherwise few (if any) could be saved.

All souls therefore must pass through the refining and calcining regions, prepared for their purifying, according to the measures and degrees they do attain to in herein this life; and the more they do suffer here, the less they will have to do and suffer in the life to come, where the difficulty will be much greater.

Whereupon, at the first delivery of this doctrine, these express words are found: *How numerous years may you abide in these purging and frying furnaces? One day here, while in the body, would have set forward your work more than years in those centres, where you are to be confined. Therefore let this be an acceptable, etc.* Enoch Wal. p. 16.

And thus all souls having been created by God to be happy, after their purification by such ways and methods (in such regions) as the Divine Wisdom shall see fit, shall in the end be eternally so. Who being first truly humbled are they made capable to love God, and to enjoy God for ever, according to the order of their creation, which will be in the unity and harmony of his own life and light in them.

But this is not generally to be, *but after some considerable time beyond the thousand years reign of Christ*, when the high and great saints of all ages of the world, shall sit as counsellors and judges with him, and by virtue of his authority demand all such condemned souls as are captivated in the infernal prisons, and set them free from the dominion and tyranny of the dark prince.

And this Universal Jubilee of mankind will be the bruising of the head of the devil, which he shall never be able to move more. It will be taking away the sting of death, the seizing the prey of the mighty, and the treasures of darkness.

After which jubilee, the angels, also, which fell, shall attain to the end for which they were created and designed by God, and shall recover again their primitive state, beauty, and lustre. For seeing themselves now divested of all their might, and become so weak and poor as to have no place, nor subjects to exercise any authority upon, they will be deeply pierced.

When they are thus abased, then the eternal and pure nature which ingenerated into them immediately from God at the first, and could never be either corrupted or lost, will be stirred up and awakened for their recovery.

This will be done by the Father of all spirits, the eternal UNITY, who will not fail to gather to himself what is of his own, and to annihilate whatever is not derived from him; that so the contrariety may finally cease in Nature, all things being re-united to their original, from whence they branched forth in the beginning, through the eternal Word. So that whether they be things in heaven, or in earth, or things under the earth, they must bow and pay their obedience to the ONE Supreme Being.

Yet until the wonders of the mystery of iniquity be fulfilled in all lapsed worlds, the disobedient angels will refuse to surrender up their kingdom, or to humble themselves before the throne of God and of the Lamb, that they may be admitted into their ancient thrones, or new thrones then erected.

And when this mystery shall be filled up in all its wonders, then will the end be: the end finding the beginning, and Christ becoming (manifestly) the Alpha and Omega of the whole creation, and as the first so also the last.

But as the order of the transgression of the angels was different from that of men, so also shall the order of their restitution be.

For as the restitution of man was more proper to the Word made flesh, so *their* restitution is more proper to the Father of their spirits, as he is the Spirit of Eternity. And as the Father there moved in the Son, so the Son here will move in the Father, by the same Spirit. And as Christ was the creating Word by which they were created at first, so again the second time will he be: First consuming and devouring all the diabolical nature, by an impregnable fire of Love from the breath of the Almighty, invisibly blown up: and then reintroducing himself by the eternal generation of the Father, into their eternal essences; that so being created new, they may be recovered to their primary existence in the Deity, and inseparably united with their true original.

Moreover, as God did introduce himself again into the fallen human nature, in a corporeal manner, for that its depravation was chiefly in the outward birth, called the third principle of nature; so will he into the fallen angelical nature in a *spiritual way*, for that its *tartarization* was chiefly in the inward spiritual root of their essences, called the first principle of nature. And therefore their fall having been so deep, it cannot be recovered, but after an universal and radical dissolution, in the second death.

Which death must have its resurrection, as the first death had its, by a new creation and new generation from the Virgin principle of Wisdom in perfect nature:

Since the foundation of God being in them, can never be annihilated, but must abide for ever, and so cause in them this angelical resurrection and new angelical creation. For which they are to be prepared, and made to believe the same, by the ministration of Michael, and the rest of the holy angels commissionated by God for this end; who cannot but have a sympathy of nature for their fallen brethren, and desire that they also should be happy, if it be the will of God, in loving him, and ministering before his throne, as they do?

This is the sum of her doctrine concerning the general restitution of the creation, as far as I do apprehend it. I have endeavoured only to represent it in its true light, as delivered; and having done so, I leave you to judge whether it do indeed give that favour to libertinism, which many think.

I would also ask you, whether you believe it altogether unreasonable and precarious? or whether the contrary be so expressed in Scripture, as that it is not possible for sober and considering persons to fall in with this sentiment?

I do not vindicate it, or think it necessary so to do; but if it were, there is hardly one doctrine about which Christendom is divided, for which more can be said.

This plucks up Manicheism by the roots, and so also Gnosticism, or the false magical knowledge of the ancient heretics, it having been a fundamental doctrine, you know, of Simon Magus their head, that the

God who created Adam was not the supreme God, but an impotent demon only, for that he was not sufficient to preserve his work from being marred, or to hinder his will from being disobeyed. This puts an end to many otherwise inextricable controversies, throws down the foundation of many ancient and modern opinions very destructive to mankind, reconciles the sentiments and decrees of persons and churches one with another, that have been thought most inconsistent, and above all, promotes catholic love and universal peace. And supposing once the truth of this doctrine, there are besides these several other advantages, too visible to be denied, which will hence flow. Be it as it will, this may be enough to excite any rationalist impartially and unprejudicately to enquire into the same.

XXVIII.—Now whether it be true, and the revelation for it be likewise true, are or different consideration.

I may be convinced of the one, but not of the other: I may be convinced of one by the other: and lastly, I may be convinced of either by divers mediums. But if both should be found to be true (upon a free and just enquiry), then will this be an unquestionable evidence, as for that spirit which was the author of such a revelation or revelations, so for the person taken up to be the instrument for their conveyance to others.

For though an evil spirit may reveal a truth, yet it is not to be believed that he will ever reveal a truth to any that is capable of doing so much good in the world; or that he can take satisfaction in foretelling the final destruction of the devil's kingdom. And though a person may also receive a revelation from a good spirit, and not understand it, yea even mistake some part of it: as did, say some, the very Apostles, who had a revelation of angels, that they should see Christ return in like manner as they had seen him to ascend, and did misapprehend it, as if his return was to have been during their lives, or very suddenly; and did misapprehend Christ himself, in relation to the exit of St. John. I say, though a revelation which is from a good spirit be not understood, or even misunderstood, yet is not the instrument through which this passeth, therefore to be undervalued, but God alone to be adored and admired, who knows how to make use of the meanest instruments for his praise.

Let this now suffice for the charge of heresy, as also for that of enthusiasm.

XXIX.—There remains still the first and last charge to be considered, which is *Schism*. But here, also, the best way will be to represent the state of the case nakedly as it is, and then to search out what is the proper nodus of the question.

The society whereof I profess myself a member are not of one ecclesiastical communion, nor under one civil government. But they are of different communions, and are under several jurisdictions, temporal and spiritual. They are not for dissolving any obligations to the princes and states they are born under, nor for transferring their allegiance to another whose right it is not, on the account of this alliance: but notwithstanding it, they think themselves bound to the same civil obedience, as if such an alliance had never been.

So likewise they are not for destroying the obligations hereby to any rightful or lawful authority in the Church, that is derived from Christ and his Apostles, so as either to assume the same to themselves, or to transfer it where they please: but they are for maintaining the same spiritual obedience still, which could any ways be antecedently claimed, either from the principles of primitive Christianity, or the common motives of ecclesiastical peace.

Hence in Lutheran countries, there are many aspiring with us after the renovation of the angelical spirit and life, and the restitution of the Church, and yet do not therefore break off from the communion whereof they are subjects, or withdraw their obedience there, where they are permitted to pay it without violating an express Divine command.

The same is also in some kingdoms of the Roman communion, and even in Rome itself. Nor is the same altogether unobserved by our friends that live under the reformation of Calvin.

The true members of this Society, wheresoever dispersed they are, and under whatever kind of government in state or religion they live, are never for opposing the established constitutions or acknowledged rights of any, except where they are directly against the law of Nature, or the light of the Gospel. But they had rather bear with many things, and submit themselves for conscience sake, than to run the risk of disturbing the peace and rest of the public, by withdrawing from their true superiors, and denying them that obedience which Christ hath commanded. Yet the object of this obedience may be very easily, and is very commonly mistaken. Of which in the Roman Church itself, where the practice of this virtue is most eminent, several have greatly complained; as particularly Father Baker and Gertruda More, writing expressly against that servile obedience which the Jesuits generally required.

These explicitly declare that the true object of obedience is God alone, and that none can live in true obedience without attending to the internal Divine call, whatever their superiors may persuade to the contrary, or their spiritual directors dictate. And herein we cannot but concur with them; yet do not for this think that we separate from the church whereof we were before members, any more than they did separate from theirs, unless that church that claims us should either deny this Divine call or prohibit the obedience to it.

But I have a far better opinion of the Church of England, in which I have hitherto lived, than to believe that it be ever guilty of such an excess as this. Since from its very liturgy, I have sucked in those very principles, which oblige me to act as I do at present. And this in my answer to Philalethes I have fully declared, and could yet declare more abundantly. But let this be as it will, the principles of our society are compatible with all due subordination to rightful superiors: and the members of it are not for levelling all communions, as if there was no difference betwixt them much less *for overthrowing the establishments of our   for settling and establishing the true communion.*

For though it would be for them a great absurdity, and wholly incompatible with their design, to take on them peremptorily and immediately to determine the right of the many contending parties, yet they do not by this their refusal allow any right to an heretical or schismatical communion to take any from the true communion (wherever that is). But they do leave all things in the same state, without interfering with any, but where it is absolutely necessary, and then, too, with all imaginable candor, still reserving to themselves a liberty to join these, where truth doth most balance.

They profess with the Catholic Church a true veneration for all the positive institutions in the Gospel; which gospel they say is everlasting, both as to this world, and as to the next also.

They think it very warrantable to labour after an evangelical perfection; but then they do not evacuate the means which are subsidiatory to it, under pretence of being in it. If they had lived in the age of the Apostles, or at least before the Church was poisoned under nominal Christian emperors, I dare say there would be very little difference betwixt them and you, about the regular subordination of the gifts of the Spirit, and consequently about the trial of spirits. *Since God*, according to your own most true observation, *was pleased so to distribute his gifts, that the supreme governors were endued with the highest gifts, and the most undeniable credentials.* For they cannot so easily persuade themselves that this is so in every true communion at this day, or in every communion that is by you acknowledged to be a true one.

They say, that though there have been, and are even still, some excellent persons, and endued with the Spirit of God, in the chiefest dignities of the Church; yet there is no general example for this in any one church at this time whatever, from which a conclusion may be drawn, that the true

Spirit of God must needs be subject to the decision of the majority of them that are so advanced, as if to them of inseparable right did belong the gifts of *γυβερνησεις*, and *διακρισις πνευματων*.

And they suppose, that the worst persons being always the most forward to prefer themselves, even under all kinds of constitutions, civil and sacred, and there being no possible security against the intrusion of such but a constant miraculous gift in the governing part of the Church, of spiritual discernment; therefore, none ought to challenge the subjection, without more than human credentials for being possessed thereof, or allow that to be a fair way of proof now, which would not have been so in the Apostolical age, when none was admitted to be a presbyter, much less the head of the presbytery, or a bishop, without an express Divine call, and without a real and sensible communication of the Apostolical spirit by the imposition of hands. And albeit Christ never has, nor ever will withdraw his Spirit from the church, or suffer it to be totally eclipsed by the powers of darkness, they cannot but think that there is a great degeneration at this day in every part of it: and that God seems to have included all parties under evil, even they that are, above the rest, most catholic, that so all being left without excuse, he might have mercy upon all.

And particularly as to the legal Church of England; they do not so much object to the evils of the times, or the corruption of particular persons, as they do the heavy load of sacrilege and Erastianism which entered into its very constitution, and which some do call the original sin of the Church, lamented both by the governors and subjects, but never yet cured, or like to be cured.

And therefore such as are more immediately herein concerned, do want to be convinced, how a superiority of the Divine Spirit in the governors of the church, can be universally and constantly claimed under such a constitution as this; which even those themselves do lament as imperfect.

Now, no arguments that it *must* be so, will be sufficient, unless it do actually appear that it is so. And if even the contrary do besides appear *de facto*, in some cases at least, then all reasonings *de jure*, concerning the perpetual succession of the Apostolical spirit, will be here insignificant.

But that this doth not actually appear, but rather the contrary, we think is evident (if not demonstrable), from the communication of baptismal Spirit to all the Christian proselytes in the first churches, whereby not only the ordinary graces, but even the extraordinary gifts of this Spirit were conveyed, compared with the present ministration of the holy initiatory mystery, in which the gifts are never, and the graces thereof but rarely, transmitted. The which is confirmed by sad and general experience, there being of ten that are baptised (whether infants or adults), hardly one found that can so much as be pretended to have received the Spirit in baptism, as a permanent principle of spiritual life: many of them never receiving it during their whole lives, and the most of them that do receive it, receiving it a long time afterwards.

This appears also from the communication of the *Pastoral Spirit*, as it was heretofore practiced, compared with what is now succedaneous to it in the very best reformed Churches, as well as in the Roman and Greek. And seeing that, *de facto*, the succession both of the pastoral and baptismal Spirit is not perpetual, there being evidently many baptised with water, who are not baptised with the Spirit, and many ordained to the pastoral function by the imposition of hands, who have not received thereby the Holy Ghost; therefore, as many as are of the spiritual society, cannot presently yield to own a superiority of spirit in the pastoral and episcopal order, as their peculiar and inseparable right. But they think themselves obliged to be faithful to that measure of the Spirit of God in them, which they either mediately or immediately have received, and which is not at all different from the Spirit which is in the true pastors of a true Church, but is the very same with it, and with that which ever has been in all the true pastors and governors since the Apostles.

They think that the Epistles of St. Paul and St. Clement to the Corinthians do bind indeed spiritual persons to a due subordination to their spiritual governors; but then they also suppose that this subordination was not merely (or chiefly) political, but that it was according to the various distribution of the spiritual gifts, the lower gifts being made to give way to the greater, according to St. Paul's enumeration; whereby all the members of the mystic body were both distinguished from each other, and united together into the same band.

Thus have I represented to you the case of the Unity of the Church and of Schism, as it is understood not by myself alone, but by many persons of good will in other countries, with whom I have true spiritual correspondency and union.

And the sum of all is this, that the Unity of the Church is the unity also of the Spirit, (et vice versa,) and that there may be a political unity in a true communion without a Spiritual Unity, (et vice versa.) And that they who are of the *nearest* spiritual unity in the same communion, or in different communions, are not to break themselves off from their respective political unity, so long and so far as they can maintain the spiritual. But where political and spiritual cannot be both preserved, or so well preserved together, there it is safer to recede in some things from the political unity of the Church, than from the spiritual, which is the ground of the political relation of Church members.

XXX. —We of England observe not just the same measures, as they that are abroad; but our principles are the same; only our reasons of appearing in a more outward work are different.

And even several of us here, that have not a sensible, internal call to such an appearance, do choose rather to retire privately, and wait in peace for the powers of the Holy Ghost to descend, and the kingdom of Christ to come into souls duly disposed; and so to pray and wrestle together in spirit with us for the times of restitution; than to declare and proclaim openly the external manifestation of what they enjoy secretly, without a positive command for so doing. Which some having received, do meet together twice every week, as a religious society, for the free exercise of spiritual gifts, and for the better manifesting to others our faith and hope; without raising up altar against altar, or setting up a divided church or communion. In pursuance whereof we do not come together on the Lords day in the morning, which is a solemn time of public worship and communion every where over the whole world. Nor do we oppose either the doctrine, the discipline, or the worship of the established communion of this nation; or seek to withdraw any from it, that we may gain them to ourselves.

But on the contrary, we have hitherto acted as friends, while we have been counted as enemies.

Some of us are so far from giving any just occasion of offence, that willingly they would not have met on the Lord's day, or at least not till all the whole service of the day was performed, and could not be prevailed to dispense in this point, but upon some considerations that absolutely necessitated them.

The doctrine of the general restitution, as it is not an article of faith, or term of communion amongst us, nor even generally understood, or maintained by our English Society, so it is not opposite to the established doctrine of an eternity of future punishment in a scriptural sense, nor to any of the articles agreed to in the beginning of the reformation.

It is not condemned by any of the four general Councils, which are received by the Church of England, though it was known before them all; nor by any of her convocations, as far as I can learn.

Nay, the doctrine of praeexistence, which falls in with it very near, has been publicly asserted by some of her learned members, without incurring a censure or being so much as struck at by a decree of an university.

The doctrine of the guidance of the Holy Ghost is indeed carried much higher, than what is vulgarly taught in her pulpits; but it is not a doctrine contrary to what she anywhere delivers; but seems rather most conformable to her principles, or at least easily deducible from them.

The doctrine of the Spirit of WISDOM, and of its being distinct from the WORD, as well as one with it, is no less than Apostolical tradition, if we may credit so ancient a writer as Tertullian. And, (being rightly stated,) has never been condemned, as I know, either by the Catholic Church, or this particular church.

Neither do we oppose the discipline of the established Church, any more than the doctrine. The private discipline of our Society doth not interfere with that, or very easily may be kept from interfering.

And the discipline of the Church, being confessedly defective, we have begun to revive among ourselves privately some of the Apostolical constitutions of the Catholic Church.

And that we do not oppose the established worship of this communion, may be made evident from many matters of fact, and not only from our solemn declarations; which in the *Reasons, Propositions* and *Constitutions* of our society have been published.

Some assist at it with much sincerity and devotion: and even at the more solemn parts of it, are not less zealous than the most rigid confirmists. We do not hence claim the name of a *Church*, but are contented with an inferior title. We say indeed that this Church is imperfect, and so cannot be accepted of Christ as his true bride. But at the same time we own ourselves to be yet imperfect, and therefore we wait to be of that perfect Church, which we surely expect to arise in this nation, and to be gathered both out of the *episcopal* communion, and out of *others* that have separated themselves from it, with a design at least (as we hope) of a greater purity. And thus it is mentioned in the first *Message to the Philadelphian Society*, by way of parable: in which the defect of the Reformation, and of all the sub-reformations in this kingdom, is pointed at, as by the Spirit of Christ sitting in judgment.

But since we do *at present only wait for the manifestation of a pure Church, which is there described*, and do not name ourselves that Church, but only a Society preparatory to it, therefore though indeed we do excite others, both publicly and privately, *to join with us in the same expectation:* yet is not this to make them separate or divide from the present communion, notwithstanding imperfections in it, for the sake of greater perfection in discipline or doctrine, but rather to *embrace all that is good and true*, and pass over what is not so in an imperfect church.

This is what we have declared again and again, all manner of ways, and upon all occasions, and do hold to, except where there is a clear Divine authority to preponderate the judgment, and some *evident and eminent mark of the Divine will.*

And though we may seem perhaps to allow no prerogative to the true communion, yet it is because we think there is no great fear that, if truth be set on *equal terms* with error, that she must turn her back to her adversary. Nay, we desire no greater prerogative for the truth, that we court, than that she may be upon equal terms with whatever may contend with her for that name. That is, we require only impartiality and indifference.

We are not for dissolving either spiritual or the political unity; but since there may be the political without the spiritual unity even in a true communion, and also the spiritual sometimes without the political, therefore we think it our duty, never to recede in the least from the spiritual unity, however the political may occasionally be dispensed with. For to prefer the case before the jewel we have not learnt. This is the state, and these are the pretensions of this Society in England.

XXXI. —Now as for my own part, I believe the communion of saints in the holy catholic Church, and whatever my present engagements are, or may seem to be, I hope I shall ever study to preserve the same, to my utmost ability, wherever it is truly, and never be found to violate it in any part of the church.

I do also believe that this communion will be better understood than it has hitherto been, (the Church of Jerusalem itself not excepted, where it did not continue long in the saints, but began to cool,) and that the church will be more catholic and more *holy* than it is now, or has at any time been.

And, in acting according to this belief, consists the whole Philadelphian Design. As for irregularities, seeming or real, may have been committed by myself or others, through human frailties, in the prosecution of this design, I am not unwilling to take shame upon me, and I hope, never shall be. But as these do not concern the substance and foundation thereof, I presume that no persons of any ingenuity or candour, will be very severe in charging them. And whatever irregularities and anomalies there may remain for a while, they are perhaps not more to be minded than the scaffolding work to some royal structure.

I am far from having the least natural propension to what I am now engaged in. And whoever thinks it can proceed from passion or interest, I leave him to enjoy his own thoughts, till the truth shall vindicate or condemn me. Nay, did I consult with flesh and blood, I know, I should not find a greater natural aversion in any, than I do in myself, against what the love of God has constrained me to in these late proceedings; and with respect to which, I hope I may be said with the apostle, to die daily. For truly it is such a cross, as to all outward considerations, that *to speak in confidence to you*, I were of all men most miserable, if I had not a more than human support to bear me up under it, and the sensible communion of that Spirit, which none can take from me, to comfort, and assure me, that I am yet a true member of the Israel of God.

But because you will doubtless say, that this may be nothing but my own warm imagination, though it doth bring along with it that peace, which is not only above all imagination, but also above all understanding, therefore I beg the favour of you to consider,

Whether there can be proved both de jure and de facto such an Apostolical spirit in the governors of any Church at this day, which may not only oblige every member in all cases ordinary and extra-ordinary to hold communion with it, but also to hold communion with no other, even where nothing but what is manifestly Apostolical is required for a term of communion, and wherein no part of the discipline doctrine or worship of the said Church is opposed.

Or otherwise. *Whether a person who doth not oppose the discipline, doctrine, or worship of a Church which is imperfect; but is willing to hold communion with it, so far as he can with an imperfect Church, may not in some extraordinary cases, as where he really and truly believes a Divine call for it, be permitted to have fellowship with a religious fraternity* (not separated, and) *that requires nothing to be believed or practised, which is not clearly Apostolical, without incurring thereby the sin against the Holy Ghost, or rebelling against the Apostolical spirit, as resident in the governors of the said Church.*

With whomsoever the credentials of such a Spirit shall be found, that can oblige all the members of its communion after this manner, I shall heartily acquiesce, and entirely submit myself to their guidance in all cases.

But then these credentials must be very convincing, and the matter-of-fact solidly established, as well as on ancient Divine right vindicated. Which right, be it never so well vindicated, if it be not made yet evident by facts, is like to faith without works.

Now if this be a dead faith, that possibly may be a dead right, or if it be not altogether dead, it may be paralytical even in a proper sense of the word, whereof to find instances would not be hard.

Whence the stress of this article of Schism, as it is here applied will lie in this proposition, viz. There is an uninterrupted succession of the Apostolical Spirit in every true communion perfect and *imperfect*, which doth without *reserve* oblige every one living in such a district, to the exclusion of any other spiritual communion, even while not inconsistent with it.

The consideration of which, and of the consequences thereof, will put an end not only to this, but to many momentous disputes besides. But till they who claim a right by *succession* to this Spirit of the Apostles, can show it also by real *works*, that is, by the acts of the Apostles, I am afraid the matter will not be brought to any issue.

XXXII.—In the mean time, whatever may be the censures not only of evil, but also of good men, I cannot easily recede from those principles and practices, which the sincere research of truth against the contrary bias of education and constitution, yea, and of interest too, as well as of honour, has made me to embrace. And if you on your part, require an external evidence, I think it no less reasonable, that the same should here be given to me; the pretensions being so very great and the pretenders also many. So I heartily pray that the good Lord would illuminate all Bishops, Priests, and Deacons with true knowledge, and that they being filled with the Apostolical Spirit, may he able to demonstrate it by *gifts* and *powers*, agreeable to their respective stations in the church of God: which will be the fulness of my joy and triumph; and for which I could not only be content to be the least amongst the Nethinim of his glorious temple, but even to have no lot at all in the joys and glories of the first-born, or of perfect spirits before the final judgment. If it be His will, you will see where I stand; and that nothing can separate me from being Hogsdown, Easter morning, 1699.   Your true brother, Francis Lee.

P.S.—I beg your pardon and Mr. Cherry's, for this tedious delay. It is a mistake that I should ever put you off to any of the *Theosophic Transactions*. I know not whence it should arise, except from this, that somebody might suppose that letter to be yours, which came to me from an unknown hand, and is answered in the state of the Philadelphian Society. I have several times confessed that I was indebted to you an answer, but was not willing to show what I had written in this letter, before you yourself had seen it. This I thought myself obliged to by common decency, besides that special value which I have for your dear person. Whom I pray God long to bless for the good of his church, and for something greater in it, than has yet appeared.

I fear; not but I shall be treated by you as a friend, and that the lesser slips that are not of concern to the main subject, you will candidly pass over. Some passages I thought to have struck out, that will appear to have been written with a certain warmth, that I was not master of; but I have left them in, that you might have a true clear view of my inward parts. The faults also of the transcriber I beg you to pardon, and to believe, that none is, or can be more sincerely and cordially yours, than your old friend

[The following are notes by Walton and material by others directly related to the controversies treated by Dodwell and Lee. –Ed.].

*Along with Dodwell's papers, among Lee's MSS., the writer found the following letter from Edw. Stephens to Lee, dated 8th September, 1702. Whether its contents, coupled with the repealed exhortations of Dodwell, and his numerous old sober devout friends, might not have had some influence in inducing the breaking up of the Philadelphian Society, in the year following ; or whether Lee might not have begun to perceive nothing extraordinary in the times and seasons, notwithstanding the high flights, expectations, and prophecies of Mrs. Lead, and some of her associates, and so his views began to change *in some degree*, whereupon that result ensued,—are points that cannot now be ascertained. However, as we learn from Lee's history, and the date of his published works under the patronage or name of his dear friends Hickes and Nelson, as well as from some papers hereafter inserted, the unabateable ardour or his noble and divine soul did not leave him to sit down, in ease, or despair, but put him upon pursuits and employments adapted for more universal benefit. He was, truly, "in labours more abundant" for the edification or souls; and to promote the cultivation of the highest philosophical science, according to the most perfect discoveries, vouchsafed of God to mankind. For the pleasure of the reader, we propose to give a few more extracts from his papers; whereby, with what is above furnished, a general notion may be formed of this most estimable character, and most ingenious, learned and devout man.

The letter of Stephens to him, proceeds thus:— "Mr. Lee,—I received your letter, with the enclosed, but last night, and have hardly leisure at present to peruse them, the hand being small and not very legible ; much less return any long answer, if I would ; but I think it needless. It is now above a year since I took notice of what concerned me in the *Transactions*, and though I immediately thereupon made my remarks upon it, yet I never troubled myself farther about it. Whereby you may perceive how little I was concerned for myself in that matter. And I assure you now, you cannot be more ready to crave my pardon, than I am free to give it. For I reckon that no man can hurt me, but he more hurts himself. And the hurt, which I am principally concerned for, is what is done to a good cause; and so far as that, you are concerned for yourself to make restitution. There is one thing in these papers, wherein I must desire so much satisfaction, as to be informed of the particulars wherein I am thought to have used too great severity, to the prejudice of a good cause. For to be plain, I much suspect their sincerity, who censure it, and that it is nothing at the bottom but formality and a vain affectation, no better than that of the Ruler of the Synagogue. (Luke xiii. 14.) And, indeed, I observe so much such affectation, ostentation, and self-recommendation in what I have seen in print of your Society, as alone would make me suspect what the concurrence of other observation assures me of, that it is so far from being any true Christian spiritual society, that it is no better than a new sprout of an old sect of enthusiasts, set up under a new specious name. About three weeks since, I writ one morning a discourse, to convince some persons how far short they were of a right understanding of the spiritual life. And when afterwards we came to our morning service, the first lesson for the day was Ezekiel xiii, when, after a reproof of the false prophets, he is commanded to prophecy against the false prophetesses, the daughters of his people, who *prophecy out of their own hearts:* whereupon, when we had done, I added what I think might be proper for your consideration; but I have not time at present to transcribe it. I can only tell you now, in answer to your questions, that it is not only possible, but usual, for God to permit souls, as sincere as you imagine, when they presume to follow their own imaginations out of the ordinary way of humility which he hath prescribed, to eat the fruit of their own doings, for correction of such as are corrigible, and in judgment upon —the rest for example and warning to others: and admonish and advise as a friend, and in the name of God, to consider better what you do; have a care how you proceed farther in this Society; and apply yourself speedily to the proper means of recovering out of the snare of the subtle enemy. I do heartily wish you well, and should very willingly take any pains to serve you; but at present I am otherwise engaged. If you resolve to come hither, let me know the day two or three days before, lest I should unhappily be absent. Your affectionate, faithful friend, Edw. Stephens.

The following was part of Dodwell's Letter to Lee, of 27th Feb. 1700. which perhaps ought not to be omitted:—"I have now long expected your answer to my first letter upon the argument, but could never have the favour of one, though I have again importuned you by a second letter, with new evidence on the particular case of your mother in law: no not, though you promised Mr. Cherry that you would return an answer. I hear that when you have been urged to it by others, you put me off to your *Theosophical Transactions:* I wonder how you can do so. I have seen them, and can find so little pretence for your having answered me in them, that I do not find so much as the materials insisted on by me considered in them ; my arguments are, that private spirits cannot be proved genuine, but by their dependence on those gifts of tho Spirit which are given to governors of the Church, on account of their station, for governing that whole body which is connected by the unity of the Spirit : withal that the style used by Dr. Pordage and your mother in law, (which even you have not the command of, nor do I think it the least disparagement to you that you have it not,) is very well accountable from other originals, distinct from that of the Divine Spirit, from pagan and Rosicrucian philosophy, from Magic, from popish Mystical Divinity, from Familism, Behmism, from the disorders of brain that have befallen persons of very contradictory and false communions, and who could have no claim to that Spirit which was given by our Saviour's baptism. In what *Theosophical Transaction* can you pretend to have considered these things? Yet you still go on, as I hear, to propagate the contagion in your College of St. John's. This may oblige me, if you will not favour your old friend with an answer, to challenge one, at least for the sake of the public. And you will have reason to excuse it, when you consider it as done for the sake of your own soul, as well as of the proselytes whom you may involve in the same dangers. Give me, dear Sir, the joy of subscribing myself, as I could formerly, your most heartily affectionate Brother, Henry Dodwell. — Shottisbrook, Feb 27th, 1700." Lee's address, "at Mrs. Lead's, Hogs den (Hoxton) Square." This Letter, as will have been perceived, was embraced in Lee's replies.

But although the Philadelphian Society scheme was dissolved in 1703, Lee did not abandon his opinion of Lead's understanding of the Divine mysteries, and of her mode of obtaining the apprehension thereof, as being assuredly the right way, viz. by constant prayer, deep introversion of spirit, and silent waiting before God, (the soul being in a high degree of regeneration,) until the idea in its birth and development, arose in her mind, and so the truth became apprehended. For however plainly and clearly deep truth may lie described, (as it is done in Behmen, in a manner that for simplicity and fullness may be termed miraculous,) the theosophical student can only obtain the apprehension of the sense, by the eternal innate idea of the truth rising as a vegetation in the mind, when only he first *understands* it. By the *theosophical* student, is implied one who has made some considerable progress in the divine life ; for as truth is the most inward thing of all, nothing less than the immediate powers of the Spirit of God could touch the centre of the idea, and awaken it into life. —If Lead had solely meant by her 'visions and revelations' this circumstance of the *apprehension* of the deep points of Behmen's philosophy, (which also applies to Pordage) then the writer would fully approve of the term, though by no means of the Muggletonian fanatical parabolic garb in which she invests them : for the knowledge of a deep point of metaphysical truth, is a real *revelation* or mental *vision*. But if therein be intentionally embraced any *prima facie* un-scriptural *new doctrines*, then he would reject her assumptions. And how possible is it for even a most devout woman, by reason of the present disordered imperfect state, to deceive herself, in taking her conceptions, imperceptibly combined as they are with the truth in her imagination, to be equally of one origin.

Selection Two.

[Comments on the Seven Spirits of God].

On another slip, in his hand-writing, is found the following:—

I. —The Seven Spirits of God are so many eternal Divine emanations, whereby his Essence is manifested, as well in the Archetypal as in all created worlds.

II. —Their subsistence and circumincession is in the Holy Ghost; which is as their body, wherein they are all united as One.

III. —They are Seven and One: and their Unity is the original of all harmony in the world; even in all worlds whatever.

IV. —This Septenary of Divine Spirit emanated from the very essence of God; and subsisting in it, may fitly be termed the Divine Harmony.

V. —This Divine Harmony is to be known both in the Archetypal world, as before nature; and in the ectypal world, as in nature.

VI. —In the Archetypal world it is the eternal Sabbath, or the sabbath of the Still Eternity; wherein God takes up his rest within his own Eternal Habitation of light.

VII. —In the ectypal world, it is properly the Sabbath of Nature.

Selection Three.

Preface to the First Volume of "A Fountain of Gardens" vol. 1, Jane Lead's Spiritual Diary.

After what has already been given, in illustration of Lee's genius and mystical erudition, this POSTSCRIPT will hardly be complete without the superaddition of the discourses with which he prefaced the two first volumes of Lead's work of the "Fountain of Gardens," published by him A. D. 1697. We therefore now insert them, with a further specimen of his sanctified poetic talent, (if space allow,) taken from his own printed copy in the writer's possession, corrected and improved by his own hand. These prefaces, in connection with what has been already given, will doubtless to some readers, be of much greater acceptation than the writings of the individual which he thereby introduced to the world in such highly eulogistic terms : who, herself, judging from certain passages of the work in question, (pp. 327,8.; p. 143, etc.) and her preface to the "Theologia Mystica," would seem to have been as enamoured a woman-devotee of Pordage, in his theosophic contemplations, conceptions, and devotions, as Lee of them both.

The *Fountain of Gardens* is by no means an unsuitable title to this work, as with Lee's embellishments, it may be considered a kind of garden of spiritual recreations, for such as are conversant with transcendental exotics and nomenclatures; though still but a *pleasure* garden, and that for a few privileged *savans*. The letters of Bromley and Pordage at the end of the first volume, are solid and just in sentiment: and the only thing that seems to be wanting to them, is a resolution of the natural question, *What is the shortest, simple, most direct road to the blessed state, therein described;* an answer to which might have been profitably inserted if given in Scripture ideas and devoid of peculiar mystic phraseology. As to the Letter preceding them (which is by Lee,) addressed to a Physician, on Gerlach Peterson's published Letter (which had been translated by Lee,) it is evidently much below the standard of Christian experience ; and as it was written only two years previous to his present Discourses, it confirms what is above supposed, concerning the author's being but a *recent convert* to Lead and Pordage. Which circumstance will partly account for his enthusiastic eulogies of their writings, and his receiving their performances, so much of them as respects the philosophy of the Divine Wisdom, and Eternal

Nature, and the unmanifested depths of the Divine Mind, as immediate revelations to them by God, rather than as conceptions and deductions of their own peculiarly complexioned minds, from Behmen's ground and declarations.

The Preface (by Lee) to the First Vol. of the "Fountain of Gardens" is as here follows:— "There having been a promise made in the Preface to the *Ark of Faith*, that the *Diary* of this Author should follow, the First Volume of the same is now accordingly published for an universal good. For the author, or the instrument rather, made use of by the Divine Wisdom, is known to be of so universal a spirit, that nothing less hereby can be designed. And howsoever what is herein delivered, as well as the manner of the delivery itself, may come to be opposed, either on this hand or on that, I think I can say, that I am more than morally assured, that the All-wise God hath hereby ends to bring about, which the most acute and *vulturous* eye of the greatest rationalist shall never be able to dive into: and that all will serve but to a fuller breaking out of the Truth, and the Divine Light; that true light which enlightens every one that comes into the world, so far as it is not resisted, and according to the degree of purity in the vessel for the reception and reflection of its rays.

This is an age that thinks itself to excel all that have ever went before it, in the discovery and improvement of truths : and it cannot be denied, but that of these late years, mechanical knowledge hath been brought up to a very great height, which hath had both its good and bad effects in the world. But notwithstanding all the fancied or real light, in matters either physical or theological, which the present age doth so much boast of; it may perhaps not unfitly enough be said of those that make the chiefest cry, that *the veil it still before their eyes*. And let these imagine what they please, and pride themselves in the penetration of their sight, they must all sooner or later be convinced, that it will be impossible, without the immediate hand of Christ, to rend away the veil, or to penetrate through it into the sanctuary of God, or of Nature; without the great High Priest, bearing the oracle of truth upon his breast, do make a way for them to enter in, and do both open their eyes and ears, that seeing they may see, and hearing they may hear, whatever is written by his finger, or spoken by his mouth. Let not the blind think they see, or the deaf believe they hear; but especially let both take heed not to be offended at those little ones (as the Jews were of old) whose eyes or ears have been opened by the word and power of JESUS.

And that there may be some such even in this day, wherein materialism and sadducism do certainly no less (if not much more) eminently, than in the first day of Christ's appearance in a low corporeal form, reign and triumph, will not seem perhaps so very strange or incredible, as to many it may at first appear to be, when what is now here published, as well as what hath been already published of this nature through the same hand, shall come to be thoroughly examined, and scanned into, by any impartial inquirer. Yet indeed such are justly to be esteemed worthy of all commendation, that shall not from any evil propension, but purely from an holy jealousy for the honour of God, and out of a true tenderness and veneration for the sacred Scriptures, (which undoubtedly do contain his revealed will to man,) withhold giving their assent hereto; if they yet oppose not, what they may not at present comprehend. Who, if they do indeed take heed to that most sure *word of prophecy*, and do suspend any positive determination in this matter while they have no other but this light, as of a candle or torch shining in a dark place, are in a good disposition to receive whatever further manifestations of himself the most wise God may please to communicate: and will be then fully satisfied, when *the day* shall *dawn, and the day star arise in* their own *hearts*. Which it will not fail to do, according as they shall be found true to what they have already received, and believing in the promises that are therein given for their sakes, from him who is the faithful witness, and that is the same *now* as he was *yesterday*, in the days of the patriarchs, the prophets, and the apostles; and will be the same for *ever*, the *yea* and the *amen*.

For in all ages of the world God hath had some special friends, though perhaps hidden for the most part from the world, because they were not of it; with whom in a more familiar and intimate manner he hath chosen to converse and manifest himself. In all ages God hath been known to be *the God of the prophets:* and for his honour some have been confident to say, that he never did any great thing in the economy of his Church, or in the kingdoms of the earth in order thereto, but that he hath always before *revealed his secret unto his servants the prophets;* and given express manuductions, and rules, for the effecting of every such work, as particularly in the days of *Moses*, of the tabernacle with all its vessels; in those of *Solomon*, of the temple; in those of *Ezra*, of the restitution of that, and of the law ; and in those of the Apostles, of the foundation of the spiritual kingdom of Christ: which is now in the fulness of time about to be revealed, at his second expected coming, in the power and glory of the Father, to judge both the quick and the dead, according to everlasting righteousness and equity, and to put down all enemies under his feet; that so he may not only for a thousand years, which are to him but as one day, but for ever sit upon his holy hill of *Sion*, governing all worlds with a sceptre of holiness, as the LORD of LORDS, and KING of KINGS.

Wherefore the Spirit of the Lord, which hath more or less in all ages thus moved (as in *a particular treatise on this subject shortly to be published* is at large proved) upon the face of the meek and deep silent waters, in the souls of such as have been first made clean through the washing of the Word; will certainly not fail to move upon them in this last age, in order to a new and glorious creation of new heavens and a new earth. *And the inspiration of the Almighty*, which *giveth* man *understanding*, may with some reason be hoped not to have been quite exhausted in the former ages, but that he will appear even unto us, as he did appear unto them; opening variously the springs of all spiritual, and even natural knowledge: and will thereby renew also those noble works, and deeds of royal power, that he did in the days of our fathers, the holy prophets and apostles, and in the old time before them, even in the beginning of the creation of God; before man had corrupted his way, or had alienated himself from the image of the everlasting light, and the unspotted mirror of the power of God. While not having cut himself off from the pure streams flowing from the glory of the Almighty, he might, as his representative, oversee, and govern all the creatures of this globe, whether in the earth, or in the water under the earth, or in the air above it by virtue of that sovereign charter committed to him, Gen. i. 28.

Which charter having been forfeited, the Divine character expunged, the seals broken, all the ensigns of royalty defaced, the virgin image deflowered, and the angelical life and might exchanged for that contemptible weak form, which we now wear, that is subject to the curse of mortality and sin is again renewed to us, much more strongly than at first, through the pure humanity of Christ, which is exalted above all the principalities and powers in the heavenly places; the express character of the Father afresh imprinted, as in the very forehead; a new and everlasting commission established, to go forth and act in the tri-une name of Father, Son, and Holy Ghost, which is sealed with the heart of Jesus: all the royal ensigns are redelivered, the crown of immortality, the sceptre of righteousness, and the love imperial standard of JEHOVAH ; the violated image is restored, the image of the beast ground to powder, and his number perfectly erased. So that the bestial and antichristian kingdom being hereby brought to an end, a new *AEra* of the kingdom of Christ doth thereupon commence; first in particular souls, then in the whole family of the first-born, after that in the great assembly of the after-born, and so on, till the whole mass be leavened and transmuted by the ferment of the Divine Nature, passing through the glorified body of JESUS, that is able to subdue everything unto itself. This verily is *that kingdom*, which is so much talked of, and so little everywhere underwood, but still less *pressed after;* which is in this book, and in that also of *the Revelation of Revelations* (published now ten years ago,) so essentially and fundamentally declared, as nothing higher, nothing deeper can upon this subject be ever laid down, whether in time, or in eternity.

And because *Solomon*, (whose reign was as a faint *sketch* or type of the glorious reign of the true *Jedidiah*, or beloved of the Lord,) built himself a royal palace in *Lebanon*, which was a fruitful and a well-watered soil, and most beautiful for its situation, where he made gardens and orchards, planting in them trees of all the variety of most excellent fruits, also cedars and fir-trees for building; with great water-works, pools of water, and fountains; with a fair tower also looking toward *Damascus;* and with a vineyard of red-wine, where he entertained his *Shulamite* Queen, and her honourable women: therefore, is the palace, or mansion-house of the great King, the true *Solomon*, or prince of peace, here parabolically represented to be raised up as in a new *Lebanon*, whereinto the tabernacle of the eternal Wisdom, coming down from God out of heaven, with all its furniture, is brought: and the children of the Lamb's bride are figured out to grow up by the sides of this house, as the branches of a fruitful vine, or as so many several lilies from one stock, or olive-plants from one root; according to the manifold proportion and diversity of the Divine seed cast into the ground of nature, by the great seedsman. Whence the expected kingdom of the Messiah in restored nature, which is called the *Kingdom of God*, and the *Kingdom of Heaven*, is according to the Spirit's mystical dialect, compared to a vineyard, to an olive-yard, to a garden of lilies, and to a corn-field: and is expressed by the various figurations of a new *Eden*; of a new *Canaan;* of new heavens and new earth; of fountains, and trees, and plants of all sorts; of canals, aqueducts, and rivers of pleasure; of tents, palaces, and temples; of a mountain, of a rock, and of a city; of *Sion, Lebanon,* and the hills of spices; of new found countries descended out of the heavens, or by the creating Word in the Divine Magia made to appear, as a new *Sharon*, and a new *Havilah*, and a *Beulah;* of *Jerusalem*, of *Bethel*, and of the *Southland* of eternity; of the pleasures and grandeur of a rich, powerful, and wise prince, such as *Solomon*; and of all the badges of royalty, and scenes of magnificent glory, that do, as in a shadow, precede, attend, or follow the marriage and reception of a royal bride. But this heavenly kingdom, this marriage-supper of the King, this inauguration and coronation of the Lamb, and of his bride, to the kingdoms of the earth, and to the *lost dominion and sovereignty over the whole six day's work*, it not to be expected but after very great and mighty preparations; many forerunning signs of the Son of Man coming to us in his Father's glory, and the six ascending steps to the throne of the great *Solomon*. All which are most difficult to pass: so that few, if any, have been able in many centuries to hold out to the last degree, or ascension-step to this throne. But they have fallen short of the Philadelphian crown, and of the high prerogatives thereof, viz. the being made pillars, and principal supporters, in the descending temple of the most high God; the bearing the name of JEHOVAH, by an essential communication of the properties, powers, and dignities of their eternal Father, opened to such in Jesus, and by a most real, intimate, and vital penetration of that most glorious wonderful name, burning in the bush of their humanity, and putting forth itself in imperial acts and deeds; their bearing the name of the new *Jerusalem*-mother, that free woman which is above, and demonstrating livelily its inscription, by an utter defacing of that of the mother of *Babylon*, and of the beast upon which she rides; and by a majestic environing brightness as of the sun, a subduing the moon, with all that is sublunary and mutable, under their feet, and a wearing upon their heads a crown of twelve stars, wherein so many royal pre-eminences and ghostly powers are contained; the bearing the names of the foundations of this city, the names of the tribes of *Israel*, and the names of the apostles of the Lamb; and the bearing lastly the new name of JESUS, that no man knoweth but he himself, who with his own finger hath written it on their vestures, and on their thighs, that so in all things they may be made like unto him their Head life, by the all-powerful working of his Spirit, with which they are sealed.

There are but few found, who have so much as *an ear to hear what the Spirit saith* to this church of *Philadelphia*, the first-fruits of the Lamb: or even but to receive the promises of the *holy* and *true* one, who is now at this instant with *the key of David, opening* gradually this blessed state in a few chosen names; so that none shall ever *shut* it more. And he is *shutting* up in such the dark abyss, and wrathful depraved nature; so that it can never be again *opened*. But still fewer are they, who have not only an ear to hear, but also an heart and hands to act whatever the Spirit saith: and who dare to adventure on, to the laying hold of such a weighty crown, as is that of the first-born. And even of those that do so adventure forward for this most high prize, some do stop, having attained to the first degree, others rest in the second, and others in the third, as thinking that they are already got to the sixth, and so want nothing but to be taken presently to sit with their Lord in his throne. Some are willing at the end even of the first day's work of regeneration, or spiritual creation, to enter into their Sabbath: and without having passed the works of the other five days, to sit contented with the first productions of Divine Light upon the soul. Some who have beheld one, or two, or perhaps three signs of the coming of the Son of Man, have not had patience longer to wait for all the signs: but have thence peremptorily concluded that he was come to them, and that his kingdom was in them, before a redemption has been wrought out from the lapsed nature; or before the very head of the serpent has been bruised in them, and slain by the Virgin seed of the Wisdom of God, in the meek second Holy Principle of Light and Love: which by the inspired penmen of old, is expressed by that most soft, and yet most victorious name, JAH, Hallelu-JAH.

For the prevention, therefore, of all such miscarriages, and for the undeceiving of those who think it a *light thing to be a king's son*, or a *king's daughter*, it hath seemed good to the most wise God and *Father* of our Spirits to raise up, according to the necessity of this present day, an instrument by him fitted, through many fires and waters, and through all manner of temptations, both in the heights above, and in the depths beneath, and immediately instructed at Wisdom's Oracle, for so great a work, as the education of the king's children, and the leading them up step by step to their Father's throne, that they may be kings and priests upon the earth unto God, and unto the Lamb for ever; and may from the righteous Virgin Earth spring up as plants of mighty renown in a well-watered Paradise, and as *Olive branches*, continually *empty the golden oil out of themselves*, and drop their fatness, for maintenance of a perpetual light in the Sanctuary, that was before darkened.—

This will easily be seen to be the drift of these writings, by any one that is but a little skilled in their dialect. And it is no contemptible providence of the All-seeing Eye of Eternity, that this book, after having laid so many years as in the dust, should now come to be brought forth into the Light, in such a critical juncture of time, and in this very year, which is full of great expectations on this hand, and on that. To which nothing is given me in particular to say, but only this word of caution to the greedy expectants and waiters for some outward visible revolution in church or state: *Let such be sober in their hopes, and take good heed to themselves of their observations, or calculations: and let them not lay too great a stress upon any external deliverance how great soever, or upon the rise or fall of any earthly monarch, potentate, or state: neither let them seek for the Kingdom of Christ in their own will, nor according to certain preconceived notions and images, nor binding it down to any sect or party in the (so called) Christian world: for they shall find it nowhere but in the triumphant resignation of Jesus Christ. When, therefore, they shall be certain that they have drunk of the very same cup which he did drink, that they have passed through the straight and wrestling gate of death, that they are entirely passed from all their own, into the liberty of the Divine Will, and have broken down every image and boundary, that man, as man, hath set up; then let them know that the Kingdom of Christ is near to them, and upon its very breaking forth in much glory, majesty, and power. And when they themselves are thus got without the walls of the great city,* Babylon; *then, and not before, let them expect the descent of the* New Jerusalem *out of heaven.* For most assuredly, to none but Virgin souls; to the true Nazarites, that for the hope of *Israel* do wait in the inward temple, day and night, with their lamp-spirits ever burning, that so they may be ready to go forth at their bridegrom's call, to meet him; to the lilies of the valley, who, though they *neither reap or spin* for themselves, are yet arrayed more gloriously than *Solomon,* in the immaculate robe of the Lord their righteousness; yea, to none but the undefiled doves, that are in him made all beautiful and fair, and that having washed themselves seven times in the pool of his blood, are thereby set apart, and redeemed from the earth, to be his companions,—will this beloved city come down. Of the truth of which, every one must necessarily be convinced, that doth but consider seriously the process that this author hath been led in, according as the same from these ensuing memoirs may be gathered, in order to the drawing down the powers of the heavenly worlds, and the unsealing the fountain of the Holy Ghost, and the book of the resurrection. Neither can this *Jerusalem glory* be discerned by any others, or after any other method than is herein laid down from the opener of that principle, let them look never so long about, crying, *Lo here,* in the *East!* or, *Lo there,* in the *West.* For this high promotion of Wisdom's children cometh neither from the *East,* nor from the *West*: neither out of the *North,* (as some are gazing after it at present,) nor yet from the *South.* But the Lord cometh from TEMAN, where the glorious Virgin principle is unlocked; whence the warm, holy, supernal *South-wind* doth blow upon the Gardens of *Lebanon,* and cause the spices to flow out; whither the patriarch *Abraham* always directed his travels; and where *Jacob* saw the ladder of heaven, and the gate thereof. The key of which gate is there presented by the hand of Divine Wisdom to all her children, to whom she crieth aloud, standing at the entry of the celestial city, and proclaimeth the Joyful JUBILEE; inviting them to return now from their captivity, and presently to come forth from the tottering *Babel,* which is founded upon the sands, and to enter with her key into this city, *which hath foundations.* For this, she standeth in the top of the heavenly places, and putteth forth her voice to them at the coming in at the doors ; for this she meeteth them in every path, layeth hold on them that, having tried them with her *laws,* they may enter in hereby, and feast at the table which she hath furnished for them. But, alas! I see, that the most even of those that have been enrolled under her discipline, will be not a little afraid to lay hold on this key of the kingdom, when it is reached out to them: and will shrink from it, beholding how large it is, and that it is made full of all solid gold; even as this very author did at its first presentment, as thinking it impossible for any ever to bear the weight of it. Besides this, there is a mercurial serpent which twineth himself about it, whose life can be destroyed no otherwise but by the royal antidote of the unicorn's horn.

Let not any therefore think it a light thing, or easily attainable, to bear the key of the government on their shoulders. But let them examine thoroughly the several progresses and steps of this author, in order to its attainment; that are recorded for the space of about six years, in this present volume. Of which it must be confessed that much has been lost; so that the links of Wisdom's chain may often seem to be broken. But as the greatest architect, statuary, and painter of these last ages, is said to have become so excellent, merely by his observations drawn from a most imperfect maimed statue, or bust, being the work of a most exquisite and masterly hand: so it is not at all to be despaired, but that there may be found also in this day some of rare and excellent abilities of spirit, who, notwithstanding any imperfections or maimings of this spiritual register, or any defects in its exterior habit of language or style, may by the assistance of their supreme tutor draw forth, even from the disjointed parts of this work, such an excellency of *knowledge and skill in all* true *learning and* solid *wisdom*; that they may be *found ten times better,* and more skilful, *than all the magicians,* and men of fame, that are in the universities throughout all *Europe*. For when Wisdom's key is obtained, and her book unsealed in any, according to the process here described; then may all the depths of philosophy, as well as of divinity, and all the hidden treasury of Wisdom, in all worthy arts and sciences, be successively broken up. And thus, as from one foot of the *Rhodian* Coloss, (which is to this day preserved,) every one that is but skilled in the proportions of the human body, can exactly calculate what the whole should be, and know thence how to frame one accordingly: so every one to whom God has given some good degree of understanding in the symmetry and proportions of the spiritual body, will, notwithstanding any intervening breaches, or abrupt transitions, be able hence to frame some suitable idea of the whole design and oeconomy of God, in the manifestation of his kingdom to separated and virginized souls.

Now the manifestation of this divine kingdom is various in several persons, and in the same person at several times. Whence this variety in the descent of the heavenly and ghostly powers, (whether in this principle, or in another,) and of the joys of the world to come, is here not unfitly symbolized out by a *garden*, or *paradise*; as it was by the king thereof, himself, in his truly gracious answer to the penitent thief. And yet more expressively is this flourishing state of the lamb's elect bride cyphered to us by a *fountain of gardens*, or *paradises*, planted with all trees of frankincense, myrrh, and aloes, and with all the chief spices; out of which the royal ointment is prepared for the consecration of such priestly kings, as are to reign upon the earth in the Lamb's nature, and name. Which shall make all the wild beasts of the forest to fly into dens and lurking holes, and every venomous creature to hide itself from the great Attic Jomin, in his representatives, and from the fiery stream issuing out of his mouth; by which the spirit of Antichrist, that huge *Leviathan*, shall be utterly destroyed.

So will the kingdom of Christ manifest itself, by a gradual, but total overthrow of that of him, who has usurped all the kingdoms of the earth; until all that which he has caused to be as a wilderness by the blast of his poisonous breath, be again renewed, and made to be as the garden of God, filled with wells of living water, and streams from the upper *Lebanon*: a garden giving forth all the variety of flowers and fruits of life, according to the seasons, and according to every one's essential ground, and internal soil: a garden in which there is not any mixed tree, existing from the root of the outward elements, containing good and evil, truth and falsehood, light and darkness; but all whose trees are trees of life, all whose plants are plants of righteousness, all perfectly good and true, all-beautiful and lustrous.

How various the manifestation of this *Lebanon-kingdom* will be, no pen can describe, no tongue can express. That is various indeed: but the manifester all the while is but one; and the essential Word of God, *which is the worker of all* these *things*, is most uniform. The manuductions, illuminations, and inspirations are very different, but still there is but one way, one light, and one spirit; one Lord, and one God and Father of our Lord Jesus Christ, and of us all; who in these last days is about to appear yet more fully to us by his Son, setting him openly upon his holy hill. Thus he who is the ABYSSAL UNITY of all beings, clotheth himself as with several names, rideth forth in several powers, weareth on his head several crowns, and glanceth from his eyes several lights. And yet there is but one crown, one power, and one name, as there is but one light; which *diffuseth itself* in all the variety of *colours*. Which *unity* and *variety* of light is well to be heeded in the reading of this book, and of all other spiritual treatises whatever, of what rank or degree soever they be. For God sometimes appears in the darkness, and yet in that darkness there is light: again he appears in the light, and yet darkness may be mixed with this light, till the perfect day do spring from on high. Thus he appears to some at a distance, as in a *great and strong wind;* to others in an *earthquake:* in both which forms he eminently manifested himself through some, about the beginning of the last century. Then after this, approaching still nearer, he appears to a third sort in the *fire*: as at this very day he powerfully doth to some, that are known to Wisdom's disciplehood. And lastly he demonstrates his presence to some, as to this his chosen vessel, in a *still small voice*, and in a sweet, gentle, lambent flame. Sometimes God manifests himself to the eye or ear of the receptive heart, according to the several properties, operations, and influxes of this or that name, which he puts on; of this or that attribute, which be communicates; of this or that sphere, in which the living wheels of the creatures before the throne of God do move. Thus was he manifested to the unregenerate spirit of *Balaam*, according to the efficacy of the name *Shaddai*; who saw the vision of him in this similitude or vesture, falling into a trance: and this is the lowest sort of true divine prophecy. Then was he manifested unto *Abraham*, unto *Isaac*, and unto *Jacob*, by the name of *El-Shaddai*: which is a much higher degree than the former; as that whereby is expressed, not only the paternal property in the absolute sovereignty of his will, but also the meek love-principle co-joined with it in a federal rite. After this he was manifested under the law, at sundry times, and in divers manners, by the most essential, and great name of the covenant, *Jehovah*; but still according to the variety of the vessel, and its fitness to receive the emanations thereof, either in a high or low degree. Then lastly he was made known, under the gospel, to the apostles, to the evangelists, to the prophets, and to other ranks mentioned in the apostolical epistles by the name of *Jesus:* which name doth unseal and open that of *Jehovah;* whence the miracalous powers did so abound in the early days of the church, while there was faith in this name. But still it is the same One Holy and True God that revealed himself both to the vile son of *Beor*, and to the most heroic father of the faithful, though not by the same name. And he is nevertheless One, and having appeared after manner, and in that name, to the prophets of old, and then speaking after another manner, and by another name to their successors the prophets, Neither would he be the less so, should he even speak to us, after another manner than he hath yet spoken either to the prophets, or to the apostles: or should he make himself known to us by a none, whereby he *was not known to them*. He is still the same, let the vessel be never so different, and is equally to be adored and believed, whether he takes up an honourable or dishonourable vessel, learned or ignorant, noble or plebeian; whether the instrument be a priest or Levite, Israelite or proselyte, male or female, young or old. Some has he called from the plough, others from gathering of sycamore-trees, and others from their drag-nets; whom he has set over the nations and over the kingdoms, to root out and to plant, to throw down and to build up, by the mighty power of his Spirit, according to its various operation and manifestation. It matters not what the subject is, into which the divine influences are received, and through which they pass: even though it should be an heathen, as in the case of *Jethro*; or a brute beast, as in that of *Balaam*. The gradation, nevertheless, of these influences may be computed according to the situation, and according to the proximity and remoteness of the subject which is to receive them, from the source, or centre of Divine light, and according to the several channels and ducts that they must first pass through, before they are therein received. But the all-wise God is never wanting in the preparation of such vessels as may be suitable for the reception of such degrees of his light, as he designs to communicate. And this beautiful variety is in the writings of the Old Testament, and also in those of the New most remarkable. For it is one degree of inspiration that *Moses* had, and another that *Isaiah* had, and a third that *Daniel* had. Neither is the inspiration of the writer of the *Chronicles* the same with either of these three: and yet both the one and the other are all from the true inspiring breath of God. The like may also be observed in the New Testament. But to treat of this would require a large discourse. What has been here already said, will suffice for the wise in heart; that they may understand the voice of the Lord their bridegroom, when he shall call to them *in the cool of the day,* and present himself *walking in the garden;* that they may not seek to hide themselves from him, but may walk therein, leaning upon his breast, and refresh themselves with its flowers and fruits, that do there present themselves to be plucked.

As for the removal of that great millstone, which is thrown in the way, *That God hath ceased to reveal himself to man since the days of the apostles, and that all pretensions to the same are but illusions, and at best but the dreams and fancies of a natural enthusiasm,* I am not very solicitous; as well knowing that the same God, who hath already appeared in a most wonderful manner to give his testimony to souls concerning what hath been hitherto published from the same spirit and instrument, will not be wanting now to give his seal to this, or to what hereafter may come to be published: and even in a more ample and fuller manner to vindicate his honour, than he hath been yet known to have done since the primitive days of faith.

But howsoever the Wisdom of God may, with respect to these particular writings, show itself at present, this millstone must shortly be cast into the sea. Otherwise the kingdom of God, which we daily ought to pray for, can never come: and it is little better but a mockery of his name to solicit him for the calling of the Jews, and the fulness of the Gentiles, and for unity, peace, and concord to all nations; till this beam be removed from before the eye of our spirits. For which end there hath been, somewhile since a *treatise* writ to prove not only the *possibility* and the *expediency*, but even the *absolute necessity of divine revelation, both private and public, as in the ancient times, so no less in the present line, toward the restitution and winding of all things;* which the author of it undertakes to evince from plain and evident principles, not disputed by the very deists; and having done with them, to clear up many passages throughout the prophets, and throughout the whole New Testament, which are impossible, as he holds, to be accounted for by any other principles. But how successful such a new and surprising attempt may be, is entirely submitted to the disposal of the infinitely wise God, when he shall order it to come forth, for his honour alone, and for no other aim whatever. And unless he gives this order, and by his blessed Spirit do accompany it, let it never see the day. And whatever disagreeable to his glory, or inconsistent with his truth, may have at any time been sent abroad of such a nature, let it moulder away in perpetual obscurity, and let it not be remembered by him, when he maketh inquisition, or even known among men. But whatever is consistent with his eternal truth, and makes for his glory upon the earth in this latter day, let that break forth with mighty and irresistible power, to the confusion of all flesh.

Wherefore I do bow my knees continually before the God of my fathers, that he would give me who write, and thee who readest this, wisdom that sitteth by his throne: and reject us not from among his children, the children of his kingdom, and of his right-hand; but seal us against the great day of temptation, which is coming upon the face of the whole earth, with the spirit of truth, the Spirit of *Jehovah*, the spirit of wisdom and understanding, of counsel and might, and of a sound Judgment; which is the testimony of JESUS. That so by the inspiration of this his Holy Spirit, we being preserved against all the illusions of the false prophet, and the subtilty of the twisting serpently spirit, for the day of his appearance; may *perfectly love* him, walking with him as *Enoch,* or as *John,* in this paradisical garden, the entrance whereto, that has been shut up, is setting open: and may *worthily magnify His holy name,* even as in heaven it is magnified by the high principalities and thrones, and by the harpers upon the *sea of glass.*

To which burning sea of LOVE these secret spicy walks will lead thee; while the holy angels and perfected saints will accompany thee all the way, reaching out to thee such fragrant immortal flowers, and such refreshing, transforming, and transubstantiating fruits, as do spring forth from the very root of the Deity. Here, therefore, I would gladly leave thee. If thou art not already entered, Wisdom calls unto thee hereinto to enter, and to pass quickly the sword of the cherub; which she will assist thee to break. But if thou art entered, then here abide, and walk, till thou art brought to the shore of that sea, by this experimental traveller described, which will waft thee over to the *New Jerusalem*. Where, I with thee, and with all those that follow the Lamb, do long to sing, *Glory to God in his highest*, etc., and to publish the glad tidings of the kingdom of our God and Saviour; flying in the midst of the heavens upon the wing of the Dove-spirit, and proclaiming with a loud shout, FEAR GOD; AND GIVE GLORY TO HIM; FOR THE HOUR OF HIS JUDGMENT IS COME. Rev. xiv. 7.—TIMOTHEUS.—*January 1st.* 1697."

—Thus the preface to the first volume of the "Fountain of Gardens:" which, on further consideration, we find will suffice for our present purpose, without the insertion of the preface to the second volume.— With respect to the most interesting subject, alluded to by Lee, p. 213, and by Law, at the head of p. 94, of the distinction between God *in* nature and God *above* nature; or in other words, concerning Nature (our universal mother) in her *eternal birth*, and *standing relation* to the *super*-natural Divine Being, it will be found to be embraced under the next following head and selection of extracts.

Selection Four.

Excerpt from "Theosophical Transactions",

[Originally published in "The Astrologer of the 19th Century", in 1825 reprinted in "A Sorcerous Anthology, Magical and Occult Writings from the publications of Robert Cross Smith", Topaz 2017. The annotations were made by the anonymous "Philadelphus", who supplied the text.— Ed.]

SINGULAR EXTRACTS
RELATING TO SPIRITS AND DEMONS, AND THEIR POWER OVER MANKIND,

Communicated by Philadelphus in a Letter to the Mercurii.

PHILADELPHUS TO THE MERCURII GREETING, SENDETH THEM WITH MUCH GOOD WILL—"A RELATION OF THE APPARITION OF A SPIRIT KEEPING THE TREASURES OF THE EARTH, AND OF HIS DELIVERY OF THE KEY OF A CERTAIN MOUNTAIN IN GERMANY TO A CONSIDERABLE PERSON, AND WHAT THEREUPON ENSUED."
—*Abstracted from the Theosophical Transactions by the Philadelphian Society*, 1697.

"We received advice about two months ago from the Marquisate of B—g, by a person of undoubted reputation and great worth, who was pleased to consult with some of us about what was best to be done in this matter. How that in a place called N—n, there was a little man, seeming of about 15 or 16 years of age, who came in the night to the bed-side of a certain person of quality, telling him he must go with him; and, as the gentleman refused, he was severely threatened by the other, menacing him that he would wring off his head if he still refused. Whereupon, being greatly terrified, when he had put on a coat which the little man had brought to him, the gentleman went along with him, and was led up out of the castle wherein he lived to a certain mountain ; the little man then proceeded to open the mountain, and having done so, gave the said person the key to it, saying,—'He would do' wisely to take great care of this key, for that otherwise it would not go well with him.' As the person awoke, early in the morning, he knew not whether it was a dream or a fact. But, nevertheless, he put his hand into his pocket, where he finds the key that was given him by the little man, and it was signed with three crosses. He looked also for the money which he had put in his pocket, but he remembers that he put it into the pocket of the coat which the little man had brought, and carried away with him again. He beheld also his shoes, which, according to his own boy's saying, the evening before were cleaned, but he found them now quite dirty. Now, after he had considered this a great while, and contriving what he should do with the key, he shows it to his companion; but, as he put his hand out of the window, the key slipped out of his hand; both of them saw where the key fell, but when he came down to fetch the key away, it was there no more. A little while after this, in the morning, when he was walking through a certain alley, he felt somebody give him a grievous stroke in the face, and yet he perceived none to be near him; but his cheek was swollen very much thereby, there arising up a great black and blue nob, and hereupon he sickened. But he is chiefly afflicted with the fallen sickness, wherewith he has been ever since troubled, notwithstanding all medicines and remedies used, yet not altogether so grievously as at the beginning. Likewise, as he not long ago was at prayers, in the church, (he being always very sedulous at the public devotions) he saw upon his hand these words—'He is dead!' No further particulars we have yet received; but, as it is already related, several questions may be put, that will deserve to be considered."

Query 1. What is to be thought concerning those treasures that are by many believed to be concealed in some mountains and caverns of the earth?

Q. 2. Whether there be any peculiar order of spirits that do preside over them, and of what rank?

Q. 3. What can be the end of keeping such treasures, and what must be their design in revealing them to any?

Q. 4. Whether this gentleman could safely have refused to attend the spirit, and what method he should have taken to have secured himself?

Q.5. Whether it is not possible that there may be *real* apparitions and transactions, both good and bad in sleep?

Q. 6. Whether the obedience to this spirit was voluntary or involuntary, and how far the liberty of the will may be supposed to be constrained, or let loose in this night action ?

Q. 7. What was the meaning of the coat brought by the spirit? Was it a real coat, or only imaginary?

Q. 9. What was it that occasioned the loss of it, and gave such an offence to the spirit?

Q. 10. Whether natural distempers may not sometimes be caused from spirits? And whether evil spirits are not good natural magicians to hurt and destroy?

Q. 11. What is meant by the words—"He is dead," or "the man is dead?"

Q. 12. What is to be understood by Isaiah ch. xl. v. iii.—*I will give thee the treasures of darkness, and the hidden riches of secret places!*

An answer by Dr. Lee to certain queries proposed upon a relation of the apparition of a spirit, keeping the treasure of the earth, and of the delivery of the key of a certain mountain in Germany to a considerable person.

QUERY I.

What is to be thought concerning those treasures that are by many believed to be concealed in some mountains and caverns of the earth?

That there are really hidden treasures in several mountains, caverns, and other places of the earth, many relations do confidently attest. What ground there may be for such an attestation, and how far the evidence of the witnesses may deserve to be relied upon, will not, perhaps, be altogether unworthy of our present inquiry. These witnesses are not only dead, but there are also living ones, and some of them persons even of very great sagacity and penetration of judgment, as well as experience. The great mutations of the revolutions that have been in the world, but especially the terrible incursions of the barbarous nations, from the fourth century downward, and the dissolution of monasteries in the last age throughout the protestant part of Europe, may incline one to believe that much of what is related as to this matter may not be quite improbable, though intermixed with relations that are either wholly or in part fabulous, and set off with some unaccountable circumstances and superstitions. The writers *de Re Metallica,* may hereupon be looked into.

It is related in the life of Jacob Behmen, that whilst "he was a herd-boy, in the heat of mid-day, retiring from his play-fellows, to a little stony crag hard by, called the Land's Crown, where the natural situation of the rock had made a seeming enclosure of some part of the mountain, finding an entrance into it, he went in, and found there a great wooden vessel, full of money, at which sight, being in a sudden astonishment, he did, in haste, retire, not moving his hand thereinto, and came and related his fortune to the rest of the boys, who, coming up along with him, sought often, and with much diligence, an entrance, but never found any; though some years after, a foreign artist, as Jacob himself related, skilled in the finding out such magic treasures, took away the same, and thereby much enriched himself, yet perished by an infamous death, that treasure being lodged there, and it seems, laid covered with a curse to the finder and *taker away*."

And it is the opinion of some, that here, in England, there were formerly deposited such treasures in some of our churches and monasteries, with a curse upon whomsoever should find them, or should possess them, or any thing else appertaining to the said churches or monasteries, otherwise than by such a way of devolution as was originally designed. It is also by some believed, that several of our monasteries were at first founded, either from such magic treasures, or from something of an equivalent, if not superior nature.[1]

And it has been said, that the walls of the fairest and richest monastery in the west of England were thus built by one who was afterwards brought to an infamous death; he having too much enriched himself by a treasure hid in the church thereof, which he was taught how to have access to, whenever he pleased, by a strange artist, who led him into it, and in his sight, carried away thence a jewel of an inestimable value, though with great hazard, because of the opposition that was made. And there is one known to our society, who doth aver, that when he was at Rome, in the year 1693, he was there told by a person of good intelligence, how that there died, then (in or about the month October), an unfortunate gentleman, in the hospital of St. John Lateran, whose death was chiefly imparted to a great fright, though the occasion hereof was said by him to have been concealed, till he opened the same in confession. Wherefore the name of the person was kept secret, but the matter of fact was said to be thus: — He having been

---

1 See Dr. Campbell's "Hermippus Redivivus."

engaged in a duel or rencontre, had slain a man, for which he was obliged to fly; and the fear of justice everywhere pursuing him, he absconded himself in very melancholy and lonesome places, and one night as he was endeavouring to rest himself in the porch of the church of St. John Lateran, he was suddenly terrified by the apparition of a skeleton, who commanded him to follow him, and to fear-nothing, for that he meant him no hurt, but a great deal of good, if it were not his own fault. So a little recovering himself, he said he followed the spectre into a certain ground belonging to the hospital, where the spectre stopped, and the earth opening, there was discovered to him six earthern pots full of money, which were encompassed about with flames of fire. Then, said the spectre unto him, "Friend, all this money that you see, I will now give to you, if you will but take possession of it; *be of courage, fear not the flames, for they cannot hurt you, fear them not, I say, they shall have no power over you, for therefore only do they appear, that you may be terrified from laying hold on what I now freely do offer you: But what you do, must be, done immediately, otherwise, I must deliver up this very hour all this treasure to the* SPIRITS OF THE EARTH, *who are waiting just now to receive it; accept what is offered, if you are wise; it will not be longer in my power to transfer the same to any, and when it is too late you may repent.* But notwithstanding all the persuasions of the spectre, this poor man could not be prevailed on to accept the offer of the treasure at such a peril as presented itself. Only he made a mark where the spectre disappeared, and being left as it were half dead, was the next morning received into the said hospital, where he remained in a deplorable state for several days, being fully restored to his senses, in which time he made the aforesaid confession, with many other circumstances (some suppressed and others forgotten), for the truth thereof the curators of the hospital making a diligent search in the place to which they were directed, found just so many and such kind of pots as were named to them, but which were all empty.

That in Italy, there is great abundance of such treasures, some curious' inquirers do pretend to determine, from many reasons. And there is not wanting a catalogue or book that is kept very secret in some few hands wherein all the said treasures are said to be registered. And we are credibly informed, that some persons have been employed and pensioned for this cause, by those that are of a very high degree in the world, in order to make such a discovery. Accordingly some of them (the least guarded) we are told, have been discovered, and taken away by these artists, and particularly from out the ruins and antiquities of Rome, and also about Naples.

Now it may be demanded, whether all these hidden treasures be of the same nature and order? To which, it is answered in the negative, that they are not. For, according to what the persons were, unto whom they did originally belong, if they did ever belong to any, according to the manner and design of the concealment, and various other circumstances, and lastly, according to the secret laws, rules, and orders, of the divers inhabitants of the invisible worlds, to them any wise related so is the property and nature of these concealed treasures very much altered and circumstantiated.

QUERY II.

Whether there be any peculiar order of spirits that do preside over them, and what rank?

Some think they do enough when they cast all upon the devil that is of this kind. But let us do justice even to him; not ascribing to him more than he is rightly chargeable withal; or making him the refuge of our ignorance, as well as the butt of our ill nature. Yet, however, some cannot conceive or credit any intermediate orders and degrees of spirits, betwixt the blessed angels in the kingdom of light, and the adverse ones in that of darkness; others of an inquisitive and philosophical genius, both among the antients and moderns, do suppose that this would be to introduce a mighty chasm or breach into the creation of God, and therefore they do maintain there are many intermediate degrees betwixt these two, in the scale of the spiritual creation, and that there is no less variety in the invisible than in the visible system of nature.[2] Neither are they at all shocked herein by the objected silence of the Holy Scriptures; for they answer immediately, that by the things that are visible, those that are invisible are made clearly known. And therefore, say they, Moses had no need to describe the creation of the spiritual, and (to us) invisible world or worlds; for that, by having described that which is material and visible, we may thereby arrive to the discernment and knowledge of the other, which is in it shadowed forth; and they think that Moses speaks fully enough of this to any that are skilled in the oriental and

---

2 See Dr. Cheyne's "Five Discourses on Regimen," &c. also Dr. Nicholas Robinson's "Christian Philosopher," vol. 2.

symbolical way of writing.[3] They say, also, that David was not only a poet, but also a philosopher, or rather a theosophist, when he called upon all the creatures to praise the Lord. And indeed the ordinary interpretation of the 148th psalm, and some other places of Scripture, seems but flat and low, and very inconsiderable, if compared to that high and exalted sense which they would have given to the same with respect to the grand hallelujah of the whole creation.

Now they would give us to understand, that these middle ranks of spirits were all put into subjection under man, so long as he should remain in the Paradisaical state, that is, should be a true and loyal subject to God, his Creator, by virtue of the blessing pronounced upon him, Gen. i. 28. and afterwards prophetically renewed, Ps. 8th. wherefore they do suppose that not only the fowls of the air, the fishes of the sea, and the beasts of the earth were made subjects of man, in his original constitution (as he was the true *representative* of God, bearing his character and image) and were in all things obedient at his commands, as to their Prince and Lord; but *also* all the elementary spirits, or the natives, and spiritual *aborigines* of such or such class in the inferior or elementary worlds, whether they be of an aerial, aquatic, or terrestrial kind (according to the three grand divisions of these spirits there *typically* hinted at) were all made subservient to him from that word of blessing essentially spoken forth from the *central fountain* both of his and there being; though he be not after the same manner so to them as to him; whence say they, both angels and men, may not improperly be called the *offspring* of GOD, and the *sons* of GOD, but that neither of these expressions is at all appropriable or communicable to such inferior orders of spirits, who, by their birth, are put under the feet of Christ, and (consequently) of man also, before he was degenerated into a servile and *bestial form*, sinking into it from that imperial and divine one, wherein he was first constituted. And from this ministration, subserviency, and subjection of theirs to man, they may be called servants, or hired servants, as some that are learned in the Hebrew cabbalad—do think that they are called in the parable of the prodigal son. Now as the servant is not the heir, but the son, so likewise, these kind of spirits are not the heirs of GOD, neither can they be, being born under servitude; and as an hired servant receiveth his wages, so doth every one of these from their Supreme Master; and though

---

3 See the Chevalier Ramsay's "Philosophical Principles," 2 vols. 4to.

they may not inherit with the son, yet may they possibly receive portions or gratuities, and be encouraged with suitable rewards, according to the fidelity and diligence of their service. These, say they, were to have been the *satellites* of the human race in their Paradisaical purity and power, and would thereby have been with them partakers of the heavenly favours and blessings which they enjoyed, as a good servant whom his master loveth is with him partaker according to his degree of the plenty which the master possesseth. But the fall of man (who was the master) was not only a tumbling down of himself into death and misery, but it has also subjected these subordinate classes of spirits (who were his servants) to the vanity and the bond which they now lie under, by constraint, and "not willingly." Whence there is hopes to them of a future deliverance from the bondage of the corruptability and impurity of the elements (wherein they reside) as man shall come again to be restored to his Paradisaic state and kingdom; wherefore, also, some do think that when the Apostle mentions the whole creation's groaning, and being in pains of child-birth for this *deliverance*, he might have, in the first place, an eye towards these ranks of intelligent creatures. And some relations there are that do seem highly to favour this interpretation.[4] Now as there is a very great variety, and even contrariety in the birds, the fishes, and the beasts, which we behold at this day, the which were yet created by God in a most beautiful and perfect harmony, so the like may be supposed concerning those invisible elementary inhabitants, that there is at present not only a great variety, but even a contrariety too among them. And though we are not able to behold them with our *outward* eyes, we may be allowed to judge concerning them, from that which is visible and sensible to us, when we shall consider all the orders of creatures that have terrestrial bodies. Some of which may seem to have partaken with man very little in the curse, others more, and some so much, as it may well be doubted, whether any particle of the divine blessing remain in them, and whether they be not rather generated wholly from the curse. In like manner some of these elementary *spirits* may have suffered very little in comparison of what others have done by the fall of mankind, whereas others may have fallen under an exceeding heavy weight by the entering of the curse hereby into nature. So that, being *naturally* the subjects of man, they stand

---

4 Particularly in the singular work of Count de Gabalis, from which Pope acquired the machinery for his "Rape of the Lock."

with him in the corruption, discord, and wrath of the elements. And they must stand so, as long as the *elementary strife* shall remain, or until it come to be swallowed up into the holy heavenly quintessence, or *divine element*, the undefiled womb of the morning, the fire-water of life, which the Eastern Magi have named their HASSHAMMAIM.[5]

But if there be indeed such middle ranks of spirits, that do remain with man until the day of judgment in the contention of the elements and astral effluviums, it maybe queried in what rank of these do you place those spirits which are reported to guard the hidden treasures of the earth, whether in the mountains or in other places? To this it may be answered, that none of them are of the first or second, but all of them of the third grand division, and though amongst these there may be those of various kinds or tribes, yet that all are of a terrestrial generation.

Hereupon it may be further demanded, if there be such a peculiar order of spirits that do preside over the treasures of the earth, that of these there be various degrees, (some whereof are much better than others) whether upon supposition of the possibility, it may be lawful for man, while clothed with this gross and terrestrial body, bearing the marks of the fall, to maintain any kind of intercourse, society, or conversation, with all or any of these degrees? Some have earnestly endeavoured to converse with any of them indifferently, without examining first of what degree or station they might be. Others, not so easily satisfied, have yet consented to a correspondence with some of them who have appeared to be of the best sort. But whatever the practice of any may have been, either for a good or an evil end, we cannot but think such a correspondence, *of what nature soever it be, and after what methods soever it may be carried on, to be extremely dangerous;* for man being *naturally* their superior, and they *his subjects*, until man shall regain again his *natural* superiority over them, the danger may be exceeding great of passing away the right of nature, his true birth-right, and so of making *himself subject to them*, whose master he ought to be, and will be; if he be not kept down by a magnetical or magical force in some or other region below Paradise. Hence the rise of idolatry in the ancient heathens, who were much better learned in great part of the *intellectual system* of the world than the moderns are, under what denomination soever they may pass, or be called by. Hence the Egyptians, from whom *Polytheism*

---

5 See Law's "Spirit of Love," part 1.

was derived to *other nations*, when, in their temples, they worshipped towards the image of a calf or of an onion that was made out of this or that metal, were not so stupid as to imagine that there was any deity either in a calf or in an onion; but through these images they had respect to some spirit, or perhaps order of spirits, that was figured or shadowed forth in visible and corporeal nature by one or the other of these; and that, in their sacred worship, was presented unto them in such or such a metal as might most aptly express such or, such a planetary influence, according to that *astrological* and *talismanical* knowledge in which they were most eminent.[6]

QUERY III.

What can be the end of keeping such treasures, and what must be their design in revealing them to any?

Ans. According to the nature of the treasure kept, and of the spirits or demons that keep them, so must be the end of their concealment. And whereas these terrestrial demons can hardly be supposed to conceal them solely (if at all) for themselves, it has hence been concluded, by most, that they do it for man; for being in their *essence* somewhat allied to him (as has been declared) they desire that he should be caught into their principle; hoping hereby more to complete their essence, feed their life, and satisfy their nature, if they can but anywise make themselves masters of him, whose subjects originally they were. But as these are subordinate spirits, which are under the government of higher orders, so according to these, rather than the former, is the end to be sought for; and as this is extremely difficult to know, so likewise is the uncertainty of the end. For the invisible kingdom have their politics in like manner as the kingdoms of this visible earth, and they have doubtless as various designs to carry on, and may make use too of as different measures to compass them. However, there may be one grand end or design (under which many subordinate ones will be contained) common to the princes and subjects of this or that empire in nature whatever, whether good, bad, or mixed. And

---

6 See Gaffarel's "Unheard of Curiosities," but particularly the letter written by the Rev. Mr. Beford to a Bishop of Gloucester, respecting the great mathematician who had communion with the spirits of the earth. This letter Mr. Sibly has introduced into the 4th part of his "Occult Philosophy," and it was previously published in Beaumont's "History of Spirits," &c. a work of considerable merit.[Reproduced here, pg 408—Ed.]

forasmuch as there is great reason to be afraid, that the *apostate* principalities and powers of the angelic world have here very far extended their usurpation, there may be a great design of them laid, which may not break forth till toward the latter end of this world.[7] Well, but what can they mean in offering to reveal these treasures to some particular persons? *Ans.* If the end and manner of their concealment, the laws, or pacts, respecting the same, and the qualifications of those persons to whom these offers are made were perfectly known, then might we be able distinctly to resolve this query. But till this be, it is enough to be satisfied in general, that all such kind of offers are dangerous to the utmost to accept, or so much as listen to, without there could be such an impregnable armour obtained, as it were impossible for any evil (or mixed) spirit to penetrate. And further, it may not unreasonably be presumed, from the most deplorable history of our countryman, Dr. Dee, as also from some other relations of good credit, that *certain subtle Luciferian spirits have been carrying on, for above this hundred years past, some great intrigue, in order to grand alterations in the outward governments of the world, for the establishing somewhat that may run diametrically counter to the spiritual Kingdom of Christ, which they, foreseeing, do, and will continue, by all methods, to war against.*[8]

But we know that Michael, the Prince of Israel, shall stand up to fight for the children of his people in the latter day. When the various centres and principles are unlocked, spirits of all kinds do go forth, *some to teach, others to deceive man;* some to minister to him, others to domineer over him; some for this end, and others for that, according to the great diversity of their nature, degree, or office. Wherefore it highly behoves all men to be exceeding careful in an affair of this nature; since the soul of man is so framed, that all are capable of being acted upon by them, visibly or invisibly, sleeping or waking, in one form or another. And if the *true spirit*

7 See Dr. John Pordage's Account of the Principalities of Hell, &c. in Beaumont's "History of Spirits."

8 It will be discovered by this, that the spirits that inspired the late Joannah Southcote were of the *lowest* order of these elementary spirits, and those that taught Baron Swedenborge, of the *highest* order, both, however, under the direction of Lucifer, to mislead two orders of men, of very different signatures, thus mightily warring against the *true* spiritual kingdom of Christ, by spreading in many directions (gross and refined) false doctrine; and these infatuated spirits will now effect more than ever, on account of the near approach of that period when such wonders will be manifested in all nations, as were never before witnessed.

shall reveal itself towards the latter end of this world in a more than ordinary manner (as many do believe,) it may well be expected, that there will be sent out at the same time, from opposite and intermediate kingdoms, both wicked and lying, as also vain and trifling spirits,[9] of various ranks, orders, and offices; and that, as the *true spiritual* Christianity shall begin more and more to exert itself, as in the most primitive and apostolical churches, so there may, on the other side, *start up along with it,* many impostures or delusions, whereby even well-meaning persons shall be captivated[10]; whence we ought to be very sober, and to examine into the grounds of all such appearances (if real) and constantly to hold fast to the true spirit of revelation *and of prophecy,* and by which alone the hidden treasures of the deity, and of the invisible worlds, are *manifested to the humble* and prudent of heart.

A perilous day draws nigh, *and is even now,* wherein the false prophet and his emissaries *shall exceedingly prevail!* And as it was in the days of the Apostles, some may live to see sundry Antichrists setting up themselves, and calling themselves "the mighty power of God," upon whom the God of this world will not be wanting to bestow those riches and honours which he claims as his own. However, the bank of wisdom, no evil or unclean spirit shall be able to draw near to [11].

QUERY IV.

Whether this gentleman could have safely refused to attend the spirit, and what method he should have taken to have secured himself?

Ans. If his mind were already captivated with a strong imagination after such hidden treasures, it was then altogether impossible (though we should suppose him at the same time to have the perfect use of his senses) to refuse such an attendance as this demon did demand, at least without the imminent peril of life itself. But if his mind *were not before* thus captivated, it doth not appear but that he must have been at his perfect liberty either to obey or disobey this troublesome spirit. For though the exercise of will seems to be absolutely bound up in sleep, yet every one can

---

9 To wit the followers of Joannah Southcote.

10 As was most deplorably exemplified in that late excellent engraver, Mr. Wm. Sharp.

11 A work has been recently published that will throw immense light on this interesting subject, entitled, "The Jugments of God on the Apostatized Gentile Church,"&c. It is a reprint of a book written originally by a friend of Dr. Lee.

more or less testify, that this is not perpetually so, but that they can perceive sometimes a liberty of following the free inclination of their wills, just as if they were awake. And it is the judgment of some philosophical and experienced heads, that could the imagination of man, (wherein the original evil and curse doth properly reside) come to be thoroughly defeated and cleansed, *all the scenes that pass before him in sleep would be real and substantial* and all his actions relating to them would be free and voluntary. But the apostacy and degeneration of the imaging part of the soul is so deep, that this is not to be expected of any, without a perfect renovation of the *lapsed* adamical nature. Wherefore, since this is so, and that the renovation and restitution of human imagination to its original seat, and subordination to the mind and wisdom of God is so great and difficult a work, it will deserve to be inquired what method he should have taken under the present imperfections of his nature, to have secured himself against the impertinencies and importunities of this terrestrial spirit? And the answer to this is very plain, that every one ought to free themselves from all covetousness *and the love of this world*, if they would expect to be secure from the machinations of all these orders of spirits, whether infernal or terrestrial, whether aerial, or else the inhabitants of the fountains of waters, who can take up various forms to act in, and are no less (if not more) dangerous when they transact their plots after an invisible manner, than when they do it after a visible manner. This is an effectual remedy against the insults and surprises of any spirit of this rank. And another remedy that is like to it, and not to be disjoined from it, is earnest and real prayer for the divine protection against all the illusions of darkness, with frequent aspirations, (after the custom of holy David) that so hereby there may be such an habitual delivery of spirit, soul, and body, into the hands of the Almighty, that it will be impossible for any other seizure to be made, either secret or open.

QUERY V.

Whether it is possible that there may be real apparitions and transactions both good and bad in sleep?

This is already answered in the *affirmative*. And not only this single instance, but many others do confirm the same, but especially the apparition of an angel to St. Joseph in a dream, warning him to fly from the intended persecutions of Herod, and the apparition of another angel to the magi, in like manner warning them which way they were to travel. Now here it ought well to be observed, that it is quite a different thing to *dream* that I see an angel, and to see an angel *in* a dream as this righteous man did: the former is phantastic, the latter is real. Here also a distinction is to be made betwixt substantial and symbolical apparitions, which last are, in some degree, real, but not so properly as the first. Of this kind were the dreams of the patriarch Joseph and of Daniel, and of several others mentioned in Holy Scriptures; whence the interpretation of these dreams was anciently a *divine science*, that was not bestowed upon any but such as were highly favoured and beloved of God. But as soon as man would go to make an art of it, it was presently defiled with a thousand superstitions, follies, and impertinences. Thus came in the Chaldean oneirocritics, which the Greeks afterwards mended according to their manner, *as the superstition of the vulgar in latter ages amongst us hath done since*, partly from their custom, and partly from strained allusions. Now it is certain, that these symbolical dreams are transacted in the soul by the ministration of angels (of one kind at least or other) and where the imaginative faculty is purified from drossy and earthly matter, there is an entrance opened for good angels to administer, and to step in at certain seasons for assistance and succour, many undoubted instances whereof are not wanting in history, but amongst which I know none to be more remarkable than that which is related concerning the deliverance of a certain congregation of Protestant Christians, in the reign of Mary I. Queen of England, by the timely securing of the catalogue of its members, which must otherwise have been seized, and would have involved them all in the peril of their lives; and it is not at all to be doubted but that if men did live generally better lives and more depend upon the providence and leadings of God, such sort of admonitions might be more frequent than they are. Though there be also some natural signatures, with which some are marked, *whereby they are rendered more apt for, and susceptible of such impressions* than others are, or can be.

As for the other sort of dreams (if they can properly be called so) *which are so very real and substantial* as to be transacted after the manner that in this narrative is recorded ; they are much more rare than the former. But yet these real apparitions in sleep *are not so very rare as they may be thought*, which is because they are sometimes not heeded, or believed to be so. But were men possessed with a right notion of the manner of the soul's working during the sleep of the body, *many secret and hidden things might possibly come to be revealed to them by the apparitions of spirits* or demons connatural to them, and also of the *souls of their departed friends or relations* ; for the state of the soul doth then most nearly approach to that which she finds after her solution from this elementary body, and is therefore most capable of a true and real intercourse with spirits and souls of *her own rank*, if she be fitly instructed for it, and be also rightly qualified and prepared *according to the instructions given*, especially if she have a strong magical signature, or a violent magnetic drawing of her will, which *to some is peculiar*, and is exceedingly dangerous, *until it be regulated*, for that it associates itself more easily with the inhabitants of the dark and middle worlds, which it also not seldom mistakes for the holy inhabitants of the light angelical world.[12] But such a soul, *when it is brought into true order* and harmony by an *entire submission* to the divine will, is a vessel fitted for all the divine influences, and is itself such a wonder in the mystery of God, as requires the pen of an angel to describe.[13]

QUERY VI.

Whether the obedience to the spirit was voluntary or involuntary, and how far the liberty of the will may be supposed to be constrained or let loose in this night action!

This is already answered in the solution of the fourth query, for thence it appears that this obedience was partly voluntary and partly involuntary, and that the liberty of the will is not so constrained, or bound up even in sleep, as to endamage any one that has not *first by a previous consent*, some way or other, surrendered itself; upon which many reflections *might* be made relating to diabolical suggestions and temptations in dreams.[14]

---

12 Whosoever will be at the pains of reading the life and leadings of Joannah Southcote or Baron Swedenborge, will see how strikingly this applies to both of those well-intentioned, though highly-deluded persons.

13 See the last Discourse in Bromley's "Way to the Sabbath of Rest," and particularly Tryon's "Mystery of Dreams and Visions Unfolded."

14 It is to be regretted that the answers to the other six queries were never published.

Selection Five.

[Questions to Edward Hooker concerning John Pordage].

The following is a Letter addressed to Dr. Edward Hooker, in Lee's own hand-writing, (probably a copy):—

"Peace be with you: and blessing, and mercy from the mercy-seat of the Lord Jesus Christ in heavenly places. Amen.—Sir,—Though I would not do anything in the least to discompose you in your near preparations for a blessed eternity, yet since it has pleased Divine providence to put into my hands some writings for which you have declared the highest esteem, as well as for the author thereof, your friend, with much regret for the will of the deceased being not fulfilled herein; I think myself obliged to propose to you a few questions concerning them, which none perhaps in the world but yourself, can answer me in. And, therefore, notwithstanding that I am a stranger to your person, I must take this boldness with you, for the honour of God, for the interest and propagation of truth, and for justice to the dead, to entreat your resolution hereof, so far as you are able. Which, if you please to grant me, and to allow about an hour's time for declaring your answer, distinctly and severally to what is here propounded, I trust that it shall not be accounted to you for loss: and shall heartily pray that God may bring you into the great light of his everlasting kingdom, being first thoroughly purified in the blood of the Lamb. Amen.

The Questions are these:—

I. —From what copy was Dr. Pordage's *Mystica Theologia* printed; I having one much larger under the Doctor's own hand?

II. —Was that general *Scheme*, prefixed, of his own invention, or of anothers; I having also two schemes in the original MS. both which are different from the printed one?

III. —Were all the Three Courts of the angelical world ever described by the said Doctor? for I find not any description either of the second or third court, as there is of the first, in the MSS. which I have in my possession. Have you any copy of the Angelical World that can supply this defect?

IV. —Do you know whether the Doctor did ever write anything concerning the *Fire-world*, or the severe world, and its inhabitants?

V. —Did you ever hear him discourse concerning it? If you did, pray what might be his sense hereof?

VI—Did he ever write anything concerning the *Fireless world*, or the merciful world; it being not so much as mentioned in either of the schemes, or the general introduction, which I have?

VII. —That being created, according to the order of the printed scheme, after this four-elementary world; can you inform me what he means by it?

VIII. —Was the Treatise of Eternal Nature put into the same order in which it is printed by the Doctor himself, or by his son S. Pordage, or by any other?

IX. —Did you ever read a treatise of his, concerning *Christ's birth in us, and ours in him?*

X. —Did you ever see another of the *History and Mystery of Christ*, in six parts; I having only the first: which is about the *incarnation?*

XI. — Do you know who it was, to whom the Doctor gave his MSS. to be reviewed, who has written severe animadversions upon them?

XII.—Hare you any of his MSS. or Letters, by you; or do you know any one that has? Can you remember what became of the copper-plate of his effigies, etc. ?" "Francis Lee."

Selection Six.

Concerning Wisdom

[Transitional work between Lee's Philadelphian and post-Philadelphian period, prefaced by remarks by Walton on Lee, Lead, and authorship questions. —Ed.]

We propose, for the gratification no less than the edification of the reader, as well as with reference to our subject in hand, (and also as reflecting upon what was inserted in the note of pp. 234-7, as to the way in which Behmen's profound verities should be explicated and illustrated,) to present one more extract from the MSS. of the recondite and pious Lee, and then to proceed with our narrative.

The reader will bear in mind that what has been remarked concerning Mrs. Lead, and her visions, as being merely her own idiocratic conceptions from Behmen's ground, and how Lee became her learned apologist and defender with Dodwell and others: and also how he made her acquaintance, and became enamoured of her as an original transcendental spiritualist. The writer conceives that the first of her books, in the publication of which Lee interested himself was "The Laws of Paradise," a small 18mo. published 1795. Upon this treatise many ingenious and critical remarks and inquiries were sent to him by his friends (some of the originals being now before the Writer), to which he penned answers. The same also with respect to her subsequent works. In reference to these the writer finds an interesting MS. by Lee, headed " CONCERNING WISDOM," being answer to two queries of deep interest. It is this piece (forming, indeed, an ANNOTATION, in the "GRAMMAR OR WISDOM,") which is now proposed to be given, as follows:—

Q. I.—*What conception or idea is to be had of Divine Wisdom, to conciliate with it that personal apparition of her in the figure of an human Virgin, that performs several personal transactions, as instructing, leading, giving laws, &c.?*

ANSWER.—How strange soever this may appear, yet is it no more than what may be well defended from the best and most authentic authors, if a due examination be made of them. And, in short, it cannot be unknown how this figurative idea of the Divine Wisdom is warrantable from the sacred writers, as that also of human wisdom is in like manner from profane writers. Not only Solomon in his Proverbs and Mystic Song, with the Sapiential book by us called Apocryphal, but certainly held by the Hellenistical school and primitive Christians in the highest veneration: and the Visions of Esdras (who seems to be cited, even in the gospel itself, for a true prophet).

But Christ himself represents to us Wisdom under the very same conception, attributing to her a personal act, and giving us an idea of her answerable to that of a mother, by making mention of her *children*. The disciple who lay in his bosom and best understood his mind, is perfectly agreeable hereto, being confirmed by what was shewn to him in heaven of this nature; and has left the church an account of two such personal apparitions, the one of the heavenly woman impregnated by the Divine seed, Rev. xii., and the other of the Divine bride and mother of Jerusalem, descending from God to pitch her tabernacle on the earth. Rev. xxi. And what need is there after this to mention the apparition of such a female to St. Hermas, an immediate successor of the apostles, at the beginning of his prophetical visitations; and the Laws of Admonitions, with the parables and visions which were afterwards given him? Or what need is there to show how in succeeding ages some holy and separated souls have been visited by God much after the same manner; though they themselves may not perhaps have apprehended, or may even have mistaken, such Divine communications and appearances, which are pourtrayed forth according to certain eternal schemes in the heavens? Such a disquisition as this might be very curious, but there is no necessity for it; there being an higher and greater, and more uncontroverted authority, to vindicate this manner of writing concerning *Wisdom;* if we have but an ear to hear her voice, as a speaking in the Scriptures. The authority of which being allowed of, what occasion is there for any other subordinate reasons? or what necessity to declare the (deepest) ground, either of the whole Church (Jewish and Gentile) being always represented under the figure as of a single female person, and thence called *Our holy Mother the Church*, or of the great abuses and superstitions which have sprung up with respect to the mother of our Lord, the blessed Virgin Mary; the titles, both in the Greek and Latin churches (at first) truly given to her, but misunderstood afterward and misapplied, and the veneration which is due to her from all generations, as distinguished from that false one which the ignorant seal of many have prompted them to give? For without entering into such particular inquiries, it is I suppose, sufficiently evident both from what has been here and elsewhere delivered as to this point, that the personal apparition of Wisdom in such a figure, and her performing several personal transactions, is in no wise inconsistent with the sacred writers, but very conformable to their sentiments and modes of expression.

And as for the same representation of Wisdom by profane authors, much also might be said. But there is one instance of this so full, so particular, and so significative, as to add any others after it would be quite superfluous: it is that Platonical piece of Boethius, which may deservedly be called his philosophical masterpiece, wherein, as a perfect Deist, he handles, in Five Books, the matter of *Consolation*, without any regard to the principles of Christianity. Human wisdom, or philosophy, is here represented as a grave and majestic matron; is made to perform the part of a mother, or tutoress; and is introduced not only in a personal figure, but many personal actions are attributed to her, as giving forth counsels and monitions, instructing, confuting, reproving, and the like: the whole being nothing else but a continual intercourse and communion betwixt her and her disciple. And whether he be considered as expressing herein the sentiments either of the Ethnic or of the Christian theology, the matter will be much one: for if the former, then have we the sense of the Gentiles, as according to the light of nature; with universal tradition delivering down this figurative idea of the inward teacher as of a female principle, or as a passive form of supersensual light irradiating the mind, and a soft gentle affluence from the Divine Being, transforming, and even *deifying*, the soul, so as the wise man becomes a god *by participation* (see prop. X. of the iiid. book.[)]But if the latter, then is there no doubt to be made whether this be a new upstart conception of the heavenly Wisdom, or whether it be an old one, entertained by the Christian church from time immemorial. To say that this is an *emblematical* representation will avail but little; for if that be even supposed, we must grant at least that what is represented under it must answer to that which represents. And herein does lie the key which reveals the true origin of the Gentile divinity, and gives us to see whence sprang the great and horrible abuse of their secret mysteries. For what more ridiculous absurdity can there be, than to make Wisdom a Goddess, generated from Jupiter alone, and leaping out of his skull, so soon as cleaved asunder for that purpose; if we understand this *grossly*, as the words at first do sound? But if we shall look upon the Pallas, or the Minerva, of the Pagans, barely as an emblem of the Divine generation of Wisdom in human souls, and of its original pre-existence in the Divine intellect, before the descent thereof and manifestation in nature; then all will be very instructive. But this cannot be easily explicated as it ought in a few words; and therefore, here passing it over, I shall only hint in general that the idea of a Divine Virgin subsisting in God, and proceeding from God by outward manifestation, to teach and enlighten souls, by the assistance of the separator of nature, (or of a spiritual and vital flame which may break asunder the thick saturnine compaction which is in every fallen birth, thereby to make a passage for the Light, as a pure virgin and Divine essence to burst forth, and to be clothed in a personal figure of glory,)—whence soever this was derived, was really known to the wise Heathens, and must needs have somewhat more in it than is vulgarly apprehended. Human wisdom indeed may be mistaken for the Divine, but this alters not the case at all; though the consequent of such a mistake be in itself most fatal. So this is sufficient to show, that such a figurative idea of wisdom is no strange thing, but warrantable from sacred and profane writers. Which being premised, let us then consider what is the true conception of Divine wisdom, which answers to this figurative idea of a Virgin, and to her personal appearance, not only to this illuminated author, but to sundry others also. The conceptions hereof being exceeding various, whereby the greatest confusion does arise, for want of attention, I shall endeavour to enumerate the more principal, that so a just and adequate conception may be formed from them all.

    1.—By Divine Wisdom we may understand the unmanifested Divine intellect, the unoriginated and ungenerated light, the abyssal mind of the divine Unity. Thus Wisdom is not distinct from the Father, but is both in him, and one with him.

    2.—By it we may understand the manifested Divine intellect, the originated and generated light, or light of light, and the abyssal mind of the Divine fecundity, whereby all things are made. Thus the name of Wisdom is attributed to the eternal Word, or Son, and is both in the Son, and one with the Son.

    3.—By it we may understand the manifestation itself of the intellect, light, and mind of the Deity; or the revelation of both Father and Son to the Spirit (or most central ground) of the soul. And thus it most properly belongs to the Holy Ghost, who is thence rightly called a Spirit of wisdom and revelation.

    4.—By it we may understand the abstract Idea of the whole Divine Being, as manifesting itself through a tri-unity of principle in Father, Son, and Spirit; or as the intellectual conception of the Deity in itself, according to all its essential relations, whether this conception, or idea, be original and uncommunicated, as in the fountain, or originated and communicated, as in the the streams.

5. — By it we may understand this very idea, as passing through, and invested by pure and incorruptible Nature: or the total Divine idea corporified; which is by a more outward substantialising thereof in the creation. Thus it is the same with what some do call the *one element*, and others the universal body of the λόγος. It is called also the *heavenly humanity* of Christ, the tabernacle of God, and by many other names.

6. —By it we may understand the Image of this corporified idea; or the individuation thereof as in a personal form, or figure, being clothed upon with the angelical nature.

7. —By it we may understand this individual image, as descending in its own personal form, and representing itself even in a true human Virgin. Which virgin is thereby properly made the representative of Wisdom. And this representation may be either in one or more.

Besides which, there are two general conceptions of the Divine Wisdom, either as before, or as in Nature; answering to the twofold conception of the Deity, or to the Divine *tri-unity* before nature, and the Divine *trinity* in nature. According to the first of which this holy Principle is fitly represented by an *eye;* and according to the second by a *mirror;* of both which abundance of instances might be brought, that are nowise inconsiderable, from the *Revelation of Revelations*, and from most of the other books set forth by the same author.

Now if we do not distinguish so many different conceptions, it is not at all to be wondered at if we fall into very great confusion, and either take offence or run into some gross abuses hereby, through the mistake of that which is in itself most true, and most honourable likewise to the Divine Being; by the misapplication of this or that idea, which we may have taken up, and which, though never so true in itself, may not yet contain in it the whole truth, or be perfectly true according to such certain relations whereto it is applied. The first conception of Wisdom, for instance, is most clearly and undoubtedly true in itself. But nothing would be more absurd or of more dangerous consequence, if I should therefore deny the second to be true, and oppose myself to the Nicene Fathers calling Christ, as *God of God*, so also *Light of Light*, or Wisdom of Wisdom. And should I grant the second, and not allow the third also, what do I but contradict the Holy Ghost himself, as speaking in the scriptures? If Wisdom be a spirit, and be called the Spirit of wisdom, both in the Old and New Testament, then is he one with wisdom, as the Son and Father are one therewith. Or if I should allow all three, but oppose the fourth, what do I else in effect but deny the Creation, or the first manifestation of the Deity in nature; which cannot be, without the Divine Idea of it be supposed to pre-exist? This one, universal, all-comprehensive Idea is called the E σοπλεον ἀκηλιδωτον, or the immaculate virgin mirror of the Divine energy, by the Book of Wisdom, and the Εικων or the portraiture of the omnipotent goodness, ch. viii. 26.

It is this idea which the Lord possessed, as within himself, in the beginning of his *way*, which is his process into Nature, before his works of old; and which was manifested by the eternal Word, going forth triumphantly in the same.

It is this which was set up both *from everlasting*, that is, before any manifestation of nature, or in the silent eternity; and *from the beginning* of all time, as preparatory to the said manifestation. It was before ever the earth was, and when there were no depths &c., for according to it was the earth made; as likewise the depths &c.

It was the matrix of all lives, seeds and forms, in the three kingdoms of nature; and that great Exemplar of the world, co-extended infinitely with the Divine Being, according to which therefore, both the *heavens* were prepared, and the *abyss* encompassed at once. Whence it is described as God's most familiar friend, or intimate consort; and as the Divine *delight* and *sport*. For all which see Prov. viii. 22 to 32. This conception then of Wisdom is no less real than any of the former three; and is only to be deduced at large from the words of Wisdom's greatest favourite, and from the wise Siracides also, if it were thought requisite. But if we go to confound this conception of Divine Wisdom with either of those, we must not expect otherwise but to be lost quickly in a maze of our own imaginations. And should we also stop here, and castaway the three remaining ones, the danger will not be found much less upon an important consideration of the whole. For if there be no corporification of the Divine idea, then must the creation have necessarily stopped in the very beginning: and there must nothing have been brought forth creaturely, out of the supreme Fountain of Being, besides simple and naked spirits; the existence of anything else in *rerum natura* being an utter impossibly, if that supposition be allowed of. If also there be no individuation of the prolific Divine idea, when corporified, manifold absurdities cannot but thence follow, and consequences most highly derogatory to the unity and simplicity of God, as also to the order of beings; and even destructive of the principles of individuation in every creature. Lastly, if this individual Idea of the Divine glory, being thus invested with a Divine corpereity, or an ἀπόρροια of the one heavenly and omniform substance, may not personally represent itself, wheresoever it shall choose, in such vessels of the Divine light snd grace as are made fit to receive, and able to bear the same; then must the hope of Christ's kingdom be at an end, and we shall never be made *virgins* to follow the Lamb. Were this not so, the marriage of him and his bride could never be celebrated; as will appear more evidently, when we come to consider the next question. So long now as we keep these conceptions of the Divine Wisdom according to the gradual manifestations thereof, and descent into nature, distinct from each other; there is little or no difficulty that is considerable. But if we blend these together, there is nothing in the world so preposterous and absurd which would not hence follow. A thousand instances might be easily given in the three or four first; and hardly less perhaps than ten times as many in the last.

To form now a general conception of Wisdom out of all these, I consider it as an eternal Divine principle (or most holy energy) of fecundity in the Godhead, which is before, in and after Nature; whereby the Godhead having first beheld and comprehended all within itself, does afterward image forth itself in all whatever it thus beheld and comprehended ; bringing forth by it from eternity its first begotten image, and out of that innumerable subalternate images, from the beginning of time, and so forward; for an eternal spirit of Divine joy and harmony in the creature. Which principle, or energy, originally subsists in the Father, and is one spirit with the Father, being as the Eye or intellect to the Spirit of Eternity; by which there is eternally generated the Word, as the only begotten Son of the Father, in whom the fulness of his wisdom substantially dwells; and by whom the triumphing light of his intellect is eternally manifested, through the virtual powers of the Holy Spirit, as proceeding from the Father by the Son, into every created image, addressed according to the capacity of each. Thus is Wisdom truly to be considered as the Idea and Glass of the blessed Trinity, as also of all creatures which are thence originated; and as such it may descend and clothe itself, both with an universal and particular body, and personate its glory in a proper subject. Whereupon it may well deserve to be heeded that the original of Wisdom, or her pre-existent state in God, is expressly distinguished from her nativity, or manifestation in a glorious female figure, by those very Writings which have been censured so much, on the account of introducing a female personality into the nature of the Divine Being: for in the *Manifestation concerning the Eight Worlds*, Wisdom's *eternal originality* is there clearly declared to be *from the tri-une Deity*, being a Virgin *hid in God from all eternity;* but her *nativity*, or manifestative glory in the form of a female virgin, not to be so; for that as to *this*, she was *brought forth in time* (§ 16, p. 31). And this is afterward explained by an example taken from Adam; who for certain was created after God's image: and therefore as Eve must have pre-existed in him originally, before she could be taken out of him (if the image do answer to the archetype, or life); thus also it must have been in the very case concerning the origination and manifestation of this virgin of Divine Wisdom—the one being necessarily before nature, and the other as necessarily in nature. Now concerning her personal apparition in the figure as of a human Virgin, there can be no manner of question made according to which of these this was; for *out of* nature certainly there can be no figurative manifestation, nor appearance of any distinct personality. And if it were in nature (as most certainly it was), there can no real difficulty remain why God might not, if he pleased, thus presentiate himself; and through such a living embodied idea transact all what is recorded, and reveal in the human nature the mystery of the *three-sealed book*, as it was shewn in the vision.

Q. II.—*Whether this Divine Wisdom is another thing than that Spirit of God which dwelleth in sanctified souls, and communicated to them the gifts of the Spirit,* Isa. xi. 2; *and produceth in them the fruits of the Spirit?* Gal. v. 22.

Answer.—Divine Wisdom and the Spirit of God are inseparably united together: Wisdom cannot be without the Spirit, neither can the Spirit be without the Wisdom. Yet are they not one altogether, in whatever sense of those which have been mentioned this be taken; but there is a real distinction betwixt them, notwithstanding the union of essences: and therefore we ought not to confound their substance for the sake of this unity; which is also betwixt God and his angels. For this union of essences is very well consistent with the truest distinction: even as the angels of God are united with God in their essence, who are thereby commissionated to go forth in his name, and are yet nevertheless most truly distinguished from him. And so also there is an union of essences and natures betwixt God and man, as in the person of the Lord Jesus Christ; and by consequence hereof likewise in the persons of all his saints, as members of him. But as this union is without confusion of substance both in Christ, and in the saints; so also is it in the present case of Wisdom and the Holy Spirit: who are indeed undivided, but not the same in the ground of their being. For the Holy Ghost as essentially united with the Wisdom of God enters to holy souls; making them friends of God, by a communication of his *gifts* to them, and a production of his *fruits* in them. The Divine Wisdom doth not properly and of itself communicate these gifts, or produce these fruits; but does only infuse her nature into man, as by irradiation: to which nature of wisdom infused, the gifts of the Spirit are solely communicable, and in which alone the fruits thereof are producible. And as to every generation there is required (1.) the seed, and (2.) the nature: so likewise must there be in the regeneration of the human soul a concurrence of these two; by the Holy Spirit's producing therein the birth of Love (that is, Christ within) through the nature of Wisdom, as the principle of Divine fecundity in everything, and that without which the seed of God would be as dead, and quite shut up. To this Divine generation of souls, or their new-birth, the seed is properly conferred by the Spirit; and the nature into which the seed is received, and by which it is made to fructify, proceeds from Wisdom: and thus we are to understand that Christ, according to the flesh, was conceived by the Holy Ghost of the virgin Mary (blessed for all generations); not as she was an earthly virgin only, but as the heavenly virgin of God's wisdom had chosen in her to represent herself outwardly (according to the seventh and lowest acceptation of the name made mention of in answer to the first Quaere), for the bringing forth again, after the eternal pattern in the heavens, the highest birth of God, in the lowest manifestation thereof, under the covering of vile and corruptible nature. Therefore was that Holy One who was born of her, most truly (according to the words of the angel) called the *Son of God;* inasmuch as in this his *temporal* generation he was conceived both from a Divine seed and a Divine nature: even as he was in that which was called *eternal;* whether by it we understand his generation in the *bosom of the Father* from all eternities of eternities, as manifested to the Father alone; or else his generation *from* the said bosom of his father in eternity indeed, but yet in the beginning of time, whereby he was brought forth into a figurative image and personality, as the first born of all creatures, for the creation as well of the angelical, as of this world. Now this *bosom* of God is no other than the virgin spirit of Wisdom, the holy and eternal principle of Divine fruitfulness, and that Womb of eternity, which is alluded to in Psalm cx. 8, where the Hebrew word RECHEM, translated the *womb*, which the Jewish writers do also call *Beth-ha-Rechem, i.e.* the house of mercy, is very emphatical and proper; and doth most livelily set forth the Divine compassionateness, as manifesting itself in Christ. And hereupon it is observable what the most learned of the Jews do write upon those words of the Law, *Sanctify unto me all the first-born, whatsoever openeth the womb,* Exod. xliv 2, That all the first-born do appertain to *Cochmah*, that is, the Wisdom of God; as being the first emanation from the Divine Being, through which the Supreme Unity (which they call the Crown) descends down into nature and creature, for manifesting the heavenly kingdom of the Messias throughout, by and in all the archetypal numbers and modes of being: and moreover that to the kingdom itself (which is the archetypal number), is given the name of the *first-born*. The reason of which is that the primogeniture of the kingdom, according to the mystic scale of the Divine forms, proceeds out of the opening of the virgin fountain, or womb, of the Divine Wisdom;

by which the *Paternal Unity* in manifested in glorious variety, and so exhibited in all the descending forms, as the only immortal King. And again, upon that place of the Prophet which says, *The first of all the first-fruits of all things...shall be the priests*, Ezek. xliv. 30, they tell us that the ground of birthright belongs to God's Wisdom, or to this opened and unsealed fountain of the Divine goodness; and that the first-born, or the first-fruits of all things are the peculiom of God, and of his wisdom. Which Wisdom, having the right of primogeniture, confers thereby a kingdom; and with it the Priesthood also: according to which they interpret the name of *Melchisedech*; making it to be the same both with *Malcuth*, the kingdom, and *Dobar*, the Divine oracle, or the *word of the Lord,* Psalm cx. 4. Accordingly also they interpret what is written in another Psalm of a *joyful mother of children;* after which it is immediately added *Hallelu-IAH,* or Praise ye the Lord. Psalm cxiii 9. R. Isaac said, "It is written in the Psalms, the joyful mother of children, Hallelujah: what is to be understood by the mother is known. But who are the children?" "Come, observe! (said R. Simeon) we have been taught that there is a twofold issue, the one male, the other female &c." and so proceeds to prove that by the male is meant the Divine Word, which he calls *Tiphereth*, or the fulness of all the Divine emanations, and the beautiful image; and that by the female is meant the bride of this divine Word, which is the Church, that is, the body of this fulness, and the bright mirror of all the perfections of this image, whence she is called the *kingdom;* also the queen, and the *king's daughter;* the sister-spouse of the great Solomon, the princess, the heavenly Sarah, Jerusalem, the Virgin of Sion; and by sundry other names corresponding with these! Furthermore they tell us, that the opening of the womb signifies the kingdom of God and the Messias, and specially the manifestation of this Divine kingdom in the new formation, disposition, and configuration of the vessels (that is, the creatures), or in the redintegration, restitution, and regeneration of all things under corruption.

Which *opening*, say they, is made by the Law, in the obedience to all its *affirmative* precepts; the number whereof they calculate to be exactly the same with the number of the Hebrew word which is used for the *womb*, that is 248: thereby expressing how that it is by the opening of the heavenly matrix in the fallen nature, that there is an influx received from the Father of Lights; whereby we are enabled both to fulfil his commandments, walking before him in all holiness and righteousness unblameable, as the *undefiled* ones of Sion; and also to bear that exceeding great reward which is prepared for the children of the kingdom, or of the Sarah who is above. Hence then it appears that, according to their parabolical manner of writing, the right of primogeniture to a priestly kingdom, or a royal priesthood, doth consist in the opening of a virgin womb; and that there is also a womb of eternal or incorruptible Virginity in the heavens, from which proceeds a twofold birth, male and female, in the perfect image of God, which are re-united together in one eternally, by the highest nuptial tie, the Spirit of God. And thus the bridegroom and bride, or Christ and his Church, are both made to be truly the offspring of God, and to image forth in like manner his glory by means of heavenly generation; with this only difference, that as Christ is the living portraiture of the *Divine Essence,* which is the more inward and radical notion of the Deity; so is the Church the similitude, and representative of the *Divine Nature,* which is somewhat more outward, and as the byss, or ground, of the Spirit of eternity, or Supreme Unity. For the better comprehending of which mutual relation, it may not be perhaps amiss to set down here a short Scheme thereof, according to the more principal names which the Hebrew Mystics do generally attribute to each of these, viz. the Messiah and his church or kingdom , or do at least reduce to one or other class: since also it will serve to form some conception by, of that original distinction which is in the Divine Being itself, whence this is derived; and by consequence hereof to discern likewise the Spirit of God, which is an active and masculine power, from the holy Virgin of Divine Wisdom, which is a passive and feminine power, which therefore by some is called the *Divine Corporeity,* and also the vestment of the Deity.

Besides these several others might be brought, and observations raised from each of these in particular, which would afford perhaps no contemptible light to the matter in hand, and wonderfully set out some things little heeded, or understood, concerning the marriage of the Messias and his Church, as represented both in the old Prophets, and in the Revelations of St. John most fully. But we shall content ourselves with one only observation which seems to us most material; that we may not be carried out here into a more accurate or particular disquisition about the sense of the Jews, and the Sages of the Eastern nations concerning the Divine matrimony of heaven and earth, God and Man, than is at present needful. And which is this, "That the marriage of Christ and his Church, in the descent of the New Jerusalem on earth, can never be consummated without there be such an essential relation pre-existing in Heaven, and flowing from the very Divine Nature itself; and that the souls which are made his bride, cannot otherwise be called *virgins,* but as the heavenly Virgin, and corporified idea of the Divine Being in the superior Jerusalem, doth impersonate itself in them, and so becomes to

Tiphereth	Malcuth
1. The Supernal Man, or Heavenly Adam.	1. The Virgin of Israel, or heavenly Eve.
2. The Bridegroom.	2. The Bride.
3. The Husband of the Church.	3. The Church and Congregation of Israel.
4. The King.	4. The Queen of Heaven.
5. The Great Priest.	5. The Sanctuary.
6. The Sun.	6. The Moon.
7. The Glass of Illumination.	7. The Glass Illuminated,
8. The Law.	8. The Tables of the Law.
9. The Covenant.	9. The Ark of the Covenant.
10. The World to Come.	10. The Ark of Noah.
11. The Tree of Life.	11. The Earth of Life.
12. The Root of the Tree.	12. The Branches.
13. Heaven.	13. Earth.
14. Spirit.	14. Body.
15. The Throne of Judgment.	15. The Tabernacle of Judgment.
16. David.	16. The House of David.
17. Metatron.	17. The Schechina, or Glory of God.
18. Melchisedech.	18. The Temple of Peace.
19. Jacob.	19. Leah, or the Mother of Seven Children.
20. Israel.	20. Rachel.
21. Solomon.	21. The Shulamite.
22. The Voice.	22. The Echo.
23. The WORD.	23. The Speech.
24. JEHOVAH-	24. ELOHIM, the Angels, or Souls made partakers of the Divine nature.

them the true *tabernacle of God*, Rev. xxi. 3." For Christ and the Church are but one complete image of GOD : he is indeed the head; but as the head is not completed without the members, so neither is Christ without the incorporation of the Church, which is truly his body; being flesh of his flesh, and bone of his bone, in a sense that is no less real than that wherein it was first spoken concerning the terrestrial Eve the bride of the terrestrial Adam: wherefore they are not to be accounted twain but *one*. This is the highest ground of the *unity* of the Church, and why it is even called *Christ*. Acts ix. 4, 5. And great is the mystery of this marriage: which is no more in truth than a re-union of what was antecedently *one*, even as Adam was one before the formation of Eve, being $\dot{\alpha}\rho\rho\kappa\bar{\upsilon}\sigma\theta\eta\lambda\sigma\varsigma$ (as some of the Ancients did call him) or a complete Angelical Virgin, both male and female within himself; as possessing both the principles of self-multiplication in him individually concentrated, after a spiritual and heavenly manner. Now this most essential relation of two such principles in Adam (and these also in themselves distinct from, however united with the inspiration of the Almighty, that *breath of lives* mentioned, Gen. ii. 7), while he stood in the original (and most perfect) constitution of nature, as created after the likeness of GOD, doth not only suppose (1.) a pre-existent harmony thereof in the creation according to the highest degree of Unity, which may be termed *individual;* (2.) a separation or division thereof after the creation, or a procession of the Unity into a Duality, which duality is proportionable to and concordant with it; and (3.) a re-union of the duality, in and through the harmony of the principles thus separated, by the mystical knot which reconstitutes them one, as they were at first, though not perfectly in the same manner and degree : but it doth also suppose somewhat analogous to each of these three to have had a previous subsistence in the Divine Archetypes; and likewise that the eternal marriage eternally celebrated in heaven betwixt GOD and his immaculate consort of WISDOM, cannot make the latter to be fully one with the Holy Spirit, however inseparably hereby united therewith. And therefore this essential and most intimate relation both of the first Adam to his Eve, and of the second Adam to the second Eve, his heavenly bride, must needs flow from the very Divine nature itself, and without there had been brought forth from God a corporified Idea of his being in the virgin mirror and matrix of the celestial Jerusalem, there must have been no production either of a first, or of a second Eve; and consequently the marriage of the Lamb and his bride must never be celebrated : yea what is still more, there could have been no such thing even as human generation upon the earth. But let even one and the other be granted, yet this possibility supposed, the actual celebration will not follow of this blessed marriage, without all that are to make up the bride be first made *virgins*, and then made *one virgin*. For he who is himself a Virgin will not admit any but virgins into his nearest conversation; hence are they all virgins who follow him in his kingdom of Mount Sion; thence do the virgins love him because of his name poured forth upon them, whereby they are assimilated to him by the oil of consecration wherewith they are in like manner anointed, and so are impulsed to run after him by the savour of his good ointments, typified by that sacred and most mysterious composition under the Law, which was not to touch man's flesh, Exodus xxx. 32; and thence was it that the High Priest was obliged to marry a virgin, and that too without the least manner of blemish. And then secondly, as the bride of Christ can be but one, wherefore he says, *My undefiled* (that is, my virgin) *is one*, Canticles, vi. 9; so unless all these virgins, who are the daughters of the heavenly Jerusalem, do become one, as their mother is one, they cannot be made the bride prepared for her husband; or be one with him who is one with himself, and one with the Father. Now it is impossible that they should ever be made virgins, in the highest and truest sense of the word, without that virginity which was originally in Adam before the formation of Eve, be restored again: but (according to what has been before laid down) this can never be restored, without them was an heavenly pre-existent Virginity, according to which that was imaged forth in him. And much more impossible would it still be to have all these numberless virgins to be re-incorporated, ἀνακεφαλαιοῦσθαι. Eph. i. 10, recapitulated, or gathered together in one, without they had all proceeded out of one. If they be not born of the one undefiled womb of the everlasting morning, the pure corporified Idea and bright mirror of the Divine Tri-une Being; if they be not generated from above, or regenerated, as well of the living virgin *water* of God's Wisdom, as of the *fire* of the Spirit, which is the masculine and active power that is comprehended by the other in all angelical generations; this holy virginity of the saints, and their consequent re-union and re-incorporation both with one another, and with Christ, in that express and full sense which the Scripture gives, would be in vain expected by us: and our hopes of the kingdom of Christ, with all the patriarchs, prophets and apostles, would be no better than a pleasant amusement. Wherefore it follows, That a virgin spirit must necessarily descend from God out of heaven, as the blessed womb of all heavenly and angelical births; and that this may so presentiate and impersonate itself in man, as man thereby may truly become the tabernacle of God, for the solemnisation of the nuptials of Christ and his bride. Also it hence evidently appears that this, however united indissolubly with the Holy Ghost, is yet really distinct from him.

The one is more active, the other more passive: the one gives the angelical fire in the new heavenly generation, the other gives the angelical water. So there need no more to be added to this observation that was intended upon the descent of the new Jerusalem in the kingdom of Christ, among many others that might be made from the precedent Table; which to some may possibly afford no despicable light. And the twofold birth, male and female, from Divine Wisdom, or the generation of the Messiah and his Church (or kingdom) being thus in some measure explicated, according to principles acknowledged by the most learned among the Jews, this might be sufficient alone to take away all scandal and offence from among the Christians on this head, if the matter be but duly weighed by them. Notwithstanding which, for the fuller elucidation of what David has spoken in spirit concerning the everlasting womb of the heavenly day-break, or the Aurora of the angelical kingdom, when beholding the generation of the Messias from the same, he called him *Lord*, who yet was to be his *son;* and also because I do not know that this matter has been yet by any fundamentally handled, I shall offer some farther thoughts to the consideration of the wise in heart, about this great and holy secret of a Virgin nature, both as subsisting in God, and flowing from God: that so every one that will but incline his ear, may easily come to the understanding of it, and see how and wherein it is distinguished as from the essential Word, so likewise from the Holy Spirit, as properly taken. Nevertheless it ought still to be remembered, that by reason of their inseparable union, the operations, affections and offices of the one may be attributed to the other; so that that which properly belongs to Wisdom may very well be predicated of the Spirit of God, as may also what belongs to the Spirit more properly be predicated in like manner of Wisdom, which is as the Divine vehicle and chariot wherein he rides triumphantly into Nature. The same thing also may be said as to Christ, with respect as well to one, as to the other of these: which is a caution well to be heeded, for the sake of greater distinctness, in the reading of most spiritual writers. The considerations follow:

Consideration I. The Hebrew word *Rechem* wheresoever it is found in Scripture, whether it be interpreted for the *womb*, or for *mercy*, when it is applied to God, may be said to express not only a principle of paternity, but also of *maternity* existing in the Deity, with respect to the superior orders of created beings. And wherever the same is used plurally, as most frequently it is in relation to the Divine Being, it may fitly signify the super-excellence of this most holy principle, as not possible to be expressed by any singular; whence also the most common name of God in this language is of a plural termination, as is well known : which *primarily* denotes the super-excellent Majesty of the omnipotent Creator of all things, without detracting at all from the Unity of the Godhead thereby; as this in like manner, the super-excelling glory of the Divine benignity towards his creatures, that would comprehend them in the unity of life. And by both we are to understand the communicativeness and fecundity of the Divine nature, without which no creation or generation could be in any of the worlds, visible or invisible. Now there cannot be a more refreshing and delightful consideration than this, That the very principle of Divine fecundity, by which, and out of which, all things whatever are produced, is no other than the fountain and womb of LOVE; yea the womb of all tender loves in the creature, and of all mercy both in God and in it; the *beginning* of the creation of God, whence heaven and earth first sprang forth, the male and female offspring whence numberless births were to proceed; the universal and original womb, the womb of wombs! It was from this holy womb, eternal fountain, and most essential principle of Divine Mercifulness, that judgment was swallowed up by mercy, as but from one bright sudden glance thereof, even when the terrors of the Law were thundered forth in such astonishing majesty. For it was from this the promise was at first made to the woman's seed, that it should *destroy the curse in nature;* and from hence not some, but all generations were to be blessed: whence the curse of the Law for idolatry was to terminate in four only, but the covenant of mercy was to be extended even to a thousand generations. Now in a thousand there are all comprehended. Therefore also does the Scripture so very much inculcate the *eternity* of the Divine mercy: and God is not only pleased to attribute to himself the bowels and affections of a *mother*, but even to declare the most eminent perfection of this principle in him, both as to the intensiveness and extensiveness thereof, above all that can be found in a natural mother; and the impossibility for him to forget, or cast away utterly and eternally that which is his offspring: Wherefore the Prophet Habakkuk in his most lofty psalm calls on God, in the midst of *wrath* to remember RECHEM, or the womb of mercy (ch. iii. 2). With which, many places both in the Law and in the Prophets do sweetly harmonise; but specially in the Psalms, as particularly xc., cvi and cvii.; Lam. iii. Hence is he said to repent him of the evil, according to the multitude of his *mercies*. And hence also, as Christ according to his terrestrial nativity is said to have been born of the *mercy* of God, as of the most tender and maternal principle of Divine life: so are we according to our celestial paternity said to be regenerated thence in like manner; that is, out of the same abyssal womb of Divine Compassions, and through the visitation of that heavenly dayspring, or blessed Aurora, which opens the *light of the world* on those that live in these shades of mortality, brings forth the *ever-lasting day*, and ushers in amongst us who sat in darkness the first begotten image of the Father of lights, called therefore most properly the *Sun of righteousness*. And here also we may observe that as the MERCY of GOD, both in the generation of his Son (whether eternal, or temporal) and in the regeneration of all that bear his image and name, doth chiefly express to us the illustrious prototype of all *maternity*; so doth the WILL of GOD in *both* these, express to us the most illustrious prototype of all *paternity*. Hence we cannot receive power to become sons of God in the new birth, but by the united manifestation of both as one; by being born *of the will of God*, whereby he becomes our father in heaven; and *according to his abundant mercy*, whereby he shows towards us the tender bowels of a mother: and his love to the church is compared to that of a mother to her firstborn. All this may be implied in the word RECHEM, according to the true interpretation thereof, as the same is referred to God; which by a diligent comparison of Scripture could easily be further elucidated. But I must forbear: and shall only, to conclude this First Consideration, mention one passage, which is not the least considerable; as wherein is declared how the fountain and womb of the Divine mercy comes to be opened in the covenant of blessing, by a separation from the *cursed thing*, and how there must be in God a great prototype and exemplar of all maternity and fecundity. *There shall cleave naught of the cursed thing to thine hand, that the LORD may turn from the fierceness of his anger, and shew thee mercy, and have compassion upon thee, and multiply thee, as he hath sworn unto thy fathers. When thou shall hearken to the voice of the LORD thy God, to keep all his commandments, which I command thee this day, to do that which is right in the eyes of the LORD thy God, Ye are the children of the LORD your God, &c.* Deut. xiii. 17, 18; xiv. 1, 2.

Consideration II. The most common name of God, and which in the very history of the creation alone is used no less than two and thirty times, is even asserted by the Jewish writers who have written most learnedly upon it, to be of a *feminine* nature; and that the repetition thereof so many times in the first chapter of Genesis, doth answer just to the xxxii *Paths of Wisdom*. Whence the ancient book of Jetrivah, attributed to the Patriarch Abraham, thus begins, *By the two and thirty wonderful paths of wisdom hath the Lord of Hosts framed and imaged forth his world*. Also in another cabalistical treatise, called the *Gate of Light*, the name of God whereby the world was created, is thus interpreted: and the feminine signification of it declared expressly. And as the womb of eternity out of which all things are by God produced, is most *hid*, therefore are these paths called by a name which signifies *hidden;* and Wisdom herself is called the most high path of all, which comprehends the rest within it, and to which ought to be referred that place in Job, *There is a path which no fowl knoweth, and which the vultures eye hath not seen*, ch. xxviii. 7; from which the other one and thirty draw all their influence, in the various modes of the corporification of the Divine idea, by the omnipotence of the eternal Word. Therefore are all the works of God's creation made accordingly to proceed from this secret womb, and pure ideal fountain, called the *door of the world;* and to be outwardly manifested and wrought out from their invisible forms (agreeably to the doctrine which some deduce from Heb. xi 3), by the opening of this wonderful matrix in nature, according to all those secret channels and ducts of Divine wisdom, which they call PELIOTH, that is *concealed*. * * *

Consideration III. The *morning* which is mentioned in the generation of Christ by David, is properly that *redness* which is betwixt the darkness and the light, or the night and the day: which is well to be heeded, if we would understand the ground whence not only the creation, but *judgment* also is attributed by the mystical doctors of the Jews to that Divine Name, which is both the first and most frequent in the whole Bible. For though it may seem harsh in them to ascribe judgment and severity to the female nature, rather than to the male: yet herein they have respect to the gradual manifestation in nature of the firstborn of the creatures; to his triumphant exit against the fallen princes and angels at the creation; and to the restitution of lapsed souls from darkness into light, through the red fire of Divine judgment, whence the glorious light doth break forth, as out of a hidden womb, and with exulting joy spring out visibly to run the course of the wonders of God in love. This morning redness is called the bride chamber, or the secret CHUPPAH in which the bridegroom was to prepare himself, which is mentioned Ps. xix. 5: It is that out of which the Divine Word, as a glorious sun, arises; coming as a bridegroom out of his chamber, and rejoicing as a giant to run his race, through the whole circuit of nature. For this answers exactly [to] the meaning of the word SHAIHAR, which is not the light itself, but the triumphant breaking forth of the light from and out of the darkness: whence among all the Divine goings forth, which are many, that of *victory* is peculiarly ascribed to it; as the opposition of the powers of darkness is thereby conquered, and subdued. And forasmuch as this conquest of the day, in outward nature, always begins in the East, therefore is the east held sacred to the eternal dayspring of Wisdom; and the Magi, who are the children of wisdom, are said to come out of the East. And agreeably to this are all the kingdoms of the earth commanded to sing praises to Him who rides upon the heaven of heavens *towards the east*, Ps. lxviii. 33; not only according to the *Septuagint* and St. Hierom, but other ancient versions: whereby is described the victorious outgoing of the Divine Word from the paradisical East; as might clearly be made to appear from the whole drift of the psalm, as also from that particular name of God here used, which is universally accounted by the Jewish nation the manifestatrix of the ineffable Name; even as the light of the Son manifests the light of the Father, which is otherwise inaccessible, appearing to the creature as thick darkness. This most high East is called in another psalm the *beginning of heaven*, and in the Mosaical Genesis of the world seems to be supposed as the BEGINNING not only of *heaven*, but of *earth* also, that is, of the universal system of things. And therefore not unfitly by the prophet Zacharias may the name of the EAST be applied to the Messiah, as this very WORD incarnating itself by a power from the Divine East; whence also his star was seen to appear in the East. And perhaps this may have been understood by the Syriac interpreter, in whom there is found, *From the east hath he sent forth hie voice:* which is for certain applicable to the eternal Word, that by the most ancient Chaldee paraphrast on the Pentateuch is significantly expressed both the *Word of God*, and the *Word which is God*. But this *Beginning*, or *East* from on high ($\dot{\alpha}\nu\alpha\tau o\lambda\grave{\eta}$ $\dot{\iota}\xi$ $\zeta\psi\chi\grave{\iota}$, in the prophetic song of Zacharias), must be distinct both from the *Word*, which went forth saying, Let there be, and it was so; and from the *Spirit of Elohim* which moved upon the chaotic matter. Nor is it perfectly one either with the *Light*, which arose in the east, being clouded under the veil of mortal flesh; or with the *Holy Ghost*, who overshadowed the Virgin for the bringing forth of this *Light of Life* in such a form, in order to the manifestation of the wonders of God's wisdom and grace. As the Word and Spirit are not the same with one another, but distinct: so neither is the *Beginning*, or Divine day-spring, the same with either; notwithstanding that the former is in it, and the latter *with* it eternally and inseparably.

In visible nature there is no difficulty at all to discern the redness of the morning from the full day: and if we cannot make this discernment in invisible nature also, may we not rather suspect a defect in ourselves, than peremptorily proceed to conclude that not to be at all, which we cannot so presently understand? The Hebrew word which has been mentioned, and which is chosen by God's Sprit to express the generation of Christ from the womb of eternity, as an eternal Priest and King, is no less distinguished in sense from another word, which without the least distinction is translated the *morning* also; but imports the perfect light of the day, whence, as the *victory* of the Divine name is attributed to that, so the *glory* of it, or the triumphant pomp of Christ's kingdom, is allotted to this, according to the scale of Divine numbers. This word is found in the account of the creation throughout; and may have more perhaps of a mystery in it, than is ordinarily heeded. Now as in *redness* there is a mixture of darkness and light, or of the light hidden and the light manifest, so is it to be supposed also in some sense in the womb of the Divine Aurora, the eternal seminary of light. And from this commixture it is called the measure of *judgment:* and, according to it, this world is observed to have been created, in the going forth of that Divine Name which is communicable to all the administrators of *justice*, both angels and men, both supreme and subordinate.

Consideration IV. This Morning-redness, which the wise men have watched for in all ages, and sought to understand and behold, that they might know thereby the mystery not only of the creation and generation of all things from a Divine Beginning, and out of an holy Virgin Materiality and celestial womb, but also their regeneration from and out of the same: and which is to be considered both as the fountain of mercy, and as the measure of justice in the Deity introducing itself into nature, and is the true heavenly Day-spring and East from which all the Divine measures do descend; is further represented to us under the name of PLACE. And hence it is that some of the Ancients may have been grossly misunderstood, as if they did really assert the co-eternity of *place* and *matter* with God, according to the vulgar conception of those terms. It is true that some philosophers of no mean consideration, and nowise atheistical, have maintained the pre-existence both of place and matter from all eternity: but their meaning herein was altogether different from what many of their *dull followers* have thought it to be. It is manifest that *the philosophy of the Ancients was extremely corrupted from that purity wherein it was originally delivered by the founders of schools, (several of whom were persons of a Divine genius, and highly enlightened with the Spirit of Wisdom from above,) through their successors and disciples;* sometimes for want of attention or penetration, and perhaps at other times even through maliciousness itself: as the history of the Atomical Philosophy alone may serve abundantly to make out, together with the origination of the sect of the Sadducees among the Jews, and most of the ancient heresies among the Christians. Nor is it less certain that in this most ancient philosophy, after the fullest and freest inquiry made into it, there must be understood by their eternal place, which includes the *eternal matter* filling it, the very same thing which the Hebrew school means by that Divine Name, whereby they used to express the omnipresence of the Deity, even the name HA-MAKOM, *i. e. the Place.* By which holy Name of God they would teach that the world is not properly the place of God, but that God rather is the place of the world; and that all place is in God, and from God alone, all creatures being circumscribed by the Divine essence and nature; so that He may super-eminently be called *the place*, or universal receptacle of all beings, wherein they exist, live, and act. Now this Divine title, or name, is attributed by them to the *wisdom* of God, which is also called for the same reason BETH HA-OLAM, or the *House of the world*. And it is favoured likewise by the very original of the word, which is from a radix that imports to *rise*, ascend, stand up, or awake; and from that particular mode of it wherein the Hebrew language is so elegant in expressing that which makes or effects a thing to be, with but one word. Whereby is insinuated That the Divine Beginning, Day-spring, and East of the heavenly Wisdom, as in God *before Nature*, is the true *awakening* principle of all generated and created beings; out of which as their eternal matrix they have proceeded, in which they do actually subsist, and by which they are continually comprehended: and that all intellectual and material creatures do first *rise* and *ascend* from this beginning, which is in God and with God from all eternity; and do *stand up* out of their ideas, being brought forth into real existence. And this may not be very distant from what some, greatly illuminated in the mysteries of God and Nature, within the last generation, have called (as I remember) *the field of the great potter*, into which the Holy Ghost, for the creation of all things is said to descend, going forth from the Father (who is the *potter*) by and through the eternal Word or Son ; according to the Father's will, manifesting itself in the *voice* of the word, which is the outflown FIAT of the Son. It is not perhaps quite the same, but it is at least included in and depending on it: it is a different consideration of it from the former; and may comprehend not the whole, but a part of it, that is, with respect to this or that relation. This it truly called the *Field of wisdom*, which being filled and impregnated with the Divine magical breath, or Spirit, brings forth thereby the wonders in Nature; and so must needs be distinct from the Spirit which fills and impregnates it, whether this be in the fire, or in the light. Therefore this eternal Place, or field, is in its originality to be distinguished from the Spirit itself, which flows upon it; and consequently also in its operations. It is the highest and most secret Garden of God, according to the cabalistic theory, which the four winds of the heaven of heavens do continually breathe upon, from the cherubinical angels of the throne of the Divine Majesty; and hence there is nothing could have sprung forth without its fruitfulness. It is also called to the same effect *Beth Ho-Jotrer,* the house of the potter; wherein the furnace is generally attributed to Wisdom alone, but the wheel both to eternal Wisdom and eternal Nature. In this house of the great potter, by means of its holy magical furnace, which is eternally burning, the Spirit of God manifests its omnipotence; but the Spirit is not one with the furnace, but feeds it incessantly. Let him that has wisdom here study to become still more wise, and by descending into this abyssal House, or place, where the immortal fire is kept, to consider the origination of all the vessels of nature, according to the various circumnotations thereof; and to behold the restitution of the broken vessels, by the light of the everlasting morning arising still brighter and brighter! And further, some have thought this notion aforesaid absolutely necessary to defend and explain the Unity of the blessed Trinity in the Divine Nature, as in one mutual common Schecina or dwelling; so that the Divine Wisdom, as the heaven of the glorious Trinity, is the everlasting *Hammakom*, place, or *ubi*, both of Father, Son and Spirit, the house and temple of God in the supernatural East: it is *Domus Sacro-Sancto Trinititatis*, the residence of the most holy Number Three. Which may be set forth under several emblems; but the most ordinary seems to be that which is the manner of writing of the great name of God, everywhere found in the Jewish writings. Which is this ד ; and it may deserve well to be heeded. For whoever might be ד ד the first inventor of this manner of expressing the ineffable nature of the Divine Being, it appears more than probable that he must have been acquainted with something above the ordinary apprehensions, not only of Jews, but even of Christians, But the explication hereof may lead too far."

From these and similar papers, extracts and notices, interspersed throughout this treatise, (with equally lucid representations that might be offered of the pure cabalistic and other forms of dvine science,) the reader will now be enabled to obtain a conception of the gems of theosophical literature which Mr. Law possessed and contemplated in his retirement. Having by his side the sublimest discoveries, and (according to the elucidation of the spiritual scope of the patriarchal histories, in Behmen's "Mysterium Magnum,") the most standard and scriptural forms of divine knowledge: all clustering instinctively around the one grand central object of the gospel, the earnest pursuit of regeneration, and perfection of the divine life in the soul.

Selection Seven.

Short Reflections on the First and Secondary Universal Matter.

We also present the following MS., entitled "Short Reflections upon the first original and secondary universal matter—

I.—The invisible God has brought forth out of himself, in the beginning, a visible matter that was capable to receive all ideas and forms: to which we may fitly give the name of a subtle spiritual matter, that does penetrate all other more gross matters.

II.—In this first original matter were all qualities, elements, and properties virtually comprehended, in the highest degree: for as much as God out of the same has created in the six days' creation of this our universe all globes and visible creatures: and this indeed in such a glorious order, that the infinite wisdom of the Creator is hence clearly laid open before the reasonable creature.

III.—This original matter did fill up and occupy, before the creation of this world, the whole place from the heavenly waters above down to the centre of the earth. In which place there now is the created heaven and earth, the Almighty God having in the six days of the Creation, divided distributed, and diffunded this first matter into all those globes and several creatures.

IV.—Now, like as this first matter was pure and luminous; so were the creatures and forms that were created out of the same also, every one in their kind, luminous and perfect: but because the increase and support of the creatures must follow out of the original matter, out of which they were created, and that the same in the place of this world already was reduced into specified forms; therefore the eternal Creator wrought out, and effected, by the co-operation of the earthly and heavenly created influences a second, in all things agreeing with the first, upon the same manner as in the present earthly defiled world, a vegetable that grows out of a grain is altogether like to the same whence it did grow forth, and as in the animal kingdom, out of the seed is again generated such a seed as that was whence the living creature came forth. And after this manner, all creatures materially are resolved into the matter whence they were produced as into their quintessence, for the bringing forth their likeness.

V.—To this second matter are also given many names, and for that we *rely* the most upon the Holy Scripture; among other it is called by the patriarch Jacob the blessedness from heaven, with the blessedness out of the deep, the which otherwise is called the fatness of the earth and the dew of the heaven.

VI.—By this second matter the material creatures were maintained in their property and perfection, till the curse through the sin came into the world; by which the will of the Man did then make partakers of the curse all other sublunary creatures and subsistences. Therefore also now this second matter is no more to be obtained pure, but mixed with filthinesses as this our sublunary globe.

VII.—But this curse consists properly herein, first of all that the Creator has transported the earth out of its situation more remote from the sun, as the true centre of the universe, so that the sun cannot with his meek and gentle fire-water-rays so directly and overflowingly enlighten the earth, and operate upon and into it, as he did before; of which the earth's remoteness and distance are a mighty hindrance. In the next place, the earth in and for itself is, by reason of the inherent curse, no more the former subject as it was, not capable and pure as before; so that now the sun, according to the several dispositions of the defiled subject, and earthly lump, doth produce out of it more terrestrial and intemperate fruits and nourishments, which is not done by fault of the sun, but only through the failing of the earth; and this is also the reason why the earth shall be again reposed in its former place and situation before the thousand years. Read Isa. xiii. 13, where it expressly is written; as well as Joel, ii. 10, Isa. ii. 21, Hag. ii. 6. 27, and Matt. xxiv. 29, although these places are not altogether so express.

VIII.—Now, this curse extends itself not over the whole creation of the six days university, but only over the sublunary globe of this earth. Therefore the sun after the curse, as well as before, remains in and for himself a large and spacious ocean of the first original matter; who, as the heart in the man, is placed in the centre of the whole world's university of the six days, that he might give life and strength to all creatures.

IX.—Although now the globe of the earth, because of the curse of sin upon it, is driven far back from its refreshing centre that must enliven and enlighten it, and is also become eccentrical and sublunary, as we do alas! enough feel; so cannot the sun with his sweet and powerful beams, make the earth participate in the same manner as he did before the fall, by reason of his great remoteness, nor bring forth out of the corrupt lump pure fruits; nevertheless he doth not cease to operate upon the earth with his remote rays, and to enlighten it as well as he can, that so the animals, vegetables, and minerals may out of them take their increase and nourishment. Accordingly as all the created armies of the stars do in like manner cast their beams on the earth by reflection of the firmament; which firmament is a firm body, beneath the heavenly waters, that does separate the waters above the heaven from the under-firmamentary, or under-heavenly waters.

X. —All these powers together are drawn and drunk in by the earth, as water by a mushroom. As then the rays of the sun and stars do carry with them, and convey into the earth a salt, that is full of spirit, of little holes and pores (and consequently apt to receive the influences) for impregnation of the earth.

XI. —The heavenly rays, or influences, do penetrate even to the very present centre of the earth, where they are again by the central fire repelled to the surface; that so the animals, vegetables, and minerals may obtain their nutriment." [and so forth, to § XVIII.] Thus the MS.

Selection Eight.

[On the Book of Revelations]

"I. —There is a *mystical* and *magical* sense of the Revelations of St. John, as well as a *literal* and *ecclesiastical* sense.

II. —It is called *mystical*, as it relates to the hidden MYSTERY OF GOD IN THE SOUL: and it is called *magical* as it relates to the KNOWING AND SETTING ON WORK THE FORMS OF NATURE BY THE HOLY GHOST.

III. —Which sense is not penetrable by human reason, but only by the divine Spirit in man.

IV. —This divine Spirit is universal, and subsists in every man; but is in many, not only obstructed, but even perfectly hidden.

V. —The cause of this obstruction and hiding is the aversion of the will of man from the will of God; and the removal thereof is therefore the conversion of that will into this.

VI. —The conversion of the will of man into the will of God is not instantaneous, but by a gradual process.

VII. —This process is made through all the forms of nature, and through all the divine spirits or divine forms.

VIII. —These forms of nature, and these spirits of God, are seven; which natural and divine Septenary is a manifestation of the Trinity, as the Trinity is of the Unity.

IX. —This manifestation of the divine ternary, or Trinity, in the septenary, both natural and divine, or in nature and grace, is from the Centre, which is the quarternary.

X. —The divine Quarternary is the number of the *New Jerusalem* (therefore represented as *four square*), or of the angelical world; which is the divine *bride*, and the *mother* of all that are regenerated after the spirit angelically. *Rev.* xxi. 2; *Gal.* iv. 26.

XI. —In every human soul this quarternary, or Centre, is to be found, as standing in the midst, betwixt the two principles of darkness and light; and from thence begins the manifestation of the Spirit in light.

XII. —This manifestation, or emanation of the Spirit of the soul in light, is made in the blessed *quinary*, or the holy fifth number of Christ JESUS, who is the light of the world.

XIII. —The Quinary reveals the souls under the altar, receiving from God their white virgin robes; but who are not yet perfected, and therefore are to wait for a *little season*.

XIV. —The altar is the Cross. The souls under the altar, are the souls under the cross, or those that are crucified with Jesus: these having passed the mystic death in the fourth central number, where the light is generated from the cross, begin to arise in the next holy number, till at length they attain the Sabbath of their rest in the seventh; in which the divine Spirit is fully manifested, and the soul fully perfected.

XV. —The soul's perfection is in the full manifestation of the divine Spirit in every form and property thereof, through a real formation and generation of Christ within the same, as the true life and light of the soul.

XVI. —Every human soul is a spiritual substance, having just seven forms, neither more nor less, for the imaging forth therein of the divine nature in Trinity; and when all these are perfected, then is the triune image perfectly restored, and the kingdom of heaven made manifest in the soul.

XVII. —The seven seals are the seven forms of nature in the soul; and are the seven spirits which belong to the Father, as considered without the Son, that is, to the power of God in his anger and severity.

XVIII. —As the seven seals represent the *Father's* nature, thus considered; so the seven candlesticks represent the Son's nature.

XIX. —The soul being sealed up in the justice of God, under the seven seals, there is none able to break open these seals, and to enkindle light in the soul, which may overcome death, but the LAMB that was slain, and is alive.

XX. —As the *seals* obstruct the manifestation of Christ's kingdom in the soul, and in the church; so the opening of them by the Lamb is the revelation of his kingdom, and of the angelical world, which cannot be without his generating the soul in, and through himself, into the light.

XXI. —The new generation of the soul is a passing out of darkness into light, through the power of the Lamb raising up himself therein, and redeeming it from the wrathful source of nature, in its dark and fiery properties.

XXII. —This internal resurrection and redemption brings the spirit of the soul through all the seals of nature, into the very substantiality of Christ's universal body, the principle and centre of light eternal, where Wisdom reigns in the wonders of God.

XXIII. —The regenerated spirit draws after it the soul, and that also draws the body, without which it cannot be perfected, and so the soul is clothed upon with the heavenly body of the inward Christ.

XXIV. —This inward Christ, or CHRIST FORMED WITHIN, is the *new creature*, and is one with Jesus Christ, sitting in the heavenly places, at the right hand of the Father, being spirit of his spirit, and flesh of his flesh.

XXV. —Thus the saints are one body in him, and he is this body in God: they enter into his humanity, and he becomes man in them.

XXVI. —By this new generation, or New Birth, of spirit, soul, and body, is the new man perfected in Christ, and reigns with Christ, in the new garment of his body, completely put on by virtue of the *seventh seal* broken up in the Lamb's nature.

XXVII. —The *seventh seal* opened, shows the holy temple of God, in which are the seven candlesticks, or the seven lights of Christ in the soul.

XXVIII. —The two apocalyptical *seas*, which are the fountains and seats of two contrary principalities, are the *seventh seal*, considered either as *shut* or *opened*.

XXIX. —The seventh seal considered as *shut*, is the fountain and seat of the antichristian beast, arising out of the sea of corrupt nature; or the properties and forms of nature in their impure state.

XXX. —The seventh seal *opened*, is the fountain and seat of the peaceable lamb-like kingdom; and the throne of Christ in the soul, as standing upon the sea of uncorrupt nature; or the properties and forms of nature in their pure state, and fully harmonized.

XXXI. —The glassy sea is the seventh spirit of the eternal incorruptible nature, in which is the Joy and delight of the divine Majesty; wherein the blessed Trinity triumphantly manifests itself, and beholds the true angelical world, with the holy harpers of God.

XXXII. —This sea is the '*water-stone*,' and the '*water-spirit*' of the wise; it is the very substance and corporiety of the Divine nature, in eternal nature, and compaction of all the eternal divine powers, properties, and forms: and herein are the burning lamps of love revealed, which are the seven spirits of the *Lamb*.

XXXIII. —The conquerors that stand upon this sea, are such as in whom all the seven seals have been broken up, all the seven holy lights of Christ have been unsealed, and all the angelical thunders have been heard to utter their voices; whereby there is such a perfect conversion gradually wrought out of the human will into the Divine will, as they being fully passive to every Divine influence and motion in the harmony of the angelical world, are made as it were the *harps of God*.

XXXIV. —The process of this conversion and transportation is through the mystical death and annihilation: which is comprehended under the seven seals, being only consummated under the seventh, or last.

XXXV. —The process of the *mystical death* properly consists in a *sevenfold* purification and refining, according to the number and order of the *seals*. Yet chiefly herein are the four first concerned.

XXXVI. —The process of the *mystic resurrection*, and the *first resurrection*, (which follows immediately hereupon) and of the manifestation of it, is to be looked for under the mystery of the *seven thunders*.

XXXVII. —The *ladder of mystical ascension*, which is a true manuduction to the *Divine Magia*, is set forth according to the *gates* of the *New Jerusalem*, which are supposed successive.

XXXVIII. —The *glorification*, or *descension*, is the *New Jerusalem* itself, that is, such a state actually introduced into the soul, as may answer to the pattern of that city *descending* from GOD, in a full consummation of the Divine nuptials.

XXXIX. —In this consummation of the nuptials betwixt Christ and the soul, the true *Divine Magia* breaks forth, by the soul's unipotency with him; whereby nature's secret forms are set on work from the Holy Ghost.

XL. —The angels of the *Revelations* are the angels of time, being consummated after this manner: who are all Divine magi in the power of *the Holy Ghost;* and the *anointed priests* of the third and highest order, which is called the *order of Melchisideck*."

Selections Nine and Ten.

[On Moses]

And this consideration by the way, may serve to shew to us how wonderful a man Moses most have been, to write such a book; how full of God, how light his mind, and how pure his heart! Upon which point we find a MS. fragment by Lee, wherein he alludes to Moses, in the following terms :-

"The Holy Scripture is a wellspring of life and light. And what St. Paul has said of the essential Word of God may be said also of his written word, viz., that all the treasures of the wisdom and knowledge of God are therein included. The first of the books of Scripture is Genesis; and the author who has written it is Moses.

If we consider the person of this holy man of God, we shall find nothing in him but what is great and extraordinary. He was educated as the adopted son of a princess, who had a design of rendering him worthy to be king; and he was instructed in all the sciences of the sages of Egypt, whose reputation was then famous among the learned.

If we have regard to antiquity, he was without comparison more ancient than all those authors so illustrious in the world, who have acquired Greece the name of the mother of science and arts. For he was near five hundred years before Homer, eight hundred years before the philosopher Thales, who was the first that treated of Nature; nine hundred years before Pythagoras, and more than eleven hundred years before Socrates, Plato, and Aristotle, who were as the chiefs and masters of all the wisdom of the Greeks.

If we consider what appears of greatness in his writings, and in the whole course of his life, we shall find that without having been able to borrow any light from all profane antiquity, or reap any assistance from it, as having flourished before it in the world with great lustre, he was at the same time an orator, a poet, a historian, a philosopher, a lawgiver, a divine, a prophet; more than a prophet; more than sovereign pontiff, for as much as he consecrated the high priest; the minister of God, with whom he treated as one friend treats with another; the leader of his people; lastly, to say all in a word, the master and arbiter of nature, the interpreter of heaven, the vanquisher of kings, the God of Pharoah.

All these qualifications, both human and divine, were collected and united in Moses, to the end he might possess an authority to which none should be obliged to pay the same deference, as to that of God himself.

The Scripture says of him, that he *was mighty in deed and in word*. His deeds were his miracles, by which * * * "

[Paragraph on Mystical Theology]

* The antiquity of Mystical Theology (writes the Editor of the *Theosophical Transactions,* in commenting upon the above treatise, of ASCETICKS,) is here derived down from Noah; and the instances or Melchisedec, Abimelech, the two Pharaohs, Jethro the Midianite, Rebekah, Balaam, and Job, with his friends, are adduced to prove, that it was anciently believed in all nations, that there were means whereby men and women might come to have some acquaintance and communication with God. The tradition and succession hereof through the Colleges of the Prophets, among the *Jews;* through the Priestly colleges of the eastern Magi, among the *Egyptians, Chaldeans,* and *Arabians;* and through the *Pythagorean* and *Platonic* schools,—were it accurately and judiciously done, would be a considerable work; but this is not to be expected within a few sheets. And as for the *media* which the Gentiles did use, to attain the intimacies and communications of their peculiar Deities, or of the Soul of the world, or of the supreme Demiurgus and Creator, a particular and distinct explication thereof, would necessarily lead us into a disquisition concerning the ancient *Theurgic* mysteries.

What was the spirit of *Plotinus* and *Iamblicus,* what also the spirit of Porphyry, cannot thoroughly be understood without a more than ordinary insight into these. The *Porphyrian* spirit is a very great mystery. But as it is in witchcraft, or in demoniacal obsessions, so also is it here. The evil daemons are able to do nothing of themselves: it is Nature that works all, and produces those strange and wonderful operations. They also know how to apply *actives* to *passives,* and leave her to bring about what they design; to which the present *corrupt state* of nature is subservient, and wherewith they fail not to add somewhat of their own malice.

Selection Eleven.

An Hundred Queries upon the Mosaic Cabala

The next paper we propose to give, (as indicative of the high science of this individual,) is headed, " An Hundred Queries upon the Mosaic Cabala," which it would appear he had drawn up as an exercise upon the first and second chapters of Genesis, either for himself or some other deep-searching Christian philosophical student; which are these:—

I. —Wherefore is this word *Elohim* used in this first chapter of Genesis, and how shall it be properly interpreted? Because it is set in the plural number, why is it constructed with a singular? What also is the reason that these two names, *Jehovah* and *Elohim*, are found together in the second chapter, after the accomplishing of the seventh day, and not before?

II. —Wherefore was the earth created before the sun? and why doth it now (with all its creatures) desire and thirst after the sun's power or virtue, notwithstanding it could at that time, as the sun was not existing, bring forth all its growths, with its seeds, which it can do now no more?

III. —Since there was yet neither summer nor winter, nor spring time nor harvest, what is to be accounted of those queries that desire to know in what time of the year the earth was created.

IV. —Wherefore must the sun have been created, there having been such a power in the earth already, that it could bring forth all things without the sun? Hath the sun then taken its power out of the earth? And if so, why doth now the earth take it out of the sun? Because this power, to beget from itself, and to fructify, did originally be in the earth, (which must be done by the mediation of the sun,) whither is this power gone; and how is it come from the earth to be now in the sun?

V. —This power first having been in the earth, where was at that time the place of the earth, which doth now turn itself about the sun? How could it turn then about the sun, when the sun was not yet created? What was this thing which at that time the earth was longing for? What was there then for a sun? How is it to be understood that the sun, which is created later, hath now more power in it than the earth, which had not only the same power as the sun hath now, but hath had also more? If the sun were a child of the earth, how hath this child deprived his mother of her life? But if the fountain of light did spring alike through the earth, and in the place of the sun also, which light was now the greater of the twain? What was it particularly for a light, which the earth had? Was it visible or invisible? Out of what fountain did it spring, because every light which may be seen by outward eyes, cometh now from the light of the sun? Wherefore doth this light open itself no more through the earth, as it did before?

VI. —What is the *Haschamaim*? What is the letter ה and what signified the letter ש? Wherefore is this word compounded out of the ש which is fire, and מים which signified water? In what subject or matter may the nature of the spirit of the fiery waters be known? With what covering are they now covered and hid? Where may they now be found in the mystical earth, and in the natural earth? Are they yet together in the centre or not? Are they one thing with the earth, or are they different from it? Wherefore is the firmament afterwards called by this name *Haschamaim*?

VII. —Wherefore is here, in the first chapter, the earth called *Haaretz*? when in the second, after the finishing of the seventh day, the earth is called *Haadamah*, whereof no mention was made in the first chapter. What is the reason thereof? Is *Haadamah* created with *Haaretz* together, or was it created before *Haaretz*?

VIII. —What is *tohu*? What is *bohu*? How far doth this *tohu* extend itself? And wherefore is this *tohu* not attributed to the heavens also? Were the heavens full or replenished? Did not this *tohu* extend itself even so far as the heavens did extend themselves? And how may it then be said the heavens were created? If now everywhere was *tohu*, where the earth was, where was the place of the earth?

IX. —But if the heavens were not void or *tohu*, where have they been before they were created visibly? Were they in the same place, wherein to they came thereafter as they became created and manifested? Did they not fill this place full wherein they had been before like as nothing? Hath not then the earth filled full also this place, wherein it before was as nothing? How far did reach this full filling, or this plenitude of the heavens and the earth, in opposition to vacuity and nothing? If the heavens are not pure before God, what is their impurity? From whence cometh that *chosech*?

X. —Wherefore is the creation repeated or rehearsed, Gen. ii. 4.? And wherefore is the creation of the third day repeated, Gen, ii., 4, 9.?

XI. —Wherefore is there made no mention of the tree of knowledge of good and evil, in Gen. i. 11? What was for an earth out of which this tree was created? And on which day was it created?

XII. —Wherefore in Gen. i. is there no mention made of the metals, and nevertheless there is made mention of gold, Gen. ii. 11.? Wherefore is there in Gen. ii., made mention only of the third and of the sixth day? And why of the fowls, and not at all of the fishes, nor of the creeping things?

XIII. —Wherefore is it, in Gen. i. 26, said, that the man is created after *the image of God*, and in the second chapter, that he is created out of *Haadamah*; and that *Nischmath Chajim* is breathed into him? Wherefore in Gen. ii. 19., is set this word *Haadamah*, and in Gen. i. 24, this word *Haaretz*?

XIV. —Wherefore in Gen. ii. 19, is the creation of the beasts repeated, which was yet before in the first chapter made mention of?

XV —Wherefore were the fishes not brought before Adam to be called by him, as the beasts of the earth and the fowls of the air?

XVI. —Wherefore is this word *Jezar* used concerning the man, Gen. ii. 19, and v. 7? And why is another word, viz., *Tudshe*, used Gen. i. 11.

XVII. —What is this word *Zela?* Why, is it, in Gen. ii. 21, interpreted a *rib*, signifying properly a power?

XVIII. —Wherefore Gen. ii. 9, is used this word *Jizmach* concerning the production of trees, when Gen. i. 12, is only used this word *toze?*

XIX. —What is this word *abhid*, Gen. ii. 6? Is it well interpreted to till the ground? Wherefore is the earth here called *Haadamah*, and not *Haaretz*? And wherefore is this same word *Haadamah* not to be found, Gen. ii. 8?

XX. —Wherefore did the tempting tree not grow before the *second creation* came?

XXI. —What is this word *Eden?* Is it not the tempting ground, as a *lust*, whereby the man could become entangled?

XXII. —Wherefore came the mist not sooner than Gen. ii. 6? And what is this to say, that it went up, or that it is gone out from the *Haaretz*; and that it hath watered, or given to drink the whole form of the *Haadamah*?

XXIII. —Wherefore followeth immediately hereupon, the second creation, and the tempting tree, and the tempting earth, and Adam's being put into the garden, and the tree of life, (viz. such a power whereon Adam should hold him fast,) and the commandment?

XXIV. —For what longed or thirsted *Haadamah*, that it must satisfy its thirst from *Haaretz?* What is this ascending or going up? What is the mist? What is *Shekah?*

XXV. —What was this essence wherewith *Haadamah* was clothed, ere this mist from *Haaretz* did put another form upon it?

XXVI. —Wherefore had it not rained upon *Haaretz*, that now there must come a mist to water, or to give drink to the *Haadamah*? Or why is it that this mist must overwhelm or cover the same with its grossness?

XXVII. —Wherefore saith Moses only thus briefly, there went up a mist from *Haaretz*, and covered *Haadamah*? Wherefore saith he not, that *Jehovah*, or *Elohim*, commanded this mist to go up? Hath this mist generated, or brought forth itself, after all things were created? Was this mist not also within the idea of the Creator, because there is made no mention of it, neither in the first nor in the second chapter?

XXVIII. —Wherefore followeth this mist immediately after the repetition of the creation? Which is the true and proper interpretation of the fourth and fifth verses of Gen. ii.? How is *Haadamah* become covered by this mist? And why is it there said, The face of *Haadamah* was covered by it? What is this face or faces of *Haadamah*? From whence came this mist, and whither went it? Was *Haadamah* within *Haaretz*?

XXIX. —What was this mist, that so immediately after it the tempting tree came forth out of *Haadamah*? Was *Haadamah* not pure, before this mist came? Was *Haaretz* not pure? Did the tempting tree grow out of this mist?

XXX. —Wherefore maketh Moses mention immediately after this mist, of some bondage, or tilling of *Haadamah*; the man being before settled to be a governor or lord over all things?

XXXI. —Was there not come a twofold quality into *Haadamah*, after this mist was gone up from *Haaretz*, because there did grow a twofold fruit from the earth, in opposition against each other, viz., a tree of knowledge and lust or longing, a tree of life or power? Was the serpent also brought forth out of this mist?

XXXII. —How came the longing for this mist into *Haaretz*, and how came it from *Haaretz* into *Haadamah*? Why was *Haaretz* wanting a rain, having before brought forth all things without rain?

XXXIII. —Did Adam also mind, or settle his imagination into this mist or grossness, that there did fall a deep sleep, or an impotency and languor upon him? What is a mist? Is it not a covering of the clearness, an obscuring of the light, and often also venomous? Is it not an image of the dark world? A darkening of the sun? A cloud, and often also black and unhealthful?

XXXIV. —How should Adam have behaved himself concerning this mist, and concerning all those things in which this mist was? Should he not have retired himself to the tree of life?

XXXV. —How came it to pass, that his feeblest power, which did go out from him, did behold this same tree, wherein thus powerfully this mist of death was lying, and that he regarded and minded it? Was he not (when he consisted yet in his fulness, and when he had yet liberty to take what he would) touched or infected by this same mist, and so enfeebled, because his imagination did leave the tree of life?

XXXVI. —What was the very ground, or source of this mist? Was it not the *desiring* or lust? Was it necessary that Adam must be tempted by this desire, or lust, also? What was that thing which stirred up some other desire or lust in him, besides those whereto he was of God created? Wherefore could he not overcome this lust in his strife and temptation?

XXXVII. —Wherefore did not Adam eat of the tree of life in the midst of the garden, before he went to the tempting tree; being this tempting tree was forbidden unto him, and the tree of life not? Wherefore could he not come more to the tree of life, after he had eaten of the tempting tree? Was not this tree of life the Divine Power out of the Son, or the Word of the Lord, which became thereafter typified by the rod of Aaron?

XXXVIII. —Was this mist in the tree of life, and in the other trees also? Or was only the tempting tree of lust tinged and infected by it?

XXXIX. —What was this thing, which did so vehemently draw the most feeble part in Adam, viz., his imagination, that he looked backwards after the forbidden fruit of knowledge? Why abode he not with his will under God's will, yea, under the will and obedience of the Word?

XL. —Why arose his hearkening out of his looking backwards, and why further his desire out of his hearkening?

XLI. —Could he not have overturned and vanquished this looking backwards after the earthly lust and knowledge, by the power of the tree of life? And can he not do it yet now, by a strong, earnest looking forwards and towards the tree of life, viz., the true brazen serpent lifted up upon a pole, as a character of the curse? Will not the power of the tree of life willingly help him in this strife? Is there not now set before him a greater and more fixed glory, which he may expect after that he hath held out his trials, and hath overcome?

XLII. —Must not all the angels have been proved and tried also? Wherefore did the fairest of them not keep his stand? What was the thing which he looked for?

XLIII. —How could Adam have prevented, and how may he yet now prevent, that he may not be caught or entangled by this lust and mist of the tempting source on this tempting earth, by his longing and looking for other things, except the Word of the Lord?

XLIV. —What is this other source which is shewed him by God, to be an opposition and antidote against this tempting source? Or can there be found any other way to be delivered from this strong tempting source of his lust and self-desiring, which is entered into all things, except only by a fixed denying of his own will, and laying it down under the will of God?

XLV. —What meaneth this saying, Gen. ii. 18, *not good?* For was it not said, Gen. i. 31, *all things were very good?*

XLVI. —Wherefore, in Gen. ii., is no mention made of this word, *be fruitful and multiply?* Being this same was said, Gen. i. 22, to the fishes and fowls; and 28, to the man also? Wherefore is this same not (v. 11) neither to the beasts, nor to the men, after their fall, till, Gen. ix., it is said again unto Noah?

XLVII. —Wherefore are the beasts not given unto Adam to be his food, Gen. i. 29., like as they are given unto Noah?

XLVIII. —How is this first chapter of Genesis to be reconciled with the other Scriptures, viz. with Job, Proverbs, Psalms, and Wisdom?

XLIX. —Wherefore is there no mention made of the meteors, but only of this mist? Gen. 1. and ii.

L. —How can the waters above the firmament be the clouds, since necessarily they must have either fallen down in drops of rain or hail, by reason of the cold region of the air, and the efficacy of the moon: or at least they must have remained there congealed?

LI. —Since the earth was everywhere full of waters, had then the sun at that time no efficaciousness to make dry, and to draw up the waters, like as it hath now?

LII. —How could the herbs and trees then live; because now without water, all these things must presently die?

LIII. —Wherefore is there no mention of the place, towards which the river Euphrates doth flow?

LIV. —Where was Adam ere he was introduced into the garden of Eden? If this garden be the very Paradise, how could the serpent and the devil enter into it?

LV. —What is this to say, that after this word, *not good*, followeth immediately the creation of the beasts out of *Haadamah*, and that these were brought before man? Had Adam looked after the beasts? Because these followeth immediately, they are brought before him, and this word *Esen Kenegdo*, (a help meet over against him,) twice becomes repeated. Whence was Adam in want of a help meet? And what is this emphatical word *Kenegdo*, to show us? Had Adam minded the bestial lust and multiplication?

LVI. —Wherefore did Adam and Eva cover *their privy parts*, having sinned by their *mouth?*

LVII. —Was Eva already within Adam, when the commandment was given unto him?

LVIII. —What manner of form would Adam have retained, if he had not eaten of the forbidden fruit?

LIX. —How could Eva sin, the commandment being given before she was?

LX. —What is this to say, Gen. iii., They could hear the voice of God, walking in the garden, and that in the cool of the day? What is the cool or cooling? What anger was there kindled, that it must be cooled?

LXI. —How was the human nature in Adam become a whore? And how was he become great with child? And with what? Who was his midwife, to bring forth this birth? Which would have been the best for Adam, to behold the beasts, or to withdraw his eyes from them? Was this a temptation to him or not? What were these for names which Adam gave them? What signifieth this giving of names, powers, or puissances?

LXII. —What was this for an help meet, which Adam looked for? And what did cause him to look for it?

LXIII. —How many degrees hath his fall? How is he successively fallen deeper and deeper from one degree into another? And how is he now to return again?

LXIV. —Would God have had Adam be advanced unto greater glory, then why could he not hold out his proving? How long time was Adam proved, was it not forty days? Were the angels tried also?

LXV. —What was that drink sucked in by *Haadamah*, that made it lust for the mist from *Haaretz?* How is *Haaretz* become waterish, which before could be and consist without rain? How came the mist into it? How came the mist out of *Haaretz* into *Haadamah*, and so further into Adam? Why is it thereafter called *Tardemah*, a deep sleep, or grossness? What is *dam*, or blood? How came the grossness in this spirit, that now raiseth up the life in men?

LXVI. —How would it have been, if Adam had holden out his trying, as the good angels did, who are not fallen? And how will it be, if man yet now hold out his trial?

LXVII. —After how many manners may this first and second chapter be explicated?

LXVIII. —By how many vails or coverings is every word covered, all which first must be rent, or taken away, ere we can behold the true signature of it? How far is the knowledge of the Hebrew language able to help us thereto? How far doth this language reach? And when ceaseth the understanding which may be given by it unto us?

LXIX. —What difference is there between the sensual, intellectual, and magical understanding of the words?

LXX. —By what kind of languages, and from what sort of men, may we now, at this present age, be understood? How far reacheth our common language by its expressions, and whereto may it not reach?

LXXI. —What is that *sensibility* beyond all languages, whereby the fellow sensibility alone is able or sufficient, without any speech, to communicate our understanding unto another?

LXXII. —Of what use are the outward letters? How much of everything can we declare or utter by our speaking thereof?

LXXIII. —How may we reconcile all the different interpretations, or how may we bring them into one only understanding and harmony?

LXXIV. —How may we find out the very ground of contrariety in every disharmony? And how may we separate it, to bring that which is good into the harmony again?

LXXV. —What light and opening doth there arise out of the concordance of all the harmonies? Causeth there the multiplicity any hindrance, or is it profitable?

LXXVI. —What is this that causeth the disharmony, and the contrary senses in the intellectual life? How may the multiplicity of the concording harmonies bring again into concordance that which is not concording?

LXXVII. —How may we find inwardly, by waiting, the divine power of the harmony of all harmonies drawing nigh to us, which openeth more in one moment, than all the studies and labours ever might reach to, though they were employed for the life-time of a thousand men?

LXXVIII. —May there any other way be found, except denying every lust and desire, whereby man is to be brought into this light, and fixed in it, either in this lifetime or after it?

LXXIX. —Would it be ill done, if one should forsake all the curiosity that is in desiring after knowledge in this life? And if he should only be careful for the renewing of his heart, by pawing willingly through sufferings and purifications; till the time of God's mercy might appear, which is alone able to help him after all his waiting and striving? Wherein would be the inconvenience of this?

LXXX. —Are the fig leaves able to cover the corrupt and fallen reason, and the shame of disobedience, and of the looking and longing, which is for any other thing but only for God?

LXXXI. —Could the great gifts, given unto Lucifer, preserve him & true humility, wherein only everlasting happiness doth consist?

LXXXII. —Shall not the pure *spirit* after death become troubled by these things, whereinto he is entered here, and become entangled therein with his lust? Shall not the *soul* after death, if not purified, and having not killed all its lusts and desires, experience this self-same thing, which Adam experienced in the tempting garden? Shall not the soul fall into great sufferings by reason of its unwillingness, If it hath not a fixed ground to sink down willingly into death?

LXXXIII. —What is the Cherubimical sword, which is to cut off all our own reasoning and ownhood?

LXXXIV. —How may we come again from all the things of our own into nothingness? From ownhood into universality? From the figure into power? From the separateness of the tinctures into the one element? From materiality into the divine transfiguration? From difference into unity? From our own will, or unwillingness, into the one will? From grossness into subtlety and divine corporality?

LXXXV. —How may we distinguish that which is divine in us, from that which is earthly? That which is of the human reason from that which is of the divine power? That which is natural from that which is supernatural? That which is gift, only given us by mercy, from that which is a gift, not only given unto us, but also by death and regeneration fixed and made our own, for to abide ours for evermore?

LXXXVI. —What are those gifts which are only transitory, or transmigrating, and must become tried again and again? And what are these gifts which are abiding in us for evermore, and which by the strife and in the strife, and in all trials whatever, are fixed and abiding?

LXXXVII. —Whither come or go those persons that in the temptation held not fast on the power of Jesus, but make themselves to be entangled by the same source or ground, whereby the devil, by reason of his false heart, was catched?

LXXXVIII. —May this tempting source effect anything, or be of any effort to those who are of a pure heart and integrity of conscience?

LXXXIX. —How may those, who have received the pure sap out of the tree of life, abide conquering all the venom of temptations, and remain immutable as the gold in the fire?

XC. —Is this tempting source bad to them who shall have received power from the tree of life? or must it be only subservient to their greater glory, and clearer manifestation of the Divine Lights-power which is in them?

XCI. —Could not Adam have eaten also of the tempting tree without any danger, if he had but had power first out of the tree of life? and how more glorious would he have become thereby?

XCII. —Can the tempting tree cause any hurt or annoy to the man that hath a perfect power of Jesus Christ wherewith to overcome? or must it not rather be only subservient to him for a greater glory?

XCIII. —Did not God shut up Paradise, and all the glory thereof, for this same end, that so Adam might not become tempted yet stronger, if he were to be here more glorious?

XCIV. —Was it not God's great mercy and pity, that he did set man, who was not found faithful in the least things, on a way of *humility*, for to learn thereby obedience, that so he might help him up and restore him; there having been otherways no possibility for it, if a higher power or station here were given unto him?

XCV. —Would not Adam's fall have been deeper than the fall of the devils, if the day were not become cooled by God's mercy, that so Adam could hear his voice?

XCVI. —Wherefore is now Adam settled in this life under lowlinesss, under the commandments, and under the burden and cross of Christ? Is not for this one only end all his might taken away from him, that he may not fly *on high* like Lucifer? And is it not then only God's mercy to give no knife to his hand whereby he would kill himself?

XCVII. —When man in his desire putteth to wrong use that might which is yet left to him, and when he stealeth the things that are God's, and abuseth them, and cometh so into perdition or undoing, to whose charge is his undoing to be laid?

XCVIII. —After what manner must we now be tried and prepared, that we may use our gifts, in all purity, to our happiness; humbling ourselves, and not attempting to fly on high by them?

XCIX. —Was not this the devil's fall, that he would be like as *God?* And doth not the man this same thing yet also? Hath he who is the tree of life taught us so to do? Hath he not appropriated all things to their very ground, and hath he not himself denied all things, yea, even the things which he himself had right and access to? Why should not we then hearken unto him, more than to our own lost?

C.—After what manner must we now, by continual exercising and striving, set ourselves against our nature, and all the lusts thereof, and so continue or go on, till we may get victory from the power of the tree of life, such a grace, which by God's mercy is to abide in us substantially, and which either in or after this life, is to keep us in all our trials, and to protect us and preserve us from the venom and attracting power of perdition, and which is to give us strength or power to reign over it, according to that degree by which temptation or trial will fall upon us? Which trial surely will come upon us, because all whatsoever shall abide in God eternally, must pass through trials, either in this life's time or after it. But in this life will it be the better and more easy, and after it will it be infinitely more hard and grievous.

To him that understandeth aright, and findeth in himself these queries, not only this first and second chapter of Genesis, but also the whole Scripture, and whole nature will be opened, and he shall not want to seek anything without himself in any book or any man." Such the Queries.

We give the answer to the first of these Queries, viz. :—"This name, *Elohim*, is of all the Divine names alone made use of in the Cosmopœia, or Genesis of the World, by Moses, as expressing in it a sort of plurality or fecundity : and by it is to be understood, as the eastern sages declare, the glorious creator or executor, as containing in himself ideally the world to be created; or, as God one and many, or one and all,—with regard to that divine omniform power, which is one and the same in all the manifold productions thereof. And this therefore being always expressed in the plural number, is yet constructed with a verb singular, to signify the Unity both in God and Nature, under all the multifarious effects and phenomena ; and that as all things do orderly spring up from a centre into multiplicity, by the going forth of *Elohim* into manifestation, so likewise all things are by him to be reduced through the variety back into an Unity. But when the heavens and the earth were perfected in the full harmony of all beings, and *Elohim* had on the seventh day, finished all his work, as the executor of the incomprehensible substance or abyssal ineffable Deity, by blessing and sanctifying the day of his rest; then was the great and venerable Name, which is beyond all expression, as peculiarly respecting the Divine essence, or essence of essences, added to that of *Elohim*. And thereupon mention it made of the *generations* both of heaven and earth, as immediately succeeding their creation. Which is well to be observed."

The answer to the second Query runs thus :— "The creation of the earth is excellently represented to us as prior to that of the sun, that we might not be ignorant that the light which is concentrated in the sun, is the very light which was before concentrated in the earth: and that there must have been a certain igneous and luminous substance in the earth, from the impregnation of the spirit of Elohim irradiating those waters wherein it lay immersed for some time; which substance was perfectly of a solar nature...."

Selection Twelve.

[Lee on the Contemplative Way]

[This is prefaced by two pieces by Walton. The essay was originally broken up into two parts, with a comment by Walton before each part. These two parts have been put together before Lee's —Ed.]

ANNOTATION.—The following extract from a letter of Dr. F. Lee, found among Law's papers, touching some of the objections made against the Contemplative Way, and representing the true nature of that way, may be acceptable to many readers of this treatise:—[...]

The reader has already had an opportunity of perusing some of the effusions of this highly gifted soul, and brilliant devout genius, Lee. Commencing with the faithful practice of the pure Anglican church piety, as exhibited in her Order of Common Prayer, which he carried to its highest proficiency; and thence ascending, through the gate of a sensible regeneration, the mystic ladder of the progressive births and growths of the divine life—(by the use of true and assured means, discovered by him in the mystical spiritual writers, and consisting equally in a daily dying to self, and an actual rising on the wings of importunate faith and prayer, watchfulness and recollection,)—Lee presents a fine example of an ingenious high cultivation of the spiritual life, having a constant reference to, and virtual experience of, the process of Christ : though the unmortified propounders of a merely elementary Christianity vainly imagine, that in the more advanced or mystical stages of christian experience, (where the crucifixion of all self is to be carried on by the incentration of the spirit of humility,) the patient (yet active) subjects of this state, lose sight of Christ as their mediator and high priest before God. This point was particularly referred to by Lee, in his letter on " Passive Contemplation," inserted p. 91 ; the conclusion of which, on account of its relation to the subject of our present observations, we purpose now to present to the reader, and should an opportunity occur to insert also some further additional illustrations of the author's pious erudition, mental power, and poetic talent. From which (awaiting the publication of his MSS.) the reader will

[After a lapse of near twelve months, the printing hereof renewed, Feb. 1851.]

doubtless feel still farther induced to agree with the learned Ockley respecting the genius of Lee, as being the grand eagle spirit in evangelical matters of his age (immediately preceding and introductory to that of Law); philosophically searching into and proving all pretenders to Divine illumination, and allowing none, however seemingly recondite, a place in the category of theological *savans*, unless his principles and daily practice were characterised by the ancient spirit of devotion, and that holy mortification, humility, and self-denial, which are implied in it. Being a first-rate Arabic scholar, he made great researches into the religious Christian literature existing in that ancient language, and wrote translations of several very interesting pieces, which are now in the possession of the writer, some of them being copied in the handwriting of Mr. Law : (when convenient, a list of his MSS. will be herein inserted.) The continuation from p. 173 of the piece on "Passive Contemplation" then runs thus:—

"Without apologising for myself. I am immediately carried to consider the great point of Passive Contemplation, wherein I find that you have been much shocked by some considerable objections from a great and active genius. You shall hear, then, my free sentiments upon the matter; and after such a long term of silence, it may be concluded that they are my fixed thoughts, and not the hasty eruptions of any natural or preternatural fire in my spirit.

It must needs be confessed, that several of the admirers and followers of the Passive State do seem to show too little a respect for the sacred Scriptures, and that some of them do even very slightly pass over the mystery of salvation by the death of Christ, and do seek to find God without and above the blessed humanity of our dear Mediator; which is the ladder of Jacob, whereby the angels of God and all the Divine influences do descend from heaven to earth, and re-ascend from earth to heaven. But after I had discoursed with Mr. Coester, and had heard him fully, I found that it was the unbounded activity of his genius that had transported him too far; and that it was hardly possible for any one (how acute soever) to reach the punctum of the question, without having first learnt to moderate the active faculties or powers or the soul, or without having had (at least) some lesser experiences concerning this subject matter.

The *way* of Contemplation ought in the first place to be understood; and this is to be learned either from the Philosophers, or else from the holy Scriptures and the Christian Mystics. The Philosophical Contemplation is then evidently misunderstood, when the exercise of it is condemned in those who were never acquainted with the history of the Gospel, or convinced of its truth: for certainly it can be no fault in any one who never heard of Jesus Christ, (or, which is all one, could never be satisfied, after his best and sincerest endeavours made for that purpose,) to go as directly as he can to God, in the deepest self-abasement, and the most perfect surrender of his will into the hands of the omnipotent Creator and Father. And no less evidently is it so, when the exercise of holy Contemplation is censured in such who are both acquainted with and convinced of the truth of the history of the Gospel: for as much as every Christian contemplatist, that is truly such, doth not ascend in his spirit above Christ, or put himself anywise without Christ; but in the very exercise of Contemplation, doth most truly and properly sink himself down into the heart of Christ, and even more truly and properly than he could possibly have done it by all the meditations and reflections imaginable upon the life and sufferings of Christ. This, every one that hath had any experience thereof must needs declare. These meditations indeed, and reflections of the soul, are not to be neglected, for they are most useful and beneficial in their order: and by these when rightly pursued we may arrive to Contemplation; and thereby lodge ourselves as in the bosom of this our Beloved, in contemplating whose beauty we can never be weary, of the beauty of Him in whom all the treasures and beautiful forms of the Deity are laid up, which are never to be manifested but to the single and contemplative eye. The devout and active contemplation of what Christ both did and suffered for us, will naturally lead us into that divine and Passive Contemplation which transcends all meditation and self-action whatever, and which he by the merits of his precious death and sufferings hath purchased for us. It will bring us successively into that divine peace, which passeth all understanding and ratiocination: it will not cease to carry us on, beyond all that the activity of our intellectual abilities is able to arrive to, or apprehend: and then it will suffer us gently to fall as asleep in his dear arms, and to cease from every motion of our own spirit, that so we may be perfectly passive to all the motions and inactions of that blessed Spirit which through his merits is given unto us; and which, in the highest degree, is given to us when we are denudated of all acts of our own. And being so under the conduct of this Spirit, we do not then lie exposed to the subtlety of malicious spirits transforming themselves, but are quite delivered from them. None of the powers of darkness are able to hurt or supplant a soul that continues in this passive and silent state: for it is therein actually surrendered up into the hands of the Father of our Lord Jesus Christ; and, under that consideration too, it is truly animated by the Holy Ghost, (no less than the body by it,) and is made indeed a partaker of the Divine nature in Christ. And Christ, indeed, is the true and proper way of Contemplation, (I say to us Christians,) and I come not to the Father but by him: for it is the Son that cometh to the Father, and they that follow the Son must come to God in like manner as he cometh; that they may even, in a degree, behold his face, and, beholding it, be irradiated by the light of his countenance, lifted up and reflected upon them. But he that teacheth me to come to the Father, hath taught me not only to see the Father in him, (as if that alone were permitted,) but also to see and contemplate him *in the Father*.

The six last chapters of Cardinal Cusanus in his manual *Of the Vision of God, by the means of simple abstraction*, (which I have only seen in the English translation of it,) lay this down *ex professo*. The book of *the Idiot* doth the same: and many others of the best and wisest of the Mystics will be found perfectly to agree in this point, when they are thoroughly examined into. Yea, I believe I am able to shew even from Dr. Molinos himself, that there is no other way to the quiet of the soul in God, but through Christ; and that in the very laying aside of all sensible images, he is not laid aside, but may then most truly be beheld in the Father. Nor can I think anything more absurd, or self-contradicting, than that he should write a Book purposely for *Daily Communion*, and yet not exalt highly the merits of the death of Christ; or that he should undertake to prescribe this as a proper mean for the preservation of this internal quiet, unless that he did believe that this quiet of the recollected soul in God, was both to be acquired and preserved by an union to the humanity of the blessed Jesus, as well as by a communion thence arising of the Divine Word. This must have been the ground of his writing that little treatise; which is not otherwise considerable in itself, and will sufficiently vindicate him from the charge of Deism. And I am certain that the French lady, Madame Guyon, is not so great an heretic in this matter, as the cabal in France would make her. Her *Moyen Court*, which was burnt at Paris, has many express passages, some of them very excellent, that do set forth Christ as the *way:* and in the article which speaks of the mysteries of redemption, she briefly and fully shews, how her method of simple prayer, or of passive Contemplation, doth more effectually honour them than any other method which is more compounded and active; and how it imprinteth on us the very stigma of our Lord Jesus, so that we are truly said hereby to *bear his marks*. The method of the Jesuits has been always against this, for which they press the very same argument as our friend doth; preferring therefore meditation in their *Spiritual Exercises*, that they may not put themselves out of the protection of Christ by too much abstractedness and silent recollection: and upon this score they made in the last age such a violent opposition against Father *Austin Baker*, and against Dame *Gertrude More:* whose reasons, which they bring in vindication of their simple and plain way, are not perhaps unworthy of consideration. The articles of Issy, which are drawn up by the present Bishop of Meaux against the little book of that (give me leave to call her so) great woman just mentioned, do run in their beaten track, and fall into the same mistake with them. I have written some reflections upon them, and have in some measure laid open the fallacy of that manner of proceeding, by taking them into pieces, and reducing them into mere propositions. These I have some thoughts of printing with the discourse itself to which they belong, and which I have had by me a pretty long while translated, but is now providentially called for after I had laid it aside. This hath given me a surprising satisfaction as to the universality of that method, which is so subtlely attacked; and no less therefore as to the security and facility of it, the whole interior process being made hereby direct and linear: and it hath laid open a field, which others may prosecute with good success.

Many notwithstanding must be alarmed at it: but in the end you will see that *truth* shall be justified of her children. And after all the janglings that are in the world, there will be found no other way to arrive to the *truth* but this. It is Contemplation and Abstraction that must lead us through the veil into the Sanctum Sanctorum, where the originals of truth are preserved, even in that ark of the Divine presence, which is Christ, the Alpha and the Omega of every creature. And it is through him that we can come with boldness, (being first purified by the blood of sprinkling, which cleanseth us from every pollution of the flesh through faith.) to the throne of Grace, which is the everlasting mercy-seat in the third heavens, and inmost sanctuary, where this great High Priest ministreth continually, and presenteth such pure Contemplative souls as do ascend hither upon the wings of the Divine eagle, to his God and their God. He is the way, and he is the truth of contemplation : though we may not be always reflecting upon the way, while we are in it; nor reasoning about the truth, while we possess it, if we are so happy. And Christ being the truth of Contemplation, or that Truth which the contemplator beholds, and beholding possesses,— every one in such a state, or frame, is necessarily under the protection of the truth, and so by consequent, can be in no danger of falling into errors, or of being blinded by delusions; because the truth itself *dwelleth in him*, and he *dwelleth in the truth*, being possessed by it in silence and passiveness of spirit, and *walketh in the truth*, then when he putteth forth what he hath learnt in this internal silence as under this divine possession by the *word of truth*, by passing from rest into action, and so bringing forth all the fruits and powers of the Holy Ghost, in the life of the blessed Jesus, both active and passive; and the truth shall be with him *for ever*, as an inward principle of life, and of the resurrection from the dead. He is now in the truth, and the truth is in him; he is vitally united with the truth, and of this union (as it is made truly out of time,) there can never be a dissolution: so that all the subtle and intriguing spirits of darkness are hereby effectually shut out, and they have no power to deceive, because when they come they find nothing of their own to mix with; for as much as the creature being silenced, God alone in Christ speaketh, moveth, and doeth. And I think that this is a state both warrantable, and Christian, and what everyone would do well to press after; there being few incapable of it, and none but may be made capable of it. Before we arrive to it, we are not yet in the Truth, but are only advancing toward it; neither is the truth (properly speaking) in us, but instead thereof, there is a shadow only, or image of the truth, which being followed, will lead us into that of which it is a shadow and an image, as we shall silently introvert our souls into the fountain of the Divine Being. And then may we be said to worship God in truth. The more spiritual, and the more perfect our worship of God in Christ is, it must of necessity be so much the more near to this state of internal silence and rest: that so Christ our Lord in like manner as in the Heavens, may in us also come to enter into his rest, and to sit down in the soul as" [break in the footnote] "——on his throne. He hereby becomes our everlasting priest and king as well as a prophet, to reveal unto us the whole will of God, and the length and depth and breadth of his love to us wards. He offers up in us *pure incense*, in which there is nothing of man's composition: and he commands in us both as the King of Righteousness and also as the Prince of Peace, with an absolute sceptre, and without dividing his dominion to any. All this is nothing but the natural result of that Passive Contemplation which I am contending for, as you will easily find by a little application; because that Christ himself, as he is the union of God and man, is both the *way* and the *truth* of it.

Moreover, as he is the way and truth, so also the *life* of pure Contemplation, and the soul that shall arrive to it, may then truly indeed cry out, it is no longer I that live, but Christ that liveth in me. For the soul being in it doth not properly live its own life: it doth not reason; but he who is the eternal reason reasoneth in the soul, or giveth himself, and in himself all things to be seen. It doth not will; but he who came into the world to do the will of the Father, is come into the soul to do his will, and he alone willeth there, in such a manner as the will of the Father, of

Christ, and of the soul are all three but one will: it doth not remember, for all old things are passed away, and is as redeemed (for that season) out of the earth and temporal nature; only the spirit of Christ bringeth to remembrance whatever pleaseth him: it imagineth not, being lifted out of and above all images, by being brought into the possession of the truth itself; but the truth imageth itself upon the soul, in which all the ideas of the archetypal and angelical worlds are contained, and will spring forth; and so this divine imagination of the truth maketh all things new in the soul, as likewise in all nature internal and external, and is the proper medium or instrument of the new creation, and of the new Jerusalem descending out of heaven: it doth not perceive, being out of the bodily senses, ravished into a state that is altogether supersensual, which no eye hath seen, neither can tongue express; but the body of Christ being the body of his whole church, and no less of every particular member, the soul, after its purification, is taken into the body of Christ, and in that it seeth, heareth &c. the heavenly objects, sounds &c. by a free and passive reception of the same into the mind, which is become the *mind of Christ*. But till souls be purified from the mortal body by the prayer of simple abstraction, there can be no such free and pure reception of the divine objects, lights, voices, tastes &c.; but there must be some impurity and mixture still adhering to them, which will remain so long as any activity of their own remains, or so long as they are not perfectly separated from the body of sin, in the exercise of Contemplation, and so united to the body of righteousness, which is Christ. So that herein is the greatest security; and the life of Contemplation is a most strong fortress, against which none of the gates of hell shall be able to prevail, forasmuch as it is the very life of Christ in the soul. He who is arrived to the blessed state puts forth no acts of his life, but is led and acted wholly (yet freely) by the divine life in him: he has no ratiocination, volition, memory, imagination, or sensation which he can call his own; but all is surrendered up, and all proceeds again from a new spring of life; which is not his but Christ's. And in this new life, which can never perfectly be attained without Contemplation, is the will of our God to be done by us upon earth, as it is done by the angels in heaven, who though they are continually contemplating his face, yet are also always ready to be sent forth as ministering spirits from him, to execute all his commands. Hereby likewise we feed upon the hidden manna, we sup with Christ and Christ with us; the door being opened to Him by naked faith, in a total abstraction from the flesh, and the senses thereof. So that there is an end of iniquity and transgression, and we are cleansed from all sin by the blood of the Lamb, to walk with him in white. And then following him in white we are made priests with him, and intercessors for others, that they likewise may obtain mercy and be purified from every evil that so easily besets them, being brought into the same state of holy contemplation, and called up again into their primitive inheritance of the divine light. Thus we come to live as translated out of the wilderness of this wicked world, and are secured against all temptations, having our conversation in heaven, where the malice of the evil one (τῦ πουνεχ) cannot reach us: and the kingdom of God is made manifest in our souls, and his power is revealed, and his glory is spread forth to the utter confusion of the creature; and then is that new name given upon the white stone, whereby the name of our Heavenly Father is no less hallowed in the earth than in the heaven. For it is the very name of this our Heavenly Father (whom we can now most truly call so) written, and sealed, upon us invisibly and visibly. And having once obtained this name, there is nothing which we shall ask in it either for ourselves or for others, but it shall be perfectly and fully answered: and we shall not pray afterwards in vain, any one petition of that prayer which Christ has taught us, but shall see the complete fulfilling of the same both in ourselves, and in all them that we pray for and with. Thus it appears that the life of Contemplation is the life of Christ in the soul, the life of God in man, and the wonderful gate of the Holy Ghost, and the powers thereof: and that it is not only warrantable, but laudable to wrestle against the senses, and even against all the imaginations and thoughts of our own hearts, by means of the highest and most perfect abstraction; and to press after the mark of this life, to believe and pray for it, to retire and wait much in the pretence of God, and so by ceasing from all operations of our own, and all self-willings, though never so apparently good, to stand still and see what Christ, our life, will do for us, and in us, so soon as we shall hereby have given up ourselves to his sole and immediate conduct. And if this be unchristian, I know not what is Christian; it is the way that I desire to be found in, and the truth which I court, and the life which will not make me ashamed before the face of my righteous Judge.

If now I have cleared this point to you, or am made rather an instrument to direct you to Him who alone is able to clear it, and to clear it fully, I shall heartily rejoice in *Him*; and you will have cause to say that. Great is the truth: but I have made use only of one topic, whereas I could have made use of many others. However it is that which I take to be the most considerable, as it was also the first which came to my mind; there being nothing more strongly imprinted in it than this axiom of my blessed Lord, *I am the way, the truth, and the life;* or than this dear salutation from his adorable mouth, 'I will be thy way, thy truth, and thy life:' and this is so far from being exhausted by what I have said upon it, as I doubt not but you will be able to say much more, and to draw thence beside many corollories both delightful and profitable in the Christian race. As for other arguments it would be quite unnecessary to heap them together, if this one be able to bear the shock: and if this will not, a multitude will not help, or help but little. I find arguments not a few both in the Gospels and in the Epistles, that do establish the doctrine I have been pleading for, and serve to remove that grand objection of our friend (and with it all other objections too), and such as do it unanswerably, if I understand them: which you also of yourself will easily find out by the key that has here been given. But not only the New Testament, but also the Law, the Psalms, and the Prophets will be found after a just inquiry to patronise and recommend to us the state of Silent Abstraction, and to lead us in the noble path of Contemplation, after Enoch, Moses, Elias, David, and other great worthies. What is contained under the institution of sacrifices, and the whole Levitical Law, hath all a reference to this matter, either near or more remote: the tabernacle and the temple are never to be understood without it; the office of the high priest will be still little better than a riddle, even after all the history which we have of his antitype; and the establishment of the Colleges of the Prophets will be most absurd and unaccountable. The truth of all is within the veil: and there is no passing there but by the contemplative soul; and none can assist the soul in breaking through the veil, by the deepest abnegation of her own power and the most profound exercise of Contemplation and silent watchfulness, but Christ alone. Therefore as Christ is the fulfilling of the Law and of the Prophets, so also is Contemplation the key which leads us into their inward cabinets, and the mirror in which we may behold all their wonders.

But notwithstanding all this it must be confessed, that the too early affecting and endeavouring after this state may be highly dangerous to many souls: for that not a few would be glad to be at the end of the journey, before they have gone perhaps two or three fair steps in it. And souls that come to it unprepared do very often overset themselves, and make shipwreck of the death of Christ, and of the resurrection from the dead; putting themselves out of his protection, as not being led by his Spirit, but by their own. Wherefore if we have a longing to enter into this most excellent path, we must not fail to pray the Father assiduously and confidently that he would give us his Holy Spirit that may purify us in spirit, soul and body, that so we may be fit to walk therein. And especially ought we never to let go out of our mind the word of our Lord, that it is the *pure in heart* that shall contemplate God; and therefore no other can contemplate him. For the blessing has a regard both to this life and to the next; as also the rest of the blessings. We are taught from the mount that *purity of heart* is necessary to the attainment of the vision of God, in this blessed state of the kingdom of heaven upon earth, this silent path of peace and joy inexpressible: and without *this purity* all Contemplation that can be pretended to, how glittering soever it may appear to some, is nothing but mere rantism and madness. Wherefore, Dear Sir, I do not fear but you will *seek after holiness*, and wait at wisdom's gates, and be obedient to *her discipline*, that after a due term of days you may be admitted into her palace, and advanced to this state; which is so very lovely and desirable, as every hour (if your heart be struck, as I believe it is) will appear a year until you can attain. So it did to the ancient hermits, and to the holy fathers (whose names they that are most against us have so due a reverence for), who never thought that they could do or suffer enough, that they might be made partakers of this heavenly gift, which was very far from being a relict of Paganism in them, as is pretended; unless the belief of a Deity may be called so too. And supposing that it were so, it must have introduced of necessity whole Paganism again; forasmuch as they did still represent this state as a state of communion betwixt the Divine Word and the soul, which must have been (upon that supposition) nothing else but a state of communion with impure demons and the malicious spirit of darkness, presenting themselves to them in the name of Christ, the heavenly Word. The consequences whereof I leave you to consider, being too many for me to mention. So that these holy men did not retain this as it was part of the Ethnic religion, but only as it was a true (and precious) relict of the *patriarchal* religion which the Ethnics had transferred and corrupted; and they therefore did restore and bring back with them according to the primitive design, and according also to the clearer Light which was now revealed to them in the race of Jesus Christ, manifested in the truth.

There is a book of Benedictus Angius which for the settling you fully as to this matter deserves to be recommended to your perusal, if you can procure it in either Latin or English, which bears for title *De Triplici Voluntate Dei;* whose two first parts do make in English *The Rule of Perfection*, and the third *The Bright Star*. I have found much benefit by it; but the last part in the English wants of that union which is found in that of the two former. The sum of all is contained in the exercise of the *Divine Will*.

Now the activity of a soul that is arrived to this state, will not be less, but greater than it was before; it will be more central and deeper but not so sensible and outward. For by being made passive to the divine energy, it loses nothing of those forces which it had in its first creation, or constitution, but being renewed it becomes by many degrees, more quick, powerful, and penetrating than it was before. Of which I have several special observations to make; but am prevented by the female Qutetist of France [Madame Guyon], who has said enough upon this matter: I think better cannot be said.

As for the author of the *Parrhasiana* your remarks I find to be very solid, and his treatment of Mr. Poiret very disingenuous and *à la cavaliere*. If the *Divine Economy* of this learned man be but one piece of enthusiasm from one end to the other, they that know Mr. Clerc will be apt to say, from the specimens that he has hitherto given of his skill, that he is not able with all his reason to do anything upon the subjects there treated of that shall agree better with good sense, or with itself. And some will conclude, who have taken the pains to examine but a little, that notwithstanding all his self confidence, he will find it a hard matter to write a book upon any subject whatever but a tenth part so large, that shall not have quite as many enthusiasms, and ten times the inconsistencies.

Sir, what I have written to you, you may communicate as you please, but with all due caution; and in what else I can further serve you, you may assuredly command-Your most affectionate servant in Christ.—F. Lee. Hogsden (Hoxton), August 9th. 1700. I have desired Mr. Blundell to do me justice to my friends, and the friends of truth."

Selection Thirteen.

[Two Commemorations and Three Prayers by Lee].

We append, as a close to this Note, the following prayers and devotional commemorations, having regard to the author's friends Hickes and Nelson: the deep, fervent, orthodox piety, natural tone, and classical beauty of which compositions, may not be deemed unworthy of the compilers of our beautiful Church Service, any more than of the author of the "Feasts and Fasts" or of "Hickes's Devotions," or of "Hickes's Kempis," or "Nelson's Christian Exercise," &c. And thus will conclude our annotatory elucidations of the profandity and versatility of pious erudition of the highly gifted Lee who was, manifestly, in the generation next preceding Law, one of the great 'preparers of the way' for the renovation of the Gospel spirit, and *evangelical prophet* proclaimers of the latter days' glory under the still light of theosophical truth; as described in some of its experimental diversities in the above Preface to Lead and the accompanying poems, and generally hinted at throughout the present Treatise.—The first of these papers being a commemoration of Nelson, commences and proceeds thus:—

GAM-ZO!—A Commemoration. Jan 16, R. N., of blessed memory, my familiar friend and brother. The righteous shall be had in everlasting remembrance. Psalms: xli. xlii. cxii. cxvi. Lessons: Wisdom, iv. 10.—to v. 17. John, v. 29, 30.

O ye spirits and souls of the righteous, bless ye the Lord. Praise him and magnify him for ever. Praise him, O my soul, with these, and magnify him for *ever and ever.*

O my brother * * * bless thou the Lord, praise him and magnify him for ever. Yea, magnify him, O * * * for *ever and ever.* Halleluiah!

Holy! holy! holy! Lord God Almighty, who wast, and art, and art to come! glory be to thee in all thy saints: and praise be given to thee by all the souls redeemed from the earth, whom thou hast called up into the courts of the heavenly sanctuary. But more especially let glory and praise be given unto thy name in and by thy servant our dear brother R. (surnamed after the flesh, N.), whom thou didst here adorn with thy grace in an eminent manner, and whom thou hast now called hence, that where his heart was, there he now also may be. Thy will, O Father, is done in him: and because his soul pleased thee, therefore didst thou remove him in peace from the evil to come, and hast glorified thy name both in his life and in his death, which is precious in thy sight, and in the sight of thy angels.

Thou gavest him unto me for a friend, and for a companion in my pilgrimage: and my soul cleaved unto him, because I found thine image in him, and rejoiced in it. Thou gavest, and thou hast taken: and blessed be thy name both in him and in me, even in thy poor servant left behind, and unworthy of the least of all thy benefits, and therefore unworthy of such a friend.

And now that thou hast taken him, O Lord; and having loosened the bands of the vile and corruptible body, which weighed down the soul which was musing upon thee, and the joy of thy presence, hast set him at liberty, to fly with the wings of the dove to the place where thine honour resteth; I render thee most humble and hearty thanks for the riches of thy grace conferred on this thy servant, in the days of his flesh, and for all the consolations which thou hast at any time given me through his means. All love, all glory, be to thee, in whom our brotherly friendship was founded, and in whom it hath been carried on from the beginning, and never therefore to to be dissolved. Blessed be the fountain of love eternal: blessed by us for ever, world without end.

I praise thee, I bless thee, I magnify thee, for all the good which thou hast done through this thy chosen servant and instrument, and the last victory wherewith thou hast crowned him. All love, all glory be to thee!

And I admire the wisdom of thy providence, in separating him after such a peculiar manner as thou didst, in honouring him with the true honour which cometh from thee, and in richly qualifying him for that lot and post to which thou hadst ordained him.

And as I render thee adoration and praise for thy many and great benefits conveyed through this vessel of thy grace elect and precious, unto multitudes of all ranks in this kingdom, and elsewhere: so I meekly beseech thee, that all they who have received the same, or have been partakers of thy mercy thus communicated by him, may be assisted through thy Spirit, duly and rightly to honour thee for these thy gifts, and to follow the steps of thy dear Son in all virtuous and Godly living; so as he, together with us, may have joy in thee, beholding the fruits of his labours, and may perceive the increase thereof rise up even to an hundred-fold.

Now forasmuch as there is no multiplication, either in nature or grace, without a previous mortification and solution, or without the grain that is sown do first die, I acknowledge it to be thy goodness, O Lord, that thou madest him pass through the gate of mortification, melting down as it were the will, by a radical solution thereof, and quickening and resuscitating him by the light of thy presence.

Lord, lift thou up the light of thy countenance upon all faithful souls, and more particularly upon all who have been confessors amongst us for truth and righteousness, especially this our dear brother, thy servant and the delight of my soul, and let the cry both of him and of all the other souls lying under the heavenly altar with the seal of faith, together with the prayers of all the dead Israelites, from the faithful Abraham down to this day, come up before thee and be accepted; that thy long expected kingdom may come speedily, and that thy glory may dwell upon the earth, and both mercy and truth may here meet together, while justice and peace do kiss each other, according to the heavenly patterns.

And in order to this, let a double portion of that Spirit, which lately rested on the head of this thy servant, beloved and faithful, fall now upon some or other, who shall be found fit by thee to succeed him in the same ministration. And do thou prepare and qualify many others also to be herein assistant and minstrtng, that so his righteous soul may rejoice to see thy work go prosperously on, notwithstanding all the rage and malice of evil spirits; may exult in thee his Saviour, beholding the mighty increase of the fruits of his toll and sweat; and that charity again recovering herself, and faith being found, his peace may abound more exceedingly.

Remember, O Lord, yea, remember the days of his sorrow in the flesh, and the temptations wherewith he was tempted, and all the evils which he wrestled against, by confessing thy name, thy great and glorious name: And bearing a noble testimony in a most corrupt generation for the cause of righteousness, and for the glory of thy kingdom upon the earth. And let not the secret mourning of his soul, for the high crimes and sins of this nation, and of all the orders thereof, be forgotten of thee.

But have thou regard to all the supplications and intercessions which he here poured forth in thy Spirit at any time, but more especially in his last hours, for the state of the world and the Church at this day: that so a new generation may rise up, which may declare thy glory and praise; and that thy work, O God, may be now received amongst us, and thy word go forth as in the beginning.

But for as much as the heavens are not pure in thy sight, O Lord, and the very heavenly sanctuary itself had therefore need to be purified with the sprinkling of the most holy blood of our great High Priest himself; and as the very greatest of thy saints thou canst justly charge with folly, while they lived in the mortal body; look thou upon him, even as thou hast done upon them, because his chief delight was towards thee, though he could not serve thee as he would, for the infirmity of his flesh; which was his burden.

And if it be appointed that he should rest yet for a little season, until he be perfected with his fellow-servants and brethren, yet let him be so thoroughly washed in the blood of the Lamb, as to appear in the congregation of thy saints without any spot: and let a white robe be given unto him with the candidates of the first resurrection, that in the beauty of holiness, he may wait in the courts of thy heavenly temple, till the sound of the seventh angel shall awake his dust.

In the mean time, now that he is called to rest, let his works follow him, even all the works which thy good Spirit hath wrought in him: and as with the unrighteous mammon he hath made himself many friends; both of those who went before, and of those who are left behind him, let not only the former be ministering spirits about him, to receive and entertain him in the everlasting habitations by thee prepared; but let also all the rest in their course be gathered unto him, for the continual increase of his joy, and for completing the crown, wherewith he is to be crowned in the day of retribution.

Until then, let thy right hand cover him, and let the light of thy countenance, and thy glory from betwixt the cherubims be lifted up on him; O lift thou up the light of thy countenance upon him, that with the holy patriarchs and apostles, and with all the souls of the righteous in their chambers, he may worship thee according to his heart, even according to thy heart, in all the beauties and splendours of holiness, and may praise thee among the *living*, who art the God not of the dead but of the *living*. It is the living, the living that praise thee; and I know that he liveth, because thou livest in whom his life was hidden, but which shall be manifested in that day before all the world. O that our souls might be bound together in the bundle of life eternal; and that in our lot there be no parting; that so I also with him, and with all the living who live evermore, may praise thee the living God, as I do at this time, in full unity of heart and soul, casting myself before thy footstool, and saying *Holy, Holy, Holy*, etc."

The next paper is thus:—

"For Dr. Hickes.—Whereas our dear father and brother in God,

N. N.—who departed this troublesome life in a good old age, upon the 15th. of December, in 1715, in the communion of the Catholic Church, with the sign and seal of the faith, once delivered by the apostles, in the sure and certain hope of the resurrection of the body, and of the life of the world to come, after a pilgrimage in this valley of mortality of years, and the end of the fourth week of years, wherein he was an eminent sufferer for the sake of righteousness and truth, and an encourager of others not to be ashamed of the doctrine of the cross, or of the truths of God; —according to the accustomed practice of the purest ages of the Church, did communicate in confidence his designs to some, whom he perfectly knew to be agreeing with him herein, that be might, both in the body and out of the body, have the prayers of his true Christian friends offered up in the most precious atonement of the Lamb of God, and in the unity of the one holy catholic Spirit, together with all faithful souls, whether in the flesh or out of the flesh; recommending him in faith to the great High Priest in the Heavenly tabernacle, who maketh intercession both for him, and for us, and for all that look unto him as the way, the truth, and the life."

To which is added —"For Dr. Hickes whilst sick.—O Almighty God and most merciful Father, who art the health of thy servants, and a strong tower in the day of trouble to all that put their trust in thy name, look down now from thy heavenly sanctuary; behold, visit, and relieve thy ancient servant our spiritual superior and father under thee, at this time grieved with sickness, and afflicted with great bodily pain, whose soul is also oppressed with many heavy weights, both public and private, and whose righteous spirit is vexed day by day, with the iniquity of an ungodly and rebellious generation: incline thine ear unto him, and hear all his prayers, and deliver him mightily for thy mercy's sake. O thou that hast upheld him ever since he was born, against the raging of Satan and of the people, on every side, and hast made him valiant in the cause of righteousness, and in the defence of thy truth and honour; quicken him now at last with the abundance of thy grace, and give unto his fainting soul the wings of an eagle, that he may mount up, and his heart and mouth be filled with thy praise. Deliver him, we beseech thee, from all fear of death and of his ghostly enemy; take out the sting of death; repel all the fiery darts of the accuser; pour into his wounds the most precious balsam of life, even of thine own life; be thou his stronghold, whereunto he may in this evil day resort; let him be made strong in thy righteousness, in his infirmity, let the mightiness of thy power appear, to rid and deliver him. O cast him not away in the time of his age, neither forsake thou him now that his strength faileth him; but haste thou to help him, according to thy accustomed goodness and mercy; and put into his hands the banner of salvation, that he may not go hence till he shall have declared the great things that thou but done for him, and shall have shewed thy strength unto this generation, and thy power and the victory of thy truth to all them that are yet for to come; and that when thou tellest, he may readily and cheerfully go forth in the strength of thee his Lord and his redeemer, and being thoroughly purified by these refinings, which thou graciously sendest him here, may be without spot and blemish presented unto thee, through thy Son Jesus Christ our Lord, and his and our only Mediator and Advocate. Amen."

The following prayer is without title

"Almighty God, Father of Mercies, and God of all Consolation, who dost after sundry manners correct those whom thou dost love, and chastise every one whom thou dost receive, we beseech thee look down in pity and compassion at this time upon thy poor afflicted servant, now desiring our prayers, against whom evil angels have been permitted by thee to send a fire, and whom thy hand hath touched in all that he hath: behold now, therefore, from heaven, visit and relieve this man of sorrow, with his desolate family; yea, after the multitude of thy mercies, look upon him and them; turn again, and be gracious unto them; be favourable unto them, O be favourable unto them, good Lord; forgive them all their sins, and let not Satan approach to hurt them; comfort them with thy salvation, both outward and inward; give them faith and sure confidence in thee, that so submitting themselves wholly to thy will, this short affliction may be to their exceeding profit, and may help them forward in the right way which leadeth to life and joy everlasting, through the merits of thy most dearly beloved Son, Jesus Christ, our Lord. Amen.

O God, who despiseth not the sighing of such as are of a contrite heart, neither rejecteth the tears and desires of those that mourn before thee; favourably accept, we pray thee, the supplications which we now offer unto thee, for thy poor troubled and afflicted servant, whom thou hast called to pass through a most sharp and fiery trial, and hast in thy righteousness stripped of all things in this world that he might nakedly depend upon thee, with whom is the fulness of all things both in heaven and earth: hear our prayers for him in this adversity and tribulation which oppresseth him; bow down thine ear to his cry; consider his necessity; send him help from thy holy place: support and comfort his distressed family; stretch out thy right hand to succour and deliver them; and all that are sufferers together with him; carry them through all difficulties, as upon thy arms; O make thy face to shine again upon them; and so break to pieces all the designs of the destroyer, who spitteth out fire and indignation against thy servants, as they putting their trust in thy name, and bowing their wills to the wisdom of thy providence, may be hurt by no manner of evils, and being delivered out of this their   trouble and anguish, and established upon a rock, may joyfully give thanks to thee, O God, in thy holy church, and glorify thee in their lives, and in their death, through the mediation of Jesus Christ, thy Son our Lord. Amen."

With the same MSS. was the following letter, which in the true order, ought perhaps to have been placed at the commencement of the present series of devotional papers. It is headed:—

"To Mr. Nelson in his last sickness.—GAM-ZO!—My dear friend, and the gift of God to me! O how doth my spirit embrace your spirit in the spirit of our Beloved! O my friend, in the highest root of friendship, my heart floweth at this time to you, as in and from the heart of our dearest Jesus: whose love therefore, constraineth me to write to you, whom he hath set his mark upon; and hath called now to the foot of his cross, and me together with you. *This also is good.* This day, my friend, I heard it sounded in the lesson, *Lord, behold he whom thou lovest is sick.* Thus, thus prayeth my soul. And oh, that I could but now hear the voice of our Jesus, sounding also this gracious answer, *this sickness is not unto death.* Be comforted, be comforted, dear sir; for as you have been a comforter to many under God, so much comfort remaineth for you both here and hereafter, when your warfare shall be accomplished. All then will undoubtedly be for the glory of God, what lieth so much at your heart. I was once near to the gates of death, when I cried to the Lord, and he sent his word to heal me, bringing before me in a manner extraordinary, that most sweet and powerful passage, Ps. cxviii. 18, 19, 20. May he that then spoke to me, speak in like manner to your heart! And though even the very sentence of death, should be gone out against you, according to the inferior dispensation of God in nature, yet there may still a surplussage of years be added to you for the perfecting that which is *behind*, and for the filling up the measure of all that good which God hath put into your heart to do. This I may be certain of, that all this is for your greater purification, and that the Son of God will be glorified in you by it, even as you desire that he should be glorified. You are now, therefore, called to make a sacrifice of all to him: and if at any time you have been too much pleased with the good that you have been made an instrument of, by grace, or with the applause that you may have received for it by men of good will, or may unwarily have taken any part of the glory thereof to yourself, and now you are to cast all at the feet of Jesus, that so he alone may have the glory. This I doubt not but you do: and whatever you thus part with, you shall receive again an hundred-fold. God knoweth what he may have further to do with you, and with us all: the clouds are at present very thick;

but I no more doubt of the sun's breaking through them all, than I can, of what we saw and felt together, when I was with you last in your chariot in the park, the which I then looked upon as a faint emblem of what you might in faith expect and hope for. May the cherishing and breathful beams of that holy intellectual sun, which is your light and life, descend upon you more and more vigorously: and may you find healing thereby to your whole man, through that faith which is most powerful, and is of his operation. To whom, dear sir, I always commit you, with most affectionate sympathy of heart, resting in hope, Yours, in that friendship and service which hath no end. Francis Lee. Nov. 19, 1714. TO THE BEST OF FRIENDS." [From the MOST AFFECTIONATE of FRIENDS?]

Selections Fourteen and Fifteen.

[Organizational Proposals by Lee]

[These consist of Lee's proposal for a publishing company, and two proposals for Christian study groups. —Ed.]

And now to return to Lee : whose indefatigable efforts and incessant schemes in the cause of truth, of religion and heavenly wisdom we have alluded to. The following two papers are transcripts from his rough MSS., the latter of which is dated 1703 ; the first is headed,—

"PROPOSALS for the raising a STOCK to print BOOKS of MYSTICAL DIVINITY, PHILOSOPHY, and HISTORY. In order to the advancement of the most ancient and universal religion, as professed by Christ and his apostles, and of the most curious and solid learning, throughout all the ages and parts of the world. And it proceeds thus:—

"There being at present but very little encouragement in this kingdom for all books of such a nature, they being known but to very few, and coming into the hands of fewer, and there being like to be in the beginning a great expense, because many hands will be employed (both natives and foreigners), and many books successively published, of which no suitable return can be expected for some while; it is therefore proposed,

I. —That whosoever shall contribute towards a stock for such an end, shall be repaid his money deposited, in books, as they come forth, according to the number they subscribe for. And that the performance hereof shall be secured by such trustees, as some of the principal subscribers shall agree upon.

II. —That the books shall be printed carefully, on a fine paper, and with a very good letter.

III. —That the return which is made by the sale of the books, beyond the original stock, shall be made a bank for charitable uses, and services most agreeable to the carrying on of this design; and shall be in the regulation of the said trustees.

IV. —That from the said stock there shall be printed upwards of an hundred sheets the first year; and so on till the contributors and subscribers shall be fully satisfied.

V. —That every term there shall be published one or more books, papers and stitched tracts excepted.

VI. —That the ancient Christian Mystics, Macarius, Nilus, etc., shall be set forth in the English tongue very advantageously, with proper annotations.

VII. —That the best of the Heathen Mystics shall be set forth also after the same manner: with a just parallel betwixt them and the Christian, and a demonstration of the excellency of the latter.

VIII. —That whatever can be collected of the true ancient Jewish Cabala, shall be translated, and set forth in like manner, in Latin or English, or in both.

IX. —That the Christian Mystics of the middle age, and the moderns which are out of print, being such as are of an established character, shall be faithfully and correctly reprinted.

X. —That our English Mystics of the former ages as many as can be found, whether in print or in manuscript, that are of value, shall be diligently revised, and methodised in convenient portable volumes: and so as they may come at a most easy rate to the buyers, considering the great dearness of many of them at present.

XI. —That many originals, both of some that are lately deceased, and some that are yet alive, containing many deep and hidden discoveries, shall be published, with some account of the authors, and many curious passages relating to them, and to the opening of the Archetypal and Angelical worlds.

XII. —That the most approved writers of Mystic Theology, in Italian, French, High Dutch, and Flemish, shall be translated, revised, and methodised after the same manner, in portable volumes.

XIII. —That the same care shall be taken in printing the best and most approved books of Mystical Philosophy, according to its various kinds, for a solid promotion of natural studies, and the benefit of mankind, and of this kingdom in particular.

XIV. —That the lives of the ancient Fathers of the Desert, and modern lives, with many most curious and profitable histories, both in divinity and philosophy, shall be set forth with all impartiality and love of truth.

XV. — That every month, or two months, some account shall be given of the progress herein made, and of all that relates to the promotion of this design, in this or in other kingdoms and states; by means of a settled correspondence erected in most parts of Europe.

XVI. —That twice every year, something of the same nature be published in Latin, for the benefit of foreigners, and the maintaining and cherishing our correspondence betwixt them.

XVII. —That a beginning shall be made with a new collection of some Mystics, Catholic and Protestant, printed this year, in French, at Amsterdam, under the name of *Real Divinity*, with a letter on the principles and characters of the chiefest mystical and spiritual writers of the last ages. Also with a particular account of those of this nation, both printed and manuscript; and a Chronological Catalogue of Christian Mystics and witnesses of the kingdom of God, down from Christ's time to this day; together with some other additions."

The Second MS. is as follows:—

"A Model of A SOCIETY for REVIVING the spirit and life of CHRISTIANITY. With proposals for promoting Catholic Peace and Charity. Humbly offered to the consideration of all sober and serious Christians.

It is proposed,—That a Society, or societies, be formed out of a select number of faithful friends, being persons of a true Christian spirit, experienced in the ways of God, sincere lovers of peace and truth, without respect to person or party, and specially nowise addicted to disturb government, either in Church or State, or to speak evil of dignitaries. And that the formation of such a society or societies, having no other end but the revival of the genuine and primitive spirit of decayed Christianity, and the life of its most renowned professors in the purest ages of the church, be according to the model following:—

I. —That the members of this society do, as members hereof, distinguish themselves by no other name but that of CHRISTIANS.

II. —That they unite together purely for the reviving the life and spirit of primitive Christianity, and for promoting peace and union universally.

III. —That they meet once a week (if not oftener), and chiefly on the Lord's day; if it may be, without interfering either with the public duties of the day in the churches, or with family duties at home; unless some other time for this be found more convenient.

IV. —That the number of its members exceed not that of six or seven, both for the more liberty of Christian conversation, and for several other weighty reasons.

V. —That for the preservation of unity and order, every member hereof shall have his particular lot and service ascertained to him, besides the general, according as every one is fitted by God and Nature, for this or that.

VI. —That there be a fund of piety settled herein, according to such regulations and orders as shall be unanimously agreed on by the members, for charitable and pious ends best suiting so generous and Christian an Institution.

VII. —That this society be dedicated to GOD through CHRIST, that so he may ratify and say Amen to it, by his HOLY SPIRIT. And that the feast of the dedication hereof shall be annually kept, with a recollection of the old year's proceedings before, and with proper services and offices for the occasion.

Now, for as much as it has been found expedient, after mature deliberation and experience, that no society of this nature do contain above half-a-dozen members, or seven at the most; and that not any one be admitted into it without the full consent, and hearty good will of all: therefore that any serious Christians may not be debarred the benefit of this design, it is thought proper here to annex the specimen of an agreement for the forming of such a society; that so they may consider of it, and accordingly form themselves after some such manner, into a sacred fraternity and fellowship, with those whom they may bear a nearest relation to in spiritual matters, let their number be never so small. For, but three or four united fully into a society of this kind, having a good agreement in their tempers, and a near sympathy spiritually and naturally with each other, may be capable of doing far more than three or four hundred loosely combined, who shall be for carrying on the very same end: and may expect more of the grace and blessing of God, as they are carried on with greater unanimity and concord." [The paper thus proceeds:]

"A SPECIMEN of an AGREEMENT for the forming of a Society, or a RELIGIOUS CONFRATERNITY, in order to revive the Spirit and Life of Christianity.

In the name of God. Amen. We [N. N. or] resolve by the grace of God, out of a sense of the degeneracy of the generality of Christians at this day, and of our infirmities and temptations which beset us on every side,

I. —To unite together into a society for *reviving the spirit and life of Christianity*, under the conduct of the blessed Spirit of God, as it was in the beginning: and so by means of this union to endeavour, with our hearts and souls, the mutual promoting of real holiness in ourselves, in subordination to the power and gift of God; and the encouraging and strengthening each other in the rule and practice of true *primitive Christianity*, freely and impartially; not respecting any particular constitution, or custom, of any one society among Christians in these latter ages.

II. —To meet together once upon every Lord's day. (unless some other day shall be more convenient for the members to come together in,) and at an hour that may neither hinder the public worship, nor interfere with the more private duties of the family, and closet; in order to carry on by all proper and suitable methods so excellent an end: and therefore to cultivate, maintain and advance a spiritual friendship and Society betwixt every one and all of us, severally and jointly, by discoursing, conferring and consulting together about the ways and means proper to accomplish this our design.

III. and IV.......

V. —To consider the grounds of the decay of Christian piety; and of the mighty increase of anti-christianism, Atheism and Sadducism, with the remedy that ought to be applied to put a stop to this spreading contagion. Not only to lay to heart the rents and schisms of the whole Christian world in general, and of the reformation in particular, and more specially of that part of it in these three Kingdoms; but to be in a constant readiness to do whatever we can for cementing the same, according to our several places and stations in which it shall please God at any time to set us; and for restoring the most ancient and perfect model of Christianity.

VI. —To renounce every interest in the world that may be any wise inconsistent with this present undertaking, or be an hindrance to it by entangling or warning the affections; always supposing that this be no impediment to the necessary occasions of life, on this side or that: and therefore be greatly careful of accepting any charges, or offices, that may be apt to balance the mind, against the common interest and welfare of all mankind.

VII. —To contribute toward a fund of piety, for the promised end, and for all such pious and charitable uses as the Society shall judge fit, in cases both ordinary and extraordinary, and to agree with all such necessary regulations and orders in the management of it, and all the affairs of this Society, as they shall determine among themselves."

Part Three:
Richard Roach & Christopher Walton

Selection One.

Solomon's Porch, by Richard Roach

[This text combines the partial version of the poem in Walton with the rest of the verses in the original. —Ed.]

* We insert the poem originally accompanying the above introductory preface, (that is, so much of it as may be deemed needful,) as a note, and in this place, rather than in the body of the work. It is entitled, "SOLOMON'S PORCH; or, the BEAUTIFUL GATE of WISDOM'S TEMPLE. A POEM, INTRODUCTORY to the PHILADELPHIAN AGE :"

>   When sinful man first left the blissful seat,
>   Outcast, forlorn; from all that's good or great,
>   From virgin-purity, and virgin-love
>   Banish'd, and doom'd round the curs'd earth to
>   rove,
>   In bestial image vile; the fiend within
>   Possession took, without the beast was seen.
>   God's temple wasted lay: his image bright
>   Thick veil'd in black Egyptian shades of night.
>   That glorious Shechinah which erst did shine
>   In his clear soul; the once all beauteous
>   shrine,
>   The seat and mansion of th' eternal Trine;
>   How is it fled ! its finest gold how dim !
>   Its stones poured out, its precious *Urim*
>   Oracular no more, all clouded lies;
>   Where demons now their oracles disguise.
>   From heights of bliss to deeper woes he fell,
>   Still falling, sinking still down tow'rds the abyss
>   of hell.
>   This couldst thou not behold, Almighty Love,
>   But in compassions dear, thy tender bowels
>   move:
>   Pity and mercy move. The heavenly bride
>   *Sophia*, torn from her new lover's side,

Her bridegroom could not thus forego. Her eyes
In pearly dews distilling, as he dies
One parting glance she threw : fast hold it took,
And stop'd him sinking: caus'd him back to
    look
Repentant. Deeper then, the heavenly ray,
Wing'd with love's fires, more piercing, makes
    its way:
God's light and love conjoin'd; ere long to dwell
Within him. In the blest *Immanuel*.
Till then content in tabernacles low,
And temples made with hands, some gleams of
    God to show.
  They travel hand in hand through every age;
  In poor disguise and humble pilgrimage:
  With only types of rest at every greater stage.
  One glorious king, the Virgin did descry.
  Enamour'd, courted, entertained her high :
  She stay'd awhile; all blessings round her fly.
He would have had his deitess enshrin'd
With earth's magnificence in one combin'd.
A glorious temple-structure rends the sky :
The world's amazement: little in her eye.
Departing yet, this flavour high we deign.
Said she, be thine a *type* of our *returning reign*.
This house a draught in miniature shall be
Of an eternal temple rais'd by me.

————

  This revolution finish'd, on they go,
Now downwards, back again to scenes of woe,
Through deaths still conquering death; where
    e'er they can
Pierce deeper; and take faster hold of man.
Till in the virgin meek she found abode
More chaste; and lodg'd in her the infant God.
Here, by the o'er-shadowings of the heavenly
    Dove,
She unlocks the centre of eternal Love.
Here light and love, but scattered in the earth
Till now, unite their beams, and to a birth
Proceeding, one blest human offspring crown

With Godhead-power; whose kingdom's vast
    renown
Through infamy, anguish and death must rise;
A bleeding victor, a triumphant sacrifice.
Here a true living temple they enjoy'd;
Delighted, *rested in*, which though destroy'd
In outward frame, the grave could not withhold
From rising glorious; brighter far, ten thou-
    sand-fold.
    Hail *Sion's* joy, her precious corner-stone,
    The heavenly *Salem* a true foundation,
    The God, the Man, the Virgin all in One!
The builders thee refus'd; but thou the head
Supreme, and we're thy happy members made:
Strictly compacted into one; the whole
One body in thee, one heart, one life, one soul.
    Ere long, in th' next great revolution.
    When the fair Virgin pilgrim's stage is done.
    Her travails ended, and her garland won;
A temple-glory of living stones to rise;
Whose base shall fill the earth; whose head the
    skies.
Love yet can't triumph here, without its mate,
Till light and beauty too become incorporate.

    Thus still disguis'd, to this great stage they
        speed.
Contented still to suffer, grieve, and bleed:
Bleed in their members dear. Through all they
    move
Up hill, to triumphs hasting. Now the Dove
Assistant powerful joins; in each pure soul,
O'ershadowing, Christ to form. Spite of con-
    troul
From demon's malice, or fierce tyrant's hate,
God's image, light, and life, they here create:
Still spreading, tincturing deep; till all's di-
    vine;
And Christ in every feature, every line,
Appearing, shall e'en here through soul and
    body shine.

In vain hell's obstacles and bars oppose:
Each seal the conquerors as they pass disclose.
The last now opening, when the Spirit's day
Its powers uninterrupted shall display.
See! see! the Virgin sends a precious ray.

From thy dark cell now, great BOHEMIUS,
    [Böhme, Behmen] rise;
Tutor to sages, mad to th' worldly wise.
Wisdom's first distant phosphor, to whose sight
Internal nature's ground, all naked bright
Unveils, all worlds appear, heavens spread their
    light.
Early, thou risest glorious: but in clouds
Thick set, not sent to th' vulgar, nor the learned
    crowds
Of reason's orb, too low: none thee descry;
None but the *well-purg'd mystic eagle eye*
Of some *few anchorite* elected *magi*.
Here all past sages veil and disappear.
E'en *Malebranche* bends beneath his weighty
    character;
  To thee resign'd: and 'tis but just, for he
  Draws all from one small rivulet of thee:
  Fountain of science, art, and mystery.
    Where *Stagyrite*, *Hermes*, *Plato*, all combine,
    Descartes in ev'ry page, and *Boyle* in ev'ry line.
    And yet *alone*, by eminence, the Divine.
By whom advis'd, the firstling flocks small band
Prepare, well trim their lamps, and ready
    stand.
'Midst whom for pious seal and forward care.
Great *Pordage*, with thy generous *file* appear.
Adventurous worthies, set in th' forlorn hope
With hell's outrageous malice first to cope.
Furious the dragon storms, all methods tries,
Ev'n by false magic dark incrept
To crush the royal infant spirit's rise.
  But on they charge undaunted, strive, and
    pray,
  Believe, watch, bleed, and travel; force a way

For entrance, and foretaste the glorious day.
As the' dark breaks loose, still the light world's
    displayed,
By the *Virgin's* magic wand the cursed fiends are
    laid:
  Pure spirit breathes : new senses open fly;
  They see: and all with joint assent.
            Hail, great BOHEMIUS ! cry.
All's true; we bear thee record: hail to thee !
Fountain of science, art, and mystery.

———

  At last, great Hero, throw off thy undress:
Speak, condescend familiar. Now, no less,
A cherub-seraph, tow'ring, flaming high
Is sent thy veil to rend, thy *Gordian* knot to
    untie: [FREHER ?]
Commander sole of all the graceful charms
That flow in language, passion, harmony.
Attempered just. In sum, second to thee.
The wondrous *Taylor* now revolves again
Ardent, seraphic, and with tenfold fires:
Thunder, and fire, and love compose the name.
How should it then not breathe harmonious
      powers,
          Or want empyreal flame.
    Through whose clear style in each transparent
        line.
    Thy rough-cut, well-set, polish'd diamonds
        shine;
    Each page out-streaming light, and kindling
        love divine.

———

All bars remov'd at last, heaven's dawn appears,
The Virgin blushes round the hemispheres.
Shedding celestial rosy tincture pure,
From *Sharon's* spicy beds ; of radiant hue:
Mix'd with her own fair lilies silver dew.
  The morning star, true *Venus*, high aspires,
  Darting on ev'ry side, unblam'd and free.

Her gracious glittering, lambent, amorous
    fires.
Bright morning-star of God's eternal day!
For this we shout aloud, we sing, we pray
Amen, hosanna, hallelujah!
Ah, dear, divine *Urania*, now be kind,
Speak thou, and leave the wretched man be
    hind.

———

THE GLORIOUS ERA *now, now, now* begins.
Now, now the neat angelic trumpet sings:
And now in ev'ry blast.
                  Love's *everlasting gospel* rings.
      The glad triumphant sounds
      Through vales, o'er hills rebound;
Glory to the eternal King of Kings.
Glory to the eternal King of Kings:
The glorious era *now, now, now* begins.

———

O may through me the mighty trumpet sound;
And spread its fame the woods and plains.
            The isles and seas around.
    Let sportful echoes play,
    And dancing all the way,
Swell and intune the trembling sounds anew:
    All well-tun'd voices raise
    To great ELCHAJAH'S praise;
Peace through all lands, dear love to man, to
    God his honour due.
O way through me the mighty trumpet sound,
And spread his fame the woods, and hills, and
    plains,
        The isles and seas around.

———

Proclaim aloud the mighty jubilee,
    That sets the sin-bound captives free:
Proclaim, proclaim the mighty jubilee.
    Let all the heavenly nine
    Wreath arm in arm entwin'd;
All in one high love-labour'd song agree:

Let muse and grace combin'd
With harmony divine,
In sweetest consent, perfect unity
Melodious voices join.
Proclaim, proclaim the mighty jubilee,
That sets all sin-bound captives free;
Proclaim, proclaim aloud the mighty jubilee.
Hail morning star of God's eternal day :
For this we shout aloud, we sing, we pray.
Amen, hosannah, hallelujah.
O bless the dawn, salute the morning star.
Thrice bless the happy womb that bars
Sophia's darling child.
Lustrous, all-charming, mild;
Bless, bless, and kiss the daughter fair.
And for the nuptial bowers prepare
Of God's eternal Bride;
Bless, bless the happy lovers by her side.

―――

Arise, ye lovers true.
Arise, arise, ye wondrous few;
Apparitors divine; ordain'd, fore-sent.
Heaven's beauteous Virgin queen
To attend and usher in;
The mother to adore, the bride to complement:
Blest Virgin, Mother, Bride, in One:
Thrice sacred band of love, and mystic union !
Arise, arise, ye wondrous few,
Arise, ye lovers true.

―――

Long in inglorious ease obscur'd ye lie.
Despis'd, neglected; yet neglecting, too,
Nor caring what the impious trifling world
Could either say or do.
O'erlook'd by man, yet lov'd, and favour'd high
In heaven's regard, and God's auspicious eye.
Whom neither high preferment's charm can move,
Ambition firs, or beauty prompt to love:
And yet to love most true.

Out of the everlasting Virgin's womb.
Sons of the morn already born anew:
        Born into time.
And wing'd at will to ascend the etherial clime,
Angelic men, imbodied Seraphim.
All captives to the blest Sophia's charms;
      Through wisdom's mazes bright,
       Wandering in tracks of light.
By her still guided and exempt from harms :
        Still kept
From mazy errors tangling step.
    From paths untrue
By her fair silver-twin'd mercurial clue.
Dear *captives to the bright Sophia's charms:*
      And yet more loudly to proclaim
       Transcendent love's and beauty's fame,
Long wrap'd in the divine *Urania's* arms.
Wrap'd in the dear divine Urania's *arms,*
Plund'ring her sweets, and rifling all her
   charms.

      Ye wond'rous few, arise,
God's heralds true; throw off your mortal
   guise.
Now lift your tweet, loud, speaking, trumpets
   high.
Now let your jocund levets fill the sky;
Tell, tell the drowsy world their God is nigh.

Now let eternal song unbounded flow
With torrent deep, serene, majestic, slow;
      Disdaining art's control
       Like heaven's full spangled canopy.
        Most nice, and yet most free,
Ring'd by dame Nature's artful liberty.
    Let ev'ry point a star, each line
      In constellation shine;
        Each living world a soul:
      In thousand differing ways,

>   Varying to God new praise:
>   Now, now let your inspir'd seraphic strains
>   In mighty numbers roll.
> Proclaim, proclaim the gracious *jubilee:*
>   And set the sin-bound captives free:
> Proclaim, proclaim the gracious *jubilee.*
>
> *O way through me the mighty trumpet sound:*
> *And spread, etc.*
>
> ———
>
> And ye fair *virgin-daughters* of the morn;
> *Sion's* first blossoms; from New *Salem* born:
>   High *paradisial* nymphs appear,
> The *Virgin queen's* attendant *graces* dear:
>   Haste, haste, away.
> And join your powers unanimous to proclaim
>   *The wondrous year;*
> The great, the good, the now-revolving day:
> Full period-circle bright, of endless fame.
>   *Ye* paradisial *nymphs appear;*
> The Virgin queen's *attendant graces dear:*
> Sion's *first blossoms;* from New Salem *born:*
> Rise *ye fair* virgin-daughters *of the morn.*
>
> ———
>
>   Arise and shine.
> Illustrious troop of *heroines* divine;
> Celestial *Amazons;* untaught to yield.
> With heaven-aspiring ardours, sprightly vigour
>   fill'd.
> In this, the *Virgin's* day, most forward; bent,
> Zealous their very heroes to prevent.
> In terrible-majestic-gay parade.
> Hell's fierce imbattel'd legions first t' invade:
>   With orient beams of light.
>   Scattering the misty gloom of night.
> And chasing every black infernal shade.
>   *Arise and shine.*
>   Illustrious heroines;
> Cherubic phalanx bright of *Amazons* divine:
>   Arise, *arise and shine.*
>
> ———

Yet tho' deep skilled in spirit's war-like arts.
Nature has fram'd, love arm'd ye, too too free
Far deeper wounds, to give; and nobler darts
To fix in pore and captivated hearts.
In whose high-tinctur'd forms harmonious
    move
The fiery quick *serpentine* energy.
Charm'd by the mildness of the peaceful dove.
        Inviting still to love.
        Contraries here agree
        In strictest unity.
        Each other to improve;
The fierce and powerful *sting*, the lofty *spire*
Co-mingling to *exalt* the amorous fire.
You, at whose presence mortal beauty must
Abscond, and in confusion kiss the dust.
        Beauties too flaming bright
        To be endur'd by human sight;
Which but unveil'd would quench the inferior
    light.

———

The glances of whose eyes are lucid beams.
        In-drawn from the all-radiant One,
        Divine, *Super-celestial* Sun:
        Where his full streams.
        Pointed in central union.
Himself produce in lustrous image fair
        Of his belov'd *Eternal Son*.
        Hence darting ev'ry way
In each reflecting, subdivided ray.
        The little loves entranc'd
        With innocent and wanton dance,
Thousand enshrin'd celestial *cupids* play.

———

        From whose coralline lip
Angels their spicy draughts of *nectar* sip;
Quick darting the divine love-flaming kiss.
        In free *enormous* bliss.
In whose fair cheeks the tinctures pure com-
    bine:

The matchless diamonds sparkle *paler* bright;
      And in their orbs of light
Enchase the glittering ruby's *sanguine* flame;
In radiant blush of modesty divine,
          Exempt from mortal shame.

———

Here, re-aspiring from their humble vale
To meet the inclining vigorous scented male.
      In their dewy, fruitful bed.
Their *Sharon* rose the *virgin* lilies wed.
      Whom, as with strict embrace inwrap'd
        They lock within their flowery lap,
A stock of graces numberless proceed;
      A spring of lesser beauties breed.

———

The clear tralucent forms all shade disdain,
      Disclosing freely to be seen.
      The wonder-world within;
Each *argent* nerve, and ev'ry *azure* vein:
The beauteous *love-eye* burning in the heart;
From whence love's centres endless multiply.
As thick-set spangles of the sky,
Raising a sting or joy in ev'ry part.
      In ev'ry point a *Venus* bright;
        Each star a world of new delight,
Opening an unexhausted spring of bliss,
      Each nymph herself a *paradise*.
So fine, so pliant the external mould,
      That e'en therein the brighter soul.
      With all its graces train,
        Imprints itself distinct and plain.
      And as in fabled streams,
        Where silver currents roll
      On orient pearl, and sands of gold;
Displays her rich inestimable gems.
      Which free expos'd to view
        In their untarnish'd native hue.
      Reflex through bodies *chrystalline*.
        In their transparent *mirror* shine.
But deeper yet and more amazing fair

Outshines, outflames through her.
Express, the only Son's refulgent character.

Now, now, ye paradisial nymphs appear;
The Virgin queen's *attendant graces dear.*
   Arise, arise and shine.
   Illustrious brigade
   Of heroines *divine*;
In terrible-majestic-gay parade:
    With orient beams of light
    Scatter the misty gloom of night;
And banish *every black infernal shade.*

   Arise and shine,
   Illustrious heroines.
Cherubic phalanx, *bright of* Amazons *divine.*
   Arise, arise and shine.

   Haste, haste away,
And let your well-trim'd flowing tresses fair,
Waving in wanton ringlets, gild the air;
Out-beaming, sun-like, with pellucid ray:
   And as they loosely move,
  Fan'd by fresh odorous gales of love,
With heaven's warm, gentle-breathing zephyr's
 play.
   Haste to proclaim
The great; the good, the now-revolving day;
Amen, hosanna, hallelujah.
   Haste to proclaim
The period-circle *full; of endless fame:*
The great, the good, the now-revolving *day:*
For this we shout aloud, we sing, we pray,
Amen, amen; hosanna, hallelujah.

   Heroes, fall back again.
   Lead up the virgin train,
And hand in hand, as love-pair'd twins advance
   In sacred well-paid mystic dance,
   Tracing on holy ground,
   Circling *Jehovah's* altar round.

Where thy love-incence burns, goodness and
    grace abound,
            Whence living coals out-fly,
            Generate and multiply,
Seraphic ardors ev'ry way to impart
To each bright-flaming and love melting heart.

            The quick celestial fires
            Straight their sweet-warbling tongues
                inspire,
While ev'ry voice and ev'ry trumpet sings,
Glory to the returning King of Kings;
Love's golden era now, now, now begins,
Now, now, in ev'ry breath, in ev'ry sound
            The universe around,
                Love's *everlasting gospel* rings.
Glory to the returning King of Kings;
Love's glorious era now, now, now begins.

Fresh springing still the' inspir'd harmonious
    vein,
Tunes up to higher key and loftier strain;
            In more enchanting lays.
            Varying new hymns of praise,
Jointly the' ascending voice and soul to raise:
            E'en till they both aspire,
            And join with the seraphic quire;
            And under God's bright eye
            In influence serene they lie,
Dissolv'd in rapturous hallelujahs.

As that sweet little chorister that flies,
            And singing mounts the skies ;
            Till all his breath and song be spent.
Then down he falls, in sweeter languishment;
So do angelic souls in sounds aspire:
            They mount and sing
            Upon the dove's bright wing;
That gently fans and feeds th' ethereal fire;
All emulous to win the steep ascent,

>   The mighty mountains Seven;
> Those lily-deck'd, and rosy-flow'ring hills.
>   Form'd by th' all-bounteous hand of
>   heaven,
> Its darling sons with mere delight to fill;
>   Till in melodious ravishment,
> Their powers, their voice, their very soul be
>   spent:
>   The light
>   Becomes too blazing bright:
>   The bliss
>   Unsufferable is.
> Then down with speed they take their humble
>   flight.
> In adoration deep; yet but retire
> To' embrace more near, and be exalted higher.
> Now, love's last, sweetest *mystic death* to try,
> Rap'd in sublime exstatic toys expire;
>   Entranc'd and *silent* lie.
> Thus in soft languent slumbers sweet, true
>   sleep,
>   That rests in God's *abyssal* deep;
> The rest in visionary dreams they *see;*
>   They *taste*, they *feel*.
> What is unknown, immense, unspeakable.
> *Proclaim, proclaim, etc.*
> *O, may through me, etc.*

>   Too long, too long the wretched world
> Lies waste, in wild confusion hurl'd,
> Unhing'd in ev'ry part; each property
> Struggling, disrang'd in fiercest enmity.
>   The whole creation groans;
>   And labouring with perpetual toil.
>   In man's rebellion vile,
>   Her own hard fate bemoans.
>   But now shall nature's jar,
>   Cease her intestine war:
> Now, shall the long six working days of strife,
> Attain their line and to their crown arrive:
>   At last set free

In peaceful rest of Sabbath true.
Heaven and earth created new,
To celebrate an endless *jubilee*.

Concord divine now meets in ev'ry part.
And love subdues and reigns in ev'ry heart.
    O'er all.
   In sum or individual.
Triumphant harmony, triumphant love.
   In sweetest unity.
     Combin'd together move.
   E'en from the *zenith* high
Of the clear boundless *empyrean* sky.
    The throne of God;
Down to earth's inmost central deep abode,
All is consent and perfect amity:
    All in proportion due,
     In weight and number true:
In moods and measures of the spheres.
That never enter'd mortal ears.
   E'en from the zenith high,
    The' all-radiant throne of God,
Down to earth's inmost, central deep abode;
Nothing but love—but love and harmony.
Where every voice and every trumpet sings.
Glory to the eternal King of Kings,
Love's golden era, etc.

    Now harmless through the sky,
Let the sweet, whisking, treble lightnings fly:
   Full base from shore to shore,
    Shall in deep thunders roar,
Not death, not horror now, but melody.
Now, Mighty Bard, sing Out thy sonnet free.
   Nor doubt it true shall be.
    Come thou and join
   Thy loud prophetic voice with mine.
   "Ring out ye chrystal spheres,
   "Now bless our human ears:
For ye have power to touch our senses so:

"Now *shall* your silver chime
"Move in melodious time;
And the *deep* base of heaven's great *orb* shall blow.
    From the bright zenith high
Of the clear, boundless empyrean sky;
    From the all-radiant throne of God,
Down to earth's inmost central deep abode,
Nothing but pure consent and unity:
    All in proportion due,
    In weight and number true,
All universal love and harmony.

———

This globe terrene no longer turn'd askance,
Hitch'd in her poles shall now direct advance,
    And through the liquid ether dance.
    And on her axle spin,
    In an harmonious round,
Breathing substantial, dense, embodied sound.
    Then shall surcease the ungrateful din
Of jarring spheres and clashing orbs around;
    While this wonder-machine,
    Engine of harmony divine,
    Shall through the echoing welkin play;
    And everywhere
    Its melting air,
In clear triumphant sounds convey;
Into each obvious rolling sphere
    Mingling her ringing atmosphere.
    Which as it springs
Still more transparent, bright, and sounding clear,
    At first divides in lesser rings,
Compacted close, in voice acute and shrill,
    More to the surface near.
    Then wider waves indented, till
The circles swell, the sounds begin to fill.
    Still wid'ning more and more;
    Till with deep *gamut* roar
In fall-mouth'd peals orb within orb resound.

———

                    Here in epitome
Shall the vast heavenly spheres collected be;
And down through them transmit their har-
    mony.
Each sphere, each star shall now dispense,
            With passage free in direct line;
                And full aspect benign,
Its various powers and proper influence.
            Which in her hollow womb.
            This globe shall deep entomb;
        Where, from her central working urn
They shall arise, and into body turn :
And shoot from centre to circumference.
Her caverns dark, must now enlightened be.
            Unfetter'd, free;
As one transparent, vast, self-moving wheel
Of liquid crystal; open to reveal
            Her rich innumerable stores,
Her various wonders great, and her own acting
    powers.
These upward move, and on the surface play,
Adorn'd all beauteous, bright, amazing, gay:
            And there,
Themselves in radiant flowers, fruits, metals,
    gems, display:
All living, breathing, sounding free
Into the all-uniting element,
            The one capacious air;
Blowing from ev'ry pipe a different harmony,
Still from the lower circlets upward sent.
"Thus every grateful note to heaven repays"
        "The melody it lent."

Thus from earth's inmost central-deep abode,
        E'en to the zenith high
Of the clear, boundless, empyrean sky,
            To the all-radiant throne of God;
All is consent and perfect unity ;
        All in proportion due.
            In weight and number true:
    In ev'ry motion, ev'ry sound

The universe *around*,
All is triumphant love and harmony;
   Through all the heavenly Dove
   Breathes her eternal Love;
  Collecting ev'ry various tone,
  All acts, all powers, all hearts in one,
Center'd in beatific union.
    ———

Proclaim, proclaim the mighty jubilee.
   That sets each world of captives free.
Proclaim, proclaim the mighty jubilee.
   Let all the heavenly nine
   Wreath arm in arm entwin'd;
All in one high love-labour'd song agree :
    Let muse and grace combin'd
    With harmony divine,
In sweetest consent, perfect unity
    Melodious voices join.
Proclaim, proclaim the mighty *jubilee*,
  That sets each world of captives free;
Proclaim, proclaim aloud the mighty *jubilee*.

O may through me the awakening trumpet sound.
And spread its fame *the woods, and isles, and seas,*
    And heaven and earth around.
  Let sportful echoes play.
  And dancing all the way,
Swell and intune the trembling sounds anew:
  All well-tuned voices raise
  To great ELCHAJAH'S *praise.*
Peace to all worlds, dear love to man, to God
 his honour due.
O may through me the mighty trumpet sound;
And spread its fame the woods, and isles, and
 seas,
    And heaven and earth around.
While ev'ry voice and ev'ry trumpet sings,
THE GLORIOUS ERA now, now, now begins.
Now, now the angelic trump his message
 brings:

And now in ev'ry blast,
          Love's *everlasting gospel* rings.
   The glad triumphant sounds
Through spheres and worlds rebound,
Glory to the returning King of Kings.
Glory to the returning King of Kings:
The glorious era now, now, now begins.
For this we shout aloud, we sing, we pray,
Amen, Hosannah, HALLELUJAH.

[The poem here takes a fresh wing and direction; but we have not room for further sublimities and annunciations of this soaring *evangelical prophet* of the latter days' glory]

[Continuation of the poem,—Ed.]

Hast now my Soul, and lay thy humble Ode
Low at the Feet of thy Returning God.
Make hast to Welcome Heaven's Eternal Queen;
        She is by some already seen;
          Come here to Live,
            And ere 'tis long to Appear,
Transfus'd in Her Great *Representative*.
Sure when she leaves the blissful Seats above,
And comes to Teach, and Give us too, Celestial Love,
        None can the Rebel play
        To that dear Scepters sway:
She thinks none here can Disaffected prove.

     Great Hero's ye must now give way,
And learn a *Female* General to obey;
Led on to mighty Deeds and vast Renown,
        To Eternal Glories Crown,
By the Divine Illustrious *Deborah*;
The High-born Beauteous *Amazonian* Queen,
          Immortal Heroine:
Of all the Virgin Train most dazling fair.
Mother of All, and All compriz'd in Her.
       Who ere She Dies
Up to Mount *Sion's* blissful state arrives.
       And in Her Age,
    On the Celestial Rosie Bed
        Of fragrant Spices lies.

True *Phenix* who in Heav'nly Flames *Revives*.
           To Her
Heav'ns lofty Virgin condescends familiar;
Unlocks Her Secret Cabinet, and shows
Where Her inestimable *Pearl* is hid;
Where run the *Golden* Mines so long forbid
To Purblind Mortals; Where the *Unction* flows
Divine and where Lost *Paradise* on Earth
Restor'd, Immortal springs, and fairer grows.
She teaches Her how to Project alone
The Divine Magick-wonder-working *Stone*:
But that to purer Souls as free she may
Her Secrets, Wisdom, Stone convey.
To fix the true *Ascension Ladder* high,
        That leads directly to the Sky,
The rising Cherub Soul ev'n here to Glorify.
        And to Proclaim the Gospel Pure;
Wonders unknown of Gods surprizing Love:
        Which Firm and Sure,
Spight of fierce Demons Hate or Sins controul,
          For ever shall endure.
            To Her she gives all free
            Her Privy-Garden Key
That leads us to the *Still Eternity*:
           Which only is
The true Transcendent Virgin-Paradise.
Whence she such Flowers of various Kind and Hue,
        Imbalm'd in Odorous Heav'nly Dew,
Into her own Spicy Garden brings.
              In which each Flower,
          Indued with multiplying Power,
          Pregnant becomes of Thousands more.
Hence th' unexhausted *Fountain* of fresh *Gardens* springs.
Here living Trees their glittering Arms extend;
Apples of Gold the Silver Branches bend:
          Plenty Luxuriant without End.
           Here round the *Oak* of Strength entwines
           The softer Amorous *Eglantine*.
Which hitherto tho' wild, and barren-wast,
Here bring their proper Fruits too high for Mortal tast.
The stately *Elm* still Weds the creeping *Vine*,

Whose Branches wide-Embrac'd profusely Pour
    Their large *Escolian-cluster'd* Dower.
The Princely Cedars Heaven aspiring Clime:
And fit to build the Presence-Ark Divine,
Th' Incorruptible Trees of *Shittim*
Nor wants Improv'd that *Indian* Wonder-Tree,
    All Spices in Epitome.
Whence we the true Perfumes and Incense bring,
To Ingratiate and Attone the Offended King:
Ev'n till the Savour of our Ointments move
    The Bridegroom dear to grant his Love.
Amidst the Trees of Faith and Life aspire;
Most Virtuous-rich, and Goodly to behold:
    O see 'em Blooming fair
With Orient Pearl, and pure Ambrosial Gold.
Hail Blest *Elysian*-flowery fruitful Vale:
    Eden transplanted new.
Here Blushing Roses, *Lilies* Love-sick Pale,
High-Purpled Mourning *Violets* humbling low,
With Pinkt *Carnatians* of collected Graces grow.
    Here is the Sun-Flower true
Of steady fixt Love-Contemplation high,
That from th' Eternal Sun ne're turns its Eye.
Here the Dove-Gales in Gentle Zephirs Blow:
Here Sions Golden Rivers boundless flow;
Pure Nectare-Ambrosial Streams, that spring
With Quintessential Element Divine,
    And the New Kingdoms Flaming Wine,
From the clear *Glassy Sea*, Loves Ocean, bring:
    These are the Gardens of Mount *Lebanon*,
Where *Wisdoms Temple* can be raised alone,
    By the True second *Solomon*.
Whose Glorious Representative shall here
    Become its Mighty Founder;
Himself most radiant and Head Corner-Stone
    Next to th' Eternal One.
Hail Great and Powerful CYRUS, Thou art He
Forenam'd and Chosen from Eternity.
True *Hyacynth* who to thy *Jasper* Bright
Loves charming Queen shalt evermore unite,
Mingling thy Streams of Power with Rays of Light.

Hail Glorious King, DAVID and MARY One:
Hail Types of Greater Glories yet to come:
Hail Pledges of the Blest MILLENIUM.
Blest Pair 'tis Now, Now you begin your Days
when the Divine SOPHIA Sings your Praise.
The Rose and Lilly of th' Imperial Crown
The Flower and Beauty of the Heavenly Throne
The V and M of the Creation.
Blest Pair thrice happy now begins your Days,
When the Divine *Sophia* Sings your Praise.
Hail Glorious King DAVID and MARY One:
Hail Types of Greater Glories yet to Come.
Hail Pledges of the BLEST MILLENIUM.

Hail Powerful Beauteous Kind Harmonious V. M.

Arise, arise ye glittering Temple Stones,
Arise ye Precious *Twelve* Foundations.
Hast and your Ravisht Souls in one combine,
All in One Heart, One Life, One Glory shine:
To Raise of Spirits all compact and Pure
Wisdom's Magnificent Immortal Structure.
Each Princely Pillar Generating more,
Story on Story rais'd, with Golden Spires,
Waving their Streamers of Celestial Fires.
While the true Doves from ev'ry distant Shoar
To the Love-Windows fly, and Add their Store,
Till to the Heavens they Build her Lofty-Tower.
Then down in Love the very Heavens shall Bend:
Then shall the *Still Eternity* descend.
And shouts of Victory the Skies shall rend:
With full-ton'd Acclamation-Anthems clear
      And Love Congratulations Dear.
Thus down in Love the Heavens themselves shall bend,
Thus shall the *New Jerusalem* descend,
And God shall *Tabernacle* Here with Men,
              World without End.

And here at Rest Heav'ns Glorious Virgin Queen,
In all her Darling Beauties, Charms Divine,
Majestick Port, and Glories unconfin'd,

Sits on her Royal Throne, in her high *Fane* Enshrin'd.
And in the *Mirror* of her Heavens so clear
Presents her Lustrous *Son*, in whom Express
Outshines the Glory of his Father Dear.
In and through All the Eternal Peaceful *Dove*,
Out-pours the Burning Sea of Everlasting Love.
While loud each Arch-Angelick Trumpet Sings
Glory to the Eternal King of Kings.
                      While ev'ry Breath and Sound,
       The Ecchoing Spheres and Worlds around,
in Universal *Hallelujah* Rings.
Glory to the Returning King of Kings.
For this we Shout aloud, we Sing, we Pray,
AMEN: HOSANNA: HALLELUJAH.

MEAN while we turn our Eyes and Ears attent
To Heavens Embassadress to Mortals sent,
To shew her Virgin Mother's Love-Intent,
Through her a sweet Inchanting Ray she flings:
And purer Souls Inviting Thus Divinely Sings.

Now Open wide ye Everlasting Doors
       And swiftly Fly the Winged Hours,
Till your Great *Lebanon* Prince, the Mighty King
       In Solemn Triumph enter in:
All your Fresh Springs with Heavenly Dews to fill,
       Flowing from ev'ry Spicy Quill.
That you may Drink those *Nectarine* Draughts so pure.
       To Effect the Universal Cure.
Quint-Essence streaming from the *Godhead* Source;
       So Ravishing sweet, of such high Force;
As to transmute Man's Earth, and drossy Mold
       To Pearly Beauty, Living Gold.
Crown'd with the Sun and Star-bright Glory high;
       Clear Substance of a Deity;
Thus meetly Qualified and All Divine:
       Companions to the Glorious Trine.
Such Heavenly Virgin Souls shall free Command
       The Treasures of their *Native* Land:
Those hidden Mines, whose Springs of Golden Ore
       Shall decaid Nature full Restore.

Fountains of *Lebanons* Generated free
     Shall from this Golden Ocean be.
The Rapturous Joys whereof no Tongue can tell,
     But Godhead-Plants that in it dwell:
Who under th' shady Rocks high Banner grow,
     Whence Love's spic'd Liquors ever flow.
O come and tast what Pleasures here abound.
     Where would ye move in Endless round?
You must from Dross Refine, and Mount away;
     Mingling no more with Earth and Clay.
But as New-Risen Souls make your Ascents,
     To dwell in *Lebanon's* Golden Tents.

O *England*, Hear thy Genius loudly Call.
O Hear, and ere 'tis fixt, Prevent thy Fall.
Of Heaven thou most Abhorrd, thou dearest Lov'd.
Whom one by True Poetick Instinct mov'd
Well *Jews* has call'd, "A moody Murmuring Race
As ever tried th' extent and stretch of Grace.
Ah stop, take heed heed less thou so Head-strong move,
"As ev'n to Burst the very *Chain* of Love.
Still with Gods Prime-indulgent *Favours* Blest,
And Prov'd as oft by bitter Plagues distrest.
He cannot spare. Yet cannot thee forgo.
O how His Fury *sears*! how His Compassions slow!
Mark thy mild Saviour well; how once he stood,
Shedding at *Salem's* Gates his tender Flood,
O're thee again He Mourns, in Tears, in Sighs,
Wrung from his Bleeding Heart, and Melting Eyes,
Once more, from the Exuberant Mercy-Store,
A Glorious Day shall touch Fair *Albion's* Shoar:
Take Heed, Prepare: for if thou wilt not see
The Visitation Day-spring offer'd Thee:
If thou neglect the STAR that will Appear
First Rising Glorious in thy Hemisphere.
Thou of thy Birth-right wilt Suplanted be;
And Heavens full Shower of Blessing pass from thee.
The *Morning-Star* despis'd must Glide away;
And to a better Land its chearing Beams display.
Then at thy Loss and Folly, for a while,
Shall the Fair-sprouting *German Lilly* smile,

Yet kind and free Assist thy Labouring Toil.
Then, *Britain*, then Prepare for Scenes of Woe.
Then *Nilus* shall the wicked Land Ore-flow.
A—a's Stately Pride must tumble down,
And B—b's Lofty Towers must Kiss the Ground.
Then Happy who in *Goshen's* fruitful Land,
Sheltred beneath th' Almighties Wing shall stand,
In Safety, Peace and Plenty at Command.
Till the short Gloomy Day be past and gone:
And soon another Brighter Morning Dawn.
Gods Hand, and Will, shall be too Glaring plain,
Longer to meet Neglect, or bear Disdain.
Jealous, provok't with Emulation-Fire,
Again shall *British* Piety Aspire.
As it sunk Low; so shall it now Rise Higher.
His *First-born*, God in Thee again shall Own
And pour the Vast, the Double Blessings down.
And *England's* Monarch High, shall wear the Nations Crown.
The Fivefold-Portion-Right belongs to Thee.
Then shall the Land from Curse and Toil be free.
And *England Benjamin* Restored shall be.

Onesimus.

Selection Two.

[Richard Roach on Magical Prayer.]

[From "The Imperial Standard.", 1726—Ed.]

Chap. V.

FOR increasing and lengthening our Faith, and bringing it to more ready Act and Exercise on all Occasions, and particularly of the Inroads in Spirit upon us; consider it, First, when any Evil, or mixt Thing, or inferior Spirit, is entring, or operating upon us; where generally the first Thing that rises in the Mind is an Act of solicitous *Concern*, mixt with *Fear*; which, instead of obviating, gives it *further* Entrance. Instead of this, an Act of Faith, that God's Power and Wisdom shall overcome, and turn it to good Effect, puts a Bar to the Entrance of the Injection of Spirit so deeply into us; and engages God the sooner to answer and strike in with *His* Act, according to our present Need. Secondly ; As Faith worketh *by Love* externally, *i. e.* showing itself accompanied with Works of Charity; so consider it also as going forth to act thro' and by *that Love* of God, which thro' the first Operations of Faith, was shed forth or begotten by the Holy Spirit in the Soul ; consider Faith as actuated by and working from this Love, as its *Root* and Ground : or as *Love* varying itself, and going forth in Act of Faith, engaging Gods Superior and *General* Act in Concurrence with his own Life and Act *in us*. Faith is here the outgoing *Will of Love*, which is the Central Unity or Regent-Power of the Soul ; and is ultimately God in us. Consider then the *Active* Power of Faith thus bottom'd and founded upon *Love*, as a lesser Orb comprehended, penetrated and actuated by a greater, and following the Motion of it; yea, as an Act of God's Will, in Consent and Union with our particular Will, (understand still of the New Man,) as the Result, Egress or Emotion of our united Wills, in and from the Central or Universal Love. Thus believe in God, thus believe in Love, thus let your Faith work by Love, and no Evil shall hurt you. Thus believing in God and with God, your Will in Act of Faith will touch his Heart, will move in Sympathy of Love, and be mov'd and actuated by his Omnipotent Will, in order to bring into Act what is believed for. And thus you may do and will, and have what you will. Yet is not this to be understood as if we mov'd or wrought a Change in God : but it is our being wrought up out of our own Wills, and risen into God's, and so being mov'd and car-ry'd on in the Current of it. He that ends the Work *begins* it also : for *it is God that worketh in us both to Will and to Do, according to his good Pleasure.*

In order to the Operation of Faith in the *Miraculous* Way, to be reviv'd as of old, there must be an Opening again of the Powers of Nature in the secret *Magia* of the *Desire* and *Will*, thro' Regeneration, to become the Seat and Instrument of the Divine Powers in this Kind : which Powers of Nature in the Fall were suspended, and lock'd up in Impotence : some small Remains of which yet appear, particularly in the Case of Women's *Longing*: where the strong Desire and Imagination oft goes so far, as to produce a real outward Effect, in a *Mark* upon the Child in the Womb, and afterwards remaining. This effective Power of the Will and Desire in Nature, thro' the *Imagination*, the Instrument of it, as acting upon external Things was that whereby Man, the Image of God, *imag'd* or represented Him in his *Creating Power*. And even now the common Products of the Imaginative Faculty, or the *Images* form'd in the Mind of Man, are more real Things than they are taken to be, and will appear so, when the Soul appears divest of Body, and surrounded with the numerous Offspring of this Kind, which it has brought forth. *Eve's* Longing after the forbidden Fruit brought in Death: and so it continues to do in all her Posterity. So in the *Regeneration* the holy Souls *Longing* after *Christ*, the *Tree of Life*, in the strong Desire of the Will, thro' Faith, assenting to and closing into the Union with *His* Will, not only draws *Virtue* out of him, but his very *Life* and *Spirit* to be fed on. The common Hunger and Thirst in Nature often reaches an Effect in the *Astral* Soul, which is the Part that is waking in Sleep, so that they there meet with a Refreshment. But the Hunger and Thirst of the Immortal Soul has not only a natural *Tendency*, but the Concurrence of the *Divine Will*, and an actual *Promise* and Declaration beforehand, that *it shall be fill'd*, Matt. V. 6.

Now what is in us Call'd the Power of Faith, in this highest Sense, *viz.* of Miraculous Operation, is in God the *Divine Magia*, the Effective or Creative Power of his Will: Whence his Almighty *Fiat*, or Word of Command, going forth to execute what is his Desire and Will, becomes impregnated with the *Seed* of the design'd Product, or the Power to make it so. Here the Understanding or Wisdom of God conceives the Thing desirable; the Divine Will embraces it, resolves upon the actual Product, and re-acts upon the Wisdom in Power to effect it. This is from the Wisdom, as the Intellectual, *Conceptive*, or Divine Virgin-Nature, is communicated to the *Son* the *Word*; which the Son speaks forth in the *Fiat* thro' the *Breath* of God, which is his *Spirit*: Which Word proceeds and sounds forth descending thro' the *Seven Spirits*, or Emanative Powers of the One Holy Spirit: which we find *Rev.* i. 4. 5. put in the Place of the One Spirit, in the Blessing to the seven Churches from God, and from *Jesus Christ*, and from the *Seven Spirits* which are before the Throne. And thus the Original *Pattern* in the Mind of God is immediately answer'd to by its *Copy* or *Image* in created Nature. Thus were the *Angelical* Words at first formed, or *out-spoken* from God; thus this visible World in Conformity to the invisible ; and thus were the great Wonders and *Miraculous* Operations effected thro' the *Prophets* and *Apostles* of old : in whom these are said to be wrought by *Faith*, because what the Creator originally acted was brought forth thro' them, in their dependent Act of Trust and Reliance on him, and in the Resignation of their own Desires and Wills into Union with his. And the Way for this lies the more open and easy, by Reason of the Birth of *Christ* into our Nature; in which he now exists glorified in the Heavens; thro' which he sent forth the *Holy Ghost* at *Pentecost*; and by the near Alliance of which to us, and the *Communion* in Spirit between him, the Head, and Believers as his Members, the Way for Descent of the Divine *Fiat* into Nature thro' the Adventurers in this high Faith, is yet more facilitated. This Key, when rightly turn'd, will bring forth the *Miraculous* Operations e'er long, to the Glory of God in Christ, and the Manifestation of his triumphant Bride: who shall come forth from her *Wilderness*-State leaning upon her Beloved, and endow'd with those Primitive *Gifts* and Powers, which have so long *Ceas'd* in the external and visible Church-states.

Selection Three.

Index of Theosophical and Philosophical Terms, by Richard Roach

[From "The Imperial Standard", 1726, —Ed.]

AN
INDEX

And Explanation *of some Terms, and the manner of their Application, made use of in this Work, and in the* Great Crisis *Preparatory to it; Digested in such Order as may best serve to render the Scheme at Large more Intelligible; and be also of more* General *Use.*

It will be needful here in general to apprize the Reader, that the Terms commonly applied by the Learned to Natural or Corporeal things, are not in these Writings transfer'd or wrested from their proper Signification, consider'd in General: but are indeed often applied in a higher manner to *Like* Objects of a *Spiritual* kind, in which the same Properties or Qualities are found; but are to be understood in a manner Suitable to Things or Beings of a more Sublime, and *Spiritual* Nature, The Ground, of which is this: that Things below are form'd according to the *Patterns* of Things above, and that *Material* things are *Figures* or Shadows of *Immaterial:* whence it follows that the *Immaterial*, and Heavenly things to which the Inferior bear Relation, Exist more in the *Truth* and Reality of Essence; and Consequently, that the *Terms* common to Both when applied to Them have also a Signification more according to the Truth and Reality of the Thing. This was not unknown the Ancient *Philosophers*, as may appear from that famous *Axiom*, said for its great Import and Excellency, to have been written in the *Smaragdine* Table, (*i.e.* of *Emerald.*) viz *Omnia Coelestia sunt in Terris; sed modo Terrestri; Omnia Terrestria sunt in Coelis; Sed Modo coelesti.* i.e. *All Heavenly Things are found on Earth, but after an Earthly manner; All things on Earth are found in heaven; but after a Heavenly manner.* The Terms then thus applied from the Figures or *Copies* to their *Originals* are not only *Metaphors*, as they are generally taken to be; but, as before, more Truly, and highly Significant, than as commonly us'd. To give an Instance or two. There is an Internal *Spiritual Space*, as Well as an External *Local*; and of which the Latter is a Figure: *viz. That* in which the Spiritual Worlds exist, and in which Angelical Beings Live, move and act; the Root whereof, or the Inmost *Ultimate* Space is the Infinite *Being* of *God* himself, in whom all Worlds have then Foundation and Existence. There is *Spiritual Dilatation*, in Inlargement of Soul, and Capacity of Comprehension: as whereby it can take in still greater degrees of Knowledge, and open still more and more in Participation and Enjoyment of God the Fountain of it; also whereby in Thought or Mental Act it can stretch it Self to a View of the whole System of the Earth and Heavens. And there is a *Spiritual Contraction*, whereby it can settle down again to the Consideration of a Single, or of the most Minute Object. So there is *Spiritual Generation*, and *Divine* Generation, and the *Marriage* of the *Lamb* with the Church: his Bride; all most true and Real in their Sublime and *Spiritual* Sense. I have Inisted the more on this Point on account of the great Usefulness and Weight of it, and as it is indeed in it self, and may be found in the right Application of it, a *Fund* of *Endless* Knowledge.

I shall also in this *Index* for the use of the Unlearned Reader give the Explication of some Scholastick Terms, in Use, and some more common, in which Distinction may be needful on account of the Ambiguity, or where the full Import of 'em may not be generally apprehended;

§ First then *Essence* in the strict Sense, denotes the *Being* of a Thing in general, *Prior* to the Consideration of the *Substance* and *Nature* of it: And so is oppos'd to *Non-Entity*, or not Being. It is us'd also in a more loose and general Sense, including the Substance and the Nature also; as usually in the Term *Co-Essential;* and as we say All *Beings* in Heaven and Earth.

Substance, strictly taken is the matter of which any Thing consists: and is consider'd *Prior* to the Modification or *Form* introduc'd into it: And is sometimes more generally us'd, as including also the matter so modified and form'd.

The *Nature* of a Thing denotes the Modification or Form introduc'd into the Matter or Substance, constituting it in such a Kind or Class of Beings, whence arises its *Act* and *Product*, according to its Kind.

Existence, Implies a Thing in Act, or in *Actual Being*. *Essence* in the strict Notion of it may be applied to a Thing yet in its Causes, or Seed of Production; as the Ear of Corn in the Grain Sown, or a Son yet in the Loyns of his Parents; but *Existence* implies the Thing brought forth in a Distinct Being of its Own, as the Product or *Effect* of those Causes.

Life; is the First general and constant *Act* of the Nature or *Form* in the Being so constituted; the Central Spring of Motion and Operation therein, actuating each Part or Organ in its proper Office. It arises from the just degree of Heat, or Participation of the Active Element of Fire concurring in its Constitution; and chiefly in Natural Beings from the Influence and Genial Warmth of the *Sun;* which as communicated and wrought into the Animal Texture or Composition, and Seated in the Heart is by some call'd the *Archeus*, and the *Archeal* Power, which imports the Principal *Regent* and actuating Power of the Whole: And is by some also Subdivided into *Inferior Archeal* Powers, Regent of the Principal Parts of the Body, as the Head, Stomach, *&c.*

Idea. It signifies a Thing Seen: but is translated to the Mind, as a Thing *seen* therein; and so imports a *Mental Conception,* or a Representation of any thing in the Mind; which is either by the pure *Intellectual* Power as conceiving a Thing, or a Truth of a more Sublime and Spiritual Nature; or in the *Imaginative* Faculty forming an *Image* of a more gross and Spiritu-Corporeal kind, by Aid of the *Animal Spirits;* as of a House, a Tree, or the Outward Form of a Man. The Word *Idea* is oft applied to both, tho' more strictly and properly to the Former, and Word *Image* to the Latter.

Prescinding, Precisively. Where of several Parts, Properties or Qualities that are conjoin'd in any Subject some One or more are taken, and attended to apart from the rest. The Word signifies a *Cutting off,* and as applied to a *Mental* Act, a *Distinction*, or Distinct Consideration.

Transcendent, Transcendental. Passing the common Bound, Use or Sense. Where applied to a Term or Expression, the taking it in a Higher, or a Spiritual Sense.

Analogy. The *Proportion,* or just Agreement of One Thing or Part to another; or of a Part or Parts to the Whole. So where we speak of *Scripture Analogy*, or the *Analogy of Faith*, the Interpretation of any Part or Portion of the Former, or Explanation of any Article of the Latter is to be judg'd of by its Agreement or Disagreement to the main Scheme and Design, as the *Proportion* or *Disproportion* it bears to the Whole.

Nature, at large, is the Whole *Frame* of created Beings, Consider'd as under its *Immediate* Regent Power; and *Superior* Regency of its *Author*. This is call'd Temporal Nature, as diftinguish'd from *Eternal Nature:* which is the whole Frame of the *Heavenly* created Worlds, in like manner consider'd under their Immediate Regent Powers; and with relation to *God*, the Supreme, as manifested in 'em, and acting in and thro' 'em.

Archetypes, or *Prototypes*. The First, Original *Patterns* or *Ideas* in the *Mind* of God, according to which all Created Things were form'd.

Ectypes, the Things Outwardly or visibly form'd or accordingly to these *Ideas* and Original *Patterns*.

Inchoation. A Beginning.

Binary, Ternary, Quaternary, Quinary, &c. to the *Denary*. These here us'd to denote in the Numbers proceeding on from the Unity, *viz*. Two, Three, Four, Five, &c. to Ten, the *Variations* of the *Divine* Powers explicated in the Process of Simple or Single Numbers. These Terms have their Signification *Abstractedly* or *Substantively, i. e.* as expressing the Import or *Power* of the Number by it Self, without connoting or implying the Subject in which they may be found. They are also otherwise applied to the Process of *Nature* tending to its Perfection, or as bearing an Impression of the Divine Powers, operating in or thro' it.

Ten Sephiroth. The Powers of the Deity explicated in this Number or Order, according to the Jewish *Cabbala*: (the more Secret or Mystical Knowledge and Writings of the *Jewish Rabbins*, or chief Teachers.) The Word *Sephiroth* implies *Numbers*; and may also denote *Books*, as so many Volumes of the Eternal *Word*, Truth and Wisdom, thus Expressing and unfolding the Divine Powers and Properties.

Virgin Wisdom. The Divine *Intellectual* Power, *Original* in the *Father, Derivative* in the *Son*, and *Processive* in the *Holy Spirit:* and thence going forth with the *Divine Word* to Creation, and Manifestation of God to, and in his Works.

Super-Coelestial Planets. The Original *Planetary* Powers in the *Heavenly* Creation; to which the Planets in the Outward Visible Heavens correspond, or Answer in their peculiar Properties: as they (the *Super-Celestial*) answer to, and are under the Regency of the *Seven-Spirits* of God, mention'd Rev. i. 4.

Seven Spirits, or *Holy Septenary*, the Out going Powers or Emanations of the One *Holy Spirit* of God.

Emanation. A Flowing forth, as of a Stream from its Fountain: applied Spiritually to the Procession of Divine Power or Virtue, and the Influence of the Holy Spirit. Emanation and Influence import the same Thing, only the former respects the Origin or Term from whence the Power or Virtue comes; the Latter the Subject into which it is receiv'd.

Sublunary Things. Such as are beneath the *Moon*; in the Air, or on the Earth.

Quintessence, Quintessential; Signifying a *Fifth Essence*. In a more loose and *Chymical* Sense a pure *Extract* of *Spirits* drawn from a more gross Matter. And more strictly and properly an Essence in which the Properties and Powers of the Four Elements are so Combin'd as to lose their Contrariety to each other, and concur to the Perfection or Happiness of the Subject in which they are thus combin'd

Hence, *One-Element*, and *One Elemental*; denoting the *Four-Elementary* Powers in *Eternal* Nature combin'd in perfect Harmony and Unity.

Elixir. An *Arabic* Word, importing a pure or Quintessential Extract in the former *Chymical* Sense, of Spirits drawn from grosser Matter.

Grand-Elixir. A more Perfect Extract or Composition; a Universal Restorative of Health.

Homogeneous. Of the same kind.

Heterogeneous. Of a Different kind.

Coalesce, Coalescence. Where Distant or Disagreeing Things accord, close, or grow on together as it were in One Substance or Body.

Defecated. Purified, purg'd from its Dross.

Sublimate, Sublimated. Refin'd, and Exalted to a high degree.

Arcanum. A peculiar Secret.

Grand Arcanum. The Great Secret of the Chymical Philosopher for Transmutation or changing of grosser Metals into Gold; and for Universal Medicine.

Adeptical. Belonging to *that* Art.

Adept, Adeptist. One that has attain'd that Art.

These Terms are sometimes us'd, as applied to Matters or Subjects of a Higher or Spiritual kind.

Archives. Places in great Libraries where Books of more Recondite or Secret Knowledge are kept from publick View, and for the Use of such as may be capable of it.

Theosophy, Theosopher. As the Common *Philosophy* by the Faculty of Humane Reason, or a more peculiar Talent therein, considers Things chiefly with Regard to their Second or more immediate Causes, tho' with a General Eye to their First; *Theosophy* in a more Intellectual Way, and from a peculiar Talent or *Gift* of the Divine *Wisdom* in order thereto, has its chief Regard to the First Cause of all Things and its Act upon and Operation in and thro' both the Invisible and Visible Creation; and that both in their first Constitution, and also in the Government of them in the State wherein they now are. It gives a more Fundamental Discovery of the State of Faln Nature both *Angelical* and *Humane*, and the Influence of God upon them in his strict Justice or Anger only, or also his Grace and Love: As also of the Deep Mystery of our Redemption by *Jesus Christ*; the Regeneration, New Birth, and Restoration to the Divine Image again: and gives further and deeper Manifestation of the Nature of the Soul, the State of the Heavenly Worlds, and of the Nature or God Himself, than can be attain'd by Humane Reason and Learning. This chiefly relates to the Works of *Jacob Behmen*, who is call'd the *Teutonic(German) Philosopher* and by way of Eminence the *Theosopher*: but it is also applied to other Writers in the same Way.

Magia, or *Divine Magia*: so call'd to distinguish it from both the *Natural* and *Diabolical* Magic. *Natural Magie* is perform'd by the Agency of Middle Spirits residing in, or Regent of the Air or Elements: and by determining, and combining the Powers or Virtues of the Elements Planets, and Constellations to the Product of uncommon Effects: not Lawful, especially under the *Gospel*; because of the Danger of Mixture and Intrusion of Evil Spirits, not easily to be discern'd; and because of That being a Dispensation, in which the Operation of the *Holy Spirit* it Self is found: whence Books of this kind were brought and burnt at the Feet of the Apostles. *Diabolical Magic* is by the Concurrence and Operation of Wicked and Infernal Spirits, acting upon and in the corrupt Part of, and thro' the Curse in Nature; also Perverting the Powers of the Elements and Stars to wicked Ends and Purposes. The *Divine Magia* then is the Operation of God Himself by the Agency of his *Holy Spirit*; in the Efficacious Power of his Own Will and Word; or the Power of the Divine *Fiat*, Saying Let it be done, and it is done;

viz. by the Outflowing Virtue of and from his Word, as a *Seed* to the Design'd Product: by which the Miracles both of the Law and Gospel were brought forth.

Seven Forms, or *Properties of Nature*.

The Seven Principal Operative Powers and Movements in Nature in order to its various Effects and Products: these Answering to the Properties and Operations of the Seven *Planets*.

The First *Astringent*, binding, close comparing, *Attractive* towards the Center: in the Property of *Saturn*.

The Second *Opening*, Dividing, Dilating and Elevating ; *Abstractive* from the Center: in the Property of *Jupiter*.

The Third *whirling* in a dubious or Mixt Movement, partly *Spiral* as a Screw, or a Worm in a Limbeck; but forwards and backwards; and sometimes direct forwards with a quick Return backwards again, so making sharp and pricking Angles, as in the Motion of *Light'ning*. This is the Property of *Mars*.

The Fourth comprehending these Three as farther advanc'd into a *General* Motion of all its Parts, and so producing *Fire*. These four consider'd as not reaching further in the Process of Nature, are in Discord and contrariety; and the Cause of Pain and Suffering (in Subjects capable of it,) or of Corruption and Dissoulution (otherwise.) But where they reach the *Fifth* Form they combine in Amicable Unity. This Fourth Form is in the Property of *Sol*; and as it is the Center of the Seven is consider'd in a Twofold *Aspect*; First Backwards as receiving the concurrent Influence of the Three first Forms, and so as a Body of *Fire*: and Secondly with its Aspect Forwards, and so receiving the Influence of the Three latter Forms; by which all is reduc'd to Concord and Harmony. Here indeed *Sol* is consider'd as the *Sun* in his Central Position and due Distance, giving forth Light and kindly Heat for Vegetation, Life, Generation, Production; and adding Lustre and Beauty, or also Comfort and Joy to Beings partaking of his Influences. And *thus* the Fourth Form is consider'd as *Light* producing *Love*.

The *Fifth Form*, then, is the *Love* thus produc'd, and moving thro' the Union of the proceeding Forms or Properties, in a gentle, *Lambent*, and delightful Flame.

This accordingly in the Propertie of *Venus*.

The *Sixth Form*, in the Propcerty of *Mercury*, gives the *Voice*, Speech, and Musical Tone, and the Mutual Intercourse, and more External Expression and Celebration of the Love-Harmony thus attain'd.

The *Seventh Form*, in the Property of *Luna*, gives the Compaction into *Body*, and forms as it were the House or Palace wherein all the other Properties, having reach'd their End, acquiesce and rest, or dwell together in perfect Accord and Unity.

There is to be observ'd in these *Seven Forms*, as also in the *Seven Planets*, an Agreement or Likeness in Properties between the First and the Last, as *Saturn* and *Luna*, both in degree binding or close compacting; between the Second and the Sixth as *Jupiter* and *Mercury* both Abstractive, Dilating, and Volatile, between the Third and the Fifth as *Mars* and *Venus*, the former being in the nearest Advance to the Fire, the latter advancing the Fire into the Love-Flame. Hence 'tis that *Mercury* has been by some put here in the Place of *Jupiter*.

These *Seven Forms* have their Operation not only in the Material World, but in the *Spiritual* also; and not in Temporal only but also in *Eternal* Nature or the Heavenly Creation; and they are consider'd as under the Supreme Conduct of the *Seven Spirits* of God. In the Soul of Man they may be consider'd as acting in their Bad or divided Properties, or in their Good as temper'd into a degree of Harmony and Union. Thus the First in the Astringent or binding Property tends to produce, in the bad Part, Covetousness, Immoderate Desire for Self-Ends, or Self-Love; also Moroseness and Stinging Saryr; and in the good Part, Frugality, Recollection, and Staidness of Mind, Smartness in Reproof. The Abstractive and dilating Property produces, in the Bad Part, Prodigality, Looseness or Dissolution of Mind and Manners: in the Good Part, as in the Union with the other Properties, Openness, Generality of Mind, Liberality. The Third Form in its Whirling and mixt Movement, *&c.* causes, in the Bad Part, Uncertainty, Doubting, Anxiety, Anguish of Mind, violent Movements, strong Flash, with sudden Turn of Passion: in the good Part, Activity, Boldness, Martial Courage, Point or Emphasis of Joy and Delight, also Langour of Love.

The Fourth or Fiery Property produces, in the Bad Part, Wrath, Enmity, Rage, Destructive Intent: in the Good Part Magnanimity, Nobility of Mind, Capacity of Government, Friendship, Love, Love Flame; *viz.* from the *Light's* giving Knowledge, Wisdom, Discovery of Beauty and Excellence, and consequently producing Love; Hence also the Poetick Faculty. The *Fifth Form* as in the Property of *Venus*, gives in the good Part, Inclination and Determination of Will to Marriage Union, Generation; also Spiritual Union or Communion of Souls in Sacred, or ev'n *Divine* Love; where they are highly Sanctified. The *Good* Part is here, *viz.* the Latter Forms, *First mention'd;* because in the

Regular Process thro' the four first into the *Fifth Form* the Contrariety and Evil Ceases; but without that, or in Disjunction the Property here Declines to Unlawful Love, Lust, Fornication, Adultery.

The Sixth or *Mercurial* Property gives the Faculty of quick and ready Thought and Expression, Facetious Wit, Dextrous Application, and Musical Genius. But where without the Temperature, it tends to the Perversion of these Talents, Readiness to Mischief, Lying, Tricking, Stealing, *&c.* The *Seventh Form*, in the *Lunar* Property of Compaction into Body, gives in the *Mind* Solidity and Gravity, due Care of the Body, and Outward Concerns: and in the Divided or Bad Part, Heaviness, Dulness, Sloath, and Immersion of the Soul into Low and Earthy Things. *N. B.* These Properties in themselves tend to Good; the Evil Part is only where the Band of Harmony is *Broken*, as in the State of *Faln* and Corrupt Nature.

I have Inlarg'd on these Forms of Nature as they are the Ground of the deepest *Natural* Knowledge, and of the true *Theosophy*.

Mystical Theology, or *Spiritual Divinity:* Distinguishd from the common Systems or Bodies of Divinity in the Way of Humane Reason and Learning, First as it depends more Immediately on the Conduct and Illumination of the *Holy Spirit*. Secondly, As to its Subject; chiefly the Inward Operation of the *Holy Spirio* upon the Soul rooting out the most Secret Vices and Corruptions, and carrying it on in the *Perfective* Part, to Divine Contemplation, Union, and Communion with God. Thirdly, As it contains the Rules, Doctrines, and Experience of the most Advanc'd and Spiritual Christians both Antient and Modern, in their Process towards Perfection. It is as to the Substance of it the *Same* in the Writers of all Ages, however differing in External Profession or Denomination.

Aera: Deriv'd as some think from the *Latin* Word *Aera* or Money paid for Tribute at such Time Impos'd ; or as others from an *Arabic* word Signifying to Compute or count. It is us'd for a Time made Signal by some Remarkable Action or Event, from whence particular Countries *Date* their Account of Time : as the *Romans* from the *Building* of their City; the *Greeks* from the Institution of their *Olympick Games* in Honour to *Jupiter Olympius*; the *Turks* from the Time of *Mahomet's* Flight from the City of *Mecha*, which they call their *Hegira*; the *Christians* from the *Birth of Christ*. From *Aera* comes the English Word *Year*.

Epocha: signifies also such a *Date* of Time; only connoting or implying the *Stop* or Interruption of the Former General Computation by the Introduction of a New One, and Particular to such a State or Nation.

Dispensation, Ministration, Oeconomy: (as of the *Law*, the *Gospel* or the *Patriarchal* State, *i. e.* of the Fathers before the Law.) These agree in a General Signification, denoting a Course or Appointment of God in such an Order, and under such Rules, Suitable to the Degree of Manifestation of Himself to Mankind, in such a Time or Age. Yet they have some Difference in the manner of Denotation, and in the Particular Application of them; grounded on the immediate Signification of the Words themselves. Thus the Word *Dispensation* has regard to Gods Dispensing or giving out his Rules and Institutions, and his Assistant Grace therein: and is Applicable also to a Less or more Private Providential Course. The Word *Ministration* bears Respect to the Administration of Government therein: which may be referr'd to the Spirit of God as Supreme Regent, or the Administrators under it.

The Word *Oeconomy* imports the Government of a *House* or Family according to Laws or Rules proper for it: and so has its First Signification more Restrain'd: But with Respect to *God* the Universal Father and Governor, it may be extended more largely, and denote either his Government of a Chosen People, as the *House* of *Israel*, the *Household* of Faith; or of all the Families of the Earth, or even the whole System or *Frame* of the Universe.

Denisons Indenizon'd: made Free, and Having Right to all the Privileges of a City, Community, or Ministration.

Central Pass. A Middle Passage, or Transition from One Ministration to another: here applied to the Time of Preparation of the Kingdom of Christ, as between the Gospel Suffering State, and the Gospel Triumphant. This is Two fold; First, the Preparation in Strict Justice and Judgment. Secondly, in Grace and Love, or the For-eshooting Powers and Foretasts of the Kingdom.

Intermedial: What is contain'd between two, Terms, Extreams, or Ends.

Center, principle, or *Region*: Often taken as *Nature* before in its full Sense for both the Origin, Source or Regent Power, and its Product at Large. So in a transcendent Sense we say the *Fathers*, or the *Sons* Centre or Principle. Also the Principle of Eternal Nature, the Principle of this World, the Worldly Principle. And sometimes the Principle or Region of Pure-Deity, *i. e.* as above or beyond all Created Beings or Worlds.

Central, Circumferential. These Words are often us'd in a transcendent and Spiritual sense. They are also in Ordinary Speech sometimes translated from the *Mathematical* Sense, *viz.* of a Middle *Point*, and the

Circle or Globe round it, to other Natural things of different kinds; as where we say the Centre of *Motion*, the Centre of *Life*; *i.e.* whence the Motive or Vital Power Springs, and communicates it Self to the most distant Parts as its Circumference. So with relation to *Time*, the Present Now is the Center between Time past, and Future: and even Time it Self between the two Eternities consider'd as before and after it. The Mystical Divines, and also Philosophers, (as the *Platonists*,) have gone further in the Application of these Terms to purely *Spiritual* Objects, and been censur'd sometimes by the common Learned; as particularly for that Expression of the *Centre of the Soul:* which yet has a deep and Solid Meaning, *viz.* the *Spring* of Spiritual Life, Thought or Act, Originally in the *Will* as the First Mover: and as *That*, the Will, is consider'd in Conjunction with the purer or Superior *Intellectual* Part, distinct from the Ratiocinative Faculty, it is as the *Gate* of Emission or giving out its Influence, and of Admission or Reception, both with Respect to *God* the Fountain of its Being, and to others; or as the Navel String or Medium for Communication with Them also. These Terms of Centre and Circumference are also sometimes applied to the Divine Being, and may represent the Spring or Origine of the Divine Life and Power, diffusing and varying it Self to Infinity; or otherwise of the Divine *Unity* Explicating it Self in Endless *Variation*. These Terms indeed according to their natural Signification import a *Limit*; both of the Littleness and Greatness; but as here Transcendentally applied, *viz.* to God, they denote a Central or Original Power *without* Determination to a *Least*, and a Circumferential without the Bound of a *Greatest*. Had we the Proper Terms in which an Angel might be suppos'd to speak of the deepest Spiritual and Divine Subjects, there would be no need of representing them by their *Ectypes* or Figures in Nature, as for Want thereof we are forc'd to do: and for the same reason those who for Want of Knowledge in the Mystical or Theosophical Way censure and reflect on this manner of Expression, are themselves oft constrain'd to do the Like in their Own Way and Sphere.

Kingdom. This Word has Several Acceptations. First the *Place* or Country wherein a Government is administer'd. Secondly, The *Subjects* over which such Dominion is Exercis'd. Thirdly and most fully, as including the two former Senses, a State wherein a *King*, in such a Place, and over such Subjects, is found in the Actual Administration of his Government.

Hierarchy. A State, Principality or Kingdom, as under its Chief, and Inferior Rulers. The Word Originally denotes a *Sacred* State; but is us'd Indifferently: as where we say, the *Luciferian*, the *Roman* Hierarchy.

Kingdom of Christ. This is here taken in the full Sense, of a King in his Kingdom: and is understood of his *Millennial* Kingdom; which is to begin according to the Revelation Prophecy of it, upon the Sounding of the *Seventh Angel*, and the *Finishing* (and Manifestation) of the *Mystery*, *viz.* of Gods Secret Conduct of, and Operation in the Process of the Church Periods in order thereto, till at last Satan is Dethron'd and Bound, and the Kingdoms of the Earth become the *Kingdoms of the Lord and of His Christ.*

Millennial. Belong to, or continuing for a Thousand Years.

Millennial Doctrines. Relating to the Thousand Years Reign of Christ.

Extraordinary Powers and Operations:

These are Acts and Influences of the *Spirit* of God in the same Kind and Nature as those experienc'd by the *Prophets* and *Apostles viz.* by Voice, Vision, Dream, Impulse, Union and Communion with God: as thus Differing from the *Common* Operations of Grace, experienc'd in a more Secret and hidden manner in the Souls of the Good and Pious. They are call'd the *Charismata*, or *Gifts* from the peculiar Grace and Favour of God: and are to be consider'd First with Relation to the Persons possessing them, as given to carry on the Work of Regeneration in them to higher Degrees, in the more Perfective Part of Religion; and Secondly for the Edification of Others: They are also consider'd here as *Reviving* again in this Age, in *Preparation* of the Kingdom of Christ: as found, in various Degrees in the Souls of the Elect hereto, according to their Growth; and in some more Eminently to Qualify them to give forth the Manifestations of the Kingdom; or to warn, instruct, and Prepare Others for it.

Again the *Extraordinary* Powers of this Day come forth and will proceed with some Difference both in Kind and Manner from those in Former Times. Those under the Gospel differ'd from those under the Law; and those of the Third and last Ministration will differ from those under the Law and Gospel, both in kind, manner, and Degree; And that on the account of *Christ's* coming therein more peculiarly and Eminently in the Power of his *Father*: in the Opening of whose Principle together with the *Virgin Wisdom*'s, to Prepare and Establish the Kingdom of his Son, this Difference will chiefly consist.

Those *Internal Extraordinary* Powers may be call'd, in the General, Miraculous Operations, as proceeding directly from God, and Evidencing his Immediate Prefence in the Spirit: But what is more Particularly call'd *Miraculous* Operation or Outward Miracle and Sign, refers to those that are Without, as 1 *Cor.* xiv. 22. for *them that Believe not,* i. e. upon other Sufficient Evidence. For *such* Appearance of the Power of God the present Day and Dispensation, like that of *John Baptist*, is not Ripe. Tho' for Excitement of Faith, and as a *Sign* of the Times, God has been pleas'd to give forth the few instances of *miraculous Healing,* as in the Case of the *French Maid, Susannah Arch, Lydia Hills,* and others, fully attested before, and the Attentions *Sign'd* by, the publick *Magistrate*. Several instances have been also given in private among the Waiters for the Kingdom, both in Way of the Effect of Faith, in the Persons themselves Restor'd, and also by the Mediation of Others in whom the Divine Power has open'd: which will be known more generally as the Work of God and Progress of the Preperation of the Kingdom in this our Age shall be further inquir'd into.

Spiritu Corporeal; or *Spiritual Bodily;* belonging to a *Resurrection* body; or to the Internal *Spiritual* Body of Christ, with which he cloath'd himself externally and visibly at his *Transfiguration*. Applicable also the *Internal* Body gradually form'd in the *New Man*; also to the Figures and *Images* of Things form'd by the Soul by the Mediation of purest *Animal Spirits* supplied from the Brain.

Internal or *Spiritual Senses*. These Terms are sometimes used more generally and indistinctly, to denote the Perceptions of various kinds, in the Regenerate Soul, in the Extraordinary Way; as the Soul has in it Powers of Perception purely *Spiritual*, yet answering to those of the *Corporeal* Senses: But, more properly and distinctly Speaking, these Internal *Senses* belong to the *Internal* and *Spiritual Body;* which under the Extraordinary Powers and Influences is gradually Form'd, and becomes the immediate Vehicle and Organ of the Soul or Spirit; and by Means of which, as disintangled from the Clog and Fetters of the Inferior Body, the Spirit obtains Ascent or *Translation* sometimes into the Heavenly World. And these in a *Spiritu-Corporeal* manner Answer to the *Outward* Senses of the Natural Body. This Inward Spiritual *Body* with its proper Senses is form'd by feeding on, and being cloath'd with the *Body* of Christ, in its *Diffusive* Virtue.

And by these purer Senses the more compared and Spiritual-bodily Powers of the Heavenly Creation are receiv'd and enjoy'd; and a more *External Converse* maintain'd by and with pure Departed Souls, and Angelical Spirits; while a *higher* is carried on in a purely *Spiritual* and Intellectual Way.

Spiritual Union, and Communion. This Experienced by many under the Extraordinary Operations, or Preparatory Powers of the Kingdom at this Time of the so near Advent of the *Bridegroom*, giving Holy and separated Souls the *Foretasts* of the *Marriage Feast*. It is experienc'd sometimes in Influences from *God* himself, and sometimes between highly Regenerate Souls under the Operation of the *Spirit*; and is the Primitive *Communion of Saints* again reviving. It is, interiorly to the Spirits Operation, facilitated and carried on by the *Medium* of the *Spiritual Body*, that also concurring in it.

Thus far the *Index*, thus dispos'd: to which it may be needful to add a short One, of the Words only therein explain'd, digested in their *Alphabetical* Order, to be consulted as Occasion may require.

Selection Four.

[Comments by Christopher Walton on Freher, Lee and the Philadelphian Society.]

[pg.200] * It will not be forgotten, that this writer became afterwards the ingenious author of the 'History of Montanism'— By the way, Fenelon's 'Maxims of the Saints explained,' was omitted to be particularly recommended to the student of Mystical Books, in regard to the orthodox and spurious of Mystical Doctrines.

[pg.330]* Note, and in continuation of the note of p. 200, so far as relates to Lee ; as also concerning the 'Treatise' referred to, p. 252, 3.

But first we take occasion to observe, (though such an announcement belongs more appropriately to a Preface, if one shall be found needful,) that this treatise, to be duly apprehended, should be perused regularly from the commencement, it having been drawn up in the intervals of daily commercial avocations, from only a general scheme or conception of its form and contents, just as the sheets were demanded by the printer; the editor, moreover, not being possessed of literary talent, and having no other preparation for the work, than the singularly providential possession of the MSS., treatises, and almost all the books of reference necessary for the compilation of a biography, such as is thereby sought to be obtained. Wherefore as in such cases, there will not be found a logical uniformity in the arrangement and composition of the work. On account then of these circumstances, of the editor's not being a practical master of logical composition, (clearness of conception, and perspicuity of expression, having been his sole aim,) and his having to get together and decisively arrange the matter as it has been required by the printer, it is recommended to the reader, not to satisfy himself with dipping here and there into the work, but *to give it a regular perusal from the commencement.* The printing of it began in the month of November of the last year, and has continued up to the present time, the month of September, 1848, and is intended to be proceeded with, until the circle line of the scheme be drawn round all the points needful to be embraced in a treatise of such a character; which is designed as an index to the quintessence of all orthodox metaphysical, spiritual or mystical science, (the science of the saints, enlarged to its true philosophical extent,) and to the direct attainment of all that is experimental therein, from the lowest to the highest supersensual degree, scholastically accomplished, naturally developed, square, straight, unidiocratic, Christlike, standard mind of William Law. Which general directions or rude outlines can be hereafter filled up to their full proportions for *universal benefit* and practically applied, by such as shall be qualified and called to the work.

With respect to the reference of p. 252, 3, the writer, a few days ago, met with a work which, on examining more closely its matter and style, he has no doubt of being the 'Treatise' there in question, and written by Lee. The title-page runs thus, "The General Delusion of Christians, touching the ways of God's revealing himself, to, and by the Prophets, evinced from Scripture and Primitive Antiquity. And many principles of Scoffers, Atheists, Sadducees, and wild Enthusiasts, refuted. The whole adapted, as much as possible, to the meanest capacity. In four parts.' Prophecy came not [οὐἠνέχη was not, or is brought] at any time, by the will of man; but holy men of God spake [φερομένοι] being violently moved by [υπο, under] the Holy Spirit.' 8vo. London, 1713."

To come now to the chief purport of the present note, or continuation of the note of p. 200, where is observed concerning Lee, that notwithstanding what he had there above written to Dodwell, in defence of the Philadelphians, their principles and proceedings, he became afterwards, in the year 1709, the author of "Hickes's" History of Montanism. Upon which, the editor of this treatise, as incumbent upon him, would additionally remark, That it appears to him quite paradoxical, how Lee, so eminently devoted and spiritual an individual, so experienced in deep communion with God, and so cognizant of the super-rational operations of the Spirit, could have written (even anonymously) the history of the Montanists as he has done in the above work; after what is contained in the above-mentioned letter to Dodwell, in his prefaces to Lead, and in his other writings in connection with the Philadelphians. Contrasting the spirit of these latter, with the cool, semblant-impartial, yet, in effect, condemnatory tone of the same writer, in the above-mentioned work, an ordinary reader would suppose the author to have been a menial crafty advocate, acquainted, as a backslider, or growing lukewarm professor, with the spiritualities of high Christian experience, and, at the same time, with what may be plausibly urged against them by sober orthodoxy and rationalists, and yet ready to write on either side, as hired. It is strange, we say, that the pious and devout Lee, could be induced to write at all in *judgment* upon so super-rational and delicate a subject as is implied in the history of the Montanists, or indeed upon any devoted individuals, whose lives were characterised by a strict practice of gospel piety outwardly, and by great self-denial, total separation from the spirit of the world, and earnest continual prayer, in their private walk and conversation.

How differently does the divinely wise and apostolic Freher speak and write, in the passages to which these remarks are a note, as on every other occasion. And who that knows anything of experimental religion, is not aware, that a man must become a fool to the world, to be truly wise, in the sight of Christ and God? 'And though *human prudence*, (under the character of sober orthodoxy) may talk mighty wisely about the necessity of avoiding *particularity*, (and, whether in synod or individuals, will judge and condemn accordingly ;) yet he that dares not be so *weak* as to be *particular* in his religious course, will not only fail of the attainments of evangelical perfection, but be often obliged to avoid the most substantial duties of Christian piety.'[...]

[...]Amongst the most warm hearted of the admirers of Law, and collectors of the aforesaid MSS., was a Mr. Edward Fisher, of Bath, to whose philanthropy we perhaps owe the preservation of Freher's inestimable productions. Freher was a profound philosopher, (by birth a German,) of great learning and piety, and of amazing capacity, originality of genius, and strength of mind. The latter years of his life he spent in London, where he died, in 1728, aged seventy-nine. He appears to have been altogether taken up with his MS. demonstrations and illustrations of Behmen's writings, having also continually with him a friend, of the name of Leuchter, a draftsman, to execute the beautiful drawings and symbols with which his demonstrations are so abundantly illustrated, as well as to make copies of the same for others. Freher lived on intimate terms with the Rev. Mr. Waple, and other admirers of J. B.'s writings ; among whom might, perhaps, be reckoned some of the remaining members of the Philadelphian Society.——This latter society, which began publicly in 1697, and terminated its meetings in 1703, having correspondence with individuals of similar sentiments in Holland, and various parts of the continent, owed its existence, originally, to one or two devout persons of the complexion of piety peculiar to the Cromwell times, giving up themselves to the study of Behmen's writings, which had then just been published in English; and then fancying themselves to be the subjects of visions and revelations, which they also published in print, till, in about a dozen years or so, the Philadelphian Society was formed. This society, the writer considers, however, was more immediately brought into existence and kept together by the pious zeal of the learned Francis Lee, who was then the son-in-law of the chief heroine of the society, a Mrs.

Jane Lead. She being a very devout woman, [a *seeker* of visions, Mr. Law seems to intimate, while he at the same time deprecates the folly of such attempts, as knowing that it is God who selects his prophets, and not for man to take that office to himself, which truth does not appear to have crossed the minds of these Philadelphians.]—her admirers were probably thereby induced to conclude that what she termed her visions, being by them found to be in harmony with Behmen's principles, with which they might have been acquainted, were true revelations to her from God. And as to her style, whatever the *modern* reader might say to it, they professed it to be quite consistent with her pretensions, and fully equal to that of *Hosea*, or other second-rate ancient prophets; nay, they found a beauty in it which was admirable, if not inimitable! Her published visions, would we obtain a general idea of them by a modem illustration, may be described to be such as we should expect from the devout and sincere, *moaning, quawking,* unknown-tongue professors, had they been dipping largely into the transcendentals of Behmen's philosophy, and thereupon turned prophetesses. And as these obtained abettors of their innocent self-deceptions as to their 'extraordinary vocation,' in sincere and pious, though, as respects theological knowledge, partially informed individuals; so did this Mrs. Lead, in her day, make her converts, though not of the simple only, but of some very respectable persons of the University of Oxford: for she captivated the very learned and ingenious Lee, Fellow of St. John's, and that to such a degree that, for a time, he would seem to have given up his brilliant talents entirely to the propagation of her views, or, as he considered, the interests of Divine truth. The purport of the Philadelphian Society may be ascertained by a reference to their periodical of "Theosophical Transactions," 1697, of which five numbers only were published, to Roach's two publications, and others, up to 1727. Without Lee, however, the thing would perhaps never have been heard of, as the other members, including Dr. Hooker, do not appear to have been very eminent in literary ability. But how great were Lee's talents, and the devotion he brought to the cause, may be inferred from his defence of Mrs. Lead, in a long letter he addressed to Mr. Henry Dodwell, who had reproached him for encouraging her groundless enthusiasm, and thereby bringing a reproach on the university; as also from his writings in connection with the Philadelphian Society. If an opportunity offers, we hope at the conclusion of this section, or elsewhere, to afford a few sparkling illustrations of the genius, ability, and Christian science of this celebrated individual—that "most pious, ingenious, and ready writer," as Dr. Hickes is supposed to call him in that observation. After the dissolution of the Philadelphian Society, Dr. Lee returned again to his wonted sober occupations of practical philanthropy, and incessant activity in the promotion of learning and piety, and of general good to his fellow-creatures. He was *supposed* to be the author of "Nelson's Feasts and Fasts," of the second volume of "Kempis's Christian Pattern," with the preliminary dissertation therein, and of "Kempis's Christian Exercise, by Nelson;" also of the translation of Fenelon's "Pastoral Letter," besides being the editor of numerous other ingenious and devotional publications, translations and originals, and, perhaps, partly of Nelson's "Life of Bull." For any one who has read his prefaces to "Lead's works," (which he edited,) his poems therein, his writings in connection with the Philadelphian Society, and the above-mentioned works in the order of their appearance, may perceive the identity of style, and when he compares them with Nelson's own undoubted letters, dedications, etc., will recognise the difference in the authorship.

Among other "revelations" which this Mrs. Lead published abroad, was one which she termed the "Everlasting Gospel," which was to be preached to the devil and his angels, after the restoration of the whole human race; for she gave out that the whole lapsed creation, both of men and devils, should return to their original state, as brought forth by God, the immutable God of Love and Goodness, whose designs by the creation should not be eternally frustrated, but rather his glory be the more infinitely glorified in triumphing over every opposition and self-will of the creature, all which, after having expended itself, and been conscious of its possibilities, should return to the unity and harmony of the Divine life. To overturn such a bold assumption, Freher wrote a deep grounded philosophical treatise, illustrated with elaborate symbols, demonstrating from Behmen, in accordance with Scripture, the absolute impossibility, according to the known powers and possibilities of eternal nature, of the restoration of devils. But when Law, in after life, had obtained a clear philosophical apprehension of the whole subject, he declared that both sides stood in the same position, viz. in a necessity of neither affirming nor denying the thing,—that neither Behmen nor Scripture sufficiently reached the question, that it all depended upon the *possibility* which at present could not be *proved*, but if it was possible it would surely come to pass.——Another celebrated character, who will deserve notice in connection with Freher, Law and others, immortally identified with Behmen, is John George Gichtel, the original compiler and publisher, in a uniform German edition, with notes, of Behmen's works——a man of the deepest practical piety, and at the same time highest scientific and theosophical abilities. His life, in German, was published at Leyden, in 1722, entitled, "The wonderful and holy Life of that elect instrument and man of God, John George Gichtel;" as also his "Theosophia Practica." These should all be translated into English, preserving their theosophic idiom.—But to return.

Selection Five.

[On Enthusiasm, by Christopher Walton]

* Here we obtain a clear view of the ground and nature of 'ENTHUSIASM.'—In *will, imagination,* and *desire,* as already observed, consists the life, or fiery driving of every intelligent creature. And as every intelligent creature is its own *self-mover,* so every intelligent creature has a power of *kindling* and *inflaming* its will, imagination, and desire, as it pleases, with shadows, fictions, or realities; with things carnal or spiritual, temporal or eternal. And *this kindling* of the will, imagination, and desire, when raised into a *ruling degree* of life, is properly that which is to be understood by enthusiasm: and therefore enthusiasm is, and must be of as *many kinds* as those objects are which can kindle and inflame the wills, imaginations, and desires of men. And to appropriate enthusiasm to religion, is the same ignorance or Nature, as to appropriate love to religion; for enthusiasm, a kindled, inflamed spirit of life, is as *common,* as *universal,* as *essential* to human nature, as *love* is? It goes into *every kind* of life as love does, and has only such a variety of degrees in mankind as love hath. And here we may see the reason, why no people are so angry at religious enthusiasts, as those that are the *deepest* in some enthusiasm of *another kind.*

He whose fire is kindled from the divinity of *Tully's* rhetoric, who travels over high mountains to salute the dear ground that *Marcus Tullius Cicero* walked upon; whose *noble soul* would be ready to break out of his body if he could see a *desk,* a *rostrum* from whence *Cicero* had poured forth his thunder of words, may well be unable to bear the *dulness* of those who go on *pilgrimages* only to visit the *sepulchre* whence the *Redeemer of the world* rose from the dead, or who grow devout at the sight of a *crucifix,* because the Son of God hung as a sacrifice thereon.

He whose heated brain is all over painted with the *ancient hieroglyphics;* who knows *how* and *why* they were *this* and *that,* better than he can find out the customs and usages of his *own parish;* who can clear up every thing that is *doubtful* in antiquity, and yet be forced to live in doubt about that which passes in his own neighbourhood; who has found out the sentiments of the *first philosophers* with such certainty, as he cannot find out the *real opinions* of any of his contemporaries; he that has gone thus high into the *clouds,* and dug thus deep into the *dark* for these *glorious discoveries*, may well despise those Christians, as *brain sick visionaries*, who are sometimes finding a *moral* and *spiritual* sense in the bare letter and history of Scripture facts.

It matters not what our wills and imaginations are employed about; wherever they *fall* and love to *dwell*, there they kindle a fire, and that becomes the *flame of life*, to which everything else appears as *dead*, and *insipid*, and *unworthy* of regard. Hence it is that even the poor species of *fops* and *beaux* have a right to be placed among enthusiasts, though capable of no other flame than that which in kindled by *tailors* and *peruke-makers*. All *refined speculatists*, as such, are great enthusiasts; for being devoted to the exercise of their imaginations, they are so *heated* into a love of their *own ideas*, that they seek no other *summum bonum*. The *grammarian*, the *critic*, the *poet*, the *connoisseur*, the *antiquary*, the *philosopher*, the *transcendentalist* the *politician*, are all violent enthusiasts, though their heat is only a flame from *straw*, and therefore they all agree in *appropriating* enthusiasm to religion. All *ambitious, proud, self-coneceited* persons, especially if they are *scholars*, are violent enthusiasts; and their enthusiasm is an *inflamed* self-love, self-esteem, and self-seeking. This fire is so kindled in them, that everything is nauseous and disgustful to them, that does not offer incence to that idol which their imagination has set up in themselves. All *atheists* are dark enthusiasts; their fire is kindled by a will and imagination turned from God into a gloomy depth of *nothingness*, and therefore their enthusiasm is a *dull burning* fire, that goes in and out through *hopes* and *fears* of they know not what there is to come. All *professed infidels* are remarkable enthusiasts; they have kindled a *bold* fire from a *few faint ideas*, and therefore they are all zeal, and courage, and industry, to be *constantly blowing* it up. A *Tyndal* and a *Collins* are as inflamed with the notions of infidelity, as a St. *Bennel* and St. *Francis* with the doctrines of the Gospel.

Enthusiasts therefore we all are, as certainly as we are men; and consequently, enthusiasm is not a thing blameable in *itself*, but is the common condition of human life in *all its states;* and every man that lives either *well* or *ill*, is that which he is, from that *prevailing fire* of life, or *driving* of our wills and desires, which is properly called Enthusiasm. You need not, then, go to a *cloister*, the *cell* of a *monk*, or to a *field preacher*, to see enthusiasts; they are everywhere, at *balls* and *masquerades*, at *court* and the *exchange:* they sit in all *coffee-houses*, and *cant* in all assemblies. The *beau* and the *coquet* have no *magic*, but where they meet enthusiasts. The *mercer*, the *tailor*, the *bookseller*, have all their wealth from them; the works of a *Boyle*, a *Shaftsbury*, and a *Cicero*, would lose *four-fifths* of their astonishing beauties, had they not keen enthusiasts for their readers.

That which concerns us, therefore, is only to see with what materials our *prevailing fire* of life is kindled, and in what *species* of enthusiasts it truly places us. For either the *flesh* or the *spirit*, either the wisdom from *above*, or the wisdom of *this world*, will have *its fire* in us: and we must have a *life* that governs us, either according to the sensuality of the *beast*, the subtilty of the *serpent*, or the holiness of the *angel*.—Enthusiasm is not blameable in religion, when it is true Religion that kindles it. We are created with *wills* and *desires* for no other end, but to love, adore, desire, serve, and co-operate with God; and therefore the more we are inflamed in *this motion* of our wills and desires, the more we have of a God-like, divine nature and perfection in us. Religious enthusiasm is not blameable, when it is a *strong persuasion*, a *firm belief* of a continual operation, impression, and influence from above, when it is a total resignation to, and dependence upon the *immediate inspiration* and *guidance* of the Holy Spirit, in the whole course of our lives; this is as sober and rational a belief, as to believe that we *always* live, and move, and have our being in God. Both nature and Scripture demonstrate this to be the true spirit of a religious man, Nature tells every one, that we can only be heavenly by a spirit derived from heaven, as plainly as it tells us, that we can only be earthly by having the spirit of this world breathing in us. The Gospel teaches no truth so *constantly*, so *universally* as this, that every good thought and good desire are the work of the Holy Spirit. And therefore both nature and Scripture demonstrate, that the *one only* way to piety, virtue, and holiness, is to *prepare*, *expect*, and *resign* ourselves up *wholly* to the influence and guidance of the Holy Spirit, in every *thing* that we think, or say, or do. The moment any one departs from *this faith*, or loses *this direction* of his will and desire, so far, and so long, he goes out of the one only *element* of all holiness of life. —There is nothing that so sanctifies the heart of man, that keeps us in such habitual love, prayer, and delight in God; nothing that so kills all the roots of evil in our nature, that so renews and perfects all our virtues, that fills us with so much love, goodness, and good wishes to every creature, as *this faith*, that God is always *present* in us with his *Light* and *Holy Spirit*. When the heart has once learnt thus to find God, and knows how to live everywhere, and in all things, in this immediate intercourse with him, seeing him, loving him, and adoring him in everything, trusting in him, depending upon him for his continual Light and Holy Spirit: when it knows that *this faith* is infallible, that by thus believing, it thus possesses all that it believes of God; then it begins to have the nature of God in it, and can do nothing but flow forth in love, benevolence, and good will towards every creature;

it can have no wish towards any man, but that he might *thus know*, and *love*, and *find* God *in himself*, as the true beginning of heaven and the heavenly life in the soul.

On the other hand, no error is so hurtful to the soul, so destructive of all the ends of the Gospel, as to be led from this faith and *entire dependance* upon the Holy Spirit of God within us, or to place our recovery in anything else, but in the operation of the Light and Holy Spirit of God upon the soul. It is withdrawing men not only from the easiest, the most natural, the most fruitful, but the only possible source of all light and life. For every man, as such, has an open gate to God in his soul: he is always in that temple where he can worship God in spirit and truth. Every Christian, as such, has the *first fruits* of the Spirit, a *seed* of Life, which is his *call* and *qualification* to be always in a state of inward prayer, faith, and holy intercourse with God. All the *ordinances* of the gospel, the daily *sacramental* service of the church, is to keep up, and exercise, and strengthen, *this faith;* to raise us to such an *habitual* faith and dependence upon the Light and Holy Spirit of God, that by thus seeking and finding God in the *institutions* of the church, we may be habituated to seek him and find him; to live in his light, and walk by his Spirit in ALL the actions of our ordinary life. THIS is the ENTHUSIASM in which every good Christian OUGHT TO ENDEAVOUR TO LIVE AND DIE.

Selection Six.

[Walton's Recommendations for Readings on Magic.]

[MAGICAL AND CORRELATIVE STUDIES.—*The next following Six Divisions are an accompanying scientific and practical study, of high importance.*]

1. *Tryon*. *The Knowledge of a Man's Self;* being a Second Part of the *Way to Health*, etc. 8vo. 1703. Also, *The Way to Health*, etc. 1697. (All grounded on J. B's. philosophy.) Also, *Memoirs of T. Tryon*, 18mo. 1705.—*The Phalanstery, or Moral Harmony ; the Preface*, by Lady Chichester, 12mo. London, 1841.

2. *Pure Foods*. Here to read some judicious treatises on the necessity of pure diets, or a pure fuel for the fire of life, and indeed of an universal cleanness, in order (in common with the spiritual exercises of earnest religion,) to the regeneration, or purification and sublimation of the humanity, according to the true scope of the gospel. Also, to examine some works treating of high *Boodhist*, and other *Oriental, Druidic*, etc. religious science, virtue and piety : and likewise, concerning the real *purificative* rites, and *inductive* physical and mental training of the ancient *vestal pythonesses, sibyls, priestesses*, etc., etc.

3. *Popular Experimental Transcendentalism*, or *Animal Magnetism*, with its *subsequent Inductions*. To peruse, in this place, Dr. Haddock's *Psycheism* and *Somnalism*, 12mo. London. 1851.—Also, Dr. Gregory's *Letters on Animal Magnetism*, 12mo. London, 1851. With *Newnham, on Human Magnetism*, 8vo. 1845. Dods's *Philosophy of Mesmerism*, 1851, (American,) and *Philosophy of Electrical Psychology*, 12mo. 1852.—Townshend's *Facts in Mesmerism*, 8vo. 1844.—*Night Side of Nature*, by Mrs. C. Crowe, 3rd ed. 1852.—*Deleuze. Histoire Critique du Magnétisme Animale*, 2nd ed. 1819. And *Practical Instruction in Animal Magnetism*, 8vo. Balliere, 1850.—*Zoist*.— Dupotet, *Introd. to Study of An. Mag*. In French.—Reichenbach. *Researches in An. Magnetism*, 8vo. 1852—Ennemoser's *History of Magic*, 2 vols. 12mo. 1854;—with other sober treatises, both German and French, elucidatory of *spiritual developements* and accidental openings of the Magic philosophy. And along therewith,

(N.B.) TO WITNESS SOME REALLY GOOD CASES OF MAGICAL SLEEP OR TRANCE, WITH LUCID CLAIRYOANCE,

4. *Works on Modern Spiritism. The Spiritual Herald*, 8vo., (Monthly,) London, 1856 —*Yorkshire Spiritual Telegraph*, Keighley, 1855-6.— American *Spiritism* Newspapers, and Periodicals ; *New York Spiritual Telegraph* ; *New England Spiritualist*.— Judge Edmond's *Preface* to his book : etc.— Ballou's *Exposition respecting Modern Spirit Manifestations*; with a *New* [and N.B. MOST ENLIGHTENED] *Preface*, 16mo. Howell, Liverpool, 1853.—(With works advertised in the American *Spiritism* Newspapers.)

[Jung-Stilling's "Pneumatology", hand-written marginal note by Walton—Ed.]

NOTE.—After having gone through the present division of study, (referring likewise again to the Notes of pp. 522–24, 549, 550, 553,556, 559, and of 467–9, 464, 449, 495, and to the text of pp. 320, etc.,) the student will perceive its scope and object; as opening out to him a glimpse of the whole field of the *natural* and *divine magic,* and of the accidental entrances therein made by the astral spirit and by faith, up to the present time ; besides enabling him to advocate with superlative force of reason and earnestness of zeal, the necessity of the establishment of *Theosophic Colleges*, in regard to the perfect triumphs of the Gospel. Which should be, not mere elementary schools of the prophets, nor yet as the ancient *philosophical academies* : but brilliant evangelical seminaries, worthy of the age, for the rearing or training of children of God, up to the *highest perfection* of sanctity and wisdom, according to the lights of this work—even to the matured apprehension and exercise of those *angelical arts* and *powers*, which are the prerogatives of the regenerate humanity.

The considerations that will ensue upon a review of this particular of study, will also elucidate the original doctrines and mysteries of Christianity, of *imposition of hands*, (by a regenerate and official medium,) of *baptism*, of the *supper of the Lord*, etc.,—yet, even of the *supplementary* sacraments of the Romish church. [...]

5. *La Philosophie Divine, appliquée aux Lumières Naturelle, Magique, Astrale, Surnaturelle, Celeste, et Divine ; ou aux Immuables Vérités que Dieu a révélées de Luimême et de ses Œuvres, dans le Triple Miroir analogique, de l'Univers, de l'Homme, et de la Révélation Ecrite*. 3 vols. 8vo. 1793. To peruse the judicious Notes of the first Volume, and a few of the second Volume, containing the author's experience and judgment of the *astral* magic, somnambulic, Swedenborgian and similar delusionism.

[The reflective reader may in this place, further conceive respecting the glorious manifestations that might be expected in, and by the *duly trained,* (see again, *New Preface* to Ballou's book,) divinely illumined subjects of a right Theosophic College.]

6. *The Hermetic Mystery, and Alchemy*. For references to treatises thereupon, see *A Suggestive Inquiry into the Hermetic Mystery*, 8vo. London, 1850.—*Query*, Prof. Molitor, of Frankfort, *on the Cabala*? End of MAGICAL INTERSECTION.]

Traité du Discernment des Esprits. Par Cardinal Bona. 18mo. Paris, 1675. A judicious work.—*General Delusion of Christians touching God's Revealing Himself*. 1713, 1838; supposed to be written by the Author himself of the *History of Montanism*, 8vo. 1708, which also especially peruse; and this latter to have been a strained work, drawn up to oblige friends.—*Lead. A Fountain of Gardens*, 4 vols., 12mo., 1697, and *Revelation of Revelations*, 4to., 1683.— [*Apologetical Letter of Lee to Dodwell*, pp. 188–258.] To glance over Roach's *Great Crisis*, and *Imperial Standard*, 8vo., 1727.— Bromley's *Sabbath of Rest*, 12mo. London, 1730.—*Mrs. Pratts Letters*, pp. 587–91 seq., etc.— Kelty's *Spiritual Fragments, the Preface*, 18mo., 1838.

Theosophical Transactions, by the Philadelphian Society, for the Advancement of Piety and Divine Philosophy, pp. 294, 4to., 1697. The close perusal of this Work, is highly recommended, especially pp. 248–268, though indeed, it is full of spiritual gems, the editor being the celebrated Francis Lee, author of *Ketllewells Life*, &c., &c-Lee's posthumous *Dissertations*, 2 vols. 8vo., 1752.

[Freher's *Abstract of the 'Second Part' of P. Evangelista's Kingdom of God in the Soul*, pp. 623–627.]—Also Canfield's *Rule of Perfection*, the *Third Part*, viz. *Of the Essential Will of God, wherein is treated of the Supernatural Life*.—Also, *Eckart's Discourses, Tauler's Sermons*, and *Rusbrochius, Of the Perfection of the Children of God*, all in German and Latin. And *Jean de la Croix's* sublime experimental writings, the *Ascent of Mount Carmel*, &c.— And again, Böhme's *Supersensual Life*, p. 43, seq.; *Divine Contemplation*; and *Abstract of the Mysterium Magnum*.

The object of this *sixth division* of study in the series, has already been sufficiently intimated, viz., to afford to the so advanced student, a knowledge of all the science and art, which has hitherto been revealed and discovered, in regard to the high sublimation of the human life ; and of the true and lawful mode whereby to advance steadily to the very central throne of the divine revelation, even to become a *holy artist*, a lord, a prince over nature, to the praise and glory of God. For the humanity, as before observed, being now fully redeemed, man is therefore capable of a transcendently *exalted* spiritual renovation and illumination : (and if of a spiritual why not of an outward and physical—even of an *Enochian life* on earth?) And therefore it ought to be the aim of the enlightened Christian, to press on to this high regenerate perfection, or *glorified resurrection state** of the inner man; to prove the arts of *paradisical horticulture*, first in himself, with his own life and intellect, and then to raise up others to the same faith, and inward glory. Which attainment according to its degree, it is, that restores to man his original prerogatives of *dominion over all temporal creatures*, and to open the latent powers of God, and *scientz* of the Divine Wisdom in everything. Our Lord spake to his wondering disciples to this purport,—Ye seem surprised at what I now effect, deeming it a *miracle : Verily far greater works than these shall ye* (my faithful, theosophic disciples,) *do*, after my ascension. St. *Paul* also, in the same scope of apprehension, observes, *Henceforth know we no believer after the flesh* .... (but rather as members of a God of glory in heaven.) And again, *But ye are come, &c. Hebrews* xii. 22–24. And what St. *John* declares, respecting the *paradisical glories* of the New Jerusalem, *i. e.* of that Christianity, in which we are all *set* and *growing up*, if of the regeneration, needs not to be particularized in this place.

**Philip.* iii. 11-16.

Appendix

Appendix.

Jane Lead and Franz Hartmann documents.

"Marks of a True Philadelphian" by Jane Lead compared point by point with Franz Hartmann's "Secret Signs of the Rosicrucians". Lead's work was originally published in her "Third Message to the Philadelphian Society", while Hartmann's was published as an appendex to "In the Pronaos of the Temple of Wisdom."

THE MARKS OF A TRUE PHILADELPHIAN
According to the Description of the Blessed Apostle St. PAUL

THE SECRET SIGNS OF THE ROSICRUCIANS.

There are sixteen signs by which a member of the order of the Rosicrucians may be known. He who possesses only a few of those signs is not a member of a very high degree, for the true Rosicrucian possesses them all.

1 A PHILADELPHIAN SUFFERS LONG

The first victory of the True Philadelphian hero may be said to consist properly in suppressing the irascible emotions of the soul: or in stopping the mouth of that Roaring Lion, which watches all the travelers to the City of Brotherly Love, how he may surprise and devour them. For the two great Boanerges, the most beloved brothers had like to have fallen into the jaws of this Lion; and the most masculine champion of Christ, and most zealous of all His disciples was bitten by him, and had much ado to escape with his life. Therefore having these examples set before him, he is exceeding cautious to guard himself against this wild and furious beast. And he strives to imitate the longsuffering and patience of the Deity towards evil doers. He studies to conquer his adversaries with Love, and to bring them over to him by kind offices, or by presents, as Jacob did his brother Esau. He is not for calling down fire from Heaven upon them, or anathematizing them; but for heaping coals of love upon their heads. He is not for prosecuting heretics or recusants with the faggot, or with the sword: but is for suffering the tares to grow with the wheat, till the Day of the Harvest: when everyone's work shall be purged by fire.

1. The Rosicrucian is Patient.

His first and most important victory is the conquest of his own self. It is the victory over the LION, who has bitterly injured some of the best followers of the Rosy Cross. He is not to be vanquished by a fierce and inconsiderate attack made upon, him ; but he must be made to surrender to patience and fortitude. The true Rosicrucian tries to overcome his enemies by kindness, and those who hate him by gifts. He heaps not curses, but the burning fire of love upon their heads. He does not persecute his enemies with the sword, or with faggots, but he suffers the weeds to grow with the wheat until they are both matured, when they will be separated by Nature.

2. A PHILADELPHIAN IS KIND

As courtesy and kindness is a moral virtue, so in him it becomes a Christian grace. Therefore he cannot be austere, or starched up to any little formalities. His religion makes him not sour or uneasy to others, but renders him more sweet, affable, and easy, if there be but the least opportunity for him hereby of doing any kind or generous office to any. And though he uses himself much to solitude and retirements, with his blessed Master and Pattern, yet whenever he appears in the world, he affects not a singularity, or to be taken notice of, but freely converses with it, and accommodates himself to the manners of it, so far as innocently he can. Thus the True Philadelphian is the most obliging person of the whole world: not only inoffensive in his carriage, but even pleasant, and nobly exercised in the most advantageous parts of human conversation, as well as the most delectable. And as different as the address of a Master of the Ceremonies to a strange minister, is from that of one brother to another most intimately endeared to him; so is that of this Philadelphian, when he converses with any, from that outward, formal, and ceremonial way which is practiced by the world. In short, none better (if so well) understands all the solid delights of conversation, and the permanent pleasures of a true and masculine friendship; not confined, but extended to the very utmost capacity of his sphere.

2. The Rosicrucian is Kind.

He never appears gloomy or melancholy, or with a scowl or sneer upon his face. He acts kindly and politely towards everybody, and is always ready to render assistance to others. Although he is different from the majority of other people, still he tries to accommodate himself to their ways, habits and manners, as much as his dignity will permit. He is, therefore, an agreeable companion, and knows how to converse with the rich as well as with the poor, and to move among-all classes of society so as to command their respect; for he has conquered the bear of vulgarity.

3. A PHILADELPHIAN ENVIES NOT

When he has thus slain the Lion and the Bear, he next proceeds to cut off the head of that most cunning twisting Serpent of Envy, that would insinuate himself even into Paradise. And it is much more easy to vanquish, subdue, and harmonize the fierce wrathful, and the rough unmannerly properties of a disordered soul, then to eradicate this more secret and lurking evil, which lies gnawing on the very vitals of religion, in any great and specious professors. But the true Philadelphian is one perfectly content with that state or lot, in which he stands, through the wisdom, justice and goodness of God. He thinks not much at any advantages or privileges which another enjoys: but rather congratulates them. He is certain that the Master whom he serves, if he be faithful, will not fail to prefer him: and therefore he is not at all solicitous after any preferments, honors, or riches, which this world can give, or in the least envies those who possess them. And much less does he repine at any favors conferred by his Master, upon any of his fellow-servants: but is pleased thereat. And will not presume to bind up His Majesty to act thus or thus, and to confer His favours and graces upon none but those that are of this or that body, or society, that he likes best. No: he dares not do so: he prefers others before himself; thinking himself unworthy of the very least grace, or gift of His Holy Spirit bestowed upon him. For,

3. The Rosicrucian knows no Envy.

Before he is accepted into the order he must go through the terrible ordeal of cutting off the head of the snake of envy ; which is a very difficult labour, because the snake is sly, and easily hides itself in some corner. The true Rosicrucian is always content with his lot, knowing that it is such as he deserves it to be. He never worries about the advantages or riches which others possess, but wishes always the best to everybody. He knows that he will obtain all he deserves, and he cares not if any other person possesses more than he. He expects no favours, but he distributes his favours without any partiality.

4 A PHILADELPHIAN VAUNTS NOT HIMSELF

He will take no glory or honor to himself; but will ascribe all to the Supreme Majesty, which he serves, the sole fountain of honor, and the origin of whatever is glorious, or praise-worthy. He is free therefore from all ostentation: and being inconsiderable in his own eyes, he cannot be over-forward, temerarious, or precipitate in any design, but will wait always for the call and command of his Master: that so he may not dishonor, instead of honoring Him. And this also teaches him to weigh his words in the balance of the Holy Sanctuary, and not to speak rashly for God.

4. The Rosicrucian does not Boast.

He knows that man is nothing but an instrument in the hands of GOD, and that he can accomplish nothing useful by his own will; the latter being nothing but the will of GOD perverted in man. To GOD he gives all the praise, and to that which is mortal he gives all the blame. He is in no inordinate haste to accomplish a thing, but he waits until he receives his orders from the Master who resides above and within. He is careful what he speaks about, and uses no unhallowed language.

5. A PHILADELPHIAN IS NOT PUFFED UP

For he avoids all manner of ostentation and impertinence: this is a certain sign that there must be in him somewhat substantial, and that he is not a vessel filled with wind. He is neither elevated with any applause, nor dejected with obloquy or contempt. He is contracted within a very little compass, and is not blown up as a bladder, either with the vanities and pomps of the world, or with any spiritual attainments, fancied or real. But the more he receives, natural or supernatural, he is still the more humble, more passive, and more resigned to the divine will.

5. The Rosicrucian is not Vain.

He proves thereby that there is something real in him, and that he is not like a blown-up bag filled with air. Applause or blame leaves him unaffected, nor does he feel aggrieved if he is contradicted or encounters contempt. He lives within himself, and enjoys the beauties of his own inner world, but he never desires to show off his possessions, nor to pride himself on any spiritual gifts which he may have attained. The greater his gifts, the greater will be his modesty, and the more will he be willing to be obedient to the law.

6. A PHILADELPHIAN DOES NOT BEHAVE HIMSELF UNSEEMLY

He takes care to do nothing that is indecorous: but is a most strict observer of the Eternal Law of Order. Which law is the rule of all virtue: and therefore though he is not solicitous about the niceties or punctilios of ceremony; yet having this Law written in his heart, all his actions proceeding must needs be regular, orderly, and decent. There will therefore be seen a decorum in all his conversation, that is not superficial, but essential; that is not counterfeited, but natural; that is not transient, but permanent; as derived from that Root which abides ever, and fails not. There is an inexpressible beauty in his behavior, both to the Children of Men and to the Children of God; that is insensibly conveyed from the Supreme and Infinite Beauty. And this he calls the reflection of the light of God's countenance upon his soul.

6. The Rosicrucian is not Disorderly.

He always strives to do his duty, and to act according to the order established by the law. He cares nothing for externalities, nor for ceremonies. The law is written within his heart, and therefore all his thoughts and acts are ruled by it. His respectability is not centred in his external appearance, but in his real being, which may be compared to a root from which all his actions spring. The interior beauty of his soul is reflected upon his exterior, and stamps all his acts with its seal; the light existing in his heart may be perceived in his eye by an expert; it is the mirror of the Divine image within.

7. A PHILADELPHIAN SEEKS NOT HIS OWN

There is nothing more that contradicts the beautiful Law of Order, than a narrow contracted spirit, which is always seeking its own, and not that which is for the good of the whole. Therefore a true Philadelphian is the most public spirited person that can be described. He seeks not his own private interest in the public: but tramples the former under his feet, even with the utmost disdain, so he may but promote the latter. And he not only lays hold on every opportunity that is presented to him, for the exercise of this public, merciful, and beneficent spirit: but even sedulously watches for, and catches after opportunities, after the example of his blessed MASTER, continually going about doing good.

7. The Rosicrucian is not Ambitious.

There is nothing more injurious to spiritual development and expansion of the soul than a narrow mind and a selfish character. The true Rosicrucian always cares much more for the welfare of others than for his own. He has no private or personal interest to defend or foster. He always seeks to do good, and he never avoids any opportunity which may present itself for that purpose.

8. A PHILADELPHIAN IS NOT EASILY PROVOKED

It is not otherwise to be expected but that a person of public spirit, whose study it is to do good to others, and to advance the honor and interest of his great and glorious MASTER, will meet with many affronts, misrepresentations, and provocations from the unthinking or ungrateful part of mankind. But a true Philadelphian will not be hereat in the least provoked or irritated. He lives above the censure of the world, as being the spectacle of God and of his holy Angels, and of all the great and good men now made perfect, who have ever lived upon the face of the Earth, and been the benefactors of human kind. Therefore looking steadfastly upon such as these, he matters not either the good or bad report of the present age; but is resolved to break through all, that he may be serviceable to it, and to posterity. He will not be provoked to lay down a good and noble design, whatever clamors may be raised against him: and will hazard both his reputation and fortune a thousand times over in this life, rather than not to do what he knows to be for the honor of his GOD, and the benefit of his neighbor; and more specially if for that of a kingdom. In short, he is so great a master of himself, by the grace and Spirit of Christ, that should all mankind set themselves against him, they could not be able to cast him even into one paroxysm.

8. The Rosicrucian is not Irritable.

It is evident that a person who works for the benefit of the whole will be hated by those whose personal advantages are not benefited thereby ; because selfishness is opposed to magnanimity, and the claims of the few are not always compatible with the interests of the community. The Rosicrucian will therefore be often resisted by narrow-minded and short-sighted people ; he will be slandered by calumniators, his motives will be misrepresented, he will be misjudged by the ignorant, ridiculed by the would-be wise, and taunted by the fool. All such proceedings, however, cannot excite or irritate the mind of the true Rosicrucian, nor disturb the divine harmony of his soul ; for his faith rests in the perception and knowledge of the truth within himself. The opposition of a thousand ignorant people will not induce him to desist from doing that which he knows to be noble and good, and he will do it even if it should involve the loss of his fortune or of his life. Being able and accustomed to direct his spiritual sight towards the divine, he cannot be deluded by the illusions of matter, but clings to the eternal reality. Being surrounded by angelic influences, and listening to their voices, he is not affected by the noise made by the animals. He lives in the company of those noble beings, who were once men like others, but who have become transfigured, and who are now beyond the reach of the vulgar and low.

9. A PHILADELPHIAN THINKS NO EVIL

Candor is the most peculiar Philadelphian characteristic: by which he is distinguished, visibly and eminently, from all the parties, sects, and external denominations of religion whatever. He is ever willing to take things in the best sense: and when two opposite constructions may be put upon the same matter, he constantly remembers the council of that good natured philosopher, who charged his pupil never to take up a vessel by the left handle, when he could hold it by the right. So the True Philadelphian, considering how all things have two handles, and how the very same person is made both an hero and a monster, according as the painter is pleased to draw him; will suspend his assent, till he can be fully ascertained, and will incline still to the more favourable part. For,

9. The Rosicrucian does not think evil of others.

Those who think evil of others see merely the evil which exists within themselves reflected and mirrored forth in others. The Rosicrucian is always willing to recognise in everything that which is good. Tolerance is a virtue by which the Rosicrucian is eminently distinguished from others ; and by which he may be known. If a thing appears to be ambiguous, he suspends his judgment about it until he has investigated its nature; but as long as his judgment is not perfect, he is more inclined to form a good opinion than an evil one about everything.

10. A PHILADELPHIAN REJOICES NOT IN INIQUITY

He sets not up for a critic upon the failures of others: nor would establish to himself a reputation of a wit upon the weaknesses or mistakes of any. It is the common vice of the world to take a pleasure in discoursing of the folly or knavery of others (without which topics perhaps nine parts in ten of ordinary conversation would be nothing), and to censure these is taken up as the most easy method to be thought a man of sense, or a man of probity. But the true Philadelphian genius is quite otherwise: it minds not the impertinent or insignificant buzzings of a fly, or the ridiculous gestures of a monkey; it finds no delight in calling over the political fetches of a cunning fox, the hypocrisy and treachery of a crocodile, or the rapacity and unmercifulness of a wolf; nor is diverted in raking into dung and ordure. The Philadelphian Spirit is far too noble for any such employment as this: and therefore, living above the genius of this world, converses much with the blessed inhabitants of the superior worlds; who think no evil of one another; neither rejoice in iniquity, or the failings of any of their fellow creatures; but rejoice in the truth, and in the conformity of things below with things above, or with the heavenly patterns. By whom being instructed,

10. The Rosicrucian loves justice.

He, however, never sets himself up as a judge over the faults of others, nor does he wish to appear to be wise by censuring the mistakes of others. He does not enjoy gossip, and cares no more about the foolishness committed by others, than he would about the buzzing of a fly or the capers of a monkey. He finds no pleasure in listening to political or personal quarrels, disputations, or mutual recriminations. He cares nothing for the cunningness of a fox, the dissimulation of a crocodile, or the rapacity of a wolf, and is not amused by the stirring up of mud. His nobility of character lifts him up into a sphere far beyond all such trifles and absurdities, and being above the sensual plane, wherein ordinary mortals find their happiness and enjoyment, he lives with those who do not think evil of each other, who do not rejoice about an injustice done to their brother, or make merry about his ignorance, and enjoy his misfortunes. He enjoys the company of those who love the truth, and who are surrounded by the peace and harmony of the spirit.

11. A PHILADELPHIAN REJOICES IN THE TRUTH

Calumny is the very nature of the Devil himself, who never rejoices more than when he find matter for his accusations. And its opposite virtue is a ray from the divine nature communicated to blessed Angels, and blessed souls. Hereby the True Philadelphian is made most like to the Deity, which is truth, and therefore never rejoices but in the truth, or in the reflection of His own immaculate Light. Therefore the Philadelphian rejoices not alone, but with the best company: with the Holy Majesty of God, with the whole Court of Heaven, with all good men on Earth, and more particularly with injured and oppressed innocence, that comes to be vindicated by the truth.

11. The Rosicrucian loves the truth.

There is no devil worse than falsehood and calumny. Ignorance is a nonentity, but falsehood is the substance of evil. The calumniator rejoices whenever he has found something upon which to base his lies and to make them grow like mountains. Opposed to it is the truth, it being a ray of light from the eternal fountain of GOOD, which has the power to transform man into a divine being. The ROSICRUCIAN seeks, therefore, no other light but the light of truth, and this light he does not enjoy alone, but in company of all who are good and filled with its divine majesty, whether they live on this earth or in the spiritual state ; and he enjoys it above all with those who are persecuted, oppressed, and innocent, but who will be saved by the truth.

12. A PHILADELPHIAN CONCEALS ALL THINGS

As his great care is to do nothing against the truth, so since the world is very little able to bear it, he is forced to enjoy it by himself, together with this secret blessed society, rather than to prostitute it, to such as would trample it under their feet. Therefore a true Philadelphian will bear and keep all things in his heart, that are not to be communicated to any but to the wise; according to the most express command and caution of Christ Himself, and His own practice, with that of His holy Mother and Apostles, and indeed of all the Prophets, Wisemen, and Scribes of the Kingdom in all ages. This gift of taciturnity, and holy silence is most absolutely requisite for him, as he stands engaged in great undertakings for the glory of God. For if the secrets of princes ought to be sacred, then much more, thinks the true Philadelphian, ought the secrets of HIM by whom princes reign. And yet even His secrets are with them that fear Him (Psa. 25:14). However this taciturnity or reservedness must not hinder, but that he be bold as a lion to declare and promulgate all that he is commanded by his supreme LORD: and thus to bear up, and support as it were, under HIM, the pillars of His government. For,

12. The Rosicrucian knows how to be silent.

Those who are false do not love the truth. Those who are foolish do not love wisdom. The true Rosicrucian prefers to enjoy the company of those who can appreciate truth to that of those who would trample it with their feet. He will keep that which he knows locked up within his heart, for in silence is power. As a minister of state does not go about telling to everybody the secrets of the king; so the Rosicrucian does not parade before the public the revelations made to him by the king within, who is nobler and wiser than all the earthly kings and princes ; for they only rule by the authority and power derived from Him. His secrecy ceases only when the king commands him to speak, for it is then not he who speaks, but the truth that is speaking through him.

13. A PHILADELPHIAN BELIEVES ALL THINGS

On the part of GOD, he believes that He is faithful and true to perform all His promises, even to the minutest title of them: and that he is no less ready now to assist them that truly believe in Him, than He was to assist all the ancient worthies, and great heroes: who are left as a cloud of witnesses (Heb. 12:1), for us to follow their steps. And on the part of man a true Philadelphian will also believe all things, that upon any probable motives of credibility can be produced either for vindication, or alleviation.

13. The Rosicrucian believes that which he knows.

He believes in the immutability of eternal law, and that every cause has a certain effect. He knows that the truth cannot lie, and that the promises made to him by the king will be fulfilled, if he does not himself hinder their fulfilment. He is, therefore, inaccessible to doubt or fear, and puts implicit confidence in the divine principle of truth, which has become alive and conscious within his heart.

14. A PHILADELPHIAN HOPES ALL THINGS

On the part of GOD he hopes both for an ordinary and extraordinary appearance of His Majesty. The ground of this hope is upon a Rock: and nothing is too great for it to reach after, in advancing His glory. And on the part of man, there where the notoriety of evil is too plain for him to believe good, yet he despairs not, but hopes that even the most diabolical sinner may at length repent, and become a very great and glorious saint; loving much, because much is forgiven.

14. The Rosicrucian's hope is firm.

Spiritual hope is the certain conviction resulting from a knowledge of the law, that the truths recognised by faith will grow and be fulfilled ; it is the knowledge of the heart, and very different from the intellectual speculation of the reasoning brain. His faith rests upon the rock of direct perception and cannot be overthrown. He knows that in everything, however evil it may appear to be, there is a germ of good, and he hopes that in the course of evolution that germ will become developed, and thus evil be transformed into good.

15. PHILADELPHIAN ENDURES ALL THINGS

This heroic faith and hope makes the true Philadelphian to endure and suffer all things in his Master's cause, and for His sake. For always expecting Him to come quickly, he will never flinch back, but will keep the Word of His patience, and will remember to hold that fast which he has, that no man take his crown. Therefore,

15. The Rosicrucian cannot be vanquished by suffering.

He knows that there is no light without shadow, no evil without some good, and that strength only grows by resistance. Having once recognised the existence of the Divine principle within everything, external changes are to him of little importance, and do not deserve great attention. His main object is to hold on to his spiritual possessions, and not to lose the crown which he has gained in the battle of life.

16. A PHILADELPHIAN NEVER FAILS

But when all other names of distinction shall fail, and be burnt up, this shall abide. The Name of a PHILADELPHIAN shall endure forever: it shall be continued as long as the Sun: and all nations shall call him the Blessed of the Lord.

16. The Rosicrucian will always remain a member of his society.

Names are of little importance. The principle which presides over the Rosicrucian Society is the truth ; and he who knows the truth, and follows it in practice, is a member of the society over which the truth practises. If all names were changed and all languages altered, the truth would remain the same ; and he who lives in the truth will live even if all nations should pass away.

These were the Marks that were given to a certain Traveler toward the heavenly city of PHILADELPHIA, by a strong Angel that descended from there, who having taken out his heart, left as it were a flaming coal in the room thereof; which burns incessantly with most vehement desires, for the good of all His brethren, that is, of all mankind.

These are the sixteen signs of the true Rosicrucians, which have been revealed to a pilgrim by an angel who took away the heart of the pilgrim, leaving in its place a fiery coal, which is now incessantly burning and glowing with love of the universal brotherhood of humanity.

John Madziarczyk is the editor of Topaz House Publications. A native of the Midwest, he briefly attended Earlham College, and has a bachelor's degree in political science from The Evergreen State College in Olympia, Washington.

www.ingramcontent.com/pod-product-compliance
Lightning Source LLC
Chambersburg PA
CBHW070902300426
44113CB00008B/918